THE PATH OF
INITIATION

THE PATH OF INITIATION

SPIRITUAL EVOLUTION AND THE RESTORATION OF THE WESTERN MYSTERY TRADITION

J. S. GORDON

Inner Traditions

Rochester, Vermont • Toronto, Canada

Inner Traditions
One Park Street
Rochester, Vermont 05767
www.InnerTraditions.com

Text stock is SFI certified

Library of Congress Cataloging-in-Publication Data

Gordon, J. S. (John S.), 1946–2013
  The path of initiation : spiritual evolution and the restoration of the western
mystery tradition / J. S. Gordon.
    pages cm
  Includes bibliographical references and index.
  Summary: "Details the process of spiritual initiation from aspirant to the highest
Adept" — Provided by publisher.
  ISBN 978-1-62055-173-8 (pbk.) — ISBN 978-1-62055-174-5 (e-book)
  1. Spirituality—Miscellanea. 2. Occultism. 3. Consciousness—Miscellanea. 4.
Self-actualization (Psychology)—Religious aspects—Miscellanea. I. Title.
  BF1999.G6295 2013
  203'.82—dc23
                                                                          2013011422

Printed and bound in the United States by Lake Book Manaufacturing, Inc.
The text stock is SFI certified. The Sustainable Forestry Initiative® program promotes
sustainable forest management.

10 9 8 7 6 5 4 3 2 1

Text design and layout by Brian Boynton
This book was typeset in Garamond Premier Pro with Helios and Palatino as display
typefaces

This book is dedicated to the Rational Soul of the World, to the memory of both H. P. Blavatsky and A. A. Bailey, and to all who are truly working toward the practical unfoldment of the impending New Age of Enlightenment for humanity as a whole.

CONTENTS

ACKNOWLEDGMENTS

In being able to produce this book my grateful thanks are due to several people, but primarily to my wife Helena, whose enthusiasm for the subject knows no human bounds and whose capacity for remembering and finding useful references is beyond imagination.

Others to whom I am most grateful for their helpful comments and suggestions include Alistair Coombs, Ron Wallwork, Barry Thomson (Librarian of the Theosophical Society in London), plus Christine Morgan and Laurence Newey of the Lucis Trust for their continuing enthusiastic support and also for consenting to the use of extensive references from the works of A. A. Bailey. My thanks also to the Fintry Trust library and the Theosophical Publishing House in Adyar, Chennai.

Finally, I would also wish to add here an "in memoriam" mention of Professor Nicholas Goodrick-Clarke, an academic colleague and friend to many of us, whose sudden and unexpected passing from our midst at such an early age (in 2012) has sadly deprived the worldwide community of esoteric studentship of one of its brightest and most prolifically informative lights.

PROLOGUE

In this exploration of the subject of spiritual initiation, our overall concern is to derive a completely new and objective understanding of what the subjective world of consciousness (and its evolution) is all about—leading all the way to divinity itself. In a very real sense, this book concerns itself with what the concepts of God Immanent and God Transcendent (i.e., the microcosm and the Macrocosm) actually involve. But, in practical terms, these have to be blended synthetically together before the associated parts can be studied or analyzed separately with any real degree of intuitive understanding.[1]

The whole (originally sacred) subject of initiation and Adeptship has, most regretfully, been traduced over the last century by foolish or unscrupulous individuals and groups wishing to elevate themselves spiritually at absurdly great speed and at little personal cost, or otherwise to benefit financially from these same ingenuously-minded types. The author thus approaches this subject with more than a little concern about it being presented in the most objective manner possible, such that it can be seen to follow a fundamental logic, accessible to all with an open mind and clarity of thought.

Extensive reference and cross-reference has correspondingly been provided so that the reader can follow the associated psychology without the constant need to jump to unsubstantiated conclusions. These cross-references are also quite deliberately taken from historically and geographically very different cultures so that readers can see for themselves that the central principles have always been recognized as universal in application throughout the ages. In those instances where I have otherwise put forward my own speculative suggestions, I have hopefully done so in a manner that clearly indicates that this is the case.

The book itself is based upon a mixture of personal experience (over some thirty-five years) plus fairly extensive literary reference to the works of others who have evidently experienced and understood a great deal more than I have in this lifetime. It is therefore presented merely as a reasoned perspective for general consideration. If anyone reading this work comes to believe that I am making claims or suggestions beyond provable reason, that is up to them. They are entitled to their own views. All I am trying to do is advance the cause of practical esoteric philosophy in such a manner, with reasoned logic and supporting reference, that it is seen to be both useful and even fundamental to the further evolution of human intelligence and spiritual enquiry in the modern era. I would otherwise like to make it clear that I make no claims whatsoever as to the involvement of Adept influence in support of what I have written in this or any other work. The rationale of their existence as a rather more advanced kingdom in Nature than the merely human must stand or fall on the combined basis of necessity—through the logically natural and progressive workings of spiritual evolutionary development—and the factual testimony of direct observers working with them in many lands, the world over, through many past centuries and millennia.

The issue of the Adept Brotherhood is dealt with at some length toward the latter end of the book, in an attempt to put the whole subject of Adeptship in due context. However, in that regard it is worth pondering upon the following reported comment of one lesser Adept to the effect that

> the Masters of the Wisdom Who are advanced enough to work upon the larger areas of the spiritual plan are oft amused at the importance which the disciples and aspirants of the world attach to Them, and at the manner in which They are overestimated. Can we not realize that there are members of the Hierarchy Whose grasp of truth and Whose knowledge of the divine Plan is as much in advance of the Masters known to us as They are in advance of the savage and of the undeveloped man?[2]

The originating idea behind this book derives from many years of listening to two groups of friends talking about initiation and the Mysteries from completely different and equally conflicting viewpoints, as though they were in the same place, looking forward but standing back to back. One group involves those so fascinated with the subject that they glamorize it (and their own adulatory relationship to it) out of all proportion. The other group involves those so modestly concerned not to be seen as pushing themselves forward that they present themselves as being unable to consider the subject in any sort of detail for lifetimes to come. But there is also a quite separate third group, comprising those minds that see the Mysteries in general as mystical flim-flam, to be considered only as a historical phenomenon. None of these opposing approaches is at all helpful in trying to attain to an objective perception of what initiation and the Mysteries were (and are) really all about.

This work is really aimed at two other groups, however. First, those who realize that they have somehow come to be affected (they often know not how) by deeply esoteric influences that keep peculiarly reemerging into their lives, despite their wish to avoid them; second, those who have become so familiar with the consistency of such experience that they recognize there to be something good and useful leading them in that same direction. They thus want to know more through reason, without being completely taken over by mere fascination. Of these two, the second group will probably draw far more from this book, because of their natural common sense directing the way. However, I hope that it proves useful for others as well.

One other consideration involves the difference between the approach to derivation of knowledge adopted by esotericism on the one hand and orthodox science on the other. In rather simplistic terms this difference is the same as that followed by neo-Pythagoreans and neo-Platonists on the one hand and Aristotelians on the other. The former approach is that of always deducing from the universal to the particular, following an interdisciplinary system of applied universal principles, which concerns itself with essential (that is, qualitative) function in the greater continuum. The latter endeavor is to draw conclusions by a reductive process of systematic classification that separates and diversifies through focus on mere forms of appearance. That is why Raphael's famous painting of Plato and Aristotle emerging from the Academy depicts the former as pointing heavenward and the latter, in opposition, pointing earthward.

Fig. P.1. Plato and Aristotle at the School of Athens

Notwithstanding this, what we are trying to do here, essentially, is to get away from the old-fashioned-mystic approach and instead to start consciously using a combination of reason and applied intuition, the latter being to some degree flexibly anchored by the former. Without a reasonably strong sense of the usefulness of the intuitive function and the need to pursue it, the individual will get absolutely nowhere, for reasons that will become increasingly apparent further into the book. Correspondingly, without the use of reason—whether academically, scientifically, or psychologically based and applied—the individual's consciousness will merely fly off on all sorts of uselessly misleading tangents.

This book is oriented toward essentially practical work. Those pure mystics whose sole aim is heightened subjective experience will therefore be unlikely to take much positive interest in what it has to suggest. Correspondingly, it should become increasingly obvious to all of an academic persuasion that initiation is not in any way the same as the mere acquisition or expansion of knowledge.

In concluding, may I perhaps mention (in case of irritation to any reader) that throughout the work I tend to use the words *kosmos* and *kosmic* rather than *cosmos* and *cosmic*. The reason for that is based upon the fact that the former deal with the visible and invisible (that is, the objective and subjective) universe, whereas the latter are concerned purely with the objective version. It is my personal hope that my readers will follow and extend this usage in their own lives because experience has shown me that it makes quite an impact on the many who have never even thought of the cosmos itself having an invisibly subtle or subjective nature. As the whole book is based on the idea of an "organic" kosmos involving the principles of Unitary Being and Universal Consciousness—there being no such thing as "dead matter"—it follows quite logically that this should be so.

I should otherwise add that while I generally use capitals to signify a universal principle, such as Mind, I perhaps paradoxically decapitalize the word *gnostic* by virtue of regarding it as either descriptive of a much larger field of esoteric/occult knowledge, or otherwise as a particular type of mystic experience. As my fellow author David Fideler quite rightly comments, *Gnosticism* with a capital *G* is merely a scholarly concept evolved (in the West) during the last two centuries.[3] It is as misleading as the wholly erroneous modern (also scholarly) belief that esotericism and occultism too are merely modern Western concepts, or ways of thought.

Again, like David Fideler, I otherwise focus on the issue of gematria (the esoteric use of number and numerological significance), although in a rather more limited fashion. This is solely with the intention of explaining the altogether rational basis of metaphysical structures or progressions and those sequential dynamics of the kosmos. These themselves appear to have been well known to the spiritual cognoscenti throughout the ancient world, although having slightly different cultural overlays. The latter forms, however, were due entirely to the vagaries of environmental and social change throughout human history and not to any really fundamental difference.

For those wishing to pursue the study of those subjects dealt with here, a full bibliography is to be found at the back of this book. For the reader's convenience, terms of particular significance to our topic, such as *gnosticism, esoteric,* and *occult,* can be found in a glossary, also at the end of the book.

In addition five appendices are provided, which deal with complex issues associated with aspects of the whole (psycho-spiritual) evolutionary process. They are really intended only for those already having some degree of familiarity with occult metaphysics, although many of the principles described will be reasonably understandable or even familiar to others as well. They deal with the following subjects, in necessarily somewhat generalized terms, all to be considered in far greater detail in the works of both H. P. Blavatsky and A. A. Bailey:

Appendix A: Planetary Chains and Rounds

Appendix B: The Issue of Shamballa

Appendix C: The Evolution of the Human Racial Type

Appendix D: The Three Solar Systems and the Failure of the Moon Chain

Appendix E: Spiritual Avatars

The intention in these appendices is to provide a wider degree of context for the description of the universal evolutionary process than is perhaps clearly apparent in the chapters of the book. While this may prove a complex step too far for some—which is always a danger to be faced in dealing with subjects of a truly radical or revolutionary nature—it is a risk that must be undertaken. And what is described here merely involves bigger perspectives than those already described, following exactly the same principles. It should be clearly understood that they are presented as subjects for objective consideration and discussion, not for unquestioning acceptance or rejection.

INTRODUCTION

In our present day and age we face a curious schism in public thinking. On the one hand there is an absolute fascination with the increasingly self-evident "occult" world behind the veil of Nature, itself possessing all sorts of supposedly "magical" capacities, which all too readily draw the unwary. On the other, there is media-induced thought that only scientists really understand the "unknown" and what scientists don't know is not worth knowing. However, orthodox science does not believe in the occult, and thus very few scientists have made any seriously objective study of the subject; nor have most journalists, many of whom nevertheless like to write pontifically and disparagingly about it. This is something that I have rather regretfully confirmed time and again, at first hand, over more than three decades. Despite the interest that has translated itself into the superficial field of literary, TV, and film-based science fiction, there is a great deal more yet to be said about the real subject of occult science* and its philosophy by way of actually quite rational explanation. It is, after all, available to all willing to make the necessary effort involved in studying and understanding it on its own terms.

There are fundamentally two approaches to the subject of the psycho-spiritual world. The first—that of the mystic—is wholly concerned with the pure intensity of associated inner experience and its repetition if at all possible. For the mystic that itself is quite sufficient, with the expectation of anything more being regarded almost as an intellectual impertinence. The second is that of the esotericist-occultist, the dissatisfied mystic who

---

Occult science is the study of "the concealed or secret knowledge of Nature's energies and forces and how they can be controlled and manipulated."

Fig. I.1. Magus looking beyond the objective universe

has gone a major step further in questioning "Why?" "How?" and "In what context?" (see fig. I.1) so that a completely fresh world of subjective meaning comes into quite natural perspective behind and supporting any such experience, no matter how high or apparently beyond description.

Thus what is to the mere mystic a moment of sublime unity with the Absolute is revealed in fact to be no more than a purely partial perception of something far greater. With persistence and careful discrimination, that "something" will gradually re-present itself in far better and greater detail, en route to an even more amazing and more enlightening range of perceptions. And so on. In other words, the true esotericist sees and recognizes the "inner world" as a progressive theophany (subjectively visual perception of divine organization) of far greater extent and reality than the objectively visible world. There, gnosis involves the consciousness of the seeker becoming at-one with the essence of the object of his or her search. With this very attainment—even in its early stages—comes the realization why sacred metaphor and allegory plus paradox are necessary (even essential) in the outer world to describe what is, in the spiritual world, completely indescribable in a purely objective sense because of its qualitative nature and unimaginable magnitude.

This book is aimed at those willing to make that extra effort, their number in the world being far greater than commonly imagined. With that in mind, it is presented as a merely partial explanation or range of suggestions as to the dynamic rationale behind the whole historical range of mystical and psychological experiences (for there are many) of seers over the ages. This is in the hope that occult science and its partner, esoteric philosophy,* will come to be more openly acknowledged and seen by those with open and questioning minds as providing a thoroughly and logically reasonable field of causal knowledge, worthy of our deepest attention and study.

In some respects it is perhaps unsurprising that both occult science and esoteric philosophy have been vilified over the centuries. Originally, for thousands of years, they had been contained by a wall of protective silence and of misleadingly paradoxical sacred metaphor and allegory. These were generated within and surrounding the Mystery Schools of ancient times, the latter being found all over the world, not just in the Middle East and Europe. However, following the preliminary modernizing efforts of Gautama Buddha and Pythagoras (both apparently born around the late seventh or early sixth century BCE), and subsequently Plato (428–347 BCE), a wholesale destruction of Middle Eastern social and religious culture was wrought by Alexander the Great (356–323 BCE) in the fourth century BCE. That then unwittingly led, following his death, to the open internationalization of scholarly thought and discussion. To begin with, sacred knowledge began to leak out in the form of *gnostic* (that is, theophanically and metaphysically structured) thought, through the widely varied agency of increasingly independent initiates, mystics, and quasi magi, now largely freed of the sometimes lethal summary justice so often meted out to independently minded initiates by the Mystery Schools themselves.

Eventually, however, in the eclectic intellectual crucible of Greco-Egyptian Alexandria, these scholars, magi, and other savants in the associated schools of esotericism and occultism began to come together (not by mere chance, however) from all over the then known world, in a meeting of minds, to learn more about each others' areas of knowledge. Following that, the hitherto unified, ancient system of philosophical and metaphysical knowledge became

---

Esoteric philosophy is devoted to the study of "that which is *spiritually* obscure for intentional reasons related to protecting its sacred nature."

(superficially at least) increasingly fragmented and distorted. This took place partly due to simple, literalistic misinterpretation of sacred metaphor and allegory in other traditions and partly through cultural repression based on spiritual ignorance. The latter occurred largely because of the political intervention of the Roman Empire on behalf of the Christian Church (and later by politically emergent, doctrinaire Islam). That in turn led to the general suppression or corrupted absorption of gnostic thought in general, but of neo-Pythagorean and neo-Platonic concepts in particular, as we shall see later in this book.

That same fragmentation continued for a thousand years because of the unenlightened pursuit of a paradoxically mystic-dogmatic Christian theology following an Aristotelian process of reductive (hence naturally divisive) academic thought. This continued until there occurred an apparently sudden major restoration of interest in the subject of occultism, as a natural science of spiritual origin, in the Renaissance. That took place because of the dramatic reappearance in 1460 CE, at the court of Cosimo de Medici (1389–1464) in Florence, of ancient Hermetic texts, which explained in some detail the relationship between esoteric reason, occult science, and the emergent "natural philosophy" being pursued by humanists.[1] These texts, once translated and published (in 1463), transfigured the already humanistically influenced intellectual culture of the time. That led progressively (but again, not by chance) on to what we now call the Christian "Reformation" and then "the Enlightenment" of Western thought during the seventeenth and eighteenth centuries. This was then schismatically followed by a just as dramatic descent into the materialism of the Industrial Revolution in the mid-to-late eighteenth and the nineteenth centuries.

Following a relatively brief interlude involving a mixture of fascination with mesmerism, spiritualism, and "romantic philosophy," the underlying spiritual nature of this schism was then highlighted, during the latter part of the nineteenth century, with the dramatic appearance of modern Theosophy. This was introduced first of all by H. P. Blavatsky (1831–1891) and then followed up some three decades later, in direct continuation of her pioneering work, by A. A. Bailey (1890–1949) during the first half of the twentieth century. It is their work above all (or rather, one might suggest, that of the Adept teachers behind them) that actually gave rise to the so-called mod-

H. P. Blavatsky
(1831–1891)

A. A. Bailey
(1880–1949)

Fig. I.2. H. P. Blavatsky and A. A. Bailey

ern "New Age" movement. It also enables us today to make some coherent sense of the ancient mystic-cum-metaphysical traditions with which the early theosophers and neo-gnostics of the Renaissance and the subsequent four centuries struggled so hard to come to terms.[2]

We shall look at aspects of this fascinating historical background in further detail in chapters 6 to 7, where we shall concern ourselves quite generally with the historical development of Western esotericism, as a prelude to the appearance of modern "rational" science in the eighteenth century. However, we should keep in mind that the nature of modern scientific thought itself has, without actually being aware of the fact, already wandered into the continuum of occult science, in the fields of psychology and quantum physics particularly. As a result, it now finds itself face to face with the greatest conundrum of all—that of squaring orthodox scientific thought with how to rationalize consciousness. The latter is now very widely recognized as the next great "frontier" to be crossed in the field of scientific research. However, the present method of approach is little less than chaotic because of being based upon a complete lack of familiarity with and understanding of those basic metaphysical principles known to the intelligently open-minded and trustworthy few since ancient times.

By virtue of working analytically from the universal to the particular, ancient philosophical and metaphysical thought were Platonically deductive from first principles in both nature and practice. However, modern science—taking its cue from the religious theological environment (both Christian and Islamic) in which it had its roots—works in exactly the opposite way. Its technique is largely that of deriving concepts from reductive empirical classifications of outward appearances or forms, following the method of Aristotle (384–322 BCE). He himself, curiously enough, was the teacher of the teenage Alexander the Great, later accompanying him on his great military conquest of Persia. It would seem that while Alexander laid waste to the objective structure of Middle Eastern civilization (already by then in near-terminal decline anyway), Aristotle did the same subjectively for the Western world psyche, albeit unknowingly. He had already been dead for several centuries by the time fragments of his writings were found and put together (not always accurately) by early Christian theologians looking for a supporting world of "rational mysticism" to offset that of the neo-Pythagoreans, neo-Platonists, and other gnostics of the time.

Fortunately, modern science was to some extent prevented in pre-Victorian times from becoming totally materialistic in its nature. This occurred first of all by the progressive insemination into the Western mind of Eastern philosophical thought during the seventeenth and eighteenth centuries, for example, by the literati of the East India Company; secondly by the later discovery of radioactivity and its progression into the world of atomic physics. Paradoxically, both of these widely differing influences showed quite conclusively that the "objective" world was actually based upon illusion.

Since then, it has become increasingly apparent to more intuitively observant scientists—notwithstanding the curiously inverted assumptions of neo-Darwinism—that the world of phenomenal causation has to be based upon a nonphysical reality specifically associated with (or actually derived from) consciousness itself. At the present stage, however, the associated linkages are still not readily apparent. That is for the simple reason that modern physics is not yet capable of dealing alone with what is, in essence, a field of metaphysical reality. That same principle applies also to the world of astrophysics but, again, in a manner that is not yet readily acknowledgeable in terms of current scientific paradigms. However, the latter are still evolving and we thus have plenty of time ahead of us.

As metaphysics has all sorts of religio-mystical connotations because of the absurdly literalistic way in which it was dealt with by Christian theologians during the Middle Ages and even later centuries, we now find that today's scientists are very wary of it. That is simply because they tend to classify everything historically associated with theology as mystical and antimodern science. They tend to forget—although academia on the humanities side is beginning to remind them—that modern science was itself originally derived from the "natural philosophy" of highly intelligent and careful observers of long past centuries. They themselves followed a "philosophy of esoteric enquiry" plus a regime of absolute intellectual integrity, itself based on the highest objectivity. The latter fact is clearly proved by studying the very nature of the intellectual dialectic and metaphysics of pre- and post-Socratic thought.

Notwithstanding this, there is clearly a need for a new type of metaphysics, to be set in a modern context, with current scientific associations wherever possible. This is so that it can again be used as the main technique of analyzing and understanding the (as yet largely invisible) background world of psychospiritual causation. It is also with that firmly in mind that this book has been written, in the hope that some apparently ancient ideas can be shown, through graphic illustration, to have a directly modern (in fact, timeless) application.

The main basis of the modern conflict between humanists and religionists is that the latter believe in a supreme Creator-God whereas the former do not—hence the divergent attitudes to the subject of evolution. What this book concerns itself with, however, is the proposition that both are only partially correct in their beliefs, because neither actually understands the subtle background rationale that is common to both. That rationale is based on the metaphysics of the idea that our universe and everything within it lies within the consciousness of a structured spectrum of Intelligence, a celestial organism itself beyond all human conception, hence impossible to identify as "God" per se. This same structure, however, gives rise to what ancient Hermetic philosophy saw as the "as above, so below" principle. That in turn refers to the principle of universal sympathetic association, inevitably generated by the repetitively organized relationship of Macrocosm to microcosm, which lies behind the much-misunderstood idea that "man is made in the image of God." It also refers to the fact of real causality existing beyond and preceding the physical state, as suggested by what the Hindu calls the Law of Karma and known in the West for centuries past by other names.

It is interesting to speculate in passing upon the possibility that the word "God" was itself derived from the kabbalistic term *Hod* (pronounced "khod") meaning "the (Universal) Mind principle." As mind was what clearly raised humans above the animals and as the human was gnostically regarded as the microcosm to the divine Macrocosm, this would make clear sense. However, in the same sort of way, it is metaphysics that just as clearly gives rise (and historically gave rise) to the modern sciences of physics, biophysics, and even astrophysics. We shall explore this in greater detail in the earlier chapters of the book, where we shall examine (in simple terms and purely in passing) some general aspects of modern physics in relation to aspects of consciousness, including the true nature of the Mind principle as the creative projection of a consciousness.

The metaphysics of the occult world, however, is itself derived from the workings of abstract thought and reason, an abstruse field of apparent uncertainty that tends to scare many people because they see themselves as wholly unfamiliar with it. In fact, this is actually not so. Modern higher education frequently involves the teaching of the same systematically reasoned logic in which occult metaphysics "clothes" itself. Nevertheless, the actual world of spiritual causation lies beyond even this state of abstract logic in the field of what we misleadingly like to call "intuition," it having been confirmed that all the world's great scientific discoveries have been made by scientists in moments of sudden, often supposedly irrational yet causally intuitive illumination. The "rational" basis of such insights has then only subsequently been put together. The whole process seems then to involve a progressive accessing of a latent field of already preexistent thought or knowledge—what C. G. Jung called "the collective unconscious"—which lies permanently beyond the purely objective human thinking state. However, while this same field of higher perception has for centu-

Fig. I.3. C. G. Jung

ries seemingly been accessed merely by mystics—who have thus been able to give only their necessarily nebulous perceptions of it to the world—it now becomes increasingly possible for the rational intelligence to do the same through increasing familiarity with use of the higher (abstract) mind. Thus any new and practically useful insights achieved will have to be of a correspondingly rational nature.

What this book also hopes to do (at least in part) is show what this "intuitive" field of thought actually consists of and how and why the techniques of esoteric (or gnostic) philosophy and occult metaphysics provide access to it. It will then be seen that the process of what has for millennia been called "occult initiation" involves (is in fact) a quite natural but nevertheless systematic progression in the evolutionary development of pure (that is, spiritual) intelligence, which only secondarily uses the brain. That evolutionary progression is, nevertheless, determined by intermediate (and again quite natural) experiential "tests" that the intelligence has been able not only to absorb but also to safely and wisely employ to contain and utilize the information already provided, before any further and yet more subtle information is made progressively available. That in turn infers the existence of both highly knowledgeable Adept teachers and a "perennial spiritual philosophy," a tradition that has existed unchanged in its essential nature and trusteeship since well before the very dawn of known historical time. As one such Adept teacher has commented:

> Initiation is in truth the name given to the revelation or new vision which ever draws the disciple onward into greater light; it is not something conferred upon or given to him. It is a process of light recognition and of light utilisation in order to enter into ever clearer light.[3]

The close connection between knowledge and light has been openly acknowledged by human beings since ancient times. To some extent, this perception has become distorted by the misperception of modern science that there is but one form of light—that experienced on our planet as part of the electromagnetic spectrum. Yet it has been shown again and again by psychic sensitives to extend much further, well beyond the range of our best technology and with an associated spectrum of vital, complementary colors. However, the ancient view that the substance of the universe is qualitatively based in both nature and organization is as yet a puzzle to modern science. The further suggestion that such knowledge and its intelligently rational usage were actually known to highly advanced human beings at a time when modern history still views humanity as mere "hunter-gatherers" who had not even invented the wheel, seems incredible. But that is only so from the self-limited viewpoint of modern science's own paradigmatic assumptions, as we shall also see.

The overriding concern of this work is to demonstrate and explain why the principles of esoteric and occult philosophy, as described in relation to the process of spiritual initiation, are in fact a completely normal part of human evolutionary experience. The features of psychological safety and altruistic orientation found throughout the process will then be seen as central to the way in which they operate (and have always operated) for the greater good, not just of humanity, but also of Nature at large. This might sound a rather grandiose proposition but it is hoped that its truth and rationale will become self-evident as the book progresses. However, as many of the descriptions in the book—although extensively referenced—are not immediately capable of proof, the work is presented merely as a working hypothesis, a referenced paradigm if you will. It is thus hoped that the systematic logic followed will suffice to show all "unbelievers" that, underlying Nature's processes, there perhaps exists a definite and intelligently causal rationality, which is itself the basis of Universal Order in the kosmos. To all others, it is hoped that it will offer a sequence of provisional explanation, which may encourage them further in their own personal researches toward spiritual self-development, while also showing to their fellow humans a greater tolerance of their views, as well as of their apparent psychological shortcomings and failures. If that were to take place, even in small degree, our world would be a changed place indeed.

One of the primary constituents of the paradigm described in this book is the ancient idea that evolution on our planet (as also in the universe generally) is guided by intelligent beings who have long since evolved beyond the human stage of existence. It is accompanied by the correspondingly ancient idea that their organization is hierarchically structured in nature. This, together with the concept that our universe itself exists within the dynamically structured consciousness of a Being beyond all conceptualization, forms the very basis of the idea of our inhabiting an intelligently ordered kosmos. Consequently, we shall return to it frequently throughout the book.

Creationism (and much orthodox religion) interprets this in a very limited way as indicating the idea of an altogether abstract single "God" (plus an equally unsupportable "Devil"). However, the now scientifically registered fact of the universe functioning according to consistently self-repeating patterns of order confirms that there has to be a general and mutually reciprocal principle of intelligence (but not a God) extending throughout Universal Nature. This also, quite naturally, incorporates and involves a vast spectrum of semi-intelligent (elemental) life extending from the infinitesimal atomic particle and the unseen biological germ right up to the animal nature, which has yet to reach the human state. But it extends in a yet greater spectrum of intelligence far beyond the human, as we shall also see.

As our concerns in this work are focused on the psycho-spiritual evolutionary causal process rather than the merely Darwinian one of side effects, we need to understand the "mechanics and dynamics" of that spectrum of intelligence in terms of process. Accordingly, the first part of the book deals with the structures and sequences inherent in consciousness itself—as seen from the viewpoint of esoteric philosophy. This is essential reading because it explains the rationale of the hermeneutic process, which involves progressive but apparently separate states of being and consciousness. For some people this subject often proves initially difficult because of their relative unfamiliarity with the imagery of abstract thought. However, patient persistence with its wholly sequential logic will generate its own reward and insights.

There is one further issue that needs to be raised at the outset, before we get down to any sort of detail. It is the suggestion made by some modern commentators that the very ideas of initiation and hierarchy are purely elitist. This is fundamentally wrong and based upon a highly misplaced sense of what we like to call "democracy," which Plato rather interestingly placed but one step above anarchy. However, why that is so needs to be explained, as follows. Although it is true that many exponents of esoteric and occult philosophy create initiatory cults that instinctively seem to generate or require hierarchical forms of internal structure, which set them aside from the external masses, that is because all human social, political, and economic groups instinctively do the same thing, but for different reasons. It is the core of the organizational function, arising out of the common recognition that effective management requires delegation and different levels of process and function. However, any sense of elitism that arises out of such organization derives merely from ignorant self-centeredness.

In fact, the apparent separativeness of esoteric and occult groups derives fundamentally from an awareness that they are dealing with a highly specialized area of human experience involving very real powers of an intelligent or semi-intelligent nature. These the uninterested and untutored masses fear, on account of their own ignorance as to their real nature. It is because of this fear that they thus historically react to any of its associations with uncontrolled destructiveness. There is also no doubt that many such groups, although perhaps starting out with the best intentions, tend to fall into the trap of self-induced, psychically based glamour. Instead of adopting an objective, quasi-scientific position, they imagine (through supposed revelation) that they understand more than they actually do. Some then make the further mistake of looking down on others whom they believe to be less advanced than themselves.

The true esotericist or occultist, on the other hand, recognizes (and ever holds firmly at the front of his or her perceptions) that all fields of consciousness are essentially transitory (hence illusory) and that all form permanent traps for the even momentarily unwary or ideologically inflexible. This goes along with the realization that the moment any of us believe that we have achieved a full and complete understanding of something (in fact anything of an objective nature in particular), we have "lost the plot." An inner form of humility and modesty is thus crucial to an awakened subjective nature and this necessarily involves a recognition that every "spark" of the Universal Life is actually on the very same evolutionary Path. Any even faint sense of elitism would instantaneously destroy the higher powers of reason and inner perceptual faculty. It is thus wholly unacceptable.

It could perhaps be inferred, from one viewpoint, that the central orientation of this book might be regarded as theosophical in nature. However, the word *theosophy*—first used by the sage Ammonius Saccas in ancient Alexandria—means a structured, gnostic philosophy of psycho-spiritual existence; hence the worldwide theosophical *movement* and not just any particular theosophical institution. So what is said here has to be seen in a much wider context. Indeed, many of the references used to illustrate or support the points made or suggested are derived from very varied and widespread other sources of a gnostic, religious, or philosophical nature over the last three or four millennia, as well as from modern scientific ones.

The literary works of H. P. Blavatsky and A. A. Bailey, however, are so well presented (and so well known) in terms of a modern systematic logic (Blavatsky's in particular having a frequently scientific or quasi-scientific background of historical reference) that—despite their occasional complexity—they are perhaps among the most immediately effective for much cross-reference here, in a foundational sense. They are thus extensively, but by no means exclusively, used in this book. However, in relation to all the quotations from or references to passages in the Bailey works, I have made it clear that it is her Tibetan Adept mentor who is making the statement. That is because she herself confirmed that, unlike Blavatsky (having had no correspondingly deep and prolonged occult training in this lifetime), she was only acting as his stenographer.* Readers must, however, decide for themselves whether the various references used—supported as widely as possible by other given authors—are adequate enough to prove their overall case, where felt necessary.

---

*In the case of Blavatsky herself, although there is no doubt that her own mind was being impressed by one or more senior Adepts during the writing of *The Secret Doctrine,* it is not at all clear which of them was actually involved, or when, although it is clearly inferred that it was the two who subsequently became known publicly as the Mahatmas Morya and Kuthumi (pronounced Koot Hoomi). It seems, however, that the Tibetan Adept Djwahl Khul (otherwise known as "DK") was at least partially involved in helping her as well—something that the most ardent of Blavatsky disciples are apt to reject outright. However, the corresponding quality of the written material speaks for itself. DK (himself well known to Blavatsky and then on the point of achieving Masterhood) was the Master Kuthumi's closest disciple, his name or a version of it being mentioned several dozen times in *The Mahatma Letters to A. P. Sinnett.*[4] So as the original idea behind the direct explanatory correspondence with Sinnett itself seemingly came from the Mahatma Kuthumi, there is at least a strong probability that DK was also involved in the authorship through assisting Kuthumi as a literary go-between.

I should perhaps add here that this book takes direct issue with those authors like K. P. Johnson, who seem to start out with the prejudice that the very concept of the "Adept Hierarchy" or "Brotherhood of Masters" is based on mere storytelling artifice or mystic wishful thinking. It does so, however, by explaining the rationale of both spiritual existence (as opposed to objective existence) and of the powers of those capable of achieving access to such subtle states at will. Once these are properly recognized in due context, there will never again be the need for any associated cynicism. However, it is hoped that the same context described here will also help to rid us of the foolish guru-worship that attracts the naive many and simultaneously puts so many others off further consideration of the whole subject.

In concluding, I should perhaps suggest a particular approach on the part of the reader to the (sometimes apparently complex) nature of what is being suggested in this book. This is irrespective of reference to the accompanying pictorial graphics, which I hope will prove to be helpful where mere words fail. The reason for apparent difficulties in the interpretation of terminology is that a few areas of what is being described are necessarily of a highly subjective, abstract, or metaphysical nature. Their consideration sometimes requires quite intense and sustained concentration from an almost meditative angle. My suggestion is, therefore, that the reader should read through each chapter at a completely normal speed, without worrying or being deflected in the slightest degree by any specific points not fully understood en route. Their own subconscious mind will quite naturally pick these up and begin putting them into an order and context, which will make later understanding more possible. It follows that a second reading will then be necessary, at rather slower speed, in order to take full advantage of the way in which one's own subjective intelligence works. Under no circumstances should readers allow themselves to become frustrated by an initial failure to grasp in full what is being discussed or described in any particular area.

That leads me to make one final point, regarding education in general but with particular emphasis in relation to study of the fields of esoteric philosophy and occult science. It is this: the real purpose of any such teaching is to introduce the individual to an ever-widening yet ever-subtler perspective of inner vision, this through demonstrating the underlying working interrelationship—hence true significance—between all things. As a result of this, the individual arrives at a direct perception of the fact that what was originally thought of as complexity was actually a result of wrongful association through limited perspective. Realization of the greater perspective thus always results in recognition of an essential and beautifully coordinated simplicity—what the scientist calls "elegance." However, if we strive to oversimplify concepts at the outset, we actually render this process far more difficult (and far more frustrating) for the individual to understand. It is therefore essential, through patience, to learn and understand the structural A-B-C and basic numerological significance of things (plus associated terminology) before we attempt to progress further. This is something that these days—in the West in particular—is far too often forgotten; and in relation to esoteric philosophy and occult science, it is fatal as far as any real depth or breadth of understanding is concerned.

Time is also essential to allow the natural process of progressive assimilation of any structural concept. This is more especially so in the case of a concept possessing a dynamic or abstract metaphysical function as well. What is being discussed in this book concerns itself with the very nature of what our subjective range of experience is all about in both a microcosmic and a Macrocosmic sense. So until we come to grips with a commonly acknowledged technique of bridging and thus interconnecting these, we shall learn nothing. With that in mind, the first five chapters primarily concern themselves with explaining consciousness itself, from both a human and a suprahuman viewpoint, before we go anywhere near the actual subject of spiritual initiation and associated spiritual evolution.

The reader therefore should be aware from the outset that we shall be working from certain fundamental propositions, the rational basis of which should become increasingly self-evident as we progress, namely:

1. That the energy of Universal Life itself is the only reality in the omniverse; therefore, there is no such thing as "dead" matter.
2. That sentience and intelligence are the naturally accompanying aspects of the Universal Life, thereby generating Universal Consciousness and Intelligent Adaptability in which we all participate, whether knowingly or not.
3. That these three accompanying realities give rise to a universal and

intelligently organized spectrum of states and fields of being, which can be progressively accessed through the intelligent use of esoteric knowledge.

4. That the true human intelligence exists in a contemplative orientation at all times within what we call the spiritual state and that our objective human consciousness is therefore only a partial projection of this.

With the third and fourth of these propositions particularly in mind, the reader is invited to consider fig. I.4 along with fig. 1.2. The latter seeks to depict the progressive spiritual development of the human being within the

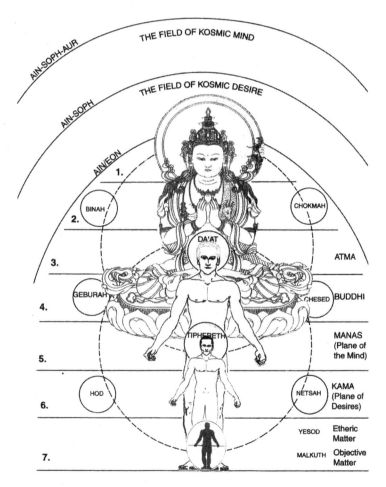

Fig. I.4. Evolving human intelligence

coherent structural arrangement of the states and substates of consciousness comprising the octave of Being contained within our particular solar scheme. It is this same dynamic structure of kosmic Being to which we shall make constant reference throughout the book, thus hopefully enabling the reader to identify the "geography" of the vast field of kosmic consciousness within which all lives in this solar system are functioning at all times.

In fig. I.4, which deals with the personal spiritual development of the individual, the contemplative Buddha figure represents the true nature and latent potential of the human being within the overall planetary scheme, while the small dark figure at the bottom represents the merely objective human organism. The figure with the Tiphereth halo represents a person with fully developed triple personality and psychological faculties while the figure with the Da'at halo represents the evolved Master Adept. It is hoped that this picture will serve as a useful foundation to the whole of what will be discussed in this book.

PART ONE

Consciousness
and the
Evolutionary Instinct

ONE

ON SPIRIT, SOUL, AND CONSCIOUSNESS IN GENERAL

As already suggested in the introduction, our concern in this book is to consider the issue of spiritual initiation as one directly related to the question of evolution. However, unlike in Darwinism, our focus is specifically on consciousness. This is on the grounds that it is adaptable consciousness that gives rise to forms throughout Nature, not forms to consciousness. Having said as much, however, we need to explain why and how that should be so before we go any further, so that the reader is clear on the issue from the outset. We can then go into further detail concerning initiation itself, on the basis of established parameters.

Perhaps the first thing that we ought to deal with is the ancient idea that the omniverse (Space) exists within the oceanic (but nevertheless sevenfold) field of consciousness of an Intelligence of which the human mind can have no faint conception, but which many still misconceive of as "God." This is the logical basis of the paradox—already recognized by the more far-seeing modern scientists of our time in various fields—that the omniverse and its major and minor forms are all derived from Chaos but are nevertheless coherently maintained by consistent, patterned Order.

The ancient Egyptians recognized the principle of consistent Order, ascribing it to the wisdom of the metaphorical goddess Ma'at (see fig. 1.1). Ma'at is a slight variation on the Sanskrit *Mahat*, itself signifying the Kosmic (or Universal) Mind and memory, symbolized in Egypt by her husband-god Tehuti. However, as such consistency can only be the product of intelligence (and not a product of mere chance, as Darwinian extremists would have it), it follows that Universal Nature itself must possess a vast spectrum of intelligence, perhaps involving what Jung called the "collective unconscious."[1] From this viewpoint, what we call "evolution" takes on a much greater sequential perspective than provided by mere Darwinism, which deals only with objective local effects.

Fig. 1.1. The Egyptian goddess Ma'at

What we call "initiation" itself follows suit. It implies a progressive sequence of subjective development, specifically concerned with consciousness, of which Mind is but a projection. Hence we may suggest that "inner reality" has a definitely structured or hermeneutic nature, which relates the human microcosm to the macrocosmic Logos or celestial Intelligence within whose manifest Being all solar and planetary Nature is contained. This correlation is as depicted in fig. 1.2, which endeavors graphically to

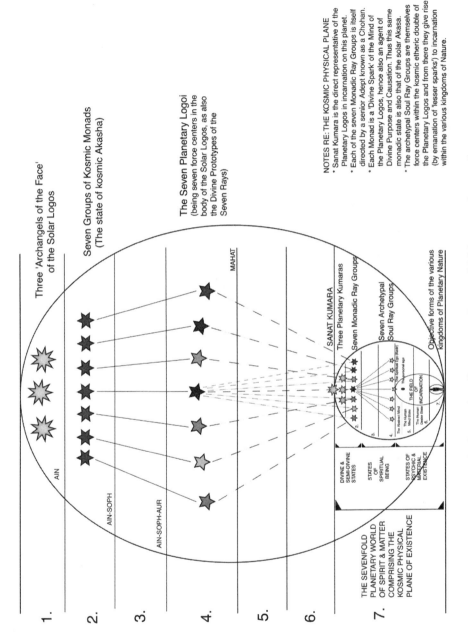

Fig. 1.2. The hierarchically organized, sevenfold kosmic scheme of Creation

1. Three 'Archangels of the Face' of the Solar Logos

2. Seven Groups of Kosmic Monads (The state of kosmic Akasha)

4. The Seven Planetary Logoi (being seven force centers in the body of the Solar Logos, as also the Divine Prototypes of the Seven Rays)

AIN

AIN-SOPH

AIN-SOPH-AUR

MAHAT

SANAT KUMARA
Three Planetary Kumaras
Seven Monadic Ray Groups

Seven Archetypal Soul Ray Groups

THE FIELD OF INCARNATION
The Spiritual Ego (Soul)
The Abstract Mind
The Human Mind State
The Human Gross State

Objective forms of the various Kingdoms of Planetary Nature

DIVINE & SEMI-DIVINE STATES

STATES OF SPIRITUAL BEING

STATES OF PSYCHIC & MATERIAL EXISTENCE

7. THE SEVENFOLD PLANETARY WORLD OF SPIRIT & MATTER COMPRISING THE KOSMIC PHYSICAL PLANE OF EXISTENCE

NOTES RE: THE KOSMIC PHYSICAL PLANE

* Sanat Kumara is the direct representative of the Planetary Logos in incarnation on this planet.
* Each of the seven Monadic Ray Groups is itself directed by a senior Adept known as a Chohan.
* Each Monad is a 'Divine Spark' of the Mind of the Planetary Logos, hence also an agent of Divine Purpose and Causation. Thus this same monadic state is also that of the solar Akasa.
* The archetypal Soul Ray Groups are themselves force centers within the kosmic etheric double of the Planetary Logos and from there they give rise (by emanation of 'lesser sparks') to incarnation within the various kingdoms of Nature.

illustrate the concentric nature of consciousness as a dynamic sequence of states, as well as mentioning some of the entities contained within or controlling each greater and lesser field/state of existence. We will deal with the latter in greater detail a little later on when we will refer back to this same illustration.

Now, before we start to discuss initiation itself in any detail, we need first to consider those background structures and potentials of consciousness as universal principles, and how they are developed from a fundamental state of generalized awareness in Nature. It is as yet impossible to do this from a purely scientific viewpoint, simply because our modern Western science does not begin to understand what awareness and consciousness actually are or even might be, other than in terms of effects caused by a possibly symbiotic collision of neurons. Thus mainstream biophysics and biochemistry are as yet unprepared to face the idea and practical effect of consciousness as the intelligently organized awareness inherent in matter. However, functional awareness is an attribute of all organisms, as well as being qualitatively organized and entirely subjective in its causal origins.

NEW AGE AND SCIENTIFIC CONCEPTS OF SUBTLE STRUCTURES

A consideration of some of the modern approaches to the structure of consciousness may help to provide a helpful context for our exploration. The New Age approach to the subtle worlds of existence behind objective reality is quite varied. This is despite a number of commonly accepted principles such as that Earth life is intended as a "school" for the learning of higher values and perceptions through rejection of materialistic values and paradigms; also that humanity has to learn to live in harmony with Nature rather than merely trying to exploit her, so as to produce the idealized world on which modern "holism" is based. Parallel to this, many neopagan and shamanic views appear curiously materialistic because they see everything in Nature as sacredly derived from the "World's Mother." But in so doing they seem largely confused as to the distinction between the higher, spiritual world scheme and the merely psychic nature of the objective one. They also reject the objective or scientific approach in favor of learning what they see as a mystically instinctive perception of Nature's subtly adaptive capacities. This, however, is fundamentally regressive. It is vastly different from the concept of developing a truly spiritual intuition in which the perception of other, far higher states of being becomes accessible to an expansively evolving human consciousness.

In direct contrast, we have the neo-gnostic "escapist" view, which has been derived from many and varied misconceptions of Alexandrian "New Age" thought two thousand years ago; it sees the objective world as the disastrous result of mistakes made in the spiritual world by highly intelligent Beings "who should have known better." However, we will not go into this here as it is dealt with in far greater detail in the later chapters of the book. Nevertheless, it is fascinating to contrast it with the modern Sethian approach in relation to which Wouter Hanegraaff (professor of Western Esotericism at the University of Amsterdam) curiously describes Jane Roberts (its founder) as "the Muhammad of New Age religion and Seth as its angel Gabriel."[2] The Sethian approach basically takes the view that the Eastern focus on the Absolute and the eventual nirvana of absorption into it is a complete waste of time. Hence one should instead be directing oneself to learn all about the spiritual creative principle so that one can become a co-creator with God and thus have a much more interesting eternity to face. However, this is based on a clear misconception of Eastern thought, which we shall also explain in greater detail later on.

Many of the ideas within modern science that are concerned with arriving at a unified understanding of consciousness and the universe are related with what is often called the "holographic paradigm." Perhaps the best known of those ideas based on holographic structures are those of neuroscientist Karl Pribram (whose concern, however, is merely the brain function) and the theoretical physicist David Bohm. The central idea with these two, however, is that "the form and structure of the original object are enfolded within each region of the photographic [or visual] record and can in turn be unfolded from each region." Hence Bohm's suggestion that here lies a causal, "implicate order," quite distinct from the merely mechanistic order that orthodox science presupposes.[3] There are, nevertheless, various presuppositions associated with this general concept that are in fact based on a merely more subtle but psychic background activity, which is not truly spiritual at all.

Another popular modern concept is that formulated by Ilya Prigogine, who—in a manner interestingly parallel to that of the Sethians—takes the view that the "ever becoming" nature and character of the universe is far more important than the issue of its underlying "being." He is thus highly critical of the concept of eternal laws suggesting a fundamental cosmic harmony.[4] But this approach in turn falls prey to the objective world view that Plato referred to as the "ever changing" or "different"—hence unreal, because it is ever-generating new prototypes and their offshoots—instead of trying to understand the world of spiritual archetypes that provides the truly causal reality behind everything that exists in objective and even subtle Nature.

SPIRITUALITY AND EVOLUTION

This is an area where few seem to want to tread because of associated uncertainties. The work of two modern researchers in this general field provides us with a clear indication as to where and why modern science itself has gone astray. First of all, the biologist Dr. Richard Dawkins—known worldwide for his much televised scientific materialism, atheism, and public evangelism on behalf of neo-Darwinism—has nailed his colors to the mast on the basis of a mere assumption. That completely unfounded and poorly researched assumption involves the idea that the views of Creationists and Darwinists are the only alternatives available to consider the problem of human biological causation and subsequent development; hence that there is no such thing as a spiritual state of existence. He consequently sees the (equally prejudiced) Creationist approach as baseless and founded on mere superstition. That his atheistic view is itself based on myopic prejudice and lack of awareness of other available and quite well known perspectives should become very apparent well before the end of this book. To some extent, however, I have already dealt with some of the related issues in my previous book, *The Rise and Fall of Atlantis.**

The second person to base his whole theory on a basically flawed assumption is the also internationally known and really remarkable "mindsmith" Ken Wilber. His area of research lies not in biogenetics but in the

---

*London: Watkins, 2008.

combined fields of physics, psychology, and parapsychology, where he has become particularly well known for his approach to "the integral theory of everything." This involves the attempt to relate everything of a subjective nature in human experience to everything of a physical nature by way of what we might see as a web of "intellectual artifacts." Just as Dawkins sees everything in his field from only two points of view, Wilber tends to do rather the same—but much more interestingly—from the angle of "constructive post-modernism." Even so, his criticism of the holographic paradigm and of the supposition that there are close connections between science and mysticism represents a lone view within the New Age movement.

However, despite his many valid psychological insights, Wilber's own viewpoint is itself surprisingly anthropocentric and restrictive. For him, despite the extraordinary extent of his own subjective experience in the fields of transpersonal psychology and mysticism (which latter he curiously and mistakenly associates not only with religion but also with metaphysics), there is essentially only the physical world and the spiritual world. These are then holistically connected by a relating mass and variety of what he calls "integrals," seemingly derived from his third factor—Mind. However, much of the latter, as described and explained by him in his immensely complex books, involves (to the esotericist) quite definitely no direct connection with the spiritual world at all. They too are rather associated with an intermediate, merely compound psychic state of existence, which science does not (yet) recognize and to which most New Age groups pay curiously little if any attention, because they do not choose to understand its distinctive nature either.

As regards the view of science itself, we hear in Wilber's own words that "modern physics neither proves nor disproves, neither supports nor refutes, a mystical-spiritual world view," this apparently being on the altogether illogical basis that "If today's physics supports mysticism, what happens when tomorrow's physics replaces it? Does mysticism then fall also?"[5] Curiously, he does not see this as a complete non sequitur, despite the fact that all such interpretations of perception, in whatever field of concern, are themselves based on constant and inevitable mutation.

Wilber's further suggestion that all of the greatest physicists of modern times—Einstein, Schrödinger, Heisenberg, Bohr, Eddington, Pauli, de Broglie, Jeans, and Planck—are "virtually unanimous in declaring that modern physics offers no positive support whatsoever for mysticism or transcendentalism of any variety (and yet they were all mystics of one sort or another . . ."[6] fails to acknowledge that for them actually to have done so in public would have led to an early end of their scientific careers. In fact, Pauli (like Jung) believed that psyche and matter were composed of the same substance.[7] Wilber also fails to mention that Eddington, for example, long before Koestler, had suggested that elemental particles could be intelligent matter. This was a view later pursued not only by physicist D. F. Lawden, who held that "the continuity of Nature entails that consciousness or intelligence be a universal property of matter," but also by astronomer V. A. Firsoff, who was of the opinion that "Intelligence is an entity or universal interaction of the same nature as electricity or gravity."[8] Other well known scientists like Einstein (see fig. 1.3) have expressed similar (actually highly occult) views. We might thus suggest that the outwardly apparent result (conditioned by

Fig. 1.3.
Albert Einstein

its environment) does not necessarily coincide with the truly causal hypothesis. Wilber also pays no attention to the fact of occult science, rather than mere mystical experience. These two will be defined in accompanying detail in the next section so that we can better understand where and why there is a common failure to understand real connections.

There is no intention here of criticizing Wilber specifically. However, he is undoubtedly one of the best and foremost examples of our times of someone who started out with the most beneficent combination of a first rate academic intellect in tandem with a mystic nature, who then rejected the former; then, despite (or perhaps because of) several forced mystic or other experiences brought about by his own asceticism or other personal experience, he has become progressively mired in his own subsequently attempted intellectualization of the objective and subjective worlds of human experience. His descriptions of the hermeneutic structures of consciousness—while acknowledging the existence of and necessity for progressive planes or states of being—lack any real metaphysical understanding of their essential natures or interactive dynamics. That is largely because—in his attempt to rationalize the duality of objectivity and subjectivity—he mistakenly tries to shoehorn ancient subjective perceptions into modern psychological and scientific concepts. However, he does so without the use of true metaphysics, the latter itself being a very far cry from the so-called metaphysics of medieval or even modern theologians. In short, he has attempted to "take Heaven by storm" in purely theoretical terms, by progressing the Path of spiritual initiation in an altogether unnatural, back-to-front manner. In addition, he completely fails to understand the practical difference between the esoteric and the occult—which we will now deal with in greater detail.

ESOTERIC PHILOSOPHY AND OCCULT SCIENCE

Like nearly all modern scientists, Wilber tends rather simplistically to follow the neo-Darwinian line by assuming that consciousness is merely a product of historical and biological experience. Esoteric philosophy on the other hand states quite unequivocally that consciousness precedes the development of its own objective organs of perception. For most scientists, this appears nonsensical. How can there be percipient faculty without an objective organ? The Cartesian answer to this would be to state that mind and matter are quite separate, thereby generating that attitude that distinguishes between quantum physics and classical physics. The former is seen as dealing only with the subatomic world, while the latter deals only with so-called "objective reality." However, quantum physics has itself shown us that the objectively visible world is in fact an illusion and this has in turn led to the development of a rather newer and more inclusive (but still incomplete) view of what consciousness itself might perhaps be all about.

This view, as expressed by the scientist Amit Goswami in his books *The Self-Aware Universe* and *The Visionary Window,* involves what is called "monistic idealism." It posits the concept that ideas and their associated consciousness are considered to be the basic elements of reality and that matter is secondary even though, paradoxically, consciousness is itself composed of matter.[9] Thus, whereas mainstream science of the last two hundred years or so has viewed mind and consciousness as epiphenomena of matter, monistic idealism takes the reverse view. According to monistic idealism, forms derived from matter are themselves the epiphenomena of consciousness. Hence Goswami quotes his fellow scientist Henry Stapp who interestingly suggests that the message of quantum nonlocality is that the fundamental process of Nature lies outside space-time but generates events that can be located in space-time,[10] although he does not add quite how this might be so.

Although this overall view appears to coincide with the way in which esoteric philosophy sees the process, it is only partially correct, because it fails to explain or suggest the real basis of both perceived and perceptual identity. Because of its scientific belief in the modern anthropic principle (the idea that the universe evolves toward life and sentience[11] or for the purpose of creating sentient beings[12]) it also fails to explain, or even to examine, the most fundamental axiom of esoteric and occult philosophy: *that there is not, nor ever could be, any such thing as dead matter in the first place.* This concept (that "dead" matter exists) is in fact a bizarre product of nineteenth and twentieth century reductionist thinking never wholly accepted, however, by the world's leading scientific minds. In practical terms, all existence contains and expresses (to a greater or lesser extent) the three basic universal principles of Being, Knowing, and Doing, or Livingness, Sensory Capacity, and Intelligent Adaptability.

This takes us back to the issue of the important distinction between esotericism and occultism (occult science to be more precise). *Esotericism* involves the study of the essential nature and interrelationships between all aspects or expressions of existence, whereas *occultism*—whether conscious or not—concerns itself with understanding the associated energies and forces of the omniverse and the manner of their natural implementation, hence with the law of cause and effect (referred to in Sanskrit as *karma*). It is for this reason that esoteric philosophy always works "from the universal to the particular," whereas the accrual of purely intellectual knowledge or personal experience works in precisely the opposite direction, thereby resulting in natural friction between the two. We shall return to this same subject frequently throughout the book.

SO WHAT EXACTLY IS MATTER?

What the ancient wisdom tradition has always stated and what modern science has confirmed for us is that energy and matter are but varying phases of the same essential phenomenon (hence $E = mc^2$). In practical terms, energy-matter is infinitely variable in expression while paradoxically being composed of nothingness; yet it is the source of all life and objectivity. How can this be so? Well, esoteric philosophy—as symbolically indicated by the Great Seal of Solomon (see fig. 1.4)—answers this by suggesting that energy and matter are but the two *objectively* complementary faces of the one Life or Universal Spirit that pervades the omniverse, there being nothing else in the whole field of existence. But esoteric philosophy goes a step further in suggesting that the variability of self-expression is due to the Spirit's essentially qualitative nature. However, as the spectrum of quality is itself infinite, so the forms of self-expression must inevitably, in parallel, involve a systematic degree of repetition, although themselves differing in quality.

The essence of what is being suggested here then is that this infinitely qualitative spectrum of being or existence necessitates all qualities existing side by side, yet with each somehow retaining an independence of state. Thus a being of a particularly refined state could pass through a much denser state or series of states without even being aware of them as such. In practical terms, because matter is essentially invisible, esotericism refers to

Fig. 1.4. The Great Seal/ Symbol of Solomon, from Eliphas Levi's The History of Magic

it as the "universal ether." Hence it is possible to have a *kosmic* or a *celestial* ether, a *systemic* ether (related to the life of our solar system), and a *planetary* ether. This trinity of existence is the compound that we shall adopt in this book. Hence also we shall find ourselves referring to *kosmic* beings, *solar* or *systemic* beings, and *planetary* beings, all of these being "spirits," considered either individually or, as we shall see shortly, as hierarchically organized groups forming a parallel spectrum of fields of consciousness.

SO WHAT IS CONSCIOUSNESS?

Some of today's more open-minded scientists may intend to explain consciousness (hence also matter) in terms of scientific quantum theory, but their approach in doing so usually fails to consider the rationale behind the spectrum of Universal Being, of which consciousness is itself merely one of two aspectual expressions. Consciousness involves sentience, but sentience itself involves a preceding foundation of being and generalized awareness. So it is the latter that logically needs to be considered first. In fact, the esotericist explains this by positing Universal Being—that is, Life itself—as the true, qualitatively organized foundation behind all existence. Hence the use of the ancient Hermetic axiom "as above, so below" to describe its repetitively complementary nature—in terms of underlying principles of expression.

The esotericist uses this axiom to describe how consciousness involves a subtle duality of percipience derived from the progressive limitation of Universal Awareness into a sequence of concentrically organized fields of limitation, as we saw earlier in fig. 1.2. That is to say, consciousness arises through progressive macrocosmic emanation. It does so through the Macrocosm projecting a partial, germinal aspect of itself (as Mind) into a lower field of existence in order to produce a form of phenomenal self-expression (such as a planet or a kingdom of Nature). That projected aspect involves a group (or groups) of lesser beings or entities (commonly referred to in esotericism as "sparks") whose task it is to generate that self-expression as accurately as possible before returning to their Source to report on the effectiveness of what they have achieved. Hence there inevitably occurs a simultaneously higher and lower consciousness arising out of this experience. This results from the intelligence of the emanated group eventually recognizing its own experiential field as one of subjective self-limitation. The same group then progressively realizes that this field can be breached by expansive movement back into the already existing and larger parent field of consciousness that was its own Source (involving a greater reality) in which another, far more advanced (and far more subtle) degree of intelligence already exists.

The "monistic idealism" of Goswami derives from the seemingly curious theoretical concept formed by quantum scientists that the collapse of the quantum wave to produce a visual actuality is based on the intervention of an embodied consciousness, hence that consciousness has no material basis.[13] However, esoteric and occult philosophy state quite categorically that Life itself is the basis of all matter and that—as there is nothing other than Life in the omniverse—everything, including both awareness and consciousness, has a homogeneously "material" basis in essence, albeit posing as an infinite spectrum of qualitatively different light in outward expression.

It is here then, in relating microcosm to Macrocosm, that we discover another distinction between esoteric philosophy and occult science. *Esoteric philosophy* deals not only with perception as to the widely varying interrelationships between subtle organisms and beings at every possible level of objective or subjective existence but also their causes. *Occult science,* however, deals very specifically not only with the characteristic nature of all the energies and forces in the universe—again whether objective or subjective—but also the techniques by which they work or can be controlled. The former, while not exactly theoretical, does not concern itself with quite the practical, "hands-on" involvement of the latter. This distinction is highly important and needs to be kept in mind, as does the fact that esotericism and occultism, if properly practiced, work hand in glove with each other as the expression of intelligent purpose. In reality, they cannot be approached from a merely academic or intellectual viewpoint, because the intellect only succeeds in cloaking and disguising them.

MIND, INTELLIGENCE, SPIRIT, AND SOUL

One of the most fundamental aphorisms for those "on the Path" (of spiritual evolution) is that "the mind is the great slayer of the Real"—hence the direction: "Let the disciple slay the slayer."[14] A second most important principle is that *intelligence* and *mind* are quite separate. True intelligence actually uses the mind (involving the emanation of a field of knowledge) by working "from above downward," not "from below upward." The range of modern human intelligence is considerable but the whole process of evolution is actually based upon persistently necessary self-sacrifice (by the higher nature) of that which is the very basis of past experience, when no longer of real use. However, many are those who mistakenly seem to believe that one can eat one's cake and still have it. They fail to recognize the fundamentally important occult difference between living "causal essence" and past "experiential effect." As a result, they personalize all experience rather than realizing that they are, in a very real sense, merely observers of a constantly changing spectrum of existence that ever surrounds them.

One other highly important issue that needs to be considered here—although it is not recognized by academics, scientists, or theologians (or journalists) in general—is that in considering esoteric and occult philosophy, the very first thing to be understood is the entirely rational distinction between *spirit* and *soul*. Without this recognition, there will be no real understanding of anything else.

First of all, in acknowledging the ancient metaphysical concept that there is but one Life and one Intelligence in the ocean of the omniverse (there being nothing else in existence), it behooves us to recognize that all substance and energy comprise, in essence, what we rather blandly call "spirit." That fluidic spirit, however, is made up of a qualitative infinity of huge and tiny monadic "sparks," or germs of living awareness, each with its own innate potential intelligence. It is these that periodically separate and recombine in a multitude of different ways to produce those temporarily differentiated states of being and consciousness that we call "souls," which in turn give rise to "planes" or "states" of matter, involving kosmic, solar, and planetary systems, plus all the various kingdoms of Nature within them.

Soul, on the other hand, consists of the coordination of a huge group of spirits coming together through a common sense of identity (or "selfhood") and thereby forming the periphery of a field of isolated existence that then acts as a space within which creation/incarnation can take place. This periphery is akin to the "brane" of the quantum physicist and the "event horizon" of the astrophysicist.

Each soul is itself but an expression of a hierarchically greater and more knowledgeable soul, which, in turn, is itself a cellular expression of something far greater still that nevertheless embodies the same principle. (Please refer again to fig. 1.2.) In other words, each soul entity is but a partial emanation or projection of a far greater and more powerful parent soul, an all-soul or "Oversoul" as the Greek philosopher Plotinus (204–270 CE) put it.[15] (See fig. 1.5.)

Thus the Oversoul of the Earth is itself a cell derived from the yet greater Oversoul of our solar system. The Oversoul of our solar system is in turn a cell derived from the vastly greater Oversoul that contains the stellar

Fig. 1.5. Plotinus

nebula within which our solar system exists, and so on. In each case, the soul in question is composed of groups of spirits of a particular quality and force, and it is their composite range of faculty and power that then characterizes them, together, as a greater or lesser form of individuality. Similarly, the human psycho-spiritual organism involves a parallel concentricity, as illustrated (but not to scale) in fig. 1.6, which depicts the three human soul bodies: terrestrial, causal, and spiritual.

The derivation and nature of the three human soul bodies is of

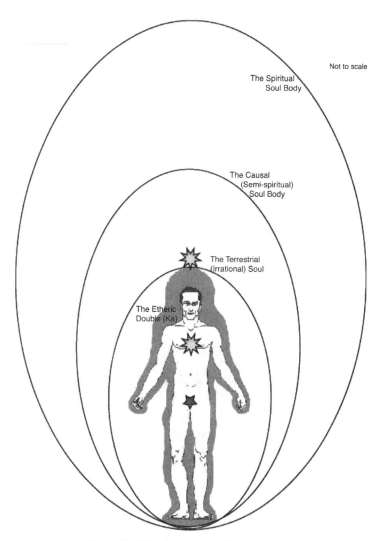

Fig. 1.6. The three souls of the human

fundamental importance to our esoteric considerations, and we shall deal with related issues in greater detail in chapter 2. For the moment, however, let us define the Spiritual Soul as the offspring of the Oversoul of our solar system, embodying its instinctively intelligent (hence rational) nature. The terrestrial or "astral" soul is correspondingly the offspring of our planetary Oversoul, embodying its natural instincts—those of the animal and plant kingdoms in particular—which is why it is also known as the "irrational" soul. The intermediate Causal Soul is, however, semi-spiritual and purely human in nature, hence human consciousness acting as a reasoning bridge between the other two. However, let us now spend a moment considering the issue of what the soul body sets out to contain and generate in terms of form, remembering that it follows the "as above, so below" principle. In other words, the greater gives rise to the lesser, not the other way around.

Each soul coming into a fresh cycle of (re)incarnation seeks to contain lesser matter of a particular quality, which it then conditions with its own nature and (temporarily) uses as its servant. For example, the terrestrial (or "astral") soul borrows such matter from the reservoir of substance maintained by the planet. This then becomes its physical elemental "shadow" or "double" (the Egyptian *ka*), which generates a corresponding organic body form out of itself. This "etheric double"* (see again fig. 1.6) thus becomes a sort of battery-transceiver (constantly recharged by the vital electrical tension of the soul), which maintains and sustains the coherence and functionality of the physical body. Like the soul organism, it too is composed of light, although not of so subtle a nature.

However, such is the symbiotic closeness of the relationship that develops between the terrestrial soul nature, the elemental "double," and the physical body form and its processes that they appear to be one. Consequently, once the terrestrial soul has managed to bring about this inward coordination (in early childhood), it then begins to pursue a parallel outward process of elemental coordination as well, thereby progressively developing what we regard as our subjective nature—comprising the emotions and the lower mind. This development leads to the sense of "self." Hence we may suggest that the extraverted projection of soul influence is itself the very basis of selfhood. Self is actually founded in the soul nature.

One often hears the suggestion that the soul resides "in the body." This

---

*The etheric double is the same as Rupert Sheldrake's "morphogenetic field."

is technically wrong, as it is the soul—held in place by the Mind principle, acting as a restraining sheath[16]—that contains the physical body form, which it generates within and from the massed matter of the etheric double, as we shall see in more detail later on.[17] It is again the soul that, via the chakra system,* emanates its own psycho-spiritual nature, thereby generating its "anchorage" in the etheric double. From the chakras are then produced those microcosmic organisms known to us as the organic cells that, in the form of flesh and blood, make up the different limbs and organs of the physical body.

However, the terrestrial soul has no capacity for entirely self-engendered function. For that, it relies upon the directing influence of the mind, which (emanated by the higher soul—that is, the Causal Soul) contains and controls it. The union of the mind sheath and the terrestrial soul generates an entity that has a direct parallel to what in modern quantum science is called an "event horizon." It is within this that all knowledge or information is found in a two-dimensional state that, upon emanation, gives rise to three-dimensional forms. Quantum theory, however, makes the error of suggesting (in its current paradigm) that, due to its highly magnetic nature, light or other matter never escapes from within this entity. It does indeed do so, for it ultimately (following the evolutionary process) becomes luminescent and then colorfully radiant, by virtue of liberation of its animating essence.

THE SOUL PRINCIPLE

An increasing number of scientists today are already toying with the idea that the animating consciousness of the human organism originates "outside the body." That has occurred purely because the observed physical processes more and more clearly confirm that consciousness cannot be a phenomenon with a purely physical cause. The question then arises, "What exactly is the outer organism that might contain or generate consciousness?" Fortunately, the (at least hypothetical) answer to this has actually been known for many past millennia. It is the soul entity that, as H. P. Blavatsky reminds us, expresses exactly the same principle in Nature as both the cell and the atom,

---

*Chakras are psychic force centers in the etheric body of an organism; in the human being there are seven main centers and a variety of lesser ones.

but on a substantively larger scale.[18] Hence it is—by virtue of the greater always giving rise to the lesser—that the soul (which is itself immortal)[19] is itself parent to the cell, which is in turn parent to the atom. Once again, as above, so below.

Modern science, as yet, has this particular principle back to front by virtue of its limited reductive perception and fascination with the concept that all objective forms are merely composed of atoms. The fact that it is still in total confusion as to whether the atom involves a wave or a particle, or both, merely confirms the problem. But let us now look at the same problem from a wholly different angle, to see if it can be better explained.

This same soul principle, it is suggested, involves an ethereal ovoid or spheroidal field of subtle light and of being, without gender[20] but incorporating a vortex of living energies rotating at varying speed on its own axis. At the microcosmic level (that is, as an atom) it apparently comprises types of two different polarities (see fig. 1.7). Its outer membrane contains its memory and intelligent functionality. It is then the inward and out-

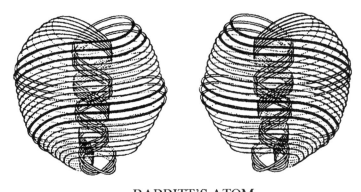

BABBITT'S ATOM

The 19th century clairvoyant, Thomas Babbitt, was the first to recognise what was subsequently called by Besant & Leadbeater 'The Permanent Atom'. Still unacknowledged by science, it involves a vortex of energy of tiny size, perceivable only by clairvoyant magnification, taking the shape shown above. The two atoms shown are each revolving on their axis in different directions, hence generating different polarities. There seems to be a possibility that the soul - the same but higher principle - not only follows the same activity of intense axial rotation in different directions, but that this somehow gives rise to male:female gender in the physical body created within the field of the vortex.

Fig. 1.7. Babbit's atom

ward emanations from this cellular (or soular) organism that by extension give rise, respectively, to the biological form of its own self-expression and its neural sensory mechanism. Hence, as the ancient philosophers Plotinus and Iamblichus were able to agree, "the body is contained by the soul"[21]—that is, the terrestrial or "irrational" soul. However, this in turn gives rise to those personalized, subsidiary environmental projections that we call desires and emotions on the one hand and experiential mentality on the other. These are well known to modern theosophists, and others familiar with theosophical books, by their respective Sanskrit names—*kama* and *manas*.

It is perhaps curious that our modern science acknowledges the fact of the spheroidally based cell as the primordial organism in the objective body of a plant, animal, or human, yet solidly refuses to even contemplate the idea that the very same principle might have its own higher and lower counterparts. But cells—which multiply from themselves not unlike the flame of a fire—must themselves originate from germs in a sympathetic environment (i.e., a "culture") in order to survive. The ancient philosophical and metaphysical traditions unequivocally recognized all this to be so, even if they did not describe it in modern scientific terms.

For example, Pythagoras (see fig. 1.8) held that the Monad (i.e., the metaphysical sphere or field of being that corresponds with the Higher Mind principle animating the lesser soul principle)—and later referred to as the

Fig. 1.8. Pythagoras

"Indefinite Dyad"—was (like the germ) the self-emanated, causal originator of all objective existence, without having any objective existence itself. Yet every field of objective existence contained within itself a septenary constitution; hence the Hermetic "as above, so below" principle. In addition, geometrical relationships between a given number of macrocosmic points (i.e., celestial souls or stars) had to be considered by reference to the interactively rotating fields of limitation in which they existed.

The more modern philosopher and mathematician Wilhelm Leibnitz (1646–1716) (see fig. 1.9) concentrated on the emanating points themselves, also seeing them as "living essences," which acted as the agents (as either window or mirror) of the mind, but he did so without taking the axially rotating soul sphere into his philosophical considerations. These points—his "living monads"—had previously been described by Pythagoras under the generic term *monas*, which was actually derived by him, while in Babylonia, from the Sanskrit term *manas*, meaning (a "spark" of) Mind.

Modern academic researchers of ancient mathematical philosophy have consistently failed to recognize this fundamental basis of hylozoistic philosophy. So how do we go about proving the issue? Can it be done in a manner that will satisfy scientific or other rational criteria? Well, with the rather arbitrary limitations which modern science seeks to impose upon experimentation—that is, the need to work under unnatural laboratory conditions—this would never be straightforward. We must therefore look

Fig. 1.9.
Wilhelm Leibnitz

to ancillary approaches, recognizing—as some scientists already do—that cross-corroborated psychological experience alone (without technological support or intervention) is a valid field of scientific research. In other words, we must apply forms of ruthless self-discipline to our own subjective experiences and then cross-examine these with those of others. This is already being done in a somewhat restricted manner in the fields of psychology and parapsychology, although neither of these has as yet recognized as such the existence of deva and elemental nature—which we shall deal with in chapter 3.

PLANES AND SUBPLANES OF EXPERIENCE AND FACULTY

Let us remember that every level works according to the Macrocosm-microcosm relationship principle. At the outset a celestial entity (the Logos*) emanates its Oversoul, the vehicle of the "Demiurge," a group entity that we shall explain and deal with in greater detail later on. From this a spectrum of yet lesser soul hierarchies are then emanated. Thus, we might suggest, the demiurgic Oversoul of the solar scheme (known as the Aeon) provides the hierarchical groups of what we call "Spiritual Souls," whereas the planetary Oversoul and Demiurge provides the many hierarchies of "terrestrial souls." These, in turn, give rise to all the various forms of the kingdoms of Nature on Earth. From each of these Oversouls and souls a vast range of spirits then circulate within the solar and planetary system, so giving rise to all their characteristic functions and ranges of consciousness.

Thus each soul organism is the emanated offspring of a yet greater Oversoul, which is what enables the soul entity to generate what we call the sense of self. The soul entity contains a restricted field of awareness and function—hence its characteristic consciousness, but it is the human "spark" inseminated within the terrestrial soul nature (from a yet higher soul) that endeavors to cause the expansion of that field. That first impulse

---

*The Logos is the intelligent light emanated by a divine being in charge of a planet or solar system.

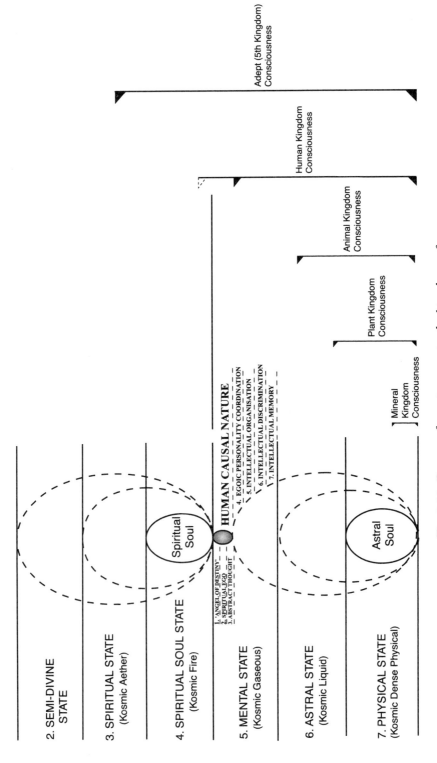

Fig. 1.10. Ranges of consciousness in the kingdoms of nature

toward expansion is generated by sensitivity to external influences. This results in desire for reexperience; hence the auric area immediately surrounding the terrestrial soul becomes progressively conditioned by that same quality of desire-energy. This then develops the "astral" or "feeling" function, which otherwise acts as the sensory awareness of the animal nature. However, by virtue of its further, subjective orientation in the human (which the animal has not yet developed*), it evolves into the human phenomenon of the astral "e-motions," or outwardly sensory emanations.

From a metaphysical viewpoint, today's less well developed humanity only uses the grosser matter of the astral soul field, that is, the emotions, in its subjective workings. The lowest two levels or substates of this comprise a reactive emotional nature and acquisitive personal desires, which lead to an idolistic or fetishistic nature. The third and fourth levels then comprise the personal and impersonal ambitious senses respectively; the fifth level comprising the idealistic nature. More developed types progressively add to this the various qualities of the four lower subplanes of the mental state—that is, egoic personality coordination and intellectual organization, discrimination, and memory—usually in conjunction with matter of the astral-emotional state. That thereby generates slightly higher or subtler forms of the same trinity involving idolism, ambition, and idealism.

This same usage of subtler quality subjective matter by more developed individuals derives from the unconscious polarization of self-association with the yet higher spiritual nature. That, in turn, gives rise to the mystic and religious frame of mind, which is, however, largely psychic in nature. That purely psychic orientation is nevertheless now changing due to the formal recognition of the distinction between the Higher Self and the lower self by transpersonal psychology, pioneered by Abraham Maslow and Roberto Assagioli.

The gradual outward projection of astral energies in the practical

---

*Contrary to what was suggested by the seventeenth-century philosopher René Descartes (1596–1650), the animal does indeed possess a soul, but only one (the terrestrial soul, or psyche), which is derived from the World Soul of our planet. However, the World Soul only emanates group souls, so the animal (and the plant before it in the overall evolutionary sequence) only possess a group consciousness associated with its particular species, although a promise of future individualization is evident in some of the higher mammals.

experience of a human being generates residual memory-forces—hence the base nature of what we may call the "lower mind." The latter then forms the next auric subfield. The increasingly intelligent manipulation of those memories then, in turn, generates a general sense of organization, the second of the lower mind faculties. That then leads to a sense of the need to organize these distinctively different memories into recognizable categories for potential re-use; hence intelligently analytical discrimination forms the third of the lower mental faculties. Finally (at the present stage of highly developed human evolution) there is derived the fourth lower mental category and capacity. This involves actively intelligent coordination and control of all the so far developed subjective faculties, which coordination thereby forms the basis of what we call the human personality. That, however, is as far as the lesser (terrestrial) soul develops. We shall deal with this again in further detail in later chapters of the book.

All these qualitatively different categories of elemental (astral and mental) substance—although intermingling with each other in the objective and subjective nature of the human being—are thus metaphysically described by modern theosophy as hermeneutically structured, in graded subplanes or substates. These are of immense importance and are in accord with a recurrently underlying sevenfold principle, for reasons also to be described later on. This same principle was known of in Plato's time—and long before that too.

We human beings (although mostly unconsciously) then choose and use amounts of such substance as is deemed necessary for each subjective task, just as we unconsciously use specific muscles for each objective task. If this approach is kept in mind, the student of the subject will not go far wrong. The current tendency, however, is for people to have a merely static concept of the hermeneutic structure. In practice, this is largely useless. That is because it separates the objective and subjectively theophanic perceptions. These, as suggested from the outset, need to be involved in working together, rather than apart, simply because the purely intellectual viewpoint—in modern scientific terms—causes disintegration of the wave flow.

THE DIFFERENTIATION OF
HIGHER AND LOWER MIND

As suggested earlier, the principle of Mind involves an emanation from one field or state of consciousness into another. Thus within the purely human experience, the downward emanation of the human Causal (semi-spiritual) Soul generates the field of the "Higher Mind." Correspondingly, the upward emanation of the terrestrial soul nature generates first of all the emotional nature and then the "lower mind" faculty. It is then the problem of the individual to bring about a harmony between these Higher Mind and lower mind aspects in order to enable the uninterrupted downflow of higher soul consciousness straight into the physical brain via the limpidly expectant terrestrial soul. However, both the higher and lower Mind emanations involve substates and associated subfunctions amounting to a septenate—four in the higher and three in the lower, as shown in the Pythagorean system defining the Quadrivium and Trivium (see fig. 1.11). The sequentially progressive nature and quality of each substate is quite different, as will be explained in rather greater detail later on.

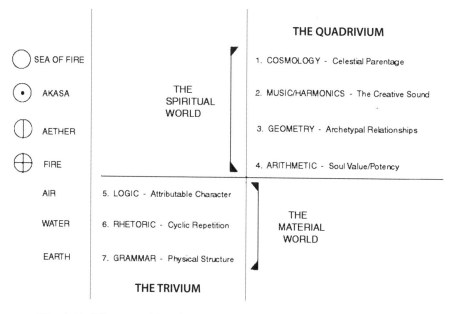

Fig. 1.11. The seven liberal arts and sciences in relation to metaphysics

The expansion of human consciousness in the mass of humanity has, so far, extended to include the four lower mental substates shown in fig. 1.10, although without bringing them under firm control. That is the next stage, leading to full coordination of what we call "the integrated personality." Further developed humanity then begins to become psycho-spiritually aware of something beyond even this. That "something" involves a fifth mental substate consisting of a completely different quality of matter, derived (as explained above) by downward emanation from the next higher soul organism. This "causal" state we would associate with the generation of abstract mental forms, or archetypes. These are necessarily interdisciplinary in nature and highly ethereal in form. They are also extremely volatile and thus very difficult to work with. Consequently, a truly self-disciplined and highly sensitive human nature is required to be able to perceive or control matter of this fifth mental subplane.

However, the vast majority of human beings are as yet wholly incapable of even approaching that capacity. The reason that this is so derives from the fact that such perception and control comes from an instinctive sensitivity to the nature of the next higher soul organism, which itself controls all activity of higher mental subplane matter. Consequently, in order to achieve this, the individual's self-polarization has to turn completely about. It must now reorient itself to function from the higher to the lower and no longer upward from the selfish terrestrial soul nature.

As each soul entity is but a partial emanation or projection of a far greater parent soul, in order to access any higher consciousness, it is quite logical that the orientation of awareness must first change in the same way. We can then better understand (as Plato reminds us) why "all learning is nothing but recollection."[22] The omniverse is the playground of a perennially active and emanating Universal Consciousness, the progressively higher reaches of which can only be accessed gradually and sequentially by a process of subliminal sensitivity and reassimilation, in other words, through subjective contemplation.

Rather interestingly, recalling what has already been mentioned regarding his view from the perspective of "quantum yoga," Amit Goswami believes in "upward causation and continuous change" on the one hand and, in addition, "downward causation as consciousness collapses the possibility wave into an event."[23] From the viewpoint of esotericism the former involves merely karmic action, that is, action derived from sensory reaction (which is not actually causal), whereas the latter involves dharmic action, that is, purposeful action derived from higher soul consciousness. That, however, leads on logically and sequentially to our next point, as follows.

The scientist Bruce Lipton—although concerning himself largely with cellular development and evolution—has a rather interestingly occult view on his own field. Showing how the genetic determinism of Crick and Watson (although still widely accepted) has been completely disproved by science itself in the field of epigenetics, he otherwise describes how environmental influences conditioned by our own personal attitudes of mind are actually the true determining factors behind all cellular change in the human organism.[24] Recognizing also that consciousness exists outside the body—hence the telepathically morphic field theory of Rupert Sheldrake—he too is of the belief that the surrounding "field" is of the most crucial importance as a transceiver of information or knowledge, circulating within a given "horizontal" continuum.[25]

However, while also making clear his perception that the human mind is very capable of transmitting commands that the cell or cellular groups will obey, thereby effecting all sorts of biochemical change, he does not take into consideration the interface of the terrestrial soul, or of the etheric double. The esotericist and occultist, on the other hand, both recognize that these sequential interfaces are themselves the main "environmental" determinants.

THE NATURE AND STRUCTURE OF THE SOUL AURA

Within the terrestrial soul field, there is a light-filled aura, a literal web of psychic force interpenetrating and extending beyond the body of the human organism. This is as well known to clairvoyants as is that surrounding the cell, the latter having been made visible to us all through the agency of the electron microscope. In order to answer the question as to why it appears as it does, let us look at the situation rather more sequentially as follows.

First of all, meditative contemplation confirms that knowledge is contained in the outer auric envelope of the soul (the latter being paralleled by the "brane" of quantum science and the "event horizon" of astrophysics, as we saw earlier), expressing itself in the form of subtle vibration. Hence the same might be said of the cell. This is due to the fact that the outer membrane of the cell is highly sensitive and in a state of constant tension, as can to some extent be seen using an electron microscope. In addition, science already acknowledges that it is the outer plasm of the cell (hence also that of the soul) that contains its memory and driving mechanism.

In other words, the nucleus is secondary to the outer membrane; it is not primary or causal. Yet we still tend to think of the center of anything as being causal, with everything else gathered around it. This, however, is a fallacy based upon pure misinterpretation, through following the Aristotelian method of reductive analysis. Yet both clairvoyants and scientists are equally uncertain as to the real nature of these phenomena. There is a general ignorance about what constitutes the fundamental difference between the outer plasmic membrane and the inner plasm (the cytoplasm) of the cell, which may or may not contain a nucleolus.

What is it then about the cellular membrane of the atom, the cell, and the soul that thus gives it its faculty of coherence and instinctive knowledge? What also causes so many of them to rotate around their own axis? The very same question could be asked by the astrophysicist contemplating the fields surrounding each galaxy. These somehow manage to contain all of the galaxy's constituent dark matter and dark energy, thereby arresting them from being centrifugally ejected into outer space, as the world of astrophysics has already acknowledged. But how and why? The answer to the question in both cases lies in yet another completely misunderstood word—Mind.

THE TRUE NATURE OF MIND

From the viewpoint of occult science and metaphysical philosophy, spirit, matter, and energy are one and the same in essence, although periodically presenting themselves phenomenally as one or another of these. The same happens with energy and force in the objective world, in accordance with relativity theory. Yet the same philosophical tradition puzzlingly states that the spirit (or monadic life-essence) is everywhere and nowhere at the same time, that it exists and yet does not, that it is no-thing but yet gives rise by self-emanation to all phenomenal existence, of which it is itself the germ. By virtue of its primordial nature, preexisting that of even the soul, what then is it? And what does the soul itself then comprise?

It follows quite logically that if, in the beginning, there is/was nothing but spirit (this being the substance of the universal *nous*), soul must itself be composed of it. Indeed, this is perfectly in accord with the ancient wisdom tradition. Thus the cystic or auric periphery of the cell's or soul's field must itself be composed of spirit-matter in some or other form of coherent inter-relationship with itself.

It is thus the "spark" of spirit—the germinal no-thing (the Pythagorean monas and the monad of Leibnitz)—that essentially provides the causal nature of soul-consciousness by virtue of some kind of mutually sympathetic group activity. That same activity must then necessarily comprise or involve a coherently sympathetic vibration, which results in the generation of mutually self-constricting wave patterns. It is these latter wave-fields, one might suggest, that then combine to produce the outer membrane, the peripheral field that in esotericism is known as the "ring-pass-not," thereby engendering the cell or soul entity. Hence Plato tells us very graphically that the human body is carried about by us "like an oyster in its shell."[26]

With that in consideration we might then ask what causes this apparently self-containing activity that results in the formation of an outer membrane? The answer to this lies in what H. P. Blavatsky described as "Fohat [the dynamic electricity of Mind] digging holes in Space."[27] Hence also the often-repeated gnostic principle that the universe is concentrically organized.[28] That is to say, as already indicated, each soul entity is the off-spring of a parent soul, or Oversoul, that contains it. That containment results from the inward or centripetal emanation of the Oversoul, which we call the descending "Mind" principle. Thus the Mind itself is effectively that intelligent force, which generates and contains the lesser soul in a sort of vortex (referred to by the ancients as a "whirlwind") through a form of electromagnetic containment and then impregnates it with its own higher essences. As the early theurgical philosopher Iamblichus comments: "For Soul is brought to completion by intellect [Mind] and Nature by soul."[29]

SOME ANCIENT CORRESPONDENCES

The ancient Greeks explained the generation of the lesser soul by the Mind allegorically in the story of the Titan god Ouranos, a name derived from the compound *aura-nous*—meaning the "sphere of celestial Mind." Ouranos thus enfolds the Titan goddess Gaia (Gaia being a portion of Space itself, not Earth as commonly misinterpreted) within his mighty embrace. He then forces himself upon her "sexually," emanating the Eros principle, thereby causing her to become pregnant with six pairs of lesser Titan gods and goddesses, all of whom are described as (titanic) "forces in Nature" rather than discrete entities. The actual essence of what is being described here is that the Mind—emanating from the higher and purposeful Intelligence—separates and thus contains a field of space within the overall field of Universal Consciousness and then, within this, generates creative activity. (This is also precisely what we humans do when we "think.")

In the first few verses of the biblical Book of Genesis, shared by Jews, Christians, and Moslems alike, exactly the same principle in the Macrocosm is described, albeit in a slightly different way. Here the Elohim (the hierarchies of the Demiurge known in Hindu philosophy as Dhyani Chohans and in Christian terms as archangels) separate the "waters (of space) above" from the "waters (of space) below," thereby generating a spheroidal "firmament," which they then turn into a heaven world. From this all the germs of life in the various kingdoms of Nature are then made to emanate in due cycle into the field of containment thus formed.

The kabbalistic Zohar follows exactly the same line in the definitive statement:

> One is the source of the sea. A current comes forth from it making a revolution which is Yod [the first letter in the name of God]. The Source is one and the current makes two. Then is formed the vast basin known as the sea, which is like a channel dug in the earth and it is filled by the water issuing from the Source. This vast basin is divided up into seven channels.[30]

In fact, Kabbala refers to the Source as Keter and the primary emanation as Hokmah (perhaps meaning "true magic") or Chokmah (a phonetic corruption of the ancient compound *Shu-Kumar,* meaning "divine virgin light"). Binah (derived from ben-Yah, that is, "son of Yah") is then the great "sea"—that is, the Oversoul—containing the lesser seven. Later Lurianic Kabbala (conceived by its founder Isaac Luria in Egypt) tells us exactly the same thing. It does so by describing how the Deity limits itself by a creative process called *tzimzum,* thereby generating a second Creator-God (the Demiurge or Oversoul). The latter then emanates all the seed-essences of the world-to-be out of itself. The Greco-Egyptian literary work *Hermetica*[31] correspondingly tells us that:

> The Mind who is God, being androgyne and existing as life and light, by speaking gave birth to a second mind, a Craftsman who, as god of fire and spirit, crafted seven governors; they encompass the sensible world in circles and their government is called Fate.

The neo-Pythagorean philosopher Iamblichus also confirms that: "Soul is defined by the divine principle of limit, and participates in this in a partial mode."[32]

Yet another example, which takes into account all the various aspects just mentioned involves the emblematic metaphor known as the sacred Tibetan "Wheel of the Law" (see fig. 1.12), described by Evans-Wentz as: "The eight-spoked Wheel on a lotus throne and enhaloed by Flames of Wisdom . . . symbol of the symmetry and completeness of the Sacred Law of the Dharma."[33] In relation to the ten characteristics thus described, drawing a direct parallel with kabbalism, the lotus throne is akin to Keter, the enfolding flames of wisdom to Chokma (or Hokmah) and the eight-spoked wheel to Binah, the Oversoul of Creation, or Demiurge.

Fig. 1.12. Tibetan Wheel of the Law

It is otherwise worth mentioning in passing the parallel Hindu symbol of the god Siva Natarajah (see fig. 1.13) with his six limbs (seven including his head), dancing on the waters of space, surrounded by the sacred flames of the great god Agni. He and his six limbs constitute an esoteric heptad, while the halo of flames constitutes the enfolding Ogdoad of the yet greater divine Mind, of which the rest are but partial and temporary expressions.

Fig. 1.13. Siva Natarajah

THE UNIVERSAL PRINCIPLE OF "DIVIDE AND RULE"

One could go on almost endlessly justifying what has just been stated here by citing the different allegories of Creation in all the ancient traditions. However, in every case, without exception, the gnostic principle follows exactly the same course, in which Creation is caused by the self-limitation of kosmic consciousness, thereby creating a celestial Oversoul. This is then followed by a segmentation of that field into seven lesser fields or states; following precisely the same principle, the human is the microcosm of the Macrocosm. As our neo-Pythagorean friend Iamblichus again comments:

It is by the action of the superior beings that the inferior are produced, by the action of the incorporeal that bodies are produced, and by the action of creative forces that there are produced objects and they are given guidance through their all-embracing direction.[34]

This is, of course, yet again in direct contrast to modern scientific orthodoxy. The latter still holds to the irrational idea that matter coming together in molecular form by pure chance eventually gives rise to simple organic and then coherently complex biological forms, which eventually generate consciousness and intelligence out of their combined range of experience. This has been amusingly described as akin to the rather ludicrous suggestion that given enough monkeys with enough typewriters and enough time, one might expect the works of Shakespeare to be produced by them.

We thus return to the issue of what exactly comprises the internal field of the soul/cell. This might be described as a generalized, protoplasmic substance, "captured" from the mass of what the nineteenth-century magus Eliphas Levi (1810–1875) (see fig. 1.14) called the "astral light" of the planet.[35] It is this underlying plasmic "ether" (as yet still not accepted by modern mainstream science, although often referred to as "dark matter")

Fig. 1.14. Eliphas Levi

that subtends (and also preexists) the gaseous atmosphere of the planet. It is then electrically magnetized by the polarity induced in it through the constriction of the cell by the enfolding Mind principle, which "descends from above." The result is equivalent to the piezo-electric effect induced in a crystal when squeezed.

It is as a result of this electromagnetic induction that the captured matter is further induced to generate forms out of itself. These are then coordinated to produce a single visual organism, as evidenced in the scientist's use of a cathode ray tube or holographic projection. This same principle applies in the microcosm, the macrocosm, and the yet greater Macrocosm, these being respectively known in theosophical terms as the astral light, the Buddhi, and the Maha-Buddhi, the latter Sanskrit term also otherwise being known as Mahat.[36] H. P. Blavatsky tells us of the ancient tradition that this was the first stage of proto-human development on this planet (something which is further detailed in appendix A at the back of this book) a concept correspondingly described by Plato. He openly referred to the first men as being "spheroidal in shape and fiercely ambitious,"[37] only later developing the complex biological form with which we are familiar today.

PLATO'S CAVE

While mentioning Plato again, it is interesting to note here his analogy of the cave[38] in which the mere shadows of sunlight or firelight thrown upon the cave's internal walls are taken for reality by those living within it, with their backs to the cave entrance. The "cave" is itself an esoteric metaphor describing the internal enclosure of the terrestrial soul organism within which the human experience takes place. However, keeping in mind that the real light is emanating from outside the "cave," that is, from above, we can readily understand why a form of magnetic polarity should be involved in the organism by virtue of its relationship with its own parental source. That is to say, the parent Oversoul contains the lesser soul within itself, its own electrical emanation being what we like to call the Mind principle, as earlier described.

The Mind principle is projected like a sort of electrified coil of living essence that enfolds a field of space like an aura (derived from Ouranos/

Aura-Nous) for purposes of ideation, but which can be withdrawn from this activity by the Oversoul at any time. Rather like the string of the puppeteer, the controlling influence of this "coil" is to be found at the upper or "northern" pole of the auric soul field (the "cave entrance") where there exists a depression caused by the vortex of force being drawn down into the field, as described in Babitt's atom (see again fig. 1.7). The congruence of Oversoul energy and soul-matter to be found in this area generates a very real and fiery light, one that gradually irradiates the brain consciousness with insights and intuitions according to the invocative focus of interest to be found there. This too we shall deal with in greater detail somewhat later on.

The principle involved here is already well known to physics: energy imposed upon a captured field of inertia gives rise first of all to vibration, then to heat, and then to light. The generalized ethereal substance "captured" by the soul body is itself a field of relatively material inertia, as already described. Hence, when made to vibrate, this merely generates a generalized awareness to begin with. However, when this constraint is intensified, the localized consciousness of the individual (in the heart chakra or center), when first exposed to a higher influence, responds by generating heat—that is, highly emotional (i.e., "astral") passion with a mass of associated colors.

The individual's impressions and responsive reactions are initially more full of heat and color than light. However, this gradually changes through further experience and imposed crises of decision forcing the person to learn self-discipline. That in turn leads progressively to the appearance of an illuminating and then discriminating sense of reasonableness. Hence it is that compassionate tolerance is a characteristic associated with the heart. That same faculty eventually leads to a subjective reorientation to the consciousness of the crown chakra with its range of influence on the human brain, particularly via the brow and occipital subchakras.

THE APPEARANCE OF SELF

The preliminary effects of this psychological evolution is that the soul entity is made to generate two secondary fields of qualitatively personalized consciousness around it, as earlier described. The first of these fields contains energy and force conditioned by personal sensitivity, giving rise in the human case to the formation of reactive desires and ideals. This constitutes the individual's emotional world. The second field—that of the "concrete" or form-building mind—contains energies and forces involving more coherent and longer lasting personal memories of both a "good" and a "bad" nature. Both these aurically enfolding fields then progressively tend to "fill up" with the elemental condensate of the forces thus generated. That thereby creates a further densification through which the higher (that is, spiritual) energies have to penetrate to have any real effect on what lies below.

This perhaps aids in understanding the logic of the ancient tradition that humankind was originally much more naturally "spiritual" in its consciousness—that is, when the two outer fields (the Oversoul and the lesser soul) were still in the early stages of development and coordination. It was only as human beings became more self-concerned that the two outer fields joined together in producing within human nature a progressively more defined persona and associated sense of individuality. This self-centeredness was an inevitable outcome of the evolutionary process and of course it led to (and still leads to) all sorts of iniquity as a result of latent elemental influences stored up in the lesser auric memory of the terrestrial soul, impelling the physical human entity to behave in certain rather animalistic ways.

It is perhaps easier for us to understand this process in terms of the colors that the clairvoyant sees in the aura of the individual. The inherent vibratory quality imposed upon matter by any particular energy will result in an aggregation of force with an attendant color and hue, plus a characteristic intensity (or lack of it). A grosser desire or experience will thus inevitably lead to darker, murkier colors being generated, while less self-centered mental or emotional activity will produce much lighter colors and far less in the way of psychic condensate. Thus, in the case of the less self-centered, there will be a far more prolific response to incoming spiritual energies. However, with those who are less experienced in discriminating the qualities and forces inherent in the incoming energies, desire and the mind faculty tend very quickly to become overenergized and thus subject to psychic illusion. It becomes very easy for them to become carried away with a light-filled imagery, which is actually only psychic and not of a truly spiritual nature at all.

MYSTICISM AND THE FACULTY OF SIGHT

It is this latter type of situation that leads to one type of mysticism. In this, to begin with, because of the tremendous sense of expansion and power thus occultly experienced, the individual very easily feels in tune with what is assumed to be God or the archangels/angels, or even at-one with the Universal Mind. No amount of rationalizing will persuade the person to the contrary; in fact, the apparently very wondrous nature of the subjective experience will, when recounted, tend to lead others into the trap of devotional adulation or supposedly spiritual hero-worship that has no real justification at all. This is endemic in the Roman Catholic Church in terms of the so-called "beatification" of individuals of the same faith in order to approve them as "saints." That is, in fact, a brilliant political device for the church's own self-existence, as well as ensuring its own political control over the laity.

From the occult viewpoint, however, it follows quite logically that the true types of spiritual training associated with real initiation concern themselves first and foremost with teaching the individual how to use the intelligence to recognize these pitfalls and, eventually, how to avoid their self-creation altogether. As we shall see later on, it is this that enables the true spiritual vision to develop as a very real faculty within the individual's nature, leading to a progressively more reliable inner illumination.

It might also be worthwhile mentioning here what Plato had to say about the question of light, bearing in mind what has already been suggested about the correlations between light and the spiritual fire that forms the apparent "body" of the soul. He tells us first of all that fire is of several types[39] (esoterically there should be seven) and that one of these involves a nonburning radiance or "pure fire," which emanates from within the soul of the individual outward through the eyes, this being essentially of the same nature as that of sight, along which the stream from within strikes the external object.

> [Thus] the whole so formed is homogeneous and the motions caused by the stream coming into contact with an object or an object coming into contact with the stream penetrate right through the body and produce in the soul the sensation which we call sight. But when the kindred force disappears at nightfall, the visual stream is cut off.[40]

What Plato is actually saying involves the basic occult principle that only like recognizes like in complementary fashion, for all essential qualities of matter. Hence, because the inner spiritual being is essentially a solar entity, the emanations of the two must fuse to some degree before a given faculty becomes apparent in a particular state. Vision is ever the third faculty to be developed—after hearing and touch—hence it is that we find the faculty and organs of sight first manifestly apparent in the third kingdom in Nature, the animal. However, the human—the fourth kingdom in Nature—then adapts this faculty and turns it inward. That generates the subjective vision that we call "imagination," plus the "mind's eye," with an associated ability to produce conscious memory. This the animal entirely lacks, although astral vision in some animals is apparent in a very rudimentary and unconscious state.

It is also important to be aware that the psychic condensates generated by human imagination and memory not only block the incoming spiritual influences but at times also cause them to be refracted—like light passing through a crystal or water—or reflected. As a consequence, they give rise to all sorts of distortions, literally "bouncing" off the walls of the soul aura in question. This, in passing, points to the way in which the visual faculty itself works—something which science again believes it understands but which it actually does not.

The faculty of physical sight, perhaps curiously, works essentially through soul faculty, not—as science teaches us—because of sunlight or artificial light passing through the pupil and retina, causing a biochemical reaction in the rods and cones at the rear of the eyeball, which then transfers itself to the brain. Instead—because of the internal light-energy generated by the soul (known to Platonists as "the single eye")—the human eye actually projects outward a beam of invisible light that comprises five streams of force[41] of which modern science yet again knows nothing. It is this very principle that has given rise to fears of "the evil eye" on the part of peasant or native communities, who are much more in natural tune with psychic phenomena than city or town-bred folk who have learned to distrust what they believe to be the mere absurdity of folklore.

It is this same principle of a psychic "lever" that, when properly harnessed by simply (occultly) altering the attitude of mind in a certain way, enables some people to be "natural" hypnotists. It is again this that causes people, usually inadvertently, to attract the attention of others by merely staring at them. However, what is not generally realized is that a higher psycho-spiritual influence is involved and that the coordinated energies from two chakras are being used to project it. We might add the suggestion that it is because of these two chakras that the animal organism of the human body has two eyes.

THE PHENOMENON OF LIGHT

We might otherwise suggest that physical sight actually works as much through the agency of the iris as it does through the pupil and retina. That is because every external form has an accompanying etheric "shadow." But to explain this we first need to explain one or two other things that are not quite as they appear, or as we have been taught. The first of these is that there is no such thing as "sunlight" per se. The sun at the center of our solar system does not itself generate light, but only a highly powered energy; when that energy comes into contact with our Earth's atmosphere, it causes it to vibrate intensely and thus generate light out of itself. Even this, however, is a simplification of what actually happens, because different types or qualities of solar radiation are due to the auxiliary assistance of other influences.

To recapitulate what was explained earlier: the Earth possesses its own Oversoul, which contains, by entrapment, a field of chaotically unorganized ethereal substance (from solar space), which is known to occult science as "the astral light"—a term first used, as mentioned earlier, by the nineteenth century occultist Eliphas Levi. This substance—otherwise known as the Earth's etheric double, which is a lower correspondence to the Buddhi (the kosmic etheric double)—underlies the gaseous and watery atmosphere of the planet, these being merely its condensates. This ethereal double is a sort of plasma, an invisible mass of subtle matter carrying a latent electrical energy of a particular quality and force, rather like a battery solution.

This latter solution is constantly reenergized by solar activity, sometimes even becoming overcharged and causing all sorts of technical problems to modern electronic equipment. It is also charged by what we would today call "gravity" and "levity," two (fundamentally similar) forces generated by the core of the Earth and the ionosphere respectively, although mainstream science has not yet quite recognized how and why. The electromagnetic "loops" seen emanating from the Sun's surface give some idea as to the former, for "gravity" is merely the returning energy (hence the limitation of its objective force, as noted by modern science), which originally emanated from the core of the celestial body, as I have suggested in previous books.

The individual human being, by possessing a terrestrial (or "astral") soul organism derived from the planetary Oversoul, also contains, by entrapment within its auric field, a proportion of astral light. This the human soul "personalizes" and uses to generate and maintain a physical body of incredibly complex organization. Consequently, it is the interaction between the soul, the etheric double, and the physical body that enables the human being actually to exist and survive. But this is not the whole of the story, because what we have described so far merely involves the intermediate psychic nature of the human being. The spiritual nature, which gives humankind the faculty of self-consciousness, is something quite distinctively greater, derived from the fact that the inner person is a solar being, working within the kosmic etheric double of the Logos.

CONCERNING ANGELS AND DEVAS

We shall deal rather more fully with the subject of angels and devas in chapter 3 where we shall see how and why they are fundamental to this same subject of consciousness. However, a few preliminary remarks at this point should be useful in correlating the human soul nature with that of the deva, or angel. Devas—a hierarchy of being that is complementary to the human—are essentially the partial and localized expression of Universal Memory, while the soul is itself the container of a necessarily limited field of knowledge (as light), a holographic fragment of the Universal Memory. It is then the concentric nature of the soul principle, which we have already described, that enables the macrocosmically "local" containment of consciousness throughout the universe through the agency of a celestial being known as an "Aeon." This, in unfolding its own essential nature as a sequential stream of reexpressed memory through a cycle of manifestation, is itself neither beginning nor end, but both.[42] Hence the consciousness of the Aeon and infinity are essentially synonymous terms.

An "infinity," it should thus be noted, merely signifies a celestially localized perfection or limitation of Universal Memory innate in the nature of a kosmic organism. The aeonic "body" itself comprises the Oversoul of whatever celestial organism is under consideration. Any transfer from this entity to a lesser entity then occurs as a result of groups of spirits (previously contained within the peripheral membrane of the Oversoul in question) "descending" to a lower sphere of being in order to impose upon it the will and purpose of the higher Oversoul entity. Hence it is that we have the purely allegorical story of the "fallen angel," found in so many different religions throughout the world.

Higher beings require "vehicles" of a lower order in order to take up a phenomenal existence in the lower world scheme in order to effect their duty, in pursuit of logoic Purpose; hence it is that individual spirits of a higher order are forced to incarnate in (or through) lesser soul organisms in order to carry out their appointed tasks in the pursuit of that same higher Purpose. According to the ancient traditions, where such a situation arises, there we find the human being. But what then is the soul organism that does not contain this higher "spark"? And what is its purpose in the general scheme of things?

This other type of soul organism (or rather, its "bodily expression") is what ancient tradition has made known to us as that of the "angel" or "deva"; its predominant subjective characteristic is that it possesses a distinct range of knowledge and faculty but has no sense of choice or alternative. Its consciousness is completely instinctual, although highly intelligent—far more directly so than that of the human, even in the higher reaches of the latter's mundane social hierarchy. The sole concern of the angel/deva—often mistakenly known as a "nature spirit"—is the perfect reproduction of the "divine plan" in the mind of its parent Oversoul. It might thus be considered in the mass as the instinctual "memory" of the Macrocosm or Logos—that which maintains the "status quo." The human, on the other hand, may be described as the lesser agent of the imagination of the higher Logos (and is thus the instigator of all change in the kosmos)—hence the Macrocosm–microcosm relationship to which we constantly refer. This idea will perhaps be more easily understood as we deal rather more specifically with human consciousness in the next chapter. Of that the *Hermetica* has this to say by way of an introduction to the idea of an emanating higher consciousness "ensouling" a lesser one.

> The Mind cannot naked and alone take up its abode in an earthy body; a body of earth could not endure the presence of that mighty and immortal being, nor could so great a power submit to contact with a body defiled by passion. And so the Mind takes to itself the soul for a wrap.[43]

TWO

HUMAN CONSCIOUSNESS

In this chapter we shall take a more specific look at human consciousness, rather than consciousness in general. In doing so, however, we shall build on what has already been suggested in the first chapter concerning the nature of the soul principle and the fact that, as a universal principle, it is the concentrically higher counterpart in Universal Nature to the cell and the atom. To begin with then, let us consider the principle and process of concentric emanation from the greater soul (the Oversoul) downward into a lesser field of consciousness. This, as already described, deals with the Higher Mind and lower mind, hence also with the fundamental nature of the Macrocosm–microcosm relationship, that is, between that which some call "God" (i.e., the Logos) on the one hand and the human on the other.

Fig. 2.1 shows us (but not to scale) the greater Oversoul and a lesser soul emanated (inward) from its outer membrane by a spiraling yin-yang projection of its mind-consciousness. This same yin-yang projection (which Blavatsky describes as Fohat—the electricity of Mind) not only instinctively envelops a portion of intended working space within the field of the Oversoul, it also contains within itself the essences of that inherent duality, which we otherwise know as spirit and matter. This projected mind-envelope is fundamentally the same as the kabbalistic Hokmah, which generates and contains the lesser soul or Binah principle. This is also the same as the gnostic Sophia (itself derived from *Suf-Ea,* the "breath of the higher Aeon").

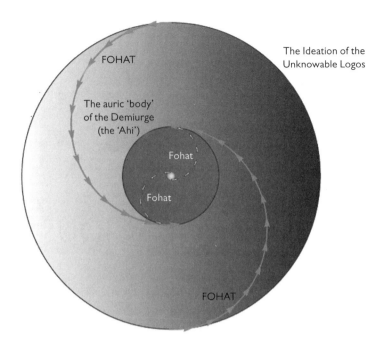

Fig. 2.1. The generation of the Demiurge

Thus, as the *Hermetica* tells us, soul is joined to the membrane of the spheroidal Mind[1] thereby forming a fiery "ring-pass-not."

In relative terms, the greater soul is akin to the field of consciousness of a high archangel (archon), whereas the lesser soul is merely that of an angel/deva. The latter's animating consciousness, derived from its parent, nevertheless involves the three fundamental instincts of all possible existence mentioned in chapter 1: Being, Knowing, and Doing. From these the philosophical and theological Trinity found in all ancient and modern mainstream religions (except Islam) is derived. Below the three are shown as they are referred to, respectively, in Christianity, Hinduism, and Babylonian religion.

1. The Will-to-be (vitality)—the Father/Siva/Anu
2. The Will-to-know (perceptual sensitivity)—the Son/Visnu/Ea
3. The Will-to-create (adaptability)—the Holy Spirit/Brahma/Bel

By virtue of the fact that these are derived from the logoic Oversoul, they are archetypal in nature, thereby comprising what Plato calls "the Same." However, the lesser soul responds by instinctively trying to reproduce (by emanation) the same trio of forces within the field of elemental nature

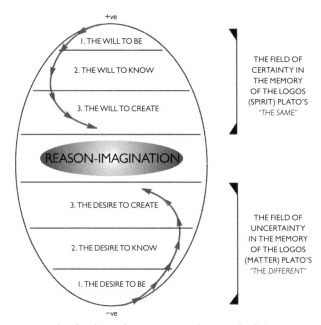

Fig. 2.2. The duality of memory in the mind of the Logos

that it in turn contains and influences. However, by virtue of its lesser experience, it fails. Instead, it produces a mere reflection (see fig. 2.2) based on desire, correspondingly expressed thus:

3. The desire-to-create/regenerate
2. The desire-to-know
1. The desire-to-be

As we can see, the effect is still a trinity of expression. However, it lacks the sustained power of the archetype, so it is evanescent. It comes and goes. That is why Plato refers to it as "the Different," that is, the ever-changing. From our viewpoint, however, the Same and the Different are but synonyms for that relativity otherwise known to us as spirit and matter. Additionally, bearing in mind that both of these are representative agents of the consciousness of the parent Demiurge, which is itself merely the instinctual memory of a greater, parent Logos, we might more usefully refer to them respectively as "certainty" and "uncertainty"; for these latter two are the two aspects of any consciousness, our own included.

THE TWIN SOULS OF THE HUMAN BEING

In discussing human consciousness, we necessarily consider the fact that the average human being works through two souls—a higher, semi-spiritual or Causal Soul and a lower, terrestrial soul (often and misleadingly called an astral soul) (see again fig. 1.6). As mentioned earlier, the terrestrial soul is provided by the World Soul of our planet and its capacities are of a very limited nature. It basically provides the human (as also the animal) with five physical senses—hearing, touch, sight, smell, and taste, plus a synthesizing sixth sense that we call "instinct." This terrestrial soul generates cells and maintains the human physiological form in response to the purpose imposed upon it by the Causal Soul.

The Causal Soul is of a rather different and more complex nature. Just as the terrestrial soul is generated by the planetary Oversoul, so the Oversoul of our solar system generates solar (that is, spiritual) souls. These too are deva entities, but of a far more evolved type. Then, in a form of spiritual "pregnancy," some Spiritual Souls maternally contain the emanation of a yet higher Oversoul, that is, an evolving divine "spark." However, in the process of the "individualizing gestation" of the Spiritual Soul, the deva generates within its own nature a sort of "fetal sac," which is the source of the human being's individuality. This then is the Causal Soul, into which the maternal deva then pours the influences of the higher, spiritual world—very slowly to begin with. Within the Causal Soul, the "fetal" spiritual nature of the human being then develops over countless lifetimes until its consciousness is that of the advanced initiate of a certain degree (as will be described later on).

The individual's developing spiritual independence eventually ruptures the Causal Soul from within and, in so doing, enables the person to emerge self-consciously into the light of the spiritual state itself. In this way the human being recognizes himself or herself as a solar being rather than a merely planetary being, with the capacity to generate a "personal" soul identity at will. However, just as a human infant has to come to terms consciously with objective planetary existence, so the advanced initiate of this degree has to learn how to deal consciously with the spiritual state, its quite different influences, and all its many and varied hierarchies of life. In other words, the person embarks upon a higher rung of the evolutionary process altogether as will be described in chapter 11.

Nevertheless, by virtue of the symbiosis inherent in the duality of spirit and matter within the yet greater (kosmic) system, the human being continues to have a role to fulfill in transmitting higher influences down into the lesser field of planetary being. This thereby aids the continued evolution of consciousness of the lesser kingdoms of Nature (including the human). As we shall see, this transmission takes the form of what we rather misleadingly call "intuition."

INTUITION AND THE BRIDGING PRINCIPLE

The certainty and uncertainty inherent in an evolving consciousness involve a duality that cannot be resolved, precedent to onward progress, except through the agency of a completely different, third factor. In order for an archetype to give way to a yet better archetype, it has to become involved in a form of experience devised by that third agency. It cannot change its own instinctive nature by itself. That third agency or factor is imagination, a faculty possessed only by a self-conscious entity, that is, a human being. The angel/deva does not possess imagination because its instinct to repetition of the "status quo" memory of its parent Oversoul absolves it of any sense of doubt. It then follows that human consciousness (at least in potential) is, in essence, "higher" than that of the deva's Oversoul. In other words, humankind is the agent of a yet higher (logoic) Purpose, which necessarily "falls" into the consciousness of the Oversoul specifically for the purpose of reorganizing it.

However, the faculty of imagination in the human being is itself merely representative of only dimly sensed higher possibilities. Though spiritual, humanity forgets its own higher, original nature because of its distraction by and self-association with the lower forms and forces provided by the planetary Demiurge. That is why the ancient Greek tradition refers to the lesser gods drinking of the cup of Lethe, which gave rise to spiritual sleep. Yet there remains something within the inner nature of the human being that instinctively seeks to reach upward and outward, back to a sensed higher possibility. This is what will eventually trigger the intuitive process.

However, to begin with, the person attempts to bring together the forces of certainty and uncertainty in his or her own mind, by imposing upon them the "shadows" of what is sensed by his or her own higher faculties. This produces an initial faculty of somewhat cursory creative inventiveness and opportunism: the dawning imagination. In due course of time, that itself evolves—in conjunction with memory of failure or of only relative success— into a practiced faculty involving a discriminatingly organized higher memory. As the occult process is actually described: "The creative activity of the imagination is the first organising influence which works upon and within the ring-pass-not of accumulated energies held in a state of tension by the intention of the individual."[2]

This same intention is achieved by the faculty of visualization, which can be defined as: "the process whereby the creative imagination is rendered active and becomes responsive to and attracted by the point of tension on the mental plane," in the process of which "a current of force is set up between these pairs of opposites (astral-buddhic) and—as it passes through the reservoir of force upon the mental plane—it produces an interior activity and an organisation of the substance present."[3]

Eventually, however, even fascination with this faculty begins to pall and the innate higher consciousness again begins to reimpose itself, only this time more directly and distinctively. It is this latter "pull" to which we misleadingly give the name "spiritual intuition." Ultimately, however, even this gives way to a more direct faculty of conscious insight, which we might perhaps call "spiritual reason" based on direct perception. At this point, the whole of the lesser human consciousness comes under the direct sway and control of the overshadowing logoic Purpose. The individual has already recognized by this stage that he or she is, in fact, no longer a merely "human" being. Thus the individual "spark," or spirit, reawakens to that which it already was at the outset, only this time it possesses a higher Self-consciousness and a true spiritual individuality. Now the "spark" takes on its own creative identity within the higher world, with a newly and more widely individualized range of soul faculties for a "vehicle."

It is interesting to note the way in which the ancient Egyptians expressed these same ideas symbolically, through the various types of headgear and colors worn by the pharaoh. The best known of the former were the Red Crown of the North—with its long butterfly-like proboscis, the latter representing the lower mind and the upward projected imagination—and the

White Crown of the South (see fig. 2.3 with the two crowns combined). The latter correspondingly represents the inner, "ever virgin," spiritual nature. Although understood by Egyptologists merely to represent the northern and southern halves of the country, their actual symbolism of the coexistent material and spiritual human states is far more esoteric.

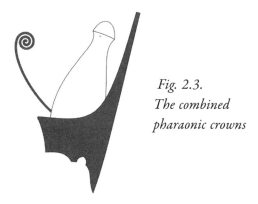

Fig. 2.3.
The combined
pharaonic crowns

The distinctively different blue of Osiris's body, on the other hand (like Ptah and Krisna), is much more specifically associated with the Monad or "divine spark"; it symbolizes, it is suggested, the divine spark's "fallen" nature—that is, that of the Kosmic Higher Mind, of which dark blue is, esoterically, the associated color.[4] Correspondingly, the Eye of Horus or Ra (see fig. 2.4) with its downwardly curling proboscis symbolizes the spiritual consciousness extending its Mind-projection down into the yet lower world of objectivity, which the divine nature cannot directly reach.

Taking into consideration that Platonists and Neoplatonists used the terms "Essence," "Same," and "Different" in the same way that we use "divinity,"

Fig. 2.4. Eye of Horus

"spirit," and "matter," it is interesting to note how they saw the increasingly evolved human soul as being made up of different combinations of these. As one of the main later Neoplatonist philosophers (Proclus) describes:

> When Essence vanquishes Same and Different, then according to the mixture of the media, a divine soul is generated. . . . But when Sameness and at the same time Essence vanquishes Difference, then an angelic soul is generated; when Sameness alone predominates, a daemoniacal soul is produced; but when Sameness together with Difference have dominion over Essence, then an heroic soul is generated; and when Difference alone prevails, a human soul is produced.[5]

THE NATURE OF THE DEVA
AND WHAT HUMANKIND CALLS "GOD"

We referred earlier to the parallels between the light-filled aura of the soul and the rotational, radiant nature of the cell under the electron microscope. What we might now do is take a look at the way in which the soul exercises control over the human body form and some of the effects this produces. The next few remarks to be made, however, may well cause some astonishment or even disbelief on the part of some readers. Notwithstanding this, they are based on a systematic logic, which should at least be considered on its own terms.

First of all, as we suggested at the outset, the terrestrial soul is a deva or angelic hierarch emanated by the planet's archangelic Oversoul. The latter is itself a composite mind-intelligence of a greater hierarchy of far more highly evolved solar entities called in the East *Dhyani Chohans*. These latter beings are (from the planetary viewpoint) fully developed Intelligences of archangelic status. As exponents of the memory of the Logos, they have complete freedom of movement within the solar system as a whole. From one angle, they are themselves the intelligent projections of the Oversoul of our solar system, and it is they (collectively) who constitute what most people regard as "God" or "the Mind of God." However, they are themselves merely the aspectual expressions of the logoic memory. They thus comprise what the ancient gnostics called "the second god" (the creative "architect") or Demiurgos. Of their origin the *Hermetica* correspondingly says:

> The Mind who is God, being androgyne and existing as life and light, gave birth to a second mind, a craftsman who, as god of fire and spirit, crafted seven governors; they encompass the sensible world in circles and their government is called Fate.[6]

These "governors" are the archangels responsible for containing within their own nature (by way of an infinite stream of lesser angelic hierarchies) the various planes or states of our solar and planetary systems.

As we shall see later on, the higher "Mind Who is God" takes the form of a hugely advanced hierarchy of fully liberated spirits called *Dhyani Buddhas*. The inner "divine spark" of the human is of exactly the same nature as these entities,[7] but, still possessing a mass consciousness, does not yet have their faculty of self-realization together with all the knowledge and powers that generates. Before full SELF-realization—to begin with as a human being, then as an Adept—one must first of all develop a merely psycho-spiritual Self-consciousness and then a semi-divine SELF-consciousness, these being derived from progressively higher Oversoul faculties. The average human has as yet only developed an egoic self-consciousness attached to the terrestrial soul nature, which provides a merely human sense of individuality, far advanced though this is above even the highest of the animal types.

The Spiritual Soul entity containing the human consciousness-to-be is itself a deva "cell" emanated by the Oversoul of our solar system, which is itself merely the objective vehicle of the Solar Logos. Within it is to be found a group of divine (potentially human) "sparks" from a yet higher celestial scheme. The latter is said to involve seven solar systems, of which ours is but one. This spiritual group soul entity might perhaps be crudely described as fastening around our planetary Oversoul like a limpet and from here projecting subaspects of itself (those same "sparks") into local terrestrial soul entities, which themselves descend from the "firmament" of the Oversoul, down to Earth. A graphic (see fig. 2.5) from an ancient Egyptian wall carving symbolizes what is intended here, the scarab beetle itself signifying the principle of self-resurrection or reincarnation.

Fig. 2.5. Human soul self-emerging from the firmament

Each such terrestrial soul entity, thus "overshadowed" by the Causal Soul nature, then generates the human form from out of the matter of the astral light (the etheric double) of the planet, which it has "captured." The terrestrial soul projects seven types of psycho-spiritual force into the human etheric double; these are the origins of the seven primary chakras in the human entity with which we are so familiar. From these seven are then generated forty-two lesser chakras. Then, following the radiant transmission of energies and the forming of dynamic interrelationships between primary and subsidiary chakras, the organs of the body—and the body itself—come forth into objective existence. Hence the objective body is the creation of the soul.

HUMAN PSYCHIC CONSTITUTION

As we have already seen, the outgoing and incoming cycle in the lower world takes place in the three lowest of the seven planetary states—those we associate with the physical, astral, and mental planes of consciousness. (See again fig. 1.10.) As each of these are sevenfold in nature, the lower world scheme effectively comprises twenty-one substates. In the ancient Sufi tradition (now reclothed as the esoteric part of the Islamic religion) we correspondingly find the idea that human incarnation in the lower world scheme is accompanied by twenty-one angels, separated into a higher trio and eighteen lesser angels. The higher trio of solar angels represents the three highest mental substates. Considered in descending order, they are of a purely impersonal, semi-spiritual quality and have the following functions:

1. The guardian angel of life and death
2. The recording angel-cum-conscience
3. The angel that (via the abstract mind) directs human higher intelligence

Together, these three constitute the Higher Mind or Spiritual Ego/Self of the individual, which we have already described. The lesser eighteen angels constitute the merely elemental (and thus transitory) personality of a human being and rely entirely upon the three angels of the Higher Mind to regenerate in them the reincarnating sense of individuality. From this description it should become readily apparent that the cycle of each human lifetime is also entirely dependent upon the three angels of the Higher Mind. They themselves are the temporarily emanating agents of an immense spiritual group to be found on the buddhic plane of being, having a particular relationship with one or another of the Seven Rays (see chapter 9) via the human monad, or divine spark. They are thus to be considered as the direct influences on the individual of the Purpose emanating from the kosmic Mind of the Logos. This suggestion needs to be considered very carefully. It will be mentioned again later.

Three of the eighteen lower angels are clearly and immediately visible to modern theosophical esotericism as the three "Permanent Atoms" (of the physical, astral, and lower mental states), which are the seeds of reincarnation. In combination, the three Permanent Atoms guide one's evolutionary progress from lifetime to lifetime and accordingly contain one's personal karma or psycho-spiritual heredity. Of these three, the mental "Permanent Atom angel" is of particular importance, as we shall see later on, for it involves that faculty par excellence that coordinates all the other seventeen lower elemental substates and thereby gives the individual human being his or her integrated personality.

THE TERRESTRIAL SOUL
AND ITS ORGANIZATION

Having thus briefly considered the overall constitution of the human entity (excluding its truly spiritual nature), let us next consider the lesser parts in greater detail, commencing first of all with the terrestrial soul organism (refer again to fig. 1.6), which contains the seven elemental substates of the overall physical being. Modern research shows these seven to be organized as a duality involving a progressively dense lower trio (comprising the gaseous, liquid, and dense elements of the objective body form) and a higher quaternary of ethereal substates, which need to be considered in further detail as follows.

1. The luminescent soul entity, or fiery ring-pass-not
2. The outer rays of personal electromagnetic life force containing the instinctive knowledge faculty
3. The aura of vitality radiations (*prana* in Sanskrit)
4. The etheric double (Sanskrit *linga sarira*)—containing the chakras

First of all, let us deal with the completely false notion that the etheric double (pictured in fig. 1.6) is an extension or extrusion of the dense physical body. It most definitely is not. When the terrestrial soul commences the cycle of incarnation (enfolded by the Higher Mind principle projected by the Causal Soul), it does so as a field that contains only a homogeneous mass of etheric (i.e., pregenetic) substance within its enfolding auric embrace. This is itself borrowed from the "astral light" of our planet. That then separates into a duality as the "sparks" projected within it form a web of interrelated geometrical relationships as major and minor chakras, or emanating centers of vital force. The lesser part of the duality takes the form of a denser continuum, which then coalesces around these major and minor chakras, thereafter generating the foundational cells and then the bones, muscles, organs, and so on of the physical body. We can thus say that the dense body organism with which we are familiar is itself "hung" on the underlying etheric web. The pranic vitality aura indicates just how healthy the web is. The outermost rays, however, are those of really dynamic surplus, hence liberation.

They are so powerfully radiant that, in some cases—for example the extreme mystic state—they can be physically seen.

THE CHAKRAS AND
THEIR EVOLUTIONARY FUNCTION

The chakras themselves are vortices of semi-intelligent psychic force that take up their existence within the substance of the etheric double. The major ones are distributed as shown in fig. 2.6. Like all vortices, they draw down, and it is from them that the animating and maintaining energies of the physical body are themselves constituted and distributed. The pranic (that is, surplus energy) radiations, however—notably in the very healthy individual—appear to emanate from all over the etheric double. The outermost rays are of a singularly distinctive nature, for they are indicative of a certain stage of spiritual development. When they are apparent, the whole "physical" aura takes on a completely different and far more radiant appearance, which extends in diameter far beyond the norm for the average human individual.

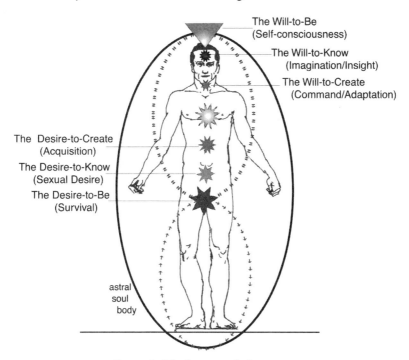

Fig. 2.6. The human chakra system

In the case of the relatively undeveloped or little evolved human being, the majority of activity is to be found in the vitality aura and the lower chakras—the solar plexus, sacral plexus, and base of the spine. These three are respectively associated with emotions, desires, and sexuality, plus the survival instinct. In the more advanced type of human being, a greater degree of activity is to be found in the heart, throat, and brow (ajna) centers, although reflex activity in the lower chakras is still evident. In these types, where the natural intelligence in the heart chakra is constantly and often violently being pulled in either direction, the individual frequently tends to suffer from heart disease or heart-associated difficulties or abnormalities. Where any particular center is overactive but nondistributive, cancers are frequently to be found.

The underlying problems here are differently polarized, although both derive from an overabundance of self-concern, with heart problems being due to uncontrollably fluctuating stress, and cancers deriving from unwillingness to let go of those energies and forces associated with desire and fear. Hence it is that the process of spiritual initiation necessarily requires the psychological abolition of self-centeredness. It is this that ultimately provides the perfect health of the evolved Adept.

As the spiritual development of an individual progresses, the appearance of the terrestrial soul entity itself changes, in concord with the nature of the overshadowing Causal Soul. Instead of its originally quiescent ovoid nature, the soul periphery becomes more spheroidal in shape and its periphery develops (through intensified vibration) a much more self-evident wavelike appearance, through the points of which radiations project. This produces a remarkable harmony of colors both internally and externally. The etheric double—which originally has the appearance of a smoky grey overlay on the physical body (although actually extending right through it)—develops a violet or rose-hued nature.[8] This can actually be seen "from the inside," as it were, by the individual during meditation.

At a certain stage of spiritual development, in the area of the crown chakra, a very real and literally sparkling iridescence and radiance become visible. The image of this "crown," together with the violet "cloak" of the spiritually empowered etheric double, gave rise to the ancient philosopher-king's vestures of majesty, adopted by the Roman emperors and seen to some extent in the regalia of the British monarchy today. As we shall see later on, the third initiatory degree in the Mysteries conferred this (and associated powers) on the individual, thereby admitting them to the true "aristocracy."

However, let us now take a look at certain of the main chakras within the human organism and endeavor to understand what part they play in the bigger evolutionary perspective. This should help to link up and explain the corresponding rationale of the overall psycho-spiritual organism.

The solar plexus chakra, to begin with, might be regarded from one angle, as the lower counterpart to the throat chakra. Both are concerned with self-expression, but the solar plexus is of a purely astral or astro-mental nature. Less evolved yet dominant human personalities use the solar plexus chakra in a positive manner, to generate their feelings and make their personal presence felt. However, they do so only psychically, through the response of others to the potent magnetic field generated by this center. The throat center, in such a case, is secondary to and dominated by it. However, in a gentler type of individual, the function of the solar plexus chakra (which is itself dual in nature and function) tends to relapse into a passively functional psychic sensitivity. Such psychic sensitivity usually remains of an unconscious nature, despite the constant resonance with the psychic projections of other individuals, which results in constant emotional fluctuations of whose source the individual is unaware.

The other notable use to which this solar plexus chakra is put is that of generating and expressing devotional idealism, hence its importance in all religions where it often results in the production of very apparent mass fields of (psychic) electromagnetic influence. Interestingly, such fields are also sometimes generated by response to great orators. That is because the throat chakra, through the use of compound, modulated sound, generates a vibratory energy that powerfully interconnects or interrelates different qualities of emotional or mental substance. It does so in a much more obvious and self-consciously potent manner than the unselfconsciously operated solar plexus chakra and its purely personal type of energy.

The ajna or brow center is the higher counterpart to the sacral chakra. The "desire-to-know," in a sexual or biblical sense, is generated in the latter, whereas the brow chakra generates the "Will-to-know" energy. Both are concerned with projection and the derivation of experiential knowledge. In a very real sense they are associated with the generation of the soul principle, for, as we have already seen, it is the soul organism that contains all knowledge. Hence also the fact that these two centers are concerned with the transfer of knowledge, or a state of being, from one organism to another and also with the principle of fertility.

THE THREE SOULS OF THE HUMAN

As we saw from fig. 1.6, the objective human being (at least, at a certain stage of development) is surrounded by three soul bodies—the spiritual, the causal, and the terrestrial. Much later, an individualized divine soul comes into being. Interestingly, this same idea is apparent in the gnostic teachings of two thousand years ago. Then, Christian theologians condemned as heretical the concept—as described by the early Christian bishop Origen, whose ideas were clearly gnostic—that, after the "Last Judgment," the arisen soul of perfected man would have an ethereal and spheroidally shaped body.[9] However, in the vast majority of individuals, the true Spiritual Soul is nonfunctional because it is still dormant. It only becomes active when the individual has reached a certain highly advanced stage "on the Path." All this is perhaps more logically understandable if we now take a look at the positioning of the three main chakras—the spine base, heart, and crown—in the pictures. In doing so, we shall see that these are seemingly located at the center of each of the three soul bodies, in ascending order. However, by virtue of the fact that the concentric principle does not work in quite such a simple manner, but rather by sympathetic vibrational response, the image (which is not to scale) is only intended to be indicative of certain issues, as follows.

The spine base chakra is directly associated with the mineral kingdom (hence the planetary or terrestrial soul), the heart chakra with the human kingdom (hence the Causal Soul), and the crown chakra with the spiritual kingdom (hence the future Spiritual Soul). The association in each case is one of sympathetic vibration, involving consciousness at a particular turning point. Hence it is that the sacral/genital and solar plexus chakras—associated with the plant and animal kingdoms respectively—are merely indicative of intermediate evolutionary stages. When the spine base chakra becomes objective and constitutionally coherent, physical manifestation becomes possible because of the terrestrial desire-to-be. Correspondingly, when the crown chakra does so, psycho-spiritual consciousness—involving the spiritual Will-to-be—comes into play. A far higher transition takes place. Thus the brow and throat chakras are also of an intermediate nature, expressing the Will-to-know and the Will-to-act/adapt respectively.

The heart chakra, in a curious sense, stands alone, although specifically associated with the semi-spiritual Causal Soul nature of the human, as we shall see later, in greater detail. It is found in the animal although possessing there only a vital, circulatory function, while in the human it contains much more highly developed sensory faculties. The human form has an animal-like appearance in certain respects, because what is esoterically called "the solar angel" has, on behalf of the monadic spirit, generated a terrestrial soul that only has the instinctive knowledge of how to produce an animal-like form. Like the human faculty of acting as the imagination of the Demiurge, the human heart chakra contains an intelligence of its own, uniting the three lower and three higher chakras in one single (but sevenfold) organism. The animal nature on its own is incapable of doing this.

It is perhaps worth mentioning here that the self-conscious nature of the human is derived from the focalization of consciousness being in the heart center. From there (until the initiatory Path is attained), energies are instinctively projected mainly downward to the solar, sacral, and spine base chakras, as already described. In the animal, the primary anchor or focus of consciousness is still in the spine base center (hence the intensity of desire for survival), from which upward force is generated and projected to the sacral and plexal centers. This is by virtue of influences emanating downward from the animal group soul "located" (with other major group souls) within the buddhic state of consciousness.

EVOLUTIONARY TRANSITION

Finally, let us take a look at the principles behind the transitional evolutionary development that takes place between the various kingdoms of Nature. As we shall see, these are quite different from what Darwinists fondly imagine. Development according to these principles also bears little relationship to what Creationists assume in their wholly literalistic interpretations of what the Bible has to say on various related issues.

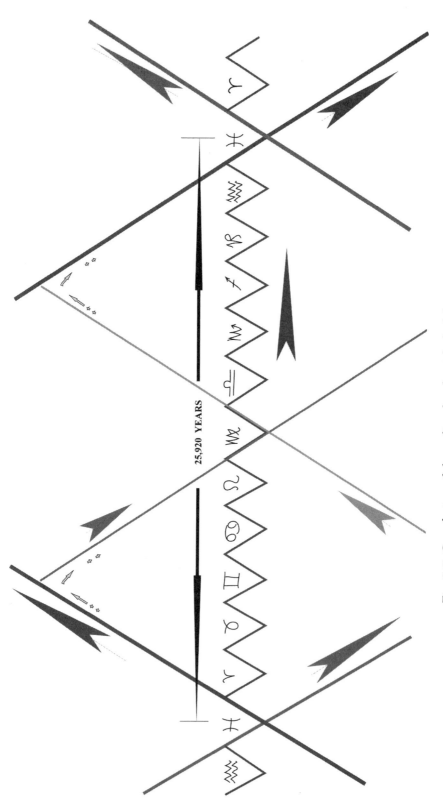

25,920 YEARS

Fig. 2.7. Correlation of the zodiacal cycle with the life wave

To begin with, fig. 2.7 provides us with a graphic depiction of wave-like sequences in the unfoldment of our planetary consciousness. Within this, a zodiacal cycle of 25,920 years (otherwise known as the "precession of the equinoxes") comprises twelve subcycles (shown by the purple lines), each of 2,160 years, each subcycle consisting of an involutionary (outward) and evolutionary (inward) progression. The overall cycle has, however, to be seen predominantly in the context of the giant carrier wave of kosmic consciousness that gives rise to it.

Each sequential part of the overall wave gives rise to the appearance of a particular subkingdom or subspecies (not all objective), but it is also shared between kingdoms, qualitatively speaking, just as the senses of the animal have higher counterparts in the human being. However, whereas Darwinism imagines the evolutionary change to take place only at the physical level, esoteric philosophy takes the stance that it actually occurs within the purely psycho-spiritual field. It only then translates itself, later on, into a complete change of objective form. Thus it is that there is no such thing in evolutionary terms as a purely physical "missing link" between the human and animal kingdoms, or between the animal and plant kingdoms, or between the plant and mineral kingdoms either.

Notwithstanding this, there do appear to be anthropological "throwbacks," which confuse the issue. For example, esoteric philosophy tells us that the anthropoid apes are in fact interspecies degenerates, brought about by wrongful (but purely temporary) sexual liaisons between early humans and proto-simian ancestors, many millions of years ago.[10] These, fortunately, could not take place today, although some misguided scientists working in the field of genetics would doubtless like to believe that they could achieve such things. Despite their having learned that the structure of cellular matter is spiral (one might suggest that DNA is actually spiral-cyclic, by virtue of its rotation), they have far to go before coming to any real understanding of what life itself actually is. Correspondingly, as to what extent life's appearances and disappearances are dependent upon other vital factors, modern physical science as yet knows absolutely nothing.

THE CONTROL OF THE LOWER NATURE
BY THE HIGHER

One such vital factor in the appearance of life is the way in which the Higher Mind principle drives and conditions the terrestrial soul, thereby engendering self-consciousness in the human being. However, in relation to those people in whom irrationality takes over consciousness, the *Hermetica* tells us:

> Mind often flies out of soul and in that hour soul neither sees nor hears but acts like an animal without reason—so great is the power of mind. But in a sluggish soul mind cannot endure, it leaves such a soul behind as clinging to the body, held down and smothered by it. Such a soul . . . does not possess mind and so one must not say that such a thing is human.[11]

From this it is quite clear just how important some form of public education is, involving a definitely higher moral or ethical aspect. Without this the less developed natural intelligence of humankind tends to be overcome by the elemental nature of the terrestrial soul. The result is a mixture of creative vacuity on the one hand and instinctively selfish (even vicious) behavior on the other, varying degrees of both being extensively self-evident among humanity today. This is so, paradoxically, particularly in the urban environment and more especially in the peripheral urban slums of those major cities where great financial wealth is to be found accompanied by little or no real social conscience. The *Hermetica* adds the following advice for the benefit of those willing to listen:

> [The higher] Mind displays its own splendour to those souls that it commands and it opposes their predilections. As a good physician, using the cautery and the knife, causes pain to the body overtaken by disease, in the same way mind causes pain to the soul, withdrawing it from the pleasure that gives rise to every disease of the soul.[12]

THE IMPORTANCE OF CYCLES

One of the primary factors that our modern science also fails (as yet) to take into consideration in relation to these issues involves what esotericists call "the law of cycles." These periods of duration (not *time* per se, for time does not actually exist) actually comprise unfolding periods of consciousness within the minds of celestial Intelligences both inside and outside our immediate (solar) system. These thus involve astrological influences, for the simple reason that the planets and stars are themselves, so we are told, the "vehicles" of endless hierarchies of celestial Intelligences (the Dhyani Chohans and Dhyani Buddhas already mentioned) of greater and lesser potency. Their constantly changing interrelationships, in response to Divine Purpose, give rise to the very structure and fabric of the universe.

The issue of cycles is of enormous and fundamental importance when we come to the study of esoteric philosophy, where we find that the whole issue of initiation is inextricably interlinked with it. The connections between greater and lesser cycles—as cycles of consciousness—give rise to the sympathetically organized appearance and disappearance not only of new forms in the species of our planetary life but also of old and new impulses in human civilization. Hence the true underlying nature and importance of initiation. As the ancient wisdom tradition has it, all in the kosmos takes place in accordance with intelligently managed order.[13]

EVOLUTION AND THE SPIRITUAL PATH

Let us now take a closer look at the developing inner experience of the individual as he or she progresses on what is called "the spiritual Path." That is the name given by esotericists to the ascending stream of consciousness that individuals must generate for themselves in trying to connect with a correspondingly willing descent of higher consciousness. This, interestingly enough, was allegorized by the ancient Egyptians in the Creation story told to Herodotus of the two phoenixes (see fig. 2.8) that descended from heaven as the primeval mound of Earth (*Atum*) first rose above the waters.[14] One phoenix (the supposedly "dead" one), evidently representing past *karma*, is buried by the other "live" one, representing *dharma*, the

Fig. 2.8. Egyptian phoenixes

duty inherent in the purpose of the present lifetime, as imposed by the Higher Self.

Our first consideration is to remind ourselves that consciousness is qualitatively organized, with its own fields of limitation. Hence, in order to access a higher quality of consciousness, the individual must first correspondingly relinquish that which is grosser and unable to coordinate usefully with it. This natural separation comes about as a result of the far greater power generated by higher consciousness, relative to the seductively magnetic but less forceful power of a lower form of consciousness. The higher has an astringently vital, cleansing effect, which requires the willing cooperation of the soul through which it must pass. The soul that prefers the status quo sticks with the old and crystallized forms of energy, which eventually lose all their force and turn to elemental corruption. It is thus the intelligence of the individual that—via control of the mind—uses the soul as a transformer of higher energies. It does so by steadying its tensile nature in order to render it more sensitive to external influences. That thereby causes in the first place the development of the desire nature (the externally sensory emanation of the terrestrial soul), which later evolves into a field of higher aspiration. This is of really fundamental importance and therefore needs to be remembered at all times.

PLANES AND STATES OF BEING AND CONSCIOUSNESS

If we once again consider the structure of the human persona from the viewpoint of the esotericist (shown in fig. 2.9), we find what was described earlier, in line with the kabbalistic Zohar. Here are shown the four lower (of seven) planes within the overall field of consciousness associated with our planetary scheme. A projection of spiritual radiance (taking the form of Mind-force, or intelligence) is emanated from the spiritual state on the fourth plane. This emanation, as already described, contains within itself that which will give rise in matter to the three aspects of desire: (1) the desire-to-be; (2) the desire-to-know; and (3) the desire-to-create/adapt. These thereby generate the three primordial soul states—the physical, astral, and lower mental—which together form the reincarnating human entity, as already described.

The descending emanation (synonymous with the theosophical Fohat, the gnostic Sophia, and the Greek Eros)[15] continues on its way, eventually giving rise to an entity (that is, a soul entity) containing the seven grades of substance of the physical or terrestrial plane (see fig. 2.10). In the kabbalistic tradition, these ten stages in the Macrocosm are referred to as *sephiroth*. In fact, exactly the same set of principles holds good in the appearance of the microcosm, the human. For, as we saw earlier on, Keter is the primary emanating source, which we refer to as the "Spiritual Ego," Hokmah (meaning "great magic") is the spiral-cyclic emanation of Mind itself, while Binah is representative of the terrestrial soul, the "great sea" that contains the other seven as substates. In biblical terms, Binah is also the "Great Mother," the manifest heaven world of the firmament (i.e., the Oversoul), which is generated by the Elohim, thereby containing the "waters below," separate from the "waters above," as biblical Genesis has it.

The spark of intelligence that "falls into generation" from a higher field

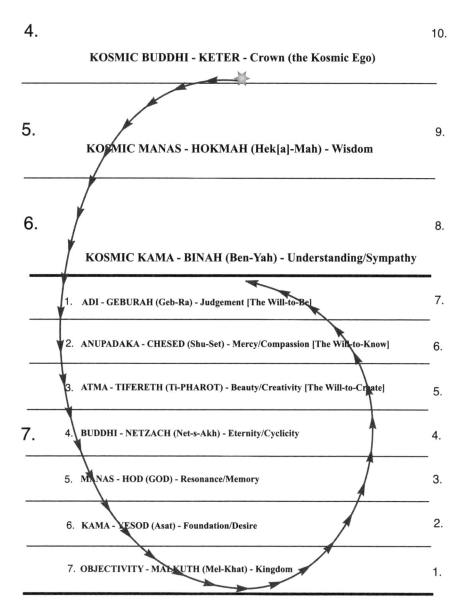

Fig. 2.9. The theosophical Kabbala

of consciousness has to return to its emanating Source. In doing so, it adapts the consciousness of the astral/terrestrial soul, thereby generating an external field of desire and a further field of mind-memory based on experience, as described in the previous chapter. As a result, the human persona consists of: (1) the physical senses; (2) the field of desires and feelings; and (3) the lesser

Mind field and its associated faculty, comprising four substates. In addition, however, the original highest three mental substates mentioned earlier still exist. These are the local, microcosmic equivalent of the Christian Trinity, which are described in the Moslem faith as the three angels that accompany all human beings during each incarnation, as we mentioned a little earlier. To reiterate, the highest is the "angel with the sword" who guards the "Gate

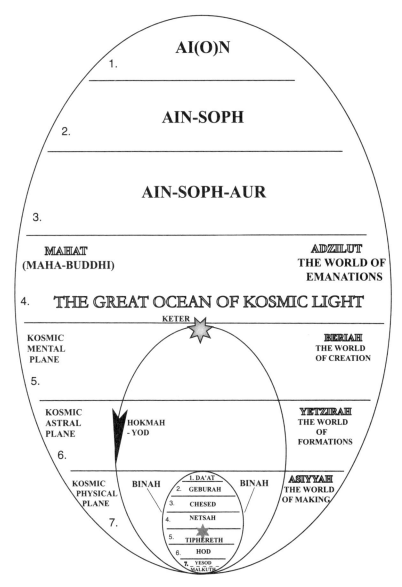

Fig. 2.10. The Kabbala relative to planes of consciousness

of Heaven" itself; the second is the angel recorder of all life experience; and the third is the angel of *karma* and *dharma,* or higher memory and purpose, which guides the lesser human life.

Interestingly, in the modern theosophical tradition, the evolved human personal ego takes the part of the third angel, while the Spiritual Ego takes the part of the second angel. The first angel remains the "guardian angel of the Presence." In terms of human reincarnatory experience, the third angel is "punished" by being forced to contain and regenerate all the accumulated karmic deficiencies of previous cycles.

Thus, in the modern theosophical tradition, the fourth mental angel thereby becomes what is esoterically known as the "Dweller on the Threshold"—a potentially malignant egoic entity that must ultimately be entirely subjugated and its sense of self-centered independence then destroyed beyond reanimation, as we shall see later on. The second angel meanwhile accumulates all the positive essences derived from the spiritually oriented "good deeds" of each cycle of incarnation. It thus becomes the future creative spiritual individuality, which, with the first angel, will eventually generate a form of Self-conscious existence within the fourth (spiritual) state of the planetary scheme. It is thus that the whole process of spiritual evolution proceeds on its way, because the third angel is esoterically related to the third initiation in the sequence of seven. This will be described in greater detail later on.

GLAMOUR AND ILLUSION

One of the things that modern psychology as yet fails to recognize is that the field under discussion deals with the interaction of very real energies and forces—much more real than those externally visible. With that in mind, it is perhaps worthwhile pausing a moment to deal with the issues of glamour and self-indulgence, which so malignantly infect our world today in so many ways. A large part of this is due to psychologists and psychiatrists in general (excluding only a few) lacking any real understanding of the concept of hermeneutically arranged planes of being and consciousness. As a direct result, they are themselves easily confused, because they are unable to define logically where actual problems might exist or arise in the subconscious nature of their patients. They also have little or no sense of consciousness being qualitatively organized, which reduces their accuracy yet further. It is thus hardly surprising that every psychiatrist has their own psychiatrist! But the fact that this is regarded as "normal" is indicative of just how out of control the situation really is.

Human beings, in using their day-to-day consciousness, tend to function rather chaotically (usually out of habit or fear). As a result of the lack of use of their discriminating or qualitative sense, they are easily disorientated and frequently unable to discern rationally on the basis of complementary behavior. They "hear but do not listen." They therefore tend to react irrationally rather than to respond intelligently. They then compound the problem by revisiting such experiences through reliving them in their imagination, thereby further weakening their own subjective constitution. All such reaction is based on either glamour or illusion. As the individual on the spiritual evolutionary "Path" has to learn to conquer these two, amid much unavoidable suffering, it would perhaps be helpful to describe what they essentially are and how they come about.

Very basically, glamour is the result of astral desire, whereas illusion is the result of (lower) mental projection. Together they constitute the very basis of the human predisposition to like and dislike, which causes us so many problems in our social interaction with others. As we have already seen, both of these are founded on the characteristic nature of the terrestrial soul. In the vast majority of animals where the polarity of consciousness is still entirely physical, glamour as such does not exist. Such astral desire as exists is wholly orientated toward the satisfaction of the purely physical senses, involving self-preservation, food, sexual procreation, and so on.

In the higher animals, however, a rudimentary form of glamour does exist, partly by virtue of their astral attraction and devotion to humanity and partly because of the preliminary development of a semiconscious use of the lowest aspects of the lower mind. This is not emotion as such, although some mammals—elephants, for example—are said to suffer emotionally as a result of a sense of bereavement from deaths in their herd groups. The glamour factor in higher animals is largely based on a willingness to follow and is consequently related to the herd instinct—as it also is with human beings.

However, by virtue of the lower mind also being somewhat expertly developed in humans (unlike animals), its union with glamour produces a tremendously supercharged potency, which mere animal consciousness cannot begin to match. Hence it is that humans are so easily glamorized by the potential or actual ownership of "things," by reference to purely subjective factors, including how other folk actually react to the same range of "things" and also how the individual believes other people will react to their own such ownership. The latter effect is of course derived from the work of the imagination, which the animal does not possess, not having yet evolved it. Despite the practice of colorful mating rituals, social "one-upmanship" does not exist in the animal kingdom except as leader of the herd, although a crude sense of "ownership" of territory and even of artifacts is evident in some mammalian species for practical, physical reasons.

POLITICAL CORRECTNESS

One of the other foolish phenomena practiced by human beings today (in the West at least) is that of so-called "political correctness." This actually involves a technique of allowing people to feel psychologically superior by very openly pointing the finger at others' supposed social failings and inviting others to join in general condemnation. This entirely pernicious practice—totally contrary to the Christian admonition "He amongst you who is without sin, let him cast the first stone"—positively invites and encourages our fellow humans to engage in reckless and wholly unnecessary social vindictiveness. It is thus deliberately mischief-making.

It undermines personal confidence in those taking a real moral or ethical stance and is always pursued only by those with little minds who themselves lack any real depth of character. In short, it (unconsciously but still dangerously) seeks to drag human intercourse into the viscous mud of a common mistrust, which eventually destroys the very foundations of human sympathy, culture, and civilization. It is precisely this sort of general mistrust that has characterized all modern totalitarian political regimes since the French Revolution in the late eighteenth century. However, it was also found in earlier religious regimes leading, for example, to thousands being burned for witchcraft.

Nobody of real natural intelligence (and by that I do not mean the merely intellectual) would practice political correctness because their Higher Self would immediately perceive its entirely vicious and self-seeking nature. Those who quite rightly disapprove of perniciously antisocial behavior would instead seek to arrest it by other means, whether direct or indirect, but always by taking personal responsibility. They would, in short, seek to arrest the cause at source rather than merely seeking to bury the mere symptoms under a cloud of supposed public disapproval in the hope of distracting attention from their own shortcomings. Dishonesty and lack of psychological integrity lie at the base of all political correctness. Thus anyone truly "on the Path" would reject it outright. Even those who do find themselves caught up in it feel a real sense of personal shame at their own weakness.

THE INNER VOICE OF THE SILENCE

The "voice of the silence" is at once our personal "guardian angel" and our teacher, through the use of both conscience and intuition, which both emanate from the Spiritual Ego, the very source of our innate evolutionary drive. It is the very real voice of the Higher Self in us all—hence the fact that it has for so long been regarded in religious terms as the "Word of God" speaking directly to the individual. However, until an individual learns to recognize it as the direct influence of the Spiritual Ego and to make a point of listening and acting upon it, the momentum of his or her own spiritual evolution will not be maintained. Spiritual evolution requires an ever-increasing degree of self-applied personal integrity, which is not psychologically negotiable.

Thus it is essential that we try to understand what exactly the "voice of the silence" is and how it works. While we can only hear it or feel its influence during the earlier stages of our development, there will come a time when we actually come face to face with it, recognizing it for our own true Self. We have already seen that the whole process of evolution works "from the top downward." Hence it is that the Higher Self stays exactly where it is (in the spiritual state) and merely projects a tiny aspect of itself downward into the terrestrial soul nature. This "spark" of natural intelligence anchors itself in the heart chakra of the individual, but its influence is extended gradually throughout the body, via all the lesser chakras. Thus it is that the heart is the true center of human intelligence. The logical follow-on from this is that the whole process of what we call "death" merely involves the projected "spark" being withdrawn back to its semi-spiritual source. In reality, there is no such thing as death because there is a factually permanent continuity of consciousness. Death merely involves the separation of the animating consciousness from the objective body form.

Once the intelligence in a human being recognizes this logic, a process of inner reorientation starts gradually, yet irrevocably, to take place. That process will undoubtedly take many lifetimes before it becomes thoroughly embedded in the waking consciousness as a living paradigm of near certainty. It will then take a few more lifetimes before the individual actually arrives at the point of factually recognizing the Spiritual Ego and being able, at will, to call upon its influence and power. This—as we shall see in a later chapter—takes place when the individual has undergone the third of the seven main initiations, which pertain to the evolution of purely human consciousness.

The individual has to constantly practice a top-down orientation from an early age—hence the importance of its inculcation both in the home and at school—otherwise the inner nature will steadily weaken, through drifting backward toward the instinctively selfish focus of the terrestrial soul nature. From this viewpoint we can perhaps understand the suggestion that adherence to practically applied ethical standards through education is vital to the very quality of our human civilization and its various cultures.

THE GREATER PERSPECTIVE

Curiously enough, however, the Spiritual Ego is not the highest Self in the human experience. That is because this Ego is itself merely a secondary aspect of a far higher and more powerful Intelligence still, which theosophists call "the divine Monad," already mentioned earlier. Just as the Spiritual Ego in the human projects a tiny egoic aspect of itself into the terrestrial soul nature, ending up in the heart chakra of the human individual, so the spiritual EGO of our Logos is said to do the same from its much higher (kosmic) plane of existence. This emanation generates seven "Ray Groups" of divine Monads, of which we shall hear much more later on, in relation to their individualization on the "Higher Path." They—even though we may not understand quite how—are themselves "divine sparks" of the kosmic Mind and, in

Fig. 2.11. The gnostic ABRAXAS

conjunction with other such "sparks" (which motivate the other kingdoms of Nature), are responsible for the intelligent animation and purposeful coordination of the whole physical body of the Logos. Therefore, when we talk about evolution, what we are actually discussing—even if we are unaware of it—is the progressive incarnation of the Logos "in Whom (as St. Paul puts it) we live and move and have our being."

For those interested in gnostic philosophy, it might be worthwhile pausing here to indicate one or two parallels with which very few are familiar. Working "from above to below," we start with the idea that the field of Kosmic Buddhi* is the same as the Ain Soph Aur of the kabbalist and the Pleroma of the gnostic. The primordial emanation from this—the kabbalistic Keter, or first sephiroth—gave rise to what the gnostics named ABRAXAS, which appears to mean, quite literally, the emanating heart center (the Egyptian AB'R), which is the pivotal polar axis (hence AXAS) of logoic manifestation. This has been defined by C. G. Jung as: "the fiery force which acts as the primeval union of the opposites at the foundation of psychic life."[16] It is a deity symbolically presented as a triad having the head of a cockerel, the body of a man, and serpents for legs (see fig. 2.11).

This deity is itself equivalent to the kosmic Persona of the Logos,

---

*Here, *Kosmic Buddhi* is to be understood as "the kosmic etheric double of our greater celestial system, the higher, spiritual equivalent of the astral light of the planet."

hence its triune nature. By virtue of its own self-emanation, it duly gave rise to a secondary god—that known to gnostics as Ialdabaoth, meaning (as Blavatsky tells us) "the child born in the egg of Chaos."[17] This projection is thereby synonymous with the aeonic Demiurge—having a sevenfold nature and responsible for endless cycles of existence in which the celestially fallen Man (the "divine spark") became trapped. The planetary Demiurge thus emanated within itself that hierarchy of lesser hosts given the name *Sabaoth,* which, as Stephan Hoeller tells us: "is represented as a power who repented of the dark deeds of his demiurgic father and came to worship *Sophia* (Wisdom) and her daughter *Zoe* (Life) and was rewarded by receiving light and becoming the ruler of the seventh heaven."[18]

In practical terms, the Sabaoth are "the Word," the "hosts" of monads or "divine sparks" projected en masse into the lower world scheme (the Underworld) in their ignorance, there to learn how to overcome that environment en route back to the consciousness of Abraxas, before entering the higher Pleroma itself. It is interesting to note that the name *Sabao* was much used by the gnostics, representing one of the hosts of Sabaoth. The ancients were very keen on wordplay to imply concealed (hence esoteric) meanings, which could thus be used safely in public. Thus the name Sabao, is (I suggest) derived from the compound *seb-iao, seb* or *sab* being derived from the Sanskrit *sabda,* meaning "word" (here the "sacred word"), while *iao* derived phonetically from the same root as *yoga,* meaning the collective or gathering force of the kosmic Mind—which we have already otherwise referred to as the Fohat of esoteric Buddhism. Thus the Sabaoth—which eventually escaped from the supposed clutches of their parent the demiurgic Ialdabaoth, lord of cycles—also escaped from the tyranny of cycles of rebirth.

We see in all this superficially complex sacred metaphor and allegory the very way in which true esotericism works. Far from being an invention of Western mystics, as some modern academics suggest, esotericism deals with the inner, archetypal (i.e., causal) realities that lie behind all objective manifestation. Thus the true esotericist is concerned with the world of meaning derived from subjective realities. These he (or she) comes into contact with by skillfully observing and following the intelligently functional side of Nature, which is throughout life ever present and available to the esotericist who is ever-watchfully employing interdisciplinary powers of interpretation. As we are otherwise told:

> Esotericism involves also comprehension of the relation between forces and energies and the power to use energy for the strengthening and then for the creative use of the forces contracted [thereby] bringing down to Earth those energies which emanate from the highest Sources and there "grounding" or anchoring them.[19]

This latter point is of immense significance in relation to the human role in the whole process of creation. That brings us to the subject of human reincarnation—something which we tend to think of in purely individual terms as concerning our personal future. That, however, misses the point. By virtue of the fact that we are all agents of the kosmic Mind (of the Solar Logos), it follows quite logically that we are all here for a higher Purpose that extends far beyond our own purely personal issues. The latter are of purely secondary consideration, irrespective of just how serious they might appear to us in terms of life and death. It also follows quite logically from what has already been said that reincarnation is itself a group activity in order to fulfill a particular function or range of functions within the body or organism of the Logos. This is much easier to understand when we take into consideration the teaching that the spiritual nature of the human functions within the kosmic etheric double of the logoic body, in fact within one or another of the seven kosmic chakras within that same vehicle. It is here that the esoteric teaching about the Seven Rays becomes so important. The Higher Self of each one of us belongs to one or another of the seven Ray Groups, the latter being emanations of the kosmic Mind (of the Logos).

Just as each of our own chakras channel energy and force into our own etheric double—and thence to the physical body—so too do the logoic chakras channel higher Purpose (via these Rays) to groups of Spiritual Egos within them. These groups then project or emanate lesser "sparks" (conditioned by an aspect of that same purpose) from their own nature, which are forced into a new cycle of incarnate life. In so doing, they gather together matter of the lowest three subplanes of the logoic body and, in coordinating them intelligently, give expression to that Purpose. Thus the social and cultural interaction between all human beings is, to some extent at least, part of this same process that gives rise to a definite logoic physical sensitivity and function. In a very real sense, the human is the lynchpin required for logoic incarnation. It thus follows quite logically from this that the more spiritually sensitive and capable the individual human being, the more capable is the Logos of full physical manifestation.

As we know from what science tells us, the different parts of our own body are in a constant process of renewal. For example, the bones are renewed every ten years; the skin is renewed every seven years; each cell exists only for a day. Thus everything is involved in an ongoing, cyclic process of change. That is because the emanations from our own etheric double—in response to the cycles sensed by our planetary soul body—ensure that this takes place. To us this appears instinctual, but coordinated instinct only occurs as a result of overshadowing intelligence.

The planetary soul of each human being is acting in response to the directed purpose imposed upon it by a Higher Self, acting through the Causal Soul. Hence it is that more intelligent groups of human beings find themselves trying to achieve (through group effort) larger and larger scale activities involving common purpose, quite often of an altruistic nature. Thus the existence today of so many aid agencies and welfare agencies, financially supported on a personal, national, and international scale. These had their humble origins in the soup kitchens and workhouses of philanthropic Victorians in the early to mid-nineteenth century, themselves responding to a fundamentally spiritual compassion arising out of a recognition of our common humanity.

LOOKING TOWARD THE FUTURE

From an evolutionary viewpoint, such instinctive mass altruism involves a major step forward. Who could have imagined it only two hundred years ago? Yet the more advanced human intelligences of our time are already looking ahead, on behalf of humankind as a whole, to a prospective time when human hunger and disease no longer exist. Such an idealistic advance has only become possible because the larger part of humankind has achieved an inner realization that this is possible; that international cooperation is necessary for the very survival of an increasingly intelligent and ever more powerful humankind. The evolution of that international realization has itself, in turn, only become possible because of the mass crisis of human consciousness that took place as a result of the two World Wars. These extended historically from 1914–1945.

The first World War, we are told, was viewed by the Adept Hierarchy as a sort of purifying surgical catharsis needed to save humanity's life and promote its future possibilities.[20] As the Tibetan Adept DK has pointed out, it was this subjective "surgery" that resulted in humanity in the mass making that huge psychological reorientation recognized by the Adept Hierarchy as involving the initiation of "probation" preceding what is otherwise known as "accepted discipleship."[21] However, although this pertains to the larger proportion of our humanity in general, it is not universal; nor is it yet a fully "anchored" instinct that prevails at all times and under all conditions.

It has only occurred because a sudden subjective coordination has taken place between the Spiritual Egos of humankind and the "spark in the heart" of each human being, which we associate with compassionately reasoned intelligence. To have responded so unilaterally and with such coordination under intense stress, humanity (at the psycho-spiritual level) has managed to achieve a spiritual–physical link, which has effectively generated a linkage of function in the body of the Logos that never existed before. From this viewpoint it can perhaps be seen why and how the initiatory process and the evolutionary process blend into one. From this viewpoint also we can perhaps see why the phrases "universality of existence" and "universal consciousness" are not mere ideals in the minds of philosophers and esotericists. They are facts in Universal Nature. With that in mind, we can perhaps move on to our next chapter, in which we take a rather more detailed look at the nature and functional character of the deva or angelic hierarchies and their part in the same overall process, while remembering St. Paul's admonition "Know ye not that we [as initiates] shall judge angels?"[22]

THREE

THE UNSEEN KINGDOMS OF NATURE AND THEIR ROLES

In the previous chapter we took a brief initial look at the kingdom in Nature that parallels the human—that of the angels or devas. In this chapter we shall take a closer look at their overall hierarchy and function, in general terms, ranging from their archetypes right down to the lowly nature spirits of the plant kingdom and the elementals* of fire, air, water, and earth to be found on our own planet. In keeping with our main theme, however, we shall be considering them in relation to the whole principle of evolution and initiation. First of all then, because the very mention of devas or angels tends to draw decidedly sideways looks in the West, we need to explain their nature and function as logically as possible so that it can be seen why and how they are fundamental to the whole process of creation and not just imaginary beings derived from the minds of mystics.

In the last two chapters we have explained how Creation is said to be generated and maintained within the sphere of consciousness of a Being beyond all conception. As with the human, the consciousness of this great Being is dual, comprising on the one hand reflexive memory and, on the other, a higher and intuitively derived imagination and reason. The angels

---

Elementals are low-grade psychic entities working their way along the involutionary scale of consciousness development.

98

Fig. 3.1. Ocean deva (courtesy of Theosophical Publishing House, Adyar, and the trustees of Geofrey Hodson)

or devas are the agents of the former, hence they are bound to go on repeating the status quo of form-building in Nature, always in due cycle albeit in progressively better quality. However, human beings (even if unconscious of the fact) are the agents of the latter and are thus the essential cause of all evolutionary change.

The spirits of both deva and human are nevertheless monads (that is, "mind-sparks"), and the two together form the soul vehicle of the Planetary Logos.[1] They are united on the highest plane of the solar scheme (thereby forming what is esoterically called the "sea of divine fire," which contains all the monadic "divine sparks"). The deva and human spirits begin to emerge into dual function on the second and third planes, out of the *akasa*.* The deva beings of this latter state are of archangelic status and they then form the souls of each of the lesser five planes, within which they emanate lesser hierarchies of devas in septenary sequences, these and all ethereal forms within the lower world scheme being generated out of their essence.[2]

All the devas that exist within the solar scheme are known esoterically as

---

Akasa is the spiritual essence that pervades all Space.

the "Army of the Voice." That is because they are the agents of "the Word" (of the Logos), which becomes the Demiurge. Although the concept would as yet be laughed at by orthodox science, the devas emanate from themselves the animating germinal essences within all objective forms in Nature (hence their sustained coherence). Thus, by virtue of their existing as three groups—which are electrically positive, negative, and neutral[3]—they are also the source of all electrical and magnetic activity or potential in Nature. They are its builders.

Hence it is, as Blavatsky tells us, that "the universe is really only a huge aggregation of states of consciousness."[4] With these various suggestions in mind, let us take a look at fig. 3.2.

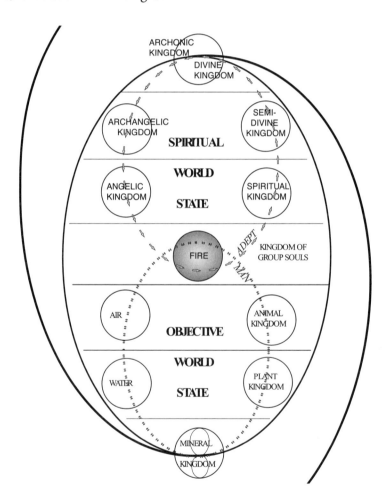

Fig. 3.2. Kosmic physical involutionary/evolutionary progression

The terms *involutionary* and *evolutionary* used here are of fundamental importance and, before we go any further, they need to be clearly understood in relation to what they signify. *Involutionary* means the unfolding particularization of essential types and faculties, leading to the generation of different forms of expression and a consequent limitation of consciousness. *Evolutionary,* on the other hand, refers to the development of understanding of the limitations generated by those forms, thereby resulting in their being gradually transcended. Hence, evolution develops an expansion of consciousness, resulting in a diminution of the sense of importance attached to the form. In short, *involution* is concerned with developing self-expression through limitation, whereas *evolution* is concerned with transcending limitation through conscious knowledge, or understanding.

Fig. 3.2 depicts the involutionary and evolutionary states and cycles of both spirit and matter in the complementary fields of solar and terrestrial existence, which together comprise the lowest kosmic plane. Within this structure of our local universe, the four upper planes are regarded as solar, hence the related deva entities are known as solar *pitris* (Sanskrit for "ancestors"). Correspondingly, the three lower planes—although comprising our terrestrial Nature—are regarded as being inhabited by "lunar pitris." That is because their nature is seen as that of the first (now nonexistent) solar system, of which the Moon is seen as the last in the chain of planets. (Our present solar system is regarded as the second in a progressive, evolutionary series of three such systems.[5] See appendix D for further detail.) Each of the seven planes shown are contained by a great deva of archangelic status, while each of these in turn actually manifests through seven great deva groups of lesser status, these forming the actual vitality and consciousness of each subplane.[6]

In relation to the three lowest planes or states associated with the elements of air, water, and earth, the manifesting deva essences are all considered esoterically as aspects of the centrifugal fire (Sanskrit: *agni*). Hence they are known in the Hindu tradition by their Sanskrit names: *agnisvattas, agnisuryans,* and *agnichaitans.* The suffix *chaitan* in the last of these is the origin of the much abused and misunderstood European word Satan (*shatan* in the Hebrew, meaning "adversary"), which is not fundamentally demonic or evil at all, the latter idea being merely due to a misinterpretation.

A passing point of clarification might be made here concerning the fivefold sequence of the elements that, in most instances, is aether, air, fire, water, earth. In this instance "air" is equivalent to the "atmosphere," which is actually supported by the common etheric state—what Eliphas Levi called "the astral light." However, as we know from science, many gases are non-combustible and much more prone to condensation—hence their moisture content. It is only when gases dry out that they become electrified or ionized in nature. It is only then, through their combining with the etheric state, that combustion actually takes place. Thus, the more appropriate sequence of elements would be aether, ether-fire, air, water, earth.

INVOLUTIONARY AND EVOLUTIONARY PROGRESSION

In the ancient wisdom tradition, the involutionary and evolutionary impulses and cycles were seen to be influenced and guided by the most advanced Intelligences forming the two aspectual branches of divine consciousness. These were the archons (superior archangels) and the Dhyani Buddha gods respectively—the "guides" of our planetary life—each having its own progressive subhierarchies. These we shall be looking at in some further detail in this and later chapters. In the meantime, it will be seen (again from fig. 3.2) that what we are primarily focusing on are two seemingly parallel fields of existence. The upper spiritual one is that of the involuting deva or angelic hierarchies, consciously imposing (in archetypal form) the established Will and Purpose of the Logos as agents of logoic memory and divine law. In the lower one it is that of the involuting elementals and evolving nature spirits responding in each case to unconscious instinct.[7]

With the elementals and nature spirits, involution is the chaotic instinct to generate gross matter and form of different basic quality, while evolution is the instinct to perfect the subjective form, thereby leading to a development of semi-intelligent consciousness and basic types of functionality. Correspondingly, in the upper register, the involuting devas are concerned with the maternal aggregation of spiritual substance to generate light forms of different quality, while the evoluting devas are concerned with the development of spiritual intelligence within the forms of light thus produced. In

*Fig. 3.3. Volcanic deva (courtesy of Theosophical Publishing
House, Adyar, and the trustees of Geofrey Hodson)*

short, the former involves aggregation of forms, while the latter involves an increasingly subtle aggregation and definition of consciousness.

Esoteric philosophy places considerable emphasis on the distinction between *Man* and *(hu)man*. *Man* is an evolving "god" from a yet higher dimension, which projects a mere aspect of itself down into the lower world of the devas to enable each incarnation as a *human* being. The spiritual Man remains ever in situ, while the projected fragment becomes the lesser "spark" of intelligence buried within the nature of the objective human individual. For this reason we can see how and why it is that the intelligence within each of us is always being watched over, protected, and influenced by its mentor and parent, the spiritual Man, who can also perceive all the surrounding activity of the lower world. Our personal experience as a human being—in the lower world scheme of elementals and nature spirits—is far less than that of the developing Man-god that we really are, simply because the human intelligence of any particular lifetime is merely a partial expression of the Man-god's developing identity. That in turn leads to forgetfulness until the experiential crises of the evolutionary process force a radical reawakening and consequent reorientation.

The spiritual identity in Man could in a sense be considered as an evolving "germ" impregnated within the bodily nature of a particular deva hierarch. However, not all deva hierarchs contain this evolutionary germ. The vast majority of them do not and are thus concerned only with maintaining the involutionary status quo. As we can see from the diagram, the Man-germ or "solar angel" stands right at the center of the four different influences (two involutionary, two evolutionary) described above, hence the deeply ancient association of spiritual experience with the crucifix.

In a very real sense, the evolved human being is the simultaneously apparent product of all the seven states and stages in the lower register. He represents the seventh stage yet contains all the other six within his bodily form on the one hand and within his sensory faculties on the other. He is, relatively speaking, a junior macrocosm, physically made up of all the elements and with all the elemental characteristics as well. A very large proportion of his overall makeup is thus instinctively involutionary. Yet the other (evolutionary) half, while not only possessing varied characteristics of plant form and organic function, also has integrated animal sensory characteristics and instincts. However, over and above all these, the human being has self-consciousness and objective thought through the perception of duality. This in turn produces a very different and independently characteristic nature from that of the deva. That self-consciousness and the creativity generated by it derive from the overshadowing influence of the demigod-nature just described.

By virtue of objective human experience taking place in the lower register (despite the perennially overshadowing influence of the higher, spiritual register), we are influenced and conditioned by three main factors. These are: (a) the elemental world—only a small part of which is visible as the elements of fire, air, water, and earth; (b) the world of nature spirits—only a small part of which is visible within the bodies of the plant and animal kingdoms; (c) other human beings whose spiritual nature is as deeply concealed within their personae as ours is within our own. As we are really quite familiar with the objectively visible world and its influences, we shall not concern ourselves overmuch with these in this book. We shall instead concern ourselves with the apparently invisible world and its influences around us that, these days, are rapidly becoming more perceptible to us through the agencies of psychology and scientific analysis. In addition to this, we need to remember:

- The elementals (which, in their entirety, comprise the *Anima Mundi* or World Soul) and nature spirits of the lower world system are themselves directly controlled by the deva hierarchies.
- Our own terrestrial soul organism is itself a deva.
- Our Causal Soul (within which our spiritual nature develops) is itself the "fetal sac" within a yet greater deva organism.
- Our subtle and dense bodies are composed of a vast mass of interlocking energies provided by tiny elemental beings, all selfishly concerned with their own specific instincts.
- The intelligent function that actually guides and maintains the physical body is provided in the system of chakras, which act as local command centers for the higher and lower soul organisms; they project their influences (via the etheric double) more directly through the endocrine glandular system.
- The three primary chakras are those of the crown, heart, and spine base; they are the respective human expressions of the Will-to-be, the Will-to-know, and the Will-to-generate/adapt, which provide the basis of all existence.

CENTRIPETAL AND CENTRIFUGAL SOUL FUNCTION AND FACULTY

Let us now return to the issue of soul faculty. Remembering that sensory consciousness is essentially contained within the peripheral membrane of the deva-soul, what is being shown in fig. 3.2 is that there are three fundamental types of emanation for any soul entity or sphere of consciousness:

1. From the peripheral membrane inward and back to it
2. From the center of the sphere and back to it
3. From the peripheral membrane outward and back to it

The first of these is centripetal, while the other two are centrifugal in nature. It follows that each of the three generate characteristic forms of light of widely different quality: the latter two both develop an expansion of conscious awareness and perceptual range, while the first continually recirculates the existing range of knowledge internally, in line with Divine Memory, always improving its quality of expression.

Within what is being described here on the larger scale, the sphere itself represents the planetary Oversoul, containing the totality of consciousness of our planetary Life. Centripetal emanation from this then represents the deva or angelic hierarchies whose sole purpose is to maintain (by serial repetition) the status quo in Nature, thereby acting as archetypal agents of the divine Law. The outward or centrifugal emanation from its center then represents the elemental kingdoms of Nature—the expression of the Anima Mundi of our planet. The further outward emanation from the outer periphery then represents the expansive, evolutionary urge, which is spearheaded by Man. However, our immediate concern here lies with the first two emanations and their functions. The centripetal emanation results in the production of the deva forms of the spiritual world, while the centrifugal emanation from the core results in the production of elemental forms, leading to the appearance of the objective kingdoms of Nature; it generates increasingly dense atomic and molecular forms, eventually resulting in the objective appearance of what we regard as "living" organisms. That which emanates from the periphery develops purely psycho-spiritual forms of increasingly coherent light. Some of this is already known to modern science, albeit unconsciously.

GODS, DEVAS, AND HUMANS

As already suggested, the deva hierarchies essentially comprise the Divine Memory of the system. Thus, so ancient tradition has it, deva and human, when united in one fully coherent self-consciousness, comprise the nature of a demiurgic god. That is to say, they are the cause of all cyclical and forward motion in space and, between them, they generate both kosmic necessity and its fulfillment. The expression "a god" is, however, a very relative term. On Earth, the human is a god because (at least at a certain stage of development) the human maximizes both aspects of the involutionary–evolutionary equation in relation to the lesser kingdoms of Nature. Because of the faculty of imagination, the human is the "thinker" and the "maker." Hence, as the *Hermetica* says: "For the human is a godlike living thing, not comparable to the other living things of the Earth but to those in heaven above who are called gods."[8]

In the local kosmos, the consciousness of Man (the divine spirit) is united with that of the highest archangel (the archon, in planetary terms), and so becomes a planetary god of (to us) unimaginable power. Man thereby eventually becomes at-one with the planetary Demiurge, before proceeding yet further and higher in the process of celestial fulfillment. In this greater kosmic environment the highest devas/archangels are known (theosophically at least) as Dhyani Chohans,[9] a term literally meaning "meditating princes of the kosmic light"—those who hold objective existence together by the very power of their combined will-force.

Let us otherwise remind ourselves of the fact that the angel/deva hierarchies possess an essential group (or even mass) consciousness and that it is by virtue of this that they are responsible for the production of all forms in Nature. They are thus the cause of all illusion. Hence they are in a very real sense the Brahma or reproductive "Holy Spirit" nature behind the kosmos in its entirety, just as Man is the "Son" or Visnu aspect—that which expresses the further reaching "Will-to-know." They are thus responsible for the balance in Universal Nature, ensuring that all cycles are rigorously maintained and also that all is compensated for. From that viewpoint, the angels/devas are the direct agents of the universal Law of Karma, which Man sets out to upset in the overall quest for change and improvement through the "Will-to-know." Contrary (or complementary) to Man, the nature of the devas (with the exception of the greater ones who have already passed through the human kingdom in an earlier cycle) is focused on acquisition of greater feeling rather than greater knowing.[10]

The devas, by virtue of their function as the memory of the solar universe, are solely concerned with the perfection of its expression. Hence, when Man causes change to take place outside due cycle, the devas are responsible for applying those forces that cause sensory equilibrium to be regained. It follows that the spiritually Self-conscious human being (i.e., the true Adept) takes great care not to generate personal causes revolving around himself or herself (as humankind in general does) by going outside the established order and cycle. Human self-centeredness brings its own unfortunate "rewards" of a karmic nature, whereas unselfishness brings liberation. However, self-consciousness (at whatever level of being one wishes to consider) is the crown of the evolutionary process.

Consequently, we have the paradox that the deva evolves through yielding to realization of the need for qualitative change (at the correct moment in each cycle), whereas Man evolves by yielding to realization of the essential illusion of change in form. Both then progress in parallel until eventually reaching a divine reunion. That same reunion is itself the expression of a realization in the consciousness of their parent Logos. It takes the form of Man becoming a SELF-realized god.

It follows from this that the angel or deva possesses an instinctive sense of functional necessity. It has no sense of choice because it has no experience of or desire for alternatives. As the agent of Divine Memory, its sole concern is to carry out the purpose of its hierarchical superiors, as best it can.[11] It is thus by virtue of this unquestioning obedience to Universal Law that the universe functions according to strict order—the ancient Egyptian Ma'at—which leaves nothing to chance. While this suggests that everything is preplanned, thereby allowing even Man no sense of choice, it needs to be acknowledged that, like all engineering principles, tolerances are allowed as of working necessity and are thus inherent in the system's innate flexibility. In other words, despite the inborn limitations of the soul nature and the restrictive feeling consciousness of the angel/deva, there always exists a range or spectrum of available possibilities within which a relative "freedom" of thought and action must continue to operate.

SEVENFOLD HIERARCHIES

Because of the serial confusion caused by mention of the term *angel* or *deva*—particularly in the West—we perhaps need to understand something more of the structural rationale connected with their functions. These functions, involving the generation of states of being, are of a far wider nature than commonly imagined and we can probably do no better in setting them out than by following the format adopted by that individual known to modern historians as "pseudo-Dionysius" (not "the Areopagite" friend of St. Paul), who is said to have brought their names (from Assyria) to Western Christianity in the third century CE. These are as shown on the left-hand side of fig. 3.4. We might mention in passing that they macrocosmically parallel the seven hierarchies of Elohim found in the Judaic system (itself borrowed largely from the Chaldeo-Babylonian scheme). This same graphic can be compared by reference to other ancient metaphysical systems in which there are also seven kosmic states, the seventh and lowest comprising the seven substates of our solar/planetary world scheme. The correlations between these systems are thus of very particular importance.

For example, in the esoteric Buddhist metaphysics of H. P. Blavatsky (as shown on the right-hand side of fig. 3.4) we also see the seven kosmic planes, this time comprising the nature of seven hierarchically organized groups of Dhyani Buddhas, hugely evolved Intelligences. These (again just like the Elohim) contain the various world systems of our overall solar scheme within their nature. We can similarly turn to the ancient Greek and Egyptian systems, in the latter of which the seven kosmic planes correspond with the seven aspects of the great god Ra. The lowest of these comprises the world of the Demiurge, Atum-Ra, who, within his own nature, gives rise to the Heliopolitan Ennead of lesser gods concerned with "the Underworld."

In the Greek system, the three Titan brothers, Zeus, Poseidon, and Hades, respectively represent the constantly interfering kosmic Mind, the "ocean" of kosmic Desire, and the again sevenfold kosmic Underworld. The latter (completely misunderstood by most scholars) is our world of spirit and matter at the center of which is to be found the metaphorical "forge" of Hephaistos, the "blacksmith" god, himself an esoteric metaphor for the Spiritual Ego that "creates" the compound human organism from the "sparks" generated within the "forge." A further direct correspondence is found in the much more modern concept put forward in the early twentieth century by Alice A. Bailey (as essentially illustrated in fig. 1.2, the sevenfold kosmic scheme of Creation). This defines the structural makeup of the seventh and lowest kosmic plane in a manner that much more easily confirms for us the Macrocosm–microcosm "as above, so below" rationale that we have already discussed.

The basis of the sevenfold scheme, within the nature of a field of

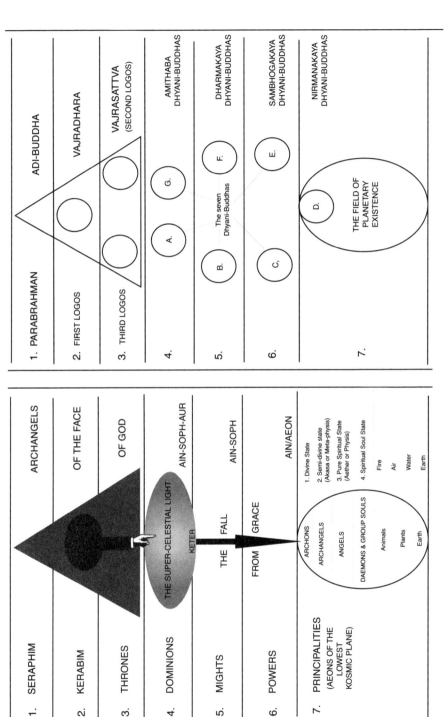

Fig. 3.4. The Dionysian and esoteric Buddhist hierarchies

consciousness, was explained for us in chapters 1 and 2. However, unless that explanation has been fully understood, the reader would be advised to reread it before moving on, because it now becomes fundamental to comprehending the rationale behind all the hierarchies in Universal Nature with which we are about to concern ourselves. In very simple terms, the three highest planes in any overall system are archetypal, while the lowest three merely involve its evanescent expressions or passing reflections.

The intermediate fourth plane is that "bridging" state in which Man (in the form of the Spiritual Ego) perennially exists and, like the lesser Greek god figure of Hephaistos, "forges" the forms of the lower world. By virtue of representing the evolving Mind principle, Man has to be seen in a dual sense as both the massed impulse of the imagination projecting its influence downward and as the individualized spirit that has realized its higher role, despite being immersed in the lower field of Nature. To begin with, it is not easy for the individualized spirit to realize its higher role. However, with persistence, it eventually becomes possible, as the Spiritual Ego is the emanating agent of the divine Monad, working through and from within the kosmic etheric double of the Logos.

DEVA NATURE AND PLANES OF BEING

Every single plane or state is that of a deva nature, using the term *deva* in a purely generalized sense. Each such plane consists of a soul (or Oversoul), which, as we know from chapter 1, is itself definable as a group of spirits of a particular evolutionary status with a common (i.e., mass) sense of their own functional identity. What we are studying, therefore, is a metaphysical structure of major and minor soul states (and substates). To, from, and within these, groups of spirits, the creative artisans of the Army of the Voice, are constantly passing upward and downward as telepathic messengers of the consciousness of the given Logos, the latter comprising all the massed hierarchies of soul states within its unified consciousness. Within our nature as individual human beings—and thus demigods of rather lesser degree—the very same process is taking place. We are, after all, microcosms of the greater Macrocosm.

Our concern here is therefore twofold. First of all we need to understand the sequence by which—through the auxiliary agency of the devas—the kosmic imagination is said to manifest itself in and as Man (the Spiritual Ego) and then as human. Secondly, we need to understand the role of the higher deva/angel and the lower nature spirit in bringing this about. Therefore, referring back to fig. 1.2, we can see that the seven Ray Groups of the kosmic Mind are emanated downward into the local planetary Oversoul, which contains the seventh and lowest kosmic state. Here they merge with the Oversoul, thereby forming an auric sea of fire from which two separate monadic groups then emerge, within the lowest kosmic plane. These two groups comprise deva monads and Man monads, the former outnumbering the latter by a vast proportion because they represent the status quo of Divine Memory.

Despite this joint emergence, the group of Man monads do not begin to exert themselves noticeably until the fourth stage of unfoldment. Then they begin to emanate their own "daemonic" offspring (the *maenads* of Greek mythology) into the lower world of planetary existence, where they undergo innumerable cycles of incarnate experience in the various elemental kingdoms of Nature, learning how to control them. As a result of this experience, they eventually learn how to generate human forms out of the elemental morass within the terrestrial soul nature provided by one of the lesser deva hierarchies. In relative terms, the coherent set of states formed within the terrestrial soul field is as follows:

1. The homogeneous atomic state   the sea of living fire, or "lesser divine flame"
2. The subatomic (germinal) state   the daemonic maenad, or lesser "spark"
3. The vital, radiatory state   the aether, or prana
4. The fiery plasmic state   etheric fire/light
5. The airy/atmospheric state   air
6. The liquid/colloidal state   water
7. The dense, molecular state   earth

As described in chapter 1 (see again fig. 1.2), there are seven kosmic states, of which the lowest is the sevenfold solar state; within this, the again lowest state forms the terrestrial state, which consists of the seven states described above. Within the solar state, however, we find the duality of spirit and matter. The former comprises the various angelic or deva states, while the latter comprises the various elemental and nature spirit states.

"INHABITANTS" OF THE UPPER SPIRITUAL WORLD

In the gnostic system of the philosopher Iamblichus we find the sequentially evolving "inhabitants" of the upper, spiritual world to be as follows:

Involutionary	Evolutionary
1. Archons	7. Gods [Human Buddhas]
2. Archangels	6. Self-conscious Demigods [Chohans]
3. Angels	5. Heroes [Human Master Adepts]
4. Spiritual Group Souls	

Archons, Archangels, and Angels

Of the involutionary deva groups, Iamblichus comments[12] that there are two types, that is, "the kosmic and supra-kosmic." Our present interpretation here would designate them respectively as "the solar and dual solar-kosmic." In technical terms, the latter (the archons) are the highest angels/devas on the involutionary arc, that of unfoldment. As Blavatsky's work *The Secret Doctrine* confirms, those highest Intelligences that comprise the nature of the Demiurge are actually dual in character, containing within their own nature both the "brute energy inherent in matter" and the cosmic or extra-planetary energy and consciousness that controls and directs it.[13] They are thus, in a very real sense, the equivalent of the Greek demigod Dionysus (a name agglutinatively derived from the compound Sanskrit *dhyani-dhyaus*), who is described as being in control of the maenads (the lesser monads, or "daemons"). These are the elemental hordes that wreak vengeance on those humans who do not pay due deference to Dionysus, that is, those who do not abide by natural law, which involves the Law of Karma, or of cause and effect, which we shall learn more about in the next chapter.

It follows from what has just been described that the lesser archangels and angels have an organizational and distributive function regarding those same forces and influences within the system. A correspondence can be seen in the more mundane terms of a human corporate environment in which the most senior management deals with intercompany relations while junior management deals with departmental issues and associated considerations.

Spiritual Group Souls and Daemons

The *group soul* is an Oversoul—literally, a (deva) soul organism containing a group of lesser souls. In other words, it is a more senior deva hierarch (sometimes known as a "greater builder") containing within its aura groups of less senior deva organisms.[14] Each of the latter, in turn, is made up of massed ranks of elemental spirits under the control of a lesser deva. *Daemons,* on the other hand, are individual spirits, usually "guests" from a different deva soul organism. Hence the "divine spark" (or daemon as the ancients termed it) of the spiritual Man inseminated into a higher deva entity is itself a higher daemon. However, there are also lesser daemons. One of these is the lesser "spark" (Sanskrit: *jiva*) emanated by Man into the terrestrial soul to initiate each cycle of incarnation. It needs always to be borne in mind that context is everything in the use of esoteric terminology.

Higher daemons (in groups) appear to perform a function within the body of the solar scheme that is equivalent to the seven main chakras within the human organism. In one sense they can perhaps be considered as emanations of the Oversoul of the solar system, just as the lesser, terrestrial soul is the emanation of the Oversoul of our planet. This is perhaps easier to understand if we work from the periphery inward, following the "as above, so below" principle. Thus we see the deva monads contained within the planetary Oversoul, which is itself contained by the sphere of Mind projected by the higher consciousness of the Logos. As the sphere of Mind concentrates, so the Oversoul is put under stress. That in turn creates polarity and causes it to generate centripetal force, thereby creating a yin-yang effect, as we saw earlier in fig. 2.1. However, the concentration also results in a counter reaction of centrifugal force generated from the planetary core. As we saw earlier, this is the Anima Mundi.

The centripetal and centrifugal emanations then overlap at a point where their combined influences generate the crust of the physical planet in celestial terms and the epidermis of the body in more mundane terms.

Further (cyclic) pressure applied upon the Oversoul by the logoic Mind then forces the former to generate persistent sequences of force as "spiritual quanta"—those cellular entities that the esotericist calls "group souls." These are themselves then projected down to the Earth's surface, there to generate those multitudes of forms that we call the "kingdoms of Nature."

The terrestrial soul entity is thus a holographic microcosm of the planetary Oversoul. The higher "divine spark," however, is a germ of the logoic Mind, a partial aspect of which becomes inseminated into the soul organisms formed by the Oversoul as a direct result of the external pressure applied upon the latter. The spark/daemon is thus a dissociated fragment of the (kosmic) Mind of the Logos. Because of its dissociation it becomes contained within the terrestrial soul nature and is thus esoterically regarded as "falling" into a state of ignorance, while still maintaining an unconscious instinct as to its parent state. By virtue of the Mind's intention to change the lower status quo, the daemon is also inherently destructive in its nature, until it reaches a certain stage (as a human being) when it learns to work with and within the soul organism and the deva nature instead of against it.

Let us next take a brief look at the terrestrial group soul that contains within its deva nature masses of those lesser daemons, which will cause it to produce an objective form such as a herd of deer, or a flock of birds, or a shoal of fish, moving and functioning according to a mass group instinct. As these lesser daemons accrue wider experience through being eaten by and consequently assimilated into a higher form of terrestrial soul, so they very gradually develop an increasing sense of independence. In this way, by becoming the predator rather than the prey, they move away from the mass group soul consciousness into that of a more isolated animal family group. Ultimately, the consciousness of the spark/daemon becomes so developed that it moves out of the animal kingdom altogether and into the human kingdom. Quite how this transition takes place we shall consider later on.

Daemons, Heroes, and Demigods

As Iamblichus confirms, two classes of beings exist between the extremes of the gods on the one hand and souls on the other: daemons and heroes. Their function is that of "giving expression to the ineffable and causing the formless to shine forth in forms."[15] Heroes are "just above the level of souls,"[16] while daemons are described as being "more immediately dependent upon the race of the gods" [and "far inferior" to the heroes]. In summarizing the work of these two classes of beings Iamblichus also tells us:

> These classes of being then, bring to completion as intermediaries the common bond that connects gods with souls and causes their linkage to be indissoluble. They bind together in a single continuity from top to bottom and render the communion of all things indivisible.[17]

Hence we might say that *heroes* are essentially "those individualized 'divine sparks' known to esotericism as Self-conscious Adepts." They are those who have already passed through the daemonic human stage and have now become part of the fifth kingdom in Nature—the superhuman— thereby becoming "clothed" in an individualized Spiritual Soul body. In a sense, they are Self-realized daemons, who have just begun to appreciate the true nature of the kosmic Mind with which they are themselves imbued. Consequently, whereas the daemons functioned unconsciously but instinctively within the logoic body to produce its forms, the Adept Heroes now function consciously within the kosmic etheric double of the Logos, generating and distributing its creative forces.

In these descriptions of Iamblichus we see a direct correspondence with the modern theosophical perspective, in which the logoic etheric double and the "divine spark" (the Masonic "Word") are central to the whole creative process. Just as modern theosophy describes the lesser "spark" (the daemonic jiva) as that downward emanation of the spiritual Man, which unconsciously becomes human and then (after long ages and a multitude of reincarnations) Self-consciously Adept, through monadic influence, the gnostic and neo-Pythagorean traditions were saying precisely the same thing. Hence, as the *Hermetica* puts it, "The human on Earth is a mortal god, but that god in heaven is an immortal human."[18]

Demigods are effectively one very important evolutionary stage beyond that of the heroes. Although still classified by modern esotericism as part of the same group, they belong to what might better be described as the nascent or future sixth kingdom in Nature. They have the status of Chohan or *chokhan,* an oriental term found in ancient Egypt as *choen,* in the Hebrew tradition as *cohen,* and in the Japanese tradition as *shogun.* All these terms were originally derived from *shu-khan*—a "prince of celestial light," although it subsequently degenerated over the millennia into merely meaning "a priest" or "high priest." They are, in effect "sons of the divine Mind"—effectively, minor demigods.

The Man-God

The fully Self-realized individuality in this evolutionary series is what we today would call a human or, in Sanskrit, a Manushi Buddha. The intelligence at this stage is at the stage of becoming wholly at-one with the consciousness of the planetary Demiurge, the "second God" of Platonic philosophy. Having eventually done so, it will subsequently become what esoteric Buddhism refers to as a Dhyani Buddha, a true "god" whose responsibilities and range of influence—so we are told—become interplanetary, having the freedom of the solar system, although not able to go beyond its "Ring-Pass-Not," the solar Oversoul.

As Iamblichus comments: "The gods have present to them throughout, concurrently with their essence, the measure of the [solar] universe, or the cause of this."[19] In order to achieve that function, the Dhyani Buddha seemingly takes over a part of the "body" of the archon for his own individualized use, this vehicle thus being a semi-divine soul. It is at this stage, so esoteric philosophy has it, that the fully individualized spirit becomes capable of generating, by an act of will, that phenomenon known to esoteric Buddhism as a human Bodhisattva. The Bodhisattva then functions as a semi-divine intermediary within the objective world of Creation—the physical body of the Logos. We shall deal with this in a later chapter, in far greater detail, so that it is more easily possible to understand the associated context and function.

It is otherwise worth noting here in passing that the "divine spark" of kosmic Mind referred to by oriental philosophy is the same as the "star" that is the supposed evolutionary ambition of the pharaoh, according to modern interpretation of ancient Egyptian texts. In fact, contrary to Egyptological orthodoxy, the term *pharaoh* is itself derived from *piru,* the plural or collective name for the spiritual lord (*pir*) otherwise found in the ancient Persian tradition and thus meaning "high initiates." However, this too (via the medieval Crusaders) has degenerated in the European monarchical class system, thus referring merely to the sociopolitical nobility, the so-called "peers" of the realm.

THE UNDERWORLD

In the lower sequence of evolution, as already described, we find various groups of daemons, which we might otherwise classify as those individual spirits that control "elemental subgroup souls" (of fire, air, water, and earth). Of these, the human daemon (or jiva) is the highest. All daemonic groups derive their existence from the fourth of the seven systemic states, as suggested by fig. 1.2. This fourth state is dual. From it there are projected downward into the elemental substates those lesser groups of daemonic "sparks," which constitute the evolving principle in the forms of the lower system. Hence the lower system follows the following sequence:

1. Elementals of fire (salamanders)   7. Individualized human "daemons"

   2. Elementals of air (sylphs)   6. Animal nature spirits

     3. Elementals of water (undines)   5. Plant nature spirits

       4. Elementals of earth (gnomes)

The fourth state thus acts as a bridge between the spiritual (or solar) world and the elemental (or terrestrial) underworld. The spiritual group soul not only puts down "roots" into the lower system, by emanation, but also "harvests" the results: for these minor "sparks" unfold as lesser daemons within the four elemental states of fire, air, water, and earth, to create its various involutionary kingdoms of Nature. Eventually, their efforts result in the appearance of an evolutionary drive, generating plants and then semi-intelligent animal types, these being precedent to the appearance of humans. By virtue of their instinctive "homeward" drive, the consciousness of these semi-intelligent lesser daemons eventually becomes occultly invocative.

This results in the group Spiritual Soul nature responding by radiating its own nature more powerfully downward until a definite link is set up between the spiritual state and the underworld. This link—the intermediate Causal Soul (comprising the Higher Mind nature)—thereby gives rise to the

Fig. 3.5. Earth gnome and grass elf (courtesy of Theosophical Publishing House, Adyar, and the trustees of Geofrey Hodson)

psychological and physical appearance of the fourth (i.e., human) kingdom in Nature. Thus, Iamblichus tells us, the human being has two souls[20]—a causal or semi-spiritual one plus a terrestrial one. However, not yet being spiritually Self-conscious (i.e., as an Adept), the person does not yet have a fully independent Spiritual Soul organism.

INDIVIDUALIZATION AND THE CAUSAL SOUL

As a result of many continuous cycles of experience, reincarnating "seeds" of the lower world are generated within the aura of the Causal Soul organism, as described in the previous chapter. This in turn leads to a subjective expansion, which results in the gradual individualization of a personal faculty reaching across to the spiritual world itself. Thus an intelligently coordinated yet still daemonic sense of independence (which we call "self-consciousness") within the spiritual world eventually evolves out of the mass or herd instinct (originally emanated by the deva group soul) of each mass of "sparks." The evolving daemonic intelligence has now not only conquered the lower, elemental world in its entirety, it has succeeded in generating for itself a new angelic/deva vehicle constituted entirely of semi-spiritual substance. In this it can learn to function (by a combination of imagination and reason) as if within the higher (i.e., solar) world state. As already described, this latter state covers the whole of the solar system. Thus it is that the Master Soul is able to research and understand what goes on in planetary schemes other than our own as well as understanding much better the hierarchical management of our own planetary scheme itself. It has to be pointed out, however, that this is accomplished by consciously associating oneself with a higher intelligence and thus drawing oneself into its field of consciousness. It is not possible to just draw down such knowledge into one's own.

Within the sequence of what has just been described, it can perhaps also be seen how the unfoldment of a spiritual hierarchy from the "body" of the Demiurge necessarily produces its own progressively more objective forms (of light substance). The "body" of the archon is the first such state to be produced. It is of a far more ethereally tenuous nature than that of the next deva entity, the archangel, whose own "body" is correspondingly of a far more tenuous nature than that of the angel whose "body," in turn, is less tenuous than that of the human Causal Soul. Each involutionary progression results in the generation of "bodies" of more objective light. Thus it is that the expression of Divine Purpose necessarily works downward in strictly hierarchical function and order. The archons direct the archangels, and the archangels then direct the angels, which, in turn, direct the Nature spirits and the elementals of the lowest world orders.

However, the fourth progression just described is quite different, because it is here that involution and evolution overlap, thereby producing that organism we referred to earlier as the "group soul," from which eventually emerges the human Causal Soul; but, once the spiritual nature becomes individualized by the Self-development of Man as an Adept, its further evolutionary development necessitates no new bodily form because it functions (very largely) as a formless spirit. However, it otherwise generates a considerable increase in effective power. This power becomes immediately obvious within the psycho-spiritual state itself as a very highly charged field of living Self-embodiment.

KOSMIC, SOLAR, AND PLANETARY STATES

One immediate problem facing us (as we are only using analytical reason here, rather than the visual faculty) is to discriminate between the entity and the state in which it is found. For example, how do we distinguish between a particular deva and the state in which it exists and functions? Similarly, how do we distinguish between a fire elemental and the fiery state? As each such state contains seven substates, this is particularly difficult, even in rational terms. To some extent we should be assisted by the fact (as Bailey's Adept teacher points out) that the solar planes and kosmic planes correspond exactly with each other according to the "as above, so below" principle (as shown in fig. 1.10) hence:

4. Our spiritual soul plane is simultaneously the lowest kosmic etheric subplane
5. Our mental plane is simultaneously the kosmic gaseous subplane
6. Our astral plane is simultaneously the kosmic liquid subplane
7. Our physical plane is simultaneously the kosmic dense subplane

It follows from what is described above that the densest form of spiritual light is that of fire, inhabited by the elemental salamander on the one hand and by Man (the fiery spirit) on the other. The former is an unselfconscious daemon of great power, only controllable by the spiritual nature. The latter is a Self-conscious and Self-controlled daemon. Difficult though it may be for us to understand, the daemonic elementals of fire, air, water, and earth—the essences of the salamander, sylph, undine, and gnome—are contained within Man's own psycho-spiritual nature. These, however, are the living forces behind the objective elements of fire, air, water, and earth. The phenomenal elements are a combination of these plus the substance of the astral light—the etheric double of the planet. Consequently, we can logically suggest—in line with the principles of occult science—that the full Adept or Self-realized initiate has conscious command over the elements. That is because, by sympathetic association, he has fully self-conscious control or mastery over his own nature of both inner and outer states of consciousness.

The subjective structure of the human being, however, is very little understood, particularly as far as the psycho-spiritual evolutionary process is concerned. As we shall see in greater detail later on, the physical senses of the animal nature reproduce themselves in different but nevertheless corresponding and sequentially logical guises at the various higher levels of human consciousness beyond the mundane. This "above, so below" sympathetic reproduction is entirely due to the progressively interlinked memory consciousness of the deva in which the human shares, or from which the human borrows. Thus, by virtue of the reproduction of all forms taking place in response to vibration, the first sense is that of hearing, which then gives rise to touch, or feeling, and then to sight, followed by taste and smell. However, we shall consider these again in repetitively sequential progression on the planes beyond the physical in chapter 5.

THE FIVE AND SEVEN SENSES

We might note that there are fundamentally only five senses on each plane. That is because the first and second subplanes (counting downward)—as with the first and second planes in the greater organism—are entirely abstract and thus wholly subjective. As previously suggested, the third plane manifests the first emanation from the subjective state. Hence it is that the third state is always of a homogeneous (aetheric) nature, while it is always the illuminated fourth substate that generates group discrimination, the radiance from which itself gives rise to sight and different archetypal forms.

It may (and probably will) come as something of a shock to most to learn that their outer and inner senses are merely borrowed. However, that is entirely consistent with the central idea in occult science that the human is merely a participant in the worlds of form and not their creator, irrespective of what we may think to the contrary. We need to remember that we are the agents of logoic realization and that we can only fulfill our true function by a self-aware reorganization of the status quo while in transit. The moment that we allow ourselves to become fascinated by our surroundings—no matter how wondrous—we fall once more into a state of divine ignorance and psychic lethargy.

This leads us to the axiom that the initiated Adept is only one in the use of occult powers.[21] That is to say, the individual human being who has attained Adeptship does not spend all his or her time in occult manifestations, any more than does the deva. The use of minimum necessary force is the general rule, as any use of force involves causes, which generate effects in time and space. One of the complete misconceptions about the Master Adept is that he (or she) can control Nature with a snap of the fingers. The truth is not so simple. In fact, to do so he must first of all render his human persona and organism completely inert, in a manner that enables the purely psycho-spiritual powers of the soul body to be advanced to fulfill the task in hand.

We also need to realize—as we shall again see later on—that the lesser Adept does not have anything like the same degree or extent of occult power that a senior Adept (i.e., a Chohan) possesses. Nevertheless, even the lesser Adept does have the capacity to call for the assistance of the devas, provided that there is adequate reason. However, the mere display of occult power, even of a minor nature, is forbidden. That is because it artificially stimulates the deva nature, while actually fulfilling no useful function. The true magicians— the theurgists of ancient times—recognized this, realizing also that such abuse would always (by occult law) rebound on them at a later date. Thus, on completion of any theurgical act, the deva or daemon was always ordered to depart back whence it came. For avoidance of doubt, it might be mentioned at this point that lesser occult activity such as "spoon-bending" does not require deva assistance. It is achieved purely by the focused and applied magnetism of the individual, working through the etheric double.

DEVA/ANGELIC FUNCTIONS

The correlative function between the deva and elemental hierarchies also needs to be much better understood, so that we can see how objective Nature works. Remembering that the whole system works from the top downward, it should quickly become self-evident that there are subhierarchies of archons, archangels, and devas; only the latter, however, are directly responsible for each of the elemental hierarchies of fire, air, water, and earth. At the highest level, the archons are demiurgically responding to planetary necessity within the solar system as a whole. Some of them have interplanetary concerns; others are concerned solely with the containment of matter in all its varied qualities within the field of limitation of the planetary Oversoul. In a sense they are akin to the "World Mother," symbolized by the ever-pregnant hippopotamus goddess of the Egyptians.

Fig. 3.6. The Egyptian hippopatamus goddess Ta'Urt

Archangels are concerned with transmitting their forces internally within the planetary system as organized schemes of function. Their responsibility extends to complete kingdoms of Nature. The angels, in turn, are then responsible for putting these schemes into more specifically objective effect, their work being directly concerned with the distributive manipulation of the elemental hierarchies. If one understands something of the process of management in a modern, large-scale corporation, it should become apparent that the deva scheme works correspondingly in the same sort of way. In fact, to be more precise, the modern human scheme of corporate and industrial management might be regarded a mere reflection of the overall planetary scheme instinctively run by the devas since time immemorial.

Unsurprisingly, each of the deva hierarchies have their own higher and lower echelons, according to function. For example, the higher counterparts of the element of fire involve atmospheric electricity (lightning) and the generation of what we call "sunlight" from the blending of solar energy and the planet's own etheric double—the astral light. Physical fire is itself generally of a low order. Correspondingly, the devas of the elements of air and water are concerned primarily with atmospheric and oceanic or large river currents, while the corresponding elementals—sylphs and undines—are concerned only with local conditions giving rise to more objective forms such as winds and waves.

Fig. 3.7. Deva of temple of Burhobhadur (courtesy of Theosophical Publishing House, Adyar, and the trustees of Geofrey Hodson)

INTERACTION BETWEEN DEVAS
AND HUMANKIND

One of the popular misconceptions about the devas is that they can be summoned ad lib by humans in the know. The devas, as just described, have different functions and are organized strictly according to those functions. Thus the capacity to invoke their aid—for example in healing—necessitates some degree of occult knowledge as to the use of color and carefully organized sound (as in invocative mantras), for it is by these that the deva world is summoned, not by mere words of exhortation.

For example, Luther Burbank, the early twentieth century Californian agronomist and horticulturalist, discovered, by repeated practice and the use of his intuition, that plants could be made to grow and develop much more efficaciously through the use of a mixture of harmonic sound (i.e., music) and color. That is because sound and color provide particular qualities of energy that can be manipulated by plant devas and nature spirits into the plant forms. Much more recent research has shown that the same principle applies with animals, for example in milk production by cattle.

The author has come across a variety of people in recent years who claim to be able to involve archangels (not even bothering with mere angels!) in their healing practices and who also claim how to teach other people to summon them for the same purpose. This, I suggest, is wishful thinking of a grand order indeed. That is because the knowledge and power involved in what is actually theurgy—psycho-spiritual invocation and manipulation—involves no little knowledge and psycho-spiritual discrimination. To summon an archangel would require immense power just not achievable by even lesser initiates. What in any case would be the point in invoking an archangel when the more specific function of the lesser deva/angel would be more appropriate? Why take a sledgehammer to crack a nut?

Bearing in mind the subtitle of this book, it might here be useful to mention some of those groups of devas said to be working with the Spiritual Hierarchy of Adepts in order to bring about specific evolutionary developments in human culture, in line with the influences of the Seven Rays shown in fig. 1.2. For example, we are led to understand that those particularly associated with the First Ray are gold-colored, flame colored, and white and gold in color, their work being directly concerned with helping the lesser devas responsible for vitalization and maintenance of particular thoughtforms.[22] Those associated with the Second Ray—working predominantly on the astral plane—are the rose and light blue colored devas. Their functions range from protecting and vitalizing religious sanctuaries to intensifying the devotional nature of those human beings working in the religious and educational fields for the betterment of humanity.[23] Various other deva groups of unspecified color appear to be involved with development of human psychic and psychological faculty, as well as with health and general physical welfare.[24]

APPEARANCES OF
THE SUBTLER KINGDOMS OF NATURE

Apart from the still not fully explained phenomenon of the Cottingley fairies, advanced by Edward Gardener and Conan Doyle in 1917–1918, the twentieth century clairvoyant Geoffrey Hodson is perhaps the best known of all modern commentators on the appearances and characteristics of both the deva and Nature spirit orders. The interested reader is seriously recommended to study what he has to say and otherwise to view the many illustrations in his book *Kingdom of the Gods*. From our immediate viewpoint, however, we are less concerned about appearances than we are about characteristic hierarchical function and purpose. Notwithstanding that, however, let us take a brief look at what the ancients said about the devas and other like beings as invoked during the Mysteries through the eyes of the practicing magus, the neo-Pythagorean philosopher Iamblichus. It is worth quoting at some length as follows; however, as his descriptions were rather unorganized in sequence, I have altered the text around slightly to provide simplification.

> The appearances of the gods are uniform; those of demons are varied; those of angels are simpler than those of daemons but inferior to those of the gods. Those of archangels are closer to divine principles, but those of archons, if you take these to be the rulers of the cosmos, who administer the sublunary elements, are varied but structured in an orderly manner; and if they preside over matter, they are more varied and more imperfect than archangels. . . . Those of archons are striking if they are in authority over the cosmos and actually harmful and painful to the viewers if they are involved with matter. . . . And the appearances of souls come in all sorts of forms. And again, those of gods shine benignly in appearance while those of archangels are solemn, though at the same time gentle, milder than those of angels, while those of daemons are frightening.[25]

He continues: "Order and tranquillity are characteristic of the gods, while in the case of archangels the order and tranquillity take on an active quality. But with the angels, orderly arrangement and calmness are no longer exempt from motion. Tumult and disorder, however, accompany the visions of daemons . . ."[26] He then adds further description by reference to the degree of light emanated by each type, as follows:

> The images of the gods flash forth brighter than light, whilst those of archangels are full of supernatural light and those of angels are

bright. But daemons glow with smouldering fire. The heroes have a fire blended of diverse elements and, of the archons, those that are cosmic reveal a comparatively pure fire, whilst those that are material show a fire mixed from disparate and opposed elements. Souls produce a fitfully visible light, soiled by the many compounds in the realm of generation.[27]

To draw any conclusions about any of these hierarchies of beings merely from such descriptions of apparently visual appearances, no matter how accurate, would be pointless and distracting. In any case, it is their functions that are of real interest to us. We also have no idea from what Iamblichus says, as to the conditions under which such appearances were made, or by whom they were seen. What can nevertheless be suggested is that the psycho-spiritual power and influence of each such hierarch, as experienced by the viewer, would be above all else what characterizes them. The evolved power of the viewer would necessarily affect the experience.

What Iamblichus has to say on these and all sorts of other related issues is very extensive and the interested researcher is commended to study his work at length, but only after arriving at a real sense of the "mechanics and dynamics" of the psycho-spiritual worlds. That necessitates a very real sense that although Universal Consciousness is essentially One, it is also structured. If that sense is not achieved, the individual will learn nothing of any real worth and will probably just become wholly confused or disillusioned, purely through failing to approach the subject in the correct manner.

ELEMENTALS AND NATURE SPIRITS

Let us now turn to an area that seemingly does not directly concern the initiatory evolution of humankind but certainly does so in relation to the mineral and plant kingdoms. As we can see from fig. 3.2, these two kingdoms are on the evolutionary arc within the sphere of planetary objectivity, following successively on from the involutionary unfoldment that takes place among the elementals of fire, air, water, and earth. The mineral kingdom here provides the balancing point and transition between the processes of involution and evolution in our planetary Nature, just as Man does the same on a higher turn of the spiral. Hence it is that, within the mineral kingdom, we simultaneously find both involutionary elementals and evolutionary nature spirits, the latter being in the great minority. The distinction between these two is highly important and could perhaps be described in the following manner.

Within the involutionary sequence, the manifesting consciousness is only capable of generating a mass effect, thereby resulting in the appearance of the qualitative distinctions in planetary substance. These we call fire, air, water, and earth, or vital, atmospheric, liquid, and solid activities. Of these, perhaps the most difficult to understand is the vitalizing effect of fire, although this is easier if we consider it as ionization—the transitional effect of solar electricity (taking the form of planetary lightning) upon that terrestrial substance known as the gas helium. As we know, this results in the production of carbon (the residue of fire), which (esoterically viewed, as a literal seed) itself leads to that progressive generation of "organic" life, within that part of the mineral kingdom that enables the production of plants. Thus the carbon cycle of our planet lies at the very foundation of its evolutionary and creative processes.

The further involutionary cycle of elemental activity is interesting and it is worthwhile pausing here a moment in order to describe it, from the esotericist's viewpoint, following the "as above, so below" rule as follows. In doing so we first need to remember that the third of the seven planetary substates (counting downward) is that of the homogeneous kosmic aether, the electrical energy that is common to the solar system as a whole. The fourth is that of the kosmic etheric double, an electromagnetic field of living plasma, which must itself be considered to have seven qualitative and functional aspects. These two states have their exact but lower counterparts in the purely planetary aether (otherwise known as prana) and the astral light—neither being as yet known to modern science, although the latter is increasingly accepted by some and referred to as "dark matter." It is from this that hydrogen is generated, while oxygen (like carbon) appears to be derived from the impact of solar energy upon helium. Nitrogen, the other main and much denser constituent of our planetary atmosphere, appears to be much more closely connected with the mineral kingdom itself.

While fire in the upper world state is the phenomenal result of the admixture of ether and ionized (i.e., highly solar-energized) gas, the lesser planetary substates (the liquid and dense) are merely subeffects of igneously-generated spatial movement within the lower planetary organism. Whereas fire is essentially generated by background electrical activity, (even at the Earth's core I suggest), elemental air movement gives rise to erosion, elemental water movement to sedimentation, and elemental earth movement to geological metamorphism. These are commonly recognized by modern science.

THE ILLUSION OF FORM

Given the recognition by modern science that the world of form is one of illusion, we also have to take into due consideration the fact that it still requires a steady background environment for change to take place in such a manner that a resulting evolutionary development of "organic" form and an associated consciousness—in all kingdoms of Nature—can be consistently derived and relied upon. Consequently, we might suggest that it is the deva hierarchies that provide the same steadily balanced (but still changing) environmental background, in a manner that is so discreetly harmonic that we ourselves completely fail to recognize it. The environment in question is the climate, which is itself due to the balanced interaction between the elements of fire, air, and water, in their variously triple aspects. It is of course the lower atmosphere or troposphere (the playground of the astral light) within which organic life survives and thrives in form. Yet the oxygenated vitality within this is itself held in balance by the harmonic overlap between the energies emanating jointly from the core of the Earth and the ionosphere surrounding it. I mentioned something of this in my last book *The Rise and Fall of Atlantis,*[28] suggesting that this same interaction was responsible for producing the phenomena of gravity and levity. However, it also results in the phenomenon of that fluctuating but ever-present electrical stimulation that generates organic life forms.

Scientists have discovered within the last few years a whole new field of climatologic phenomena taking place above the troposphere but having a potent effect upon it and the cloud-based weather cycle with which we are normally familiar. It involves the existence of what has been called "mega-lightning," taking place between the ionosphere and the cloud base. The different forms of such mega-lightning (the causal origins of which scientists are still trying to understand) have been given the names *elves* and *sprites*, although these are hardly adequate to describe their potency or huge size. The subject is one that could be developed esoterically at some length, to show that these same phenomena are in fact the manifestations of deva hierarchies of a particular type, related to the principle of (electrical) fire. However, that would take a chapter on its own. Suffice it here to suggest, therefore, that the carbon cycle involves these same entities. If understood from the angle of occult science, this is itself a parallel reexpression of the very same principle as described in the objective manifestation of the Monad through the agency of the daemonic jiva, as described earlier.

The interaction between solar energy (via the ionosphere) and planetary substance is thus of critical importance in the production of all organic forms. However, direct solar energy alone cannot generate productive forms. It is the interaction between less powerful reflected solar energy (that is, via the Moon) that actually draws forth the apparently dormant spark of plant life, thereby giving rise to the manifest evolutionary process. This should alert us to the fact that reflection has a magnetic effect. As is recognized by science, reflection in a mirror produces a virtual image. As is also recognized by science, a hologram (which is also virtual) is generated by the out-of-phase interaction (at a specific point in space) of two laser projections emitted from the same source. In a very real sense, therefore, the multitude of evolutionary forms generated on Earth by solar and lunar energy are mere holograms. Hence, perhaps, the ancient idea that the manifest world is an "illusion."

The whole process is perhaps more easily understood by reference again to fig. 2.1. This shows the sphere of kosmic physical existence (the Oversoul) from within which the deva Monad projects its influence centripetally inward, in response to pressure from logoic Intelligence. This is met by a corresponding, but dual outgoing (centrifugal), influence from the center, the two thus providing what we otherwise recognize as the yin-yang duality, which gives rise to magnetic polarity. At the points where the two then meet, we find a coordination of the incoming and outgoing forces. Within the field of our planetary Oversoul, as already mentioned, this meeting place becomes the Earth's crust and lower atmosphere. Here all objective forms thus find themselves generated by the involutionary process, and here also the evolutionary process commences, beginning logically with the mineral kingdom, the most objective of the involutionary elemental states.

THE CONJUNCTION OF DEVA AND MAN

Remembering that the higher deva system is both involutionary as well as evolutionary, we find that the third (Atmic) plane of the planetary scheme is particularly associated with what is called the "law of disintegration," which controls the breaking up of those unindividualized monadic groups contained on the second plane. Correspondingly, on the return cycle, it is the state in which we find the commencement of the destruction of the final demiurgic sheath that contains the evolving monad, or "divine spark." The same principle occurs on the second plane of Mind, in relation to the destruction of the Causal Soul at the fourth initiation. That is because the Causal Soul is said, in the case of more advanced human types, to be constituted of mainly second mental subplane substance. In others, still retaining a more Atlantean or emotional quality of consciousness, it is constituted of third mental subplane matter. Thus it is, so we are told, the deva and human evolutions ultimately remerge on the second plane of the sevenfold solar scheme[29]—which the theosophical system refers to as that of *Anupadaka,* a Sanskrit term meaning the "self-born monad" or, in other words, the "divine spark," of which the Spiritual Ego (on the second mental subplane) is the lesser counterpart, or agent. It is also the state otherwise known as that of the Akasa—that of All-Knowledge (within the system) from which all the essences of the various kingdoms of Nature are emanated in the first place, at the outset of so-called planetary "Creation."

This stage of development, attained by that senior human Adept known as a Chohan, thereby involves a fundamental reunion or fusion of all those original essences plus the further knowledge gained from their diverse experience in the world of our planetary Nature. Bearing in mind, as already described, that the deva nature represents the memory of the Logos and that Man represents the imagination of the Logos, we can perhaps understand, in concluding this chapter, why it should be that this reunion otherwise represents the achieved understanding of the Logos, within the kosmic physical plane. With that in mind, we can perhaps next move logically on to the subject of the universal law of cause and effect, otherwise known by its Sanskrit name, *karma*.

FOUR

ON KARMA
AND REINCARNATION

A quotation from the *Hermetica* makes it quite clear that the ancient Egyptians understood the nature of the Law of Karma just as much as did the ancient Hindus of India:

> Heimarmene [Karma] and Necessity are bound to one another by an unbreakable glue of the two; Heimarmene comes first, begetting the sources of all things; but the things that depend upon her beginning them are forced into activity by Necessity. What follows them both is Order, the structure and temporal arrangement of the things that must be brought about. For, without the fitting together of an order, there is nothing; and in everything the world's order is complete. Order is [thus] the vehicle of the world itself; the whole consists of order.[1]

By virtue of the interconnections between the various Mystery Schools throughout the Middle East, there is little or no doubt that this same law was commonly known to all—probably throughout Europe as well. However, the *Hermetica* adds the following very important reference to an associated idea, the principle of recurrent or seasonal change:

The world is Time's receptacle; the cycling and stirring of time invigorate it. Yet Time works by orderly rule: Order and Time cover the renewal of everything in the world through alternation.[2]

The concept of karma, involving the law of cause and effect, was not completely new to the West. It had roots in the god-metaphors of the Greek Mysteries, in the forms of their goddesses Nemesis, the Fates (see fig. 4.1), and the Furies. It was also well known in the later Christian Bible in the aphorisms "As ye sow, so shall ye reap" plus "The sins of the fathers shall be imposed on their children unto the third and fourth generations."

Fig. 4.1. The three Greek Fates

It was, however, the idea that the karmic penalties and benefits resulting from one's own actions in this lifetime could not be avoided in one's own next and subsequent lifetimes that really caught fire. The single-incarnation Christian theology of the time was of course (and still is) propagating the idea that all that one had to do to achieve spiritual redemption was to believe in Jesus Christ so that, by sympathetic association with him, all one's sins were automatically washed away, simply because of the power of his virtue. The humanist response to this, in defiance of theology, was that it not only defied logic and reason, it was also a travesty of natural justice. The esotericist is in complete agreement with the latter viewpoint, acknowledging that the universal Law of Karma works because of applied Universal Intelligence, resulting in the fact of a Universal Order.

The more clearly interrelated doctrines of karma and human reincarnation, however, arrived in the West during the late nineteenth century. They were brought and explained first by H. P. Blavatsky, at a time when fascination with spiritualism was already sweeping America and Europe, almost in the form of a new religion. At that time, it was believed (and still is by spiritualists today) that the spirits or souls of "the departed" could be contacted by those on this side of the "curtain" separating the living and the dead. This belief seems to have derived from an earlier fascination with eighteenth century Swedenborgian mysticism. However, the latter was reenergized through the early nineteenth century seduction of Western thought by ancient Egyptian religion, the latter following the great expansion of knowledge about it generated by scholars and antiquarians attached to Napoleon's expedition to Egypt between 1798 and 1805.

Scholars and antiquarians have ever since managed to distort the actual nature of ancient Egyptian religion in singular fashion by focusing almost entirely on its later and, by then, much corrupted culture. Most of this had already (in the intermediate and new kingdoms) degenerated into a mere shadow of its former self through the adoption of a superstitious literalism imported from other Middle Eastern countries. However, these synchronistic concepts of "parallel states of being," other than the objective physical, really caught the imagination of the nineteenth century Western mind, which, thanks to the Renaissance and Enlightenment, was then in the full flush of emerging humanistically from centuries of almost blind adherence to dogmatic religious theology.

Notwithstanding the fact that the twin concepts of karma and reincarnation have developed and spread worldwide in the twentieth century, they are still largely misunderstood. The reason for that is that they have tended to be merely grafted on to the ill-defined, spiritualistic theories of the nineteenth century, particularly the one involving the human personality supposedly managing to survive the transition we call "death." What Blavatsky taught, in deference to the true, original teaching from the East (and from ancient times in the West also), is that it is only the soul (plus the informing spirit) that survives. The compound human personality cannot do so, except under the most exceptional circumstances, which it would not be appropriate to deal with here. However, by virtue of the fact that Western theologians and philosophers seem in general to have completely forgotten what the soul and its function actually are, it is perhaps unsurprising that the largely unthinking masses of the last century seem to have developed little interest in the subject.

We have already looked at the concept of the soul in the last chapters, where we also saw just to what extent it differs from the personality, the latter being merely the temporarily integrated combination of the developed physical, emotional, and lower mental natures. In this chapter, therefore, we shall take a look at the way in which the human personality produces karma and the soul takes responsibility for it, thereby generating repetitive evolutionary experience. Before we do so, however, let us just clarify one or two other basic issues, as follows. First of all, what is karma and how does it work?

THE NATURE OF KARMA

Personal or group karma is generated by virtue of either positive or negative intention within a particular field of consciousness causing subjective reaction. It does so by intelligent or semi-intelligent desire (or will) imposing itself in some or other way upon another, separate being or entity. That intention can, however, be either self-aware or instinctive. It can be beneficent or malefic. It can come from above, from the same level, or from below, in terms of evolutionary equivalence. However, our main concern here involves mainly subjective effects generated by intent between human individuals or groups, rather than involving other kingdoms of Nature. In this manner, either "higher" or "lower" causes—whether intelligently, semi-intelligently, or clumsily directed—generate objective effects by the emanations or expressions of their influence.

By virtue of the fact that the emanating influence is projected and allowed to develop its own scheme of operation in the lower world, so it necessarily draws to itself the essences of its own experiences there. These "essences" are formless, germinal entities of a highly magnetic and thus psychically parasitic nature. Consequently, when the higher "causal" influence is withdrawn from the lower field of consciousness toward the higher one, it inevitably draws some of the most evolved essences of the lesser field along with it, in train. They then remain in a temporary state of limbo (within the nature of their parent deva entity) until called back into action by the re-emanation of that same consciousness. Once this happens, in line with the overriding deva natures between the doer and the done-to, they instinctively go back into action to rebalance the previous situation, for good or ill. It is important to remember here, therefore, that the deva natures on both sides are involved in the process of restitution. It is not just a question of reaction by one person against the other. This fact is hardly ever noted or mentioned.

THE PROCESS OF REINCARNATION INVOLVING KABBALISTIC CORRELATIONS

As described in chapters 1 and 2, it is the spiritual nature of Man that—for purposes of evolutionary self-sacrifice—originally emanated an aspect of itself (a daemonic "spark") down into the terrestrial soul. The latter is the entity that, on the lower turn of the evolutionary spiral, also gives rise to the forms of the mineral, plant, and animal kingdoms of Nature. As a result of this emanation's development, the human kingdom came into being, thereby forming a "bridge" between the fields of consciousness of the higher and lower natures of our planetary Life. The originating point of projection from the spiritual nature is known to us as the Spiritual Ego. In kabbalism it is called the principle of Keter. In the Arabic tradition it is known as Kid'r (or sometimes Kedir). The word actually appears to derive from the same root as the ancient Egyptian Kheper, symbolized by the scarab beetle god and meaning the self-regenerating faculty. It is also the protector or guardian angel.

This descending, serpentine "ray" of projected intention from the spiritual nature is, in fact, the same as what we otherwise call the Causal Soul and the Higher Mind principle. It is that which is also associated with the kabbalistic principle Hokmah. It is dual in nature, combining the vitalizing and percipient principles of Life and intelligent sensory Awareness. As also explained in the previous chapters, it contains the terrestrial soul. Holding the terrestrial soul within its serpent-like auric embrace (see fig. 4.2), the Causal Soul transfers something of itself to that lesser soul by means of tensile vibration. This (living) mass vibration thereby "falls" into the lesser soul nature and thus becomes temporarily trapped within it, or anchored to it.

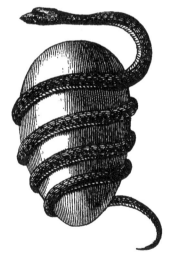

Fig. 4.2. Kosmic serpent enfolding the Egg of Creation

In the gnostic Christian system of philosophy, this union was metaphorically referred to as an "imprisonment"—that of Sophia Ackamoth—by the Demiurge, Ialdabaoth. The practical result of this union is that the originally spiritual vibration becomes diffused throughout the lesser soul's nature. This, in human biological terms, is somewhat akin to what happens to the ovum when pierced by the male spermatozoon. The resulting mass of daemonic "sparks" then begin the long and arduous task of reorganizing themselves into an intelligently coordinated unity of web-like interrelationships. This they do by gradually recognizing each other's functions and thereby banding together in mutual sympathy. That in turn causes seven major (and many more minor) centers of force (chakras) to appear. Their influence then results in the matter of the lesser field of consciousness surrounding them being gathered together in increasingly coherent forms with a functional interrelationship. Interestingly, this same idea in the Macrocosm is to be found as an allegorical story in Chinese literature, in the tale of *The Water Margin*.

Of the twin projections of the spiritual nature, the vitalizing Life principle (Sanskrit: *sutratma*) remains fully extended throughout the life of the lesser organism thus formed. The higher Consciousness principle, however, is gradually withdrawn as an autonomous faculty of upwardly projected sentience (the Sanskrit *antahkarana*) develops in the lesser being. Consequently, the latter finds itself "chasing" the former from which it was itself originally emanated. In this way, the true process of progressive evolution takes place.

THE COMPOSITION OF
THE HUMAN PERSONALITY

Eventually, the individualization of the consciousness of the "sparks" that have thus fallen generates its own persona in three stages:

1. First, it coordinates (within the field of the terrestrial soul) an organic form with a full range of physical senses. This is paralleled by the development of the mineral and plant kingdoms.

2. Second, it conveys the sense of persona into the terrestrial soul itself and extends this outward to contact other terrestrial souls of an equivalent nature. This develops the faculty of desire—of like and dislike—and thus the so-called astral nature. This is paralleled by the development of the higher plant and the animal kingdoms.

3. Third, it uses this astral experience to generate a combined faculty of qualitative discrimination (through recognition) and a "personal" associated memory, the latter being the foundation of the lower

mind. This process of development is seen in the higher ranks of the animal kingdom and also in the lowest human types.

Near the end of the final stage, the "animal soul" propensity is fully attained. However, when these three stages are fully coordinated in the form of the human individual, we have the following further development, that of the triple aspects of egoic personality: the lower mind faculty, the astral or desire faulty, and the physical senses.

In the case of the human being, the upward projection of the personality is countered by the downward influence of the Spiritual Ego, in a manner corresponding with that of the Sun on the upward growth of a plant. The plant shoots up straight in the darkness and without much natural strength as a result of attraction to lunar influence; the solar influence presses down on its "head," thereby inducing slower, but stronger (cyclically coordinated) spiral growth and innate, self-induced balance. In the human being, the radiant influence of the Spiritual Ego—itself occultly regarded as a solar entity—forces the "lunar" growth of the egoic personality to slow down, thereby likewise generating a pattern of enforced experience. It is then only when the innately developed consciousness of the human "plant" has properly "flowered" that its evolved essence (i.e., its very real psychological "aroma") is absorbed back into the causal source—that is, the truly spiritual nature.

It is therefore in the nature of the action-and-reaction between these downward and upward projecting influences that karma is generated. The process of reincarnation also parallels the nature of the plant-like instinct to reproduce itself in seed, but this occurs in the spiritual nature's intention, purely because the intelligence within the spiritual nature recognizes that the "aroma" generated by the lesser entity is not yet perfected.

THE REINCARNATING *SKANDHAS*

So then, how is it that reincarnation is progressive? The answer lies in what Buddhist philosophy calls the *skandhas*. These are germinal memory-seed forces that, between incarnations, are to be found in what we earlier referred to as the Causal Soul body. As already described, the latter is a localized, fetal sac of radiant, semi-spiritual substance; it "hangs" like a roosting bat from within the outer surface of the Spiritual Soul and is particularly associated with the emanation of the Spiritual Ego. The skandhas—described by theosophists as the "three Permanent Atoms" of the physical, astral, and lower mental natures[3]—are themselves to be found in both the Macrocosm (the logoic Life, viewed as a unified entity) and the microcosm (human) (see fig. 4.3).

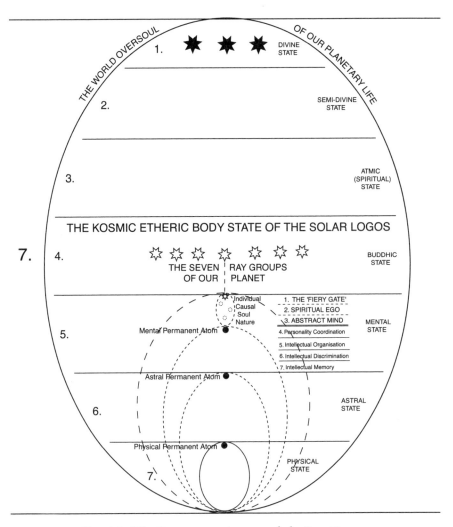

Fig. 4.3. The Permanent Atoms and the Ray Groups

The "Permanent Atoms" are highly subtle and intelligently organized germinal entities that accrue and contain the psychological seed-essences derived from past experience. When they are acted upon by the fresh impulse emanating from the higher spiritual nature, they provide the working blueprint that will cause a "new" terrestrial soul to be generated for the (re)incarnation of the objective being. In practical terms, the demiurgic Oversoul of the planet produces the new terrestrial soul in response to the reengaging influence of the skandhas. Thus, in a very real sense, the three skandhas provide the germinal prototypes of: (a) the terrestrial soul nature; (b) the astral body (incorporating the desire principle); and (c) the mental (that is, the intellectual or lower mind) body of the human individual. These, as already described, will eventually develop, through experience, that coordination of consciousness between them that we call the "egoic personality."

THE MACROCOSMIC PARALLEL

In the Macrocosm, the same principle applies, but within the kosmic planes of being and consciousness, the equivalents to the skandhas are known as Dhyani Buddhas (see again fig. 3.4), who are liberated groups of planetary gods and pure divine forces in Nature. We will come across them again in a later chapter. They too are three in number, as Evans-Wentz describes for us in his work *The Tibetan Book of the Dead*[4] as the hierarchies of the Dharmakaya, Sambhogakaya, and Nirmanakaya Buddhas. The Nirmanakaya Buddhas are responsible for the regeneration and repopulation of the physical planet. They—in concert with the Dhyani Chohans—are, in a very real sense, the operative planetary Demiurge, for they contain within their own nature that consciousness containing all the seed-beings and essences of the kosmic physical plane (that is, all the kingdoms of Nature), to be "regurgitated" during the course of the next planetary cycle and then reabsorbed at the end of it. This is akin to the Krisna nature in Hinduism, as described in the Bhagavad Gita.[5]

Correspondingly, the Sambhogakaya Buddhas contain within themselves the totality of kosmic desire related to the existence of that future planetary scheme. Finally, the Dharmakaya Buddhas contain within their own nature the totality of knowledge of the kosmic Mind principle—that which holds over all intellectual experience from one cycle of planetary incarnation to the next. When the impulse takes place to either regenerate the existing planetary scheme or to create a new one, that impulse emerges from within the yet higher kosmic Spiritual Soul nature where, it is said, a still higher Dhyani Buddha hierarchy—that of the Amitabha—exists. However, that will be touched on in a later chapter.

Such a dynamic structure of existence might perhaps sound completely abstract even to many readers and students of esoteric philosophy, who could thus be given to wondering of what use such information really is. The answer to that lies in the fact of working correspondences. In other words, when the mind of the enquirer is awakened (through training) to the fact that such Macrocosmic–microcosmic correspondences exist as influences through a matter of practical necessity, it instinctively orientates itself to "keeping an eye open" for signs of their influence. The whole essence of training in esoteric and occult philosophy is organized with this end in mind, while maintaining an appreciation of the fact that partial perceptions, although inevitable, tend to give rise to ever-increasing distortions of interpretation.

We need to bear constantly in mind that our own highest nature as individuals (of which we are as yet completely unaware) is itself that of a "divine spark" of the kosmic Mind, which must, someday in the incognizably distant future, become that of a SELF-realized kosmic god. The conscious progression toward that realization must itself, however, first acknowledge that all souls and spirits—and therefore all associated knowledge—are but fragments of the one Universal Oversoul. Hence it is, as earlier mentioned, that the universal brotherhood (of souls) is actually a general, working fact and not a mere ideal. Until this perception becomes rooted in the consciousness of the individual, nothing of any real and lasting value concerning the world of esotericism will be learned.

THE REASON FOR REINCARNATION AND ITS PROCESS

Turning back to the issue of reincarnation, it follows quite logically that, for the most part, it arises necessarily because of previous failure. That which is incomplete in one cycle must be completed in another in order for balance and harmony to prevail. In a few cases, however, it occurs through a willingness to self-sacrifice for the purposes of teaching other souls of lesser degree. Without such self-sacrifice, less evolved consciousnesses would have no blueprint to follow, no inspiration or role models to guide their ideals. It also follows that what has previously been greater may in later incarnations take a much more minor role. Thus even a sun may become a mere planet, just as a king in one lifetime may become a slave or pauper in the next. The issue of what takes place in succession is predominantly related to the greater purpose of the group to which the individual soul and spirit are affiliated. The question of the individual soul's own evolutionary development is then of a secondary nature.

Let us now briefly look at the question of what happens "on the other side of the curtain" during sleep and also following the transition that we call "death." These experiences are common to all humanity but they are pursued unconsciously until the point is reached where the individual masters his or her own lower, elemental nature and thus becomes Adept, or spiritually Self-conscious. By understanding what is involved, we will then see where the process of spiritual initiation fits in quite logically.

When the human individual falls asleep, it is due to a temporary separation of the terrestrial soul organism from the etheric double, which is itself closely tied to the body throughout the life. This takes place because of a "pull" from the Causal Soul nature, which provides the terrestrial soul nature with its faculty of self-consciousness. As it is the higher soul that provides the faculty of sensory consciousness, the sleeping body form becomes inert, other than via an autonomic awareness provided by the continuing link with the soul through what has come to be called "the silver cord." This is a living but ethereal stream of light that is anchored in the heart center of the individual's etheric double during incarnation (in the solar plexus center in the less evolved), thereby also providing a vibratory connection with the higher soul organism. Hence, wherever the soul astrally travels during the hours of bodily sleep, a fragment of its intelligence remains in situ, within the etheric double, to protect it through warning of potential danger or need. In such case, the lesser soul organism is invoked and immediately returns.

However, while the consciousness remains associated with the terrestrial soul nature, the individual's perceptions remain of an elemental nature, partly within the atmosphere of our planet, mixing with all sorts of entities, many of which are of a decidedly low nature. Many of these experiences are then remembered in superficial types of dreams and even nightmares, as also many of those experiences derived from reliving waking experiences in the purely astro-mental nature. Other experiences derive from the intelligence reliving the subjective or objective daytime experiences achieved through emotional or lower mental contacts. When the individual's consciousness becomes dissociated from the terrestrial soul nature, however, it is immediately drawn to the semi-spiritual nature of the Causal Soul. This coincides with the phenomenon known as "deep sleep" in which a constant regeneration of spiritual purpose takes place, frequently leading to the individual waking with the strongest sense of having been "told" something of great importance. This takes place through the agency of either the individual's own Spiritual Ego or, if the individual is "on the Path" and thus attached to a spiritual ashram, by an Adept teacher also known as a *nirmanakaya*.

One might suggest that in the macrocosm of our planet, during those long intervals of cyclic "obscuration" during which the various objective kingdoms of Nature are withdrawn and the planet "falls asleep" (as seems currently the case with Mars, for example), the same sort of thing happens. However, in that instance the anchorage with the temporarily absent Oversoul is provided by a nucleus of the Spiritual Hierarchy of the planet remaining in situ. It is their work in that respect—involving a slower recycling of the animal and plant kingdom lives—which results in the continuing coherence of the planetary body. It is then the return of the Oversoul (with the attendant return of Man), which generates the commencement of a new macrocycle and the return of objective Nature in the shape of the plant and animal kingdoms.

It is one of the fundamental axioms of occult philosophy that, by virtue of Man being the "bridge" between the spiritual and material worlds, the objective cycle cannot take place without Man somehow being involved at the outset. From that viewpoint, Man is *eventually* to be found in all the fully objective planetary schemes, although not in the form of earthly humans, with which we are generally familiar. The majority of the planetary schemes in our solar system are not so far advanced in their cycle as Earth. That, it is suggested, is why several of them still have rings surrounding them.

WHAT HAPPENS AT DEATH

When the individual dies, however, a far more extensive and permanent separation takes place. The life force is entirely withdrawn up the silver cord into the higher soul organism and the anchorage is thus permanently disengaged. This results in the gradual dispersal of the etheric double (likewise of the buddhic body in the Macrocosm) and the natural corruption of the dense physical body as all its cells likewise seek their own liberation. The physical sparks are withdrawn into what has already been referred to as the physical Permanent Atom, while the corresponding essences that animate the astral and mental bodies are similarly withdrawn into the astral and mental Permanent Atoms.

Before this takes place, however, there occurs a period during which the strongest characteristics of the personality have to work themselves out subjectively. This involves a "Bardo" period of constant psychic repetition of past experiences of an incomplete or maladjusted nature until the innate daemonic intelligence moves on. Correspondingly, in the Macrocosm, the masses of sparks are withdrawn into the fields of consciousness of the three groups of Dhyani Buddhas of that particular planetary scheme with which they are associated.

Care must be taken here to note the difference between the essences (the "sparks") that animate the various bodies or vehicles and the masses of substance that provide the general material of those same bodies. The latter—vitalized by the planetary Anima Mundi—have not reached the evolutionary degree required to become (through assimilation) part of the integral consciousness of the microcosmic Permanent Atom or the Macrocosmic Dhyani Buddha. They thus fall back into the general reservoir of deva substance to await another cycle of opportunity. This is more easily understood if we keep in mind that an objective body form—whether of a human being or a planet—is actually a mass of entities, all of different group potency, different group quality, and different functionary capacity.

This idea of evolutionary achievement producing assimilation into a higher organism is highly important because it gives us the clue as to the purpose of what we call "initiation." In real terms, initiation (of the individual at least) is a forced and thus unnatural process, because it is based on an artificially induced crisis.[6] In general, so we are told, it is not one that is employed within all the various planetary schemes, where instead the processes of assimilation and synthesis seemingly take place at the end of each cycle. In a few such schemes, so we are again told, it is the process currently in operation. Thus, reading between the lines, it would appear to have something specifically to do with the karma inherent in the evolution of that greater being known as our own Solar Logos.

THE CAUSAL SOUL BODY

To conclude what has already been said about the process of assimilation that follows what we call "death," we need to bear in mind that the three Permanent Atoms—the equivalent of the Buddhist skandhas, as previously mentioned—are themselves to be found contained at all times within the Causal Body (the rational soul) of the individual. As this is sometimes confused with the Spiritual Soul body, it would perhaps be opportune here to reiterate its fetal nature and function more fully.

In rather crude terms (the analogy should not be taken to extremes), the Causal Soul might otherwise be said to fulfill in the Macrocosm a function analogous to the pore of the skin, the latter itself being an expression of the etheric double of the individual. It is thus of vital importance in the process of cyclic aspiration and respiration, the latter being also associated with providing the excess radiance of what is commonly called the "pranic aura" or "health aura." The pore is of course the outer opening to a cavity within the epidermis or outermost layer of the skin. Now bearing in mind that the etheric double pervades the whole of the physical body—the latter being merely "hung" on it—and that the Buddhi is itself the kosmic etheric double of the Logos, as also previously mentioned, we can perhaps begin to see the occult (even if not the exact) parallels.

There is one final thing that might be added here, by way of providing some background perspective to what has already been said in *The Secret Doctrine* about the beginnings of humanity on Earth. It is that the appearance of the Causal Soul, generated by the downward flow of energy from the human Monad, originally occurred as a direct result of the appropriation of the dense body form of the planet by our Planetary Logos[7] through the agency of those Dhyani Chohans otherwise known as Kumaras. That in turn gave rise to the phenomenon of human individualization—the production of self-consciousness—in nascent humanity during the Lemurian era, nearly twenty million years ago.[8] The semi-spiritual Causal Body or rational soul of each human being (other than the Adept, for reasons to be explained later on) is thus the raison d'être of that person's self-conscious individuality.

In metaphysically technical terms, the vast majority of human Causal Souls are of a "fourth round" nature (see appendix A for an explanation of planetary "rounds") and are thus located in the substance of the third mental subplane, thereby inducing a "Brahma" influence. Those of the rather more advanced types exist on the second mental subplane, thereby inducing a more pronounced "Visnu" influence.[9] This, it is suggested, is principally what gives rise to the qualitatively different nature of human culture and civilization, including why the masses of humanity function predominantly within the four lower mental subplanes.

THE PERMANENT ATOMS

The three Permanent Atoms (the incarnatory skandhas) contained within the sheath of the Causal Body or rational soul organism are then, effectively, what gives rise to the human personality, their active coordination being what the objective human experience in any lifetime is all about.[10] It follows, therefore, that the inherent psychomagnetic force (charisma) of the individual is entirely dependent on that coordination by the overshadowing spiritual nature. Hence, when the spiritual nature (of the Monad) partially withdraws its influence at the conclusion of a cycle of activity, the outermost coordination quite normally ceases to exist, even though the three Permanent Atoms themselves are still held in thrall. Consequently, the outer body form of the individual dies and the integration of the derived personality naturally falls apart. However, if the coordination of the three Permanent Atoms in any lifetime is not accompanied by an integrated orientation of function with the higher, spiritual nature, which actually provides the real driving force behind its existence, the developed personality takes on a highly self-centered existence. This will be described in further detail a little later on.

By virtue of the fact that the physical Permanent Atom provides the foundation of sensory consciousness inherent in the terrestrial soul organism, it also carries the main karmic load. That is irrespective of the fact that the other two Permanent Atoms are the ones that generate the main mass of new experiences of a lifetime. In a way that would be quite complex to describe, most of the residue of past karma is dumped on the terrestrial soul, if the individual's main focus is based on the lower desire nature. Hence it is that the terrestrial soul, as the foundation of the desire nature, reexpresses that karma within the bodily form that it produces, which thus becomes conditioned by it. This is what gives rise, for example, to much innate physical disability, many of the genetic distortions discovered by scientists being merely the formative expressions of the karmic blueprint held in the memory consciousness of the terrestrial soul organism.

The memories and faculties derived from past lifetimes' experiences are not all contained in the physical Permanent Atom, however. In the more developed intelligence, where the subjective nature is much more the area of experiential concern, they are more likely to be held and retained within the other two Permanent Atoms. Consequently, some individuals are born with inherent faculties in some particular areas, although they are usually born into families where those faculties are more readily triggered into re-activity. Hence the phenomenon of certain child prodigies, like Mozart. It also needs to be borne in mind that certain individuals are born with particular faculties in order to enable them to fulfill a specific role in the objective expression of Divine Purpose. Some of these are constructive, some intentionally destructive in order to bring about innovation.

KOSMIC INFLUENCES

When considering the reincarnation of each new lifetime, it must also be remembered that the Causal Soul nature that drives it is itself driven by the influences present at that time in the buddhi, the kosmic etheric double of the Solar Logos. Hence we can perhaps see a little more clearly what is meant by the analogous association of the Causal Soul body with the skin pore, provided that we consider it in terms of its function within the logoic Macrocosm. Those influences present in the kosmic etheric double are but the partial and current expressions of the greater influences and powers held within the logoic Oversoul, an unimaginably vast deva entity, which itself sustains the logoic physical body form. Hence it is that there exists a most important correlation between these two and the seven major kosmic etheric force centers (chakras), which esoteric philosophy refers to as "Ray Groups." These were mentioned a little earlier on in relation to the question of emanating centers of higher consciousness and they too will be described in greater detail further later on.

Just as with the chakras in the human etheric double, the kosmic chakras are dual in function. They are on the one hand responsible for the channeling and distribution of new incoming energies (involving logoic dharma, or planetary purpose) and, on the other, for gathering up and synthesizing the useful essences generated by human experience (logoic karma), prior to these being transmitted back to the logoic Oversoul. In this manner, the intelligence within the logoic body functions exactly as it does in the case of the human organism. That is why the human is called "the microcosm of the Macrocosm." It is then the hierarchically organized scheme of intelligence within the chakra system—whether kosmic or systemic—which is the engine of evolutionary development.

It is for this reason that an understanding of the spiritual hierarchical scheme is so important. In fact, from what has just been described, it should by now be obvious that what we call karma and dharma are in fact but the Purpose behind the mass of redistributive energies, forces, and influences constantly recycling within the logoic etheric double and dense body organism. Within this we are but participatory agents of the Logos, despite having our own human freewill within given limits of higher functional necessity.

GOOD AND EVIL

Let us otherwise in passing touch on the subject of "good and evil," by virtue of these being seen in common parlance as fundamental to the whole process of karma. The problem of how "evil" could exist within the mind or organism of the Logos, when the latter is so vastly more evolved and perfected than ourselves, is one that has baffled theologians for centuries. Yet, seen against the concept that every aspect of Nature is but a functional process within the compound body of the Logos, the answer is immediately simplified.

Within our own human nature—that of the microcosm—we have cells that create and destroy, cells that sustain and maintain the whole sensory function, and cells that enable us to express a whole range of other faculties. All of these have a naturally balanced range of operation and limitation, which is, however, based on intelligent design. However, when that prearranged distribution and balance becomes impaired, cells that should be in one place are found in another contrary to their function; or, when too many or too few cells are to be found in a given location at any time, the local function becomes over- or understimulated. As a direct result, the body loses its naturally healthy state. From this we can infer that "good" is the natural state of balanced health in the organism—whether the microcosm or the Macrocosm.

"Evil," on the other hand, exists where there is either sustained inadequacy or surplus, leading to an unnatural imbalance that draws potent influences into wrongful areas of function. The hugely potent force that either sustains the natural balance or seeks to upset it is what we call the "attitude of mind." However, this is not the mind, per se, but rather the overall state of emotional balance, which acts as the bridge between the mind and the etheric-physical functions. If allowed to generate turbulence through holding on to energies and forces that should in fact be just passing through, the kamic or emotional field becomes a merely chaotic playground for the elemental senses. This then acts psychosomatically, partially or totally disrupting both the mental faculty and the physical sensory functions.

For this reason, the natural intelligence in a person needs to be trained (from an early age) in the actual and practical use of ideas, first through discipline and then through applied and tested self-discipline. The testing of discipline is vitally important because it confirms to any individual that they are able to control the forces within their own nature with which they normally (or abnormally) have to deal. This is fundamentally what initiation itself is all about; hence the fact that all real (that is, spiritual) initiations, which open up hitherto unsuspected inner aspects of our nature, are, in a very real sense, "baptisms of fire" that either kill or cure in a psychological sense.

Returning to the issue of good and evil, however, there is a philosophical aspect that needs to be considered. It is that all "good" (as Plato himself describes) is deemed to emanate from that source that we equate with the Spiritual Ego—whether in the microcosm or the Macrocosm. It is the downwardly emanated energy from this same source that we then call the Higher Mind principle. However, as the latter is only a partial emanation, it is not itself good, for good involves that completeness that ever remains within the source itself. Therefore, the Mind and what the Mind encapsulates for a subsidiary field of intelligent self-expression becomes, in Platonic and gnostic philosophy, what is referred to as the "second god," or demiurgic principle. In the microcosm, this becomes the terrestrial soul organism, which itself "creates" and then maintains the human form and bodily organism in its entirety. It is for this reason that it is the demiurgic nature that absorbs most karmic responsibility. It is for this reason also that it is from the demiurgic nature that the whole process of physical reincarnation takes place, whether in the Macrocosm or the microcosm.

NEW AGE VIEWS ON GOOD AND EVIL

It is very interesting to study the widespread range of New Age attitudes to this subject as it helps to explain why simple misconceptions lead to so much trouble, not only in the private life of the individual, but also in human society as a whole.[11] For that reason, it is perhaps worth mentioning one or two related ideas. The first of these is that good and evil are not metaphysical realities but merely the result of a duality of forces appearing in the illusory objective world in which we humans live. It is a result of the interplay of these forces that suffering (due to ignorance) occurs, although suffering itself (through karma) is actually the fundamentally necessary tool of spiritual education, which the kosmos provides. The background to this is that the kosmos itself provides a scheme of perfect universal order and justice, which humanity does not recognize because of mere ignorance based on self-concern. So far so good—apparently.

This first range of perceptions is, however, followed by the idea that in order to understand our own higher (spiritual) nature—and thus also the nature of the kosmos in general—we must first learn to love ourselves. That in turn will supposedly enable us to love all others, despite their many and varied faults and recurrent bad behavior. In following this idea on a general basis, compassion will supposedly rule throughout humanity. In addition, the perceptions of sin and guilt will disappear, thereby leading to a consequent loss of anxiety and fear. Thus, all we have to do to bring about this situation is to take full responsibility for ourselves as individuals, while expecting others to do the same—thereby leading to an overall self-forgiveness, which will, in turn, generate the perfect world order which we seek. Human evolution will thereby be immediately advanced.

That this approach appears naïve is quite self-evident. However, there are a number of associated errors of perception involved in it as well, all based on an anthropocentric delusion that our own human view as to what constitutes perfection is correct. In the first place, although the kosmos may indeed be based on Universal Order, that order fluctuates by virtue of Man's instinctively disruptive role within it, in pursuit of change. One might further suggest that ignorance is not endemic just to humanity, either in microcosmic or Macrocosmic terms. Consequently, not all greater beings are solely concerned with what we might regard as benevolent justice to all. Even though the Devil may be a human invention, it does not mean that evil is merely a misconception, or that what appears to us as "good" is actually "good" in the wider kosmic context.

Secondly, the idea that we need to learn to "love ourselves" involves a misperception of large proportions, again based on a purely anthropocentric view of things, plus a none-too-subtle wish for our own self-indulgence. The ancient wisdom tradition makes it quite clear that we need instead to forget ourselves entirely, in the same sense as applied by the Zen Buddhist. In other words, we have to learn the faculty of complete dissociation, thereby becoming the subjective action that leads to the objective result. Thus the actor (that is, the sense of oneself) ceases to exist and is thereby seen to be the illusion it actually is.

Then the greater Intelligence—of which we are a part—wastes no further time and effort in "personal" pursuits, because it is entirely concerned with helping to bring about the fulfillment of a far greater Purpose. Thus our Higher Self "initiates" that greater action. However, as long as we draw a distinction between our personalized human self (as the main concern) and the Higher Self (as the separate ideal), that illusory duality will continue to cause problems. But, if we instead recognize the lesser "spark" within the human individual as merely a small emanation from its parent Self, the problem is more easily resolved.

Let us finally deal with the associated issue of "altered states of consciousness," which many New Age theories mistakenly associate with a general accessing of spirituality. One related misconception is that existence involves only spirit and matter. From this arises the idea that—all objective life being unreal—all subjective life and experience must involve the spiritual nature. Hence the emphasis on the power of imagination as the invocative "key" that automatically (so it seems) opens the door to the spiritual world.

This somewhat simplistic view—which merely gives rise to fantasy—almost always involves the accessing of a purely repetitive elemental function, which is essentially psychic in nature. Despite generating a colorful spectrum of light of its own, it remains a low-grade personal product, which serves only to block and conceal the true spiritual nature. The latter is qualitatively of a completely different and far more powerful order; once experienced (very rarely), it is never forgotten because of its potently astringent cleansing nature. The seductive psychic spectrum, on the other hand, leads unavoidably into an unending miasma of karmic problems, which can only be avoided by refusing to acknowledge it. In correspondence with the old occult adage that "energy follows thought," we find (as easily proved during meditation) that a withdrawal of association from all subjective phenomena (i.e., thoughts and emotions) destroys them through attrition. That then leaves the observing intelligence (which is the real individuality in the human) to become increasingly aware of the far more subtle range of spiritual sound and light that is there in the background. That, however, requires persistent and very sustained practice.

KARMIC RETRIBUTION

One other aspect of the Law of Karma needs to be clearly understood in relation to our general consideration of initiation as an evolutionary sequence. We will see why later on. It relates to the fact that all karmic action arises out of the actions of the devas in rebalancing the forces within the overall framework of Divine Purpose, as already described. Human nature, however, is self-centered and self-concerned, thus not focused on acceding to Divine Purpose, even in the most general terms. So because the devas work strictly according to law—and thereby within the framework of the ever operative law of cycles—they are necessarily forced to carry out their karmic adjustments at the most appropriate moments, coincident with whatever "inner" cycle of activity is involved. While the higher devas are consciously aware of those cycles, the extraverted human consciousness is not.

Consequently, if we are consciously aware of having made an error of judgment, the "adjustment" appears to us as retribution, which, if we are sensible, we acknowledge. If not, we merely think of it as a form of nuisance, of greater or lesser importance, and then carry on, probably to compound matters in our general ignorance. We fail to realize that every form of mere reaction on our part generates a display of occult force, which itself provokes a counter reaction, even if we are unaware of it. That counter reaction will itself be proportionate to the force generated by us in the first place. Taking into consideration the occult principle that all energies ultimately return to their point of origin, still armed with the quality of force generated at the outset, it necessarily follows that we are largely the parents of our own many and varied miseries.

ACTS OF GOD

In concluding, some mention should also be made of those supposed "acts of God," which cause large scale disruption and damage to human society. How is it that a "good God" could possibly engage in these and the general suffering that they cause? It is this very question that has caused so many to reject the very idea of an intelligent Divinity. The short answer to the question is that such a view derives from the very limited perspective of a purely human emotional reaction, not involving the spiritual intelligence. The spiritual intelligence recognizes that there is such a thing as a higher Purpose—which we cannot possibly understand in anything like its fullness—and that all objective forms are merely the evanescent expressions of that Purpose attempting to work themselves out. The purely human organism—entirely driven by its instinctively reactive tendencies—cannot see it. Furthermore, it does not want to see it because its own highest ideals involve a supposed state of happiness based on a selfishly self-indulgent peace and quiet.

The fact is, the Law of Karma is wholly based on practical necessity within the greater organism. When a new situation is required, or when an old situation has already run its course, change necessarily comes, and any forms that get in the way of that change inevitably get damaged or destroyed. In the human case, this results in pain and suffering by self-association, on the part of either those thus damaged or those bereaved by the loss of their nearest and dearest. In the former case, this is due to the body processes involved in recovery of the physiological status quo. In the latter, it is due to an ignorance perhaps best summed up in Shakespeare's play *Twelfth Night*, when the jester asks the Countess Olivia why she is so sad and she replies that it is because her brother has died at sea. The jester then suggests that her brother has gone to Hell, whereupon she reacts strongly, saying that of course he has gone to Heaven. Upon hearing this, the jester then replies with complete logic, "Well then, more fool you for mourning his situation."

As long as human beings regard the objective world as the true world, this same situation will prevail. Curiously, however, there are many human beings who, when faced with a loss, will just accept it stoically without wanting to pursue the matter further. For them, it is sufficient as an "act of God." However, this often results in their developing a very foolish view that such an act has been one of retribution by their God for their own or their community's supposed wickedness or lack of adequate religious observance. Such an act would itself be highly inappropriate, because it predicates an equally emotional reaction on the part of the Divinity, rather than the pursuit of an extended Divine Purpose.

THE PERIODIC DESTRUCTION
OF HUMAN CIVILIZATION

It has been suggested that such an extensive act of God resulted in the worldwide cataclysms that destroyed the ancient Atlantean civilization, in response to its wickedness. However, Atlantean "wickedness" was actually based on spiritual ignorance, founded on a materialistic ideology, which, although logically derived, eventually and in due cycle had to give rise to a more definitely spiritual consciousness. Its termination—which actually took many hundreds of thousands of years to complete, so we are told[12]— was as inevitable as will be that of our own present, worldwide civilization, also still very extensively based on materialistic ideals. Consequently, the time will unavoidably come when our own society will itself experience the same karmic fate, although the means of it may well differ. In an age where international scientific concern is at its most vociferous in relation to "global warming" and the certainty that some inhabited lands will disappear under the ocean—thereby forcing assimilation of their peoples by other nations—this issue of absolutely natural cyclic destruction needs to be carefully considered and put into wider perspective. The widespread emotional fear generated by a complete failure to even entertain this possibility does nothing but deepen materialistic anxieties out of all proportion, thereby worsening the problem still further.

Thus it is that cause and effect has also to be seen in relation to the due cycle of Divine Purpose. The whole process of evolution, in all kingdoms of Nature, is based upon a process of initiation followed by experience of the new paradigm. This is then followed by initiation into a yet greater paradigm. That is as true of the Macrocosm as it is of the microcosm. However, the cycles that each kingdom of Nature faces are themselves of widely different duration, each inevitably impinging upon others and thus causing change in them as well. As long as we remember this fact of interrelated cycles and subcycles of ordered Divine Purpose, the whole issue will make far more sense. In the next chapter, we shall take a closer look at the principle of cyclic duration and the way in which the various kingdoms of Nature on our planet are themselves involved in the whole evolutionary process.

FIVE

EVOLUTION AND INITIATION IN NATURE

We can begin this chapter by quite safely reiterating that the actual process of evolution through the various kingdoms of Nature (whether visible or invisible), as shown in fig. 5.1, is quite distinctively different from that suggested by modern neo-Darwinists. It is of an underlying spiritual nature and is thus psychologically causal, whereas that of the Darwinists is purely related to the world of objective influences and effects. In order to understand how this could be so, however, we have to refer, once again, to our hermeneutic system of states of being and consciousness, remembering that this is not static but rather interconnected with the law of cycles. Following this, we shall more readily understand the associated logic as we consider the relationship (in terms of consciousness) between the Macrocosm and the microcosm.

It will be remembered that the basis of the doctrine of cycles is that, within the overall framework of Universal Consciousness, ideas—as expressions of different aspects of that Consciousness—are in a constant process of interactivity. All such ideas are entities, to be found appearing macrocosmically and microcosmically within the kosmic consciousness of Space as hierarchies of celestial Oversouls and lesser soul beings, only some having objective body forms. Transference of vital consciousness and functional

8. PLANETARY SOUL	-	8TH KINGDOM (DHYANI BUDDHAS/INTERPLANETARY SPIRITS)
7. DIVINE SOUL	-	7TH KINGDOM IN NATURE (PLANETARY BUDDHAS)
6. SEMI-DIVINE SOUL	-	6TH KINGDOM IN NATURE (PLANETARY CHOHANS)
5. SPIRITUAL SOUL	-	5TH KINGDOM IN NATURE (ADEPTS/MASTERS)
4. CAUSAL SOUL	-	4TH OBJECTIVE KINGDOM IN NATURE (HUMANS)
3. TERRESTRIAL SOUL	-	3RD OBJECTIVE KINGDOM IN NATURE (ANIMALS)
2. CELL	-	2ND OBJECTIVE KINGDOM IN NATURE (PLANTS)
1. ATOM	-	1ST OBJECTIVE KINGDOM IN NATURE (MINERALS)

Fig. 5.1. Progressively individualizing hierarchies of souls

instinct between these various soul organisms then takes place through the agency of what esoteric and occult philosophy would regard as mobile sub-hierarchies of spirits. One might suggest therefore that the whole process of what we call evolution—as with the ancient science of alchemy—lies in relation to this same constant process of transfer and assimilation of such groups of spirits from and to larger Group Oversouls.

It will undoubtedly strike some readers as bizarre that we are here discussing the issue of interplanetary consciousness when our own human consciousness is so much more limited. However, this does not take into consideration the fact that the full extent of our own subliminal consciousness has not yet been apprehended by us even though its higher reaches are said to be fundamentally celestial in origin and nature. Our own spiritual nature may be limited to function within the higher aspects of our own planetary consciousness but our divine nature is said to extend far beyond that.

All very well you might say, but how can we consider such things in practical terms? Well, one way might be to begin developing an astrological interest along even general lines. The initial approach to a greater field of existence and knowledge involves simple interest in it and its purely objective workings. That then, in due course, leads to much more defined knowledge and inner understanding. Consequently, because (esoteric) astrology leads us necessarily back toward our own celestial point of origin (as spirits), it is important for us to grasp at least a few associated points, which I shall now try to explain.

The most important feature of this doctrine, as far as evolution is concerned, is that of the interaction of greater and lesser cycles of consciousness (see again fig. 2.7) whether of a planetary or an interplanetary nature. Within these, the various phenomenal forms of self-expression to which they give rise only appear in the first half of each cycle, where they are unfolded by a process of involutionary emanation from the soul or Oversoul. That is to say, lesser cycles owe their very existence to being emanations of greater soul cycles. It follows that the interaction of a greater and a lesser cycle results in a dynamic revitalization of the latter, enabling its continued existence. The lesser cycle or subcycle then progresses until picked up by another greater cycle, which has a slightly or considerably different effect upon it.

THE DOCTRINE OF PLANETARY ROUNDS, CHAINS, AND GLOBES

As already suggested, the whole process of universally developing intelligence—what we otherwise call evolution—is taking place within the field of consciousness of hugely more advanced hierarchies of beings, commonly known to esotericists by the Greek name *logoi*. Thus our solar system in its entirety is merely the objective expression of the consciousness of a Solar Logos, who is itself one of seven such Logoi in the body of a far more evolved and exalted kosmic Logos. Hence, within our solar system we find a sequence of lesser kosmic consciousness expressing itself through the various planetary schemes with which we are familiar via astronomy or astrology.

Rather inevitably, this whole subject becomes increasingly complex the further one goes into it. However, the intention here is to keep things as simple and straightforward as reasonably possible. Rather more comprehensive detail is provided, for those interested, at the back of the book in appendix A. With that in perspective, let us just focus on the idea of consciousness always as a field of being of greater or lesser degree and mind itself as a psycho-spiritual fluid medium capable of being transferred between such fields—such as those of the various planetary schemes within the solar system.

The fact that the order of planetary globes comprising a "chain" of being and consciousness in each such scheme expresses an actual sequence of development is itself important. The general evolutionary sequence is itself triple in nature, comprising involution, evolution, and devolution. As we saw in the previous chapter, "involution" consists of the reexpression in form of the subjective achievement of the preceding cycle. "Evolution" then comprises the expansion of consciousness achieved because of the limitation induced by that form. Finally, "devolution" comprises the liberation from the repetitive lesser cycle into a yet greater cycle of being and consciousness.

This principle is the same whether considered in relation to the microcosm or the Macrocosm, the latter being associated with our solar system as a whole and the yet greater celestial system of which it forms a part. In our solar system, this triple progression involves ten planetary schemes as shown in fig. 5.2.*

Our Earth scheme, the fourth in the series of the first seven sequential planetary schemes, expresses a critical point of balance and change as between the involutionary and evolutionary functions within the nature of the physical consciousness of our Solar Logos. Correspondingly, the seventh scheme (that of Jupiter) represents a point (and a state) of balance between the evolutionary and devolutionary cycles.

THE VARYING QUALITY OF MATTER

Within the overall scheme, every physically objective planet also represents a similarly critical sequence of triple development within its own nature. Hence one might suggest that the terrestrial crust and atmosphere of the physical planets Venus and Mars, for example, which are respectively involutionary and evolutionary within the overall consciousness of the Logos, are

---

*However, in a very real and personal sense and by way of correspondence, this same triple progression also takes place in the formation of our own human ideas as memory recall and refocus, followed by dynamically sustained intention to advance our understanding, and then eventual recognition of the bigger picture.

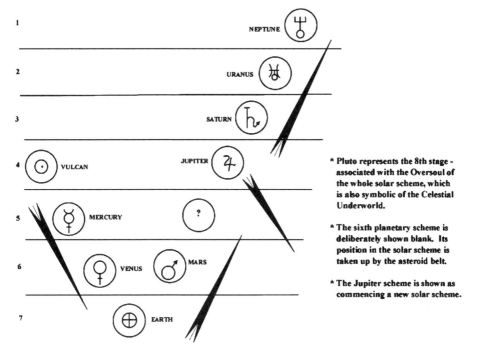

1

NEPTUNE

2

URANUS

3

SATURN

4   VULCAN   JUPITER

5   MERCURY   ?

6   VENUS   MARS

7   EARTH

* Pluto represents the 8th stage - associated with the Oversoul of the whole solar scheme, which is also symbolic of the Celestial Underworld.

* The sixth planetary scheme is deliberately shown blank. Its position in the solar scheme is taken up by the asteroid belt.

* The Jupiter scheme is shown as commencing a new solar scheme.

Fig. 5.2. Involution–evolution–devolution in our solar scheme

quite different from each other and from those of Earth in metaphysically qualitative terms, even if not in visually objective terms. That is because the mineral kingdom not only evolves but also has a slightly different purpose in each separate world scheme.

This is something our modern science cannot yet understand. That is because it is fundamentally quantitative in its analytical approach. It has not even begun to consider the possibility of qualitatively different atoms or the nature of soul being, even if it is beginning to acknowledge the qualitative difference between cellular organisms, the next higher range of entities above atoms in our world scheme.

When we consider the actual states of which each planet is composed, we accordingly find a subtle difference between them (which our modern scientific technology is also as yet incapable of registering). Thus, by virtue of every state and substate being respectively sevenfold in nature (as we saw in chapter 1), we can suggest that the gaseous, liquid, and solid matter of our Earth is—at the seventh and lowest level—the most densely organized in this solar system (apart from that of our Moon). That of Venus and Mars, however, is less so, although the arrangements and characteristics are necessarily rather different because of their differing involutionary/evolutionary functions and stages of development.

Although Blavatsky's *The Secret Doctrine* and Bailey's *A Treatise on Cosmic Fire* both go into rather greater detail on this issue, I will not do so here because, in dealing with more important general evolutionary principles, such details might only cause confusion. What I will add, however, is a suggestion that the matter of each visible planetary globe within our solar system comprises more or less of each of the seven subplanes of the seventh and lowest kosmic plane, in due correspondence. Quite apart from this, each and every planetary scheme has sevenfold companion globe-states on each of the kosmic, astral, lower mental, and higher mental planes of being and consciousness.[1] As we shall see later on, the importance of this lies in relation to the further evolution of those high initiates who pass on to greater states of being.

Each group of globe-states is known theosophically (and in esoteric Buddhism) as a *planetary chain* (see again appendix A), in each of which a complete spiral sequence of involutionary/evolutionary progression is known esoterically as a *round*.[2] The reason for mentioning all this inevitable complexity is that it helps us at least to be aware of how, why, and where Universal Consciousness is "joined up" in practical terms. Hence we can begin to understand why evolution is in fact a fundamentally spiritual process in which transmissions and transitions of consciousness always take place following the same general principles, even though between states involving widely different types of form and function.

THE IMPACT OF
THE GREATER CYCLES ON HUMANITY

Those same transitions necessarily work according to cycles taking place within the Universal Mind, each such cycle involving an expressive, logically sequential emanation of kosmic memory and Divine Purpose. Each such emanation is progressively involutionary, evolutionary, and devolutionary, as already suggested. Consequently, greater Intelligences (or rather, their auric influences) periodically pass through lesser states of being, while lesser intelligences evolve sufficiently to transcend their own fields of limitation and thus move into greater states of being. They can thus progressively access the much more highly developed knowledge associated with those same states.

The various cycles themselves derive from the relative (because constantly changing) geometric relationships of planets and solar systems in space. Hence it is that the ancient wisdom tradition conceives of the influences of greater Intelligences ("gods," relatively speaking) periodically affecting our Earth. Hence also the suggestion of divinely evolved (hence "perfected") members of our own Earth humanity systematically passing on to other planetary and solar schemes, in due cycle, in order to helpfully influence the evolutionary progress in them according to yet Higher Purpose.

As mentioned earlier, the overall zodiacal cycle of 25,920 years has to be seen predominantly in the context of the giant carrier wave of kosmic consciousness that gives rise to it and then picks it up again, much later. This kosmic consciousness is that of unimaginably evolved Intelligences whose own functions progress in sequence through greater celestial systems of which our solar system forms only a small part. In fig. 2.7, we can see that the giant wave passes through the zodiacal framework during the latter or evolutionary part of the Age of Pisces, thereby giving our planetary consciousness a huge evolutionary jolt. At the end of the Age of Pisces it continues upward into a prolonged period of what appears to be subjectivity, only to reappear in active, involutionary mode at the beginning of the subsequent Age of Pisces, some 26,000 years later. This brings into form (very temporarily on our planet) literal "gods," walking among the humankind of the time.

The cycle of precession has to be seen as parallel to the orbital cycle of our Earth around the Sun, although on a hugely greater scale. Thus, there are celestial equinoxes and celestial solstices. So by virtue of precession involving a seemingly regressive cycle (although this is itself based on an illusion), the 12,960-year period between its two celestial solstices (from Virgo-Leo to Pisces-Aquarius) is predominantly involutionary. In other words, it is concerned with unfoldment in form of the range of planetary consciousnesses evolved in the last Great Year cycle. During the latter half of the Great Year (i.e., from Pisces-Aquarius back to Virgo-Leo) the overall process is evolutionary. That is to say, there is a progressive dying out on Earth of many of the subsidiary species and types of body forms generated in the involutionary cycle, leaving evolutionary development potential to those left. Only those forms and organisms remain that are definitely concerned with and able to provide the vehicles for development of a new consciousness within each kingdom of Nature. This is the basis of the much-misunderstood "Day of Judgment" concept found in the Christian Bible and a few other religious works.

THE CYCLIC RETURN OF THE "GODS"

Turning back to fig. 2.7, those "gods" within the greatest wave who are not of such a developed nature that they can follow that wave to its natural epicycle would "drop out" of it at a certain point; in continuing their own lesser cycle, they rejoin the lesser, zodiacal cycle on our planet at the beginning of the Age of Virgo, at its cusp with the end of the Age of Leo. They would thereby give rise to the appearance of a secondary race of "gods," or demigods, whose (again temporary) involvement in our planetary consciousness heralds the upturn of the 25,920-year cycle. These beings would remain in subtle objectivity within our planetary aura throughout the Age of Virgo and then depart, en route to their own rejoining of the greater kosmic Life Wave. We see then that one hierarchy of gods has a cycle of reappearance on our Earth of around 26,000 years, while another has a cycle of only about 13,000 years.

Bearing in mind that the ending of the last Ice Age occurred some 12,500 years ago, according to geologists and paleontologists, we can therefore see the logic of the idea that certain of "the gods" are about to return to Earth. When we talk about their returning to Earth, however, it does not immediately infer that they will take physically objective incarnation. For many of them, the extent of their power, as pure spirits, is such that to do so would be impossible. They can return to the outer Oversoul of the planet, however, and from there exert their influences mainly through the deva hierarchy and the Spiritual Hierarchy of Adepts who thus act in the same way that an electrical transformer would. In other words, the higher devas and the Adepts "step down" the vast power of these great Intelligences so that their various involutionary and evolutionary influences can be safely absorbed and passed on. We are told, however, that it now becomes possible for carefully prepared and dedicated groups of more evolved human beings "on the Path" also to act in this same way, at least to a minor extent.[3] We shall touch on this too in greater detail, in a later chapter when we consider the issues of the human kingdom as a whole taking initiation and of a major change of orientation in the overall governance of our planet.

It is otherwise important to remember that these various gods (whether greater or lesser) are not concerned with the process of involution–evolution merely in relation to humankind. Their appearances present all our various kingdoms of Nature with definite points of crisis and opportunity in which old and new energies and forces are united. They bring with them other hierarchies of being and consciousness from the celestial regions through which they have passed and they eventually take with them those units of consciousness that, for one reason or another, no longer fit within our own planetary scheme of development. For example, at least some of those ex-human demigods (called "heroes" in the ancient Greek tradition) whose presence is needed in other solar or planetary schemes to aid in their particular evolutions, are removed because of their very success in this one. In this way the whole Macro-kosmos permanently re-seeds and re-harvests itself, in due cycle. But nothing happens except in due cycle—and thus strictly according to Universal Law.

THE FIELD OF PLATONIC DUALITY

Having already mentioned the intermediate states of consciousness through which the life of each kingdom must pass, before it attains to union with the next higher kingdom, let us next take a look at these states to see if we can draw any conclusions from their analysis. First of all, let us recognize that the sevenfold sequence that is described covers only the four lower states or substates within a soul/Oversoul octave. This is the field Plato refers to as the manifestly Different—that which is ever-changing. Therefore, the three higher substates comprise what Plato calls the Same, those qualitatively different archetypal progressions of the Oversoul/soul nature. So, in the lower cycle, the indwelling life of the kingdom of Nature in question passes through a myriad of different compound forms, involving experience of a wide range of constantly fluctuating energies and forces. As a result of these experiences, the indwelling life develops the power of feeling, or external sensitivity.

In the higher cycle, there is but one triple archetype of form, constituted of a homogeneous light substance, derived from an emanating center of particular quality and power. These three substates must thus be seen as three functional aspects of but one (monadic) archetype comprising the Will-to-be, the Will-to-know, and the Will-to-generate/adapt. Beyond them lies the eighth substate, the eleventh in the overall sequence of progression. This is that of the soul/Oversoul itself. Beyond this lies an emanation from a yet greater kingdom of (kosmic) Nature, an antahkarana or bridge of consciousness along and up which it has to climb before it can reach its own emanating source.

THE RECURRENCE OF THE
SENSORY FACULTIES

This type of analysis is, for most students, rather complex and it would probably be wiser to look at the issue from the viewpoint of effects in the various kingdoms on the various planes. However, before we do so, let us first consider the corresponding way in which the five senses appear and reappear within the fields of human and superhuman consciousness, in apparently different forms. These recur, as shown in the table below, within the five lower states of operative consciousness of the solar system (the first two states being wholly subjective).[4] The essence of what is being shown here is the progressive range of faculty to be found within each given state, which the aspiring human intelligence can access and take advantage of subject to the necessary effort. That same effort involves sentient perception of the associated vibratory quality followed by disciplined usage in practice. Through this combination the individual gradually develops these as readily recoverable faculties within his own nature.

Plane	Sensory Function	Quality
7. ADIC	The Will-to-be	
6. AKASIC	The Will-to-know	
5. ATMIC	5. All knowledge	
	4. Perfection	
	3. Realization	
	2. Active service	
	1. Beatitude	
4. BUDDHIC	5. Spiritual idealism	
	4. [Spiritual] Intuition	
	3. Spiritual vision	
	2. Healing	
	1. Comprehension	
3. MENTAL	7. Spiritual telepathy	Formless
	6. Response to group vibration	Formless
	5. Spiritual discernment	Formless
	4. Mental discrimination	Formless
	3. Higher clairvoyance	Possessing forms
	2. Planetary psychometry	Possessing forms
	1. Higher clairaudience	Possessing forms
2. ASTRAL	5. Emotional idealism	
	4. Imagination	
	3. Lower clairvoyance	
	2. Psychometry	
	1. Lower clairaudience	
1. PHYSICAL	5. Smell	3rd etheric state (pranic vitality)
	4. Taste	4th etheric state (astral light)
	3. Sight	Gaseous/atmospheric matter
	2. Touch (feeling)	Liquid matter
	1. Hearing	Dense matter

THE USE AND DEVELOPMENT
OF FACULTY

The sensory faculties mentioned above are, of course, described purely from the human viewpoint and we shall look at them slightly more closely later in the chapter. The lesser kingdoms too, however, share in these faculties to some evolutionary extent, in terms of response to stimulus. For example, the mineral kingdom has the crude capacity to respond (chemically) to sound, touch, sight, and taste. However, smell is not so generally developed. The plant kingdom has extended its faculty of responsive awareness into the astral state. It has consequently developed not only all of the physical senses to a greater extent than the mineral but also possesses capacity for self-generated change through now having a degree of lower clairaudience (response to sound frequencies), psychometry (external sensory faculty), and even embryonic lower clairvoyance (response to solar and lunar light). The animal goes even further through possession of all of these to a greater extent, plus some rudimentary degree of astral imagination (desire for possession), together with emotional idealism (devotional response) in the higher species. These suggestions are open to our own perceptual experience.

It is perhaps worth mentioning in passing that what we generally refer to as *intuition* is actually not that at all. True intuition is of a higher spiritual nature, involving a faculty with which even an initiated Master is only just coming to grips. What we lesser mortals experience is in fact a form of telepathic contact within one or another of the mental, astral, or physical states. In the few true cases of non-Adept consciousness picking up real spiritual contact, with its associated intuitive insights, it is as a result of the individual unconsciously using the energies of one or another of the three highest mental subplanes. These involve the faculty of what we call the Spiritual Ego, which is itself, in fact, the lowest emanation of the Monad as it impinges upon the outermost limits of the buddhic (kosmic etheric double) state. Thus it is that spiritual telepathy of the highest mental substate is not only the functional essence of the mental state itself, it is also the vibratory projection of the spiritual (buddhic) state—hence its esoteric association with occult sound.

THE ILLUSION OF FORM

The next thing to be taken into consideration is that interaction between solar energy and planetary substance is of critical importance in the production of mass forms. However, direct solar energy alone cannot begin to generate productive forms. To reiterate an earlier suggestion: it is the interaction with less powerful reflected solar energy (via the Moon) that actually draws forth by sympathetic magnetic resonance the apparently dormant spark of plant life, thereby giving rise to the manifest evolutionary process. As also mentioned earlier, reflection in a mirror produces a virtual image while, as recognized by science, a hologram (which is also virtual) is generated by the out-of-phase interaction (at a specific point in space) of two laser projections emitted from the same source. Consequently, therefore, the multitude of objective forms generated here on Earth by interactive solar and lunar energy have to be considered as mere holograms. Hence the ancient and hitherto puzzling idea that the manifest world is only a sensory illusion.

The whole process is perhaps more easily understood by reference again to fig. 2.1. This shows the sphere of kosmic physical existence (the Oversoul) from within which the deva Monad projects its influence centripetally inward, in response to pressure from logoic Intelligence. This is met by a corresponding, but dual outgoing (centrifugal), influence from the center, which we otherwise recognize as the yin-yang duality that gives rise to magnetic polarity. At the points where the two then meet, we find a coordination of the incoming and outgoing forces. Within the field of our planetary Oversoul, as already mentioned, this meeting place becomes the Earth's crust on which all objective forms thus find themselves generated. Here the evolutionary process commences, beginning logically with the mineral kingdom, the most objective of the involutionary elemental states. Having said as much, the point must be made that "Nature, the physical evolutionary Power, could never evolve intelligence unaided—she can only create [relatively] senseless forms."[5] That is to say, only by the intervention and emanation of a higher Intelligence into it can any kingdom of Nature (including the human) make evolutionary progress beyond a certain point. This we shall see, in later chapters, becomes of critical importance in understanding the nature and function of the Self-evolved human (Manushi) Buddha.

EVOLUTIONARY "MISSING LINKS"

As we have already otherwise seen, every soul state (although interrelated) is qualitatively different from all others. That distinction is manifest by virtue of the fact that the soul state consciousness generates a definite field of force, which is essentially electromagnetic in nature (but not in the limited sense applied by modern science). That is to say, it is vibrationally both attractive and repellent, depending on the psychic nature of whatever it comes into contact with. To that which it is complementary, it is attracted. However, there are definite "spaces" (synapses) between the forms generated by consciousness. Across these, curiously enough, evolutionary "ladders" or "bridges" must be built, thereby negating the possibility of any other intermediate forms. Nature firmly shuts the door on its own past creations, so we are told, and it is always so, without exception. What we imagine to be missing links never involve intermediate forms in the sense of a forward progression. However, as mentioned earlier, there are intermediate links of a regressive nature. The reason for this involves a law of retardation in Nature that, as Blavatsky describes,[6] ensures a hiatus when any new species comes into existence. This applies to humanity as well as all the other kingdoms of Nature.

Let us take as our example of the way in which the underlying scheme works, the idea of the so-called missing link—that as yet indefinable stage or sequence that links quite different main species. This is something that Darwin himself avoided by concentrating his attention on objective functional changes in mere subspecies. As we shall see, the process works through the incarnating intelligence passing out of the purely objective phase of its experience into a purely subjective phase of which modern science is as yet completely unaware but which has to do with "germinal" existence in a non-physical state.

Let us suggest first of all that there is no such thing as a "quantum evolutionary leap," as some scientists believe. When we consider this graphically, we see that the cycle of unfoldment of the various species within a kingdom of Nature reaches a natural climax in respect to potentially objective forms. For example, in fig. 5.3 (the mineral to plant evolutionary sequence) we see that the most highly evolved stage reached by the mineral kingdom involves

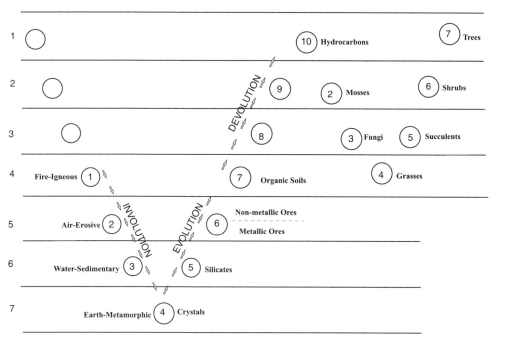

Fig. 5.3. The mineral to plant evolutionary sequence

the organic soils. That is because these provide the medium in which the next higher kingdom of Nature can objectively manifest.

From here, however, there is no immediate transition of the indwelling life into the plant kingdom consciousness, but only into its forms. Instead, we see the mineral life and its subjective consciousness extending further into two progressive states of subjectivity before becoming ready for the next stage of its own spiritually involutionary unfoldment, through merging with a yet higher involutionary influence. We then find that the last stage of objective mineral development (the organic soils) becomes the natural medium or vehicle for the first stage of evolutionary development of the plant.

Correspondingly (see fig. 5.4) we find the same principle in the progression between the animal and human kingdoms. The mammal is the most evolved of the objective animal types; yet the animal life must extend several further developmental stages into subjectivity before it attains to the first and most primeval stage of proto-human unfoldment. But before it does so, it becomes the receptor of a higher type of life with which it must unite before

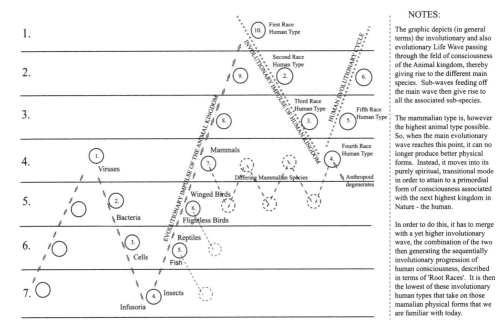

Fig. 5.4. The animal to human evolutionary sequence

being able to progress further. Yet even when this combined existence reaches the tenth stage and there forcibly unites with such a higher Intelligence, it does not begin to look "human" by modern standards of comparison. However, the most important consideration here is that the inter-kingdom evolutionary transition takes place always within the subjective side of Nature.

But then, what about the differentiation between the subkingdoms, such as the insects, reptiles, birds, and mammals? Do the same principles apply? The short answer to this is no; the reason for that lies in the fact that these are expressions of the different subfunctions found within the kingdom as a whole. They therefore appear together out of one subjective archetype, as a series of objective prototypes. It is then the latter that adapt and, in so doing, degenerate through multiplication. This, of course, is completely back-to-front as far as Darwinism is concerned. For Darwinists, multiplication is itself a sign of forward evolutionary development through adaptation. But then modern science as yet fails to take into its considerations the doctrine of cycles, which, to some extent, we touched on earlier in this chapter.

EVOLUTION IN THE LOWEST
KINGDOMS OF NATURE

If the devas/angels are only concerned with fostering the status quo and thus with promoting the same unchanging cycles of activity, how is it that evolution as such can take place within the mineral and plant kingdoms? One answer is that it is because of direct human involvement or interference. Humanity uses the products of the mineral kingdom (often blending them) for all sorts of tools and crafted artifacts. The daemonic mineral life is thereby subjected to rapid and enforced change of a type that it would not and could not generate of its own through mere vulcanism and metamorphic or sedimentary activity.

In a curious way, even human warfare follows suit. While certain elements of the mineral kingdom have developed radioactivity "organically" in small degree, humankind has accelerated this. The atomic and hydrogen bombs, despite causing immense and unfortunate destruction, have given rise to the ability by the mineral kingdom to generate mass nuclear energy and power. Although this has in turn given rise to a type of radiation that is immensely destructive to the currently existing plant, animal, and human forms found on our planet, that is because these existing forms are themselves in the process of becoming obsolescent and must, in due time, give rise to new ones, of similar shape, perhaps, but also of entirely different quality and potency. One should otherwise bear in mind that our computer age is based upon different usages of the mineral kingdom to generate "artificial intelligence." The fact of particular parts of the mineral kingdom being forced into such high-grade experience itself involves an evolutionary crisis of incredible magnitude.

Humans—being essentially self-centered creatures—would be unlikely to consider the mineral kingdom from such a viewpoint. But from the bigger perspective of planetary management, it is of vital importance. The various forms of the plant kingdom have been made use of by both animals and humans for food and shelter, while humans have also used wood for furniture, tools, and even ornately carved artifacts such as statues to adorn their homes and sacred places. The indwelling life of the plant kingdom necessarily reacts to such treatment in a variety of ways, some of them involving a merely blind cycle of repetitive experience but others involving direct sensory experience through human contact.

It is the memory of human contact—faint though it may be—that will be passed down in the daemonic consciousness of the mineral and plant kingdoms, thereby leaving a germinal impression of their greater potential, even though this memory may not fully reexpress itself for millions or even billions of years to come. In the same way, we may suggest that in past eons, ancient humanity experienced the consciousness of what we would now think of as "gods" who have themselves passed through the human cycle untold ages ago. Hence it is that the human, relatively speaking, is a "god" as far as the lesser kingdoms of Nature are concerned. The magnetic influences generated by the lower human chakras affect each in due turn. As the ancient wisdom tradition puts it, the universe is a gigantic process of ever-becoming. With that in mind, let us now take a closer look at the lives and derivation of forms in each of the objective kingdoms of Nature, as follows.

1. The Mineral Kingdom

It is commonly known, by tradition, that the Nature spirit denizens of the mineral and plant kingdoms are otherwise known to the Western world as "gnomes" plus "brownies" on the one hand and "elves" plus "fairies" on the other (see fig. 3.5 in chapter 3). As Geoffrey Hodson, the twentieth century clairvoyant researcher of the deva world, tells us, both these groups have two distinct forms of self-presentation: a spheroidal astral body, which is their permanent "vehicle" (conforming with the terrestrial soul principle) and a temporarily materialized etheric body form by which humans more usually recognize them.[7] Within both groups there appear to be numerous subtypes, comprising those with increasingly vaguer objective appearances—having a far less definable consciousness plus closer association with the underground world—and those with more coherent body forms and facial expressions. There are all sorts of other interesting human parallels, which the interested reader will discover by studying Geoffrey Hodson's works more closely.

Within the former group, in correspondence with the duality of matter and spirit, the gnomes appear to be concerned with the denser aspects of the mineral kingdom, while the brownies tend to function much closer to the Earth's surface. Hence we have the following suggested parallels, which correlate with Hodson's own view of the three fundamental processes in Nature: absorption, assimilation, and discharge.[8] They are given here in order of ascending evolutionary nature and development.

3. Human spirit—brownies dealing with mineral soils and radioactivity
2. Human spiritual soul—gnomes and brownies dealing with the extension and perfection of crystalline forms
1. Human personality—gnomes dealing with purely accumulative and metamorphic activity in relation to development of mineral compounds

Just as the human personality is triple, and primarily concerned with integration, so the gnomes dealing with metamorphic activity would perhaps be concerned with the three types of volcanic activity that give rise to the production of those involutionary compounds known to us as igneous rock, lava, and poisonous gases. These three amorphously molecular substates comprise all those atoms in the mineral kingdom that display the ability to select and thus discriminate intelligently under the law of attraction and repulsion.[9]

However, following on from these there should be seven evolutionary and devolutionary gnome and brownie types in all, paralleling in a very obscure way the seven human subtypes: (1) of the Earth, earthy; (2) the devotionally driven; (3) the mentally/organizationally driven; (4) the artistic; (5) the idealistic; (6) the philanthropic/altruistic; (7) the philosophical. We might then suggest that each of these seven groups are themselves hierarchically "overshadowed" by seven groups of devas who are in turn overshadowed by three archangelic groups.

2. The Plant Kingdom

When we come to the Nature spirits of the plant kingdom, we find similar parallels, because the organizational side of Nature always follows the same essential blueprint. Thus the three overall groups could perhaps be classified as:

3. Those concerned with photosynthesis plus smell and radiation

2. Those concerned with the phenomenal cycle of flowering and fruiting

1. Those living entirely within the plant forms and generating them out of their own etheric essences (derived from the astral light)

The seven subgroups of Nature spirits (comprising what we have come to know as the elves and fairies, the Nature spirits of the trees being otherwise known as "dryads") can perhaps be classified very roughly along the following lines of their various productions.

1. Hydrocarbons	7. "Woody" shrubs and trees
2. Fungi	6. Ferns
3. Mosses	5. Succulents
4. Grasses	

Once again, we might suggest that there are seven groups of devas concerned with watching over these and that there are three groups of archangels overshadowing them. As regards the atoms of the plant kingdom, they not only have the capacity to discriminate intelligently under the law of attraction and repulsion, as in the mineral kingdom, but they also have an embryonic sensory or feeling capacity.

3. The Nature Spirits of the Animal Kingdom

When we come to consider the process of evolution in the animal kingdom, other issues have to be taken into consideration, which are not applicable to the mineral and plant kingdoms. For here, humanity is not instrumental in changing the forms (although this does happen through specialist breeding); it is the direct experience of mingling human and (daemonic) animal consciousness that generates a very real crisis in the latter. In addition, this is the first kingdom on the evolutionary cycle where the daemonic Nature spirit becomes so fully involved in the form created throughout its life cycle that the form itself becomes a recognizably living entity. Following the same principles, the animal kingdom can be (esoterically) considered, in the following seven involutionary and evolutionary groups:

1. Viruses   7. Mammals

   2. Bacteria   6. Birds

     3. Protozoa/cells   5. Reptiles and fish

       4. Insects

Again following the same principles, these seven subgroups might be considered as overshadowed and guided by seven groups of angels/devas, while the later are themselves controlled and guided by three groups of planetary archangels. The atoms of the animal kingdom, like those of the mineral and plant kingdoms, discriminate intelligently under the law of attraction and repulsion, as well as having a materially increased sensory faculty. However, the animal also possesses instinct (partly functioning through the solar plexus chakra), which involves an embryonic mentality. This might be described as "the habitual reaction of some type of consciousness to a given set of circumstances, or of environment."[10] Thus it is that the animal possesses an embryonic faculty of anticipation but, because lacking any real range and coherence of mental faculty, it lacks the conscious capacity to preadjust to circumstances. It thus also lacks the capacity to learn consciously from experience.

Notwithstanding this, the animal group soul learns and telepathically transmits its increased knowledge to other groups through sympathetic vibration. It is this (sometimes even transoceanic faculty) that many biologists have already noted as taking place within an immediate time scale that makes physical contact impossible as an associated reason. The modern biologist Rupert Sheldrake has noted this in his published research work, as have other scientists too.

It is in the present worldwide ecological movement that humanity in the mass has begun to realize just how necessary is the balance in Nature. Interestingly also, it is the way in which our present humanity's science is experimenting with the involutionary groups of the animal kingdom, for the purpose of treating its own animal type of body, that is to some considerable extent affecting the consciousness of the animal kingdom as a whole through sympathetic association. The usage of animals for experimental science is all right up to a point, as also their training for particular purposes. However, when it takes on a purely destructive or aggressively harmful nature, either objectively or subjectively, it has gone too far and will automatically result (through the law of cause and effect) in retribution as sympathetically detrimental effects within the human kingdom.

We might otherwise pause here for a moment to consider the domesticated animals, plus those animals that various ecologically motivated groups of humans now work closely with in order to help maintain the continuing existence of their species. The training and use of animals to work with humans probably started in late Atlantean times after the "door was closed" to any further evolutionary transition of entities from the animal into the human kingdom. Although many today tend to think of such domestication purely in terms of satisfying our own physical and emotional needs, we need to consider the fact that we are also preparing the animals, well in advance, for their own next evolutionary progression. That will take place, so we are told, in the next major cycle of our planetary scheme, by which time the majority of present humankind will have reached Adeptship. Therefore, how we treat the animals that come into our care over the next tens of thousands of years will have its own karmic outcome in our own eventual ability, in due course, to help them achieve the self-conscious faculty of the human being with which we are ourselves so familiar.

HUMAN EVOLUTION

The various anthropologically distinct human types are rarely taken into consideration these days because of a misplaced sense that "discrimination is a bad thing." From the viewpoint of helping all human development, this is in fact very silly because it willfully fails to take into account quite natural evolutionary differences. There appear to be ten stages in the evolutionary development of human types, so we are told,[11] which can be classified as follows:

1. The (rare) "throw-backs" to the quasi-animal state; the lowest forms of human development whose objectivity of intelligence is almost nonexistent

2. The (also quite rare) types who have no natural skills and are completely incapable of response to even emotional training or culture generally

3. Those types who are emotionally and psychically alive and are beginning to integrate; in these "child souls" the desire nature is rampant and they are concerned purely with personal satisfaction

4. Those many types who retain the Atlantean nature; they are primarily emotional and show little sustained response to mental training

5. Those who, although still largely astral in their nature, are capable of being mentally trained and thereby showing that they can think of their own accord when the need arises

6. Those who can think of their own accord and are thus to be found forming the cultural mainstream of their age; they are classified as "the world's aspirants" who are beginning to develop the ideal of service in their consciousness

7. Those who have begun to develop the sensitive mystic consciousness, but who are as yet incapable of maintaining a sustained connection between it and the mind

8. Those who have achieved some degree of connection and are thus able to function, to some extent, as practical mystics and occultists

9. Those who have developed a very real sense of contact with their Higher Self and who are fully conscious of their various vehicles as such

10. The Self-conscious Adept

It is only when we come to the human kingdom that we find positive response to mental faculties per se and thus the self-conscious capacity to use what we call creative imagination. In fact, it might seem strange to suggest that humans possess faculties of higher clairaudience, planetary psychometry, and higher clairvoyance, although (objective) mental discrimination is more certainly recognized. However, these are generally used in an unconscious manner, while the human intelligence is perhaps more aware of having to apply conscious effort in the use of the five senses on both the astral and physical planes. The average human being is completely unaware of what is meant by (i.e., how to apply) astral clairaudience and psychometry, although the concept of clairvoyance is now commonly acknowledged. Yet, as just suggested, all three of these are commonly used all the time—unconsciously—by the individual. For example, it is impossible to use pictorial imagination (which is largely astral, not mental in nature) without the simultaneous use of astral clairvoyance and astral psychometry to produce a coherent sense of imagery. As is commonly recognized, any faculty develops or evolves through persistent practice; these faculties—although undoubtedly less common—respond in exactly the same way, preceded by the use of imagination. That is why all such faculties are self-generated.

For the vast majority of educated people these faculties might actually appear as mental constructs. Yet their use in conjunction with personal desire and self-centeredness renders them largely if not entirely astral in nature. The capacity to use these faculties consciously at the mental level are really only to be found where trained esthetics are practiced, often (curiously enough) in the field of business, because of the need for intelligently reliable application. That is why business creativity (when properly applied) has a huge potential for developing otherwise latent spiritual faculty. When business is somewhat relieved of its entirely profit-motivated orientation and returned to generating a vocational sense in the individual, this will undoubtedly start to appear. It is perhaps worth mentioning at this very point the perhaps rather unexpected but nevertheless entirely logical attitude of the Spiritual Hierarchy of our planet to the world of business, as follows:

> The development of the so-called irreligious man into a sound and creative businessman, with all the necessary perception and equipment for success, is as much a spiritual unfoldment . . . as the taking of an initiation by a disciple in an Ashram. . . . It will [one day] be realized that all activity which drives the human being forward towards some form of development . . . is essentially spiritual in nature.[12]

THE HIGHEST HUMAN FACULTIES

We turn next to the three higher faculties found in the field of mental consciousness: spiritual discernment, response to group vibration, and spiritual telepathy. It will be noted first of all that these, as a triad, are separated from the four lower mental faculties. The reason for that is twofold. First, the terrestrial soul nature reaches its optimum potential with the integration of an individualized personality, involving fourth mental substate matter. Second, the higher three substates relate to the field of group activities, involving altruism, and not to personal concerns at all. In practical terms, as we saw in an earlier chapter, these three are in fact more closely related to the next higher plane (of Buddhi, the Spiritual Soul nature) than to the lesser world of purely personal evolutionary development.

This buddhic state is otherwise (most importantly) known to esotericists as the kosmic etheric double of the Logos, as we have repeatedly mentioned throughout the earlier chapters of this book—for good reason. The field of Buddhi is itself a plane of hallowed light substance (hence of spiritual illumination) concerned with the objective expression of archetypal forms in response to what one could only call Divine Purpose. That purpose is thus expressed in ever-constant wholes (hence with groups and general influences) rather than in forever-changing elemental compounds like the human, animal, plant, and mineral body forms.

That is not to say there is no further evolutionary progress in these higher fields. However, the progress is of a purely subjective nature, resulting in increased potency and qualitative extent of influence, which are instantly recognizable as relative radiance and magnetic potency by others functioning at the same level. In relation to those of an advanced spiritual nature, their capacity to "tone down" their magnetic potency while in physical incarnation would, however, make them almost unrecognizable as such by virtually all others operating merely at the physical, astral, and lower mental levels.

THE LOWEST SPIRITUAL FACULTIES

Let us finally consider the nature of the sensory faculties as they function within the nature of the human Causal Soul itself, remembering that the semi-spiritual nature is itself still only in the process of individualization with the vast majority of human beings. That is to say, the "divine spark" that is the real Intelligence in a human being does not as yet possess the capacity for fully individualized Self-consciousness at the spiritual level (that of the buddhic state). It thus perforce only shares passively in the common life of this state as it trickles down into the mental state and thus influences the human consciousness. The lowest of the buddhic faculties is itself related to subjective (i.e., spiritual) sound and hearing, giving rise to what we know as comprehension. It is this, consequently, that incorporates the human faculty of objective understanding. It is also that which correspondingly and vibrationally gives rise (as a trinity of expression) to the three highest mental faculties involving the generation of mental archetypes and the Egoic sense of what we call "Self."

Comprehension is again that which gives rise to the next higher buddhic faculty of healing. However, this is not healing in the ordinary sense with which we are perhaps more familiar, involving for example the "laying on of hands" or "magnetic passes." It is the higher equivalent to touch/feeling on the physical plane, this by virtue of the substance of the kosmic etheric double acting as a sort of dimensionless limb. Thus the capacity for true spiritual feeling (functioning on and from that level and not from the self-induced wishful thinking of the would-be healer) involves a quasi-maternal enfoldment, the magnetic potency of which automatically gives of itself by a sort of natural "overflow." That in turn thereby (very logically) produces healing/regeneration at the lower levels of being through sympathetic correspondence.

The third buddhic faculty of spiritual vision involves true Self-consciousness within the Spiritual Soul nature. It is not clairvoyance per se, for clairvoyance merely involves the capacity to see mental or astral forms (one's own, or those of others) while still functioning in the physical body. Spiritual vision involves a fully conscious registration and identification of spiritual forms of light when fully absorbed into that state. Thus the advanced mystic may indeed experience a temporary spiritual vision through an ascetic self-abnegation that momentarily causes that total absorption, but cannot retain it. However, the true Master Adept in the field of occult science—because of a permanently ascetic lifestyle (in psychological terms)—can achieve and retain it at will.

The fourth buddhic faculty—that of the true intuition, as we mentioned earlier in this chapter—is parallel to that of taste at the physical level. However, we might also suggest that spiritual intuition is the higher equivalent of instinct. In fact, there is no conflict between these two because psychic "taste" and instinct are, in a sense, one and the same. Both carry and convey the implicit idea of a discriminating faculty of immediate insight, which generates automatic response. Hence we can see how intuition builds on the faculties of astral imagination and mental discrimination. Having said as much, however, this is a far more advanced faculty.

The fifth and final buddhic faculty is that of spiritual idealism. However, this is a long way from the quality of personal (hence astral) idealism with which we human beings are most familiar. Spiritual idealism appears to involve a direct registration of archetypal perfection and association with it. Its parallel association with the physical sense of smell may puzzle some but when the olfactory registration of beauty is taken into account, as that which fills one with the perfected essence of the flower, it perhaps makes more sense. Whereas taste without an accompanying sense of smell, or bouquet, provides us with a bland registration of mere opposites or extremes—like hot and cold, or dry and wet—smell on its own has the capacity to engender in us a sense of the sublime and of total fulfillment. It is all-encompassing.

Interestingly enough, it is only in the nose that stem cells are to be found; apparently, they do not exist anywhere else in the body. These curiously potent cells have a capacity, now registered by science, to stimulate regrowth of any other cells, however seriously damaged, even though the "why" and "how" are as yet nowhere near understood. The fact that breathing through the nose is of far greater regenerative health value than breathing through the mouth may well be allied to this same issue. In esoteric philosophy, the scientific study of sympathetic association is of huge importance and here we appear to have an example as to why that should perhaps be so.

THE ATMIC STATE

We come finally to the spiritual faculties of the fifth solar plane. However, because these are the expression of the spiritual will—with which human beings in general are totally unfamiliar—there is perhaps very little that can be said about them.

We are told that absorption into the spiritual will (and thus the Purpose of the Logos) ultimately brings nirvanic bliss by virtue of the attainment of all (archetypal) perfection and thus full release from all further need for reincarnation. However, even this appears to have a degree of conditionality about it. In terms of the spiritual evolutionary Path, the attainment of self-consciousness in the fifth solar state (the *atmic* state, using Sanskrit terminology) is that of the Master who has achieved the fifth degree of initiation, whereas the Adept of the fourth degree has only achieved a corresponding capacity for self-conscious function within the fourth solar state, that of Buddhi, the Spiritual Soul which, as we pointed out earlier, is also the state of the kosmic etheric double. It is therefore interesting to read what is said about these two achievements in *The Voice of the Silence,* Blavatsky's poetic gem of esoteric Buddhist philosophy.

Of the pathway leading to the fourth initiation—described as being entered by the gate of *viraga* (defined as "indifference to pleasure and to pain, illusion conquered, truth alone perceived")—*The Voice* warns the individual, now that the third degree of purely human self-mastery is achieved, to prepare for the temptations "which do ensnare the inner man." Here:

> [T]he lightest breeze of passion or desire will stir the steady light upon the pure white walls of soul. The smallest wave of longing for Maya's gifts illusive personal desires and fulfillments . . . a thought as fleeting as a lightning flash will make thee thy prizes forfeit—the prizes thou hast [already] won.[13]

Of the pathway leading onward to the fifth initiation, *The Voice* then continues:

> Thou hast now crossed the moat that circles round the gate of human passions. Thou hast now conquered Mara and his furious host. Thou hast removed pollution from thine heart and bled it from impure desire. But, O thou glorious combatant, thy task is not yet done. Build high, Lanoo, the wall that shall hedge in the Holy Isle, the dam that will protect thy mind from pride and satisfaction at thoughts of the great feat achieved. . . . Ere thou canst settle in Dhyana-marga and call it thine, the Soul has to become as the ripe mango fruit: as soft and sweet as its bright golden pulp for others' woes, as hard as that fruit's stone for thine own throes and sorrows. . . . When thou has reached that state, the portals that thou hast to conquer on the Path fling open wide their gates to let thee pass, and Nature's strongest mights possess no power to stay thy course.[14]

Even now, however, the Master Soul has yet much further to travel on the upward path. But this and the process of how the individual attains mastery in the first place, through human experience, will be dealt with at greater length in a later chapter. However, before we move on in greater detail to the issue of the sequentially progressive initiations of individual humankind, we shall in the next two chapters take a historic look backward over the last few thousand years to consider some of the evolutionary changes in psychological and spiritual attitudes that have taken place in human culture generally. By so doing—in relation to the hitherto unsuspected, supporting influences from the guardians of our planetary life—we may perhaps begin to see that orthodox history actually tells us very little about the underlying realities of our human cultures and civilizations.

CONCLUSION TO CHAPTERS ONE TO FIVE

By way of concluding the first part of this book, let us try to summarize the most important points in the first five chapters, as these will themselves become central to our considerations in the latter parts of the book.

In chapter 1 we started with the principle of all existence being the expression of a Universal Consciousness, which is itself beyond all conceptualization and cannot therefore be properly equated with a "God" as some religions suggest. Within this Universal Consciousness we saw that all creatures and all forms—whether visible to humans or not—are mere participants through the use of an innately percipient intelligence common to all. We also saw that consciousness manifests itself by way of that limitation, which we define as the multiple soul principle, thereby resulting in the omniverse being qualitatively and concentrically based. That consequently gives rise to what within the field of planetary existence we call the objective world state, the psychic world state, the spiritual world state, and the semi-divine and divine world states, followed by the solar or extraplanetary state of existence associated with true kosmic consciousness. We further learned that the Mind principle is itself the projection of the soul entity and that it should not be confused with Intelligence, which itself constitutes the true nature of the "divine spark" in both the human and evolving Nature generally.

In chapter 2 we considered the nature of consciousness in more specifically human terms and what is involved in the evolutionary progression leading from elemental existence through the mineral, plant, and animal kingdoms to eventually human self-consciousness. We learned how the human being, as the microcosm of the Macrocosm, derives both the lower sense of self and the higher sense of Self from his or her soul nature and how this gives rise to an eventual perception of the nature of the spiritual Path and how it must be followed.

In chapter 3 we took a look at the subtle world populated by the deva, nature spirit, and elemental kingdoms of Nature, taking particular note of their hierarchical structure, their functions, and their interactive dynamics. We also saw that the deva, as the exponent of logoic memory, thereby possesses no sense of choice, whereas Man, as the expression of logoic imagination, does possess it. The two groups—human and deva—are thus the necessarily complementary aspects of consciousness in the logoic Macrocosm. This chapter spent some time considering the interaction between deva-kind and humankind at various levels of existence, ranging from the lowest elemental state to the divine state, thereby showing how that complementary nature actually works.

In chapter 4, we considered the rationale behind the universal law of cause and effect (karma) and how humans generate karma through ignorantly obstructing the work of the devas and nature spirits. We also saw how karma underlies the whole nature of the reincarnatory process, not only in connection with human beings, but also in relation to the greater kosmic process involving planetary lives and whole kingdoms or subkingdoms of Nature. This otherwise touched on the nature of good and evil, plus the foundational criteria by which hierarchies of superior evolved Intelligence decide on the necessity for introduction or removal of groups of lives into or from the manifest state in order to fulfill Divine Purpose.

In chapter 5 we considered the actual process of causal evolution in greater Nature as seen through the eyes of the esotericist, as opposed to the materialistic view of orthodox science, which focuses on deducing paradigms from purely objective—hence transitory—effects. From this we were able to suggest that the sequential process of subjective development, which we call "initiation," is actually not specific to humans alone, but rather involves the underlying, or spiritual, evolutionary process active throughout all Nature. We saw that this is necessarily founded on the interactive law of cycles, affecting different kingdoms of Nature in different ways. We also took a more detailed look in this chapter at the functions of the various higher and lower substates of consciousness employed by humans in their evolutionary progress of developing both psychological and spiritual faculty, usually without being at all aware of their true nature.

These various issues and principles, as discussed in chapters 1 to 5, thus provide us with a coordinated foundation and sense of structure for our further considerations in parts 2 and 3 of this book in particular. In part 2 we shall take a look at how human history and its mystical-cum-religious cultures have worked out in accordance with underlying cycles and their associated impulses through the adaptive agency and influence of the Spiritual Hierarchy of Adepts. In part 3 we shall then take a much more detailed look at the actual initiatory process involving humankind, including consideration of the important underlying rationale of progressive spiritual development and its own psychological criteria.

PART TWO

Historical Background to the Mysteries and Path of Initiation

SIX

SACRED METAPHOR AND ALLEGORY IN RELATION TO THE ANCIENT MYSTERY TRADITIONS AND ASSOCIATED INITIATION

In this chapter, in line with our concern for a better understanding of how esoteric and occult philosophy has developed, we shall take a generalized (and necessarily only partial) look at certain sacred aspects of the better-known religions or spiritual belief systems of antiquity and their initiatory systems. The intention in so doing is to demonstrate that there has been a "perennial philosophy" behind all of them and to describe some of its predominant features. One central proposition of this book is that the core message of this ancient philosophy (involving spiritual identity, the universal Law of Karma, plus the nature of numerological succession and function) has actually never changed, although its outer appearances in mystic metaphor and allegory have, due to inevitable changes induced by social and environmental conditioning. Therefore, what we are about to consider here involves a mere introduction to the interdisciplinary nature of ancient esotericism and the associated role of the initiatory Path.

The first thing that we can suggest, before we move on to particular characteristics of the Creation allegories in the individual (mainly Middle Eastern) spiritual cultures, is that all of the main ones commenced with Chaos. *Chaos* is itself a word derived from the ancient composite *ka-eos*— meaning "the ethereal body of primordial universal light"—as the natural plenum from which everything is generated and to which everything ultimately returns. Within this plenum an intelligent force of creativity (the Divine Mind) emanated by self-generation; it then gave rise first to a field of self-isolation, involving a trinity of self-expression, and then a sevenfold structure of objective manifestation. Many of these ideas also used the winged disc (see fig. 6.1) as the iconic symbol of the Unknowable Logos that initiated and maintained the whole process. That in itself implies that they all shared a common religious and philosophical source teaching, although how far back this went is impossible to say.

Fig. 6.1. Egyptian winged disc over temple entrance

All of these spiritual cultures were fundamentally monotheistic, despite modern scholarly orthodoxy, although they also possessed visual imagery (in carved stonework) of gigantic greater or lesser god figures, some of which possessed animal or bird's heads on human bodies, all symbolically representing essential functions in Universal Nature, with their own inherent qualities of intelligence. All of them regarded humankind as descended from a vastly higher state of consciousness to which it instinctively strove to return via a Path of initiation. All of them seem originally to have followed a common principle of representing (also in carved stonework) the higher human initiate stages as kings, although this much later degenerated into representation of actual historical kings for political reasons as much as religious ones.

The other thing of particular interest is that the first religions of this current precessionary solar cycle seem to have concerned themselves primarily with the teaching as to celestial hierarchies of beings and humankind's own originally celestial origins. Only much later did this change, giving rise to the tradition of an inherent celestial and terrestrial duality in which the cyclic influence of an Avatar (spiritual savior) became the most important factor.

THE ANCIENT EGYPTIAN MYSTERY SCHOOL

The Egyptian Creation myth is still not understood by Egyptological scholars, who see it (or rather, them, for there are several aspects) as a hotchpotch of contrived and fetishistic superstitions generated by different tribes living along the Nile over many millennia. In fact, a clear understanding of esoteric philosophy would immediately show that the various myths of Egypt all express interrelated aspects of a single, great psycho-spiritual blueprint, almost certainly original in nature. The extent of this was so great and so complex that no attempt will be made here to deal with it, although a later book is intended on the same subject. I have, however, already touched on some of the related issues in a previous book.[1]

In one sense the Egyptian School appeared unlike a Mystery School because the subjects taught were very similar to a really wide modern academic curriculum, incorporating mathematics, architecture, astronomy, geology, cartography, botany, medical science, and so on.[2] However, the approach to the teaching of these subjects was far from merely academic. The temples in Egypt all had schools attached to them and above them all was the great university at Heliopolis, the Sacred College of the Sun. Here the curriculum taught—involving the forty-two sacred books of Tehuti—was of a very advanced nature, as one would expect. Here the initiate-professors were held in the highest regard throughout the ancient world, not just for their knowledge, but also for their spiritual wisdom. This perhaps helps us to understand why the way in which the curriculum was taught was at least as important as the knowledge itself. All knowledge was held to be sacred and it was taught on the basis that all of it comprised a seamless whole, notwithstanding the variety of subjects in the syllabus. Furthermore, because knowledge was taught as expressing the Mind of Deity, it was approached from the angle of involving an infinite spectrum of sympathetic correspondences, there being no such thing as a void or "dead matter."[3] This is as opposed to today's system, which focuses on dead categorizations based on appearances and supposed differences of form and function, in the reductive Aristotelian manner. Esoteric philosophy consequently fitted into the Egyptian academic system quite naturally, as extending the range of meaning to causal influences beyond the exoteric or objective world.

The Egyptians took the view that if one were going to explore the subjective world where such causal realities actually lay, it was first necessary for the individual to demonstrate that he was fully "grounded" in the external world, not just possessing a mystic nature. That is because the objective world introduced him to the idea of the occult principles and laws governing Nature as a whole and how to deal with them. These same causal states of existence, however, introduced one directly to extensive hierarchies of intelligent and semi-intelligent beings and the powers employed by them in the actual control of Nature from "behind the scenes."[4] Thus one had to acknowledge that "a knowledge is a power" in a very literal, occult sense. As a consequence, the individual had to learn not only what real knowledge is and how to recognize it in its many subtly varied disguises but also how to assimilate it in such a way that he himself could progressively control it and not be taken over by it. This is something that our modern academic mindset completely fails to appreciate because of its misconception as to knowledge being about something else, in an altogether literal sense.

This concept of knowledge as living powers that have to be controlled as they are assimilated is one that our modern civilization does not begin to understand, yet it was generally acknowledged by trained initiates throughout the ancient world. Modern Egyptology takes the view that ancient Egyptian culture was arrived at on an ad hoc basis, through a combination of superstition and political machination. Yet anyone who has studied esoteric philosophy on its own terms recognizes at once that there is nothing ad hoc about the original Old Kingdom Egyptian system, notwithstanding the general cultural degeneracy that progressively destroyed it from about 2500 BCE onward. It is, in fact, quite clear that the various parts of the ancient Egyptian system comprised one great whole, right from the very outset in prerecorded history. That is why it gives the impression of having come into existence whole and without any apparent "learning curve." Their inability to explain this apparent paradox is why so many Egyptologists spend so much futile time trying to prove that it cannot have been so. The very same applies in the case of the original civilizations of the Tigris-Euphrates Valley and the Indus Delta where the Chaldeo-Babylonian and Hindu religions had their origins.

The Mysteries in Egypt were ritualistically approached in three sequentially organized and presented stages, as follows:

1. The Story of Osiris and Isis (see fig. 6.2)
2. The Story of the Overcoming of Set by Horus (see fig. 6.3)
3. The Story of Ra-Horakhte and his overcoming of the forces of Set

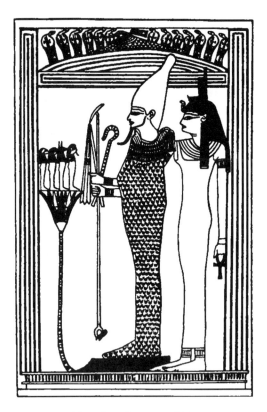

Fig. 6.2. Osiris and Isis

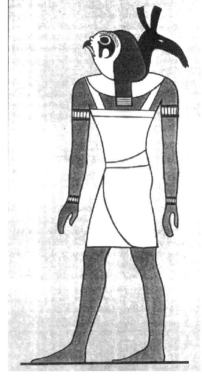

Fig. 6.3. Horus and Set

The first story symbolically describes the fragmentation of the Divine Word (Osiris, representing the human Monad) in the Underworld and the eventual recovery of the creative principle, which reunites the whole, thereby allowing spiritual self-consciousness (Horus the Younger) to be born.[5] The second story symbolically describes the spiritual self-consciousness battling and eventually overcoming the nature of selfishness (symbolized by the god Set), thereby becoming the ruler (as the Spiritual Ego) of the dual kosmic Underworld[6] (symbolized by Upper and Lower Egypt). In the third story the Divine Man-God (Ra-Horakhte) overcomes and controls all the elemental forces in Nature,[7] thereby becoming a Dionysus-like Master Spirit, effectively at-one with the Deity and controlling all the lesser daemons or "maenads." These three Mystery stories are directly paralleled by the three ancient Greek Mystery traditions, as we shall see later on.

Behind all three, however, lay another and even deeper layer of cosmological Mysteries involving the origins of the universe and the very nature of Deity itself. In this the darkly mysterious Creator-God Ptah metamorphosed into the solar deity Ra,[8] which then developed seven aspects of itself: Kheper-Ra, Amen-Ra, Mntw-Ra, Sebek-Ra, Khnemu-Ra, and Atum-Ra, the former and latter triads being connected by Ra-Horakhte. However, as a later book is intended explaining in greater detail the esoteric nature of ancient Egyptian religion and philosophy, no more will be said here on this particular issue, to avoid creating a potential distraction.

THE ANCIENT ASSYRIAN AND CHALDEO-BABYLONIAN MYSTERY TRADITION

The religious myths of Assyria and Babylon (derived from the preceding wisdom traditions of Sumer and Chaldea, originally known as the Maghdim)[9] have come down into the modern era in somewhat fragmented form. However, all of them seem originally to have been interconnected or based on a single but complex allegorical myth structure. Like the ancient Egyptian system, the Chaldeo-Babylonian system was based upon the concept of Man's origin in the stars. Like all ancient religions, the Assyrians also had a sacred tree, of sevenfold nature. The tree sheltered four creatures—a man, a lion, an ox, and an eagle[10]—representing the four astrologically "fixed" constellations of Aquarius, Leo, Taurus, and Scorpio respectively, as borrowed by Hebrew tradition in its "vision of Ezekiel" (see fig. 6.4). As I have suggested in other books, these also seemingly represent the four celestial equinoxes and solstices generated by the Great Sidereal Year cycle (otherwise known to us as the precession of the equinoxes), which also coincide with the four main Celtic festivals. Again as with the Egyptians, divine consciousness was represented by the winged disc, although the Assyrian system differed by having an archer within the disc, aiming his bow leftward, toward the outer world.

The three main kosmic gods were Anu, Ea, and Bel, whose functions

Fig. 6.4. Ezekiel's vision

exactly match those of the Hindu trinity of Siva, Visnu, and Brahma and the much later Father, Son, and Holy Spirit of Christianity. The Mysteries here seem to parallel those of ancient India, having an exoteric (but allegorical) range of epic stories for the masses and a sevenfold initiatory tradition for the selected few. The epic stories include the Great Flood and the finding of the spiritual leader, or Avatar, as a baby in a reed basket in the river, both later annexed by the Hebrews (in the stories of Noah and of Moses) for their own biblical tradition.

The Creation story here[11] involves the deities Apsu-Rishtu (the father of Anu, Ea, and Bel) and Ti-Amat (the "Great Mother" of Space) both of whom are allegorically "slain" by Merodach (seemingly derived from the Hindu, Marut-Akh—hence also Marduk), the Herculean son of Ea, in order to create the manifest world system. The great Zu bird then steals from the god Bel the "Tablets of Destiny"—containing the dharma and karma of the future world system—which have to be recovered. Thus the great cycle of existence begins as described in the legend of Etana. This involved the great Eagle (of kosmic consciousness), which had devoured the brood of the great Mother Serpent (i.e., the lesser soul-offspring of the celestial Oversoul), becoming entangled in the entrails of a wild ox (a Taurean reference) and then being thrown down into the celestial Underworld.[12]

In this system, where the higher Mysteries were concerned, the spiritual Man is represented by the heroic figure of Gilgamesh (the Babylonian Hercules). He is given tasks involving a descent into the Underworld (with his human alter ego, Ea-bani, with whom he is at first in conflict) and a later, lone ascent into the higher heaven world of Causation, across the "Sea of Death," to find his ancestor Pir-Napishtim, who represents the divine Monad.[13]

For the masses, however, the religious epic of *Tammuz* was given out.[14] Like the Greek goddess Persephone, Tammuz spent the autumn and winter of each year in the Underworld, from which he was rescued by his lover, the Goddess Ishtar. She seems to have represented Wisdom, the later gnostic Sophia, whose name, as mentioned earlier, was itself derived from Suf-Ea, the "breath of Ea." In doing so, she had to descend through the seven levels of the Underworld, removing parts of her clothing at each level until she was wholly naked. In the meantime, Pap-sukal, the hermetic messenger of the gods, hastened to the solar deity Shamash (otherwise known as Mitra, the god of destiny and justice, mediator between Heaven and Earth) to tell him what had happened. Shamash then created a man-lion named Nadushu-Namir to rescue her, this man-lion then being cursed by Alla(h)tu, queen of the Underworld.

Fig. 6.5.
The lion-headed Mithra

The man-lion is of course not only the Egyptian sphinx but also the (Persian) figure of Mithras, who symbolically represents Man himself, in dual spiritual-terrestrial form. It is worthwhile mentioning in passing, for the sake of deeper interest, that the ziggurat temple had seven stories and that the holy city Ecbetana had seven concentric walls.

THE ANCIENT INDO-PERSIAN
MYSTERY TRADITION

The greatest divinity of ancient Persia was the Unknowable and ever Self-regenerate Zeru Akerne (hence our word *zero,* actually meaning the spheroidal Oversoul and Source of all being), while the god of Time (i.e., the Demiurge) was Zurvan Akarana, the latter portrayed as standing erect on top of the world, holding in his hands the tools of the architect.[15] The religion of the masses in ancient Persia appears to have been that of Zoroastrianism, perhaps the most interesting aspect of which involves the seeming emphasis on duality. Although there is an ultimate Divinity, the divine aspect in Man is represented by Ahura Mazda (a being of divine light) while the self-centered aspect is presented in the form of the dark lord Ahriman, the latter being a tempter who constantly provides seductive distractions from the spiritual Path. As S. H. Nasr confirms, "The hierarchy of Ahriman and his six arch-daemons form an esoteric heptad"[16]—to which he adds of Zoroastrianism in general, "The sixfold order of Creation is completed by the creation of Fire."[17] It is of course the sacred nature of fire that stands (even today) at the very heart of remaining Zoroastrian (i.e., Parsi) religious ritual. This is the Divine Flame—the Christ spirit—which represents the manifesting Logos himself.

Another supposedly Persian Mystery tradition that appears to have accompanied Zoroastrianism was of a markedly different but still wholly complementary (gnostic) nature. It had a supreme Urgos (AEEIOYO) who had seven letters in his name, plus a Demiurge named Abraxas (also with seven letters to his name). He, symbolically depicted with the head of a cockerel and serpent legs, was one of the seven immortal gods of our world system. The Solar Logos figure Mithra is then born from within a cosmic egg generated by Abraxas, emerging from it as a septenary lion-headed human figure, enfolded by the seven coils of a great serpent. He is also frequently shown standing upon the cosmic sphere of the local universe holding either a key in his right hand, or a torch and dagger (representing wisdom and justice). His Christ-like lesser counterpart Mithras was born in a cave on December 25 (witnessed by shepherds), and his initiated disciples partook of an eucharistic meal of bread and water.[18] Mithras, as a winged demigod, is also described with various cosmological associations, particularly with the Taurean (thus perhaps Assyrian) bull (see fig. 6.6).

This same tradition, of celestial orientation focused on the sacred celestial kosmic bull, involved Mithras descending (by mistake) into the Underworld on seven black bulls and then having to reascend on seven white ones—allegories of respectively involutionary and evolutionary progressions. It further involved his slaying of the bull through a sword in the neck (like the coup de grace of the Spanish matador). These then formed allegorical

Fig. 6.6. Mithras slaying the kosmic bull

rituals as part of the Mithraic Mysteries, the latter involving seven initiations, seven caverns with seven gates of entry and seven stepped landings, the last cavern being decorated with the signs of the zodiac. The seven initiations, as known in much later, Greco-Roman times, were as follows.[19]

1. Corax (the Raven—symbolizing death and rebirth)
2. Nymphus (the Bee chrysalis—symbolizing the ability to recognize, collect, and carry spiritual knowledge back to the masses)
3. Miles (the Soldier—the initiate was given a crown and, casting it down, demonstrating his rejection of ego, was shown as liberated from the bondage of the material world)
4. Leo (the Lion—first of the senior degrees, signifying entry into the spiritual fire)
5. Perses (the Mithraic Perseus, son of the Father—signified by the sword)
6. Heliodromus (the monadic "Sun Runner"—the Sun being the "Eye of Mithra")
7. Pater Sacrorum (Father of the Mysteries—signified by the libation bowl and the sickle)

It is otherwise interesting to note that the Persian social structure paralleled that of the original Hindu and Celtic systems,[20] although consisting of three, not four, castes—priests (*farnabas*), warriors (*gushnasp*), merchants/artisans and food producers (*burzin mihr*).

THE ANCIENT VEDIC MYSTERY TRADITION

The Mysteries were approached in the Vedic tradition from two angles, as were later those of ancient Greece. The "lesser" Mysteries were given out openly (albeit entirely in allegorical format) in the form of the Puranas, epic stories about the many gods and goddesses and their various adventures. Among these is the story of Krisna, the greatest of all Avatars, who is also, paradoxically, represented as the expression of the Kosmic Mind principle. The latter, as described earlier, emanates Creation from itself at the beginning of each great cycle and reabsorbs it back into itself at the end of each such cycle. It is also noteworthy that Krisna, with the aid of his elder brother Balarama (himself regarded as a manifestation of Shesha, the serpent on which Visnu rests), has to rescue his six younger brothers from the Underworld, thereby confirming another esoteric soul-octave. From this it is evident that Krisna symbolizes the Christ principle that, in the *Bhagavad Gita,* teaches the human intelligence (represented by Arjuna) how to recognize and take advantage of his own highest innermost principle.

Fig. 6.7. Krisna

While the underlying teaching in the Puranas concerns the general sequence and process of Creation and the forces of intelligent and semi-intelligent Nature, the Vedas, on the other hand, involve the more detailed, sacred knowledge concerning the "mechanics and dynamics" of both esoteric and occult philosophy, accessible only to initiated Brahmins for their individual spiritual training. Perhaps the best-known source involves the Laws of Manu in which the Unknowable, Eternal, and Self-existent Being initiated Creation by forming the elements and thereby scattered the darkness of Chaos. By producing the great waters of Space from his great thought, he scattered his seed essence within them, this seed uniting to become a brilliant golden egg within which Brahma (like Mithra) was born. In another version of this story we find the demiurgic figure of Mahadeva (later renamed Siva) isolating with sacred fire a portion of Space within which the great god Visnu (symbolizing the "Great Waters" of Universal Consciousness) slept, Brahma being born from a lotus issuing from Visnu's navel.

Notwithstanding these by now quite well known Creation myths, so much of what was involved in the way of detailed occult philosophy passed by word of mouth alone, from guru to neophyte, that even today very little is known concerning the actual and associated stages of initiation. Notwithstanding this, we might mention in passing that in the *Rig Veda,* the god-man figure of Visvakarman is crucified in Space, his seven locks of hair (representing his seven rays) being cut off and replaced with a crown of thorns, following which he too is made to descend into the Underworld. From this he subsequently emerges "re-possessed of his rays" thereby becoming "Graha-Raja," king of the celestial universe.[21] The later Christianized elements of this story are rather obvious, as are others not mentioned here.

THE ANCIENT GREEK MYSTERY TRADITIONS

The Greek Mystery traditions were preceded by the far more ancient Greek Creation traditions (of which there were three—the Pelasgian, Orphic, and Olympian) involving Chaos, then the trinity of Ouranos, Gaia, and Eros, and the sequential appearance of six pairs of male and female Titans.[22] These, like the Vedic gods, represented the intelligent kosmic hierarchies of the solar universe, ancillary to which were many lesser ranges of semi-intelligent beings, all related to particular, interconnected states of being having an overall sevenfold structure. These Titans then gave rise to a second Titan generation of whom the most important were the three brothers Zeus, Poseidon, and Hades, these being given charge of the three lowest of the seven kosmic states of being. This then gave rise to the perspective of divine, spiritual, and terrestrial states of existence with which Man could associate himself through the actions and experiences of the Heroes, such as Hercules and Orpheus. Within this great pantheon, the concept of the origins of humankind (through the actions of Prometheus) was also introduced. The actual Greek Mysteries involved a somewhat different perspective, although retaining psychological reference to the gods and demigods. They were triple (and progressive) in nature, comprising:

1. The Eleusynian Mysteries
2. The Orphic Mysteries
3. The Dionysian Mysteries

The Eleusynian Mysteries were open to all men, women, and children (except murderers) and were orientated primarily around ceremonially displayed allegories teaching about the greater and lesser cycles of Nature and the greater and lesser forces associated with them. The main story focused on the snatching of Persephone, daughter of the goddess Demeter, by Hades, the Titan god of the Underworld, and how this resulted in the natural cycle of the seasons of Nature.[23] We are told that the Eleusynian Mysteries continued to be practiced in Athens until the eighth century CE, having never been entirely suppressed.[24]

The Orphic Mysteries were orientated around the journey of the human Spiritual Ego (represented by Orpheus) down into the Underworld (symbolic of human incarnate life experience) and the Ego's attempt to win back the terrestrial/astral soul (represented by his wife Eurydice) to the world of spiritual existence. In a very distinct sense, it is about the cycle of human reincarnation in the search for spiritual emancipation and liberation. Orpheus (puzzlingly to modern academia) was recognized as a lesser expression of Dionysus, despite the latter having had him allegorically "torn apart" by the *maenads*. We otherwise find that:

According to the Orphic theology, each of the planets is fixed in a lumi-
nous ethereal sphere . . . and is analogous to the sphere of the fixed stars.
In consequence of this analogy, each of the planetary spheres contains
a multitude of gods who are the satellites of the leading divinity of the
sphere and subsist conformably to his characteristics.[25]

In other words, there exists a Planetary Logos for each planetary scheme,
supported by a hierarchy of lesser but also divine Intelligences, as described
in the "modern" theosophical teaching.

The Dionysian Mysteries were symbolic of the knowledge and powers
inherent in the "divine spark" (the Monad) behind Man, the very name
Dionysus being derived from the Sanskrit dhyani-dhyaus. Although misinterpreted by modern scholarship as indicative of orgiastic license, these
Mysteries were actually indicative of the need (in the already spiritually
advanced individual) for focusing solely on the Monad and also on the
need for general spiritual asceticism. It is worth noting that the advanced
knowledge available in these particular Mysteries seems to have given rise
to that international society or sacred fraternity known as the Dionisyii, or
"Dionysian Artificers," sometimes also known as the "Dionysian Architects."
This same society seems to have been the parent of the much later Craft
Masons of Europe and the Middle East who had the exclusive privilege of
designing and constructing all temples and public buildings. Organized in
Lodges, each with its own Master and ruling group of initiates, they had
annual festivals and used systems of sacred signs for identification (as did the
earlier Pythagoreans and the later Crusaders). We shall mention them again
later in connection with the development of the first Western universities in
Spain, in medieval times.

BUDDHISM

Buddhism has to be properly considered from two distinctly different
perspectives—that of so-called primitive Buddhism and the modern form
of religion, which since the late nineteenth century has become progressively so well known throughout the world. The former—as the authoress
Alexandra David-Neel tells us from her own direct experience—comprised

a Tibetan form of mystic occultism (not a philosophy, nor a religion per se), which involved learning how to become aware of and then how to master Nature's forces from the subjectively causal side, the phenomenal world scene being seen as merely a mass of effects. This same mystical practice, however, although indescribably ancient in origin, has become extraordinarily varied over the millennia through its adaptation by Tibetan lamas—hence its more familiar name, "Lamaism"—in the practice of various forms of occult initiation. As David-Neel describes, this Tibetan mysticism involves its protagonists being animated by a sense of subjective adventure, which classified them in her eyes as "spiritual sportsmen."[26] Most such "adventures," however, were of a purely psychic nature, dealing with lesser spirits, daemons, or elementals, but having very little or nothing whatsoever to do with real spirituality.

One might otherwise mention here the highly occult *Bardo Thodol* tradition found in Tibet,[27] which finds its parallel in the ancient Egyptian Book of the Dead. The essence of the *Bardo* (itself not be considered in a merely literal way) involves teaching the neophyte how to find his way back and forth through the psycho-spiritual world, with all its terrors and fascinations. It is this that in very practical terms leads the individual to the progressive gates of initiation. It is again particularly associated with Tibetan Lamaism rather than with what we understand as Buddhism, whether exoteric or esoteric.

The solitary and rarely-found few following the truly spiritual perspective—the latter thus given the name "the Short Path" (indicating its steep "uphill" nature)—were those aiming at eventual development as human Buddhas. In contrast to the majority concerned purely with developing their own personal powers, these were concerned with compassionately assisting the progressive evolution of humanity as a whole, the development of psycho-spiritual powers being seen by them as entirely secondary in nature and concern to understanding the way Nature works through a constant process of presentational illusion. It is this form of (esoteric) Buddhism that, it is suggested, lies behind the origin of real Christianity.

The latter form of more widely popularized Buddhism originated in Nepal, from the teachings of Gautama Siddhartha, who was born in 621 BCE and is now commonly recognized as "the Buddha." His particular philosophy spread quickly throughout India and immediately adjacent lands after his death. Intended as a revision of Hindu Brahmanism and containing both exoterically mystic and esoterically metaphysical aspects, it was quite quickly crushed by the Brahmins and driven out of India generally, except in the far south, including Ceylon (modern Sri Lanka). There it has continued to thrive right up to the present day. However, in the second century BCE it was rejuvenated under the patronage of the Mauryan emperor Asoka, grandson of the legendary Chandragupta, resulting in a mass evangelical movement extending through the Middle East, to Rome, and even to Britain.

The essence of exoteric Buddhism is contained in the teaching that desire (*tanha*) inevitably gives rise to pain (*dukkha*), misery, and karmic retribution, always to the detriment of spiritual perception. Its idealistic philosophy is expressed for us in the "Noble Eightfold Path." Exoteric Buddhism is of course publicly associated with specific high ideals of altruistic human behavior toward all fellow creatures. It also includes a general teaching that the external world plus its many and varied enjoyments and sorrows are all based upon mere illusion.

Of esoteric Buddhism and its cosmological knowledge little is known

Fig. 6.8. Yellow hat Tibetan temple lamas

even throughout the Far East, except among the fraternity of those "yellow hat" Tibetan lamas initiated into the inner Mysteries, their particular following having been generated by the great Tibetan Master known as Tzon-kha-pa (of whom we shall learn more, later) in the late fourteenth century. However, the West was fortunate to learn rather more about it through the writings of H. P. Blavatsky, particularly in her major work *The Secret Doctrine*, published in 1888. In relation to the latter, it seems clear that a decision was made by the trans-Himalayan Adept Brotherhood to bring this knowledge to the West by virtue of it having been stultified in the East, through the spiritual selfishness of the Hindu Brahmin community at large.

THE JAIN TRADITION

A very close parallel to Buddhism is found in Jainism, an ancient religious philosophy practiced in various parts of India (and now to some extent in the West also), which does not believe in a God per se. Instead it has a central philosophy of truthfulness, nonviolence, essential nonownership of things

Fig. 6.9. Mahavira and Gautama Buddha

and no stealing. Its continuity of historic belief lies in the Tirthankaras (perfected human souls) who attained spiritual liberation and of whom there have been twenty-four in the current (unspecified) cycle. The last of these was Mahavira, supposedly born in 699 BCE and represented Buddha-like in a pose of seated meditation. Whether Mahavira and Gautama Siddhartha (see fig. 6.9) were one and the same high Adept, one cannot say, but their not dissimilar date of birth certainly begs the question. That Jainism was much weakened by the quite deliberate efforts of Hindu Brahmins—just as Buddhism was throughout northern and central India—tends to reinforce this suggestion.

THE HEBREW/JUDAIC TRADITION

This tradition—encapsulated in the first five books of Genesis (the Pentateuch) was actually derived in its entirety from far more ancient Zoroastrian, Chaldeo-Babylonian, and Egyptian mystic traditions and esoteric mythology. As David Frawley tells us:

> The Israelites were a religious reform movement. On the one hand they tried to get back to the more simple form of the ancient religions of the Middle East, like those of Egypt and Babylonia before their fall and corruption. On the other hand, they appear to have rejected them altogether and formed a new religion of their own.[28]

As the Israeli historian and author Shlomo Sand has otherwise described in his recent book *The Invention of the Jewish People,* detailed archeological research has shown that there is no evidence whatsoever as to the actual historical existence of any of the Hebrew patriarchs upon whom the whole Jewish religion is founded, or for certain of the supposedly main experiences of the "ancient Hebrews"—such as the Exodus from Egypt.[29] All are in fact based upon esoteric metaphor and allegory, as is the idea itself of an ethnologically original Jewish people. The latter seem to have been derived from a tribe that came from northwestern India (the modern Gujarat area) and, following the drying up of the great Sarasvati river (following huge earthquakes), subsequently settled in or close to Armenia.[30] However, Shlomo

Sand himself, as an academic professor of history, has not made any attempt to consider or explore the associated esoteric aspects of their belief in themselves as a supposedly "chosen" people. The modern academic view that the Hebrews were the first monotheists—which Sand himself seems to accept—is also wildly inaccurate. The earlier esoteric traditions—those of the Egyptians, Persians, Hindus, Assyrians, and Babylonians—all believed in a fundamental unity of all existence within the Being of an entity of which they logically admitted no mind could even conceive.

While the actual story would take too long to relate here, the founding of the Hebrew religion as such appears, quite conclusively, to derive from the work of an individual known to us as "the prophet Ezra." He—in the fifth century BCE—managed to persuade the then emperor of Babylonia, Artaxerxes, to allow a large group of Judeans to return to the area of modern Palestine-Israel under the satrapy of a Babylonian governor (Nehemiah) and to set up a new province there.[31] Ezra also took upon himself the literal creation of a tribally monotheistic Hebrew religious dogma or theology (the Torah), elements of which were borrowed from the religions of the surrounding nation-states—that is, Babylonia, Assyria, Egypt, Persia, and India. The name *Torah* itself appears to have been derived from the same root as *Tau* or *Tao* and *Taurus*—thus *Tao-Ra,* or "the Way of Ra." Some of these elements, in rather abbreviated terms, pursue the following general sequence.

The Hebrew tradition of the Pentateuch starts off with the Creation of the world in six "days" followed by a "day of rest" (i.e., seven successive cycles)—an idea borrowed wholesale from the Zoroastrian tradition of the Amshaspends. In the Hebrew theology the Amshaspends are replaced by the Elohim, an equivalent sevenfold group of celestial gods who actually appear to derive their name from the compound El-Ahi-im. El, however, was the main Babylonian deity and Ahi was the Indo-Tibetan name for the creative Demiurge (long ages before the gnostics of Alexandria). The word *im* is merely a collective suffix, indicating a group. We then hear of Adam—a name derived from either the Egyptian god Atum, or Adima (the first man of Hindu tradition)—and Eve/Heva (his second wife) and their experiences in the so-called "Garden of Eden." The latter name seems to have been derived from Ad-on—a Sanskrit name (Adi) with a Greek suffix (*on*), meaning "a primordial state of being." After they are expelled from

Eden by divine decree, they shed their divine "skins," take on lesser quality ones, and then produce their three sons, Enoch, Abel, and Cain, respectively representing the divine, spiritual, and terrestrial humanity of the lesser fields of existence.

The story of the family of Adam and Eve is followed by the story of the Tower of Babel and the supposedly forced derivation of many human languages. The tradition thereafter has the patriarch Abram (from the Vedic A-Brahm) and his wife Sarah (from the Vedic Sarasvati, wife of Brahma) first of all deciding to leave Ur (merely meaning either an "ancient" or "primordial" place, or the Oversoul, i.e., Aur), then moving south to Egypt, then itself known in esoteric metaphor as "the Underworld" of limitation (Mizraim in Hebrew). The first child, Isaac (actually As-akh, meaning "heavenly spirit"), is saved from death by the sacrifice of a ram, thereby allegorically confirming the start of the zodiacal cycle. The third generation sees the appearance of a pair of Geminian twins Jacob and Esau, more originally recognizable as Jah-khu-bel and As'r, the latter being the Egyptian form of Osiris. The fourth generation later arrives in the form of the twelve

Fig. 6.10. The Tower of Babel (Bruegel)

sons of Jacob (another zodiacal metaphor), now renamed "Israel" (or rather, As'r-El) the brightest of whom is called Joseph (actually Jah-suf, meaning the "breath of Jah") who eventually becomes assistant to Potiphar, the pharaoh's chief-of-staff.

Finally, the Judaic tradition concerns itself with the "escape" or "Exodus" from the Egyptian "Underworld" through the influence upon Moses of the God YHVE (Jahve), a name that appears, in fact, borrowed from the

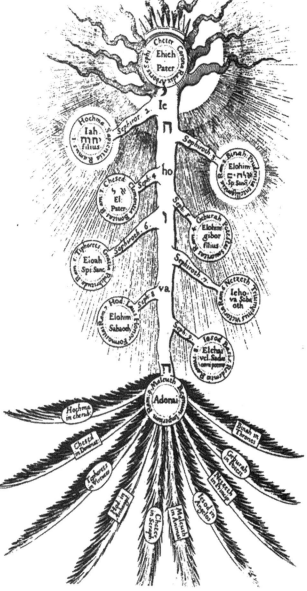

Fig. 6.11. The inverted kabbalistic Tree of Life

Sanskrit word *jiva,* meaning the lesser monad or daemon. The latter, as we saw in earlier chapters, signifies the individualized spirit or "divine spark" within the human organism, while the Exodus story itself is a merely quasi-gnostic allegory describing Man's liberation from the kosmic physical plane.

Despite what has already been said as regards exoteric Judaism, mention should also be made of its mystic side known as "Pirke Merkabah" and of its esoteric side, known to us as Kabbalism. The former provides a description of the seven heavenly temples, which must be visited in succession by the Elect before they can enter the region of the sacred chariot, that is, the all-enclosing sphere of the Aeon or planetary Oversoul. This and much else was directly borrowed from Persian Magianism.[32] As regards the Kabbala, although these days represented as a single (inverted) "Tree of Life" with its various levels and qualities associated with the archangelic sephiroth, the original description (as given in the *Sepher ha Zohar*)[33] confirms that it too is actually a restatement of the metaphysical mechanics and dynamics of the "perennial philosophy" as perhaps more clearly defined in modern theosophical terms. See also fig. 15.1 by way of comparison.

It is otherwise interesting to note that later Lurianic Kabbala—its founder Isaac Luria Ashkenazi (1534–1572) having been born and raised in Egypt and clearly absorbed aspects of its esoteric philosophy—also confirms the same principles, starting with the dictum that Creation occurs due to a self-limiting ideation (called *tzimtzum*) of the Divine Mind. The Kabbala likewise makes the following clear statement, again laying emphasis upon the sevenfold structure and also the cyclic nature of existence:

> "The seven lower Sephiroth are the children of the mother of the world ... [hence] the aeon from which everything comes, as from its mother, is also the aeon to which everything will return [hence] the bestowal on the world of one-seventh part of the primordial light." [To this is added] The Sephiroth are somehow related to the seven heavens. Each is a world in itself but also the initial starting place and the object of desire for the souls that issue from it.[34]

In fact, the use of the word *heavens* is wrong. It is the seven states of our human planetary existence that are being referred to, as confirmed and found in various other ancient traditions and as described in the earlier chapters of this book. It is otherwise interesting to note that Judaism uses the word *devekuth* (from the Sanskrit deva) to mean "communion with the gods,"[35] while the Hebrew word *ruach* (spirit) is itself derived from *ruh* (breath) and *akh* (the "fallen" "divine spark"). Hence *ruh-akh*—the "divine breath" of the Monad—is essentially the same as the Sanskrit *atma*.

PYTHAGOREAN TRADITION

Although the philosophy of Pythagoras was not (nor did it subsequently become) a religion as such—his knowledge having been derived from his time in Egypt, Babylonia, and India—it was held in such high regard (especially by Plato) and was itself distinctive enough to rate a mention here. Although best known for its concentration on esoteric relationships in the fields of arithmetic, numerology, geometry, music, and astronomy, his essentially monotheistic philosophy involved a description of God as the "Supreme Mind"—the Power, Intelligence, and One Cause within all yet behind all Creation.[36] However, as in the kabbalistic concept of Ain Soph, he described this God as "Unlimited," whereas that which emerged from it by emanation was by definition "Limited."[37] This latter God was the One, called by him the Monas—derived, as we saw earlier, from the Sanskrit term *manas,* meaning the Universal Mind principle—which itself gave rise to the existence of the Demiurge. The combination of Mind-emanation and Demiurge thus became the "Indefinite Dyad" of the later Platonists.

Pythagoras was perhaps the first (at least the first known to us) to produce an openly clear presentation of Divinity in an abstract and reasoned manner that was not religiously devotional. This is even though extreme piety was an essential part of Pythagorean working philosophy as distinct from his more abstract philosophy. The latter had what we might call "a reasoned cosmological structure," itself based on an occult approach to mathematics. Like the Babylonians (from whose esoteric philosophy Judaic Kabbalism was itself seemingly derived), his mathematical philosophy was based on the number ten—as particularly expressed in the form of the sacred *tetraktys* (see fig. 6.12), which formed the repetitive basis (in decads) of all possible existence. He regarded the number 360 (of Indo-Chaldean origin) as particularly sacred and he correspondingly described the nature and motion of Deity itself to be circular or spheroidal, its substance to be that of light, and its nature to be that of Truth.

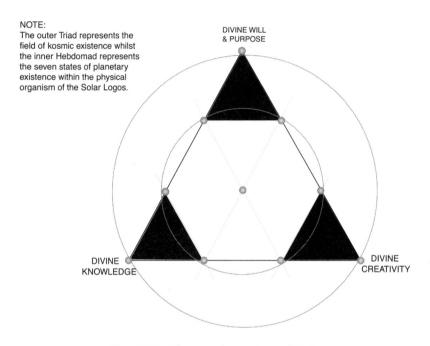

NOTE:
The outer Triad represents the field of kosmic existence whilst the inner Hebdomad represents the seven states of planetary existence within the physical organism of the Solar Logos.

DIVINE WILL & PURPOSE

DIVINE KNOWLEDGE

DIVINE CREATIVITY

Fig. 6.12. The sacred tetraktys of Pythagoras

Humanity was regarded by the Pythagoreans as the living microcosm of the Logos, hence the Logos was the mediator between the Unknowable Deity and the incarnate human spiritual Monads. The Pythagoreans otherwise logically described the Monad as the "axis" as well as the "tower of Zan." The latter—seemingly derived from the Tibetan *dzyan* (meditation)—brings to mind the "Stanzas of Dhzyan" in Blavatsky's work *The Secret Doctrine*.[38] Pythagoras also taught the principle of universal brotherhood (as espoused by the modern worldwide theosophical movement) in the form of the "natural friendship" between all beings and all things. This is of course otherwise instantly recognizable as quite logically derived from the "as above, so below" principle of universal sympathetic association later attributed to Hermes Trismegistus, as described in the *Hermetica*.

In the Pythagorean Mystery School itself there were two main groups of students, those of the *exoterikoi* or probationary *akousmatikoi* on the one hand and the *esoterikoi* or serious students on the other. Only the latter had direct access to Pythagoras himself and even they had to undergo a probationary period of five years before being allowed to listen to his teachings face-to-face.[39] There were also three initial initiations facing the latter. These comprised those of the: (1) Mathematikoi, (2) Theoretikoi, and (3) Electoi, the latter apparently corresponding with the third initiation of Craft Freemasonry, permitting the initiate access into the Higher Mysteries. Others in the Pythagorean gymnasium devoted to contemplation were called *sebastici*.[40]

As with Eastern gurus and also in accordance with the original traditions of Freemasonry, absolute obedience together with secrecy in regard to sacred knowledge were cardinal principles on the part of all disciples. As elsewhere explained, the reason for this involves the very real sympathetic, psycho-spiritual connection that results from the Adept taking responsibility for his disciples. In certain respects, their two fields of consciousness merge, thereby leaving the Adept highly vulnerable, as will be further described later on.

THE SUFI TRADITION

Despite the fact that Sufism is today purely associated with Islam, its patrimony actually appears far, far older and appears to come from the area of ancient Persia and Afghanistan, which perhaps suggests an original association with or derivation from Zoroastrianism, although it is actually even more gnostically universal. It appears that there originally were seven Sufi groups, each specializing in some particular field of interest and activity (such as healing or music) with one parent order or Tariqa—the Naqshbandi—to which all the others such as the Chistiya, Quadriya, and Mevlevi (see fig. 6.13), paid homage. This structure—that of the seven aspects within the octave of the Oversoul—is of course deeply esoteric in nature and exactly parallels that of many other Mystery traditions. This includes the kabbalistic tradition of the seven lower sephiroth contained by the "mother" sephira, Binah, as already described in an earlier chapter. However, there is also a

Fig. 6.13. Mevlevi dervishes

great focus on the development of occult powers following the second initiation, subject to the agreement of the dervish candidate's sheikh.

The first preliminary initiation in the Sufi system is that of the Aspirant or Salik, while the second probationary degree is that of the Seeker (Talib) after which the Great Oath is taken and the individual becomes a full member or Murid, meaning "disciple." The next degree is that of Tariqat, meaning "potentiality," which is the first real stage on the Sufi Path, itself known as the Safar-Ullah—the "Journey to Knowledge." The second main degree is that of the Arif, "the Knower," followed by the third, known as Fana, which involves the destruction of all personality considerations. Although there are two further, highly secret initiations rendering him a Wali (saint), the third is regarded as the furthest that most can go.[41] As we shall see, this sequence of initiations is fundamentally no different than that described in the Mithraic Mysteries or in chapters 8 to 11 of this book, although the latter provide us with much greater detail concerning the fourth and fifth initiations.

We otherwise find in allegorical form, in the Sufi romance *The*

Parliament of the Birds, the sevenfold initiatory progression involving a traversing of seven valleys. The first four of these are those of the Quest, of Love, of Intuitive Knowledge, and that of Detachment, the last involving liberation from all desires and dependences. The fifth to seventh stages then involve the Valley of Unification, the Valley of Astonishment, and the Valley of Death. In the last of these the individual finally understands the paradox of the "drop" merged with the ocean of Being yet still retaining its individuality and its sense of purpose.[42]

THE PLATONIC TRADITION

Although revered by scholars for his idealized ethics and philosophical clarity, and for his interpretations and highlighting of Pythagorean philosophy (such as the principle of Divine Limitation), Plato (428–347 BCE) is best known for having derived his deep knowledge and structured sense of presentation from his own two decades of study in Egypt. For example, in the cosmological descriptions given in his work *The Myth of Er* (showing his fundamentally esoteric approach to the subject), he mentions seven concentric celestial whorls (vortices) contained within an eighth, all moving or rotating in the same direction, although at different speeds, "the eight together forming one harmony." The eighth is of course the Oversoul of the later Greek philosopher, Plotinus (204–270 CE). Plato adds that beyond this octave lies another series of three bands of existence (i.e., kosmic planes), which he associates with the Three Fates, as "Daughters of Necessity."[43] This coincides with the theosophical idea of the four lower planes in each system (kosmic or systemic) giving rise to the cycle of objectivity—that is, of involution and evolution—as already described. It is also directly comparable with Pythagorean and kabbalistic cosmology.

In his *Timaeus,* Plato also makes the point that where the Mind manifests, there also follows the existence of a spheroidal field of being.[44] In Plato's work *The Banquet,* Aristophanes speaks of prototypal humankind having been androgynous and that "their bodies were round and the manner of their running circular. They were terrible in force and strength and had prodigious ambition."[45] This coincides with what Blavatsky's *The Secret Doctrine* has to say about the earliest prehuman types of what she calls the

"Second Root Race."[46] whose body form (derived from the First Race) was essentially that of a gigantic cell, which had not yet developed proper arms and legs, let alone a head and brain.

To try to provide a realistic synopsis of Plato's ideas here would be impossible because they are far too deep and too broad to deal with other than at some length. Not only does he deal with the subjects of human ethics and law, but also with the whole nature of human behavior in response to spiritual and divine impulsion. The fact that (even before he went to study in Egypt) he was one of the foremost disciples of Socrates, who taught that following one's own Higher Self (one's "daemon") was of greater importance than abiding by religious orthodoxy, gives us a real insight into the core of his philosophy. So does the fact that he was prepared to set up and head "the Academy," with its central focus on higher reason and insight, right in the face of the dying Mystery traditions of ancient Greece. The fact that the Platonic way of thought and many of his ideals are still held in the highest regard and widely pursued even today is itself indicative of the intrinsic quality of his philosophy.

THE HERMETIC TRADITION

Despite being regarded by modern scholars as being of late, only Greco-Egyptian origin, there is every reason (from at least the esoteric viewpoint) to believe that the Hermetic philosophy is exactly the same as that propounded in the ancient Egyptian Mysteries and that Plato accrued his own great store of knowledge from it. The whole *Hermetica*—supposedly derived from one or more of the forty-two Books of Tehuti (which provided the central canon of all Egyptian knowledge)—is essentially about the way in which Nature works in both the Macrocosm and the microcosm, through the agency of Mind. For example, in the work we find the following statement:

> And the Eternal Father took the matter that He desired to set aside and made it all into a spheroidal form with body and bulk. The matter that he invested with this special quality is immortal and its materiality is eternal. Further, the Father implanted in the sphere the qualities [essences] of forms, shutting them up as in a cave. He wanted to adorn

what comes after Him with every quality, to surround the whole body with immortality so that even matter, tending to separate from the composition of this body, would not dissolve into its typical disorder.[47]

Here we have a direct correspondence not only with ancient Greek Creation "myth" (involving the enfoldment by Ouranos of Gaia) but also with Judeo-Babylonian Genesis in which the Elohim separate the "waters [of Space] above" from the "waters below" by the creation of a heavenly "firmament."

The tradition goes on to describe the fundamentally concentric and sevenfold structure of what is being created, as follows:

The Mind, who is God, being androgyne and existing as life and light, by speaking gave birth to a second Mind, a craftsman who, as god of fire and spirit, crafted seven governors; they encompass the sensible world in circles and their government is called Fate.[48]

The "Craftsman" here is of course the supreme Egyptian god Ptah, the progenitor of the seven aspects of the great god RA, which represent his sequential manifestation within the celestial sphere of Creation. He is also the Demiurgos of later Alexandrian gnosticism who gives rise to the state of the Ogdoad, in which the highest initiate first becomes aware of the even higher celestial states of Being, as we shall see later on.

THE TRADITION OF THE CHALDEAN ORACLES

Although the actual origins of this work are not known, Michael Psellus (a Byzantine Platonist philosopher of the eleventh century CE) is known to have possessed copies in his personal library. This book—regarded by scholars as possibly the work of Julian the Theurgist (a contemporary of Marcus Aurelius)[49]—follows very closely in the same metaphysical tradition as the Hermetic, neo-Platonic, and neo-Pythagorean philosophical traditions, in both a Macrocosmic and microcosmic sense, as we can very quickly confirm from the following: "Nothing can exist or subsist on any plane or in any realm without the three principles represented by the Primal Triad" and "In every world shineth a Triad of which a Monad is the principle."⁵⁰ And again, "For the Father caused to swell forth seven firmaments of worlds, confining the heaven in a curved form [while] . . . the Demiurgus suspended six zones and for the seventh hurled into the midst the fire of the Sun," which it had already confirmed as having a sevenfold aspect.⁵¹

We also find, in parallel to the seven groups of Elohim of the biblical book of Genesis, the idea that

the One Invisible Fire of the Creative World has a septenary division [which is] . . . unfolded in the Chaldean Mysteries as the Intellectual Hebdomad, or the Seven Creative Principles, which are called the Intellectual or Noeric Fountains, the Creative Fathers or Cosmagogoi, or Leaders of the Cosmos.⁵²

THE "GNOSTIC" TRADITION

Although very incorrectly regarded by many modern historians as an early Christian or Judaic phenomenon, the true gnostic tradition was far older and appears to have had at least some of its roots in the Zoroastrian Mysteries of ancient Persia, despite the fact that a number of other concepts (including those of Greek Stoicism) seem to have been added. Hence *gnostikoi* were often regarded as those of Pythagorean and Platonic orientation.⁵³

The modern scholar Gilles Quispel agrees with Blavatsky in claiming that, although "gnosis" appears to be a primarily Western tradition, which only "began" in ancient Alexandria, there nevertheless existed in antiquity before this a worldwide "gnostic" religion.⁵⁴ A similar view was held by the Islamic philosopher Suhrawardi (mid-to-late twelfth century) who considered himself to be the reviver of the perennial wisdom, "which had always existed among the Hindus, Persians, Babylonians, Egyptians and Greeks, up to the time of Plato."⁵⁵ In contrast, their contemporary, the Greek Plotinus, regarded the Alexandrian gnostics as not being philosophers at all. However, his views were those of a purist (in certain respects, at least) and also appear to have been those of a somewhat noninterdisciplinary, academic mind, which might in retrospect be seen as having suffered from a degree of mystic "tunnel vision."

Some of the ideas of the gnostics were certainly of mixed origin and some seem also partially equivalent to those pursued by the Druzes of Lebanon and the Dead Sea community of the Essenes (who seemed in fact more orientated toward Buddhism). However, both of these were themselves clearly of far more ancient patrimony as well. The various gnostic sects that appeared included the followers of Simon Magus, the Carpocratians, the Cerenthians, the Marcians, the Basilideans, the Ophites and Naasenes, the Valentinians, the Bardisenians, the Johannites, and later the Manicheans. Some of these sects continued in existence until late in the fourth century CE, when the orthodox Church managed to drive them out of at least objective existence. In the sixth century CE, those remaining in the former Persian empire were similarly put to the sword or, later still, forced to embrace Islam on pain of death.

According to the Dead Sea scrolls the gnostic traditions appears to have had two main aspects. The one concerning a form of cosmogenesis—the Creation story—involves the descent of Sophia (i.e., Suf-Ea, Divine Wisdom) from the Pleroma (the Celestial Fullness) into the Abyss (Bythos). There she is arrested by a power known as Horos (the Limit), so forcing her to depart while leaving behind her lower nature (Sophia Ackamoth), which itself unites with or creates a Demiurge (Ildabaoth, the Artificer). The latter then generates a sevenfold kingdom of its own and keeps her prisoner until she is rescued.[56] However, as the Ackamoth of Sophia appears to be a corruption of the Egyptian Akh-Mut (meaning "spirit-firmament") and as Horos is identical to the Egyptian Horus (the divine falcon, representing the limit of percipient consciousness itself), it is not difficult to see the immediate metaphysical correlations. The other aspect of gnostic tradition deals with the initiatory Mysteries, seemingly involving nine initiations in all and concerned with an Avatar or Christ-like Savior of kosmic origin. Aspects of the latter are mentioned and described in later chapters.

THE SCANDINAVIAN TRADITION

The Scandinavian myth, as described in the *Eddas,* is itself directly derived from the Vedic tradition, as confirmed by the fact that the abode of its gods is Valhalla, derived from the Hindu god Indra's heavenly palace being called Valhal.[57] There was a fundamental duality of cosmological existence—Niflheim and Muspellsheim. There was also a central Tree of Life (Ygg-dras-il), its name clearly indicating the meaning "three heavenly eggs" (i.e., auric soul states), in which were to be found the three primary states of existence: Asgard (the fiery heaven world of the gods), Midgard (the land of the living), and Hel-heim (the elemental Underworld, "land of the dead"). The gods themselves were known as the Aesir, a direct borrowing from the Hindu term Asura, itself paralleled by the Etruscan Aesar, the Egyptian As'r (Osiris), and the Assyrio-Babylonian Asher, or Asar.

THE EARLY CHRISTIAN TRADITION
(See also chapter 13)

Given the historical uncertainty as to the figure of Jesus as described in the New Testament, and also given the fact that many of Jesus's own teachings are of an essentially gnostic-Buddhist nature, it seems more than likely that he came from an Essene community, as some have already speculated. Jesus himself made the point to his disciples that what they were secretly taught by him differed from that given out openly to the masses.[58] He also forbade the twelve to go to either the Samaritans or the Gentiles. However, that all changed with the advent of St. Paul who must really be regarded as the main reason why Christianity developed so dynamically as a mainstream religion, open to all. Notwithstanding that, the theology put forward by the successors to Jesus's apostles appears to have been derived from several sources. Most of these were Mithraic, some were Hindu, some neo-Platonic, and some even gnostic, despite the open hatred of certain early Christian bishops (particularly Ireneus and Eusebius) toward the latter two. However, bearing in mind that these bishops had a definitely political view as to how Christianity should be developed, quite contrary to that of its more spiritually-orientated adherents (including Jesus himself), its seems not unfair (and certainly not at all impossible) that Jesus might himself be seen, retrospectively, as a purely gnostic adept of the perennial philosophy, as further suggested in chapter 13.

It is of particular interest to note that perhaps the greatest of the known gnostic philosophers, Valentinus (circa 100–160 CE), nearly became Pope. Had he done so, the implication is that the whole tenor and direction of Christianity would have been more overtly in line with the principles of esoteric philosophy as now known. It is also more than likely, however, that the later Western orientation toward scientific and technological innovation would not have been so evident. It is otherwise worthy of note that esoteric Christianity had a very distinct view of the Mysteries having inner and outer aspects. Origen, one of its main exponents, taught the (Hermetic) concept of the preexistence of souls and is known very informatively to have stated:

> To the literal-minded we teach the Gospel in the historic way, preaching Jesus Christ and him crucified; but to the proficient, fired with love of divine wisdom, we impart the Logos.[59]

Origen also confirmed that many of the things described in the Gospels were merely spiritual allegories and not historical incidents.[60] Synesius (another early Christian bishop) likewise took the view that: "The truth must be kept secret; the masses need a teaching proportionate to their imperfect reason."[61]

Both of these seem to coincide with the reported view of Jesus himself, as given to his disciples in the New Testament, as mentioned in a previous paragraph. As regards the adapted Mysteries themselves, the early mystic grades in the Church (these being derived from the Egyptian rites of Serapis in Alexandria) were progressively categorized as:

1. Catecomonoi (probationers)
2. Pistoi (disciples)
3. Photozomenoi (illuminated)
4. Memuemenoi (initiated)
5. Teleioumenoi (perfected)[62]

As we shall be considering the Master Jesus as an apparently current member of the Spiritual Hierarchy of Adepts in a later chapter, and as in yet another we shall be dealing with the dispute as to the connection between Jesus, the Christ, and the Lord Maitreya, we shall leave further discussion until then. In the meantime, it is worth mentioning in passing that Rome-based Christianity seems to have survived because it was willing to act politically in taking on a very large proportion of the Mithraic symbolism already highly popular with the upper classes and the Roman army. That is why the story of Jesus, in the developing Christian theology, adopted the following already existing Mithraic attributions:

1. That he was born on December 25
2. That he was born of a virgin
3. That he was a celibate
4. That he was a savior god[63]

At the same time his followers:

1. Were baptized with water
2. Viewed wine as sacrificial blood
3. Held Sundays sacred
4. Called themselves "brothers"

These are just a few of the Mithraic characteristics of the early Christian Church once it accepted a sort of metamorphosis, which enabled it to become the formally accepted main religion of the Roman state. However, there are many more, which would undoubtedly surprise Christians today. That is more particularly so among those not familiar with the actual history of the Church's early development after it separated from its gnostic origins in Alexandria. But we shall look at that too in greater detail later on.

MANICHAEISM

The gnostic prophet Mani (216–274 CE) (see fig. 6.14) identified himself with the Christian Paraclete and Holy Spirit, as well as presenting himself as the divine successor to Buddha, Zoroaster, and Christ. He also presented himself as the ultimate "seal of the prophets."[64] He lived in Babylon under the Zoroastrian Sassanid Empire and his concepts—based on supposedly direct inspiration from God—led him to initiate his own Mysteries. These involved "the two contrary and coeternal principles of Light and Darkness and the Three Times of their original separation, future and cosmic struggle, plus their ultimate future separation."[65] This is why he is today—rather superficially but commonly—regarded as a "dualist," despite his self-evident monotheism. He perceived his mission as a spiritual war to recover the light imprisoned in the darkness of the world,[66] and his syncretistic form of philosophy was intended to generate a worldwide religion but instead acted as a major thorn in the sides of Zoroastrianism, Christianity, and Islam for a thousand years after his death.

Fig. 6.14.
The prophet Mani

In Manichaeism, Christ was held to be a divine being who did not actually assume a physical body and whose incarnation, passion, and death plus resurrection were only symbolically carried out through his influence over the son of Mary. The latter was thus the one who actually suffered death on the cross. This view was otherwise held by the Basilideans—a gnostic sect with Mithraic characteristics from Alexandria—who held that, at the crucifixion, the place of Jesus was taken by one Simon of Cyrene.[67] The same view is interestingly held even today among the Sufis of Istanbul (ancient

Constantinople), who, however, are not prepared to elaborate on the issue, according to my own personal sources.

ISLAM

Although the fact is little recognized, the religion of Islam was derived entirely from the aim of bringing peace among the Bedouin tribes of Arabia at a time when some of them were trying to move away from the nomadic desert life to a more settled urban existence. The prophet Muhammad very intelligently recognized that the Arab community held Judaism and Christianity in high regard because of having no single overall Deity of their own. This fact seemingly gave the Bedouin an innate sense of social inferiority.[68] However, by a stroke of psychological genius, Muhammad then (through a mixture of some knowledge of the Hebrew Old Testament plus an apparently divine intervention) associated the Arabic peoples as a whole with Ishmael, the son of the biblical (and entirely metaphorical) Abraham and his concubine Hagar. Ishmael had been "cast out into the wilderness," just like the Arabs, thereby simultaneously providing them with a ready-made ancient patrimony, as part of the overall Divine Plan, thereby ridding them of their sense of inferiority.

Muhammad further cemented this in two ways. The first of these was the (truly gnostic) idea that Islam meant complete surrender to the Will of God (as reportedly transmitted by the archangel Gabriel to him) and the second was the suggestion that, as Arabic had been used by the archangel in teaching him, Arabic was effectively a sacred language. Against such statements of fundamental principle, there was no ready argument from within the Arabic speaking community at large.

It is otherwise worthy of suggestion—given Islam's particular type of monotheism following that of Judaism in particular—that the Arabs owe their own name to their probable land of origin, archeologically ancient Harap-an (hence Arabia from Harap-Ea) in northwest India. This was itself adjacent to Pali-stan and Iaodheya (or Yahudheya), the latter being where the ancient Jews (the Iaos or Yahus) also seem to have originated. In addition, prior to Islam (the worship of Al-Lah, the Creator) becoming general among the Arabian tribes and spreading elsewhere, the Arabs (like the Greeks and Dravidians) worshipped a triple ancestral pagan female divinity—the "three sisters," al-Lat, al-Uzza, and Manat.[69] There is good reason to equate this same trinity with the archetypal Divine Trinity of all ancient philosophy and religion—the equivalent of Father, Son, and Holy Spirit. The second "sister" appears to be a corruption of al-Ursa (probably the Great Bear constellation), while the third "sister" Manat appears just as clearly derived from the Sanskrit manas, which is itself directly associated with the third person (Brahma) of the equivalent Hindu trinity. The fact that Al-Lah is very definitely defined as "the Creator" also confirms (despite modern Islam evidently being unaware of the fact) that he (as with the Father in Christianity and also Jahve-Elohim in Judaism) is demonstrably equivalent to the Demiurge of the neo-Platonists and sundry others of a generally gnostic persuasion.

As otherwise suggested elsewhere in this book, the religion of Islam is just at the point of beginning to experience its own equivalent of the Christian Reformation. As a result of the important research work done (and the books written) by Professor John Wansborough at the School of Oriental and African Studies in London, much written by Islamic authors over the centuries, the accuracy of which has for so long been taken for granted, is now under question by modern scholars. This includes much about Islam's actual origins and its subsequent history, and concerns even the interpretation of the Qur'an itself. Although such a detailed review is undoubtedly necessary, and will inevitably continue for decades to come (despite much resistance from within the orthodox Islamic theological community), this is not the place to deal with it. Serious students are, however, recommended to pursue their own research in order to give themselves a broader picture of this whole field of concern.

OTHER SACRED TRADITIONS

The traditions already mentioned here are merely the better known ones of today. Others involving, for example, the Chinese and the north and central American traditions can, with careful consideration, all be shown to follow along exactly the same general paths, although with their own highly characteristic variations. For example, the deeply enigmatic Chinese Taoist philosophy (the Way) system taught (in its earlier stages) the psychological reconciliation of all apparent duality based on a fundamental unity of existence, while its apparently older cosmological system—which quite possibly derived from Tibetan origins—used winged dragons (instead of more occidental serpents) to depict influences suggesting aspects of kosmic desire and kosmic mind (see fig. 6.15).

Fig. 6.15. Mystic Chinese dragon

What has been dealt with here correspondingly involves a merely outline attempt to show that the Mystery tradition, to date, has been universally twofold in nature. That duality involves a closed esoteric/occult "school" system on the one hand (for individual spiritual training of those capable) and an apparently more open religious Creation tradition on the other, involving widespread graphic symbolism and imagery, for general public use and devotional reference. As we shall see from the later chapters of this book, however, humanity now finds itself awakened to a third approach, in which, potentially, the "school" is intended to become much more open as well as rationally accessible to those willing to make the necessary effort. This derives from the sequentially combined theosophical work of H. P. Blavatsky and A. A. Bailey, each acting as secretaries to senior members of the Adept Hierarchy.

By now it is hoped that the reader will have come to a clear appreciation of the fact that all the ancient traditions saw and based their philosophies on the central metaphysical concept of the repetitive sevenfold system of being and consciousness within the octave of existence, which comprises and is expressed by the soul principle. In addition, all were based on the idea of there being but One (Unnameable and Unknowable) Divinity, an aspect of which generated the One Universal Soul from which all other souls derived their existence. So real monotheism long predates the traditions of both the pharaoh Akhenaten (who ruled 1350–1334 BCE) and Mosaic Judaism, which were essentially characterized by misguided attempts to literalize (or suprahumanize) Deity on behalf of their respective cults.

There is one final point that should be mentioned in relation to the issue of those initiations involved in the rituals of the ancient Mysteries, before we deal with the actual initiatory sequence facing the individual in his or her evolutionary spiritual development. It is that those Mystery initiations were merely representative, in order to imbue the inner consciousness with the deepest possible sense that a very real and most important spiritual progression was involved and taking place. This has been largely misunderstood by literalistic modern academic interpretation, which views these traditions as involving forms of sociopolitical elitism by which the local population was kept under psychological control by the wealthiest and most powerful. This is nonsense. The secret Mystery tradition initiations and associated rituals were of course originally devised by the Adept Brotherhood for local usage, in line with their own personal experience. However, these local organizations did not automatically lead to actual spiritual initiation, at least not in later years when these same traditions had indeed become progressively corrupted through being taken over by men and women devoid of any true inner understanding of the esoteric metaphor and allegory in the rituals being practiced.

In the next chapter we shall take a look at the historical progression that took place in giving rise to what we now call "Western Esotericism," a title given by the French scholar Antoine Faivre to the modern occidental manifestation of the ancient wisdom tradition. As we shall see, however, this historical sequence starts much further back than modern academia would generally be willing to acknowledge. That is because we shall look at it as if from the viewpoint of the progressive, behind-the-scenes influence of the Adept Hierarchy, in guiding and influencing the cultural and spiritual development of the last several thousand years.

SEVEN

THE "DARK AGES" AND THE RISE OF WESTERN ESOTERICISM

In the earlier chapters we considered in general outline terms the principles of celestial (i.e., astrological) cycles and the way in which they served to influence the involutionary–evolutionary sequences of Creation. In this chapter we are going to follow on somewhat in the same direction, but applying the principle in a rather more direct way, to the history of human culture and civilization. This is with the aim of considering why—over the last four to five millennia of recorded history at least—"things" have turned out (or appear to have turned out) in the way that historians tell us, in relation to the world's religions and philosophies in particular. However, we shall be taking into account a variety of issues and factors that the professional historian would either be completely unaware of, or would probably refuse point blank to consider. The main factor among these is that of the Spiritual Hierarchy positively influencing the course of human history as a whole "from behind the scenes."

As we also saw earlier, the involutionary sequence in any particular cycle involves the generation in new forms of whatever constituted the evolutionary development of human cultural psychology in the immediately preceding cycle. Therefore, our first question must be where we currently stand in relation to the present cycle and what that cycle might be. That should then help us to put the period of known history into some reasonable degree of focus by assessing whether known history has actually taken humanity forward in any real cultural sense.

Therefore, taking our starting cue from the spiritual tradition that all history takes place in accordance with the preplanning of the Guides of the Race, who are said to work strictly according to cycle, we can perhaps carry out some speculative dating going back even further into prehistory. This, however, will necessarily be by reference to zodiacal Ages, which correspond with the 25,920-year celestial cycle known to us as the precession of the equinoxes but which, as already mentioned, was otherwise known to the Ancients themselves as the "Great Year of the Pleiades."[1]

The beginning of the celestial year (the Egyptian Zep Tepi or "First Time" described by Robert Bauval and Graham Hancock in their book *Keeper of Genesis*) might be said to occur around the beginning of the Age of Leo, close to its cusp with Virgo, the last one being between 12,500 and 13,000 years ago.[2] Hence this celestial solstice is matched by an equivalent celestial solstice quite close to the cusp of Pisces and Aquarius, which we are currently approaching. It consequently follows that one of the two celestial equinoxes of this same cycle would logically have reached its midpoint during the Age of Taurus, about 6,500 years ago (approximately 4,400 years BCE). This date is of particular importance because our own modern historians and archeologists place the formal origins of human civilization (in Sumeria and Egypt) not very much later. Nineteenth century archeologists placed them at virtually the same historic period.

It is otherwise interesting to note the great importance placed by Judaism (itself borrowed largely from Babylonia) and by Celtic tradition on the four "fixed" signs of the zodiac, that is, Taurus, Leo, Scorpio, and Aquarius. In the Judaic tradition, the associated figures of the bull, the lion, the eagle, and man are to be found in the so-called vision of Ezekiel, representing the manifestation of Deity. In the Celtic tradition, it is in these same signs that we find the four main festivals of each year: Lughnasad, Imbolc, Beltane, and Samhain. But when we look at these same signs in relation to the angle of the Zodiac relative to our own Earth's solar orbit, it quite quickly becomes clear that our planet's own solstices and equinoxes coincide with the greater celestial solstices and equinoxes just mentioned. In fact, the celestial winter solstice appears to coincide with the Age of Leo and the celestial summer solstice with the Age of Aquarius. It is then the latter that we currently approach.

We obviously know nothing about the history of the previous precessionary cycle of 25,920 years, which would have commenced some 42,000 years ago. However, we do know that the Egyptian priests indicated to the Greek historian Herodotus (484–425 BCE) that their civilization was well over two precessionary cycles in age,[3] that is, going back between 60,000 to roughly 90,000 years. Blavatsky otherwise confirmed from her own sources among the Himalayan Adept Hierarchy that ancient Egyptian civilization of the Delta began nearly 100,000 years ago,[4] perhaps set up, as I have suggested elsewhere, by the very ancient, red-skinned ancestors of the Tuaregs or Dravidians—peoples of originally late Atlantean stock.

Now, if there is indeed a Macrocosmic-microcosmic parallel in the cyclic unfoldment of human culture and civilization, as esotericists suggest, then these numbers of years should not cause us undue anxiety. This is notwithstanding the fact that they fly in the very face of modern anthropological dating. The latter, because based on very limited archeological findings, cannot (as yet) conceive either of a *Homo sapiens sapiens* much older than 200,000 years or of even primitive human urban civilization commencing much more than 10,000–12,000 years ago. However, I have dealt with these issues already in my previous book *The Rise and Fall of Atlantis* and so will not go over them again here. Our immediate concern, after all, lies purely with the current precessionary cycle and humankind's further progressive development within it.

A FRESH APPROACH

In pursuing this idea, what I am now about to suggest will be regarded by many readers as somewhere between entire speculation and completely wishful thinking. However, it is based on a logic that is completely natural to esoteric thought and follows in the tracks of the ancient Vedic ideas of the human as a "sevenfold plant" (*saptaparna* in Sanskrit), thus that the cycle of human civilization and culture must naturally parallel the celestial year and its associated "seasons." Our own Spiritual Hierarchy would be very aware of this cycle and would thus necessarily be directly constrained by it because of the very nature of the celestial influences available or not available to them during its various parts or stages. That logic involves the fact that what happens on our Earth is merely a shadowy replay and correspondence of what takes place within the parallel psycho-spiritual (hence celestial) world of being.

Hence, we might suggest, our Earth year of twelve months is a microcosm, contained within a celestial year of far greater magnitude. The last celestial "spring" equinox having taken place around 6,500 years ago (4,400 BCE), at or around the beginning of the Age of Taurus, as already suggested, we can perhaps imagine the last celestial "winter" coming to an end a little beforehand. Within that winter period, the "germs" or "seed souls" of human redevelopment for the next cycle would, quite naturally, have been carefully protected by our planetary Guides, together with the "hardy perennials"—those already well on the spiritual Path. Thus the first external signs of the renewal of human civilization would logically have occurred at around the same time as the celestial spring equinox, as just described.

In *The Rise and Fall of Atlantis* I suggested that the two celestial solstices of the Great Year of the Pleiades were inevitably accompanied by worldwide cataclysms. These were generated as our planet responded to the acute pressure generated on it by our whole solar system decelerating during its approach to the greater equivalents of the longest and shortest days of our (sidereal) year. The worldwide disruption to daily life, agriculture, and trade would have been almost unimaginable, particularly in relation to the celestial winter solstice period. It was at around this same time, some 12,500 years ago according to Plato, that the last Atlantean island of Poseidonis (together with widespread other landmasses around the world) was destroyed by huge volcanic and earthquake activity prior to its complete oceanic submersion.[5] From what Blavatsky otherwise tells us, it was also from around this time that the ancient Mystery Schools of the previous Great Year "went underground," in order to prevent their secrets from "leaking" out in the succeeding period of inevitable social chaos.

It would be wholly unrealistic to conceive of human civilization and culture recovering and returning to normality relatively quickly after such a prolonged period of worldwide cataclysm, which would have decimated human life and property on a really grand scale. However, some monuments (e.g., ancient Chaldean and Central American ziggurats, as well as Egyptian pyramids and some temples) would undoubtedly have survived from the previous historical cycle, to be taken over by the new civilizations, thereby explaining their lack of a new archeological "learning curve."

Therefore, the natural logic following on from this is that the next 6,500 years would necessarily have involved a prolonged period of basic cultural reorganization, plus spiritual retrenchment, as well as due preparation for the next era. In other words, it would have been an involutionary period. This might then perhaps be regarded as having a parallel correspondence to the underground root development and "rising of the sap" within the plant kingdom, which takes place between the winter solstice and the spring equinox. However, the celestial spring equinox occurs in the zodiacal Age of

Fig. 7.1.
The Assyrian bull-god
(courtesy of the British
Museum)

FIG. 16 - THE ASSYRIO-
BABYLONIAN KABIRI-BULL

Taurus and not on the cusp of Pisces and Aries. Perhaps that is why the first reemergent cultures, on a worldwide basis, had the bull and its associated fertility cult at the center of their various religious symbolisms?

It makes wholly logical sense that, with a new generation of humanity, a new psycho-spiritual cycle of human culture would inevitably involve the necessity for a sequentially new re-presentation of Divinity. That in turn is based on the logical assumption that human culture and its higher perceptions must themselves evolve in due sequence within any greater cycle. So, if the worldwide Atlantean cataclysm of 12,500 years ago reduced the overall human culture of the time "to ashes," so to speak, the idea of spiritual evolution back toward a divine state would itself have had to restart using very basic sociopsychological paradigms. In line with that same suggestion, the external regrowth of human culture and civilization might perhaps have been according to a sequence such as the following in relation to religious developments.

Ages	Religious Developments
Age of Taurus (circa 4300–2150 BCE)	Reawakening of a new religious culture with an astrological/celestial orientation
Age of Aries (circa 2150–0 CE)	Awakening of an idolistic god-orientation
Age of Pisces (circa 0 CE–2150 CE)	Awakening of astral (devotional) orientation
Age of Aquarius (2150 CE–4300 CE)	Awakening of psychological (re-) orientation

As a result of this, it is suggested, we might find a parallel development of public religion perhaps coinciding with the following sort of sequence:

Age of Taurus

Celestial/star worship, generating religious imagery of kosmic gods and involving allegorical stories of their interactions and escapades to awaken the subconscious spiritual nature.

The general use of mass external public ceremonials and ritualistic worship openly led by the initiated priesthood.

Widespread religious symbolic use of the sacred bull and cow to draw a direct connection with the constellation of Taurus (and also the Pleiades).

Widespread symbolic use also of the undying Sacred Flame. At this stage the Mysteries and the public religion would probably have been kept completely separate.

Age of Aries

Solar worship, involving the symbolism of solar fire and the concept of the gods descending to Earth to interact with humans, thereby generating the Age of Heroes and Demigods.

At this stage, the Lesser Mysteries now opened to involvement by the general population.

The Ram symbolism appears in Judaism (and in Egypt), the Mosaic rejection of the "golden calf" indicating the spiritual urge to move on from the influence of the Taurean Age.

Exoteric religious priesthoods now appear.

Age of Pisces

The era of "lunar" orientation—that of the Mother aspect in Nature, this thereby generating mystic forms of religion in which the masses were able to participate in direct worship of Divinity through the mediation of their priests.

The suggestion of God-incarnate-as-Man.

The Lesser Mysteries discarded now in favor of open temple/church ritual. The real (higher) Mysteries cease to exist except in the few ashrams of initiated Adepts.

Initiation of individuals remains deeply esoteric but wider public education becomes increasingly evident as a prelude to the New Age.

Age of Aquarius

Our humankind arrives (through mass education) at the point of a
personal Self-realization of direct progressive connection with the
spiritual and divine in Nature.

Man at last recognizes himself (semi-scientifically) as an ensouled
spirit—a potential god.

Old style temple/church worship accordingly becomes completely redundant. The new mass religion is invocative, based on a "scientific" (that
is, rational) focus on the underlying group psychology of Nature.

The "initiations of the threshold" gradually become exoteric. The spiritual cycle of evolution now proceeds openly.

On the speculative basis that these concepts are taking us in the generally correct direction, let us next imagine the "flowering" of human culture in this greater cycle having taken place at some time during the Ages
of Taurus and Aries, between about 4300 BCE and the current Piscean
era, the latter commencing, so it is thought, some two thousand years ago.
This covers the academically recognized era of the great historic civilizations of the Middle East—India, Persia, Chaldeo-Assyria, plus Babylonia,
Egypt, and Greece. That would then have been succeeded by a preliminary
period of "fruiting"—during the last two millennia—eventually producing the worldwide culture of the present era. However, as every gardener
knows, not all the fruits on the tree come to full term because the tree
always produces more initially than it eventually needs or can sustain.
Consequently, at a certain point, it sheds large numbers so that the rest
can survive and mature properly. That, it is suggested, is roughly the point
at which we stand today, when the world population has reached an all-
time unsustainable high of some seven billion people—another highly
interesting septenary situation.

THE TIME OF REORIENTATION

The psycho-spiritual development of humanity since the celestial spring equinox has thus progressed under the influences of the zodiacal eras of Taurus,

Aries, and Pisces. Perhaps unsurprisingly—in view of the progression from spiritual to mental to astral—the mass religions during this time have been correspondingly orientated toward the sustaining of purely personal human values and aspirations. Thus Divinity has been increasingly seen in terms of a purely superhuman "God," transcendentally set at an inconceivable and permanent distance from humanity by often politically-motivated religious theologians, and given particular characteristics to maintain separative social mores. However, we now (in the forthcoming Aquarian Age) face an evolutionary move toward a conscious development of coordinated subjective faculties, with their much more directly spiritual orientation and focus on the wider group, involving all kingdoms of Nature.

Consequently, the general polarization of human consciousness has to shift in direct correspondence. No longer will the unfoldment of human civilization and culture be orientated from the transcendent to the immanent, but rather from the lower back toward the higher. That is why, it is suggested, the Spiritual Hierarchy must itself now (by Divine Law) externalize and mingle with humanity once again, as described in A. A. Bailey's works. It is also why spiritual initiation as a wholly natural process of evolution has had to be openly described and explained, as a preliminary to that same (necessarily gradual) externalization process. With that in mind, it is suggested, the sequence of progressive psychological preparation of humanity over the last 6,500 years by the Guides of the Race begins to make much more rational sense.

Human spiritual tenacity develops as a result of experience and frequently harsh testing. That same inner tenacity is vital to the continuity of evolutionary progress. However, without some form of helpful educational orientation, humanity has no way of knowing which direction to follow, any more than a child does at school in the earlier classes without the help of teachers. It is because of this that each new generation of humanity (taking such a "generation" as equivalent to a 26,000-year cycle) needs the help of the Spiritual Hierarchy who, in turn, devise systems of teaching and experience in the form of culture and civilization, involving both religion and sociopolitical interaction.

During the Age of Taurus, it would appear that nascent humanity's religious teaching involved a purely mystic approach. This had a definitely celestial orientation, inculcating the basic concept that divinity appears cyclically on Earth, although "seeded from the stars," and that it is therefore in this same direction that humankind must maintain its subjective orientation and psychological commitment. Unsurprisingly, it seems to have been in this era that astrology was at the core of religious worship. During the succeeding Age of Aries, very roughly between about 2100 BCE and 0 CE, we find the orientation changing to the fulfillment of human interest via more general involvement of the population in the Lesser Mysteries. During the past two thousand years, the emphasis has changed again, this time toward a theoretically transcendent Deity and a humanistically orientated sense of good and evil, although right and wrong still involve (to many) an equally theoretical Devil. To the more humanistic, this has been rejected in favor of personal responsibility and civil law. The overall emphasis in all this has been to develop in man a sense of his own inner nature and faculties, thereby gradually liberating him from the thrall of purely mystic experience and subjective superstition.

In each instance, however, the original subliminal direction has been largely misinterpreted by humanity, resulting in all sorts of distortions. The celestial symbolism of the Taurean era seems to have given rise to idol worship; the Mysteries of the Age of Aries produced the appearance of priestly politics, widespread intertribal warfare, and the dehumanization of women; the humanism of the last two Piscean millennia has produced the divorce of philosophy, religion, and political government, plus (more latterly) the rise of rational science and technological materialism. All of these, however, are now increasingly apparent as a result of our capacity to analyze history from a present-day standpoint, where past errors of judgment more clearly stand out. However, continuing with the astrological association, let us take a moment or two to examine in slightly greater detail what has taken place over the last two millennia of the Piscean Age, as follows.

Each zodiacal epoch of 2,160 years is esoterically divisible into either seven parts of roughly 300 years each or three parts, each of 720 years. In relation to the latter, the first sees the implementation in cultural form of the understanding achieved in the previous epoch; the second sees its adaptation; the third sees its disintegration, precedent to the new and forthcoming cycle. This progression is akin to the sequence of involution–evolution–devolution mentioned in earlier chapters. Thus we can see in the last third of the Age of Aries (itself a sign of renewal in the overall zodiacal cycle), the progressive breakup and loss of influence of the Mystery Schools, which would themselves have originated at the very beginning of that same Age, some 4400 years BCE.

In the current Piscean zodiacal epoch, the Christian religion—with its emphasis on theology and mystical surrender on one side and political evangelism on the other—also started to disintegrate in the final, third stage commencing in the fifteenth century with the rise of humanism and the Renaissance. Interestingly, Islam (with its own sense of mystical surrender to "God")—in its own era of 2,160 years—has just commenced its own final 700-year subcycle of synthesis and disintegration after 1,400 years. Its own "Reformation" is itself now underway with a vengeance and will undoubtedly continue for at least the next century. The fact that this is the last of the three "Religions of the Book" is also indicative of a major, all-round change in the world of orthodox religion.

The progression within these religions helps to confirm that the zodiacal cycle itself—which is only one of many different length cycles, each of different purpose and value—appears to be specifically orientated toward the progressive evolutionary cycle of human consciousness in the mass. In other words, public religion has been the main type of vehicle for developing human inner awareness. However, that is now giving way to the development of science-based psychology and a general familiarity with its use in all sorts of highly unethical ways, which themselves breed a dual sense of uncertainty and moral independence. That same general sense, it is suggested, would have been regarded as inconceivable only three to four hundred years ago.

THE SUBCYCLE OF NECESSARY DISINTEGRATION

Historians tend to regard the "Dark Ages," so called, as having commenced more or less with the eventual dissolution of Plato's Academy in 529 CE, by edict of the Roman Emperor Justinian, in deference to Christian political pressure. However, from the rather wider perspective of the esotericist, they actually started much earlier with the degeneration of the sacred Mystery Schools themselves—in particular those of India, Egypt, China, Persia, and Greece. It is difficult to date the degeneracy in India although it appears, quite logically, to have happened in parallel with the increasing rigidity of the caste system and the feudal self-isolation of the Kshatriya (warrior) and Brahmin castes as they broke away from a great and previously existing Indo-Persian civilization. In Egypt, it seemingly began with the so-called Intermediate Kingdoms beginning as far back as the third millennium BCE, when descent of the royal line was taken over by the ruling pharaoh from the previously ancient morganatic (mother-to-daughter) system and turned into a father-to-son dynastic system. In China, where the Mystery School involved the dragon religion, it apparently occurred at least one millennium BCE; in Persia, perhaps around 1500 BCE. Finally, in Greece, it seems to have commenced some several centuries before the time of Pythagoras (late sixth century BCE).

As we have already seen, the disintegration subcycle of the Age of Aries commenced some six to seven hundred years BCE with the appearance of Gautama Buddha, his spiritually reorganizing influence being closely followed by those of Lao Tse and Pythagoras in particular, followed by Confucius and Plato. That was then followed by the usefully destructive work of Alexander the Great (356–323 BCE), whose warring efforts cleared the way for major social, religious, and political changes throughout the Middle East and the eastern Mediterranean. Behind that same destructive work and the eventual creation of the entirely new city of Alexandria as a cultural and philosophical "melting pot," itself accompanied by the international Buddhist evangelism of the great Indian emperor Asoka (304–232 BCE),[6] we can see (it is again suggested) the renewed influence of the Spiritual Hierarchy. However, what happened next is, I suggest, not quite so apparent to historians who tend to see only the objective effects of underlying causes. Let us see if it can be explained, or at least suggested, in logical terms, as follows.

The purpose behind the advent of Gautama Buddha clearly involved the restoration of a subjective order in our planetary consciousness following the destruction of the last bastion of Atlantean consciousness some 12,500 years ago, as Plato describes. What Plato did not describe, however, was the much further extent of geological cataclysm around the world that simultaneously accompanied the submergence of Poseidonis, as mentioned a few pages ago,

Fig. 7.2.
The emperor Asoka

or the fact that it was due to the conclusion of a major celestial cycle. As we have just seen, the new celestial cycle duly reached its vernal equinox during the Age of Taurus and the consequent reexpansion and acceleration of human cultural growth then had to be redirected into a new (definitely post-Atlantean) channel.

It was seemingly only then that the spirit known to us as "Gautama Buddha" arrived on the scene—by divine (i.e., higher celestial) Purpose, so we are told—evidently in order to reorganize and revitalize the Adept Hierarchy of our particular humanity first of all. They naturally describe him as "the patron of all the Adepts, the reformer and the codifier of the occult system."[7] The Hierarchy itself, by that time, seems to have organically produced no initiates higher than that of the fifth degree (Master of the Wisdom). However, this latter statement needs to be explained by reference to the suggestion that each greater solar cycle produces its own humanity in response to Divine Purpose, our particular humanity having first appeared on Earth some eighteen million years ago, according to the tradition described by Blavatsky's magnum opus, *The Secret Doctrine.*

According to the same tradition (at least, as described in the later works of A. A. Bailey), the individual known to us as Maitreya Buddha was the most advanced of our particular humanity.[8] As speculatively suggested elsewhere in this book, it was probably because he (while still only a Master) and other leading initiates could make no further purely self-generated progress in their own evolutionary development, that Gautama—an Intelligence from a far more advanced Hierarchy than ours—appeared in order to make that advance possible. On that basis and also because of Gautama's own achieved subjective connection with the planetary center of Shamballa,* following his own attainment of *moksha* (liberation), this subsequently became established fact. By inference, it seemingly did so through the extraordinary and simultaneous alignment of his consciousness with that of Maitreya (the latter apparently overshadowing the body of Jesus and embodying the bodhisattvic Christ principle in fullness), which took place some two thousand years ago, thereby heralding the Piscean Age.

THE EFFECTS AND THEIR DISTORTED REPORTAGE

The effect of this—following the same logic—was seemingly threefold. First of all, so we are told, Gautama achieved full spiritual liberation as a Dhyani Buddha, or Interplanetary Spirit,[9] although still connected with our planet by virtue of that initiation still being incomplete. Secondly, Maitreya, the formative Christ or Bodhisattva, became a human Buddha, with rights of direct access to Shamballa at all times. Thirdly, the initiate Jesus (directly overshadowed by the Christ consciousness of the Chohan Maitreya) took the fourth initiation and became an Adept.[10] However, so we are also told, it was the Christ (not Jesus) who, in this manner, indirectly aligned humanity with Shamballa itself, thereby himself achieving the first stage of "God" consciousness on behalf of our humankind, in a manner that we shall endeavor to describe in further (but necessarily outline) detail later on, in chapters 13 and 14.

It would appear that a small part of this truly amazing story subsequently became available to the outer world through somehow being made known to those lesser initiates of the time subsequently known to us as "gnostics." One of these was the apostle St. Paul whose latterly derived

---

Shamballa is the fabled dwelling place of the divine Kumaras (great Intelligences who are the real Guides of our planetary Life as a whole), said to exist in invisibly ethereal substance somewhere to the north of the Tibetan plateau. For more about Shamballa, please refer to appendix B.

gnosticism is clearly evident from several of his own reported statements,[11] although he unfortunately endeavored to place undue emphasis on the concept of blood sacrifice rather than on resurrection—a legacy still with us today. In that sense, Christianity owes more to his brand of fiery evangelism than it does to the more compassionate nature of Jesus's teaching and the example of the Christ. However, even St. Paul's teachings took time to take root.

As will be explained in more detail in a later chapter, the psychological independence of most gnostics—despite involving idealism and personal behavior of the highest order—quickly came into direct conflict with much more materialistically (and politically) orientated early Christian individuals. The latter wished to set up a formal "church" with its own orthodoxy and its own internal hierarchy of bishops and deacons. It is their historical successors who were subsequently very happy to fall in with the political aims of the Roman emperor Constantine in making a literalized Christianity the sole religion of the empire, in order to help him maintain social coherence and the rule of religious law and order. Hence the origin of the Roman Catholic Church, which is essentially a political institution, despite its religious "clothing."

It is because of this partial literalization of the full story, as suggested here, that later Christian theologians became so confused with setting up their own orthodoxy. As a direct result, we have subsequently been misguidedly saddled by them with the idea of Jesus as the Christ on the one hand and, on the other, with the even more absurd concept of the "Christed" Jesus being God manifest. The other curious and even later addition to this theological "camel" is the concept of the wholly allegorical Sophia (Divine Wisdom) borrowed by eastern Christianity from the gnostics and materially translated into the humanized concept of the Virgin Mary by Roman Catholicism.

ST. PAUL AND THE NEO-PLATONISTS

The development of neo-Platonic and neo-Pythagorean philosophy centered on Alexandria also saw a separate error of judgment on the part of their protagonists, who seem to have seen it as a major opportunity for reviving the Mystery School setup. Whereas the whole essence of Platonism involved an outward movement toward greater public dialogue, which directly incorporated reference to hitherto esoteric issues (including natural philosophy, the precursor to modern science), some neo-Platonists seemed to have seen this as moving too far too fast as far as the masses were concerned. In their view, the masses did not possess the intellectual potential to follow their concepts. However, in explaining themselves in writing, they unknowingly initiated the academic movement that, from one angle, can perhaps be seen as an intermediate staging post between overt religious mysticism and covert metaphysical philosophy.

It is therefore hardly surprising that the early gnostic Christian movement, under the main influence of St. Paul (himself apparently an initiate of the Great White Lodge*), came into direct conflict with those who were politically motivated. St. Paul evangelically set about conveying the idea that there should no longer be a question of secrecy in the following of religion by the masses, that everyone should be regarded (and taught) as having direct subjective access to God. The basic follow-on from this, of course, is that priests or intellectual intermediaries were also unnecessary. However, that idea failed to materialize among the members of the early Catholic Church. It was also, in one sense, a direct threat to the then expanding, mainly male-dominated Mithraic intelligentsia of the time, the latter following a semi-secretive and hierarchically organized initiatory system.

The Mithraic and Christian movements eventually attained a roughly equivalent degree of political influence throughout the Roman Empire, with the former looking as though it would probably be the final political victor.[12] As we now know, however, the Christian movement eventually took the upper hand by virtue of political maneuvering on the part of the Emperor Constantine, who made it the only religion of the empire and banned all others. This occurred at a time when Rome was so saturated with "New Age" movements and "Mystery Schools" in open conflict with the idolized worship of traditional Roman gods that it seemed as though the whole basis of Roman social culture was in extreme danger of falling apart. It appears

---

*The *Great White Lodge* is formed of self-evolved Spiritual Adepts through the influence of the Will-to-know produced by the Planetary Logos of the Earth.

as though the very openness and simplicity of worship promulgated by the Christians carried the day quite effectively.

However, the great problem facing the leaders of the Christian movement from the outset was that Christianity possessed no obvious theology to contrast with that of the neo-Platonists, so they had to set about creating one. This they did by progressively absorbing elements of various other sacred (gnostic) traditions from India, Persia, Egypt, and Greece, with which we are now very familiar, as well as building on their sacred sites.

Among these, as we have already seen in chapter 6, were the ideas of the virgin birth of the god-man (the Christos), his crucifixion, and his rising from the dead. However, whereas all these in their original form involved sacred allegories, the protagonists of Christianity literalized them all in the single figure of Jesus, thereby giving them a huge public relations advantage when presenting their doctrine to the still spiritually ignorant and devotionally gullible masses. The other, almost inevitable, backward step was that the leaders of the Christian movement turned themselves into a hierarchy of priests, with senior bishops and deacons who then began squabbling and politicking among themselves over the centuries, over which theological issues were generally acceptable to provide a united front to the rest of the world. More of this is dealt with in chapter 13, where we also look in greater detail at the issue of Jesus and the phenomenon of his supposed Christhood.

THE EFFECTS ON NEO-PLATONISM, NEO-PYTHAGOREANISM, AND GNOSTICISM

With the rise of an "orthodox" Christianity and the fall of neo-Platonism and gnosticism in general under the Roman Empire, progressively from the fifth century CE, it is hardly surprising that publicly accessible esoteric philosophy went into a period of steep decline, lasting for several centuries. The fragmented remains of neo-Platonism and neo-Pythagoreanism, plus the equally fragmented remains of ancient Egyptian sacred philosophy, seem to have been transferred eastward, first of all to Edessa in Mesopotamia, under the Nestorian or Eastern Church. Here a scientific and philosophical school existed until the late fifth century CE, when it was closed down by order of the then Byzantine emperor, Zeno.

Such studies then progressively moved to the intellectual center of the Persian Sassanid empire at Gondhishapur, near Baghdad, where students (from Greece and all over the Middle East, even from India and China) paid particular attention to research in medicine, mathematics, philosophy, and astronomy. These subjects were later continued under the banner of Islam, possibly through the intervention or involvement of Sufi Adepts, Sufism having long predated Islam itself, as we have already suggested. What remained of "natural science" in Alexandria and elsewhere in the West consisted for a while of pockets of alchemical practice and other unnaturally isolated aspects of what subsequently became known under the general banner of "magic" and "occultism." That then diversified in the mid-eighth century CE with the extended influence of the Umayyad Caliphate into Andalusia (Iberia), as will be described in greater detail later in this chapter.

In the West, however, small isolated pockets of neo-Platonic and neo-Pythagorean thought and written works persisted here and there. The Greco-Egyptian, Hermetic *Stobaeus,* which resurfaced in the seventh century CE, remained generally well known and very popular throughout Europe particularly because of its cryptic message "as above, so below," thereby perpetuating the understanding that all magic was based on sympathetic association. Yet further west, one of the most important medieval works, *The Key to Nature,* came from the Irish monk Duns Scotus Erigena (1265–1308 CE), the first Western philosopher to use the term *theosophia* to describe any system of hermeneutically based association between Macrocosm and microcosm. Despite appearing to be an Aristotelian, he wrote about Macrocosmic Nature (the World Soul) having a structured existence based on different qualities of light; believing in God as a process of self-revelation in which every creature will ultimately be redeemed, he also taught that the human being, just like the World Soul, contained all the essences of Creation.[13]

Erigena's contemporary, Meister Eckhart (ca. 1260–1327) (see fig. 7.3), believed in Man being a trinity of spirit, soul, and body, which, as Joscelyn Godwin observes, is also the foundation of the concept of spiritual alchemy,

Fig. 7.3. Meister Eckhardt

Fig. 7.4. Paracelsus

where the process of change takes place within the soul.[14] He was followed by Nicholas of Cusa (1401–1464)—a Catholic cardinal, strangely enough—whose ideas included the fact that each level of the universal hierarchy of beings contains all possible reality, in each case from a different aspect.[15] Such a spectrum of concepts provided a highly fertile soil for the later European Renaissance, despite what Stephen Hoeller refers to as "the unholy alliance of Semitic moralising which invaded and conquered Christendom by way of the works of Thomas Aquinas."[16] They resulted in the appearance of other comparable but basically Hermetic ideas, such as those of Paracelsus (1493–1541) (see fig. 7.4), who obtained at least some of them (in the field of healing knowledge and practice) from his own travels in the Middle East.[17] However, further fertile soil had already been provided over preceding centuries from other directions.

THE POST-SEVENTH-CENTURY ERA

As suggested at the outset, the whole point of this chapter revolves around the central idea that the history of our constantly changing world culture owes much to the behind-the-scenes influence of the Adept Brotherhood. It is their concern constantly to generate a sense of evolutionary direction in the consciousness of humanity's intelligentsia. This is achieved by the incarnation of often widely scattered lesser initiates of the Spiritual Hierarchy (like Paracelsus) who unconsciously pursue certain aspects of the overall Purpose with great vigor and idealism. Such an interaction is only possible, however, through these lesser members of the Hierarchy—who are not even aware of what is taking place—being psychically sensitive to the suggestions put to them by the wider ranging Intelligences of the Adepts and responding by applying their own personal force. It is they, therefore, who are responsible for initiating and pursuing the great cultural movements, which later historians then merely record. Let us now consider (necessarily rather briefly) the efforts of some of these.

With Christianity having been adopted on a wide front by northern and western Europeans, the Adept Hierarchy seem to have turned their main attention to finding a natural block to stop its further and too early expansion. That appears to have resulted in two main effects. First of all, with the decline of Roman authority, a tremendous resurgence of the Tuareg and Berber tribes of northwest Africa took place, eventually extending from beyond the western end of the Atlas Mountains all the way to Egypt. In my book *The Rise and Fall of Atlantis,* I have described these tribes as the remnants of the empire of pre-Roman Carthage, among them the Tyrrhenian "Sea Peoples" and "Barbarians" who continually caused the Egyptians and Romans (and even Alexander the Great) so much trouble with their constant warring incursions.[18]

One such incursion led, at the very beginning of the eighth century CE, to an invasion and occupation of the Iberian peninsula by an army of Berbers and Tuaregs from northwestern Africa. They were apparently from Mauretania, hence their becoming known as the "Moors," although some modern historians irritatingly and quite mistakenly refer to this as a "Moslem" or "Arab" invasion. Interestingly, it seems to have been these same very tall, red-skinned "Tuaregs" from northwest Africa who evolved (phonetically, as well as literally) into the "Tuareks" or Turks who subsequently founded the Ottoman (originally Atum-man or Atman) Empire, which originated in Egypt. The latter fact is, however, contrary to orthodox history, which curiously sees the Turks as an oriental race, despite their non-oriental features.

When the prophet Mohammed (570–632 CE)—also apparently an initiate of the Great White Lodge[19]—managed to bring the warring Bedouin tribes of Arabia under localized control during the seventh century CE, he did so by means of the psychological constraints inherent in the laws of Islam, which he founded. One particular aspect of his teaching seems to have caught and spread like wildfire among neighboring neo-Carthaginians and others. That aspect was the idea of complete surrender to the Will of God. In addition, because Islam quite deliberately derived much of its authority from the Old Testament, shared by Judaism and Christianity alike, it is quite clear that Mohammed saw his efforts as orientated toward peace and friendship between all "Religions of the Book." This is quite clearly confirmed by the Qur'an. However, Mohammed's teaching that Jerusalem was the second most holy site in Islam—together with the Byzantine Empire's refusal to give Islam access to it—later caused war between the two to break out. In the eleventh century, Moslems took control of Jerusalem, leading to the Christian world retaliating by starting the Crusades in order to regain it.

THE MEDIEVAL ERA

In Spain and Portugal (ancient Al-Andalus), the further continuing invasion from the south—this time by Islamicized Berber and Tuareg armies on behalf of an Umayyad Caliph from Syria whose mother was of Iberian parentage—resulted in the founding of the first great scholarly libraries and universities of western Europe. That is because the Caliph sent literally hundreds of Dionysii (stone masons and other craftsmen builders) needed to construct the associated public buildings—their much later successors extending their work to the first great European cathedrals. Through his innate idealism, the Caliph gave free access to the scholarly institutions to Christians and Jews as well as Moslems from the outset. This was continued by his successors for several hundred years. This again (it is suggested) was because of the background influence of the Adept Hierarchy. It was as a direct result of this—particularly in the Caliphate of Córdoba—that

Fig. 7.5. Roger Bacon

great scholars such as Albertus Magnus (1193–1280 CE), Raymond Lully (1235–1315 CE), and Roger Bacon (1240–1294 CE) were able to bring elements of ancient knowledge of esoteric and occult tradition into the field of Western thought as science, much of it through the medium of alchemical philosophy.

Similarly, a parallel explosion of interest took place in the field of Kabbalism among the Spanish community of Jews, mostly arising out of sudden Messianic hopes.[20] This later translated itself into the appearance of a Jewish nationalism in northern Europe—mainly in Poland and Germany. Regrettably, perhaps because Córdoba under the Caliphate actually overtook Constantinople as the largest and wealthiest city in Europe, the same broadmindedness and willingness to share failed to materialize between Christians and Moslems as had happened in relation to the then still holy places in Jerusalem.

Islam having originally been generated with the idea of a religious cooperation between "peoples of the Book" (the Old Testament), as just described, it was unfortunate that humanity (in this case, mainly originating with the Christian West) yet again managed to distort the original intention through greed and suspicion. As a result, centuries of mistrust and outright belligerence between Christianity and Islam have needlessly followed. The reaction of Christianity to the Moslems and Jews of Andalusia, resulting in the former being driven out by war and the latter by wholesale expulsion in 1492, followed the same regrettably paranoid pattern of behavior. Modern historians have not helped in this matter. Their general failure to draw proper distinctions between truly ethnic Arabs on the one hand and the Berbers, Tuaregs, and other tribes of northern and northwestern Africa on the other—all because Islam requires the common usage of Arabic—is really deplorable. It has caused wholesale distortions of the true history of the Near and Middle East.

However, Judaism and Islam have also suffered extensively as a direct result of selfish distortions of original truths. Judaism (or, these days, Zionism to be more accurate) has continued to perpetuate the entirely false idea of the "chosen people" when, in fact, the "children of Israel" so-called, owe their name to the Vedic term *Asur(a)* plus the Semitic El, thus meaning the semi-divine spirits of all humanity; thus Israel being derived from *Asur-El*. The name *Zion* is itself also borrowed. It appears to have been an etymological corruption of the Tibetan *dzyan* (the same as the Sanskrit dhyan), meaning the perfected spiritual state in which the semi-divine (i.e., monadic) nature of Man is to be found. It also continues, in parallel manner, to be obsessed with the idea of "Jewishness" as a supposedly ethnic characteristic when in fact it is only a religious one, as described at length by the Israeli historian and author Shlomo Sand in his recent book, *The Invention of the Jewish People*.[21]

Islam, on the other hand, has allowed itself to remain largely stuck in a Middle Ages mentality. This has occurred by virtue of: its psychological obsession with the territorial success and magnificence of the medieval Caliphates and the Ottoman Empire; its obsession with a legal system (*Sharia*) based on hierarchically acceptable and largely feudal precedents; its largely secondary and extensively patronizing view of women; and its continuing tendency to turn a blind eye to various degrees and forms of slavery, all these being more obviously prevalent in some countries than others.

Interestingly, Islam has also unconsciously retained elements of other religious influences predating its own origin. For example, the mystic word *ALM,* which we find at the beginning of various chapters of the Qur'an, appears to have been derived from the invocative Sanskrit *AUM*[22] and was originally used to denote an initiating appeal to Allat, the "universal Mother" and immaculate "Virgin of the Heavens."[23] This is so even though the deity of modern Islam has no female aspect. Such facts, however, have been progressively overlooked by modern theological scholars because of their uncomfortable origins, just as certain originally gnostic terms and concepts have been deliberately excluded by Christian theology. It is because of these characteristics that the forthcoming "Reformation" of Islam, which has already started, will be of particular interest over the course of the next two hundred years in particular.

European civilization and culture has "grown up," not just as a result of its own largely selfish and clumsy efforts, but also because of Christianity's (often grudging) willingness (frequently forced upon it by politico-economic influences) to evolve from within and thus move on from old, self-limiting ways and past mistakes. It has also come to demonstrate (after much historical pressure) a willingness to entertain and discuss different philosophical and religious viewpoints in public. In Judaism and Islam, open discussion of such matters is, for the most part, still "not done."

For these reasons, we find that the predominantly Christian West—despite its dreadful modern tendency toward materialism—remains as yet the most generally open-minded and thus most capable of absorbing new and wider spiritual truths and of adapting ways to make them part and parcel of modern life. The way in which that has taken place, however, has been for the most part tortuous and often quite unnecessarily bloodthirsty. Paradoxically, however, it seems to be entirely because of the conflicting philosophical extremes within which Christianity has operated that European civilization and culture, in containing them, has managed to thrive and evolve.

Christianity itself has had no easy ride. Physically threatened with periodic invasion by ferocious eastern European and Mongol tribes between the fifth and fourteenth centuries, it also faced Berber and Tuareg (i.e., Saracen) territorialization from the south in Spain, Sicily, and the Balkans. The eastern expansion of European trade links (via Venice) and huge increase in mercantile wealth only really got under way in the fourteenth century. However, it is only since the fifteenth century that Western Europe has begun to develop a gradually more settled sense of its own character, once the threat of invasion from the East and West had finally been negated by concerted military action.

MODERN OVERSHADOWING INFLUENCE OF THE ADEPT BROTHERHOOD

It is obviously very difficult to even speculate about the precise range of ways the Adept Hierarchy worked behind the scenes during and subsequent to the Middle Ages to motivate western Europe toward greater political and economic unity. However, what is clear to the modern esotericist is the fact that specific psycho-spiritual Ray influences have been brought to bear since the Renaissance. These projections of archetypal kosmic influence, emanated downward into the field of our planetary Life by our particular Logos, have exerted themselves in the following general fields of human interest and endeavor:

Ray 1—Political development
Ray 2—Public education and interest in knowledge
Ray 3—Commerce and cultural innovation
Ray 4—Psychological development
Ray 5—Scientific research and technological development
Ray 6—Religious ecumenism
Ray 7—Industrial development and associated social reorganization

It would take far too long to analyze the history of the last six to seven hundred years in relation to each and every one of these, but we can perhaps suggest some examples by implication. It is also worth mentioning that the Renaissance itself was preceded by the monastic system becoming a focus of Adept attention. This involved the Hierarchy, from behind the scenes, encouraging the training of increasing numbers of young men and women in the West in the art of meditation and the pursuit of academic learning and research. Without that intellectual foundation, it is highly unlikely that the

Renaissance and the later Enlightenment could have happened. Even so, by implication, it would seem that the effects of this type of monastic tutelage were somewhat fragmentary. We are nevertheless told that, toward the end of the fourteenth century, such efforts received a major boost to motivation in a longer-term direction by the orders of Tzon-kha-pa, the doyen of the Buddhist Adepts, to the Spiritual Hierarchy. These orders were for them to make a serious, combined effort to enlighten the barbarian West during the latter part of each century. Thus followed the European Renaissance.

ORIENTAL INFLUENCES
AND THE SPREAD OF KNOWLEDGE

The sudden appearance in 1460 of ancient Hermetic texts from the Byzantine Empire in Florence sparked a Europe-wide revitalization of interest in esoteric and occult philosophy, particularly in the fields of spiritual alchemy and kabbalism.[24] Initiated by Pico della Mirandola (1463–1494), it was closely followed up in Europe by others such as Johann Reuchlin (1455–1522), Johannes Trithemius (1462–1516), and Cornelius Agrippa (1486–1535). The spread of their thought was in turn aided and accelerated by the sudden appearance of machine-based printing (by Gutenberg in Europe in 1455 and by Caxton in England in 1476), thereby allowing the mass production of books and wider access to classical knowledge, political and psychological ideas (such as humanism and democracy), and discursive cultural thought, plus the pursuit of antiquarian and scientific research, among the lay intelligentsia of the time.

The sudden reappearance of Hermeticism also gave rise to the reemergence in Europe of interest in occult matters generally. These included magical theurgy (echoing down the centuries from the works of Iamblichus and Pythagoras) plus alchemy, the latter from ancient Egypt too, although reintroduced via Spain by its Moslem rulers and sages as Al-chemiya. The latter, in Christian hands, rapidly evolved into "spiritual alchemy," visualizing man himself as the "lead" to be turned into "gold." This otherwise succeeded in reinforcing the mystical humanism of the time, which was eventually to dethrone the Catholic Church before itself developing a materialistic bent during the later Enlightenment, in pursuit of "rational" science. This same

Fig. 7.6.
Michaelspaker's
alchemical allegory

spiritual alchemy was nevertheless to carry forward the ancient esoteric teaching as to the sevenfold structure of Creation, as we can see from the early seventeenth century engraving in fig. 7.6, itself appearing with the sudden emergence of Rosicrucianism.

While all this was taking place, there had occurred the rediscovery of the Americas by Columbus (in 1492) and other voyages of discovery by Western explorers around the Atlantic and Indian Ocean rims in search of commercial trade with the Far East. That in turn led to greater and much closer familiarization with oriental religion and belief systems, which eventually resulted in a later wave of academic research that brought elements of such knowledge (particularly from India) back to the West, for example through the agency of the more mystically and intellectually orientated members of the East India Company.

Following Marco Polo (1254–1324), one of the earliest Europeans who took advantage of this opening up of oriental thought was Theophrastus Paracelsus, who created a sensation in the field of Western medical practice between 1520–1540, as a result of his display of occult techniques of both diagnosis and treatment. These he had clearly learned during his travels in the Middle East. Accompanied by his books and open Hermetic teaching, they flew directly and very antagonistically in the face of the then academically and Aristotle-orientated medical establishment, thereby initiating a completely new and more thoughtfully scientific approach to the whole field of medicine.

That in turn was closely followed by other early scientists such as Nicolas Copernicus (1473–1543), who published his heliocentric theory (already long known in oriental circles) in 1543, also to the great discomfiture of the Roman Church. That theory was of course "rounded out" by Johannes Kepler (1571–1630), who published his work on the mathematical laws of planetary orbits in 1609.

In the early sixteenth century the emphasis of Adept interest in European development seems to have moved also toward the field of religious politics, resulting in the split in the Roman Catholic Church in 1517 caused by Martin Luther (1483–1546), which gave rise to the Protestant revolution in Europe. He was then succeeded by the mystically and metaphysically orientated Jacob Boehme (1575–1624), supposedly the first of the modern "theosophers" (although in many ways Paracelsus has a much better claim to this title), who might be described as having almost initiated the humanistic psychological analysis of Deity.

Also in the early seventeenth century (in 1610) we otherwise see the sudden appearance of the Rosicrucian phenomenon, which inflamed the interest of the intelligentsia of Europe from one end to the other. This appeared to die a sudden death after only twenty years due to political machination. However, to this day, there lies a suggestion that the Adept Brotherhood—whose existence is described to some extent in the legend of Christian Rosenkreutz—were behind it and were themselves so surprised at the force and extent of public reaction that they decided to withdraw it until other balancing aspects of their program became properly and more formally anchored in the European mind. The development and formaliza-

Fig. 7.7.
Martin Luther

tion of Freemasonry in the late seventeenth and early eighteenth century is perhaps one example of the latter. Although generally assumed to be but a mystical outgrowth of European Craft Masonry, there is good reason—as A. E. Waite describes[25]—to suppose that it actually derived from the traditions of that far more ancient group known as the "Dionysian Architects." As we saw earlier, they (based in Syria) had themselves originated the great municipal building program in Spain in the Middle Ages, resulting in the great libraries and universities of knowledge attributed to Islam, although their own tradition was actually far, far older.

The seventeenth century then saw the beginnings of the real Enlightenment, with its focus on the world of semi-scientific, semi-philosophical rationalism, itself mixed with metaphysical influences to begin with. René Descartes (1596–1650) was among the first with his concept of the simple division of the world of existence into that of the human soul (the animal supposedly having no soul) plus the duality of mind and body. Baruch de Spinoza (1632–1677), one of the earliest scientific rationalists, then demolished the dualistic philosophy of Descartes with the highly occult observation: "Matter and Mind are but two finite manifestations of one infinite substance which may be capable of an infinite number of other finite manifestations of which we can and do know nothing."[26] He thereby unconsciously paved the way for the humanistic materialism of the later Enlightenment.

Spinoza was quickly followed by Wilhelm Leibnitz, already mentioned in an earlier chapter because of his fascination with "monads" and the way in which mind caused the process of individuation in matter, thereby generating forms. Leibnitz was otherwise the architect of differential calculus. At the same time, we see the appearance of Isaac Newton (1642–1727) and his objective work in various fields of physics.

THE MODERN ENLIGHTENMENT

Also in the mid-seventeenth century, in England, we find the secretive formation of the "Invisible College" by enthusiasts in the field of "natural science." This was shortly thereafter succeeded by the founding of the more formal and publicly recognized Royal Society, which in the later seventeenth century foreshadowed the beginnings of a modern scientific research establishment. We then have the age of technological invention leading to the Industrial Revolution and the rapid rise of economic materialism. We also have the American and French sociopolitical revolutions, heralding the rise of political democracy and the concept of socialism. In the late eighteenth to mid-nineteenth century we see the sudden reappearance of interest in practical occult science—via a combination of Archimedean engineering and alchemically orientated chemistry—plus various forms of Spiritualism. The latter—originally derived from the visionary researches of Emanuel Swedenborg (1688–1772)—swept the Western world like a new religion, forcing skeptical humanists to look for other and more materialistic answers to human development in the fields of geology, archeology, and anthropology. This was, in turn, closely followed by the work of Franz Anton Mesmer (1734–1815) in the field of healing and hypnotism, confirming the existence of invisibly parallel states of being and forces (electricity and magnetism), which could be accessed by rationally logical techniques once the accompanying psychology was understood.

All this and more in these same and other accompanying fields of science then heralded the dramatic appearance in 1875 of modern Theosophy, uniting East and West plus ancient and modern thought in historical,

Fig. 7.8. Swedenborg

religious, scientific, and philosophical terms. Thereafter, in the late nineteenth century, the immensely important sciences of atomic physics and psychology emerged, giving rise to the appearance of radiation and cosmology on the one hand and anthropological-cum-ethnological research on the other. These were then duly followed in the twentieth century by the equally sudden rise of the worldwide ecological movement, of internationalism, plus preliminary interest in and development of space travel.

These are just a few of the major modern impulses that appear to have been quietly initiated or inspired by the Adept Hierarchy from behind the scenes. However, their effects have been nothing short of dramatic, helping to turn western European civilization and culture from mystic medievalism to a scientifically orientated psychology and also a definitely broad internationalism within the short space of seven centuries. There are of course those who will scoff at this idea and query why one should believe that such developments would need the assistance of the Adept Brotherhood in the first place. However, careful consideration of human psychology in the mass should very quickly show that humans predominantly resist all change and that, left to themselves, very quickly revert to type. We only have to look today, by way of example, at the inward tribal psychology of the hill peoples of modern Afghanistan and Pakistan, plus those of large parts of Africa, to see how "family" politics precludes a development of society at large toward the wider vision. It should be added that the same backward tendencies lie not very far below the surface even in the supposedly far advanced cultures of the West.

We should also mention here that, by virtue of their refusal to force humanity in any particular direction, the Adept Brotherhood are in no way involved in the initiating of intrigues leading to wars. Having said that, humanity's own stupidity in generating wars (instead of sorting things out by peaceful means, through discussion and negotiation) often leads to the appearance of situations involving crisis and change, where the subsequent influence of the Adepts can be made of remarkably effective and innovative use. There have been many such events over even recent years and, although today's political organizations are not prepared to invoke their assistance, because of continuing adherence to formal religion, we can perhaps envisage a time in the not-too-distant future when this might change.

NINETEENTH- AND TWENTIETH-CENTURY OCCULT MOVEMENTS

Some passing mention should perhaps be made in this chapter of the Golden Dawn movement which, in some ways, appears to personify the modern approach to occultism, although its own interest lay in the field of ritual magic, which is a very different thing altogether, much more limited in scope. Appearing in the 1880s at the same time that Blavatsky was setting up her Esoteric Section of the Theosophical Society, its three founders— W. W. Westcott, S. L. MacGregor Mathers, and W. R. Woodham—had all previously been members of other movements, including the Theosophical Society and the Freemasons. However, their fascination with magic (and ritual magic in particular) sets them very clearly apart from both these other mainstream movements, each of which focused on the principle of brother-hood, although from different angles. The self-styled Golden Dawn "Magi" in fact applied the principle of initiation in a very limited manner by lacking reference to the wider range of spiritual concerns—as have modern Rosicrucians and Freemasons (in the short term), together with a range of far less knowledgeable "cults" of rather doubtful significance.

Some further passing mention should also be made here of Freemasonry (the English Grand Lodge having been founded in 1717), because of its core principle (like that of the Rosicrucians) of an interdisciplinary brotherhood, directly linked to the intelligentsia of the era. Within its movement, Freemasonry was concerned not only with the practice of a ritualized esoteric philosophy guiding its increasingly scientific orientation, but also with that firm sense of brotherhood, in pursuit of an altruistic as well as a philosophical ideal. However, devoid of the practical responsibilities and ideals of Dionysian Craft Masonry, its intelligentsia (more particularly in Europe) managed to become entangled in all sorts of political and financial webs of national and international intrigue. That in turn—particularly following the widespread fascination with ancient Egyptian culture in the late eighteenth and early nineteenth century—led to a more than somewhat self-centered fascination with colorful initiatory ritual and public ceremonial, just for its own sake. This is yet another area of human distortion that remains to be sorted out in the future.

Fig. 7.9. Main Chamber, Freemasons' Hall, London
(courtesy of the Grand Lodge)

In late feudal times, despite the basic Christian precept of "love thy neighbor as thyself," the ideal of common human brotherhood in Western society was a very limited phenomenon merely associated with the commercial guilds and literate intelligentsia of the time. The Theosophical Society, on the other hand, was concerned from its inception in 1875 to spread the principle of universal brotherhood throughout humankind as a fact of life in Nature and not as a mere ideal, using knowledge of esoteric philosophy and occult science as an ancillary form of proof. When we look slightly further back into modern history we can see that this idea has developed over the last few centuries (since the 1391 "Peasants' Revolt" in England against feudalistic oppression) in hitherto limited because merely political terms, leading to the appearance of parliamentary democracy and the concept of "universal rights," as put forward by the UN and UNESCO. Over the last century it has become more widely accepted on a social or cultural basis, but it would seem that it still has a long way to go before it is generally recognized in the sense intended by the Adept Hierarchy itself.

The very direct involvement of the Adept Hierarchy in the literary work of H. P. Blavatsky, leading to the publication of both *Isis Unveiled* and *The Secret Doctrine,* must also be mentioned here as it clearly had the most momentous effect on nineteenth century scientific thought, particularly in the fields of anthropology, chemistry, physics, and astrophysics. When we look at the extraordinary developments in these fields alone over the thirty or forty years after publication of *The Secret Doctrine* in 1888, by comparison with the direction and speed of scientific thought in the preceding half century, we can see just how much acceleration has taken place in human intellectual potential. However, it is only now being realized that all such development actually owes its origins to esoteric philosophy. So, as that derives directly from the knowledge of the Adept Hierarchy, is it not reasonable to acknowledge their probable influence? And, if that is so, does it not then follow quite logically that more consideration needs to be given to understanding their capacities and role in helping with the evolutionary development of all the other kingdoms of Nature, as well as the human?

THE FUTURE

The new millennium is clearly one in which the natural interrelationship between all human beings, irrespective of their politics and religions, is being seen as the basis of a new world order. Such a situation has come about, however, not just because of media technology but because the psychology of our modern humanity has broadened and deepened quite extraordinarily. The principle of universal human rights and opportunity, irrespective of caste, creed, gender, and skin color, has become so successfully enshrined in our world consciousness as a pure fact of life that now to suggest anything to the contrary is immediately seen—at least in the West—as psychologically backward and socially antipathetic.

The old, restricted Eastern mystic attitudes and Western religious theology, perhaps ideal for their times, are now clearly being seen as having had their day and needing to give way to a broader spiritual perspective. It is for this reason that the West, with its more enforcedly open political, legal, and commercial culture, was—despite the associated materialism—made to become the main theater of interest. But the new world order and its civilization will of necessity be an international one, covering the globe in its entirety and uniting all peoples in a broadly common socio-spiritual culture.

What we now see in front of us, for the next few hundred years—not just the next century—will necessarily involve the natural rooting out of remaining backward cultures (both sociopolitically and spiritually) around the world. But this in turn will result in a retaliation (which has already started) where the current of expansive modernization is crudely let loose without due thought for traditional spiritual issues being taken into consideration in concert with the needed political changes. Major change—particularly that initiated on a worldwide front by the Spiritual Hierarchy—takes time to effect and settle down. In addition, the old spirituality and maternal culture of the East needs a new vehicle to contain and nurture it. At present, the West is not capable of providing it and much damage will be done before the West (the United States in particular) realizes it. It is because of Western Christianity's sociopolitical clumsiness and lack of wider spiritual perspective that both Judaic and Islamic extremism have been unconsciously encouraged in their development over the past fifty years.

PRESENT DAY POLITICO-RELIGIOUS CONFLICT

One of the major causes of current conflict in the Middle East, for example, is actually due to extreme (i.e., fundamentalist) American evangelical literalism, which has managed to persuade itself that it has a duty to help bring about the "spiritual apocalypse" allegorically described in the New Testament chapters of Revelations, with Jerusalem as the focus. As a direct result, working in concord with equally literal-minded and wholly self-centered Zionists (much to the astonishment of the latter), they are deliberately intent upon fomenting and encouraging Israeli-Palestinian conflict in every way possible. To the Western world, as presented by the journalistic media, this is not the way the current, supposedly "political" situation is usually presented, but it is so and it poses a great threat to world religious and political peace. This, however, is where the new and more open teaching on esoteric philosophy (particularly as regards the actual basis of divinity) comes into its own and where it must play a major (but very carefully passive) role over the forthcoming seven or eight generations in particular.

The Adept Hierarchy has made it clear that the intended new religion for the masses—somewhat described in chapter 15—will be based upon a spiritual science of ritual involving invocation and evocation of planetary and extraplanetary influences for the benefit of all kingdoms of nature, not just the human.[27] For that (eventually) to come about, however, it is essential that many learn the fundamental rules of esoteric and occult philosophy—but only after they have developed the highest capacity for universally altruistic and principled behavior on a day-to-day basis. There is no doubt that the Adept Hierarchy will be watching very closely to see how the present situation improves through the influencing efforts of those already "on the Path," working on their behalf.

This highlights the fact that what will be needed in the new era is an increasingly large caucus of spiritually motivated and esoterically knowledgeable people who will be seen actually to inspire through their lack of self-centeredness and their practical approach to both local and world problems. They will also need to show that they can be relied upon by the masses for what they represent and what they truly are. That needs to be considered on an international basis—country by country in some cases—although international religious and political affiliations will also doubtless play their roles as well. Bearing in mind the widely different stages of politico-economic as well as social development reached in some Third World countries, this is not going to be a simple or brief task and will require much patience and goodwill. Furthermore, an equally great problem facing a prospective sea change of this sort is that of the attitude of natural or self-induced mystics, whose very instinct is to resist that which questions their experiences. Mystics, however, are merely ecstatics who are not really interested in the "why?" of their transcendental experience. They are merely concerned with finding and re-pressing the "trigger mechanism" that gave rise to it, or otherwise of conveying a secondhand vision of it to others who are then left to interpret what they have been told as best they can. That thereby often foments further unhelpful religious division and argument. Consequently, that approach too needs to be very firmly set aside. In what ways these particular issues might be approached will thus be considered in the next chapters, covering initiatory progress itself.

PART THREE

The Stages of the Initiatory Path

EIGHT

MODERN SPIRITUAL PROBATION AND DISCIPLESHIP

According to the *Hermetica:*

> But those human souls that do not have mind as a guide are affected in the same way as souls of animals without reason. When mind connives with them and gives way to longings, the rush of appetite drives such souls to the longings that lead to unreason; and, like animals without reason, they never cease their irrational anger and irrational longing . . . for anger and longings are irrational vices that exceed all limits.[1]

It follows quite logically that the one thing animals do not possess but which is well within the capacity of human beings, if properly applied, is conscious self-discipline. It is the latter that is then the foundation of the Spiritual Path. Without the individual being able to demonstrate the use of conscious self-discipline to some positive degree, there can be no access even to the initial gate of initiatory probation. In ancient times—as for example those of Pythagoras—spiritual probation involved a period during which the neophyte had to demonstrate absolute obedience (in word, deed, and thought) to his Master, or guru. This always involved the test of silence—of not speaking until and unless spoken to, as well as a demonstration of willingness to fit in with the rest of the group and share their burden of mundane duties. Further although slightly later probationary tests involved other sorts of psychological restraint of all the physical appetites.

In the ashram of Pythagoras—who gathered his ideas from his time in Egypt and Babylon (the latter at the same time as the "incarceration" of the Hebrews)—probation involved absolute silence for the first two years of membership. As mentioned earlier, during this time, the neophyte did not even have access to the Master and was forced to listen to any talks from behind a screen.[2] Such discipline might appear to our modern minds as "over the top," but when the real reason for it is understood, this does not appear to be so after all. The reason is that the Master of such a group—who has overcome all personal karma on his own account—is said to take on a very real psycho-spiritual responsibility for all its members, effectively taking on a proportion of their karma, in proportion to their occult "distance" from him.[3] Because of the training program set by him, he creates a very real affinity within the ashram as a group because the group itself generates a characteristic consciousness of its own, with its own spectrum of knowledge and faculty. Because of this, he would allow progressively closer access to himself only after prolonged testing had shown that each neophyte could be trusted within the limits set for him. Any sign of real irresponsibility within those limits would be regarded as endangering the group as a whole and would thus result in the neophyte being forced to leave the ashram—usually on a permanent basis.

Every such ashram develops a certain psychomagnetic "atmosphere" and character of its own that, even though the junior members may not be consciously aware of it, helps to sustain and protect them psychologically, as well as physically. That, in fact, is a quite normal phenomenon in any group of human beings involved in a mutually sympathetic purpose or way of life, but—because of the spiritual potency of the Master himself and of his senior disciples—it carries with it a quite distinctively different quality and greater force in an ashram. If one draws the analogy of two teachers in a modern school—one being good at his job because of his effective and disciplined grasp of both his subject and child psychology and the other being poor at his job because of the lack of the latter—we can perhaps understand this rather better. The good teacher is respected and often revered for his or her capacity to convey knowledge in a useful and clearly caring but firm manner; the poor teacher shows little or no such care and firmness and is consequently "suffered" by the class but gains no respect from its members. Insofar as care on the Master's part generates trust, just so far will the group manage to hold together, like a family. This is so in both the spiritual and the mundane sense. However, it is very rarely even considered by guru-worshippers.

REQUIREMENTS OF THE INDIVIDUAL

The true Adept realizes that those who come to him for spiritual teaching and leadership vary widely in their instinctive capacities to assimilate what he has to offer. That is to say, some have a natural psychological resilience and inner strength that others—for various reasons—do not, irrespective of how long they have been in such training. Some seem to learn faster than others, because of what has been achieved in previous lifetimes. Others perhaps have to take things more slowly because they are still working off old karma. To generalize about individuals in such circumstances is dangerous and rarely accurate because we are all at varying stages in our own evolutionary development. However, one thing is certain—that it is not just a question of being "good" or reasonably altruistic that brings one to the gate of initiation. One of the first principles of gaining access to the spiritual Path involves putting our good intentions into practice all the time, not just when we feel like it. Nor does it happen by just dwelling on them, or otherwise by being incited to action by hope of any reward or recognition for such service to others. In occultism, sustained purity of selfless motive is everything.

Perhaps the most important other achievement of the neophyte is the proven capacity to pay attention and listen to what he or she is being told on its own terms. This might sound rather trite, but it is of very real importance. Most people tend to listen with "only half an ear." That is to say, their natural instinct is to interpret what they are hearing in line with their own existing prejudices or desires. They consequently fail to pay due attention to what they do not like to hear and thus do not act upon what is actually necessary for development of their own increased knowledge or faculty.

One of the most important aspects of teaching—particularly with neophytes—thus involves repetition in order to inculcate a firm understanding of the general principles of esoteric philosophy and occult law. Intelligent individuals come to realize that repetition of these same principles (from different angles) is of great value in broadening their perspective and deepening their insights. They consequently tend to enjoy being able to spot the principle before the teacher even enunciates the query or point at issue. The mind of the shallow individual, however, tends to shut off when hearing the same principle enunciated on different occasions.

The reason that (particularly vocal) repetition is so important in relation to general principles is that it is essentially magical in nature. That is to say, it builds up a broad and literal, subconscious psychic pathway between the outer brain consciousness of the individual and that of his or her own inner Self. This, because of its very breadth, permits a wider inner perspective to be developed, which can then be usefully used for all sorts of purposes, in both directions. Its very range generates the sense of interdisciplinary opportunity.

However, the repetitive teaching of "facts," so-called, is of a quite different nature (being much narrower) and achieves little of any real value because it does not extend as far subjectively. It links the brain consciousness only to the lower mind, the organizationally retentive part of which has to do with the intellect and the powers of merely logical reasoning. Whereas the former training builds intelligence, the latter does not. That is why it is so often found that many highly intellectual people are not really very intelligent, whereas many naturally intelligent people are not at all intellectual.

Very few people seem to realize that intellect, reason, and intelligence are quite different and that just as reason controls intellect, so true intelligence controls reason. However, in the fully "rounded" individual, there should be a strong link between all three. That is because as reason and intellect together produce merely academic faculty, so intelligence and reason alone tend to generate merely spectacular mental abstractions, of no real value or use to anyone. The lower mind is important as part of the neophyte's faculty because it acts as the traction engine to the will and purpose of the Spiritual Ego. The exoteric world has its own requirements and the Ego cannot motivate this lower world except indirectly, through that which acts as its direct agent.

One of the main reasons why so many academics and scientists usually fail to understand the principles of esoteric philosophy is that neither they (nor the majority of would-be esotericists) actually understand what has just been suggested. Much so-called "esoteric" thought is actually based on highly fragmentary or partial psycho-spiritual insights plus a mass of ancillary wishful or purely aspirational thinking. Consequently, it is difficult for them to convey their understanding in a manner that is considered reasoned or reasonable by most academics and scientists. The latter, in any case, usually tend to interpret most things in an entirely literalistic manner, consistent with extensive intellectual retention and organization of supposed facts, such that objectively assessed "laws" and "rules" take precedence over anything else. Small wonder that they usually fail to see eye-to-eye.

The further sign of the established spiritual probationer is surely that of his or her capacity to display a reliable consistency of behavior, basic common sense, a "broad-mindedness" to others and their views, plus a strong tendency toward unselfishly positive behavior in at least a general direction. When these characteristics become evident and the individual then demonstrates a firm psychological commitment of an idealistic nature, which proves the activation of his sense of altruism beyond any doubt, he is then ready to move on to the next stage of training, involving what is called "accepted discipleship."

THE NATURE OF DISCIPLESHIP AND ITS REQUIREMENTS

The term *discipleship* possesses unfortunately strong connotations of unthinking devotion to the personality of a particular Master, or guru. This, however, is merely the unfortunate corruption of an inner reality in which the neophyte commits himself to his own inner Self, or Spiritual Ego. That is because ideals (no matter how crude) themselves confirm that such an inner contact has been made. The Master or guru is merely the external reflection or confirmation of what the neophyte has sensed or perceived in his own higher nature. Those who allow themselves to adopt the purely devotional approach to a guru—as one so often finds in India, where spiritual corruption is sadly endemic—completely miss this point and thus treat their teacher as a mere psychological prop. The approach to Adeptship is marked by an ever-increasing degree of pure Self-reliance. This is seldom understood by would-be esotericists, but it needs to be much more effectively acknowledged. As Bailey's Tibetan Adept teacher remarks: "A disciple is one who, above all else, is pledged to serve humanity . . . and to change his centre of activity from himself (as the pivot around which everything revolves) to the group centre."[4] He is thus also "transferring his consciousness out of the personal into the impersonal."[5]

However, the true disciple has to demonstrate that he or she has a mind of his or her own and is willing to use it, while still acknowledging the teacher as guide. That is because the spiritual "learning curve" is a long and tortuous one, with inevitably many mistakes being made along the way. However, we learn only from our mistakes. Successes actually teach us very little, but they rather tend to "turn our heads" in self-congratulation and pride of achievement. The moment that this happens, we lose our way in a very real sense, even if that self-congratulation is only momentary. It results in a definite loss of psycho-spiritual momentum and the individual thus finds that he has to rebuild what he has just lost. This is why the ascetic sense—that involving self-denial—is so important. As the Tibetan Adept teacher again remarks:

> Be prepared for loneliness. It is the law. This must be endured and passed. . . . [Additionally] have patience. Endurance is one of the charac-teristics of the [Spiritual] Ego. The Ego persists, knowing itself immor-tal. The personality becomes discouraged, knowing that [its] time is short.[6]

SELF-DISCIPLINE
AND THE CONDITIONING RAYS

It has to be said, however, that self-denial and pure asceticism, if taken to extremes, also work against the further development of true inner realization—again because of pride. Asceticism is a psychological faculty that, in the form of self-discipline, causes the outer faculties to be restrained to such a degree that the much subtler sounds and other "signatures" of the planes of spiritual existence can be more easily discerned. Once this can be achieved (with associated powers of subjective discrimination), continuity of higher consciousness—even when in the physical body—becomes possible. Then and only then can the higher energies be made use of through the transformative power of the initiate, who learns how—through intelligent introversion—to draw them down for particular usage, for example in true spiritual teaching and also in healing at the psychological level. This is just not possible for the neophyte because he has not yet attained the necessary degree of spiritual Self-alignment. He thus has no experience of how to either recognize or otherwise discriminate between the extremely subtle energies and forces of these higher levels of being.

One of the primary and most useful factors that individuals can bring to bear, however, is a recognition of their own Ray type. This is based upon the concept that just as there are seven colors in the spectrum, so in the emanation of spiritual light from the kosmic plane of Mind there are seven refracted Rays. These then give rise to "types" through predominant psychological characteristics. Much has already been written definitively on the subject, but for our immediate purposes here the seven Rays are characterized as follows:[7]

1. The Ray of Power—giving rise to the initiatory sense of will and purpose behind all action, as well as the sense of protectiveness needed to maintain coherence. In practical terms it involves persistence (not just determination), and it is also objectively related to the worlds of law, politics, and government.
2. The Ray of Love-Wisdom—giving rise to the instinct that generates all forms of coherent sensitivity, association, or interrelationship and the wish to understand how these function. In practical terms this is objectively related to the worlds of education and healing.
3. The Ray of Active Intelligence—giving rise to instinctive adaptability to changing circumstance and the associated capacity to see and take advantage of opportunity where necessary. In practical terms this is objectively related to the world of business and commerce.
4. The Ray of Harmony through Conflict—giving rise to the tension needed to produce an abstract focus of combined attention and func-

tion. In practical terms this is objectively related to the worlds of philosophy, psychology, and of the arts.

5. The Ray of Concrete Science—giving rise to the analytical nature based on observation and thus to the organization of conceptual ideas of function. In practical terms this is objectively related to the world of rational science, engineering, and technological development.

6. The Ray of Devotion—giving rise to the capacity to generate and maintain an ideal. In practical terms this is objectively related to the world of religion and all belief systems.

7. The Ray of Ceremonial Magic—giving rise to the instinct to group/corporate organization and function. This is otherwise objectively related to the world of structured business efficiency and its negative expression, bureaucracy.

Once the individual is capable of assessing his objectively instinctive nature in relation to one or another of these Ray influences, thereby giving rise to his main personality characteristics, he subsequently discovers (although only very gradually) that his inner nature is in conflict with the outer one, the latter being progressively recognized as crude by comparison. That is because, although the inner nature is also influenced by the same Rays, the two natures are not synchronized. By then trying to discover more about his inner nature and also to apply its more refined characteristics—thereby gradually controlling the lower (elemental) nature—the internal psychological war increases until the higher eventually overcomes the lower. The individual has then, in turn, to master the higher (deva) nature. This is the essence of what esotericism calls "the Path."

There are a great many people today holding themselves out as "spiritual teachers" of one sort or another, particularly in the field of healing, despite having an actually limited knowledge and experience of the higher worlds. Some arrogate all sorts of supposed powers to themselves in order to fascinate the gullible. Others at least have the modesty to suggest that they are merely dedicated "channels" for healing energies and thereby make themselves available (with greater or lesser achievement) for transmitting deva energies, which they thus invoke. However, many of these pay very little attention to the absolutely necessary psycho-spiritual preparation and they consequently either fail outright in their efforts, or otherwise merely succeed in attracting low-grade elemental entities. These, unbeknown to themselves, invade their personal atmosphere and delude them through self-glamorization.

There are many reasons why an increasing degree of personal asceticism is incumbent upon the neophyte and then, later, the initiate. The few already mentioned merely represent the "tip of the iceberg." In a very real sense, psychological asceticism is the only method of psycho-spiritual self-protection, because increasing degrees of progress in this field generate corresponding increases in personal magnetism, which themselves attract the interest of increasingly subtle elemental powers. Hence the idea of the "razor-edged Path."

EASTERN AND WESTERN APPROACHES

It needs to be remembered that, fascinating though the Orient may be for its colorful mass of psycho-spiritual teachings and teachers, the latter represent from one angle the "vision of the past." There is absolutely no doubt that the principles enunciated in ancient teachings and Sanskrit texts continue to provide us with our "stairway to divinity." However, too many people make the mistake of imagining that the still attendant religious ceremonies and rituals found in the Orient are the only true way of attainment and that the West has little to offer, other than corrupted religion. This is absolutely not so. The Western world in the mass is firmly in the process of moving on from the purely devotional approach to higher consciousness, to an approach that involves a more mental correspondence, which is precedent to the conscious use of the intuitive faculty. This to some extent—peculiarly enough—involves activities within the world of commerce and industry. To many, however, this latter idea might well sound absurd and even fatally materialistic in its approach. In fact, that is not so and, as the vast majority of those at the level of spiritual probation and discipleship are involved in the world of business to some extent, it is essential that the new perspective be rationally explained.

Although it is generally assumed that the primary characteristic of business (at least in the West) is the profit motive, this too is not so. The main underlying characteristics are in fact tolerance, cooperation, and mutual trust. Without these three, commerce, trade, or business cannot even begin to function. Profit is itself both financial and psychological, the latter being of far greater importance. Financial profit is merely a pecuniary excess that, kept within reasonable limits, results in its wider sharing within and outside the community. Psychological profit—again, if treated properly—results in the building of character and tolerance. Trade and commerce teach people concentration, logic, self-control, and the necessity for both foresight and rational consistency.

Within the last few years, however, we have seen both national and even global financial "crashes" as a result of lax control and naked greed. What has happened has involved many people trying to achieve their material aspirations and ambitions unnaturally quickly and thus finding themselves caught up in a potent spiral of overenthusiastic activity, which contained forces completely beyond their control. Had they exercised greater self-discipline (or been forced to do so) in the first place, this would undoubtedly not have happened. Enthusiasm would then have been tempered by natural caution; then their success, although smaller, would have been much firmer. As it is, gross failure on the part of the relatively few has resulted in financial and psychological damage being caused to the many.

In the field of spiritual initiation, the same principles apply, as they do in Nature as a whole. The plant that is allowed to grow too fast upward in the shade or in mere moonlight becomes spindly and unable to support itself. It needs the sunlight to bear down upon it, so forcing a slower, spiral growth pattern, which generates more structural strength. Darkness and moonlight here are symbolic of the shady "underworld" in which purely terrestrial acquisition of space takes place. The Sun, on the other hand, is symbolic of the downward radiating spiritual emanation that forces the growing plant into a cycle of progressive maturity. Every stage of growth and outer development has to be followed by a parallel period of subjective assessment and testing during which outer growth temporarily ceases. During this latter period, purely subjective growth and assimilation takes place.

THE DEVELOPMENT OF POWERS

The quite natural inclination on the part of spiritual neophytes is to rush into the process of "reaching for the stars" and, in doing so, absorbing everything of psychic fascination that comes their way. Part of the task of the Adept teacher or true guru is thus to slow this process down, by constantly testing, thus forcing the neophyte to develop powers of discrimination and thereby to learn to focus on priorities, while also harmonizing the influences of the inner and the outer world. The attainment of specifically occult powers in the earlier stages of the Path actually acts as a direct restraint or a potentially severe distraction to the development of spiritual sensitivity. It is therefore to be avoided if at all possible.

Such powers will actually develop quite naturally further along the Path and will then be found much more easily controllable. This also might strike some readers as strange, bearing in mind that so many Westerners head to India, or Egypt, or Central America, for example, specifically to learn of yogic powers from well-known gurus and shamans. But one must again point out that nearly all these places, in spiritual terms, have reached (many centuries ago) a very definite plateau of development. Their own further evolution has largely ceased and been replaced by the darkness of superstition and prejudice. In nearly all such instances, occidental seekers have blinded themselves by a limited expectation based upon ritualistic glamour, itself based on ignorance of the wider psycho-spiritual perspective. This has frequently taken place either as a personal rejection of materialistic Western ideals or a lazy unwillingness to apply self-disciplined principles within Western commercial culture. Both involve so-called "dropping out" (frequently involving the use of drugs) and both inevitably result in disillusionment.

It is widely accepted among those with any real experience that the Western mind-set is quite different from the Eastern one, resulting in all sorts of misunderstandings between the two. In very general terms, the Eastern is more maternal. It assimilates everything and finds a place for it somewhere. The Western is masculine in nature. It tends to focus much more selectively on what is considered necessary and throws out what it deems to be unnecessary. What is now happening (on a global scale) is that the latter is becoming more generally predominant—rightly so because of the position in the overall sidereal cycle which we currently approach. However, the idea of East and West is itself completely misleading. The psychological distinction is a worldwide phenomenon and it signals an approaching schism between the consciousnesses of the outgoing Atlanto-Aryan mind-set and that of the coming Race.* As the saying goes, "coming events ever cast their shadows before them."

The true spiritual neophyte is no longer even remotely Atlantean in the orientation of his or her consciousness. Instead of being willing to sit in the shadow of a guru, many modern neophytes want to take a firm personal hand in their own inner development, while at the same time getting on with their outer life and its attendant responsibilities. But this presents as many problems (if not more) for the Adept or guru as it does for the neophyte. As a result, the technique of approach of the Adept teacher, so we are told, has itself had to change; but this has had to be accompanied by something of an external reorientation of the Western mind away from "tribal" nationalism toward internationalism or globalism.

THE INFLUENCE OF POLITICS AND JOURNALISM

Tit-for-tat politics are no longer acceptable. Instead, there is a growing public interest in wanting to share in the knowledge of what is going on at all levels and thus also wanting to know why decisions are being made and effected, even where not being directly involved. This again presents the teachers on the inner side with additional problems, although the change is welcomed because it arises from a very real evolutionary development on the part of humanity generally. However, like anything else in life, it has to be accompanied by complementary changes elsewhere and even this has to be followed by a necessary period of assimilation and adjustment.

A major adjustment of attitude also still needs to be grasped by our political leaders and those close to them, including (very importantly) the world of journalism. We (through journalism) tend to blame our political leaders for everything that goes wrong in the fields of social welfare and public finance particularly. However, that attitude rarely takes into account the fact that politicians are not only reacting to public opinion but also to what is being said about them and their decisions (or those of their civil servants) by journalists in newspaper and magazine articles in the first place. The latter quite frequently have very little to do with real public opinion per se,

---

*Please see appendix C regarding the Races of humankind.

but rather more with editorial desire to stimulate readership demand on the back of emotive reaction to a particular (often rather partial) presentation of supposed facts. Consequently, politicians generally mistrust journalists, while also recognizing that they need them to get their ideas across to the broad public. It is an uneasy symbiotic relationship, the results of which have to be rather more carefully considered by the reading public before jumping to often unfounded conclusions.

For the spiritual aspirant and initiate, the world of journalism is a mire of potential disaster. At present, spiritual aspiration outside of mainstream religion tends to be regarded with suspicion by most journalists as of "fringe" nature. That is because of its frequent association with volatile "New Age" fads, many of which are blatantly absurd, or rather more associated with merely self-indulgent "lifestyle" ambitions. This state of affairs unfortunately has to be endured while more serious approaches to spiritual development (which are, by definition, far less visible) progress quietly in the background, without so much distraction. However, serious modern books and articles (sometimes even TV documentaries) on related subjects do keep appearing and it is part of the nature of self-development that persistent personal effort has to be made to go out and find what is worthwhile taking up and studying.

One of the things that the persistent aspirant soon finds is that while some books contain a great deal of useful material on esoteric philosophy, others have very little, sometimes only a single gem or two of worthwhile but often unexpected knowledge within a whole book. This too is something to which he or she must get used. The expectation of all necessary knowledge being found in a few books is naïve. Even were it so, the individual would still have to study far more widely in order to develop an inner sense of perspective for purposes of interpretation. The deepest truths are seldom if ever to be found presented in clear-cut terms. The most worthwhile gems are always well concealed and unexpected.

THE RESPONSE OF HUMANITY IN THE MASS

Let us now turn from the individual human experience to that of humanity as a whole, because, as already mentioned, whole kingdoms of Nature also take initiation, although the technique involved is necessarily far more drastic than it usually is for the individual. That is because the mass inertia of the consciousness of any one kingdom of Nature is so huge as to require an effort or electro-spiritual charge that inevitably lacks any sort of personal discrimination. Thus it is that the Tibetan Adept DK makes the point that, as a result of the prolonged crisis in mass human consciousness that took place during the first and second World Wars (1914–1945), "the [human] race as a whole now stands at the very entrance to the Path of Discipleship."[8] This crisis—although presented as the inevitable result of the conglomerate karma of the human race over untold millennia—necessarily generated an invocative soul appeal for liberation from conflict and general world peace. This, we are told, was so powerful that it evoked the attention of the great Lives at the divine planetary center of Shamballa (see appendix B) responsible for the overall governance of our planetary Life. That in turn, so it would appear, produced the release of spiritual energies capable of bringing it about.

This highlights the fact that any higher faculty derives purely from the most powerfully evoked sense of NEED. Thus it is that human beings generally bring karma upon themselves through the twin principles of intense greed and fear, magnified by the faculty of the lower mind. Humanity as a whole now behaves in a very different way than a mere century or so ago because of the sense of internationalism now evident in its common range of interests. Although nationalism seems to grow ever stronger in many cases, no longer is this the case on the part of the reasonably educated common man or woman, where his or her personal interests are concerned. Because of television, radio, films, and the internet, humankind's range of interests has expanded enormously, resulting in such phenomena as generous financial contributions to charities and humanitarian aid becoming commonplace.

In addition, the general attitude toward the religions and beliefs of others is slowly but progressively becoming more open-minded and interested in understanding different points of view. Even sectarian religion is tending to produce a reaction against extremism and an ecumenical willingness to pursue the path of peace on all fronts. As Blavatsky had herself cryptically foretold over a century ago, humanity in the mass has now reached a point where final emancipation (i.e., distantly eventual Buddhahood) is becoming possible.[9] Hence it is that "the race is now at the point of development which warrants a complete change in the approach to divinity as taught by the

Hierarchy."[10] In other words, the mystic-religious approach to the development of spiritual consciousness in humankind, which has been adopted for tens of thousands of years, no longer suffices. A completely new approach is necessary, although one would imagine that, for the sake of continuity, some elements of the older system will continue to be used, until they are eventually phased out, or merely die out from attrition.

THE DEVELOPMENT OF A NEW
WORLD RELIGION

The way in which the prospective new world religion has been outlined for us involves two main fronts, as further described later on in chapter 15. First of all, we are told, the Spiritual Hierarchy itself—after many thousands of years of self-isolation—will once again move out into the open. The aim behind this outward move is seemingly that resulting from humanity in the mass effectively becoming part of its overall "organism." Hence, once this has taken place, there will exist not three spiritual relationships—involving humanity, the Hierarchy, and Shamballa—but only two. Shamballa (see appendix B), being the "House of the Father" (as Christ is reported to have referred to what orthodox religion believes in as "God"),[11] will then be able to influence the future of humanity directly, instead of only indirectly.

Secondly, humanity will itself become the Spiritual Hierarchy to the lesser kingdoms of Nature, taking progressively full responsibility for their further evolution. The field of modern science might be regarded as the precursor to this. For example, the skills and knowledge of the ecologist and naturalist are concerned with the maintenance of balance in Nature as between the animal, plant, and mineral kingdoms on the one hand and humanity on the other. Mankind, in this way, is already taking on board the primary ethical principle by which the existing Hierarchy works—that of assistance-with-minimum-interference.

It is interesting to note that in 1946 Bailey's Adept Teacher confirmed that

since 1925, the Hierarchy has directed its thoughts to men, but it has not vitalised, as it will eventually do, the religious movements or churches in all lands, or the educational work in all countries, or any of the activities which are concerned with the aiding of humanity through welfare movements.[12]

Yet, despite this, we now find that (since 1975) all of these movements are now in active service. International ecumenism and family welfare—particularly in the field of child education and poverty—are now at the heart of human concerns. Wherever natural disasters occur, we find an immediate willingness to dispatch practical and financial aid from one end of the planet to the other, irrespective of differing religious or political orientation. Could anyone living in the altogether self-concerned atmosphere of the early nineteenth century have possibly imagined such an internationally altruistic state of affairs?

UNEXPECTED DEVELOPMENTS

We are told that the great awakening of the human family that took place during the first half of the twentieth century (in response to work carried out by the Hierarchy during the preceding five hundred years) produced a major spiritual reorientation far in advance of what had actually been anticipated or planned.[13] It seems that where humanity stands now had been thought possible only about 2,300 years hence, early on during the Age of Capricorn—itself regarded astrologically in ancient times as the "Gate of Entry" to the spiritual world. However, the very speed of humanity's own change of subjective orientation has apparently generated inevitable problems for the existing Spiritual Hierarchy, logically necessitating its own radical replanning for the next two millennia.[14]

As a result of the increasingly obvious shift of attitudes in international public opinion over the last two decades or so, we can perhaps to some extent envisage some of the changes that must now almost inevitably take place. That same public opinion (although still selfishly orientated in the main) now increasingly, albeit falteringly, insists upon a general fairness and openness in the worlds of politics and social economics. That will itself eventually result in associated legislation to reinforce it. Overt extremism in any form is becoming increasingly less popular, despite the glamour generated by the various media industries. The idea that any one or two countries should rule the world through sheer military or economic force or threat is increasingly regarded as the view of a bygone age. Reciprocity is now increasingly the general accepted basis of political and economic discussion.

FUTURE INTENTIONS

One of the things that the Spiritual Hierarchy is evidently keen to see brought about is the eventual reunion of politics and religion[15]—a dangerously inflammable mix indeed. However, the world religion that they have in mind is quite different from the religious states that various so-called radical groups in several nations are currently trying to bring about—supposedly on behalf of Islam and just as misguidedly in Zionistic Israel. Consequently, it is small surprise to find that this ideal is being approached very slowly indeed, with much preparatory work in advance. The latter involves not only ecumenical discussion but also practical social adaptation through the absorption and integration of religiously orientated ethnic groups into Western society. This inevitably generates some social frictions, but that is an unavoidable stage of the blending process that must take place by not allowing "ghetto" mentalities to be produced.

The fact that increasingly larger masses of humanity now self-evidently stand at the very gate of discipleship and that this development shows no signs of slowing down is itself the precedent that evokes the requirement of the Spiritual Hierarchy to come out of its seclusion. For the Hierarchy to remain in seclusion in the face of humanity's own achievement would fly in the face of general evolutionary development itself—and is thus impossible. However, the magnetic potency of the Hierarchy is such that too quick a reintegration with humanity would produce a catastrophic overstimulation of the general human psyche.

The fact that the members of the Hierarchy are merely "Elder Brothers" who (through self-effort) have passed beyond the limitations of the purely human personality has thus to be established firmly in the public mind in order to avoid those merely emotional or adulatory reactions that would inevitably regenerate a regressive culture. At present, this is still some way from achievement because of the ignorant polarization of opinion as to their very existence and raison d'être. This has to be made more public by people who have a reasonably clear understanding of what they are talking about. That in turn must arise through a clearer understanding of the esoteric philosophy concerning metaphysical planes of existence, plus awareness of the true nature of the spirit and soul, so that these become psychological issues for open general discussion and no longer merely religious or philosophical ones. This is already in the early stages of progress through humankind in general having developed a fascination with human psychology. In the main, this is still very superficial in its orientation to mere personality, but, given time, that will change.

The fact that "accepted discipleship" must and before long will become the common psychological orientation for the masses of humanity, and that members of the Spiritual Hierarchy will eventually (but only gradually) externalize in public, does not detract from the fact that humanity will continue to need spiritual leadership and spiritual inspiration. That in turn means that humanity must, in due course, develop its own new political systems of self-government, each with a (spiritually) hierarchical sense of structure. However, this brings us back to the issue of the reunion of politics with religion—a reunion in which the clash of party politics must give way to the following of inspired (because selfless) leadership by those whose intelligence, experience, and personal example alone define their right to be considered fit for government. That too is some way from taking place although we can already see the positive public reaction to the occasional political figure who exemplifies these ideals.

It follows quite logically that those who will in the future be properly representative and organizationally fit for the future leadership and government of human society will have to be spiritually (not just religiously or politically) orientated as well as being also administratively capable. That in turn means that they will have to have progressed somewhat further along the Path than the mass of humanity; it is to the characteristics and requirements of these initiated individuals that we shall pass in our next chapter. Before we do so, however, there is one very important thing that we shall need to bear in mind in considering any real initiatory experience. It is that each one is very definitely progressive. That is to say, it does not occur all at once but rather involves two quite distinct stages, separated by the crisis of initiation itself. In a very real sense, these two stages are actually more important than the initiation itself. The reasons for this are worth closer examination.

CRISES OF DECISION

The first such stage involves the individual's Spiritual Ego generating such a particular and sustained focus of idealized intent in their subjective life that it brings about an inevitable crisis of decision. That same decision involves a positive recognition of what lies potentially ahead in the way of personal responsibility. This is consciously juxtaposed with an acknowledgment of the actual limitations of past experience. If the essential point of conflict is held adequately firmly and honestly in mind by the individual, then the initiation must itself automatically follow, even if not immediately. That is simply because it has to be incorporated into a readjusted subprogram of the Divine Plan. Anyone who believes that initiation immediately follows the achievement of a certain momentary attitude of mind is merely fooling themselves. The actual initiation and passing on of new spiritual knowledge only becomes possible after the individual's consciousness has settled down to some extent following the crisis and the confirmed taking of his or her decision to move on.

The second such stage—following the decision to proceed and thus to experience at first hand the new knowledge granted—involves learning how to assimilate that new knowledge and turn it into a usefully coordinated faculty. Just how long that takes will depend on the individual. However, in the first three initiations it would inevitably take many lifetimes, simply because of personal reaction against the disciplines of the first phase and then because of generating fresh karma due to over-relaxation of the personal self and consequent self-indulgence of the subjective nature. As Blavatsky very cogently and helpfully tells us:

To act and act wisely when the time for action comes, to wait and wait patiently when it is time for repose, puts man in accord with the rising and falling tide of affairs so that with Nature and law at his back and truth and beneficence as his beacon light, he may accomplish won-

ders. Ignorance of this law results in periods of unreasoning enthu-
siasm on the one hand and depression and even despair on the other.
Man thus becomes the victim of the tides when he should be their
Master.[16]

MEDITATION AND SPIRITUAL TENSION

Before moving on to the preliminary initiations themselves, a brief word
needs to be mentioned about the necessary discipline of meditation, because
without this the individual will not progress far. That is because the spiritual
Path involves a definite, subjective sense of reorientation and the generation
of a directional instinct, which just cannot be achieved by merely following
the exoteric path of humanistic cultural standards or religious morality, no
matter how finely developed they might appear.

One of the curiously related problems that is becoming increasingly
apparent in our own day and age is that of manic depression among highly
intelligent and usually creative people who erroneously believe that their
creativity depends upon living under constant psychological pressure to produce it. Because it has such little real understanding of the subjective nature
of man, orthodox psychiatry cannot begin to understand this condition and
mistakenly seeks to treat it using chemical drugs to slow down the euphoric
condition that precedes and leads to the problem.

If practitioners realized that the real problem lies in the individual's
wildly over self-stimulated imagination (i.e., in his or her astral or psychic
nature), resulting in inevitable downward mood swings to the opposite pole,
they would instead treat the subjective nature, involving the partial use of
meditational techniques. However, the treatment will not be easy because
those suffering from the condition actually enjoy the over-stimulated state,
which is actually and progressively leading them to insanity; they thus constantly reactivate it to their own unconscious detriment. Furthermore, their
irrational belief in the use of chemical drugs to alleviate subjective symptoms
can only make matters far worse.

In approaching the first three initiatory crises, regular meditation is
highly important because it not only develops the inner faculty of perception;
it also helps to develop a very necessarily balanced subjective momentum of

which very few seem aware. For that reason it is essential that the individual learns to apply a conscious regulation of the amount of time spent watching television or using the computer. Both of these, if permitted free license, have a very definite weakening effect on the individual's ability to use their visual imagination in a properly controlled manner—something that is crucial in our development of psycho-spiritual tension.

At this stage, the crises necessary for achieving that inner tension are brought about unconsciously (and with great discomfort) by the personal life because of its inherent lack of a correct sort of discipline. In approaching the higher initiations, however, it has to be achieved, so we are told, by an objectively focused self-direction in which personal idealism, as such, plays no part. That faculty of complete objectivity (generated by the achievement of a complete inner serenity) becomes critical because, due to the psycho-spiritual reorientation already achieved, the concern about acquiring a higher consciousness no longer exists. The individual is instead concerned with detecting an increasingly subtle quality of spiritual Purpose naturally allied to his inner nature—that is, that of his higher Ray type and group—and then maintaining that contact until he becomes fully at-one with it.

Imagination might help here to illuminate the combined point about spiritual tension and the ability to attain to increasingly higher degrees of it. Let us therefore imagine a series of graphic triangulations superimposed on the human body, the latter showing the progressively expansive soul organisms that Man's intelligence works through as we saw earlier in fig. 1.6. The horizontal base lines through each of the three major chakras are then symbolic of the base of consciousness (*upadhi* in Sanskrit) through which the individual works while awake. Most human beings—although unconsciously based in the heart center—function mainly through the solar plexus and sacral centers. The triangle in their case points downward.

However, the individual on the Path who has attained to that degree of self-discipline that constitutes "accepted discipleship" holds firmly and with full self-awareness to the consciousness base within the heart and endeavors to function positively through it. The initiate of the first degree, while still consciously based in the heart center, has managed to lock firmly on to the functional capacity to work positively through the throat center. The triangle of his operative consciousness thus points upward to that chakra. The initiate of the second degree has correspondingly managed to do the same in relation to the brow center, while the initiate of the third degree has done so in relation to the crown center.

However, the next stage—that of the fourth initiation—involves a complete change of psycho-spiritual orientation. That is because the consciousness base then shifts dramatically upward from the heart center into the crown center itself. By achieving this, the individual (now a junior Adept) correspondingly becomes again an "accepted disciple"—but this time on a higher Path, which will be described in greater detail later on. His fully self-aware base of consciousness is now permanently detached from the physical, although he still functions (in downward triangular fashion) through the brow, throat, and heart chakras in his dealings with others when necessary. He also retains a coherently functional contact with (and control over) the center at the base of the spine, thereby maintaining the animation of the physical body organism. As we shall see, however, he no longer has any need of the Causal Soul organism, which, in any case, has ceased to exist by the time of the fourth initiation. His main area of concern now lies within the sphere of the Spiritual Soul nature (the buddhic state), and within this he experiences a progressively widening range of contacts of which even advanced humanity has no knowledge.

In the next two chapters we shall go into greater detail concerning the various stages of initiation mentioned here. However, from here on, the serious student-reader of this subject would do well to keep in mind the practical necessity of attaining to each stage described through the achievement of an increasingly positive spiritual focus, which naturally generates an associated inner psychic tension. That same spiritual focus is much more difficult to attain than most might imagine (and even more difficult to retain). So, quite logically, it has to be associated with fulfilling a particular subjective aim allied to an exoteric objective. Thus by virtue of personal concerns no longer being of interest, the individual is drawn to finding a particular spiritual (but mundanely orientated) task to which he can dedicate all his efforts on behalf of others, while still maintaining his own immediate personal duties in terms of family and business or career. These must not be forgotten.

In the functional achievement of all this, the consciousness base of the lesser initiate temporarily and unconsciously moves upward toward the crown center. Through it doing so, he automatically (although still unconsciously) finds himself drawn into the sphere of combined Hierarchical effort on behalf of our planetary Life as a whole, with very positive personal karma accruing from it. This is of immense practical importance and highlights the altogether rational basis of selfless service in the operational functioning of the Divine Plan. That same service must, however, be allied to the consistent practice of meditation, because it is the latter that maintains and enhances the spiritual "anchorage" that provides each individual with their own innate inner power. With that in mind, it needs to be understood that the essential nature of meditation is that of persistently trying to develop a consciously greater sensitivity to the particular "signature" of a higher and wider substate of being and consciousness. This is a never-ending process, but once each such recognition is achieved, the individual can call upon it increasingly at will until, eventually, he becomes at-one with it and it, in turn, becomes an instinctive part of his overall range of faculty. This is the true, underlying nature of all spiritual development.

By way of adding to this idea that the increasingly higher substates of consciousness play a highly important role in the individual's psycho-spiritual evolution, because of their higher correlations, we are told that "when you have therefore built into your bodies—physical, emotional and mental—matter of the third sub-plane of each of those planes, then the Higher Self commences consciously and ever more continuously to function through the aligning Personality."[17] This makes more sense in light of the recognition that all true human Personalities are of fourth mental subplane matter while the vast majority of human causal bodies (the vehicle of the Higher Self) are to be found polarized in third mental subplane matter. Hence the suggestion that it is "only when third sub-plane matter of a certain percentage is contained in the vehicles, that the Personality as a conscious whole recognizes and obeys that Higher Self."[18]

Correspondingly, however—because the Higher Self is the expression of the Monad—the Causal Body of the disciple or initiate on the lower stages of the Path (i.e., during the first three initiations) is to be found polarized in second subplane substance of the Mind state. In parallel with this (or rather, precedent to it) the individual must build into his physical and emotional vehicles matter of the highest two subplanes of those states. That is because these two substates are respectively concerned with purification and subjugation.[19] As a result of this, there occurs an increasing subjective-to-objective alignment, which gradually enables the influence of the Higher Self to be more and more strongly registered in the physical brain consciousness.

DIETARY CONSIDERATIONS

The associated issue of diet is an important one, although it is not as immediately critical as many seem to think. There are literally tens of thousands of lesser initiates now in incarnation who are not aware of their spiritual status and who still include meat and alcohol in their diet. However, for anyone consciously wishing to pursue the spiritual Path, even in the informal modern Western style, the following facts need to be borne seriously in mind at all times. Alcohol in particular, to begin with—involving highly concentrated and fermented elemental essences of the plant kingdom—is extremely dangerous. That is because these essences (themselves of a very distinctive deva quality or order) give rise to immediately progressive destabilization of the natural psychic connections between the etheric double and both the physical body and the terrestrial soul, through their inherent overactivity. Over a prolonged period of time, because the individual can do nothing to counter the degenerative process, this leads to severance— and varying degrees of insanity. Alcohol, therefore, even in small quantities, should be avoided at all costs.

Meat carries with it the low grade psychic (i.e., astro-etheric) magnetisms of the animal entity in question and these then come into direct conflict with the individual's own magnetism, within the nature of the etheric double. However, the cumulative psychic effect is not so disastrous as alcohol. That is because meat eating merely reduces the natural sensitivity of the etheric double and so also reduces the natural clarity of transmission between the Higher Self and the physical brain, so necessary for everyday usage, as well as in meditation. The low vibratory quality of animal meat will also, to some extent, affect the individual's own astral nature, thereby causing yet further sensory disturbance, or even disorientation.

One should otherwise take into consideration that modern food processing involves the use or insertion of a wide variety of chemical processes, the magnetisms of which will also work their way through into the etheric double, thus diminishing its capabilities. It goes almost without saying that the actual usage of all chemically based drugs by the individual—for whatever reason—is progressively deleterious to the etheric double, no matter whether the individual is "on the Path" or not. The same is true of plant stimulants because they too disrupt our subtler etheric nature.

To understand why it should be that ingestion of such substances causes problems with the etheric double, it needs to be remembered that their chemical essences are all picked up by the bloodstream. As we saw at the outset, atoms, cells, and souls all involve the same principle in Nature, albeit at different levels of being. The blood cells—generated at the base of the spine center—are thus themselves the intermediary "vehicles" between the etheric double and the dense body organism, just as the soul is the psychic intermediary between the spiritual nature and the objective body. The terrestrial soul nature—working through its "root base" in the spine base chakra, defines the basic vibratory nature inherent in the cell. This is then modified within a given range by its journey around the human cardiovascular system, where it contacts a spectrum of higher influences generated by the other chakras. The associated memories are then registered in the heart chakra, which, as we also saw earlier on, is at the root core of the Causal Soul. It is thus from the latter that the essences of such experiences are registered (as highly subtle vibrations) and "transferred upward" to the Permanent Atoms within the aura of the Causal Soul itself. It is thus highly important that they are not externally influenced.

THE ISSUE OF FAITH

This is one of the most misunderstood yet, curiously, most important issues that the individual on the Path will face and its real nature needs to be properly recognized so that it can be adequately used or taken advantage of. In practical terms, there are three kinds of faith: (1) blind faith, (2) faith based on experience, and (3) reasoned faith. They work in the following general manner. Blind faith, first of all, is based on a mixture of unfounded belief and pure hope and it is entirely lacking in any value whatsoever. Very often (but not exclusively), it is found in mystic or religious environments, resulting from the individual having been induced (often as part of a group), over a sometimes prolonged period, to accept an idea supporting a merely partial perception or otherwise unsupportable orthodoxy. It is more often than not associated with a sense of the most forlorn hope, acting as a curtain behind which lurks nothing other than despair.

Faith founded on experience is at least reliable. It is essentially based on memory of the individual or group having already been involved in the same or similar type of past circumstance, from which a positive or reasonably positive result emerged. It thus possesses "something worth waiting for" or "something to be fought for" on the grounds of being a historically proven reality that merely needs to be recovered or regenerated. However, there is nothing "spiritual" about this sort of faith, irrespective of the circumstances, although many fondly imagine that it is. They thus believe that, if faithfully followed, it will lead to the reappearance of a wished-for state or set of cir-cumstances that has an aura of "spirituality" about it, while also promising a materialistically happy and beneficial environment. These, however, are but idylls of delusion.

Faith founded on inner (that is, spiritual) reason, is a different matter altogether. This is based on an intuitive inner recognition (even if only faintly perceived) of certain abstract principles or influences leading unavoidably in a certain direction, if not to an obviously specific outcome. The individual "knows" with an accompanying sense of growing certainty or near certainty that this is the path that must be followed if a particular inner purpose is to be achieved.

It has to be added that the purpose in question may lead the individual onward through either successive positive achievement or successive anguish (or a mixture of both) before the associated end is finally attained. In either instance, however, it is attended by a sense of stepping forward into a sort of darkness, which, although based on ignorance, is actually liberating in nature. It is also always attended by a sense that once the first correct foot-steps are taken in this direction, there is no turning back. The path ahead seems to move forward of its own accord and to be entirely impersonal in how it deals with us.

Having said that, however, there is one related subject that the indi-vidual on the Path has to consciously recognize. It involves the difference between knowledge and wisdom. Of these we are told: "Knowledge used is force expressing itself; wisdom used is energy in action."[20] We are further told that in relation to the psycho-spiritual development of man, there are two associated "threads" that link the individual to his Egoic source. These are what in Sanskrit are known as the sutratma (life thread) and the antah-karana (consciousness thread). Initially, these two are separate, hence the dualistic sense associated with human self-consciousness. However, as definite progress is made on the Path, the two come ever closer together until at the third initiation they fuse, thereby bringing about a direct (although not fully self-conscious) connection between the spiritual Monad and the objective consciousness of the lesser self.

That fully self-conscious linkage only takes place, so we are told, after the fourth initiation when the individual attains the first stage of Adeptship, or Arhatship. This united "thread" is thereafter used by the monadic SELF to project its consciousness anywhere it wills, even without the use of an associated "body."[21] Paradoxically, it is this same faculty that enables the Adept to create a body of appearance at will—the *mayavirupa* or "body of illusion"—for particular purposes. For example, Apollonius of Tyana was thereby able to appear in two geographically distant places at the same time.

We shall deal with several of these issues again in greater detail in later chapters as we concern ourselves with the specific stages of initiatory progress. Concerning these Blavatsky comments:

> There are four grades of initiation mentioned in exoteric works [the fourth being that of Arhat]. . . . The Arhat, though he can see the Past, Present and Future, is not yet the highest initiate; for the Adept himself, the initiated candidate, becomes *chela* (pupil) to a higher initiate [i.e., a Chohan]. Three further grades have to be conquered by the Arhat who would reach the apex of the ladder of Arhatship.[22]

With that perspective firmly in mind, but very firmly remembering that spiritual initiation is merely a subjective evolutionary process open to all willing to make the effort (not something by which to feel psychologically superior to others), let us now take a look at the first stages of the initiatory Path. In doing so, we shall deal with its many and various progressive characteristics, again bearing in mind that many of these too are associated with those everyday human experiences with which, in greater or lesser degree, all intelligent human beings are familiar. Before we do so, however, it would be helpful to recognize that initiation itself (i.e., by the Adept Hierarchy) involves the opening up of the consciousness of the individual precedent to a transfer of progressively more subtle and more powerful energies into it. That such a process is potentially dangerous should be self-evident. That is precisely why the Adept Hierarchy approach it, in the case of all individuals (and now all groups), so very carefully and with much prior observation and testing, to ensure that the intended recipient is fully prepared and ready.

NINE

INITIATIONS OF THE THRESHOLD

We now come to the issue of the first two initiations of the sevenfold sequence of spiritual evolution within our planetary scheme. These are essentially the same as those of the Entered Apprentice and Fellow Craft in Freemasonry. However, to refresh our minds before progressing with them, let us remember the sequence of seven states of consciousness within the all-embracing eighth state (which comprises the first and lowest kosmic plane of being) as defined in modern theosophical terminology, as follows.

7. Divine consciousness
6. Semi-divine consciousness
5. Full spiritual consciousness
4. Spiritual Soul consciousness
3. Mental consciousness
2. Astral (desire) consciousness
1. Physical sensory consciousness

Of these seven the sensory physical state is regarded as having already been brought under conscious control, as far as the Path is concerned, during the first two preliminary stages of probation and accepted discipleship.

Fig. 9.1. Craft Mason's Regalia/Items

Therefore the remaining seven include a duality in the case of the mental state, involving the Higher Mind and the lower mind, these being respectively dealt with at the second and third initiations. In each case, as already suggested, the individual has to bring about (under increasingly testing conditions) a practical and not just theoretical display of his control over the natural elemental forces that constitute the instinctive nature of each plane of being.

In a peculiar way, however, the individual generates the very conditions that he has to overcome—hence the difficulties. The reason for this is that Nature always instinctively strives to achieve balance. Hence when we strive after something higher, Nature will find its opposite and bring it to bear in order to counteract the threatened imbalance. Thus the more subtle the higher aspiration, the more subtle is the downward dragging elemental response. The only way that the human individual can then counteract this situation is by allowing his consciousness to be brought to a face-to-face crisis of these opposites in which both of them are transcended.

It is for this reason that the Path of initiation is often referred to as the path of progressive renunciation—the way of tears and sadness. Yet this is unavoidable because the whole process of psycho-spiritual evolution necessarily involves much internal (often violent) conflict, with progressive destruction, repurification, and rebuilding or reorganization in order to better align the lower nature with the higher. All of this takes a long time to achieve properly, resulting in the correct disciplining of elemental matter of the various subplanes, then of successive readjustment, realignment, and repolarization of each "body" as a whole. Thus any attempt to rush the process unduly, outside Natural Law, can only result in problems that have to be undone before further real progress is possible. So we are told, haste is not an accepted mode of activity within the spiritual world itself.

THE SEVEN RAY INFLUENCES

The essential difference between the higher and lower initiations is that the crisis in the first (lower) three is unconsciously self-engineered by the individual's own way of life. In the higher four, the intelligence—having realized the true nature and practical value of the principle of crisis—brings it about consciously through a self-willed focus. As we are very helpfully told:

> A crisis is brought about by a certain habit of mind. . . . It is the establishing of a certain objective rhythm which produces a crisis; it is the emergence of a particular subjective rhythm which enables a man to surmount the crisis and to capitalise on the opportunity.[1]

When this is consciously recognized and adapted to prevailing circumstances much later on the Path—by the initiate facing the fourth degree (the initiation influenced by the Fourth Ray)—the sense of crisis is then felt by those in close contact with the person in a manner directly affecting their objective personality life but not in quite the same manner as with the individual himself.[2] His trial is of a much more subtle and wholly subjective nature. Having just mentioned associated Ray influences, however, it is perhaps worthwhile reminding ourselves, before we proceed further, of the teaching concerning the Seven Rays, as enunciated by the Adept Hierarchy. That is because these higher influences ever condition the individual's forward progress until he himself becomes a sixth degree initiate, or Chohan. These Rays are correspondingly described as follows:

1. The Ray of Will, or Power
2. The Ray of Love-Wisdom
3. The Ray of Active [or Adaptive] Intelligence
4. The Ray of Harmony through Conflict
5. The Ray of Concrete Science
6. The Ray of Devotion
7. The Ray of Ceremonial Organization or Ritual Magic

These same Ray influences are described as the projections of seven archetypal kosmic influences emanated downward into the field of our planetary Life by our particular Logos. However, in trying to understand them (and it is essential to do so), it is important to remember what was described in an earlier chapter about the lower three being the materialized reflection of the higher three, and of the fourth acting as a bridge between these two highly potent triads. This is of really considerable importance. One further and again most important issue related to the Rays is that each—by virtue of the manner adapted by human usage—has a higher and a lower (or a positive and a negative) aspect to it. The individual must learn to recognize both these and to gradually rid himself of the tendency toward the latter through psychological honesty and applied self-control.

THE DIFFICULTIES OF SELF-CONTROL

The individual initiate has ultimately to achieve his or her progressive subjective conquests while in the physical body, because the final initiation must involve all seven influences being spiritually synthesized back into a coherent unity. We, it must be remembered, are actually not physical beings at all. We are spiritual intelligences actually existing within the fourth of the seven solar-cum-terrestrial states, from which a portion of our nature (a lesser "spark," or jiva) is emanated into the triple lower planetary world, taking anchorage within our human heart. It is that same "spark" that must bring about the control of the lesser elemental nature, but it can only do so once it reachieves a degree of contact with its emanating Source. However, once it does so, the very potency of the emanating Source (the Spiritual Ego) that is pouring down initially serves also to regalvanize the elemental nature, making it doubly or triply difficult for the Ego to reachieve control in line with a sensed higher Purpose. Here lies the paradox and the major problem for the would-be initiate.

Having—in the earlier stages of probation and accepted discipleship—achieved an apparent degree of self-control and inner reorientation, the individual effectively now opens himself up to the first downward surge of real psycho-spiritual energies. The result is inevitably one of chaos and super-charged struggle. As St. Paul put it, "That which I would not, I do; that which I would, I do not."[3] All the physical and emotional elements of our nature, which we have managed to bury beneath our good intentions as a disciple, rise up like electrified miasmas to confront us. Being of a highly tenuous and volatile nature, they taunt us as we struggle to control them. We then begin to realize that we have to use a different method to bring about that control. Previously, we had imposed a regime of good deeds and idealistic thoughts, which appeared to have overwhelmed them by sheer volume. But now, our lightest memory of them brings them back to life with a vengeance.

TECHNIQUES OF SELF-DISCIPLINE

We realize that it is not possible to exercise dominion over our physical and astral desires by just suppressing them, telling them to "shut up" while we get on with burnishing our ideals and aspirations. As long as they continue to play a role in our ideals (no matter how subtle) they will take on a life of their own. Hence it is that imagination, inappropriately used, serves only to make matters worse. In order to bring about the control that we so desire, we have to learn the difference between indulgence and necessity. The physical senses, for example, all have their necessary cycles of influence during daily life. But the individual has to learn the technique of their restraint rather than their suppression. Eating, sleeping, sex, and so on—the appetites—all play their roles; but by restricting their associated urges to certain specific times of the day, for example, and not allowing them under any circumstances any other freedom, the first element and principle of desire control is achieved. It is that of the "cycle of necessity."

By a process of subjective "divide and rule," the individual learns that there is an inherent appropriateness in human behavior. This, if followed sensibly, allows Nature to have her part, while leaving him a period of quietude in which he can subjectively reorient himself and thus pursue his inner work altogether uninterrupted. In practical terms, he has (albeit unconsciously) started the process of detachment of his inner intelligence from his "duties" by allowing his elementals their restricted "playtime." Any parents with children of their own will recognize the general principles involved here.

Those elemental beings that constitute the lower nature of humanity merely follow their own frequently wild and anarchic instincts, hence the intense "highs and lows" of the manic depressive. They can (and must) be taught discipline, but its application has to be thought through and applied with a caring yet firm hand. As experience should tell any real esotericist or occultist, the elementals make adequate slaves but highly untrustworthy friends. They must therefore be kept psychologically "at arm's length." This is the basis of the old adage that if you want to sup with the Devil, you must use a long handled spoon. However, the idea pedaled by some "therapists" that one deliberately can get rid of bad tendencies by overindulging in them to such an extent that one becomes sickened by them and thereby rejects them is very silly indeed. This is notwithstanding the fact that one very occasionally meets people who have been through this deeply traumatic and essentially very destructive experience. As *The Voice of the Silence* explicitly warns us:

> Do not believe that lust can ever be killed out if gratified or satiated . . . it is by feeding vice that it expands and waxes strong, like to the worm that fattens on the blossom's heart. The rose must re-become the bud, born of its parent stem before the parasite has eaten through its heart and drunk its life-sap.[4]

It is interesting to note that certain cultural "codes" of social behavior have recognized these principles from far back in human history. Certain things are allowed and certain things are "just not done." Unfortunately, this inevitably develops over time into a social regime of mere etiquette, with bad behavior being concealed behind "closed doors." Then another generation comes along and, recognizing the essential falsity of that behavior, throws it over and returns to a period of overt indulgence—before realizing the mistake that it has itself made in releasing all sorts of socially damaging elemental forces. This latter situation has happened in our own times as a result of the post-war generations (those of the 1950s and 1960s in particular) mistakenly believing that "polite" behavior and established codes of conduct were "old-fashioned." Only now is the same generation of mature adults seeing the psychological damage that it has brought upon subsequent generations. However, recovering the situation always proves more than difficult and always takes many more generations to achieve.

In a curious way, each of the stages of initiatory experience covers not just one plane of being, but rather two. Those facing the tests of the first degree have to realize that it is the astral desire nature that initiates overactive sensory activity at the physical level. Similarly, those facing the tests of the second degree have to realize that it is their lower thoughts that automatically impel the astral desire nature into activity.

At the present stage of human evolutionary development there is such a high degree of automatic coordination of the personality—involving the physical senses, the astral desire nature, and the lower mind—that activity in the one will automatically set off activity in the others. This needs to be recognized and brought under control—again using the principle "divide and rule" in a psychological sense. One ever needs to bear in mind that accumulated energies cannot be annihilated. If of a low order they need instead to be recognized and consciously transmuted; otherwise they will merely take the first uncontrolled opportunity to reexpress themselves.

THE STATES OF CONSCIOUSNESS CONCERNED

As we saw earlier, the astral nature of the second of the seven planes is an expression of the desire-to-know—thus also of the imagination. Hence it is that the sexual instinct (involving the desire-to-know in the biblical sense) is itself generated at this level, although it may be set off or triggered by visual imagery arising in the lower mind. The problem of sex is probably the greatest difficulty facing humanity in general, simply because the desire-to-know and the imagination are the most powerfully developed reflexes available to man. We therefore need to touch on this rather tricky subject a little further before moving on.

Any form of sexual inconsistency, incontinence, or indiscipline will cause the individual to fall off the Path. That is simply because it shows the elemental nature either to be in control or otherwise to be powerful enough to cause constant distraction. Bearing in mind that all psycho-spiritual development necessarily involves discipline of the lower by the higher, any uncertainty in this area is a sure recipe for obstruction to further progress. The same is true of gender inconstancy in all its various forms because—whatever the reasons for it (and there are several)—it involves a refusal or unwillingness to accept the masculine/feminine polarity that Nature has in this particular incarnation given to us as individuals.

In real terms, the spirit and the Causal Soul in man are genderless. However, if the kama-manasic (desire-mind) nature of the individual becomes either overactive or underactive in particular ways (often through traumatic parental inadequacy during childhood), the confused and weakened terrestrial soul nature can become unduly influenced toward a wrongful polarization. This inevitably results in some degree of psychic or psychological conflict, which renders further psycho-spiritual progress almost impossible until sorted out in a natural manner. Even the suggestion that some types of gender confusion are a "hangover" from a previous lifetime is suggestive of the fact that sexual indiscipline in that former lifetime was already a persistent problem.

The desire-orientated matter of the astral plane is highly magnetic and reactive to suggestion. It is, in a very real sense, tied to the astral/terrestrial soul organism of the individual human being in a way that the lower mind faculty is not—at least, not yet. As a direct consequence, astral polarization is an inevitably immediate effect, giving rise to the whole range of "likes" and "dislikes" to which common humanity is prone. At the lower end of the astral range—more closely connected to the terrestrial soul organism—we find very highly charged emotions and desires of a purely personal and self-centered orientation. This generates the sense of idolism. At the higher end of the astral spectrum, we find this orientation reversed, resulting in the generation of idealism, the wish to emulate or be like someone or something else of a better or higher nature and to behave toward others in line with those same ideals. The individual is no longer purely self-centered but is now beginning to reorient to a far more widely inclusive polarization.

One very interesting example of this stage of development is that found in what is commonly called modern "show business," in which the successful individual has to make a spectacle of himself or herself in such a way that it attracts widespread attention for its cleverness, or in more subtle instances, its technique of presentation and delivery. The desire to be the "creative" center of attention and the associated psychological pressure that goes along with it, which gives individuals the "buzz" that they seek in life, is a hugely increasing phenomenon in the West, because of the effects of television and film media. This generates self-centered "idolism" on a wide scale. However, it has been counteracted to some extent by many such individuals having been persuaded that part of their wealth and part of their public effort should be given to charity or an actively philanthropic cause. Thus the energy of pure idolism can be gradually transmuted into that of a growing unselfish idealism.

THE FIRST INITIATION

In real terms, this process is already to be found active in the nature of the accepted disciple who persistently strives after a range of spiritual ideals. Yet here the factor of control by the higher intelligence is not yet manifest. That control appears only after the crisis of accepted discipleship has taken place, by which time the control of all physical appetites has become relatively automatic, if not instinctual. Then, wide-eyed idolism gives way to an actively focused ideal used in self-disciplined work for a non-self-centered, or wholly altruistic, purpose in approaching the first initiation. It is for this reason that *The Voice of the Silence* refers to the first "gate" on the Path as that of *Dana*—Charity—the active idealism and willingness to give of oneself for the sake of others. However, as it also poetically points out to us:

The road that leads there through is straight and smooth and green. T'is like a sunny glade in the dark forest depths. . . . There nightingales of hope and birds of radiant plumage sing perched in green bowers, chanting success to fearless pilgrims.[5]

All this is indicative of the sense of (inevitably self-centered) well-being felt by those individuals—even apparently very intelligent ones—who determinedly involve themselves, for example, in charitable or altruistic work of any sort. That reorientation itself comes about as a result of the individual having first (through Egoic influence) been able to overcome and largely bring under control the constant demands and urges of their own physical elemental nature.[6] Perhaps unsurprisingly, it is usually the now steady heart chakra that is particularly stimulated at this first initiation.[7] However, the throat chakra thereby receives a secondary supporting stimulus, so generating in the initiate's consciousness the emergence of a more intensely creative approach to vocal self-expression.

We can accordingly see in the masses of those widespread modern groups who merely indulge in political rhetoric and demonstrations (supposedly on behalf of others) vocally forceful idealists of lesser grade. Most of these, despite their apparently developed ideals, have not yet progressed beyond the probationary stage on the Path, or the rudimentary phase of accepted discipleship. They are essentially followers. On the other hand, the leaders of those groups involved in practical work in line with their idealisms are rarely quite so vocally willing to trumpet their own sense of self-importance. Many of these are now beginning to demonstrate more effective leadership over the former type of group by a wide margin (although there are those that still overlap). This thereby proves that a large mass of modern humanity comprises groups of provably reliable disciples or those who have taken the first initiation.

However, there are some parts of the world where those at the stage of probation and discipleship are still far more concerned with showing off their political "voice" than in becoming involved in work that is sustainable, practical, and altruistic. It is these latter types who generate politically motivated mobs, drawn to them by the magnetic power of their astral natures. These include the as yet blind masses of aspirants of even lesser development who merely become swept up in the supercharged astral currents thus unleashed.

To some degree, this is a necessary stage of development and the political common sense that seeks to allow the expression of a sense of outrage within strictly controlled limits is a highly intelligent one. Where such volatile currents are merely suppressed by force and without compassion, the results are usually tragic, as well as making the underlying situation even worse.

Unfortunately, too many of our modern politicians and social activists are still so mired in their own egoic venality and their desire to use political position as a business career rather than as a vocation that better-reasoned approaches are rarely considered. The astral nature yields to leadership by example more than anything else. Thus as long as our politicians in particular show themselves as self-seeking demagogues, the masses will tend to follow a chaotic path through their own mistrust giving rise to outbursts of anarchic frustration.

Against this we find the phenomenon of much more defined "political pressure groups" involving larger numbers of "accepted disciples" and first degree types. Many such groups are led by a second degree individual, either or both frequently (but unconsciously) receptive to the influence of adepts of the Left-Hand Path (the path of materialistic self-concern and deliberate evil to others), of whom there are many, mostly disincarnate. These are generated (again usually in a purely selfish way) to engineer public opinion and political "will" in certain specific directions for the benefit of small groups. The phenomenon is now so widespread in the West that it is becoming increasingly associated with political and large-scale corporate corruption, particularly in America.

However, it is extreme religious groups that tend to foment strife in the most pernicious manner, using subterfuge in order to get their own way, often by presenting themselves as oppressed minorities—for example, the ultra-"orthodox" Zionists of Israel and their misguided financial and political supporters in the United States, as also their extremist equivalents in the world of Islam, the Wahabi Moslems of Saudi Arabia and some of the Gulf states.

THE SECOND INITIATION

We turn next to those individuals facing the extremely difficult test of bringing under total control the astral (soul) body and thereby also beginning to integrate the combined astral/lower mental nature—that which we call the "personality." As we can see by using straight logic, it is those individuals and groups that most effectively manipulate passionate ideals in combination with intellectual idea-forms who tend to carry most "political clout" in society, particularly in the West. It is this faculty that inspires great admiration because of its self-generated power. It is also this, however, that brings about most confrontations of a personal nature, resulting in a bitterness that is far more acute and longer lasting than any merely astral conflicts.

However, our concern here is predominantly with the individual rather than the group, because it is the individual who has to learn how to recognize and then control these forces within their own nature, thereby generating a freedom from the slavery of those ideas that give rise to purely personal (hence essentially selfish) ideals. That is something that is far more difficult than might at first appear to be the case.

The Voice of the Silence refers to the second initiation as the gate of *Shila* (Faith and Hope), surrounded by the "grey mists" of doubt.[8] For the individual in the process of attempting to link and harmonize the astral and lower mental natures, doubt is a constant bystander for the simple reason that lack of focus and self-belief persists. The individual frequently finds it difficult to anchor his or her idealism to one particular aim or task when there appear to be so many others of equivalent potential importance. Consequently, there is subjective equivocation, leading to outright uncertainty and frequent disillusionment. Only when the individual has made a definite choice and then "follows through" do the doubts and uncertainties begin to lift. Even then, however, their shadows tend to persist until the individual feels more secure in his choice. He then finds himself (with some surprise and pleasure) the focus of attention and admiration by others, thereby generating one of the most psychologically dangerous interim stages on the Path.

LOWER MIND CHARACTERISTICS

As earlier mentioned (see chapter 5), the lower mind nature involves three characteristic faculties—singularity of ideas (coherent memory), organizational instinct, and analytical discrimination—along with a fourth involving purely intellectual reason and a coordinating presentational ability. The generalized ideals of the astral plane mutate into less specific ideas, which are then historically organized and subsequently defined in particular groups or categories. The capacity to use all three primary faculties together in an intelligent manner then involves the power of adaptive reason.

Those individuals who have passed the second initiation have done so by beginning to use this power of intellectual reason. However, their skill in its use at this stage is actually very limited in perspective because it is still largely self-centered. Nevertheless, such individuals learn very quickly how to beguile others of lesser intellectual capacity with the sharpness, force, and cleverness of their arguments. Here we find the skillful psychological opportunist in many fields of endeavor ranging from politics to academia to public relations and commercial marketing—and many others too. Not surprisingly, we find that it is the throat chakra that becomes particularly active after the second initiation,[9] although it is the brow chakra that receives the new stimulus.

We have each come across many human beings who have these various mental faculties in varied stages of development, all conditioned by their differing Ray types. That is because the Spiritual Ego works on all three bodies—physical, astral, and lower mental—simultaneously to improve their evolutionary quality and faculty. Yet, as we are told: "Some definite point in the evolution of each of the three lower vehicles has to be attained and held before the further expansion of the channel [with the Higher Self] can be safely permitted."[10]

Thus very few, relatively speaking, as yet possess the necessary breadth of development allied to conscious self-control to any great degree, although the modern educational system is at least making something of an (unconscious) effort in that general direction. The problem here is that the educational system insists upon academically treating information gained from experience as polarized "facts" and "non-facts," when these are themselves, for the most part, purely arbitrary in nature. The academic world is, curiously, an altogether unreal one, self-generated by minds that work, largely in the Aristotelian fashion, to systematize everything, thereby rather arbitrarily separating them from one another rather than interconnecting them.

In parallel we find the modern adage that "there are lies, damned lies, and then there are statistics." By using so-called facts (most of them actually paradigms, based on ultimately unproven assumptions), arguments can be twisted in all sorts of directions by the mind of the skillful individual. As we have already made clear, however, esoteric philosophy always works from the universal principle "downward" or "inward" to the specific fact or experience, thereby allying all available knowledge by way of the application of universal principles.

As suggested at the outset of this chapter, we find in the field of Craft Freemasonry a confirmation of what has just been suggested regarding the first two initiations, for these are equivalent to the stages of what are called the Entered Apprentice and the Fellow Craft (about which more in the next chapter). In the former, we see the novice who is learning the art of actual building (of human culture and civilization), whereas the previous stage of discipleship was only that of the committed aspirant in the same direction. In the latter, we see the individual who has achieved a certain degree of proficiency or skill in the combined use of hands-on effort and natural artistry on the one hand and applied theory based on the experience of others on the other. Later, as a Craftsman, he is held in admiration and respect for his talent and the automatic sense of control he displays over his particular field of endeavor. This gives him a very real distinction in human society, enabling him to supervise others and exercise administrative control over their relative ignorance.

ACHIEVING COMPLETE CONTROL OVER THE ASTRAL NATURE

One of the most important things about the complete attainment of the second initiation is that it is at this point that, in due sequence, there supposedly occurs the faculty of control over all astral emotion[11]—although its karmic effects continue. This "control," so we are told, "is then a complete episode and it is consciously registered. [Then] between the second and the third initiations, the disciple has to demonstrate a complete continuity of non-response to astralism and emotionalism."[12]

This, perhaps unsurprisingly, often results in unexpected displays of the very reverse, including the highly unwelcome addition of an apparent ruthlessness. However, bearing in mind that the astral body and the astral plane in general are the mere products of the imagination of the individual and of humanity en masse, it follows that the great problem facing the Egoic nature of the initiate at this stage is that of learning how to exercise complete control over the imagination and thus to lead its associated energies into higher channels. Hence he must also dominate the massed elemental subhierarchies, which he has himself generated and, curiously enough, those produced by others as well. This is far from being simple.

The great problem faced by the individual who has attained the second degree lies in that very sense of his own (partial) achievement in this same respect. It thereby quite inevitably and paradoxically generates an associated aura of self-satisfied glamour that then surrounds him at all times, fed by the attentions of others of lesser degree. As all glamour involves a crystallization of ideals and thoughts, it necessarily acts like a concave surrounding mirror, which magnifies the sense of personal importance and identity—the lesser ego—and focuses it back inward to produce a virtual image. Consequently, when others burnish the mirror with their adulations, the individual at the center feels an even greater sense of importance. When they do not, he is filled with doubt and suspicion that others are filled with purely jealous motivations; hence potential frustration and even degrees of neurosis.

The effects of this problem can be seen very markedly in the film acting and theatrical "professions" as well as in the media, where it tends to generate huge egoism on the one hand and just as huge uncertainty on the other, when the sense of confidence is even slightly threatened. Rather unfortunately, the same sense of uncertainty has been picked up by the advertizing business and quite deliberately and ruthlessly augmented (particularly in the field of personal cosmetics and fashion) in order to generate more sales. Conversely, however, this has in turn generated greater skeptical discrimination and prudence among the more intelligent minority. We shall consider in the next chapter the way in which the initiate of the second degree deals with this problem en route to the third degree.

RAY GROUP CONSIDERATIONS

In the meantime, however, let us cast our attention back to the issue of the Seven Rays, insofar as these affect or are related to the first two initiations in the following manner:

Ray	Quality	Arena	Plane
6	Devotion and idealism	The astral nature (desire)	Sixth
7	Ritualized organization	The physical appetites and senses	Seventh

The disciple facing the first initiation is one who encounters the problem of bringing sustained order into his life—something that, at this stage, can only be achieved by association. Hence the involvement of ritual and ceremonial. Such people are thus instinctively attracted toward areas of life where structured symbolism and hierarchical rank are of the greatest importance—for example, in the armed forces and the civil administration of a country, or a large international business corporation. In either instance, there is a sense of belonging to a larger and very much more powerful family group whose potency and outreach carries with it a really considerable sense of social importance and meaning. By belonging to this larger group, and by dutiful acquiescence to its internal rules and regulations, their lives are also given far greater importance and social meaning. They develop a sense of being able to achieve far more by their own direct association with the group. This of course develops a glamour, which the individual then manipulates on his or her own behalf in a hierarchical manner, but it has to be learned eventually that the purely personal association is illusory.

The Seventh Ray is accordingly concerned with the objective world—with the physical body as well as the corporate body—involving the relationship of the individual to the group. It teaches the inculcation of a sense of different hierarchical functions for different purposes. By so doing it imparts and indoctrinates all sorts of associated psychological connections, for example: that different functions can be quite general or very specific; that they necessitate different quantities of energy and force; that they move at different speeds according to circumstance, turning only very slowly when large; that they have to be approached and dealt with in different ways. In other words, this influence is one that teaches the nature and importance of discipline in general, of the lesser to the greater—in a parallel sense, of the microcosm to the Macrocosm.

When we consider the Sixth Ray influence, however, we discover a marked change in what it teaches the individual and the effect it has upon the masses of humanity. Instead of the focus being on physical order and discipline, the orientation is now shifted to the astral or desire nature much more specifically. Its effect becomes distinctively more subjective and thus also much more of a personal nature. What was previously done in the individual's mind for the greater group, to maintain its internal order, balance, and functional ability, now tends to mutate into desire for personal benefit, first and foremost. The group is still of primary importance but only to help fulfill the inner personal desire, aspiration, or sense of importance. The importance of the larger objective group becomes a lesser concern. The result is dualistic. With some, aspiration tends to devolve into ambition and in so doing becomes forceful or predominantly militant in one direction more than another. With others, it becomes merely passive, or mystically orientated.

In the intelligent individual, the generalized sense of duty already inspired by the Seventh Ray influence becomes, through Sixth Ray influence, a sense of specific, subjective orientation, thereby generating a considerable increase in force and directional motivation. In the individual, this takes the form of highly charged idealism or psycho-spiritual aspiration. Not altogether surprisingly perhaps, the Sixth Ray influence has a particular connection with all unquestioning belief systems (particularly with religion) and thus with the devotional impulse in all walks of life. However, by virtue of its instinctive orientation toward choice, it tends also to become antagonistically exclusive, or schismatic. The Seventh Ray influence, on the other hand, is fundamentally (or at least, corporately) all-inclusive and thus generally much more adaptable. Characteristically, both have the strongest tendency to impose themselves upon all comers.

SOME EFFECTS OF THE SECOND INITIATION

These same characteristics and tendencies have a very interesting effect upon the individual facing the second initiation; however, the real "driver" behind the persona is the inner spiritual individuality. The second initiation, as we have seen, involves the bringing of the personal astral or desire nature under a high degree of control. However, as the more evolved humankind of today has already brought about a fairly well-developed coordination of both the astral and lower mental natures to form the basis for the integrated personality, the problem here becomes much more complex and very much more difficult to overcome.

In a very real sense, the individual at this stage has to learn to take control of himself because he realizes that nobody else—even his nearest and dearest—actually begins to understand him. It might thus be suggested that the second initiation in fact sees the completed, full integration of the human personality (the kama-manas), thereby causing it to become (psychically) very highly charged. This, however, produces in the individual the strongest sense of isolation and personal distinctiveness from others. This characteristic sense of isolation thus generates in him, at least to begin with, a very troubled consciousness, a curious sense of being in the wrong place, plus a strange intensity, which makes him stand out from the masses in a way that even he cannot explain.

Such types often find that they possess a creative capacity to turn their hands and mind to almost anything they choose. At this stage, although not possessing a really focused spiritual orientation, some individuals become intensely creative while others, perhaps lacking quite the same focus, pour their intensity into mere personality domination of others, some becoming great or charismatic leaders. A few who do somehow retain or develop a spiritual (or at least mystic) focus often seem to withdraw from human society altogether into various forms of seclusion. All of them, however, become aware for the first time of an irresistible inner "pull," which leaves in their waking brain consciousness a permanent sense of dissatisfaction. The individual who has achieved the second degree is, necessarily, an unconventional type who cannot but help to make a definite mark on human society in some way or other.

Accompanying this, the second degree initiate—having thus fused the lower mind and emotional faculties after great psychological effort (of which he is personally very aware)—tends by way of correspondence to become potently certain of his own correctness and often quickly and violently reactive to anyone questioning it. This apparently complete lack of humility adds further color and force to an already existing unconventionality and frequently results in such persons being regarded and pushed forward as "natural leaders" by others around them, fascinated by such virtuoso displays of psychological bravura on their part. This, paradoxically, is quite often despite the initiate's own frequent personal desire to be left alone and not regarded by others in such an elevated or hero-worshipping fashion. Some, however, do fall prey to the glamorized psychic atmosphere generated by such adulation and they, at least temporarily, "go off the rails."

It was mentioned a little earlier that imagination is an astral faculty (comprising matter of the fourth astral substate), although to many this might seem odd because we perhaps normally associate it with the capacity for mental visualization. However, there is a fundamental difference between the two. Imagination is mentioned here because, in properly assimilating the incoming influence of the second initiation, the individual has to learn how to bring about complete control over what we loosely call "wishful thinking"—based on astral desire—through the use of mental discrimination, before being able to move on to prepare the ground properly for the third initiation. That control must involve a very real humility, which itself involves the visual sense of proportion, as seen from the inner side by the natural clairvoyant faculty. Thus the slightest loss of control by the Spiritual Ego over the fourth mental substate (which state, as we will recall, involves the reasoning power and presentational ability of the integrated personality) will result in loss of astral vision and a consequent display of arrogance. This is one great test facing the initiate of this degree en route to the next degree.

PROBLEMS CAUSED BY OVERINTENSITY

The individual's very intensity at this stage constitutes a major problem for him. That is because he (in the earlier stages) lacks full control over it, especially when it becomes supercharged by reactive emotion to what he regards as his own perfect insights, or the supposedly misplaced views of others. In the latter case he often quite wrongly attributes to them the deliberate desire to hurt or undermine his own well-intentioned efforts. This, in extremis, can lead to manic psychological derangement and it is therefore immensely important that the causes behind such psycho-spiritual conditioning are properly understood. Interestingly, intense depression is the direct result of just as intense elation—itself often originating in prolonged bursts of uncontrolled or overexuberant imagination. That is why so many naturally artistic individuals suffer from the problem, in all walks of life, as we otherwise mentioned earlier.

This characteristically deep depression is what the British political statesman Winston Churchill called his "black dog." It is, paradoxically, a not infrequent partner to initiatory achievement at this intermediate stage, just as it was described earlier in relation to the transitional stage facing the future accepted disciple, between idolism and idealism. However, one of the few attributes that often enables the individual to weather this stormy phase is a sense of humor that, when seen from the inner side, corresponds to a very definite sense of proportion. To be able to laugh at oneself and thus not take oneself too seriously is a spiritual gift of infinite potential, which all successful initiates must possess for their own survival and for their own further progress along the Spiritual Path. This is one of the most important things that anybody can learn in a lifetime.

THE "DWELLER ON THE THRESHOLD"

There is one final thing that should be mentioned here, and it is of the most serious concern. The individual who has passed the second initiation and is on the way toward the third has developed such a personal sense of self-control (and frequently of self-righteousness too) that he fails to recognize, to begin with at least, the great subjective danger that he has created. That danger involves the fact that by the very coordination of his multiple elemental nature and the process of its control, he has also created (unknown to himself) what is occultly called "the Dweller on the Threshold." This entity is effectively the sum of all the most developed aspects of the lower nature, evolved through all the many lifetimes of personal experience. It is aided by the analytical (lower) mental faculty and, together with it, generates that lesser and highly dangerous form of intelligence known to us as "cunning." This then is to be found in all sorts of social, political, and commercial environments.

If an intensive process of past memories is raised, with a deep sense of personal association, this entity will appear in a monstrous display of apparent strength and at least briefly overcome the good nature of even the most loving individual with a display of thorough nastiness. The individual is himself initially shocked to the core by this unsuspected parasite. Some then make the mistake of allowing an increasing fascination with it to bring about the progressive ruin of their lives, resulting in utter madness. Others, with apparently more intelligence, strive to find a way of negating its influence altogether by substituting a very loving attitude once the Dweller's influence has died down. However, even this ultimately fails, and it is eventually realized that a form of face-to-face confrontation is the only alternative. As *The Voice of the Silence* poetically but bluntly puts it:

> The Self of Matter and the Self of Spirit can never meet. One of the twain must disappear; there is no place for both. . . . Ere thy Soul's mind can understand, the bud of personality must be crushed out; the worm of sense destroyed past resurrection.[13]

In relation to that, one other thing should perhaps be mentioned concerning the period when the second initiation is well past and its influences properly absorbed. It is that only then does the individual begin to become really consciously aware of the fact that he or she is faced with involvement in a deeply occult process. There consequently comes a stark moment of choice whether to embark upon the next stage and thereby face the impossibility of going back to any form of comfortable personal existence. The result of that choice—not an easy one because of the immediate effects upon friends and family—will cause unimaginable changes that seem to threaten turning one's whole world psychologically upside down. We shall see more of this in the next chapter.

THE DEVELOPMENT OF PSYCHIC POWERS

One of the main fascinations for those on the earlier stages of the Path involves the occult powers developed by the initiated intelligence. These can range from clairvoyance and clairaudience to telekinesis, the latter being the ability to make things move through the air from one place to another, or to be disintegrated and reproduced even at great distance. However, there is nothing in the slightest bit "spiritual" per se about any of such powers, and their usage more often than not actually hinders or gets in the way of real spiritual development. In order to understand why that should be so, we perhaps need to spend a moment considering some associated issues.

As we know from science, all forms are made up of atoms that, in turn, consist of apparently infinite numbers of invisible particles that, puzzlingly, have no apparent individual existence at all. Their influence is due to the associated intensity of their vibration, relative to the environment and function in which they find themselves. In practical terms, the objective physical state with which we are so familiar is itself an illusion. "Objectivity" is something of which we are aware by virtue of partial observation leading us to forms and degrees of passing association or identification, which encourage us to believe (falsely) in their ownership by us as "personal" experience. This leads us to develop those reactions that we know as "like" and "dislike," or "good" and "bad." Eventually, however, the individual intelligence comes to realize that this personalized perception is erroneous and futile, even though it can be brought about by an act of will or desire.

The so-called "physical" world is actually part of a greater field of purely psychic existence, of which the perceptual consciousness of the individual develops an understanding through manipulation of the chakras. Each of these produces objective forms (e.g., organs) and instinctive responses through the endocrine glandular system, plus a range of subjective or sensory faculties. For example, the base of the spine center actually generates an ectoplasm that gives rise, progressively, to the blood cells and the skeleton. The psychic faculty that works through this same center provides us with our basic sense of self-preservation, while the subjective sense is one of identification. The heart chakra is essentially responsible, in objective terms, for the cyclical circulation of the blood cells generated by the base of the spine chakra and for their cleansing. Its psychic nature—involving a very real intelligence of its own, which has only recently been recognized by research scientists—involves a dualistic sense of interrelationship, which itself generates an intelligent care and sensitivity. This extends not only to the whole body but also (in certain circumstances) to other bodies. The subjective faculty is one involving the sense of self-identity, which derives from a vibratory responsiveness to the Causal Soul nature.

When we move to the yet higher chakras, however, we find rather more obvious signs of psychic faculty. The brow chakra is the basis of the objective faculty of sight. The psychic faculty involves sight at a distance (even thousands of miles) and also the capacity to see elemental and elementary entities. The subjective faculty involves visual imagination. However, when associated with the crown center above the head, a great change takes place. That is because the crown center provides direct access to the real spiritual world. Hence the fusion of crown and brow center energies enables the individual to see (although only progressively, as the faculty develops) the clear, archetypal relationships behind all objective existence. It is thus interesting to note that the ancient Egyptians symbolized the brow and crown center faculties respectively by the raised cobra and vulture heads on the forehead of the initiated individual (see fig. 9.2)—not just the pharaoh as modern Egyptologists imagine, although the pharaoh was certainly the primary symbol of the advanced initiate, or *Pir*. In fact, the individual with both the cobra and vulture heads shown side-by-side would have been an initiate of at least the third degree. Why that is so should become more apparent when reading the next chapter.

Fig. 9.2. Egyptian cobra and vulture on pharaonic head

SPIRITUAL TRAINING

There are two final points that might be mentioned here, although they are pertinent right up to the gates of Adeptship. The first is that the individual "on the Path" is given occasional insights—through particular "dreams" or moments of "déjà vu"—to spur him on his way or to point him in a particular direction in connection with work to be done. These are usually provided by his own Spiritual Ego, but occasionally also by an Adept or Nirmanakaya of lesser degree, if the situation merits it. However, such experiences become increasingly less frequent and increasingly more subtle as the individual progresses, so that he is progressively forced to develop his own powers of constant inner observation and personal drive.

The second is that, as part of the training process, the Adept responsible for any individual or group's spiritual development will from time to time (and quite deliberately) apply increasingly subtle tests involving the insertion of a distracting elemental influence into their aura. The reason for this is that both the individual and the group, by their own (usually unconscious) efforts, set up a psychic barrier to particular types of elemental influence without first having dealt with the root of the reactive problem in their own nature. This generates a false sense of security, which thus needs to be upset. Otherwise, the problem will just increase in size and force until it causes unnecessarily major problems in the individual or group environment. The Adept intelligence has to be able to recognize any prevailing elemental influence at once and learn how to deal with it quickly and effectively so that it is not allowed to develop in that manner. In this way, the Adept Brotherhood protects not only the younger initiate but also humanity as a whole.

This latter point leads logically to the little recognized fact of just how much responsibility is carried in a personal sense by each Adept. In order to form a reliable part of the "Guardian Wall" that protects our planetary Life as a whole, Adepts have to prove by demonstration that they and their faculties are entirely reliable. While they come to recognize themselves as part of a very powerfully united Brotherhood, they have to achieve this by showing just how skillfully effective they are when acting on their own. In other words, they do not "hang around" awaiting instructions "from above." They not only act (at the appropriate moment, based on spiritual principles), they also initiate new projects by influencing lesser initiates to get involved or otherwise take responsibility for them in the outer world.

It is because of this latter fact that initiates of the first, second, and third degrees find themselves (frequently despite their purely personal inclinations) taking on work involving compassionate responsibility for groups often well outside their own social orbit. This applies to the other kingdoms of Nature as well; for, as already suggested, our humanity is also learning to become the protector and evolutionary developer of consciousness and other faculties in them. In the final analysis, therefore, initiation only becomes available when the individual (or group) self-initiates his own future development by taking up action on behalf of the wider group and seeing it through, no matter what the personal cost. Understanding that in relation to the way in which Western society in particular has developed over the course of the last century might help to put in perspective two statements by the Tibetan Adept: first, that there were literally hundreds of thousands of initiates of the first degree already in incarnation by the middle of the twentieth century, and secondly that thousands of others would (in groups) be taking the second and third degrees before the end of the same century.[14]

In concluding this chapter, it needs to be mentioned that, although we have here discussed the application of the Sixth and Seventh Rays on the evolutionary progress of the individual in very general terms, the actual effects will depend on the Ray type of the Causal Soul in question. Those same effects will also be conditioned by the Ray type of the individual's astral and lower mental natures as well as by the astrological influences inherent in their natal chart. The subject of psychological conditioning is a very complex one and we can here deal only with general principles. However, we shall see more of the problems facing the thus far initiated intelligence in the next chapter, where we shall consider the very real change of subjective orientation from the psychic to the spiritual.

We shall then also begin to see why it is that the initiate has to learn that the categories and distinctions of Aristotelian thinking are but static mental representations, which must give way to progressively direct intuitive perceptions. The latter then instead reveal themselves to the developing inner faculties as expressions of pure and immediate (spiritual) reason. These in turn potently display themselves in the subtle fluid mechanics and dynamics of essential relationship and the naturally sequential interactions actually underlying all forms of life. That is why the next two initiations are of such critical importance in bridging the inner and outer worlds, thereby finally revealing the distinction between reality and illusion.

TEN

THE GREAT TRANSITION

We now come to the initiation that is equivalent to the Raising of the Master Mason in the tradition of Craft Freemasonry. It is the third degree in Freemasonry, but it is very frequently misinterpreted. That is because the true Raising of the Master in the mainstream occult tradition is the fifth in a sequence of seven. However, within its own parameters, Freemasonry has it correct because the true Master Mason—in the limited sense of the one who has been "killed" by the three rebellious apprentices and who thereafter raises himself up despite this—is indeed the initiate of the third degree. In order to understand why this is so, we first need to understand the nature of the esoteric metaphors and allegories used.

In the Masonic metaphors, King Solomon is actually symbolic of the Demiurge, while the enigmatic King Chiram of Tyre is symbolic of the human Monad, the higher divine "spark." Hiram, the Master Builder, is then representative of the Spiritual Ego (working under the aegis of the Monad), whose job it is to train the building apprentices and make craftsmen out of them. The similarity of the names Chiram and Hiram is quite deliberate, because the working Master Mason, the Spiritual Ego (the "Higher Manas" in theosophical terms) is merely the alter ego and agent of the Monad, the true "king."

We then turn to the three rebellious craftsmen in the story, these being representative of the three lower aspects of the human being—his physical, astral (desire), and lower mental natures. Together, they constitute the integrated personality that, if kept under strict control, performs well. However, if control is lax, they indeed seek through selfishness and jealousy to undermine the work of the Master (the Spiritual Ego). They then esoterically try to "kill" him in order to have their own way without his constant overshadowing and controlling presence. In other words, our own lower nature is constantly trying to subvert our higher nature from carrying out its preordained tasks. In the same tradition, the Master Mason is killed in the very entrance to the temple (i.e., the Causal Soul) using three instruments—the hammer, plumb bob, and the square—which are functionally symbolic of the three states of physical, astral, and lower mental matter respectively. The hammer symbolizes the blunt force of purely physical substance; the plumb-bob, upright emotional balance and a sense of perspective; the square, mental discipline and capacity for exactitude of arrangement or presentation.

Furthermore, we also find in the Masonic tradition the concept of the three temples of Solomon, the first one having been destroyed and the second one in process of being rebuilt by Hiram when he is "killed" by the apprentices. However, the whole allegory has been subverted into a mixed Judeo-Christian context. The three "temples" are in fact symbolic of the three souls of Man—the terrestrial, causal, and spiritual—though which Divine Purpose expresses itself. The terrestrial soul nature has to be "demolished" to make way for the much finer Causal Soul nature—the second temple. The Spiritual Soul nature, on the other hand—the future third temple—is of such grand scale and incomparable beauty that it cannot even be commenced. It must remain as yet an ideal in the mind of the Master Mason.

Hiram himself—the Master Mason representing our own Spiritual Ego—is "employed" to supervise the building of the second or "causal" temple, and for this he needs to train these three (actually groups of) potential craftsmen who constitute his own (i.e., our own) threefold personality. When brought to perfection through self-discipline, their joint skills will comprise the perfected human being, although not yet the perfected Man. The distinction between the three craftsmen and the Master Mason is that the latter not only understands the full extent of craftsmanship inherent in human nature, he also understands how to interpret the higher Purpose in conjunction with that perfected craftsmanship.

The three craftsmen working without that overall guidance and sense of higher Purpose are merely highly skilled workmen. The same is true of our own physical senses, astral desires, and intellect. All three are perfectly capable of working together as a team but, without inspiration and leadership, they will merely go on and on reproducing exactly the same artifacts—as does the human personality—without the addition of that qualitatively special "something" that comes from a higher dimension of perception. In purely human terms the difference is the same as between technical brilliance on the one hand and artistic genius on the other. It is very easy to confuse the two if one does not yet have in one's own nature the creative experience of trying to pursue an ideal beyond its own apparent limitations. It is the latter that ultimately takes our percipient faculty into the abstract realms of spiritual existence, because it is here that we find the archetypes behind all objective forms.

The would-be Master Mason or initiate facing the third degree is, to begin with, concerned with bringing about an overall coordination of his own faculties, something that results in an almost wholly mental polarization after the midpoint between the second and third initiations.[1] However, he quickly finds that the increasingly individualistic characteristics of his personality—which were described in the latter part of the previous chapter—keep interfering in the process of its effective control by his Higher Self. Thus he has to learn how to become the very process of subjective management by withdrawing his own egoic individualism and certainty as to his own righteousness. Otherwise the group of three apprentice craftsmen will themselves copy that egoism, thereby generating the very set of circumstances he is trying to avoid. Hence the recognition of the fact that the "I" nature constantly gets in the way eventually dawns on the individual as being entirely his own (even if unconscious) fault.

THE ISSUE OF INNER REORIENTATION

One of the associated realizations that comes with this is that it is actually impossible to blame others for anything that makes us feel unhappy, worried, or discontented. The reason for that is due to our needing to inject that scenario of uncertainty into our own minds first of all. We then blame others for what we have done to ourselves by a serial process of unconscious psychological associations. When we first clearly realize this, it comes as a shock at our own stupidity. If acted upon, it is then followed by an incredible sense of liberation. This highlights a point made in the previous chapter concerning the fact that the persona of the individual is the product of his own imagination, which, in psychological terms, involves his lower mind as well as his personalized feelings. Hence the candidate for the third initiation has to get rid of this self-generated, elemental parasite before he can make further progress.

A further thing that we learn on the Path is that, with the progressive spiritual development at its latter human stages, less new karma is generated by the individual. That is not to suggest that the individual of the third and fourth degrees faces less karma. He still has to work off the often long-term results of previous causes, which he has generated in this and other lifetimes, before he can—through the inner experience of palingenesis (regeneration as a pure spiritual being)—become a Master of the Wisdom. He also needs to understand that those same causes—apart from being settled in their own right—result from his own psychological reaction to elemental stimulus, both subjective and objective. When he does not give them attention, they effectively cease to exist—something that many people find difficult to understand. Once he recognizes his power to control such elemental activity, he starts to make firm efforts to limit his own mental activity. He becomes energy-selective, if one might so describe his actions. This then brings about the progressive cessation of purely personal karma, because his own insidiously reactive or judgmental thought forms die out by deliberate attrition. We dealt with this to some extent in chapter 4.

Karma, of course, extends far beyond the purely personal situation. We are all involved in various forms of group karma, such as national karma, racial karma, and even gender karma. Our own recognitions of the various false conceptions or prejudices regarding these then help to break down the thought-forms behind them. It is this type of work in which the Adept Hierarchy are themselves said to be involved on a large cultural scale, in furthering the evolutionary progress of humankind.[2] The individual facing the third degree thus has to achieve a high degree of self-control over his subjective nature. This he does using the Fifth Ray faculty—comprising that of the Higher Mind principle, combined with his natural intelligence—which combination we associate with "common sense." Thus the critical faculty here necessitates complete personal objectivity.

However, having just developed a high degree of personality coordination in the previous (second) degree, the individual now faces a huge challenge. That is because he can no longer deal individually with either his physical, or emotional, or lower mental natures. What affects one affects all the rest and all "gang up" together—hence the Masonic allegory of the three apprentices in collusion. Notwithstanding this, it is the lower mind faculty plus its organizing and analytically cunning or discriminatory functions that, uniting as intellectual reason, now constitute the main source of the problem. The purely astral imagination has by now been well and truly conquered and its magnetic, sensory, and visualizing capacities largely contained, but the merely logical, mind-driven type of self-orientated reason subjugates all, incorporating all under the direction of the dominant personality. Hence it is that "the work to be done prior to the taking of the third initiation . . . entails the complete domination of the concrete mind [i.e., the intellect] by the Ego."[3]

WAR BETWEEN THE "DWELLER ON THE THRESHOLD" AND THE SPIRITUAL EGO

The power of his own personality now becomes to his own higher nature what esotericists call the Dweller on the Threshold, which was mentioned at the end of the previous chapter. This (very real) elemental intelligence has a remarkably strong sense of its own creative potency and self-righteousness and that very sense most effectively tends to block out the far more subtle influence of the Spiritual Ego, or Higher Mind. In addition, the individual at this point finds that any attempt by the Spiritual Ego to project its influence more often than not results in that same power being absorbed by the "Dweller" (focused in the lower mind) and used to impersonate it. Consequently, good and even altruistic thoughts are quickly and subtly converted into selfish ones. The waking consciousness of the individual at this point thus becomes a very real battle ground—the Kurukshetra of the Bhagavad Gita—at the center of which he finds himself fully engaged in mortal combat.

The literal psychological war between the "Dweller" and the Spiritual Ego is a fierce and terrible one, the latter eventually realizing, however, that the former just cannot be dissuaded from its entirely self-centered path. There is only one way of dealing with the problem and that is a final war "to the death." The separative individuality of the Dweller has to be killed by direct, face-to-face rejection, beyond any possible reanimation. This recognition brings a real sense of bitter sorrow to the Ego, which, naturally enough, hesitates to destroy its own perfected creation. Yet there is no alternative and, ultimately, the Dweller and all its self-centered "baggage" must be completely cut adrift and left to die of psychological attrition. *The Voice of the Silence* describes this momentous stage in the following words:

> Beware, disciple, of that lethal shade. No light that shines from Spirit can dispel the darkness of the nether soul, unless all selfish thought has fled therefrom and that the pilgrim saith: "I have renounced this passing frame; I have destroyed the cause; the shadows cast can, as effects, no longer be. For now the last great fight, the final war between the Higher and the Lower Self hath taken place. Behold, the very battlefield is now engulfed in the great war, and is no more."[4]

THE AFTERMATH OF THE INNER BATTLE

For the Ego, this wholesale rejection of the lower self results in a catharsis of which the individual's everyday consciousness is initially unaware. To begin with, it seems as though everything worthwhile has been sacrificed and that nothing of any use is left, except a deep, deep sadness and sense of emptiness. Nevertheless, once the crisis is past, the recognition quite quickly dawns that the "temple" can very quickly be rebuilt using the creative skills, which the Ego has already developed and which remain within its range of faculty. This time, however, the recognition is accompanied by a revitalized sense of freedom and the aroused will to ensure that any future personality never gains any sufficient degree of astral or mental independence to menace the intelligence of the spiritual nature ever again. That is why the initiate of the third degree has great natural charisma but no fixed personality, although the remnants of his previous persona are of course still evident to others.

Now, however, the underlying individuality and character are quite different. As we are told: "The heart is now sufficiently pure and loving and the intellect sufficiently stable to stand the strain of knowing"[5]—thereby confirming that true knowledge is assimilated psycho-spiritual power. Here lies the inherent paradox. Without passing the really very extreme tests posed by the third initiation, the individual just does not have the psychological power to contain the real and direct radiatory influence of the Monad itself. The latter, emanating downward through the buddhic state and the Causal Soul, irradiates the brow center (via the crown center) with insight.

As already suggested, the individual is now equivalent to the raised Masonic Master. He is psychologically independent and mentally very powerful because of this freedom, but he quickly recognizes that he is now entirely "on his own." Few indeed are there who can approach him on his own level because of the sheer power of astro-mental self-discipline that he radiates. Indeed, he cares very little for what anybody else thinks about him or says of him, which adds yet further to his innate power. Yet he must continue to maintain normal contact with the mass of humanity, and this he does by adjusting his new outer "persona" to theirs, according to whatever need or circumstance he comes across. He also necessarily learns how to "dim his light" for others while at the same time continuing his own subjective development.

THE NEED FOR
SUBJECTIVE COMPARTMENTALIZATION

To do this effectively he must compartmentalize his nature, learning to live for the most part within the ascetic solitariness of his inner Self. However, for those few others (apart from second degree initiates) sensitive enough to recognize the fact, there is now a part of him that most can no longer reach, despite the fact that they are aware of its presence. In a very real sense, he has already died to this world and recognizes that as an established fact. Yet to all outward perception he continues to live as a human being. However, he no longer cares for his own personal ambition. That is because, by the halfway point between the third and fourth initiations, he has already reached the summit of purely human achievement and now recognizes with much greater clarity than before the sheer superficiality of most human endeavor.

Yet he now realizes that he must help others by teaching or training and also by his own example. He still has far to go on his own account and has a great deal more to learn in purely spiritual terms before he can himself "cross over" in the full spiritual sense. There will almost inevitably be those initiates of this degree who do not make such quick progress for one reason or another, but one would imagine them to be very few indeed in number. The real spiritual push, at this time, has considerable force and will not be slowed down for long. Any such person would naturally face considerable and fairly immediate karmic retribution as well for a sluggish response. For the majority, however, it is a time of immensely accelerated learning and understanding of esoteric and occult principles of an increasingly subtle nature.

The Tibetan Adept DK refers to the third initiation as that of the "transfiguration."[6] This draws an immediate parallel with the experience of the initiate Jesus on the Mount of Olives (before his final arrival in Jerusalem), where his three senior disciples (like the three Masonic apprentices) see him surrounded by an aura of spiritual light within which they can also discern two other figures—supposedly Elijah and John the Baptist—these being per-

THE LATE THIRD
DEGREE INITIATE

(Beginning to see into
the spiritual state above
although still functioning
from within the objective
world below)

THE REALIZED FOURTH
DEGREE INITIATE

(Now translated into the
spiritual state and thus
able to begin using his
spiritual vision properly
from within it)

THE FIFTH DEGREE INITIATE
(THE MASTER ADEPT)

(Now fully self-conscious within
the spiritual state and thus able
to use his higher faculties overshadowed by the Oversoul, as
symbolized by the red disc above
his head)

Fig. 10.1. The initiate in transition

haps symbolic of the two spiritual (atmic and buddhic) states of being. A further proof of the third initiation having been passed and of the individual's now achieved capacity for the beginnings of spiritual sight was shown symbolically by the ancient Egyptians in their picture of the head of the neophyte emerging above the open lotus flower (see left panel in fig. 10.1).

The opened lotus flower was known universally in ancient times as symbolic of the spiritual world and the head of the individual emerging from within it was suggestive of only momentary perception of that state. However, when the individual had passed the fourth initiation, the symbolism changed. Now it showed him as the naked youth seated within the open lotus flower and holding his finger to his mouth (see middle panel of fig. 10.1), denoting the need for silence as regards this achievement. However, that same necessity becomes very evident in the prelude to the initiation itself. That is because inner silence generates inner force and magnetic potency. The individual at this stage has to maintain an inner quietude, which builds up the power and focus that he will need literally to break through into the spiritual world; otherwise there would be no possibility of such initiation.

THE PRELUDE TO THE FOURTH INITIATION

For those who have passed through the third degree stage's initial trauma, the subjective benefits are considerable. Virtually all purely human anxieties (including fear) progressively cease for the simple reason that they are essentially based on losing or having to let go of all personal (even family) belongings, whether objective or subjective. For the initiate of this third degree, nothing could ever again be equivalent to what he has already just lost. So why should he worry about anything, now knowing himself to be a spiritual individuality who can literally, if he so wills, turn his hand and his creative imagination to deal with virtually anything the world cares to throw at him? Consequently, courage and foresight are now natural to his every thought and action.

As he is now, in addition, a probationer on the kosmic Path, he comes under the distantly watchful eye of the Chohan or senior Adept of his particular Ray, and the Chohan will (eventually) make this fact known to him, although interfering in his destiny in no way because he still has to prove himself before actually entering the higher Path.[7] Therefore, it is only approaching the next (fourth) initiation that the Chohan will give him a particular (and inevitably very problematic) task to fulfill, of which he is self-consciously aware—one necessarily dealing with crisis control. The way in which he deals with that task involves much subtle testing of his depth and breadth of character. However, on passing that next highly critical stage, with his inner perspectives and sense of humor still intact, he then becomes an "accepted disciple" of the Greater White Lodge and a true member of the Spiritual Hierarchy.

The individual facing the fourth initiation still has an enormous amount to learn in a relatively short space of time. While some of this will be in the way of theoretical (book) learning, the major discipline that he has to master is the fully self-conscious use of his own intuition. In a very real sense, he has to learn how (subjectively) to phrase and ask the right questions concerning esoteric and occult theory. He also has to learn to recognize and assimilate the ever-increasing subtlety of the answers (or the very occasional helpful pointers) when they are provided to him—very rarely in quite the clearly straightforward manner he might have expected or wished for. He must then convert it into appropriate form or action of an altogether impersonal nature.

It is at this point that he begins to realize that all knowledge is available and accessible to him (via the devas), provided that he asks for it in the right way. It is also now that he recognizes for the first time that knowledge carries with it a very real power—that it is, in fact, *a* power. He thus realizes that his own power is entirely dependent upon what he accesses for his own use in the service of others. The experienced initiate of the third degree thus now finds himself in a somewhat problematic and potentially perilous situation. While he still exists and functions very effectively within the human state, he realizes that it is unnatural to his true nature and that he must move on to the next stage of spiritual development. However, this is by no means straightforward. As *The Voice of the Silence* describes it:

> Ere thou canst near that goal, before thine hand is lifted to upraise the
> fourth gate's latch, thou must have mastered all the mental changes in

thy Self and slain the army of the thought sensations that, subtle and insidious, creep unasked within the Soul's bright shrine. If thou wouldst not be slain by them, then must thou harmless make thy own creations, the children of thy thoughts, unseen, impalpable, that swarm around humankind.[8]

Although poetically put, this is no even faint exaggeration. Harmlessness—perhaps only a working ideal for the lesser initiate—is an absolutely critical faculty of self-control in the armory of the higher initiate. Paradoxically, without it he is spiritually powerless.

INITIATORY PREPARATION

In brief, he now has to bring his mental processes under such complete control that they are no longer reactive in any way, for it is reactive thoughts that, even inadvertently, cause damage—both to others and to oneself. Yet human beings have come to believe that the instinctively reactive faculty is self-protective; hence its removal would appear to make the individual intensely vulnerable. This may be so in the case of the human masses, who are still immersed in their emotions or their personality-led natures, but it does not work in the case of those whose subjective focus is toward the spiritual planes of existence.

When the influence of the spiritual planes predominates, the individual begins to develop an occult prescience—the capacity to foresee where a process or chain of objective events or thinking will lead. As this faculty develops, so the individual is able progressively to perceive, through self-consciously intuitive reflex, what lies further ahead. As already mentioned: "Coming events cast their shadows before." He therefore learns to actively develop the faculty of inner observation (plus nonreactive obedience to it) and finds it much more effective than the merely reactive use of the mind and emotions, which most human beings employ. Somewhat paradoxically, however, we learn that in the run-up to each and every initiation, a sort of blindness descends on the consciousness of the individual. This is explained by the following note of caution:

From the moment when a human being catches the first, faint glimpse of the "something other" and sees himself in juxtaposition to that dimly sensed, distant reality, the blindness . . . is something imposed by the [higher] soul upon the hastening aspirant so that the lessons of conscious experience . . . may be correctly assimilated and expressed; by its means, the hurrying seeker is defended from making too rapid and superficial progress.[9]

It naturally follows from this why it is that the real seeker after Truth finds his way constantly and frustratingly blocked by psychological obstacles and why he thus often becomes subject to the "dark night of the soul." After understanding the tests of the third degree imposed upon him (which takes quite a while after actually undergoing them), this problem persists to a lesser extent. The individual now instinctively knows the way forward, even if he still has to master the associated understanding of what he comes across en route. However, his most immediate concern is the final destruction of his Causal Soul body, which provides the last obstruction. Without this first taking place the fourth initiation cannot be undertaken.

In a very real sense, the shattering of the Causal Soul body may be considered as somewhat similar to the rupturing of the fetal sac that contains the human infant about to be born. As already described, the causal body is contained within a protective deva organism, just as the infant is contained within the protective body of the mother. Also, just as the infant inverts its body prior to entering the birth canal, so as to make the actual birth possible, it is suggested a comparable reorientation takes place in the human spiritual entity about to be born. In order to understand this, it needs to be remembered that the entity to be born has undertaken its gestation within the higher spiritual nature, not within the lower human nature, even though we talk (erroneously) of the evolution of consciousness taking place within the waking human mind. The latter is merely a sympathetic effect of instinctive response in the lower organism. In a rather peculiar but interestingly suggestive way, the purely human organism has a sort of correspondence to the placenta by which the mother feeds the fetus, for it "feeds" the higher organism with the synthesis of the many lower worldly experiences that cause the higher organism to develop.

As human beings with a strong sense of our own individuality, the suggestions made in the last paragraph might well come as something of a shock. However, the logic of the "as above, so below" principle should be self-evident when it is also taken into consideration that the primary issue is actually the objective expression of kosmic consciousness (that of the Monad). The influence of the latter flows "downward" not "upward" (at least, not at this stage). Consequently, the developing spiritual entity, at the time of its "birth," must invert and enable its higher consciousness literally to descend into the "Underworld" of objective planetary existence. Thus, while it would certainly appear that the initiated consciousness of the individual moves literally "upward" (as will be described in further detail later on), it is because it becomes magnetically subsumed within the awakening consciousness of the Monad within the buddhic state. This, as already described, is the kosmic etheric double of the Logos "in Whom we live and move and have our being." Of this stage we are further told:

> By the time the fourth initiation is taken, the initiate has mastered perfectly the fifth subplane [on all the three lower planes] and is therefore adept—to use a technical phrase . . . and is well on the way to master the sixth. His buddhic vehicle [his Spiritual Soul nature] can function on the two lower subplanes of the buddhic plane.[10]

While this perhaps looks like a passingly interesting technical statement, it is in fact deeply occult in nature because it indicates to the initiate the stage of his achievement in terms of faculty. The substance of the subplane (counting from below upward) is highly abstract and tenuous in nature, thus very difficult to control consciously, although many advanced types use the abstract mind and the astral and physical equivalents occasionally and only very briefly, without being aware of the fact. Their abstract thoughts and feelings are thus largely incoherent and inexplicable.

The sixth subplane (counting upward), however, comprises what we might call the akasic "essence" of each associated plane; its conscious control (paralyzing all outward activity) allows the individual to discriminate as to the type and quality of mental, astral, and physical energy and force he should apply in any given situation. His capacity to control this type of energy and force depends, however, upon the conscious self-control of his inner attention. He thus has to bring his subjective nature to an absolute standstill in order to develop his sensitivity to the vibratory "signatures" of different types of mental, astral, and etheric-physical substance in their qualitatively quiescent states. Otherwise he will not be able to register them properly.

The capacity to function in the two lowest substates of the buddhic plane (the kosmic etheric) involves spiritual comprehension plus the spiritual healing faculty. That is to say, the initiated intelligence has now developed some basic faculty of truly spiritual discernment for the first time, together with some capacity to guide his own spiritual forces consciously from the inner (i.e., higher) world to the outer. This in turn highlights the fact that he is already working at the better development of his own future capacities on the spiritual plane of existence where his consciousness is still but that of a child, relatively speaking. Those capacities, as just indicated, and as previously described in chapter 5, involve the higher equivalents of the senses that we call "hearing" and "touch." However, the individual is as yet still working very much "in the dark." The next faculty to be developed is that of fully self-conscious spiritual sight, but that will not come until the next moment of evolutionary crisis in his life—that generating Masterhood itself.

There is one further factor that has to be recognized, appreciated, and put into practice by the individual facing the fourth initiation. It is that of patience—really intense patience. In chapter 3 we looked at the fact that the spiritual world is populated by deva hierarchies, which, as the expression of the logoic Memory, have no sense of choice. Their whole instinct is that of repetition, constantly refined and improved to sharpen the faculty of the Logos, while also developing their own faculty of sensitivity. By virtue of the fact that they have no sense of alternative (or thus of choice), their whole modus operandi is one of cyclically ordered expression. Consequently, while man in the objective lower world is able to make snap changes of thought and action in his daily life—hence the lower world being so ephemeral— within the spiritual world he cannot. Here (at least to begin with), he is entirely subject to the same rule of cyclical order, any wished-for change needing to coincide entirely with it. However, because the earlier initiations have produced in him a sense of his increasing freedom and power within the lower world to do exactly as he wishes, the recognition of how the spiritual world operates comes as something of a shock.

He begins to realize that the individualized sense of persona operated by his intelligence in the lower world cannot be taken with him when transferring to the spiritual world where he must instead conform entirely with the Law. In other words, to pass on through the gate of this initiation he must first relinquish his instinctual individuality of action—although not his self-conscious individuality of perceptual understanding, which he retains. In order to bring about the desired transition, he must therefore realign or reorient his intelligence by means of a patience that is permanently undisturbable, to conform with the perceived modus operandi of the spiritual world; for only then will he be able to operate consciously within it and to recognize the (deva and other) higher beings for whom it is the "home" environment. This, it is suggested, is the essence of the statement "Not my will but Thine be done O Lord." The latter is definitive of the consciousness associated with the seventh and highest substate and, ultimately, the all-inclusive seventh state itself.

It is worth noting that, from one angle at least, the life of the individual approaching the fourth initiation (and even after it) is one of even greater psychological hardship than he has yet faced. In order to focus on his spiritual work, he has to learn a degree of solitariness and subjectivity that most human beings would find altogether intolerable, particularly as his way of life now effectively and necessarily results in his complete loss of purely personal human friendships, even close family ties, and probably also his public status or social position. Everything of a purely personal nature has to be sacrificed in obedient readiness for the final great reorientation, even apparently his former reliance on the Adepts to guide him. Most such facts can be psychologically faced with courage, but by now he realizes that there is a further and even more frustratingly intractable problem for him to deal with as well.

He finds—on setting about the final destruction of his own Causal Soul body—that his personal magnetism and vibration do not synchronize with those of either his fellow human beings or of the Adept Brotherhood. That is because he is in a critical state of psychic transition. This remains the case until some time after he has actually taken the fourth initiation.[11] That in turn is so because, even after he has taken it, the continuing problem involves his whole body organism having to adapt itself to the new and much higher vibration. For those on certain Rays, apparently, this is not easy.

It is worth mentioning here in passing, however, the correspondence between the fourth initiation (that of accepted discipleship on the Higher Path), the Fourth Ray, and the association of the latter with the zodiacal sign of Scorpio. The keynote of the latter involves the disciple's triumphant emergence or return, following his much earlier "descent into Hell" through incarnation. There is also the seemingly further association between Scorpio and the giant star Sirius, within the aura of which, we are told, the Greater Spiritual Brotherhood exists.[12] But more about that remarkable idea later.

THE FOURTH INITIATION
AND ITS IMMEDIATE AFTERMATH

Thus we come finally to the fourth initiation itself, described by the Adept DK as somewhat paralleling that of "the crucifixion" of Jesus, in the sense of the initiate's own consciousness being crucified as between Heaven and Earth. The idea inherent in this parallel is that the initiate—his approach still conditioned by the human terrestrial experience—becomes progressively aware, at first hand for the very first time, what the spiritual state is actually like and how it feels to function semi-consciously within it. In other words, he becomes self-consciously aware at one and the same time of the nature of both terrestrial and spiritual states and the differences between them. In doing so he is shocked to his core, followed by a great sense of deep frustration until the actual transition is made. Yet he realizes—while still "transfixed" in the human state—that he has no option but to choose the spiritual world, even though he only sees it "through a glass, darkly" and cannot yet see how to penetrate it. In practical terms, he now gradually begins to see "with the eye of spirit" the factual illusion of the objective world, which makes that choice completely inevitable. However, the Tibetan Master describes the culminating experience precedent to the initiation itself, evidently from his own experience:

Little by little, the vibration of both [the higher and lower Selves] becomes stronger reciprocally. There comes then a moment when contact between the two projections is made in meditation. . . . This does not constitute a moment of crisis but is in the nature of a Flame of Light, a realisation of liberation and a recognition of the esoteric fact that a man is himself the Way. There is no longer the sense of personality and soul or of ego and form, but simply the One, functioning on all planes as a point of spiritual energy and arriving at one sphere of planned activity by means of the path of Light.[13]

The description then goes on to suggest that this experience has to be followed by periods of psychological "stabilisation and resurrection"[14] in which the initial, bridging thread of consciousness is augmented by further threads resulting from active (yet flexibly reoriented) work experience. As the same Adept adds in confirmation:

It [the new "bridge"] must perforce be used because there is now no other medium of intercourse between the initiate and the One whom he now knows to be himself. He ascends in full consciousness into the sphere of monadic life . . . [and thus] belongs to the great company of Those whose will is consciously divine and Who are the custodians of the Plan.[15]

Once he has achieved this self-consciously generated "third death," the individual finds that even spiritual aspiration per se ceases to exist, because it is no longer necessary.[16] We touched on some of these same issues at the end of chapter 8, when dealing with the transition of the consciousness-base (upadhi) of the individual caused by the motivating jiva (the lesser "spark") moving from the heart center to the crown center. Here it is further clarified, for the "sphere of monadic life" is that of the Spiritual Soul in a personal sense, functioning within the kosmic etheric double of the Logos in the wider context. The initiate of the fourth degree is thus "liberated" in the sense that, at last freed from all purely personal considerations, he now begins to learn how to work patiently within the far broader framework of logoic Purpose. With this he is at last steadily becoming consciously acquainted.

THE RAY ASSOCIATION

The fourth initiation is described as parallel to the consciousness of the (Fourth) Ray of Harmony through Conflict in another sense. The essence of the idea here is that the initiate understands for the first time the true nature of crisis (which takes the form of conflict in the lower world) in generating and maintaining a sufficiently acute state of psychological tension for evolutionary change to take place in consciousness. In the spiritual world that state of tension is permanent and natural, in the same sense as is the stringed tension of the musical instrument or of the muscular and psychological readiness of the highly trained athlete. Consequently, change within the spiritual world cannot be considered as in any way the same as that experienced in the lower or outer world of human existence.

For us this would seem to infer an intractable paradox. How can change not involve change? In the Buddhist philosophy, everything is seemingly subject to change. How then can the spiritual world be any different? How in fact can there be initiations beyond the fourth if some sort of change is not involved? The answer to this apparent conundrum lies in the nature of the life force itself. That is to say, while power is theoretically infinite, the associated heat and light generated vary according to the assimilative capacity of the instrument or agent. Human experience involves constant and wide fluctuation. In the world of spiritual experience that fluctuation is simply not possible because of its natural state of (much higher) tension. That same state, involving spiritual light, is itself generated by the very intelligence of the beings within it.

Hence it is that the mystic ascetically involved in intense and sustained devotional contemplation is sometimes (briefly) able to access and experience levels of perception within that state. However, because his own psychological "center of gravity," if one might so put it, still lies primarily in the subjective human state, he is unable to sustain the experience and thus "falls back." This in turn highlights the essential difference between the mystic and the occultist, the true initiate being the latter, even though he has long since acquired the mystic faculty and brought it under control. Hence the further advisory comment:

Each initiation dims the light already acquired and used and then immerses the initiate in a higher light. Each initiation enables the disciple to perceive an area of divine consciousness hitherto unknown but which, when the disciple has familiarised himself with it and its unique phenomena, vibratory quality and interrelations, becomes for him a normal field of experience and activity.[17]

The Voice of the Silence issues yet another warning to the individual facing the fourth initiation:

On Path fourth, the lightest breeze of passion or desire will stir the steady light upon the pure white walls of Soul. The smallest wave of longing or regret for Maya's gifts illusive along *antahkarana*—the path that lies between thy spirit and thy self, the highway of sensations . . . a thought as fleeting as the lightning flash will make thee thy prizes forfeit, the prizes thou hast [already] won.[18]

If that happens, the individual must start all over again, in order to recover the lost spiritual momentum. That momentum is very real (as is consciously recognized after the third initiation has been taken) and it is achieved by absolutely committed forward focus and tension—hence the "razor-edged path." Inevitably, if only momentarily distracted, the recovery takes less time than it did at the outset. But it is nevertheless supremely annoying because than loss of self-awareness is itself so obstructive. The *Hermetica* also makes clear the situation facing the initiate progressively arriving at this point when it says:

Since there are two kinds of entities, corporeal and incorporeal, corresponding to mortal and divine, one is left to choose one or the other, if choice is desired. One cannot have both together [when one is left to choose] but lessening the one reveals the activity of the other.[19]

This highly important latter sentence in particular needs to be very carefully borne in mind, as also the seemingly simple but curious statement that "The problem presented by the [i.e., this fourth] initiatory test is solved by the use of the reasoning mind [involving] . . . a combination of recapitulation and reorientation."[20]

THE "LEAP OF FAITH"

It becomes self-evident from this that the initiate-in-waiting finds himself here in the paradoxical situation of needing to move forward but yet realizing that such must somehow involve an overriding rejection of the lower, human world of existence. He is faced with the awful proposition that he must make a leap of complete (but reasoned) faith over this subjective chasm, without having any definite prior knowledge of what he will be stepping into. All that he has to support his faith is the inner certainty that he is himself immortal and that he has made such decisions before, always with beneficial results. He also knows within himself that on the other side of the chasm that he faces—sometimes described as a curtain of fire—he will find his own true home and those who have passed over before him. But he knows at the same time that there is no going back in real terms. This time he will be irrevocably changed. Thus, once this decision is made, he really is fully committed. For this reason, it requires an act of high courage, even though allied to a perception of there being no alternative.

In "technical" terms, so we are told, what the initiate is facing here involves his own final destruction of the Causal Soul body, as we mentioned a few pages ago. This is the psycho-spiritual organism that has enfolded and protected him since his inception as a self-conscious human being, literally millions of years before. This Causal Soul we described in chapter 2 as being made up of a "downward" extrusion of buddhic influence or radiance into the higher mental world—the same as the kabbalistic Keter-Hokmah. It is this same "fetal" organism that has provided him with certain necessary human faculties—self-consciousness, feeling, and sensitivity among them—but which are now no longer needed. That is because his awakened and spiritual intelligence now possesses power over form and has already absorbed all of these capacities within a by now consciously wider range of faculty.[21]

The initiate has thus arrived at the point of stepping out of one wholly personal, semi-darkened state into another that is full of a completely different quality of light—somewhat akin to the human infant breaking out of the amniotic sac at birth. Again, like the human infant before birth, the consciousness of the initiate facing this onward move is already increasingly aware of the phenomenon of "soundless sound" emanating from the new world he is about to enter. He is also vaguely but increasingly aware—through his already awakened spiritual sense of touch—of the restrictive field of psychic protection surrounding him, which he has to destroy in order to pass onward into the spiritual world proper. However, to describe these senses in terms that would make any real or practical sense to the average human being is regretfully impossible, other than by way of the analogy that we have just used.

Continuing with the same analogy, therefore, the initiate who thus breaks out of this environment still has to find his way "to the other side." On breaking out he finds that he still has to overcome a hiatus[22]—like the human infant literally squeezing its way out of the womb along the birth canal into the light of day. In order to achieve this, the infant has first to reorient itself and then to lie prone and still, allowing the maternal birth process itself to force him out. The initiate facing the fourth degree in a very real sense will have to do the same. Fully committed spiritual orientation is essential, followed by total subjective and objective acquiescence, involving that pure and sustained patience and persistence that is the foundational essence of spiritual Will. If there is instead a combative psychological struggle, it could result in death. That is why *The Voice of the Silence* warns:

> Stern and exacting is the virtue of *Viraga* (total indifference to pleasure and pain). If thou its Path would master, thou must keep thy mind and thy perceptions far freer than before from killing action.[23]

Just as the run-up to the third initiation involved a vivification of the brow (ajna) chakra, in conjunction with the crown chakra, so its achievement and the subsequent run-up to the fourth initiation involves a revivification plus a reorientation of the crown chakra. It was the vitalization and self-conscious control of the brow chakra that enabled the initiate of the second degree to bring about gradual mastery over the visualizing faculty and thus also the elemental thought-forms of the lower mental plane, precedent to the third initiation. Correspondingly, it is the capacity for self-conscious use of the crown chakra that enables the initiate facing the fourth degree to call down reserves of spiritual intuition pretty well at will and eventually to pass through this "gate of flame" to the spiritual state itself. The latter, as we saw earlier, is synonymous with the kosmic etheric double of the Logos where group consciousness is the primary concern.[24] Something of this was described in earlier chapters.

THE FACTOR OF SPIRITUAL MOMENTUM

One of the most crucially important issues facing the individual "on the Path" (at all stages of it) is that of his subjective forward momentum, as already briefly mentioned. That is itself derived from focused intent in relation to active work in furtherance of what he perceives as his real, immediate task or purpose in life. This is of particular significance, however, for those facing the fourth initiation—and, by logical inference also, those immensely advanced ones eventually facing the eighth, although the latter remains beyond our remotest considerations. That is because this necessarily involves a wholesale relocation into a completely new and higher (kosmic) dimension of self-consciousness altogether.

Without a real degree of sustained subjective momentum in the early stages of spiritual progress (i.e., following the attainment of accepted discipleship), the individual would naturally fall off the "straight and narrow Way"—and most, if not all, naturally do just that at one stage or another. This happens for a variety of reasons including doubt on the one hand or, on the other, fascination/distraction with things that should actually be avoided at all costs. However, even those who have developed a real inner momentum in their lives sometimes also come to grief because they lose or forget their own originally detached motivation. This occurs, for example, in the business world where we often see immensely successful people (men usually) who allow themselves to lose focus through falling prey to various forms of flattery and self-indulgence. Wherever the sense of self prevails, even briefly, potential disaster and its karmic consequences naturally ensue.

When it comes to the stage of actually passing from one continuum of consciousness to another, however, the issue of momentum becomes literally crucial. Entering the "kingdom of Heaven"—that is, the spiritual world proper—can thus only be done through "taking it by storm." The associated quality of momentum varies according to the individual's Ray type, but that does not detract from the fact that the totality of one's higher subjective nature has to be involved in the intensity of projection; otherwise the effort will not result in success. For those who imagine that such transitions can be achieved by merely intense desire or aspiration, think again, for the slightest impurity of thought or personal association will immediately slow down one's progress to a crawl, so that one feels as though one has run into a mud wallow.

It is worthwhile reiterating in relation to all this that the necessary focus that gives rise to the momentum mentioned derives from the spiritual Will, which, esoterically speaking, expresses itself as a subjective psycho-spiritual tension. This itself, as we are told, incorporates implacable determination, patient ability to wait and to preserve purity of intention, plus an orientation unmoved by anything of a personal nature that intervenes in life. This is such that the right creative action takes place at the appropriately timed moment, which the Oversoul nature ordains and thus determines to be correct.[25] This factor of tension is mentioned again and again throughout this work and the understanding of its true nature is of really vital importance in the individual's life work on the Path.

LEAVING BEHIND
THE FOURTH KINGDOM IN NATURE

As just mentioned, *The Voice of the Silence* refers to the immediate approach to the "Fourth Gate" of initiation as involving the nature of *viraga* (detachment) and describes the associated feeling of the individual at this time as one of "absolute indifference to the objective universe, to pleasure and to pain. Disgust does not express its meaning, yet it is akin to it."[26] Nevertheless, one can well imagine that, by this time, the individual has achieved such a sense of rejection of the excessive indulgences, indolence, and stupidity of much human behavior that his Higher Self—which now essentially belongs to the nascent fifth kingdom in Nature—would indeed feel disgust by way of personal association with the human state. This is perhaps commensurate with the way in which a reasonably intelligent human being would look at the altogether crude instincts of the animal by comparison to his own.

However, there is a definable subjective process that the initiate of the third degree must follow and perfect before he is actually in the position of taking this initiation of "renunciation" and thus attaining to the first stage of Adeptship. It involves the construction of the "consciousness bridge." The actual approach to the fourth initiation (commencing with the three earlier initiations) thus involves a prolonged sevenfold sequence of self-training in the same essential sequence as with the overall seven initiations:

1. Intention
2. Visualization
3. Projection
4. Invocation
5. Evocation
6. Stabilization
7. Resurrection

The first three of these involve the actual building and internal reorientation of the Mind faculty toward the spiritual Path, resulting in the generation and emanation of a line of psycho-spiritual light, which is itself the nascent bridge—the already mentioned antahkarana. The process is then completed by the use of a "Word of Power," which projects it "upward" with a potency that increases with practice. This then renders the initiate subjectively invocative, resulting in monadic energy being persistently drawn "downward" to meet his human consciousness. This also results in the Causal Soul body being progressively destroyed "from the inside," as it were.

After the two halves of the antahkarana meet, thereby generating a flame of Divine Light within the consciousness of the individual, the second part of this initiation is taken. The initiate now recognizes himself as the point of emanating spiritual Light, by which he may project himself, at will, wherever he wishes within the lower three planes of existence. It quite logically follows that the emanation from the Monad is at first tenuous and the young Adept must therefore now concentrate on building up his force in practical service of the Higher Purpose of which he is now an increasingly conscious agent. In so doing, thereby gradually gaining full control of the less evolved deva hierarchies, he makes himself powerfully at-one with this same Source of his own previous Self-hood and thus eventually becomes a Master Adept.[27]

Not altogether surprisingly because of his wholesale spiritual reorientation, the objective effects of the fourth initiation are also powerfully felt in the group surrounding the initiate or involved with him in his field of work.[28] That is because he has now become such a potent center of psycho-spiritual tension that his magnetism automatically generates self-induced crises of orientation and decision in their lives, both personally and as a group, through personal association and the power of sympathetic vibration.

This same effect was to some extent true even before he passed through this initiation. Nevertheless, it now becomes a permanent feature binding them together ever more powerfully—and karmically—even though they lack his focus and even find it very uncomfortable to put up with it on a sustained basis. Paradoxically, however, his own personal sense of higher identification is accompanied by an increasingly strong sense of what one can only call sadness and disgust at the wholly pointless miseries and needless excesses of human existence, which have led to so much personal karma.

Once the "bridge" of the antahkarana has been completed and the Causal Soul body of the individual destroyed by his own efforts at the fourth initiation, he finds himself at the point of leaving the fourth kingdom in Nature—humanity—altogether. However, before he can do this as just described, and thus fully join the nascent fifth kingdom in Nature, he must prove his total commitment to and command of the Higher Way. He does so by pursuing a yet greater subjective asceticism that, while retaining his self-conscious sensory faculties, literally destroys his purely human persona (although not his individuality of character) forever. This occurs while still paradoxically enabling him to continue taking a human body and participating to some extent in the life of humanity for purely altruistic purposes. Of this we shall learn more in the next chapter.

However, there is something else here of extreme importance that the individual now has to take into consideration. It is that the point of the "inner round" of higher involutionary–evolutionary experience, which he has now consciously entered, is also the final point at which involutionary deva influence is at its strongest in the overall cycle. This needs to be explained in rather more detail, as follows.

If we reconsider fig. 3.2, we can see that the "outer round" (of objective world experience) results from emanation from the lowest point of the inner round, that is, the kosmic etheric double. It is from here that the lesser "spark" (i.e., the jiva-daemon) descends by involutionary projection into the lower world order. It descends first of all into the various elemental hierarchies, which it then learns to organize, thereby progressively becoming part of the evolutionary aspects of the mineral, plant, and animal kingdoms, before joining the human kingdom. During the whole of this time, unbeknown to itself, the jiva is under the strongest deva influence. It is only once anchored in the human heart, as it reapproaches the Inner Round on the latter part of the cycle of human experience (i.e., the Path), that it begins to free itself from that same overriding influence. However, when the individual attains the fourth initiation, he finds himself subjectively exposed to the full force of deva instinct, even though at last free of the objective body. It is for this reason that *The Voice of the Silence* provides the admonition: "Beware, lest in the care of Self thy soul should lose her foothold on the soil of deva knowledge."[29]

As the Master Kuthumi explained to A. P. Sinnett in the early days of the Theosophical Society in India, "of those who engage themselves in the occult sciences, he who does it must either reach the goal or perish. Once fairly started on the way to the great Knowledge, to doubt is to risk insanity; to come to a dead stop is to fall; to recede is to tumble backwards, headlong into an abyss."[30] This statement involves no exaggeration.

It almost goes without saying that this stark description serves to explain why, at this point, as already explained, the individual feels literally "crucified" in time and space. He realizes that, at this crucially intermediate point in his development, he is entirely on his own and that there is but one direction to follow—involving complete death to the past, through what appears to be almost complete darkness—before he finds the inner light. In doing so, he has paradoxically to realize that the very darkness frustratingly facing him is itself the outer radiance of that higher light. However, as Mircea Eliade helpfully comments:

Death is of course an end—but an end immediately followed by a new beginning. One dies to one mode of being in order to be able to attain to another. Death constitutes an abrupt change of ontological level and at the same time, a rite of passage, just as birth does, or initiation.[31]

Freed of the purely human influence that has held him in thrall for so long, the individual now finds himself at the critical junction of the overall involutionary and evolutionary impulses within the inner round, the causal spiritual environment. On the one side lies all the faculty and knowledge of involutionary deva nature at its most objective point (a fact of which he must be most careful because of its highly attractive nature). On the other lies the far greater evolutionary cycle of divinity itself. In order to maintain his inner momentum, he has to make a determined choice by fastening his gaze and his intent on the latter, thus leaving behind all the distractions of deva knowledge while still able to direct it and thus work in harmony with it according to yet higher Divine Purpose.

With that in mind, it is perhaps helpful to remind ourselves here that the deva hierarchies are the local agents of expression of Divine Memory and its natural cycles. Consequently (whether we are conscious of the fact or not), they are the necessary exponents of all Nature's many aspects and attributes. These and the associated cycles of higher deva activity inevitably lead to the objective world of change while they themselves remain in the archetypal world of spirit. That thereby gives rise to the paradoxical phenomenon of constant cyclical movement without change within the kosmic etheric nature of the Logos, with which the Adept must become thoroughly familiar. Thus *The Voice of the Silence* further admonishes the initiate of the fourth degree not to look backward, when warning: "Beware of change! for change is thy great foe. This change will fight thee off and throw thee back out of the Path thou treadest, deep into the viscous swamps of doubt."[32]

It is for this reason that the Adept rejects any suggestion by the mystically inclined as to his being a deva or angel, with its naturally involutionary concerns in relation to the lesser kingdoms of Nature.

ASCETICISM AND PAIN

The Higher Way that now faces the initiate is thus inevitably ascetic in nature. The fifth initiation that lies before him is itself directly associated with the fifth stage of the Inner Round. However, it is only the first major stage of the upward or evolutionary Path. This is called, by *The Voice of the Silence,* the *Virya* gate. We shall deal with it further in the next chapter. However, there are two final points that need to be mentioned before we travel onward.

The first of these concerns the subject of pain. In relation to this there seems to be a general assumption—possibly arising out of the Christian association with the "crucifixion" initiation—that pain ceases to exist for the Adept after the trauma of the fourth initiation. However, this is not logical and we are also told that it is quite definitely not so, except in relation to his remaining, purely human senses, where the physical, astral, and mental elemental natures have been completely overcome.[33] Pain itself involves or results from sensitivity to resistance of an essentially electrical nature, whatever state of being is in process of response. It is thus found progressing all the way up to kosmic levels of experience, and doubtless also beyond. It is only when the intelligence has managed to pass beyond the protective "curtain" of any level of being in full self-consciousness that it can look back and see the experience in due perspective. Once that is done, the pain previously experienced is transmuted into a protective power. Our own human experience should demonstrate to us the logic of this.

The second point concerns accessibility to higher knowledge. The Adept no longer has to "think" in the way that the average human being does. That is because he knows how to invoke knowledge concerning our planetary Life as and when necessary—whether past, present, or future—from within the deva consciousness of our planetary Life. Its availability is immediate. All he then has to do is observe and direct its essence, as he considers appropriate.

This is something of which the initiate of the third degree is already becoming consciously aware from his own experience. That experience otherwise necessitates his learning to recognize the occult "signatures" of particular psycho-spiritual energies and forces, how to compartmentalize and thus control them, and how and when best to precipitate them whenever he needs or wants to. Were he not able to recognize and control them with skill in this way, he would find that their tendency would be to run amok in his consciousness. That in turn would lead to madness. It is worth noting, however, that this faculty of elemental control is not fully completed through the achievement of the fourth degree. *The Voice of the Silence* tells us: "And in [i.e., precedent to] the fifth, O slayer of thy thoughts, all these again have to be killed beyond reanimation."[34]

THE DERIVATION OF HIGHER KNOWLEDGE

When it comes to ascertaining the yet higher knowledge of the kosmic system within which our solar scheme exists, a slightly different approach is necessary on the part of the more advanced Adepts capable of extending their range of consciousness thus far. Where any new perceptual vision of kosmic knowledge is concerned, nothing is accepted as fact by the Adept Hierarchy as a whole until and unless double-checked by other senior Adepts over a sustained period of several centuries of related experience.[35]

It might be added in passing that this practice is essentially scientific in nature. It involves exactly the same general principles as used by modern scientists in the fields of their own research. The reason for this is that knowledge is of the essence of a greater Intelligence, which, by self-definition, is far greater than that of the lesser intelligence experiencing it. Therefore, in order that others of equivalent perceptual capacity can confirm that it has been accurately perceived, in due context and in due proportion, they too have to undergo the selfsame experience and report back on it. It then becomes the subject of general assimilation by the consciousness of the Adept Hierarchy of our planet as a whole.

In relation to what has just been suggested, it is said that the initiate immediately facing Adeptship is granted a momentary vision or perception of what lies ahead in the far distance. However, this itself only becomes possible because he has reached a culminating point in a series of relinquishments of all personality-driven subjective reactions.[36] No further mental reactivity occurs, thereby blocking his further vision, simply because even the Higher Mind is now under almost completely self-conscious control. This then is the first time that he is able to exercise the visual faculty on the buddhic plane, a spiritual faculty that will now inevitably develop yet further, until he has full command of it as a member of the fifth kingdom in Nature.

From the very scarce information available, this preliminary vision appears to be that of the self-concealing monadic vesture, called by the Greeks the *Augoeidés,* and by the Hindu tradition the *Atman.* To the Ancients it was also known as "the Body of Glory," which, according to St. Paul, was not a body of pure spirit but rather a body capable of manifesting the immediate power of the Spirit.[37] According to one interpretation, this "body" is translucent and "pertaining to the crystalline," while also being regarded as the point of inflow of kosmic energies from yet higher levels of Being.[38] Some of these descriptions thus infer a direct correspondence with the *Tabula Smagdarina* (the "Emerald Tablet") of Hermes Trismegistus within which was to be found All-Knowledge of both the higher and lower world systems.

In concluding, it might further be mentioned that the Augoeidés was also described as both "everlasting" and *astroeidés* by the ancient Greeks,[39] a reference to its eternal nature and its "star-like" appearance to the inner vision. It is clearly this same "star" to which the ancient Egyptian sacred texts refer when encouraging the most advanced initiates (*piru*) to "become as a star,"[40] which would then shine in the heavenly firmament, that is, the World Oversoul. With that thought in mind, let us now pass on to consider the nature and requirements of Masterhood and yet higher Adeptship itself.

ELEVEN

THE VARIOUS STAGES OF ADEPTSHIP

We now come to consider what have been described as the highest stages of initiation associated with our planetary Life. These are those associated with evolution into kingdoms of Nature beyond the purely human, even though some of the Adepts are said to maintain human physical bodies for particular purposes. Hence it is that they are widely known as the "Elder Brothers" of humanity. We shall look at the rationale of this in further detail, together with that associated with so-called ascended Masters, a term used more frequently than not by those completely ignorant of the real significance. What is suggested in this chapter, however, has to be seen as based largely on inference, derived from what little information is already available through existing literary or other sources.

Let us first of all deal with the issue of higher kingdoms of Nature than the human. This is something completely foreign to our general (at least Western) understanding, which has erroneously assumed for centuries past that the fourth or human kingdom is the highest or most evolved of all. To some extent this is the result of a misinterpretation of the ancient philosophical idea of man as the microcosm of the Macrocosm. After all, if man is made "in the image of God," how can there be anything in between? In fact, what the ancient statement was saying is that the compound psycho-spiritual organism, which is Man, is constituted in the same way as is the manifest Logos. That is to say, Man is actually a sevenfold being within a soul organism, which latter is itself the octave of logoic vibration—the "soundless Sound." The objective human being is itself merely a correspondence in this regard—a terrestrial soul with a sevenfold constitution of elemental substates, only part of which involves the objective human body, as described earlier—but also having a higher "Egoic" nature.

THE "DIVINE SPARK"

The inner human being, as described, is essentially a divine spirit, a (monadic) "spark" of the Kosmic Mind (actually from beyond the bounds of our solar system), a part of which has "fallen" into the terrestrial continuum provided by our planetary Life and taken on a quasi-animal form to provide it with a vehicle of experience and self-expression on behalf of its parent Logos. However, as we have already seen, only a small part of this divine spark is to be found in the objective human being. The real being remains within the spiritual state, merely watching over the terrestrial world scene. The parallel spiritual state within which it remains—the buddhi, or kosmic ether—is itself the fourth of seven such states, as we have also already seen in earlier chapters. However, only when the individuality in Man recognizes the greater part of itself, which exists in that state, does Man become spiritually Self-conscious.

Correspondingly, only when the individuality in Man recognizes the even greater and more powerful aspect of itself, which exists in the third of the seven states (Atma), does he become a full Master and member of the fifth kingdom in Nature. Then again, when he later recognizes the yet greater aspects, which exist in the second and first planes of solar existence, he progressively becomes a member of the nascent sixth and seventh kingdoms in our planetary Nature. Thereafter, he becomes a truly kosmic being. So, by virtue of each cycle generating its own humanity, we may also suggest that our humanity generates its own higher future kingdoms through its own efforts.

Thus what the higher initiates are effectively doing is literally paving the way for the future generations of superhuman types by developing out of their own natures an archetypal evolutionary progression. That same subjective progression, however, will only produce objective beings of an equivalent nature and quality in the mass hundreds of thousands of years hence. It is inferred by *The Secret Doctrine* that by the end of this current Fourth Round cycle, all those on this planet of our particular humanity will have achieved at least the fifth initiation.[1] That of course is quite distinct from the lesser "sparks" currently evolving through the animal kingdom, whose consciousness will by then have individualized, thereby allowing them to move into the human kingdom.

It follows from this that the fourth initiation (that of "renunciation"), which was described in the previous chapter, sees the final completion of the spiritualizing evolution of the present fourth kingdom in Nature. But as the latter is the objectively most evolved on our planet at this stage of the greater cycle, the still-evolving fifth kingdom has as yet no objective prototype. That prototype, so we are told, will make its first appearance during the Age of Aquarius. That will take place alongside the externalization of the Adept Hierarchy itself, for the latter is itself the nucleus of the fifth kingdom-to-be.[2] Hence, despite the immensity of the achievement involved, the fourth initiation in this cycle is itself merely a preparation for a form of suprahuman experience as yet unknown to us.

THE MASTER SOUL

Thus it is that the first of the higher degrees (that of the fifth) is that of the "risen (but not ascended) Master Soul." He has already passed beyond the "great transition" rather misleadingly known as "the crucifixion," which we saw described in the previous chapter and which is rather understandably associated with death. However, the Master conquers death by recognizing that it was due to association with the lower world of temporary objectivity, self-limitation, and constant change. Once the Adept consciousness is fully re-polarized in the transcendent spiritual state and is thus focused in its own true nature, the associated Self-realization produces the immediate recognition that the lower, form-based life involves an illusion, because based on a projection. Hence the fifth degree is known as the initiation of "revelation."

The Voice of the Silence tells us that the characteristic energy of the one who has achieved the degree of Master of the Wisdom is that of *Virya*, "the dauntless energy that fights its way to the supernal TRUTH, out of the mire of lies terrestrial."[3] The description goes even further in saying of the requirements of Masterhood: "Thy Soul has to become as the ripe mango fruit: as soft and sweet as its bright golden pulp for others' woes, as hard as that fruit's stone for thine own throes and sorrows."[4]

In other words, the initiate of this degree has to have conquered every purely human sense and faculty and brought them under such total control that even the cycle of personal birth and death is transcended. In fact, one of the demonstrations of the faculties thus attained is said to involve the capacity to create a completely new human body by *kriyasakti,* a Sanskrit word indicating the use of spiritual knowledge plus the (controlled) Will-force (atma) emanating from Man's own higher divinity. In short, he has to be able (through the use of higher creative imagination) to control a certain quality of light itself in order to produce a coherent human form within which he can abide for as long as he wishes. The changes that take place in the Adept's faculties following the achievement of Masterhood are described as follows:

> The five senses, where a Master is concerned, exist and are used at need, but the contact established and maintained with disciples and aspirants in the world (through whom they primarily work) is largely telepathic; hearing and sight, as you understand their uses, are not involved. The science of impression with its greatly increased effectiveness over individual contact through the senses, has entirely superseded the more strictly human method. Except in the case of Masters working on the physical plane and in a physical body, the outer physical senses are in abeyance; for the majority of Masters who still use these senses, the use is strictly limited; their work is almost entirely subjective.[5]

Notwithstanding this, we are told that as part of the future "externalization of the Hierarchy," those Masters who are themselves involved in the return to external contacts will have to relearn the use of those same human faculties. That this will involve great sacrifice and even pain is implicitly self-evident.

USE OF THE HIGHER AND LOWER SENSES

Whereas the initiate of the fourth degree has (only just) attained the capacity to function self-consciously within the buddhic state, he is still as yet only beginning to be faintly aware of the nature of atmic (purely spiritual) energy—the emanation of divine Will-force. The Master of the fifth degree, however, in order to exercise conscious association with and adaptation of atmic energy, has to have developed the capacity to generate and distribute spiritual (i.e., buddhic) light down into the "Underworld" below.

Just as a beam of light from a torch or searchlight has to be contained and then focused by a lens in order to illuminate an area properly, so the attention of the Master (now that he has spiritual sight) has to be directed according to the same general principles. He is able to draw on the will-force of his own Monad as necessary to provide power, but he must contain and project that same power while holding his own buddhic and higher mental faculties in absolute check. It is worthy of note to quote at this point a comment made by the Master Kuthumi to A. P. Sinnett regarding the very nature of Masterhood, where he says:

> An Adept—the highest as the lowest—is one only during the exercise of his occult powers. Whenever these powers are needed, the sovereign will unlocks the door to the inner man (the Adept) who can emerge and act freely but on condition that his jailor—the outer man—will be either completely or partially paralysed, as the case may require . . . no Adept can be supposed to keep his will in constant tension and the inner Man in full function, when there is no immediate necessity for it. . . . The inner Adept is ever ready, ever on the alert and that suffices for our purposes.[6]

THE RAY ASSOCIATION WITH THE FIFTH DEGREE

Although those senior initiates approaching the fifth degree will naturally be of various Ray types, the particular association of this degree is with the First Ray—that of spiritual Will. This is the "Siva" Ray, particularly concerned with creativity in relation to prototypal form, hence also with the first of the five elements, that of the quintessential aether. The latter is the emanation of the second plane or state (Akasa) in the sevenfold system, that of the Monad or "divine spark" itself—known in ancient times as the *akh,* as mentioned earlier. Hence, because the Ak(h)asa is the state of archetypal knowledge, that which emanates from it out into the lower world system is (relatively speaking) perfect. This emanation is then that of the *Atman,* the vehicle of the Monad— that which conceals the latter by its very auric radiance.

It follows quite logically that the Adept's ability consciously to associate with the powerful energies of the Atman makes him at-one with it—at least with its direct radiance. Once he has done so, he is "safe." That is to say, he has then "crossed the bridge" of the buddhic state, which, as stated several times already, is the kosmic etheric double of the Logos. As all etheric doubles—whether kosmic, solar, or terrestrial—are naturally dissipated and so destroyed at the end of their associated (Macrocosmic or microcosmic) cycle of existence, the Master Adept has overcome this danger. He is now a Self-conscious, creative agent of the Demiurge (i.e., the Planetary Logos) and a full member of the planetary Hierarchy, with a far greater range of responsibilities than ever before considered possible. These extend to the other kingdoms of Nature (including that of the devas) as well as to humankind.

THE REQUIREMENTS OF MASTERSHIP

The Voice of the Silence confirms for us what the Adept must achieve before he becomes a Master Soul. First of all, it says:

> Thou hast to feel thyself ALL-THOUGHT, and yet exile all thoughts from out of thy soul. [Secondly] thou hast to reach that fixity of mind in which no breeze, however strong, can waft an earthly thought within. Thus purified, the shrine must of all action, sound or earthly light be void; e'en as the butterfly, o'ertaken by the frost, falls lifeless at the threshold—so must all earthly thoughts fall dead before the fane.[7]

The teaching goes on grimly to warn of the consequences to the Adept if he fails:

Exposed to shifting breeze, the jet will flicker and the quivering flame cast shadows deceptive, dark and ever-changing, on the Soul's white shrine. And then O thou pursuer of the truth, thy Mind-Soul will become as a mad elephant that rages in the jungle. Mistaking forest trees for living foes, he perishes in his attempts to kill the ever-shifting shadows dancing on the wall of sunlit rocks. Beware, lest in the care of Self thy Soul should lose her foothold on the soil of Deva knowledge. Beware, lest in forgetting SELF, thy Soul lose o'er its trembling mind control and forfeit thus the due fruition of its conquests.[8]

If anything were needed to confirm to us that Mastership is not achieved by mere mystic contemplation, this surely is it. The spiritual Path is no bed of roses but a way of achievement through intense effort, while even the higher initiations carry with them threats of extreme psychological danger and potential failure. As the Mahatma Kuthumi tells us: "We are not gods; and even they our chiefs—they hope."[9] In addition, it should not be forgotten that the test has to involve the Adept continuing with his normal duties as a human being (if still incarnate) while striving to attain to the state of subjective perfection just described. In this, what is called "All-Thought" describes the capacity to be self-consciously and telepathically sensitive to literally the whole field of planetary (not just human) thought. Thus, we might suggest, the Master Soul does not himself "think" unless there is some specific reason for such mental projections. He has no further need of reactive or creative thought for himself. Such activity merely destroys his higher sensitivity, which immediately perceives the underlying (hence real) nature within all forms.

We are otherwise told that, until fairly recently in historic terms, the Masters normally projected their influence down into the higher mental state, this being the state in which the majority of the evolved intelligentsia of the human race practices their own highest subjective function. Centuries ago, at an earlier stage in human development, their focus was correspondingly on the lower levels of the mental plane, thereby encouraging human intellectual development. Even earlier, many millennia ago, the focus was on the higher levels of the astral plane, encouraging spiritual aspiration via the devotional impulse.

However, the capacity of relatively large numbers of human beings in our own day to use the faculty of the abstract mind in conjunction with the intuitive faculty has apparently resulted in the Masters being able to withdraw their primary focus yet further, back into the buddhic state itself. By virtue of their disciples—the lesser initiates—then passing on as best they can to the rest of humanity the influences received by them from the Adepts (in due proportion according to the capacity to receive), so the whole spectrum of human consciousness evolves by self-generated psychological progress.

ASSOCIATION WITH THE STAR SIRIUS

We are otherwise told that the degree of Master of Wisdom is but the first of the seven degrees associated with the Lodge of an even greater celestial Brotherhood (as briefly mentioned earlier) associated with the Hierarchy of the great star Sirius, itself supposedly a great center in the body of the greater Logos,[10] hence our third and fourth initiatory degrees being merely equivalent to probation and discipleship in that Lodge. This statement is of truly staggering proportions because it opens up a spiritual perspective beyond our wildest imagination. However, we have already been told that it lies merely within the wider consciousness of our Solar Logos. Hence it has an immediate logic once the various associated relationships and experiences are also known and understood to exist in direct correspondence to what has already been described in relation to our objective human experience.

Those relationships are said to involve a direct parallel between the Sirian Lodge of kosmic Adepts and the human Spiritual Ego. Just as the latter inspires and endeavors to control its human expression in order to develop its evolutionary intelligence, so the Sirian Lodge, we are told, concerns itself with the same problem in relation to the even more senior hierarchies of life within the seven solar schemes of our local universe and the various planetary schemes of our whole solar system. While the details of this spectrum of interactive kosmic relationships must as yet remain for us a complete mystery, it perhaps provides one answer as to why the most ancient traditions (for example in Egypt) held the "dog star" Sirius in such reverence. It perhaps also helps us to begin understanding why astronomy and esoteric astrology were considered such important sciences to the Ancients.

If the Spiritual Ego in man is the primary influence that initiates each cycle of human incarnation, it naturally follows that an equivalent cycle of far greater magnitude, emanating from the star Sirius, would perhaps lead to the very appearance of the Heavenly Men (Planetary Logoi) within our solar system. Those same Heavenly Men, so we are again told, are senior Dhyani Buddhas, some of whom are to be found comprising the Great Planetary Council of our own Planetary Logos or "Heavenly Man" at Shamballa. (More about Shamballa and its inhabitants is to be found in appendix B at the back of the book.)

These same Heavenly Men are the "Lords of the Rays," the planetary Logoi associated with each planetary scheme, the greater Intelligences who are responsible for the spiritual individualization of the human kingdom. They, so it would appear, have already long ago passed beyond the seven degrees of initiated self-consciousness of a planetary Life. However, they would themselves have provided the prototypal expressions of self-conscious human existence as the lowest possible correspondence to their own nature.

ASSOCIATION WITH THE PLEIADES
AND URSA MAJOR

So we are otherwise told, our mankind (i.e., the mass of higher "divine sparks") had its spiritual origins in the Pleiades.[11] As I have described in my other books, the fact that there are (esoterically, not literally) seven Pleiades and that the seventh was mythically described as "the missing sister" leads one to surmise that our solar system is in fact the latter. Hence there would appear to be a direct correspondence between the human terrestrial soul and its seven emanations—the seven main chakras in the body—and the Oversoul of the Pleiades system as a whole, incorporating the seven stars as its higher equivalent of the chakras. The ancient tradition extends even further, however, to incorporate the circumpolar stars in the same overall picture, particularly Ursa Major, the seven stars of which are described in Vedic literature as the seven Prajapati "husbands" of the seven "sisters" of the Pleiades.

Through the Adepts we learn that Ursa Major bears a relationship to man indirectly corresponding with that of the monad.[12] This is via the further suggestion that the monadic life behind humanity in general (together with all the deva monads) form the "body" of our Planetary Logos[13] whose own mass archetype originally emanated from Ursa Major long eons ago.[14] It was then seemingly inseminated into the Pleiades system, there to begin its long cycle of involutionary and evolutionary development. Inferential study of the esoteric philosophy propounded in *The Secret Doctrine* and *A Treatise on Cosmic Fire* leads one to believe that there must logically be a celestial progression within the sevenfold Pleiadic system. Hence, so it would appear, when *The Secret Doctrine* confirms that part of our present humanity arrived here on Earth from the Moon and that the latter was the last of a chain of planets, there is at least an implied suggestion that the Moon may have belonged to a previous solar system—as described in the appendices to this book.

Thus, logically speaking, our solar system would be the second in the celestial series,[15] our Earth playing its own particular, intermediate role within that progression. But for this author to extend the hypothesis much further than that would be utterly pointless, as it would clearly involve knowledge of realms of celestial Purpose of which no ordinary human being could have the remotest conception. All we can do is note the possible (or even probable) celestial correlations in order to infer a logical sequence of evolutionary progression in the Macrocosm, of which we are but a small part. Having said as much, let us now return to the issue of the highest initiations available to our humanity and the associated influences of control over the lesser hierarchies of our planetary Life.

UNDERSTANDING THE DISTRIBUTION OF LOGOIC PURPOSE

This whole issue of the Spiritual Hierarchy projecting its influence down upon humankind, thereby supposedly achieving "world governance" from behind the scenes, is very poorly understood. It has regrettably led to all sorts of foolish conspiracy theories (particularly concerning the "Illuminati") among those who evidently have too few useful things to occupy their waking hours. We should therefore pause a moment in order to clarify the issues involved, as follows.

The first thing to be understood—something that needs to be constantly reiterated—is that the whole of our planetary consciousness is part of the consciousness of the Solar Logos. Thus the general circulation of ideas, forms, and influences—whether higher or lower in the evolutionary scale—are all part of the psychological and psycho-sensory processes of the Logos. We ourselves are merely participants in this great kosmic drama by virtue of being aspects and agents of his Mind. We, as members of the fourth kingdom in Nature, are therefore here to fulfill a particular purpose by exercising our creative influences (on his behalf) upon the lesser kingdoms of Nature—the animal, plant, and mineral, as well as (quite unconsciously) the invisible elemental kingdoms. By our doing so, he (the Logos) manages to make his body organism function. This is our task and our responsibility as his direct agents. Similarly, the members of the fifth kingdom—that of the Adepts and Masters—have the responsibility to pass on higher creative influences to us.

However, there is a paranoid anxiety shared by some—particularly among simple-minded conspiracy theorists—that the Masters are in fact extraterrestrials who have come here from some other planet or star system merely to dominate our world. This, frankly, is a ludicrously ignorant travesty of what actually appears to be involved in the wholly natural and progressive sequence of transmission (and thus evolution) of consciousness around the greater celestial system of which ours is but a small part. Esoteric philosophy has always taught us that there is in truth but One (Universal) Consciousness in the Omniverse and that each of us is but an evolving, holographic fragment of it. It consequently follows that the sequence of creative Hierarchies extends from one infinity to another. The spectrum of direct hierarchical influence is thus dependent upon our range of inner perceptual faculty, which is not great—and is much less developed in the case of conspiracy theorists.

THE CHOHAN OF THE SIXTH DEGREE

The Master of the fifth degree, so we are told, has complete control over the elemental nature of the three lower worlds of the physical, astral, and mental planes. However, he does not have a correspondingly total control over the fourth state, that of the fourth kosmic ether, which itself, most critically, constitutes the kosmic etheric double of the Logos. Consequently, he himself is not regarded esoterically as "fully liberated." This liberation only occurs with the achievement of the sixth initiatory degree, which corresponds with full monadic consciousness. The reason why the fifth degree Master is not fully "liberated" appears to be because he is not yet fully at-one with his own monadic Source.

The initiation of the sixth degree (which, seemingly, only becomes available to groups of Masters every forty-nine years)[16] is described as that of "decision."[17] In other words, as the Monad or "divine spark" is in fact the emanating cause behind the whole projected phenomenon of human existence, full Self-consciousness at this level of being effectively denotes the capacity to project or withdraw that creative influence (atma, the "divine breath") at will. Hence its direct sense of association with a higher Purpose literally provides the power of life and death over all forms in Nature on our planet.

However, there is also a highly important Ray association, by virtue of all monadic groups on our planet being the expressions of the Seven Rays emanating from the kosmic buddhic plane of being (*Mahat*). This itself constitutes the etheric double of that inconceivable kosmic Intelligence Who informs the seven solar schemes, of which ours is but one. Hence the Chohan, through this initiation of "decision," has the opportunity of leaving this planetary scheme altogether in order to progress his own further evolution in one or another of seven different ways, thereby extending the faculty of the Logos within the greater system. Those seven alternative "Ray Paths" are as described in Bailey's work *A Treatise on Cosmic Fire.*[18]

THE INFLUENTIAL WORK OF THE CHOHANS

The last four occasions on which a group initiation of Chohans took place appear to have been in the years 1854, 1903, 1952, and 2001.[19] The second of these seemingly led not only to that pan-human crisis known to us as the World Wars of 1914–1918 and 1939–1945 but also to the great expansion in the field of nuclear physics that resulted in the appearance of atomic power, plus radio and television. The objective of the third was perhaps related to worldwide computerization (and instant intercommunication) on one side and the expansion of worldwide ecological awareness on another, as well as breaking down the social, economic, and political barriers between East and West. The latest one, in 2001, looks as though it may well have been orientated toward worldwide reorganization of the fields of international law and finance—these being primarily associated with First and Seventh Ray influences—involving the onset of long overdue major changes in these areas. It otherwise appears that the sudden "Islamic Spring," which has appeared and proliferated in the last few years, is itself a result of influences originating with the Spiritual Hierarchy. Other culturally innovative impulses of similarly large scale may well be looked for in the next decade or so.

The most senior Chohans of the sixth degree are described as seven in number, each having control over one of the seven human Ray Groups on our planet. Fig. 1.2 thus confirms that they act as the distributive "anchors" within our planetary scheme of those emanations originating from the seven planetary Logoi on the kosmic buddhic plane. Those same emanations are what the Indian esotericist refers to as emanations of Mahat, that is, the projections of Kosmic Mind. As elsewhere observed, this is the same as the ancient Egyptian Ma'at, meaning Universal (or Kosmic) Order and Truth, hence Ma'at and Shu (the god of Light and Air) are both shown wearing the feather—which symbolizes both purity and subtlety—in their respective headbands (see fig. 11.1).

Fig. 11.1. Ma'at and Shu (illustrations by Jeff Dahl)

The Chohans of the Rays are thus the primary local exponents of those energies emanating from the Kosmic Mind of the Logos that give rise to the objective manifestation of group Purpose. Hence it is that they are also able unitedly to discern and maintain contact, as necessary, with the Interplanetary Spirits within our solar system, in order to avail themselves of those higher influences, as and when necessary. Although some readers might find the suggestion preposterously akin to science fiction, something of this was explained by the Tibetan Adept DK in describing how the planetary Hierarchy invoked such influences during the latter part of the Second World War.[20] This was in order to ensure that the united triple force of kosmic evil behind the regimes of Germany, Japan, and Italy did not prevail. That such malign forces should exist in the Macrocosm just as they do in the microcosm should come as no surprise if ordinary logic and common sense are applied. That they should arise in a particular form of political power at the same time as a major forward development of human consciousness also makes sense. That is because universal deva Nature always seeks balance and does not necessarily see the difference between good and evil in quite the way that we do. Consequently, a forward or upward evolutionary surge will almost automatically invoke an equivalent counter-influence in Nature.

We are told (quite logically) that the Mind principle is the principle cause of creative separation. Hence it is that the Chohans, between them, might be said collectively to play the part of lesser creative demigods on behalf of the Mind of the Planetary Logos. In that sense, they are the arbiters of what both subjectively and objectively takes place on our planet within the various kingdoms of Nature. By invoking other systemic influences for the betterment of our planetary Life, they might also be said to take some inevitable risks, which may automatically attract the attention of negatively orientated higher powers. Consequently, we might suggest that part of their task (as essential elements of the "Guardian Wall") is to ensure the protection of our planetary Life from external "infection." In that sense, the Akasa might itself be regarded as part of the protective sheath surrounding our planet.

THE RAY ASSOCIATION WITH
THE SIXTH DEGREE

The second systemic plane—that with which the Chohans are particularly associated—is itself associated with the Third Ray and, correspondingly, with the Akasa itself. This is the state from which the essence of All-Knowledge emanates—that is to say, within our particular and necessarily limited field of planetary and solar existence. As all knowledge comprises the mass of all powers, it follows that the Chohan's primary faculty is that of decision as to what knowledge shall become manifest within the higher field of our planetary Nature—which itself comprises the etheric-physical body of the Logos. Correspondingly, the Chohans' power must include the capacity to bring about the withdrawal from that same field of activity of any group of lesser entities that they (as a group) consider to have fulfilled their originally commissioned role. However, this dual role is perhaps more evident in the nature of the Second Ray, the characteristics of which are Love-Wisdom, concerning which we shall deal further later on in relation to the Buddha-Bodhisattva nature.

Regarding initiatory access to this highly advanced state of being of the Chohan, *The Voice of the Silence* says, briefly but succinctly: "The Dhyana gate is like an alabaster vase, white and transparent; within it there burns a steady golden fire, the flame of Prajna that radiates from Atma. Thou art that vase."[21]

This may not say much to the average reader, but it should certainly do so with the intuition of the true esotericist, for the creative *prajna* (itself threefold in nature) is the very radiance of the monadic essence itself. In considering this, it perhaps makes a little more sense if we remember that, at the sixth initiation, the Chohan gains his freedom from the kosmic etheric double of the Logos. From then on he instead begins to function within the logoic vehicle of pure kosmic physical vitality, the atmic energies of which he now consciously learns to wield.[22]

THE SEVENTH INITIATION

We thus next come to the stage of the seventh initiation, that associated with conquest (as a human Buddha) of the first and highest of the seven planes. This is that of *Adi*—the "Sea of Flame," that noumenal light that is "the first radiation from the Root . . . [that of] undifferentiated cosmic substance," otherwise known as "the Fiery Serpent."[23] Of this *The Voice of the Silence* poetically has to say:

Know O Conqueror of Sins, once that a Sowanee hath cross'd the seventh Path, all Nature thrills with joyous awe and feels subdued. . . . He standeth now like a white pillar to the west, upon whose face the rising Sun of thought eternal poureth forth its first most glorious waves. His mind, like a becalmed and boundless ocean, spreadeth out in shoreless space. He holdeth life and death in his strong hand.[24]

How can we possibly describe this state, except entirely by inference? In fact, we can perhaps suggest one or two characteristics using a reversed process of logical deduction. That is to say, if the third plane (Atma) involves the energetic emanation of the monadic second plane (Anupadaka or Akasa), which is elsewhere described as comprising the mass of "sparks" within the "One Flame," the "Flame" must itself be descriptive of the nature of the dualistically unified Life within the planetary Oversoul. From that viewpoint, it must logically be seen as a plasmic "sea" of living electrical hyperactivity, the fundamental vitality of the planetary Demiurge. This is the fiery sheath originally projected (as Binah, from the kabbalistic Hokmah) from the Kosmic Mind, out of which all the monads of the many kingdoms of our planetary Nature themselves emerge as "divine sparks." This, we learned earlier, was also given the name Fohat (the vehicle of the Dhyani Buddhas) by H. P. Blavatsky in her work *The Secret Doctrine*.

There is a further interesting and very direct parallel here with ancient Egypt, for, as Jeremy Naydler tells us:

> According to ancient Egyptian Creation mythology, the birthplace of Ra was regarded as being the "First Land" that arose out of the dark primordial ocean of Nun. This "First Land"—sometimes also pictured as a lotus or an egg—was referred to as the Isle of Fire, because it was alight with Ra's dazzling presence.[25]

If one were here to substitute the Kosmic Mind for Ra and the planetary Oversoul for the lotus or world egg, the correspondence, it is suggested, immediately becomes self-evident.

For the Chohan of the sixth degree—a now Self-realized "divine spark" in his own right—to contemplate the possibility of being able to retain his independent Self-consciousness while being reabsorbed into this apparently hypercharged miasma of pure Life essence, and its direct association with Shamballa, would logically seem a trial of belief of the ultimate degree. Hence this seventh initiation (and not that of the fifth degree) is known as that of the true "resurrection."[26] Self-consciousness, so we are told, is the crown of the whole evolutionary process, at whatever level of being is under consideration. Consequently, Self-consciousness in this state would necessarily consist not only of containing the whole of the sevenfold state of our planetary Life within one's own percipient faculty but also of gradually uniting the latter with the Demiurgic nature of the Logos, which contains the whole and which also thereby forms the foundation of the whole sevenfold kosmic world "above" it. Hence the human Buddha-nature would simultaneously provide first access to the kosmic astral state.[27] With that in mind it is worth remembering Blavatsky's own definition of the Monad as of the essence of a Dhyani Buddha—hence that, at the seventh and final planetary initiation, the now full Adept comes face-to-face with its true "image."[28]

Merely imagining the potent expansion of consciousness required to achieve what has just been described is simply staggering. It is perhaps slightly more understandable, however (albeit only marginally so), when considered in relation to the following comment from the Adepts, defining monadic consciousness itself:

> When the student realises that the great universal Oneness which he associates with Monadic consciousness is only the registration of impressions localised (and therefore limited) and defined within the etheric levels of the cosmic physical plane, he can perhaps grasp the implications of the wonder which will be revealed to the initiate who can transcend the entire cosmic physical plane.[29]

In connection with this latter remark, *The Secret Doctrine* provides us with a morsel of information that is equally of really rather astounding value. It is that the visible plasmic substance of the Sun consists of matter of the lowest subplane of the highest of the seven planes in our system—what is esoterically called "Mother Substance." The root of the latter is substance of the highest subplane, which is itself the nucleus of the Sun and also "the heart and matrix of all the living forces in our solar universe."[30] Furthermore, so we are told, the corporeal substance of the hierarchy of Dhyani Chohans who effectively comprise the Demiurgic consciousness is itself of fifth subplane matter of this same highest plane.[31]

THE ACHIEVEMENT OF BUDDHAHOOD

Thus it is that the seventh (atomic) plane of the system sets the rate of vibration (that of the Second Ray) for the whole system.[32] *The Voice of the Silence,* however, tells us rather more of what is required of the initiate who has now attained to that state and thus also to human Buddhahood:

> Know, if of Amitabha, the "Boundless Age," thou wouldst become co-worker, then must thou shed the light acquired . . . upon the span of all three worlds. Know that the stream of superhuman knowledge and the Deva-Wisdom thou hast won must from thyself, the channel of Alaya, be poured forth into another bed. Know, O Narjol, thou of the Secret Path, its pure fresh waters must be used to sweeter make the Ocean's bitter waves—that mighty sea of sorrow formed of the tears of men.[33]

The Voice of the Silence then adds still more gravely:

> Alas! When once thou hast become like the fix'd star in the highest heaven, that bright celestial orb must shine from out of the spatial depths for all—save for itself; give light to all, but take from none. Alas! . . . Self-doomed to live through future kalpas [great cycles] unthanked and unperceived by men; wedged as a stone with countless other stones which form the "Guardian Wall," such is thy future if the seventh gate thou passest. Built by the hands of many Masters of Compassion, raised by their tortures, by their blood cemented, it shields mankind . . . protecting it from further and far greater misery and sorrow.[34]

For those individuals who one comes across from time to time, who imagine (and proclaim) themselves to be in direct touch with archangels or Buddhas, or even to be acting as their direct agents on Earth, these descriptive texts should perhaps act as a purgative, or at the very least a caution. However, few such seem willing to listen, having already made up their minds as to how they see their Masters and Buddhas and wish them to behave. It is perhaps for this reason that the Spiritual Hierarchy—faced with their own cyclical duty to reemerge among humankind—saw the necessity to explain these matters in such detail, some considerable time in advance of any such emergence. Respect for them as Elder Brothers in the stern face of their achievements is one thing; hero-worship is quite another and the logically last thing they would want is the development of a religion (or rather a cult) based on that.

LIBERATED PLANETARY SPIRITS

While the seventh degree is described as the highest possible on this planet, in which the consciousness of Man and deva merge at their most advanced level (hence its dualistic Second Ray association), it is made implicitly clear that there are initiatory expansions of consciousness even beyond this. These—of the eighth and ninth degrees (those respectively of "transition" and "refusal")—would seemingly turn the initiate into a Nirmanakaya or a Sambhogakaya Dhyani Buddha respectively. These two closely connected hierarchies are described as liberated "Planetary Spirits" whose aegis covers, respectively, the whole of the kosmic physical plane and the whole of the kosmic astral plane. In a very real sense, they together comprise the intelligence of the planetary Demiurge. It is thus highly interesting to note what the Mahatma Kuthumi says in relation to the achievement of (Dhyani) Buddhahood, as follows:

> When our great Buddha—the patron of all the Adepts, the reformer and the codifier of the occult system, reached first Nirvana on Earth, he became a Planetary Spirit i.e., his spirit could at one and the same time rove the interstellar spaces in full consciousness and continue at will on Earth in his original and individual body. For the divine Self had so completely disenfranchised itself from matter that it could create at will an inner substitute for itself, leaving it in the human form. . . . That is the highest form of Adeptship man can hope for on our planet; but it is as rare as the Buddhas themselves, the last *Khobilgan* (supreme Adept) who reached it being Tzon-kha-pa of Kokonor.[35]

It will be remembered that we mentioned Tzon-kha-pa in an earlier chapter as the fourteenth-century Tibetan Buddha who issued instructions to his Adept followers that, following his death, they were to ensure that a fresh cultural impulse was to be transmitted to the West toward the close of every century, to aid the progress of overall human evolution.

THE SEVENTH DEGREE RAY ASSOCIATION

In concluding this section we should also mention the close association of the seventh and highest state of our planetary world (that of the Christ nature) with the First as well as the Second Ray. As we saw earlier, this First Ray is concerned with that primary isolation or self-limitation which generates and maintains a field of consciousness and creativity—in either the microcosm (man) or the Macrocosm. Thus the Self-evolved human Buddha of the seventh degree must learn to become at-one with this First Ray energy before his achievement is complete. In association with that, it is important to remember that the seventh and lowest kosmic plane—which contains our seven solar and planetary states—is ruled by the kosmic Seventh Ray. Thus the First Ray of the lower world system and the Seventh Ray of the higher kosmic system are, in a very real sense, one and the same in occult terms. This fact is of particular importance to us in our current approach to the Age of Aquarius, because Aquarius, so we are told, is ruled by the Seventh (kosmic) Ray, focused through the synthesizing planet Uranus. Therefore, those of our humanity who attain to the fullness of the highest initiatory degree possible during this coming cycle will also bring about a permanently sustained link of consciousness between the higher kosmic system and our own.

Following sequentially on from that, the human Buddha becomes progressively familiar with the various substates and associated faculties of true kosmic consciousness. He becomes a Dhyani Buddha or Planetary Spirit (first Nirmanakaya and then Sambhogakaya) of the eighth and ninth initiatory degrees. Beyond even the Nirmanakaya and the Sambhogakaya, however, we find the hierarchies of the Dharmakaya Buddhas, whose completely liberated field of endeavor is the kosmic mental plane and whose contact with our planetary Life is said to exist only through the former two hierarchies. These three groups of Planetary Spirits are then to the Planetary Logos of our Earth what our human Permanent Atom is to each of us—the living factor of logoic continuity. Interestingly, however, we find the following further comment about the nature of the Planetary Spirits:

However ethereal and purified of gross matter they may be, the pure Spirits are still subject to the physical and universal laws of matter. They cannot (even if they would) span the abyss that separates their world from ours. They can [however] be visited in spirit; their Spirit cannot descend and reach us.[36]

By this it is meant that the Planetary Spirit cannot, under normal circumstances, physically (i.e., even ethereally) materialize in our world. However, by virtue of being able to project itself by association into other forms—such as the spiritual consciousness of the highest initiates—the Planetary Spirit would still be able to influence our humanity. However, there is an exception to the general rule, which the same source confirms as follows:

But these (the highest Planetary Spirits) appear on Earth but at the origin of every new humankind; at the junction and close of the two ends of the great cycle. And they remain with men no longer than the time required for the external truths they teach to impress themselves so forcibly upon the plastic minds of the new races as to warrant them from being lost or entirely forgotten by the forthcoming generations. The mission of the [highest] Planetary Spirit is but to strike the KEYNOTE OF TRUTH [sic] . . . The vibrations of the Primitive Truth are what your philosophers name "innate ideas."[37]

GNOSTIC ASSOCIATIONS

Following on from this, it is perhaps worth mentioning here the gnostic writings of the Egyptian Nag Hammadi texts. Although still considered generally rather opaque as to their true meanings (as far as non-esotericists are concerned), some parts stand out quite clearly if looked at from a non-personal and a non-Christian viewpoint. The two to which we can refer quite specifically at this point are titled "The Bridal Chamber" (sometimes "The Pleromic Union") and "The Eighth Reveals the Ninth," in which we find the following:

If I may utter a mystery, the Father of the All united with a virgin who came down and a fire shone for him on that day. He revealed the great bridal chamber. Because of this His body which came into being on that day came out of the bridal chamber in the manner of Him who came into being from the bridegroom and the bride.[38]

As Stephen Hoeller comments in relation to this:

The sacrament of the Bridal Chamber is in fact an initiation signify-ing individuation, the grand symbol of the restoration of the Pleroma, or wholeness, the sacred marriage of the opposites within and thus the attainment to the true and ultimate gnosis. The archetypal symbolism of the saviour as the bridegroom, Sophia the wandering soul as the bride and the state of wholeness, the Pleroma, as the bridal chamber in their personal analogues, are thus the process of individuation.[39]

THE EIGHTH AND NINTH INITIATORY DEGREES

In fact, we might suggest, the Bridal Chamber is esoterically analogous to the Oversoul of our planetary Life, which itself gives rise to the phenom-enon of duality within its own field of creativity. We saw in earlier chapters that the eighth principle contains the seven. This is the kabbalistic Binah, as the Zohar confirms,[40] although it is esoterically counted from above to below as the third in the overall sequence of ten sephirotic principles. Hence it is that the advanced initiate who passes from the seventh to the eighth ini-tiation necessarily passes beyond all sense of the duality of spirit and matter, of separated angelkind and humankind. However, one might suggest that it is in the further, SELF-conscious experience of the eighth state that the initiate comes to understand the esoteric analogy of himself as the gnostic "bridegroom." He himself becomes the "serpent" of Kosmic Mind, which enfolds the "egg" of the local universe, thereby making "Creation" possible. So what is his response? Perhaps it might be described as follows.

How shall I describe the All? I see another Nous [the kosmic Mind] who moves the psyche [the Oversoul]. I see the one who speaks to me through a holy sleep. Thou givest me strength. I see myself! I am willing to discourse! I am overcome with a trembling: I have found the origin of the Power above all powers which has no origin: I see a well-spring bubbling up with life! I have said, O my son, that I am the Nous. I have seen what discourse cannot reveal, for the entire Eighth, O my son, with the souls therein and the angels are singing in silence. But I, the Nous, understand.[41]

Before passing on, we might otherwise mention here the experience of Gautama Buddha at his final initiation, as reported in Sir Edwin Arnold's poetic masterpiece *The Light of Asia* where, we are told:

> *The Prince of Darkness, Mara—knowing this was Buddh*
> *Who should deliver men, and now the hour when He*
> *   should find the Truth*
> *And save the worlds—gave unto all his evil powers*
> *   command,*
> *Wherefore there trooped from every deepest pit*
> *The fiends who war with Wisdom and the light . . .*
> *All hating Buddh, seeking to shake his mind; nor*
> *   knoweth one*
> *Not even the wisest, how those fiends of Hell*
> *Battled that night to keep the Truth from Buddh . . .*
> *[Yet] in the third watch, the Earth being still,*
> *the hellish legions fled . . . [and] our Lord attained*
> *   Sammasambuddh.*[42]

FURTHER GNOSTIC AND KABBALISTIC CORRELATIONS

What appears to be described latterly here then is the transcendental illumination to be experienced by the immensely advanced initiate of the ninth degree, the Dhyani Buddha, who already contains within his consciousness the all-enfolding knowledge of the entire kosmic physical plane, plus parts of the kosmic astral and mental planes as well. As we have already seen, however, the Oversoul of our planetary Life is itself contained and held in sustained existence by the downwardly serpentine projection and union with it of what esoteric Buddhism calls Fohat.

This is the spiral-cyclic emanation of kosmic Mind—which kabbalism otherwise refers to as Hokmah and which the Christian gnostics of two thousand years ago referred to as the descending Sophia, which devolved into a more mundane counterpart called Sophia Ackamoth. The latter idea is symbolized in the picture of the serpent enfolding the egg (see fig. 4.2). Thus the latter is what ancient gnosticism referred to as the "Demiurgos." Hence, one might logically suggest, that this—the Demiurgic Nous, the gnostic "bridegroom"—is itself the projection of an apparently ultimate state, the originating point of projection that Kabbalism calls Keter, the very "Crown" of Being. The very same description is given (in different terms) in the *Hermetica* where it says:

And then, stripped of the effects of the [lower] cosmic framework, the human enters the region of the ogdoad; he has his own proper power and, along with the blessed, he hymns the Father. Those present there rejoice together in his presence and, having become like his companions, he also hears certain powers that exist beyond the ogdoadic region and hymn God with sweet voice. They rise up to the Father in order and surrender themselves to the Powers and, having become Powers, they enter into God.[43]

By comparison, it is interesting to note what the Platonists and neo-Platonists had to say about the same stage. As the philosopher Proclus tells us: "the Demiurgus constitutes the [Over]Soul in conjunction with the vivific Goddess and mingles the genera of it in the Crater."[44]

What is being referred to here as "the Goddess" is in fact what the Christian gnostics referred to as Sophia Ackamoth, that projection of the Higher Mind principle that enfolds and unites with the Oversoul, thereby "mingling its genera" in the chakra system (i.e., the "Crater")—the crown center in particular. In order to understand this properly, it is of course necessary to associate the statement both Macrocosmically and microcosmically, for the terrestrial soul of man is itself a "Demiurge."

The Light of Asia otherwise goes on to tell us how the Buddha, having attained perfected mastery over all the powers in our solar Nature, now achieved an extra-systemic vision

> *of insight vast, ranging beyond this sphere to spheres*
> *   unnamed,*
> *system on system, countless worlds and suns moving in*
> *   splendid measures,*
> *band by band, linked in division, one yet separate, the*
> *   silver islands of a sapphire sea,*
> *shoreless, unfathomed, undiminished, stirred with waves*
> *   which roll in restless tides of change.*
> *He saw those Lords of Light who hold their worlds by*
> *   bonds invisible.*[45]

Interestingly, so we are told, it is only at the ninth initiation that the previously "human" intelligence becomes "a full and true expression of divinity."[46] However, yet further beyond lies that point of originating emanation, which Plato referred to as "the GOOD" and which the Hermeticist consequently refers to as "God," where lies Creation's own manifesting source—the plane of Kosmic Buddhi (Mahat). This same state is described as that in which the hierarchies of Amitabha Buddhas have their existence (see fig. 3.4) and from which the Seven Rays are emanated downward into the various planetary schemes, expressing themselves as the groups of entities known as "solar angels."[47] It is directly associated with the Pleiades.[48]

It also seems to be the case (from the sketchy descriptions given to us) that the Amitabha Buddhas (the O-mi-t'o-Fo of Chinese esotericism) are thus the objectively manifesting kosmic lives of the great Hierarchy of Sirius, which was mentioned earlier as one of the seven solar schemes in the super-kosmic etheric double of the inconceivable Being known as "The One About Whom Naught May Be Said." Hence it is also this hierarchy of Amitabha Buddhas that (to us at least) represents the origin of the initiatory number Ten—that of Man's true completeness as a Dharmakaya god.

However, we might also mention here the parallel correspondence between their comprising the eleventh stage in the progressive sequence under consideration and the fact that one half of our own solar sunspot cycle is itself eleven years. Interestingly and in support of the suggestion just made, we find in the Ismaili gnostic tradition the following:

> At the end of the cycle of his individual life, at the seventh grade of his ascension, the Adept finds himself at the threshold of perfect angelhood of the Tenth Intelligence. This is the dawn of the Great Resurrection.[49]

As just indicated, the "Tenth Intelligence" logically appears to be that of the Dharmakaya Buddha hierarchy of the third kosmic plane (that of kosmic Mind), which is itself responsible for the "Round" emanations that give rise to the various sevenfold planetary "Chains" of which *The Secret Doctrine* speaks (see appendix A). Hence the "threshold" referred to is exactly as just described in the preceding paragraphs. We might add to this the further suggestion that additional corroboration is provided by the kabbalistic philosophy of the ten sephiroth emanated from Ain Soph. As earlier described, Binah is the third sephira, which contains the lesser seven. In reverse order it is thus synonymous with the Demiurge and the eighth initiation. Hokmah, the second sephira—which we have already described as synonymous with the Tibetan Fohat (vehicle of the Dhyani Buddha)—corresponds with the ninth initiation, while Keter, the "Crown" and point of primordial emanation from Ain Soph, itself completes the tenth initiation and thus returns the consciousness back to its Source—within the super-kosmic etheric double (Mahat).

From a theosophical perspective, the eighth initiation results in conscious containment of the whole of the kosmic physical plane, as already described. It follows logically from this that the ninth and tenth initiations then correspondingly result in complete containment and control of the kosmic astral and kosmic mental planes, respectively. However, these are associated with the areas of concern of the Sambhogakaya and Dharmakaya Buddhas respectively, whose consciousness is so far beyond anything of which we can even begin to faintly conceive that it is hardly worthwhile here even trying to speculate upon them.

THE TRANSFER OF HIGHER POWERS

The question of the powers conveyed through the initiatory process is also one that has excited great discussion among esotericists and would-be occultists. Many have hitherto fondly imagined that the "descent of the Holy Spirit"—the Arabic *bharaka* (Grace), which is what we are now discussing, is a fairly simple and nonthreatening event. But to those who have made any real study of the subject, it rapidly becomes obvious that this is not so. The idea that the Holy Spirit (Atma) conveys the (akasic) capacity to "speak in many tongues" has itself been grossly misinterpreted, through the failure to recognize that it actually involves the capacity to "speak" and "listen" telepathically within the psycho-spiritual states. It does not result in the altogether ludicrous outward babble that some modern Christian movements (such as the "Alpha System") persuade themselves to be the expression of the Holy Spirit, yet which reduces human nature and its creative self-expression to a derisory state of activity, which even animals would be ashamed to follow. The descent of the Holy Spirit raises human consciousness. It does not lower it.

As suggested earlier, the old adage that "knowledge is power" conceals the fact that "*a* knowledge" is the manifesting power of a higher spiritual being of some or other degree. Thus the invocative human individual is drawing down this power into his existing (deva) field of consciousness, thereby causing its immediate, expansive revitalization in response. However, he not only has now to contain it safely, he has to learn how to integrate it and coordinate it with his own existing range of powers. In other words, as his Self expands, so must his Self-discipline. Unless he follows this principle, the new powers will become destructive, leading quite understandably to lesser or greater degrees of personal insanity. That is why one of the tasks of the Master is sometimes to slow down the progress of his student,[50] so that the whole evolutionary process is safely and thoroughly achieved. This is something that one hardly ever hears about in the vast majority of books on the subject.

This in turn highlights another issue of which we have already spoken. It is the fact that, just as we have to project our perceptual faculties "upward" in order to contact and (at least partially) draw down spiritual insights into our mundane consciousness, so even the highest Adepts have to follow the same principle. While progressing their own faculty into kosmic dimensions, by way of the highest meditation, they "bring down" (by sympathetic association) essential elements of the kosmic states of being and anchor them in their own lower nature, the latter being of course far more advanced than ours. However, as their own nature is part of the organism of the Earthly state, which we all share, its magnetism is automatically passed on and shared in degree relative to the capacity of others to absorb it. In this way, the whole organism of our planetary Life is gradually transmuted according to the same principle.

MAN BECOMES PROGRESSIVELY DIVINE

The fact that the initiate is progressively absorbing higher powers into his field of consciousness helps us to understand the practical rationale of initiation and of evolution itself. By absorbing such powers from each and every plane and subplane as he ascends within the system of our planetary scheme, Man (the Divine Spirit) increasingly becomes the Macrocosm of the microcosm. He becomes a demigod and then ultimately "sits on the right hand of the Father" as the "Son of God," to use the Christian terminology. However, "God" in this sense is the Planetary Logos, the composite nature of the hierarchy of Kumaras (see appendix B), whose demiurgic natures comprise merely the kosmic physical expression of the Amitabha Buddhas, those even higher celestial Beings who are the begotten of the kabbalistic Ain Soph and are themselves the Ain Soph Aur. Thus "God" is not actually a separate Being.

As previously suggested, there is but One Life and One Consciousness, and we are all part of it in a universal process of "ever-becoming." Thus, within the solar scheme, Man gradually develops all the powers of the seven planetary states, unified within the eighth state—that of the Oversoul, or expression of the Pure Mind of Platonic tradition. He is thereby progressively able to associate with the powers of the lower kosmic states, so entering the ninth and tenth "spheres of glory" in the scale of final perfection.[51] As mentioned earlier, it is this tenfold sequence that we see in reverse in the ten emanating sephiroth of kabbalism and the divine tetraktys of Pythagoras.

It might be worth mentioning again here the gnostic perception of

"God," more particularly as expressed in the works of C. G. Jung. Here God is perceived "as an autonomous [divine] complex of great strength and intensity which is ultimately the expression of the intensity and strength of life itself," while appearing within human consciousness "as a star which glimmers in immeasurable distance above, but nevertheless represents the individual's goal, guidance, repose and even the destination of his journey after physical death."[52] This rather anthropocentric view does not properly coincide, however, with the ancient principle that the ultimate Deity is inexpressible because of its infinite universality. The latter would render any attempt at experiential description of it completely and utterly futile. It has to be suggested therefore that what Jung is seeking to describe is actually no more than an interim point of human causal emanation, no matter how supremely advanced it might appear.

This brings us to another important point, much misunderstood on a broad scale by Western philosophers endeavoring to understand the metaphysics of Eastern philosophy—Hinduism and Buddhism in particular. It is the curious idea that in leaving behind the human state the Adept Intelligence concerned quickly or progressively loses his sense of individuality through "the dewdrop slipping back into the shining sea," thereby becoming (or rebecoming) merely a part of the amorphous oceanic mass. Even Carl Jung, despite his deep insights into gnostic philosophy, failed to understand the background principle[53] that (as one of the Adepts put it) Self-consciousness is the continuing crown of the whole evolutionary process. Hence an evolved intelligence always carries with it (in its self-conscious nature) at least some of the character (NOT personality) derived through experience from its own many and varied past achievements. However, this inevitably becomes gradually secondary to the far more powerful evolutionary experiences to which further adaptation must still be made in passing into and through yet higher states of being. Yet SELF-consciousness remains.

The Adepts—no matter how advanced—are all quite different in character, as H. S. Olcott discovered to his astonishment when experiencing the use of H. P. Blavatsky's body by several Adepts, in rotation, during the writing of her first major work, *Isis Unveiled*.[54] This difference, however, is again not one of mere personality. It is immediately distinguishable in the magnetic character of the Adepts' psycho-spiritual nature, which is itself (partially at least) related to the Divine Ray with which they are or have been directly associated. It needs to be remembered that, in essence, they are (increasingly liberated) Spirits of a definitely kosmic origin who work through the agency of soul. They are not souls per se.

As already explained, the essence of the initiatory process is that Man is a hierarchy of spirit-beings that, at the dawn of Creation, is emanated en masse from the so-called Mind of God. As it "falls" into the lesser Underworld of matter, it automatically subdivides into three groups of souls—kosmic, solar, and planetary. The masses within each of the latter three groups then themselves subdivide into a variety of greater and lesser group-soul kingdoms of Nature. The subdivision continues until it reaches a point of optimum outreach consistent with the maximum development in the previous cycle. Then the unified consciousnesses of the group souls begin to fragment (or rather, to individualize), thereby generating increasingly individualized souls. These individual souls then begin—at the lowest planetary level—to reach out to the next higher soul group, thereby resulting in a sense of duality of consciousness. It is at this point that the human being is generated, with the capacity of self-consciousness. Thereafter, the human consciousness slowly starts to become aware of higher deva powers, which it then sets out to absorb and control, and so on until the highest Adeptship is achieved.

INITIATION AS A CELESTIAL FORCING PROCESS

There is nothing particularly extraordinary about the process of initiation, except insofar as—on this planet—it is representative of a forcing process, or so we are told.[55] In almost all other planetary schemes, the process of individualization apparently does not extend so far or so fast. It therefore does not result in such pain and sorrow to those involved in the experience. It is apparently only on this planet and two others that this occurs. The reason for this—again, so we are told[56]—is tied up in the past history of our solar scheme and seemingly involves the evolutionary development of Man that took place on the Moon Chain before its hierarchies were transferred to this planet, thus causing its own "death." This story—although introduced to the West (through Blavatsky and Bailey) during the late-nineteenth and early-twentieth centuries—has never been thoroughly explained and, when mentioned, usually draws an astonished reaction, which is perhaps understandable. Yet it was never intended as mere science fiction and there are elements of it that we can perhaps use to speculate logically, as further outlined in appendix D.

In the next chapter we shall take a necessarily cursory look at some of those members of the Adept Hierarchy who have become known to us through the modern theosophical movement. However, in line with our primary concern to gain a better understanding of how the whole evolutionary scheme works, as seen from the inside, we shall do so by considering them in relation to the spiritual functions they are said to fulfill, rather than in relation to their "personalities." In relation to any question as to their actual existence it is perhaps worth quoting the following statement by the academic researcher and author Dr. David Frawley:

> There is a class of human beings, perhaps very small in number, who have always looked over humanity. These are the great gurus, avatars and spiritual teachers. In ancient times they had a much greater role developing and shaping human culture. As humanity declined from the ancient ages of light, they gradually withdrew into seclusion. Today, they still exist, though they may be hard to find by the outer mind. . . . The prime area they relate to is the Himalayas. . . . While many occult teachings glorify such masters and may put up a cloak of illusion or mystery about them, there is still a core of truth about them which we cannot ignore.[57]

PART FOUR

The Adept Brotherhood and the Mysteries

TWELVE

THE "MASTERS" OF THE MODERN THEOSOPHICAL MOVEMENT

So much thoroughly misleading trivia has been written and spoken on this subject over the last century that one really wonders quite where to start on positive rather than negative issues. Paul Johnson—the most recent critic or commentator (depending on your standpoint)—entitles his first book *The Masters Revealed: Madame Blavatsky and the Myth of the Great White Lodge.*[1] Although approaching the subject with considerable academic research as to historical personalities, he in fact clearly sets out to prove a mere presupposition of his own. Because of that he self-evidently fails to provide a truly objective or even remotely reliable account. His second book, *Initiates of Theosophical Masters,* follows more or less in the same regrettably and unvaryingly prejudiced line, despite the remarkable extent of its background historical research.[2] Others, however, have written with such eulogistic or hero-worshipping description about the Adept Brotherhood, much of it as clearly based on wishful thinking as Johnson's was on a seemingly preconceived intention to disprove, that the average reader or student of the subject is no better off in approaching a conclusion as to verifiability.

While others in the past have sought to depict the Himalayan

Brotherhood of Spiritual Adepts as gods or demigods, whose main claim to fame is the capacity to extend their life spans to hundreds (if not thousands) of years, Johnson has gone completely to the other extreme, using academic research to support a distinctly limited viewpoint. Starting with a purely literal interpretation of the Adepts' own modest statement that they are but men who have developed their powers well beyond those of even the most intellectually advanced human being, Johnson has taken the view that Blavatsky merely adopted and adapted the Adept tradition in order to help publicize her new approach to ancient philosophy in the form of modern Theosophy.[3] This was done, according to Johnson, by Blavatsky describing some of the purely human characteristics of some of the people she had come across in her travels and adding to them a variety of supposed psycho-spiritual powers of her own choice.[4]

Unfortunately, Johnson has made no serious attempt in his books to examine in parallel the basis of what either initiation or Adeptship is actually all about or what it involves. Nor has he made any attempt to discuss the experiences of the many others in recorded literature who have described their meetings with such Adepts, the extent or basis of their knowledge and the rationale behind the altogether remarkable (but still logically derived) powers that they are supposedly able to wield. The net effect has merely been to widen the gulf of (mis)understanding on such issues between modern academia and reality to the detriment of all.

THE "NEED TO KNOW" OF THE ADEPT HIERARCHY

The Adepts themselves seem to have made it clear on many occasions that they are not in the slightest bit concerned about either approach to their individual personae.[5] What they have endeavored to establish in the public mind, however, is that such a thing as the "Great White Lodge" of Masters does in fact exist, partly for the purpose of explaining (and exploding) "the god myth" inherent in orthodox religion and partly otherwise to confirm the true nature of intelligent guidance that lies behind the progress of human cultural evolution on this planet. This is, we are told, so that humanity can itself become more consciously involved in the real process.

39. Mahatma Koot Hoomi
'Master KH'

40. Mahatma Morya
'Master M'

Fig. 12.1. Blavatsky's Himalayan Adepts

Interestingly, the Tibetan Adept DK states quite unequivocally that he told Alice Bailey that one of her major duties involved familiarization of the public with the true nature of the Masters of the Wisdom.[6] This, however, was a task from which she shrank because of the way in which their names had already come into such unforeseen disrepute, partly as a result of the only partial and deliberately misleading descriptions of them and their work by Blavatsky, plus the distortions of then contemporary and later theosophists. However, as the saying goes, "A little knowledge is a dangerous thing," and it was perhaps because of too little information that such distorted views arose in the first place. The Tibetan Adept goes on to make the further pertinent comment that: "The Masters, as portrayed in the Theosophical Society, [only] faintly resemble the reality; [however] much good has been done by this testimony to their existence and much harm by the foolish detail at times imparted."

He adds: "They are not as pictured" and then, rather more sharply, "They are not the spectacular and ill-bred people portrayed by the medio-cre leaders of many groups, nor do they choose (for their pledged disciples and prominent workers) men and women who, even from a worldly point of view, are of a pronounced inferiority or who deal in claim-making and in the art of attracting attention to themselves."[7]

DISAGREEMENT OVER THE CHRIST

One of the major sources of contention as regards the Masters—even within the theosophical movement itself—lies in the seeming conflict between Blavatsky and Bailey regarding the figure of Christ, or its oriental equivalent, the Bodhisattva. Blavatsky, who was no friend of Western Christian orthodoxy and its "churchianity," appears to suggest that the Christ concept has no basis in fact. Bailey, on the other hand, indicates very clearly that this is an official position within the Spiritual Hierarchy itself. Because this argument has become so contentious, I have dealt with it at some considerable length in chapters 13 and 14. There it will be seen that much of the dispute has arisen out of pure misunderstanding of terminology plus a general ignorance of inevitably necessary hierarchical function.

In reality there is no real doubt that the positions and tasks of both Christ and Bodhisattva are to a high degree synonymous. However, an associated idea put forward by Bailey's Adept teacher has to be taken into account in considering this further. It is that the position (directly associated with the Second Ray) has an inherent duality by virtue of association with the Love-Wisdom principle. Arising out of this, so we are told, Gautama Buddha had previously become the chief exponent of the Wisdom aspect, while Maitreya subsequently became the chief exponent of the Love aspect.[8] It is by virtue of this, so we are further told, that the two work together to ensure that the full Ray influence is transmitted throughout our planetary Life. It is noteworthy that Blavatsky only rejected the "Christ" function in the limited Christian perspective then current.

Bailey's attribution of the otherwise Buddhist "Lord Maitreya" (the Mi-lo Fo of Chinese esotericism) as fulfilling the position of the Christ or Bodhisattva after it had been vacated by Gautama Buddha, and her further suggestion that the Chohan Kuthumi was in line to take over the same function in due cycle, caused outrage in some theosophical and Buddhist quarters. However, one has to suggest that this is purely because the outraged did not understand the complete picture associated with the Adept Hierarchy and its responsibilities. Nor do they seem to have recalled the descriptive inference provided by the Mahatma Morya himself (in *The Mahatma Letters to A.P. Sinnett*) of Kuthumi going into deep retreat in an old temple "within whose bosom have gestated generations of Bodhisattwas."[9] Nor have they borne in mind what Kuthumi himself said about this following his return from the prolonged retreat, about it having been "on a long journey after supreme knowledge."[10] One has to realize that the view hitherto by critics of this same idea had been one based upon rigid religious devotionalism from one angle and just as rigid academic critique of that devotionalism from the other. Theosophically based occult theory has effectively changed all that and more.

We are otherwise informed that the two other most senior positions within our immediate Spiritual Hierarchy are those of the "Manu" and the "Mahachohan," thereby forming a trinitarian leadership, which is itself subject to change in the Adept personae cyclically filling such positions. Blavatsky had herself mentioned the Manu (and indeed cyclical Manus) in the context of their leadership of the human evolutionary function,[11] while the name Mahachohan had been vaguely implied by her as having no higher status or importance than that of a very high Adept. In line with this, the Master Kuthumi, in correspondence with the newspaper editor A. P. Sinnett, confirmed "we are not gods and even our chiefs, they hope."[12] However, as we otherwise know, Blavatsky was frequently keen to conceal occult detail (thereby protecting inner and more potent knowledge) and thus frequently resorted to the use of "blinds" (deliberately misleading descriptions or doubles entendres) for that very purpose.

Within the framework of human psychology, such partial admissions and explanations naturally invite unsupported speculation among those already fascinated by and even fixated with the apparently spectacular. That is a fact of life and, as we otherwise know, it leads many inevitably into the self-generated webs of unilateral conspiracy theory. Further, later admissions and more detailed explanations (for these people at least) often merely fuel suspicion that there is an intended cover-up. However, within the framework of the occult concept that "ideas are powers," which the untrained eye fails to see and which the untrained mind fails to control before the former have already chaotically possessed it, such progressively partial disclosure is seen as crucially important in maintaining intelligent objectivity and balanced judgment. After all, in the educational training of children the same principle is followed. Why then should it be different in relation to our exploration of the completely new and infinitely more compelling field of occult knowledge?

MODERN THEOSOPHICAL TEACHING AS A MERE INTRODUCTION

As this book has already suggested, the whole content of modern theosophical teaching as so far given out by Blavatsky and Bailey is by way of open introduction to practical esoteric and occult theory. One of the most important realizations to come hand-in-hand with this is that the whole subject is infinitely greater than one could originally have imagined from following a merely religious dogma or viewpoint. Therefore, it is entirely logical that the proposition that something even more important exists should be given out before any really detailed explanation is proffered as to why it exists and what range of functions it fulfills.

The positions of Manu and Mahachohan, as also those of heads of the Seven Ray Groups described in modern theosophical teaching, have no obvious place in the theological or devotional thought of established religious orthodoxy, despite the Christian and Hindu Trinity and Trimurti. Their very mention, from one viewpoint, implies an automatic disestablishment of the existing and more simple hierarchical setup of "God and his angels," as found in Judaic, Christian, and Islamic tradition, quite apart from the gods and devas of Hindu tradition. The very resurgence of the (most ancient) idea that an ultimate "God" is an unproven theoretical concept and that the universe is actually generated and run by a coordinated host of hierarchies of highly advanced Intelligences (many of them post-human) would be an understandable shock to many. Many, such as those of a Protestant persuasion, would reject it as effectively denying their more apparently direct type of monotheism. That is particularly so in the case of those of a devotional rather than a scientifically orientated nature, at least in the West. To some it will sound like mere science fiction.

To others it might suggest a more direct threat to the whole established order of civilization and culture. As matters stand at present, therefore, the worldwide orthodox jury is still out—and it seems likely to be so for quite some time to come.

By virtue of the Adept Hierarchy itself having made it clear that all humanity will eventually attain Adeptship in due cycle and that speculation about the personalities of individual Adepts is pointless and a thorough waste of time, there is really little point in this chapter pursuing those particular angles. Therefore, we shall continue by concentrating instead on the issue of their hierarchical functions, as described in theosophical terms, with a view to arriving at a rather better understanding of how these influences interact with human culture in the round. As we shall see, those influences derive from extraplanetary or kosmic sources related to the bodily organism of the Solar Logos.

THE SEVEN RAY GROUPS
(See also appendix C)

Our most effective focus here will therefore be on the issue of the Seven Ray Groups, which might themselves be described as the vehicles of expression of hierarchical Purpose. As we saw earlier, the Rays are described as the emanations into our lower world system of the (kosmic) consciousness of the Intelligence (Logos) "in Whom we live and move and have our being," as St. Paul puts it. In relation to these Rays we shall see (to some minor extent at least) which of the known Masters are described as having particular Ray affiliations, as shown in the summary below. Blavatsky herself firmly acknowledged the existence of the Rays, making the particular point that all Adepts are associated with specific Rays and thus also with specific soul groups.[13] From Bailey's later work, however, we have already outlined the Ray characteristics in rather general terms (in chapter 9), but more explanatory detail is provided in appendix C at the back of this book. In relation to what is about to be described, however, it otherwise needs to be remembered that there is a constant overlap of function and responsibility, by virtue of the interaction of Ray cycles, if nothing else.

The First Ray

The function of this Ray type is described (by reference to Vedic philosophy) as that associated with Siva, the "Creator-Destroyer," although this rather dramatic epithet needs to be put in rather more practical context. In fact, it might be more aptly described as the dynamic spiritual influence responsible for both initiation and ultimate termination of all types of form and cycles of activity (in all kingdoms of Nature) over which it has influence. It thereby expresses the Will-force of the Logos. In that sense, it is the observer-judge, the generator of the sense of individuality and thus also of leadership in man. It is otherwise the protector of Universal Law and initiator of all cycles of existence, hence also the strong protector of the actual field of Creation. In the latter sense it is also directly associated with the process of isolation that necessarily leads to the progressive attainment of increasing spiritual individualization in all kingdoms of Nature.

In practical terms, the senior Adept known as the "Manu" is described as chief of the First Ray and consequently as the perfected archetypal expression of the human type for the cycle in question, there being fourteen Manus per Round on our objective planet Earth,[14] that is, two per Root Race.* However, the work of this Ray is also said to be very intimately concerned with direction of the deva hierarchies, particularly in terms of the cyclical reorganization of continental land masses, insofar as the latter is related to the progressive evolutionary process.[15] We also need to bear in mind that the vast majority of the peoples (i.e., the ethnological types) of China, Southeast Asia, and Africa are actually of far older ethnic Atlantean (Fourth Race) origin, so it appears that they are still watched over by their own Manu. We are also told that the most organized remnant of the Fourth Race— presumably meaning the Chinese people in this particular instance—have still to produce one further great and last civilization as the apotheosis of their evolutionary and cultural existence.[16]

The current Manu of the Fifth (Indo-Aryan) Race has been made known to us by Blavatsky as Vaivasvata Manu,[17] but other than that we know virtually nothing of this great Intelligence. His reign, apparently as the seventh Manu of the overall cycle, would logically have commenced

---

*Please refer to appendix C for a listing and brief description of the evolutionary development of the Root Races.

around a cyclic point complementary to that now being approached, but during the middle of the fourth subrace of the Fifth Root Race, about 100,000 years ago. However, it is suggested through Bailey that the Chohan Morya will take over the responsibility of deputy Manu precedent to the next (sixth) subrace of the Fifth Root Race and then will subsequently become Manu of the early Sixth Root Race itself.[18] The associated logic would seem to derive from the present Manu's term of responsibility having commenced with the evolutionary cycle of development of consciousness of the present Fifth subrace—which would logically have been about 100,000 years ago, comprising some four cycles of astronomical precession. This then would be precedent to the much later generation of the requisite body form and type needed to house the involutionary consciousness of the actual Sixth Race human type, many hundreds of thousands of years from our present era.

The Mahatma Morya's external area of responsibility in the meantime is otherwise described as involving, influencing, and directing the activities of workers in the field of current world politics and government. He is also very significantly described as being in charge of all schools of occultism.[19] However, as a Chohan he would inevitably work mainly through lesser Adepts and Masters in influencing world leaders in these various fields, as well as being at least partially responsible for setting up the nucleus of the future Sixth subrace.

The Second Ray

This is described in the literature as the Ray of Love-Wisdom, or the Teaching Ray. Its function might perhaps be described as that of bringing about and advancing conscious recognition of actual spiritual relationships through knowledge and understanding. In a very real sense, it is also concerned with education generally but more particularly in all aspects of esoteric philosophy. As already described, the doyen of the Second Ray is described as the Bodhisattva, known in the West as the Christ, and in the Islamic world as the Imam Mahdi. Although historically associated with the field of religion, because of its association with developing forms of mystic and theological belief, the Second Ray's scope of influence apparently extends far wider within the field of knowledge, now apparently focusing more directly on worldwide education and social behavior prior to the development of a new, worldwide religion.[20] It would appear that the term of office of any holder of this position is roughly 2,000 years, perhaps specifically associated with a zodiacal Age of 2,160 years, although not necessarily coinciding exactly with the historical beginnings and ends of each such era as currently known. Again, the principle of overlap between cycles seems to hold good.

As earlier described, the issue of the relationship between the past and present holders of the Bodhisattva office has become something of a point of friction between theosophists of various persuasions on the one hand and Buddhists on the other. That is because, according to the tradition explained in Bailey's works, Lord Gautama Sakyamuni Buddha—the first of our humanity to reach full enlightenment, as an interplanetary Spirit—fulfilled the role of the Bodhisattva or planetary Christ until about two thousand five hundred years ago. The latter is something that the Adepts themselves confirmed while also mentioning the much later fourteenth century Tibetan high Adept Tzon-kha-pa (1355–1419), who was himself seemingly of equivalent occult status.[21] Following the Buddha's achievement, so it seems, the present holder of the office—that is, his disciple the Lord Maitreya—took over from him, once having himself taken the preliminary part of the seventh and final initiation of our planetary world system. At around the same time perhaps, the Lord Gautama seems to have achieved a yet higher initiation (as described in chapter 11), which enabled him to go at least one inconceivable stage further.

However, it would appear that—in line with all initiations—the final fulfillment of these great achievements has to take rather longer. We are thus otherwise told that "when the Christ completes His work at the time of the Second Coming, then the great seventh initiation . . . will be consummated and the Buddha and the Christ will together pass before the Lord of the World . . . and together pass to higher service of a nature and calibre unknown to us."[22] From this it is clearly implied that, at around this point—seemingly more than two thousand years hence, according to what we are being told—the being that we know as "Lord Maitreya" will himself take the first part of the eighth initiation (the fourth kosmic initiation). He will thereby become a Dhyani Buddha himself while the Chohan

Kuthumi will seemingly take over as the next appointed Bodhisattva, or planetary Christ.[23] The further presumption is that, as such, he will continue to be overshadowed in some way by his existing mentor, the Lord Maitreya, thereby maintaining the overall continuity of logoic Second Ray consciousness.

As regards the Chohan Kuthumi (a name interestingly akin to the Chaldean Qutamy), little is known of him other than that his present physical persona is apparently that of a Kashmiri Brahmin who seems to have spent some time in his youth—presumably during the eighteenth century—at one or more European universities,[24] during which time he seems to have learned to speak and write both English and French with great fluency. The founding of the modern Theosophical Society seems to have been his particular idea, although closely supported by the Chohan Morya. However, his further desire for literary communication with noninitiated Westerners (as evidenced in *The Mahatma Letters to A. P. Sinnett*) seems to have been consented to, only under strict conditions, by a far higher Adept referred to merely as "the Mahachohan."[25] It would appear that Kuthumi may himself have taken the first step to become a Chohan of the sixth degree in the early-to-mid 1880s.[26]

The Third Ray

The function of the Third Ray type—defined as that of "Active Intelligence"—might be described as that of the generation and maintenance of the particular spiritual impulse that gives rise to and subsequently maintains human civilization and culture. It is that most associated with intelligent, creative adaptability, and thus inevitably also with commerce. However, commerce and finance as we know them have to be seen (from the viewpoint of occult philosophy and practice) as merely the external manifestations of psycho-spiritual energy flows. We touched on this in an earlier chapter, when confirming that a spirituality of approach is just as much to be found in this area of human activity as, for example, in the field of religion. The idea that only religion provides entry to the development of spirituality is one of the greatest misperceptions of our times.

The current chief of the Third Ray has been made known to us as the

Chohan (now Mahachohan) Ragoczi,[27] who seems to have taken over this latter position of responsibility in the early-to-mid-twentieth century, having previously held the position of Chohan of the Seventh Ray. Quite who the previously Third Ray Mahachohan was is unknown, although *The Mahatma Letters to A.P. Sinnett* suggest that he was known as "the Shaberon of Than-La," whom the Chohan Kuthumi described as "the greatest of our living Adepts."[28] Ragoczi is otherwise known to us as the historically enigmatic Comte de St. Germain, the formidable alchemist and magician who came publicly to the fore in the latter part of the eighteenth century, just before the French Revolution. We are told that he is the only Adept of equal standing to the Lord Maitreya (thus presumably an initiated Manushi Buddha, of the seventh degree) in respect of ability to communicate directly with Shamballa.[29]

The position of Mahachohan, also known as the "Lord of Civilization," apparently carries with it overall responsibility for training and supervision of all the lesser Adepts of the fourth and fifth degrees. In relation to his

Fig. 12.2. The Comte de St. Germain (a.k.a. Master Ragoczi)

standing now as an initiate of the seventh degree (perhaps achieved during the nineteenth century) it is interesting to speculate upon the suggestion that the extraordinarily sophisticated and rapid development of the worlds of industry, commerce, and business administration over the past three centuries has in no small sense been due to his influence as a Chohan willing to involve himself very directly in the external Western world and its culture.

A further Third Ray Master, whose name remains completely unknown, is simply referred to as "the English Master" (there apparently being also a second, also unnamed "English Master"). He is, we are told, of particular importance in the field of human social relations, being described as the one primarily behind the world labor movement and the spiritual awakening of the masses. This is of course far more than just being behind the international movement for workers' rights. So we are told, he began his work "in the latter part of the nineteenth century but left it to carry forward of its own momentum when Russia entered the field and laid an undue emphasis upon the proletariat during the revolution and in the later years of the first quarter of the twentieth century,"[30] in other words, when Stalin and the Politburo sidelined Lenin and took over as a brutal, oligarchic dictatorship. So we further understand, his is now the task of bringing about worldwide cooperation (economic and financial) out of the present "democratic" chaos.[31]

The Fourth Ray

The function of this Ray type is that of the psychologist, as well as that of the artist. A moment's careful consideration will confirm why this connection should be so, and why also the influence should be known as the Ray of Harmony through Conflict. It is essentially that influence that very specifically deals with the effective and even creative handling of crisis on the one hand and with tension as an artistic and psychological attribute on the other, for example in the field of music. However, it has nothing to do with the emotional tension from which so many human beings in the Western world seem to suffer.

The only Adepts confirmed to us as affiliated with this Ray are the Mahatma Serapis Bey, Chohan of the Fourth Ray, and the (Irish-American)

Master "P." The main area of responsibility of the former lies, so it appears, in relation to the stimulation of national and international culture. We are thus told that, apart from having been the main influence behind the founding of the League of Nations in 1918 (the forerunner of the United Nations Assembly)[32]—with which we would normally associate the First Ray influence—he is otherwise particularly concerned with improving contacts between the deva evolution and humanity, hence perhaps his particular association with culture and the arts.[33] The area of responsibility of the latter (Master "P") appears to be in promoting and developing psychology as a properly recognized science. We are also told that this latter Master, together with the Third Ray English Master, is one of the few Adepts who mingle to any degree with the external world, apparently in order to lay the groundwork for the eventual externalization of at least part of the Spiritual Hierarchy during the next couple of centuries.[34]

The Fifth Ray

The function of this Ray type is described as that of "Concrete Science." That is to say, this type is concerned with influencing the development in humanity of scientific knowledge plus associated technological know-how and its application. The only Adept as yet confirmed to us as affiliated with this Ray is the Mahatma Hilarion, Chohan of the Fifth Ray (of Concrete Science) and supposedly a reincarnation of the apostle Paul of Tarsus.[35] His areas of concern, so we are told, involve both psychical research and scientific development, plus the coinstruction of those who will form the nucleus of the next great Race of humankind.[36] However, we otherwise learn that in the eighteenth century the Master Ragoczi was also involved in the area of science, influencing the discovery and development of steam power by English inventors such as James Watt.[37]

The Sixth Ray

The function of this Ray is described as that of Devotion and Idealism. It is thus associated with the stimulation and control of mass movements. Hence it is specifically concerned with religion in particular and also mysticism, as well, perhaps curiously, as martial discipline. The only Adept confirmed to us as affiliated with this Ray is the Chohan Jesus,[38] whom we have come to know as the Adept founder of the Christian religion, described in the biblical New Testament as having suffered crucifixion and death at the hands of the Romans. Rather curiously, however, the Master Kuthumi quite categorically comments as to "John the Baptist having never heard of Jesus, who is a spiritual abstraction and no living man of that epoch."[39] Notwithstanding that, Blavatsky herself acknowledges Jesus as an initiate, thereby suggesting that he merely lived at a different time.[40]

However, mention should be made of the esoteric tradition as described by the Tibetan Adept DK, the chela of Kuthumi, who suggests that, in the same way that Blavatsky's body was temporarily taken over by the Adepts in order to write *Isis Unveiled*,[41] so the body of Jesus was informed by the Christ at the time of his crucifixion.[42] At this same time, so it appears, the Christ was himself directly overshadowed by the Buddha (Lord Gautama Sakyamuni) who was, in turn, in the process of setting up a direct subjective connection with the main planetary center of spiritual administration at Shamballa.[43] One might add that this statement regarding Jesus seems totally and utterly confusing—unless the time part of the associated equation is materially altered, along with the name. However, if the true Jesus was actually Joshua-ben-Nun (as suggested by some) and the Christian "Jesus" was in fact the name given to a mythical personage in a preexisting gnostic allegory, as suggested in chapter 13, it would make rather more sense. It would also necessitate a complete reorientation of the Christian religion itself. But see also chapter 13 for a range of rather more detailed suggestions.

The Seventh Ray

The function of this Ray type is described as that of Ceremonial Order and Magic. This rather opaque nomenclature conceals the fact that its central concern is that of the strict administration of order under Universal Law. In another sense, it is said to involve the "anchoring" and "grounding" of new and higher (i.e., kosmic) influences and potentialities within the objective sphere of direct human understanding. It also inevitably has a particular concern with the evolutionary development of the mineral kingdom, the seventh and lowest of the kingdoms of Nature. The way in which increasingly subtle mineral characteristics have been adapted in the many and various fields of modern technology during the past century appears to involve just the beginning of this Ray influence, which, we are told, will last "close on two thousand five hundred years"[44]—throughout the Aquarian Age and slightly beyond it. Such technological innovation as thereby achieved will then provide the basis for the next prolonged phase of human civilization, lasting for at least the next two millennia, in preparation for the next great spiritual change at the beginning of the Age of Capricorn.

Although it would appear that the Chohan Ragoczi was the chief of this particular Ray group until about one-third of the way through the twentieth century,[45] the present chief's identity has not yet been made known. However, it would seem that this particular Ray is of immediate importance to human civilization and culture by virtue of now coming into direct cyclic operation in tandem with the imminent zodiacal era of Aquarius. One of its preliminary exoteric manifestations is, curiously enough, the growth of politico-socio-economic reorganization (and its negative side, bureaucracy) in human society. That itself is also otherwise indirectly connected with the work of the English (Third Ray) Master already described as responsible for sorting out the present worldwide chaos in the field of business finance and associated legal structures.

OTHER ADEPTS

Very few of the names of those other Adepts working in the external world have as yet been given out for the logically simple reason that to have done so would immediately have created conditions of public interest directly or indirectly hindering their altruistic work behind the scenes on behalf of humanity in general. However, those made known by Blavatsky and Bailey, together with some information as to their particular fields of endeavor are as follows:[46]

- The Second Ray Tibetan Adept DK (Djwahl Khul)—who apparently became an Adept only around 1875 and who was, so we are told, responsible for helping with much of H. P. Blavatsky's opus magnum *The Secret Doctrine,*[47] as well as subsequently dictating all of the main works of A. A. Bailey.

- The Indian Master (apparently known as the Master "Jupiter")— of whom we know little other than that he is on the First Ray, his objective persona being that of a "landowner" living somewhere in the Nilgiri Hills of southern India and that he has specific responsibility for the evolution of all the main subraces (and their offshoots) comprising the greater Indian nation.[48]

- The Masters Atrya, Polydorus Isurenus, and Robert More, mentioned as passing through New York while Blavatsky and Olcott were resident together there.[49] Also the unnamed "Venetian Master."

- So we are otherwise told, "Six of the Masters, as yet quite unknown to the average occult student by name, have already sought physical incarnation—one in India, another in England, two in northern America and one in central Europe, while another has made a great sacrifice, and taken a Russian body."[50] It is not known precisely what "seeking of physical incarnation" actually infers, although it might even suggest natural birth into a family.

- The Manu and Teaching Ray Master of the Fourth Root Race, responsible for the continuing evolution and rounding out of the remnant of Fourth Root Race consciousness on this planet. Their headquarters is apparently in China.[51] An Adept (once known as Confucius) is also mentioned.[52] However, the full extent of the Fourth Root Race generic types is not given.

THE BRANCHES OF THE HIERARCHY

We are told by the Chohan Kuthumi that "There are even at the present moment three centres of the Occult Brotherhood in existence, widely separated geographically,"[53] while the Tibetan Adept DK appears to confirm this by suggesting that there are now four main branches to the Spiritual Hierarchy.[54] These are as follows:

1. The Trans-Himalayan branch, whose specific concern is the spiritual development of Western humanity, particularly the fourth and fifth (European, Celtic, and Teutonic) subraces of the Fifth Root Race. It is this branch that was specifically concerned with initiat-

ing the modern theosophical movement through the agency of H. P. Blavatsky and H. S. Olcott.

2. The Southern India branch, which is also concerned with the second and third subraces of the Fifth Root Race, as well as having special work with the deva evolution.

3. The Fourth Root Race branch (just mentioned).

4. The coming Sixth Root Race branch, which is still in its very early and formative stages. This, we are told, is being developed under the aegis of the Mahachohan Ragoczi, primarily aided by one of the English Masters, plus the Fifth Ray Chohan Hilarion.

NIRMANAKAYA ADEPTS AND SHAMBALLA

We have so far discussed those senior Adepts responsible for the disposition and workings of particular Ray Groups. We should also mention that each such Ray Group comprises seven Subray Groups, which, we are told, are controlled by lesser Adept Brothers of the fourth and fifth degrees.[55] We are also told that many Adepts choose not to continue with human bodies but instead function in their Spiritual Soul bodies as what are called Nirmanakayas. The given reason for this is that these Adepts work purely at and within the higher levels of mental consciousness, sometimes inspiring particular human beings (or specific groups) by the process called "overshadowing," which has already been described.

Other Adepts, we are told, fulfill a yet higher function by acting as permanent intermediaries between the Adept Hierarchy and Shamballa, the highest state of planetary being. This seems to involve the maintenance of a direct telepathic connection between the two, achieved by intense and persistent contemplation, such that any even subtle emanation transmitted from Shamballa is automatically picked up and acted on by the Adept Brotherhood when prepared. The latter then step down the power and retransmit the influence(s) to selected destinations within the lesser kingdoms of Nature. The essential logic behind this seems to be related to the occult association between the Spiritual Hierarchy as the heart center and Shamballa as the head center in the overall bodily life of our planet. Given that these two centers are respectively associated with the Causal Soul and the Spiritual Soul—as described in early chapters—one can perhaps see the principle behind the higher evolutionary linkage.

The Adept DK tells us that the direct link between the Adept Hierarchy and Shamballa, first brought about by the work of the Lord Gautama Buddha in conjunction with the Lord Maitreya, is still only quite tenuous and that it needs to be magnetically recharged every Wesak Festival (at the May full moon each year). Under the astrological influence of Taurus, this is when the Buddha returns "personally" to involve himself briefly in the ceremonials.[56] The association, as described, seems to derive from the fact that the Lord Gautama is now a Dhyani Buddha, or fully liberated interplanetary Spirit, as are also the divine Kumaras who fulfill the manifold roles of world government in Shamballa itself. So we are told, the main officials there are Sanat Kumara, the Lord of the World himself (the representative on Earth of the Planetary Logos), plus three subsidiary (Dhyani) "Buddhas of Activity" who are directly responsible for overseeing the process of evolution in the mineral, plant, and animal kingdoms of Nature.[57]

With regard to Shamballa itself, while it is described as having an ethereal location or foothold on our planet "geographically" to the north of the Himalayas, it is made clear that it is no longer visible to ordinary human sight because its lowest form of existence is in the highest substates of solar etheric matter.[58] The fact that its "officials" or "inhabitants" have bodily forms of substantially more subtle and evolved substance does not conflict with this any more than does man's physical form and his much more evolved consciousness that is directly "anchored" to it. It is supposedly for this reason that the various initiatory ceremonies described by the Adept DK, said to involve Sanat Kumara himself (as the representative of the Planetary Logos), are made possible (but see also appendix B).

ADEPTS AND INITIATORY CEREMONIAL

The issue of initiatory ceremonial has been made much of in some quarters. However, the Adept DK makes the point that ceremonial per se plays increasingly less part as the process continues beyond the transition into Adeptship.[59] Prior to this, however, the first two initiations quite logically come under the aegis of the World Teacher, otherwise known as the Christ or Bodhisattva, with the representative of the Planetary Logos remaining well in the background. That is because the vital potency of the Kumara himself could not be directly used. It would be far too powerful, even with the neophyte surrounded by Adepts to protect him by acting as energy transformers. So we are told, it is only at the third initiation—after the candidate has himself already destroyed the elemental "Dweller-on-the-Threshold" beyond reanimation—that it becomes safe for the power (of Divine Will) of the Planetary Logos to come into direct contact with his still human consciousness for the first time.[60] But even then, as already described, it must first be stepped down in force by the simultaneous involvement of two Chohans, or a Chohan and a fifth degree Master.

The inference from this is that, were this same power to be experienced any earlier, the individual's consciousness, incapable of its adequate and safe absorption, would be destroyed by madness. It follows logically, therefore, that the personal sacrifice that precedes the third initiation itself produces the necessarily ascetic and individualized power of electrical resistance. It is consequently logical that the third initiation is regarded as the first of the pre-kosmic initiations. However, as we saw earlier, it and the fourth initiation merely comprise the "initiations of the kosmic threshold." They do not do more than directly impose upon the consciousness of the individual the qualitative note or "occult signature" of the Dhyani Buddhas. Notwithstanding this, it seems that the Adept Hierarchy are keen to encourage some advanced groups of their disciples (below the third initiation) to practice meditation directly orientated toward Shamballa[61] on the basis that the trained group—presumably headed up by a rather more advanced initiate—would develop the necessary occult resistance to permit their absorbing such an influence without undue danger.

THE REORIENTATION OF THE SPIRITUAL HIERARCHY

To understand the rationale of this more readily it would perhaps be useful to reiterate what we have otherwise been told, to the effect that the Adept Hierarchy is itself in preparation for objective externalization. Therefore, it follows quite logically that prepared groups that already function on the outer planes will inevitably make their own adaptation much easier to achieve. Otherwise they would have to waste needless time in educational and administrative management. The overall continuity of conscious function within the logoic body is naturally of great importance. The principle is essentially the same as it is in our own human bodies. The more our higher intelligence has to focus on sorting out purely physical problems, instead of being able to rely on healthy autonomic function, the less attention can be given to sorting out higher ones, with inevitable results. The whole system thus slows down and becomes considerably less effective.

It can therefore be seen why the Adept Hierarchy places so much emphasis on selflessly orientated group endeavor and advance planning, as well as sustained good health. What we call the Higher Mind, however, is merely the emanation of the buddhic state of consciousness, which, as has already been described, itself comprises the (kosmic) etheric double of the Logos. It therefore follows that the externalization of the Adept Hierarchy must necessarily result in a much closer connection being achieved between all elements and the seven substates of the kosmic physical body of the Logos. It also otherwise follows that when all these elements remain diffuse, the logoic body is largely dormant. What is effectively now happening, therefore, so it would appear, is that the Logos is in the process of "awakening," and it is during such periods of wakefulness (as it is with us) that major opportunities arise for the further advancement of knowledge. This otherwise puts a slightly different slant on the issue of the Divine Purpose to which the Adept Hierarchy is consciously responding.

As we saw in the previous chapter, in order for the initiate (one of the fourth degree) to become fully integrated into the yet higher state of logoic physical being as a still self-conscious but now fully spiritualized intelligence (i.e., as a Master), he must very rapidly progress one step further, by crossing over the buddhic state to the next state or phase of evolutionary progress. The field of buddhic consciousness—a large part of which is essentially that of the lesser deva (and thus spiritually involutionary) nature—must thus itself be left behind and thereby brought under conscious control, "from above." The Atmic state—that of the "Divine Breath" of the Monad—thus becomes the focus of attention. Hence, so we are told, it is the fourth and fifth initiatory degrees that are currently the main focus of attention by the most senior Intelligences in the Spiritual Hierarchy.[62]

THE ADVANCEMENT TO ALL-KNOWLEDGE

The further step brought about at the fourth initiation allows the development of an ascetic self-identification with the atma (pure spirit) aspect of logoic consciousness, which is itself the direct emanation of the Monad, or "divine spark." It is the latter that contains all akasic knowledge. In other words, through the power of the Planetary Logos acting as Hierophant, the initiate at the third initiation is exposed for the first time to the Ray of his own highest (semi-divine) nature (the akasic All-Thought of his monadic Source) sufficiently well to anchor himself irresistibly to it. This is then reinforced at the fourth initiation and completed at the fifth, necessarily by the initiate himself. The more Adepts of the fourth and fifth degree there are, therefore, it follows logically that the clearer, quicker, and more potent is the downward transmission of knowledge and Purpose of the Planetary Logos throughout his "physical" body organism. Were the initiate to fail in this endeavor of crossing the kosmic etheric state, he would unavoidably find his consciousness being absorbed or at least attracted backward into that of the involutionary, local deva world instead. This purely personal disaster would result in a complete, subjective disorientation already described to us in *The Voice of the Silence,* as follows:

> Thy Mind-Soul will become as a mad elephant that rages in the jungle. Mistaking forest trees for living foes, he perishes in his attempts to kill the ever-shifting shadows. . . . Beware, lest in the care of Self thy Soul should lose her foothold on the soil of deva knowledge.[63]

Once the Adept (now of the fifth degree) has achieved this degree of anchored Atmic Self-identification, he is regarded as spiritually "safe" and thus a permanent participant in the consciousness of Shamballa, even if only as a lesser observer to begin with. However, as an initiate of the kosmic first degree, he is now a Master Soul who is so disenfranchised from the elemental nature of the lower world that he can wield it with expertise to generate whatever forms he wishes, wherever he wishes; for geographical distance is now seen as a complete illusion. As a result, the Master is able to project his spiritual influence wherever he feels it necessary within the bounds of the planetary life, through the medium of the kosmic etheric double. By doing so he, in conjunction with the other members of the Spiritual Hierarchy, can thereby seek to bring about (by fully conscious sympathetic association) the exoteric manifestation of Divine Purpose. However, his work within the Spiritual Hierarchy now takes on progressively greater fields of responsibility and authority. Notwithstanding this, it is interesting to note that there are evidently very powerful demarcations between the consciousness of the fifth degree Master Adept and his own high superiors. The Mahatma Kuthumi refers to this when remarking in correspondence with A. P. Sinnett that "THEIR mind—as you know, is a sealed book for many of us and which no amount of 'art magic' can break open."[64] As previously suggested, the Master Kuthumi was himself at that time still not at the point of such spiritual individualization as already attained by the Chohan of the sixth degree. He was but of the first degree on the Higher Path.

THE WORK OF THE SPIRITUAL HIERARCHY

As described to us, the work of the Adept Hierarchy appears not only very extensive but also highly complex. To begin with, they are confirmed as forming a protective wall between humanity plus the other subhuman kingdoms on the one hand and excessive evil emanating from kosmic sources on the other.[65] Quite apart from this they are described as working constantly at the task of awakening the faculty of consciousness in all the lesser kingdoms of Nature, for evolutionary purposes. More specifically in relation to humanity, the Hierarchy is described as directing world events from behind the scenes "through developing adequate social, political, religious and economic world forms."[66] This work is done by impressing the consciousness of the intelligentsia of the age in question with new ideas and revelations, mainly of a scientific and cultural nature (but with a spiritual orientation), so that the civilization develops the widest human potential in the round.[67] Notwithstanding the very real underlying direction and control, we are told that even the Hierarchy itself, with all its knowledge, vision and understanding and with all its resources, cannot coerce and cannot forecast what mankind will do. It can and does stimulate to right action; it can and does indicate possibility and responsibility . . . but at no point and in no situation does it command or assume control. . . . If it assumed authoritative control, a race of automatons would be developed and not a race of responsible, self-directed, aspiring men."[68]

THE NIRMANAKAYAS

While we have already mentioned the Nirmanakaya Buddhas as those Intelligences who have developed beyond Adeptship to take the first stage of Dhyani Buddhahood, we ought perhaps to elaborate on their (highly important) function as follows. First of all, it is necessary to understand that each major group of beings within any given Hierarchy is essentially triple in nature. That is to say it involves: (1) those who are concerned with directing the evolution of the kingdom below their own; (2) those who are concerned to understand the Purpose emanating from the kingdom above their own and to generate a coherently integrated plan of action based on it; (3) those sensitives who are actually responsible for looking into the "Future," thereby confirming to the second group what range of Purpose is intended by the higher Powers. These latter are the committed contemplatives, given the name Nirmanakaya.[69]

There are, so we are told, two extant groups of such Nirmanakayas, whose whole task involves sustained meditation in the direction of the appropriate Higher Consciousness. The more senior group involves the Nirmanakaya Buddhas themselves. They act on behalf of Shamballa, projecting their receptive consciousness toward the celestial realms of Kosmic Buddhi (Mahat) in order to divine what impulses are in train or likely to be forthcoming from such regions of the consciousness of the Solar Logos. The second group, so we are again told, is gathered from out of the Spiritual Hierarchy of Adepts, their parallel responsibility being to act as the equivalent telepathic medium between Shamballa and the Hierarchy.

There is now, however, a third group, which has apparently been brought into existence during the last century or so. It has been given the name "The New Group of World Servers," and much has been written about it in the works of A. A. Bailey. From her references, it quickly becomes apparent that this (worldwide scattered) group of human intelligences comprises particular individuals whose intensity of idealism has itself become psycho-spiritually invocative, thereby generating some degree of helpfully inspirational response from the Hierarchy, even though most are completely unaware of the fact. These individuals range from those on the probationary Path, to accepted disciples, to those of the first three initiations, just as their higher equivalent group of Nirmanakayas consists of Adepts of the fourth, fifth, and sixth degrees. The latter, as we saw earlier, involve the equivalent stages of accepted discipleship and the first two degrees on the higher evolutionary Path. In logical progression, the New Group of World Servers thus involves individuals who have become, through their own efforts, creative spiritual sensitives and are now undergoing training in meditative techniques by those particular members of the Adept Hierarchy who take student disciples (chelas). By no means all of them do so, however.

Those members of the Adept Hierarchy who do not retain human bodies but who work entirely through Spiritual Soul bodies of buddhic substance are themselves generally known as lesser nirmanakayas. Their responsibility is either to "overshadow" and teach those human individuals or groups on the earlier stages of the Path, or otherwise (more generally) to act the role of Hermes, as "semi-divine messengers" of potential creativity between Shamballa and the Spiritual Hierarchy, under the tutelage of the "Buddhas of Activity" from within Shamballa itself.[70] In this manner we can see how it is that the whole process of educational evolution plus information gathering and telepathic transmission takes place in the kosmos as a whole and how incoming Divine Purpose is thus transmuted into the Divine Plan generated by the united consciousness of the Spiritual Hierarchy. If we stop to think about it, we shall quickly see that the same principles apply in all coherent individual human consciousness, to form the basis of our own creativity.

THE "CHARACTER" OF THE ADEPT BROTHERHOOD

It follows naturally from this that the way in which the Trans-Himalayan Spiritual Hierarchy behaves and operates is quite different from what modern "New Age" thought seems to believe. The latter belief is largely due to the images of cave-dwelling *sannyasis, sadhus,* and other yogic gurus in India, the vast majority of whom are involved in a not-too-subtle spectrum of exoteric self-indulgence, and who are self-evidently unfit for true Adeptship, irrespective of their achieved capacities (in some cases) for ascetic and thaumaturgical (magic) practices. European devotees who fondly imagine that their contacts with these individuals provide a sort of attractive introductory "hors d'oeuvre" prior to any major spiritual engagement are merely fooling themselves. Real Adepts do not waste their time in any sort of public or private self-display, even though they may well occasionally demonstrate these *siddhis* (occult powers) to their students as part of their training.

The writer was introduced some years ago to a swami from a major community of some three to four hundred Hindu swamis living in the foothills of the Himalayas. He had lived there for about thirty years. Apart from having a quietly well-developed sense of humor, this monk—despite his self-presentation as a guru in the West—was intelligently (and unusually) interested in learning of Western approaches to the ancient wisdom tradition. When asked about his community and whether he had ever met any real Adepts, his reply, after a few moments of thought, was most enlightening.

He confirmed to me, first of all, that while the vast majority of his fellow monks could recite the Hindu scriptures almost backward, he would only regard a literal handful of them as having a truly spiritual nature. The rest possessed far too much pride in their own academic knowledge. As regards the question of any real Adepts having ever appeared, he mentioned having briefly seen one such individual merely passing through their community very briefly many years before. However, he had been so outstandingly of a self-confident spiritual quality altogether different from any of the others that he stood out "head and shoulders" above them very powerfully and without any effort. He had also wasted no time in delaying his exit from their midst.

This characteristically self-evident potency is perhaps even more understandable when considering the essentially magnetic relationship between a real Master Adept and his pupil in the guru-chela relationship. The Mahatma Kuthumi commented on this as follows:

Few candidates imagine the degree of inconvenience—nay suffering and harm to himself—the said initiator submits to for the sake of his pupil. . . . In each case, the instructor has to adapt his conditions to those of the pupil and the strain is terrible; for to achieve success, we have to bring ourselves into a full rapport with the subject under training. And as the greater the powers of the Adept, the less he is in sympathy with natures of the profane who often come to him saturated with the emanations of the outside world . . . the purer he has become, the more difficult the self-imposed task.[71]

In contradistinction to this, and by way of encouraging the many in the external world, the same Mahatma makes the point that

[while] it is true that the married man cannot be an Adept, yet without striving to become a Raja Yogi, he can acquire certain powers and do as much good to mankind and often more, by remaining within the precincts of this world of his. . . . There are more ways than one for acquiring occult knowledge.[72]

Thus the fact that any individual may have heard about the Spiritual Brotherhood only after having become involved in a natural marital relationship would not preclude his or her being able to provide positive auxiliary assistance to the Brotherhood. In the West, there is thus no need to follow the path of the Indian sannyasin who, when his children have grown up, leaves his family for good, to spend the rest of his life as a wandering hermit in search of spiritual enlightenment.

EXTERNALIZATION OF THE HIERARCHY

In the final part of this chapter we might briefly look at the issue of prospective externalization of the Spiritual Hierarchy concerning which we are told: "At the great General Assembly of the Hierarchy—held as usual every century—in 2025 [CE], the date in all probability will be set for the first stage of the externalisation of the Hierarchy."[73] Bearing in mind what has already been said about the instructions of Tzon-kha-pa to his Adepts in the early fifteenth century, as to the Spiritual Hierarchy making a deeper impact upon Western consciousness, this timing is understandable because it will occur exactly seven centuries after 1425 CE. As is fairly obvious, this same externalization must be a cyclical phenomenon, arising out of necessity induced by Higher (i.e., Kosmic) Purpose.

Although a yet greater cycle may well also be involved in tandem, the Hierarchy's emergence would appear mainly to be aligned to the 25,920 year cycle of precession of the equinoxes during which (as I have described in my previous books) our solar system orbits once around its own parent star (Alcyone) in the Pleiades. This cycle, like the Earth year of 365 days, has two solstices and two equinoxes and, as described in an earlier chapter, we are currently approaching one of those celestial solstices as we near the beginning of the Age of Aquarius. From this one might infer certain parallels between the human and plant kingdoms, as follows.

From the winter solstice, the renewal of root growth occurs in perennial plants whereas seeds of annual plants are planted around the spring equinox. At the summer solstice we see the first fruit drop—a sort of lesser "day of judgment"—while at or by the autumn equinox we see the proper gathering of fruits. By the reckoning of this author, the celestial winter solstice took place just under 13,000 years ago while we now approach the celestial summer solstice. The parallel logic here then would be that the Earth humanity of our time—which has already reached a total of some seven billion—will shortly see a similar natural "culling" as many millions of souls deemed to be now unlikely to "pass muster" in this cycle (through lack of adequate spiritual "fertilization") will be withdrawn from active service.

Hence it is that the (gradual) externalization of the Spiritual Hierarchy will to some extent coincide with a serious fall in the total numbers of the population on our planet—the latter having increased dramatically by some four to five billion in the last century and a half alone. The assumption by scientists that the human population will just go on growing because of a lack of any apparent restraint is wholly misconceived. But why then would the Spiritual Hierarchy choose this moment to begin its process of externalization, as revealed through Bailey's Adept teacher, DK? How can we conceive of their being able, in like manner, to help bring about the expansion and ripening of the fruit? The answer to that lies in the expansion and qualitative improvement of human consciousness and the ripening of faculty in the soul nature, not in the objective persona. It is the condition of the soul nature that gives rise to the health of the outer form of the "fruit." Therefore, it is the inner or soul nature to which the Adepts will pay their attention and, if considered carefully, this also tells us why the sheer number of human beings in incarnation has to be reduced by Nature in due proportion.

But then why the necessity to come out in the open if the Adept Hierarchy already has the capacity to influence telepathically, at a distance? The answer must surely lie in the fact that their direct presence (although not immediately accessible to all) would inevitably enable other, even higher Powers (Avatars) to manifest in closer proximity to humanity. With the huge present orientation toward materialism, this would itself generate enormous problems. That is because the first effect of the spiritual or divine nature's presence unavoidably involves energizing the existing consciousness in general. If that consciousness were not duly prepared—also again by reducing overall human numbers—the result would be pointlessly destructive because of it supercharging the basest aspects of human nature as well as the highest.

We are already told that a great experiment has been made within the past century or two to expose humankind more directly to the energies emanating from Shamballa and that this experiment has, in the main, proved successful[74]—although quite what that success might have involved has not yet been explained. However, in the same way that the spiritual evolutionary process aims to unite the Monad with its human expression without the intervention of the Causal Soul, so it would appear the intention with humanity as a whole is to bring about a correspondingly direct union of consciousness between it and Shamballa. Thus humanity in the greater mass would become a living self-expression of the Logos and our Earth would thereby become one of the "sacred planets."[75] In biblical terms, "Heaven would descend on Earth." But this could only take place with at least some of the Adept Hierarchy in full physical incarnation, living reasonably openly among humanity, in order to provide the necessary psychomagnetic "anchorage," while many more move toward yet higher Adeptship themselves.

All of the foregoing, however, has to be seen in conjunction with the fact, so we are again told, that entry into the sign and era of Aquarius will coincide with the preliminary stage of entry into a greater round of the zodiac.[76] This implies that although the Egyptian Zep Tepi or "First Time" involves the involutionary cyclic commencement of the Great Year at the celestial winter solstice, that of the Spiritual Hierarchy's evolutionary drive commences at the celestial summer solstice. Such a possibility obviously lies some little way ahead in the future. However, we can perhaps see the underlying logic of what is being done and planned now in order to bring it about. There are of course those who will refuse to grant any credibility whatsoever to this scenario; but coming events will undoubtedly confirm their underlying effects, in due time, thereby altering such attitudes. Until then, the rest of us need to soldier on and keep our wits about us.

THIRTEEN

THE JESUS-AS-CHRIST MYSTERY

It has already been mentioned that the Trans-Himalayan Adept Brotherhood rejects the idea of the Christian figure of Jesus as having been a historical figure at the time suggested by the New Testament—which was written some several decades at least after that. It also seemingly rejects the idea that he was "Christed."[1] We otherwise know for a fact that the well-known Jewish historical figure of Philo (ca. 30 BCE–40 CE)—sometimes known as "Philo the Alexandrian"—who was a contemporary of the supposedly biblical Jesus, mentions him not at all, in any context. The slightly later Jewish historian Flavius Josephus (ca. 37–101 CE) does mention him, however, in his work *Antiquities of the Jews,* referring to him rather obscurely as having been "a wise man" and "a doer of [unspecified] wonderful works" who was "believed by some to be the Christ."[2] Yet it is noteworthy that Josephus gives no indication at all of how long before his own time Jesus had lived—which (added to the title of his book) suggests that it cannot have been that recent—although he does add the (by then self-evidently secondhand) story that he had been condemned to death by Pontius Pilate.

Historical details about the character of Pilate—known as the fifth Roman prefect of the province of Judea between 26–36 CE as the New Testament describes—are themselves very conflicting. They have thus given much rise to doubt about his actual existence and involvement in the events leading to the crucifixion of Jesus, as described in the New Testament. From the associated timeline—if he did exist—it would appear that Jesus must have lived during the first quarter of the first century CE. However, the historical reports by both Philo and Josephus come nowhere near confirming this. That in turn suggests that the story may perhaps have involved a historical combination of two individuals brought within the one "Jesus" figure, either through ignorance or through deliberate manipulation. Which is wholly unclear. But the modern Tibetan Adept DK refers quite openly to "the initiate Jesus" (in the books of A. A. Bailey), ratifying the tradition of his teaching and that his body was both temporarily "overshadowed" (or rather, temporarily informed) by the Lord Maitreya, the seemingly true Christ, and then later crucified.[3] Where then lies the actual truth?

When we look at the known history of the early Church, it becomes clear that the Christians were persecuted until 313 CE when the Emperor Constantine (289–337 CE) issued an edict to halt such activities, although Christianity did not formally become the acknowledged main religion of the Roman Empire until later in that century. But, most interestingly, forms of Christianity—apparently of a decidedly gnostic leaning—had already existed in the first two to three centuries BCE. It was then that an association with the impending astrological era of the fish (Pisces) was attached, to confirm that this new Mystery tradition was intended as being separate from the passing zodiacal era of the Ram (Aries), the latter having a predominantly Egyptian association. This is somewhat comparable to our today looking forward with eager anticipation to the impending Age of Aquarius, thereby readying ourselves for its influence. So, in order to see if we can deduce anything further, let us look at the early history of the Middle East area in brief outline, paying particular attention to the first few centuries BCE.

To begin with, ancient Palestine prior to the eighth century BCE consisted of three minor kingdoms: Samaria in the north, Galilee in the center, and Judea in the south. Of these, Samaria was the most cosmopolitan and wealthy because of its sea trade via the Mediterranean ports of Tyre and Sidon in particular. Inland Judea (containing Jerusalem) was of very minor political significance. However, in about 725 BCE, the Assyrian empire invaded the area, en route to conquering Egypt, and annexed it. Not surprisingly perhaps, most of the native peoples of Galilee and Judea were duly taken as slaves and assimilated into the northern Assyrian empire where they eventually became citizens. Although the Egyptian empire recaptured Palestine briefly for a few decades from about 612 BCE, the Assyrians were soon after defeated by the far more powerful Babylonian empire and Palestine was then annexed by it under the overall rulership of King Nebuchadnezzar. He—so the Old Testament tells us—destroyed the first temple of the Hebrews, supposedly built by Solomon some four hundred years before, although Solomon's actual existence has never been proved and, from the esoteric viewpoint, looks to be little more than another biblical allegory.

The Babylonians were then overthrown in turn by the Achamaenid Persians under Cyrus the Great (559–530 BCE) (see fig. 13.1), who allowed those Judeans who desired it to return to Judea, commencing about 538 BCE. The "second" temple in Jerusalem—the remains of which still exist today—was (according to tradition) then built, apparently during the reign of the Persian emperor Darius, and completed about 515 BCE. The later Persian king Artaxerxes then allowed the Hebrew prophet Ezra to return from Babylon to Judea in about 460 BCE, specifically to set up a colony with his particular monotheistic sect, whose intention was to pursue the idea of the "return to Zion" that has been at the center of the Jewish faith ever since. However, the name Zion is itself clearly derived from the Sanskrit dhyan (dhzyan in the Tibetan), which, as we saw in earlier chapters, is associated with the divine state of the heavenly world, not at all with the material one. The (allegorical) teachings of Ezra thus seem to have been derived from

Fig. 13.1.
Cyrus the Great

the Ancient Wisdom philosophy. They were learned from the Babylonians or Persians and not from a Jewish source, even though subsequently (mis-) interpreted and promulgated by the teachers of later Jewish religion, the Pharisees, the precursors of the rabbinate. However, somewhere along the line, these same teachings diverged from spiritual allegory and sacred metaphor into the distinctively territorial viewpoint prevalent today.

In 323 BCE Alexander the Great died, having already conquered the Persian empire. His own empire was then split between his three main generals, the Ptolemies taking Egypt and all the lands that had comprised ancient Palestine, up to the southern borders of modern Syria and Lebanon (the latter being associated with Phoenicia). The Seleucids then took over the lands comprising what is now modern Turkey and Syria, extending all the way to India. However, in about 200 BCE, the Seleucid empire (which contained ancient Babylonia) conquered Palestine and annexed it. At about the same time, the codification of Jewish law (in the *Mishnah*) followed in both Palestine and Babylonia, in the latter of which large numbers of Jews still lived.

By then two Jewish sects had appeared in Jerusalem—the Sadducees (comprising the upper, wealthier classes and priests who claimed major control over the temple and insisted on literal interpretation of the law) and the Pharisees. The name of the latter is derived from the Hebrew *perushim,* itself derived from the Sanskrit *purusha,* meaning "pure spirit"—the sixth element, above even the aether[4] (thus separate from all matter). Their single aim—in line with their name—seems to have been associated with cleanliness and purity in all respects of life (as with modern "orthodox" Judaism), although their approach to the interpretation of the law was rather more flexible.

Only thirty-five years later, the Judeans liberated themselves from Seleucid rule and formed their own Hasmonean dynasty of kings, which subsequently captured Samaria and thus reunited ancient Palestine. From about this time, Jewish theological orthodoxy centered on the temple in Jerusalem seems to have hardened and become much more separatively nationalistic. During all this time, however, Greek cultural and spiritual influence (not that of the Jews) was paramount throughout the whole area of the Middle East in general. This is notwithstanding the fact that many Jews had held influential public positions throughout Babylonia and Assyria for several centuries (as they did later in Rome). It is conjecturally in memory of this association with their time in Babylon (which was not a "captivity" at all in real terms) that the male Hasidic Jews of today still wear their side hair in long ringlets, evidently copying the Babylonian fashion of that time with the whole head of hair.

The Roman empire then invaded Palestine during the first century BCE, its general Pompey capturing Jerusalem in 63 BCE and transforming the area into a Roman protectorate. Then in 31 BCE, the emperor Octavian (later Augustus Caesar), en route to reconquering Egypt (which became a province of the Roman Empire in 30 BCE), put Samaria under the rule of Herod the Great, the then king of Judea. The Romans later annexed the whole area of Palestine as a province in 4 BCE upon the death of Herod—which is how, shortly after, we later find the figure of Pontius Pilate supposedly coming on to the scene. There subsequently followed the Jewish Wars of Hebrew nationalists against the Romans, led latterly by the Zealots who took over Jerusalem in 65 CE. They were, however, defeated by the Roman generals (later emperors) Vespasian and Titus, who had the Jerusalem temple destroyed in 70 CE—which effectively put an end to the existence of the Sadducees. It seems to have been from then that the main Jewish diaspora commenced and the pharisaic rabbis progressively set up their widely scattered system of synagogues.

THE BREAKUP OF THE GREEK MYSTERY SCHOOLS

Returning to our main theme, however, and going back a couple of centuries (to the time of the Macedonian Alexander the Great), we should note that with the progressive break up of the state-governed Mystery Schools of the Greek polis, two separate schools had appeared in their place, as we saw earlier. These were those of the "craftsmen" on the one hand, the artisan school, originators of the Assyrian Dionysii and the much later medieval European guilds, including the Masons. On the other was that of the "gnostics" (the knowledge school).[5] Prior to their dissolution, all esoteric knowledge and craftsmanship had been learned in the Mystery Schools, following a triple developmental progression (usually involving a seven-year period of neophyteship), which clearly parallels the seven-year apprenticeship of original Craft Masonry, before the birth of Freemasonry.

So Greek gnosticism was itself a twin, born of a deceased parent; for some reason or other (possibly through Adept influence), it found a foster home in the internationally accessible city port of Egyptian Alexandria. It is worth mentioning in passing here that Jewish kabbalistic gnosticism, derived from the Hebrews' time in Babylon, seems to have settled and initially developed in Ephesus[6] (on the western coast of modern Turkey). It did not, at that time, have any apparent interest in influencing or uniting with the mainstream Jewish theology being developed by the Pharisees in Palestine. That itself is suggestive of the fact that early kabbalism did not see Jewish "orthodoxy" as being worth any real degree of association.

THE ESSENES AND THE
EGYPTIAN RELIGION OF SERAPIS

As already indicated, ancient Alexandria became a real philosophical and religious "melting pot" within half a century after the death of Alexander the Great in 323 BCE. The Ptolemy family successor—as head of the Egyptian part of Alexander's empire (extending from Egypt into the Levant)—was Ptolemy Philadelphus (309–246 BCE) (see fig. 13.2), who set about the

Fig. 13.2.
Ptolemy Philadelphus

reformulation of a modernized and broader based Greco-Egyptian religion. This was that of Serapis, the Greek form of the dual Egyptian As'r-Hpi (i.e., Osiris, the god of the Nile), a cult that was flexible enough to absorb other eso-teric belief systems (including those of neo-Platonists and neo-Pythagoreans) in such a manner as to cause as little potential social friction as possible in cosmopolitan Alexandria. Ptolemy even treated diplomatically with the Indian emperor Asoka to allow the promulgation of Buddhist teachings in his kingdom. It was as a result of this that there appeared the charac-teristically gentle but ascetic belief system promulgated by the Essenes, one of the early gnostic sects, which seems to have commenced its existence in Alexandria itself as the *Therapeutai* and later spread to Palestine and Syria.[7]

The Essenes were a determinedly occult group whose overriding charac-teristics involved deep humility and an ascetic contempt for worldly goods, in conjunction with total philanthropy toward others (even non-Essenes). Their primary concerns seem to have lain with harmlessness to all others and to psychological and even physical purity as a sign of holiness. Their central aim in life was consequently that of becoming the literal temple of the Holy Spirit and thus, effectively, a prophet.[8] Healing and magic were arts pursued by them. It is suggested by some historians, however, that the study of logic and metaphysics (presumably in the Greek style) was regarded by the Essenes as injurious to a life of devotion, although it is acknowledged that they were deeply concerned with understanding the nature and organi-zation of the angelic worlds plus the origin of the soul and its relationship with the body.[9] Their religious observance—involving a perfect maximum of ten people—was that of uttermost devotion to the demiurgic Deity whose objective symbol (the Sun) they venerated.[10] This concern with the decad and many of their other practices have been seen by many (but not by some overtly nationalistic Jewish historians) as Pythagorean in nature.

THE NAZARENES AND THE PHARISEES

It would appear that the overall Essene community was formed of two groups. One, completely monastic in nature and comprising only menfolk (women not being admitted), involved a mystic and occult brotherhood. To enter this brotherhood, the aspirant had to wait outside it for three years, in a testing manner distinctively reminiscent of the Pythagorean and Stoic brotherhoods. The other Essene group—which one would imagine to have been by far the larger—comprised a community of married men and women plus their children.[11] One of the original Essene offshoots is now known to have settled in a community adjacent to the Dead Sea, where they later came to be recognized as the long-haired "Nazaars" or "Nazarenes." Here the latter remained in existence for several hundred years, hence their association by some with supposedly Jewish origins, particularly as the Judaic Pharisees seem to have adopted many of their doctrinal and practical rituals, especially those associated with extreme subjective and objective purity and cleanliness.

In that regard it was suggested a few pages earlier that the name Pharisee seems quite likely to have derived from the Sanskrit *purusha,* thus implying a state of development "above even the spiritual quintessence." Purusha is also to be found in the Greek as *parousia*—hence the Parousi, thus suggesting an Indo-Persian (i.e., Parsi or Zoroastrian) origin; hence perhaps the common veneration of the Sun. Despite this, the Nazaars seem to have been preceded locally by the Ebionites, who were the earliest sect of Jewish "Christians," even well before the term "Christian" had come into use,[12] as also described a little earlier.

The variety of other influences available and in widespread use at this time is notable. Clement of Alexandria confirmed that the initiates of Serapis wore on their persons the sacred name IAO (probably derived, again through phonetic corruption, as Yahu from the Babylonian god EA, i.e., as Ea-hu), apparently in conjunction with the Vesica Piscis. This was itself regarded by esotericists of the time (neo-Pythagorean geometricians in particular) as the determinant of all dimensions.[13] It is also recorded that the early Christians used the Tau cross on their tombs,[14] which—by virtue of its origin in China— gives us a clear indication as to just how culturally cosmopolitan ancient Alexandria was. There is otherwise known to historians a very interesting and informative letter of 118 AD from the Roman emperor Hadrian to the consul Servianus confirming: "They who worship Serapis are Christians and such as are devoted to Serapis call themselves Bishops of Christ."[15]

Blavatsky otherwise confirms for us that the gnostic Nazarenes were the original Christians and opponents of the later ones.[16] This is further amplified by bishop Eusebius, one of those later and decidedly political Christians who battled so hard and so ruthlessly against the Alexandrian gnostics, neo-Pythagoreans, and neo-Platonists. He commented about the Nazarenes: "Their doctrines are to be found among none but in the religion of the Christians according to the Gospel. . . . It is highly probable that the ancient Commentaries which they have [the Dead Sea scrolls and *Pistis Sophia* among them perhaps?] are the very writings of the Apostles."[17] No subsequent attempt to verify this more clearly seems to have been made, however.

By virtue of Pythagoras, Plato, and a host of other well-known Greek philosophers having spent their educationally formative years in Egypt, at a time when the Greek Mystery traditions were disintegrating and falling out of public favor, it is not surprising that so many Greeks and others of a philosophical or mystical nature gravitated toward Egypt, doubtless hoping that a completely new Mystery Religion would become apparent. As the historian David Fideler remarks:

> There can be little doubt that, among the initiates of the early Church, Christianity was seen—and consciously developed—as a reformation of the early Mysteries. . . . It is also clear that behind the scenes of the early Christian movement there existed an unknown number of enlightened scholars who were attempting to take the best elements of Jewish, Greek and Egyptian spirituality and synthesise them into a new universal expression. Exactly who these individuals were, however, we do not know.[18]

As regards the adapted Mysteries themselves, the mystic grades in the formative Church (these being derived from the Egyptian rites of Serapis in Alexandria) were as earlier described in chapter six.[19]

THE FORMATION OF THE EARLIEST CHURCH

At this point we might pause a moment to indulge in a little logical speculation concerning the social mix of Alexandria and its development, based upon an understanding of ordinary human interrelationships. To begin with there would have been the upper classes, mainly of Greek descent from Alexander's military officers, mixed with the higher Egyptian priesthood and the national aristocracy. Many from the latter would have comprised a semi-intellectual elite, due to the considerable range of academic study pursued by the Egyptian priesthood. As mentioned earlier, their academic study was based on the forty-two sacred Books of Tehuti, which would almost inevitably have been intellectually orientated (although full also of sacred metaphor plus metaphysical allegory), and thus quite definitely aimed toward esoteric interpretation. Secondly, there would have been the local merchant, artisan, and farming classes, much more naturally orientated toward the merely devotional and literalistic approach to religion and life in general, as is indeed the case even today, all around the world.

However, not all esotericists of the time would necessarily have opted for wholesale attachment to the merely devotional approach of the state Serapean religion. The neo-Pythagoreans, Stoics, and neo-Platonists are highly unlikely to have done so. They were spiritual purists and would probably have remained more self-evidently objective and intellectually detached in their approach. That in itself could well have led to an increasingly self-evident socio-religious split, resulting in the most mystically inclined (i.e., the "New Age" Therapeutai-Essenes, with their decidedly neo-Pythagorean and Buddhist inclinations) leaving the urban environment of Alexandria altogether, to migrate elsewhere to the "wide open spaces" of other parts of the Middle East, like Qumran and Nag Hammadi. But this separation was to continue. As Blavatsky comments, "When the metaphysical conceptions of the gnostics [i.e., the true esotericists] began to gain ground, the earliest Christians separated from the Nazarenes."[20]

Of those who preferred to stay in Alexandria, the more gregarious devotional types (the local merchant and artisan classes particularly) would almost certainly have come to see themselves as socially distinct from the rest and would thus have gradually evolved a more politically formal approach to their religious beliefs, thereby leading to the separate establishment of the early Christian Church. They would then have found themselves in direct confrontation with the gnostically orientated intelligentsia of the upper classes over particular religious issues. It is this perhaps that led to the first burning of the great Library of Wisdom in Alexandria by a politically inflamed Christian mob, akin to the one that murdered and dismembered the female philosopher Hypatia.

Intellectual and upper class elites of any age or era have always tended to suffer from a degree of arrogance, often involving a "looking down" on those of lesser intellectual depth and breadth, not able to comprehend the more subtle aspects of life because more concerned with the business of earning a living. Correspondingly, the merchant and artisan class just described (again of any age), in order to preserve their own social position and self-respect, tend to adopt a more regulated and even rigid code of social behavior, directly suspicious of any "religious subtlety." This frequently leads to their opting for much more literalistic approaches to religion as well as all of life's many other concerns. It is for this reason, it is suggested, that the lack of a historically specific Christ figure (to match the figure of Osiris) would have become to these Alexandrians a source of great concern, whereas it had not for either the intellectuals or the Essene mystics. Hence some have considered it quite probable that the "Christian" monks practicing the Serapean Mysteries progressively allowed the figure of the Serapean sun god to be translated into a deified human Jesus figure. This was in acquiescence with the prevailing policy of those Church Fathers trying to make their belief system more potently and more widely attractive than that of the neo-Platonic and neo-Pythagorean gnostics.

CROSS-CORRESPONDENCES

The Essenes of Qumran were otherwise later recognized as gnostics by the Church of Rome and were also known to have some form of connection with the Mysteries of Adonis—hence perhaps Christ being referred to in the New Testament as Adonai. Although not sun worshippers per se, they are otherwise known to have paid particular observance to the Sun, as mentioned earlier, and it is noteworthy that in those ancient times, the idea of a suffering celestial Messiah—symbolized by the Sun—was widespread. Being highly aware of the "Divine Builder" or "Divine Artificer" tradition, like that of Ptah in Egypt (see fig. 13.3), they would almost certainly have known of the parallel Hindu tradition in which the god Visvakarman (also the "Great Architect") crucified his son Surya (the Sun) upon his swastika-like lathe, otherwise recognized as the Jain cross.

The origin of the Virgin Mother concept is also to be found among the Nazarenes in the statement concerning the Higher Mysteries, which,

Fig. 13.3.
Ptah at the potter's wheel

PTAH MOULDING THE WORLD EGG
ON HIS POTTER'S WHEEL
(WHILST SEATED ON THE 'AUM-PHAL-OS')

in the Greek tradition, were governed by the goddess Demeter: "For this is the Virgin who carries in her womb and conceives and brings forth a son, not animal, not corporeal but blessed for evermore."[21] It is therefore not difficult to see how the mental association of Mary (a name perhaps derived from the adorational Egyptian name Meri-Isis—*meri* meaning "beloved")—the mother of Jesus—could perhaps have been derived by ignorant mis-association with the Spiritual Soul principle represented by Demeter. In the Egyptian tradition, Isis metamorphosed into the hierarchically higher figure of Hathor (Hat-Hor), the All-Mother goddess who was herself united theologically with Atum-Ra, the "grandfather" of Osiris and generator of the objective world. So it would not have been unduly problematic for the early Christian bishops, in their selective theological borrowings, to justify to themselves the concept of Meri-Isis-Hathor—subsequently shortened to "Meri" (or Mary)—being (mis)represented as "Mother of God."

CONCERNING THE CHRIST AVATAR

Reverting to the subject of the literal-minded merchant and artisan class of Alexandria, we turn next to the issue of the Avatar or Messianic Savior figure. This is the officially executed and risen Christ at the center of

Fig. 13.4. Isis and Horus compared to Mary and Jesus

Christian theology, seemingly derived from the Serapean philosophy. This laid particular attention on the figure of Isis and the Horus child she bore as the reincarnate Osiris (see fig. 13.4)—hence "the only begotten son of the Father." What now followed from all this, it is suggested, is manifold and complex.

First of all, it is widely acknowledged that in all ancient traditions the end of the astrological era was marked by surges of Messianic utopianism or apocalypticism. That is because the end of the zodiacal Age always supposedly heralded the wondrous birth appearance of an Avatar, or spiritual Savior. This then became—in the Western sense—a "son of God," to be known by the Greek name Kristos, "the Anointed One." The implication therefore (to the literal minded at least), was that, by the beginning of the first century CE—the millennium by then having passed—such an Avatar must already quite logically have been born, although to begin with it was not objectively apparent who he was or might have been. Secondly, it is clear that the majority of the early Church Fathers (who had borrowed their main core of theological concepts from the earlier gnostic traditions of Alexandria) failed to understand that the Trinity responsible for Creation of the world and humanity was in fact merely the expression of the Demiurge.

As described in earlier chapters, it was commonly understood in the ancient philosophical world that the One Divinity behind all existence was not a Creator but a kosmic Consciousness; that its primary point of emanation (the kabbalistic Keter) produced a secondary emanation (Mind, or Nous—the much later kabbalistic Hokmah); that this then gave rise to the tertiary principle (the Demiurge), a hierarchical group of advanced Intelligences, which was itself the true Creator. The latter then expressed the Will-to-be, the Will-to-know, and the Will-to-create/adapt, parallel to the repetitive Siva-Visnu-Brahma Trimurti of Hinduism and the corresponding Anu-Ea-Bel of Babylonian religion—hence the derivation of the Christian Trinity of Father, Son, and Holy Spirit. However, in the Hindu tradition— even then well known throughout the Middle East—the primary field of kosmic or Universal Consciousness was represented by Visnu (directly associated with the fish symbol), whose emanation gave rise to the decidedly avataric boy-god Krisna. One might also mention here the avataric Babylonian fish-god Oannes as another source of inspiration. One can see from fig. 13.5 of Oannes where the idea of the miter (the ceremonial hat worn by the Christian bishop or archbishop) actually arose—that is, symbolizing the gaping mouth of the fish, itself representing the crown chakra—thereby again confirming Babylonian influences on the formulation of early Christianity.

Fig. 13.5. The Babylonian ocean god Oannes (left) and the bishop's miter

Bearing these facts in mind, it is therefore suggested that some of our esoterically incompetent early Christian theologians must evidently (and quite wrongly) have taken this emanation of the Visnu principle to represent the literally emanated "Son" of the Father-God then cyclically due. In the corresponding Babylonian tradition, from which the Hebrews had returned in the fifth century BCE, their Dagon and Oannes were also "man-fishes" and presented as Messiahs. That the same historic period involved the beginning of the zodiacal Age of Pisces will almost certainly have reinforced their (erroneous) perception that the coming Avatar (of Visnu) had to be the actually historical "Son of God." The phonetic similarity of the names Kris-na and Kris-tos undoubtedly helped.

One predisposing factor specifically points to when the figure of the Jewish Jesus was actually incorporated into the early Christian theology. It is that of Roman overlordship of Judea and Palestine, which only began during the early first century BCE. The fact that the Jewish king (Herod) is reported as reacting to the idea of a great spiritual Avatar appearing with the astrological change of zodiacal era by ordering the first-born male children of the time to be killed—thereby forcing Jesus' parents to flee with him to Egypt—is (if true) also indicative of a timeline. Taking into account calendrical changes, no modern astrologer is certain as to when the actual change-over from Aries to Pisces took place. However, as Chaldean astrology was held in such high regard, it is very likely that the three Magi (although themselves probably Zoroastrian) were following the true astrological timeline.

So we can see that Christianity was actually of a Greco-Egyptian gnostic origin. However, its roughly six-hundred-year period of initial existence as such—commencing in the Serapean temple tradition—came to an end in the fourth century CE. Then it was officially recognized as the religion of the Roman Empire, with Rome having already taken over control of Egypt as a colony around the turn of the millennium. But, with the general spread of early Christianity around the Mediterranean during the first two or three centuries BCE under Greek rule and then the next three centuries under Roman rule, it is not surprising that variations arose in their various belief and ritual systems. One of these would almost certainly have been focused on the issue of human divinity. At this earlier stage, although there were localized Christian "bishops" scattered around the Mediterranean countries, looking after even more scattered Christian groups, no one such group or single individual spoke for or otherwise represented the whole. All of them supported their own slightly differing belief systems.

Thus it was that in 325 CE the Council of Nicaea was called, specifically in order to decide theologically upon the relationship between God and Jesus, the latter being regarded as the "Christed" Son of God, the second "person" of the Holy Trinity. Its decision—that they were united in a single divinity— was ratified at the later Council of Constantinople in 381 CE after much bitter theological and political argument in between. At the latter Council, the enclave of bishops otherwise agreed that the Holy Spirit was to be regarded as the third "person" of the Holy Trinity. Thereafter, it was also decided— again after much argument—that Mary, the supposed mother of Jesus, was to be officially regarded as "Mother of God." As we suggested earlier, however, this was purely derived from a combination of the Egyptian name Meri and the gnostic sacred metaphor of Sophia, the dark Isis-like figure yet to become another of the theological adaptations of early Christianity.

BUT WHO WAS JESUS?

Turing to the figure of Jesus (Jeshu[a] in the Hebrew), there appear to be several alternative possibilities in addition to the mentions by Josephus. Ea-Shu (these being the Babylonian and Egyptian gods of Light) is another, perhaps with a slight phonetic modification to the more Hebrew looking Jah-Shu and then to Jeshu(a)? It seems otherwise quite possible, from the little evidence available, that he could in fact have been a particularly successful and properly initiated gnostic teacher of the second or first century BCE, with his own following of disciples. The fact that they otherwise naturally held him to be their guru-savior and that their successors constantly referred to his sayings would probably also have become quite widely known. That one such guru figure might also have been identified by the Jewish Sanhedrin as a social troublemaker and subsequently crucified by the Romans at their behest is also not impossible. However, as the historical Pontius Pilate was well known as an overly violent ruler (warned against it by Rome), it is possible that his name was used later to engrave the memory indelibly in pliable local minds. His ready violence also fails to coincide with the way the New Testament describes him.

There are two such Jesus or Jeshua figures known to historians. The first was Jeshua-ben-Pantera. He was, so we are told, the son of a Roman soldier called Joseph-ben-Pantera who had seduced a local virgin named Miriam despite her betrothal to another man. Adopted by his uncle and having studied theurgical philosophy and practice in Egypt, this boy child (Jeshua) was recognized by the priesthood there as possessing unusual powers; he was then initiated by them and raised to high degree. Jeshua became known as a great healer and, returning to Judea, began a widespread evangelical movement, with his own retinue of disciples. He was later publicly censured by the rabbis for his teachings,[22] then later condemned to death and hung on a tree around 100 BCE. The other figure of Jeshua-ben-Nun (whether earlier or later in time) is known for no such specific history but (because of Nun meaning "fish") is in some ways a perhaps more likely candidate, due to the specific association with the incoming Age of Pisces. In support of that, the Tibetan Adept DK firmly states that Jesus and Jeshua-ben-Nun were one and the same.[23]

In practical terms, however, neither can positively be deduced by us today as the historical "Jesus of Nazareth" of the New Testament. Nor can we confirm that the two were not somehow combined into one persona by detail-careless local tradition over several generations. Notwithstanding this, as Blavatsky tells us: "Every tradition shows that Jesus was educated in Egypt and passed his infancy and youth with the Brotherhoods of the Essenes and other mystic communities."[24] In addition, by virtue of the fact that he disagreed with his teachers on several issues of formal observance, he cannot strictly be regarded as an Essene himself.[25] In fact, it is known that members of his family were Ebionites,[26] a name which (by association with the Serapean religion) may well have been derived phonetically from the Egyptian *Hpi*—representing the supremely powerful but invisible divine force in Nature that gave the river Nile its powerful and annually regenerative current—plus the Greek suffix *on*. Thus a Hpi-on became an Ebion(ite).

The first Christians after the death of Jesus believed him to be a holy and inspired prophet and also a vehicle used by the Christos and Sophia (two complementary aspects of the Alexandrian gnostic philosophy) for their expression.[27] With that as a background picture, and also taking into consideration what we have already otherwise mentioned, it is perhaps easy to see how later and more literal-minded supporters might have come to see him as an actual Christ figure. To some of those looking for the Avatar of the Age of Pisces this, it is suggested, thus meant that he logically had to be the Son, who was thereby also intended to be co-equal with God. This was apparently (according to early Christian theologians) based on the statement in the New Testament that Jesus (or rather the Christ, while overshadowing him) had made to the effect that "I and my God are One." However, this ignores the (to us) self-evident alternative of the lesser consciousness of the microcosm evolving through progressive initiatory crises to become at-one with the greater consciousness of the Demiurgic Macrocosm, which had itself passed through the human stage eons before. To the esotericist, initiates of the third degree (and higher) are in a definite sense entitled to make this statement of conscious inner union because of realizing it to be a fact in a logical evolutionary progression. In addition, it is otherwise known, as Blavatsky tells us: "in the secret kabbalistic documents of the Nabathaeans . . . after the initiation, ABA the Father becomes the Son and the Son succeeds the father and becomes Father and Son at the same time, inspired by Sophia Ackamoth.[28]

It is otherwise apparent that all the scattered groups of proto-Christians in the Levant and extending through modern Syria and Turkey were originally of a gnostic persuasion, each going its own way in terms of philosophical detail. The original groups—in Palestine and Syria at least—appear to have been of either Essene or Druze (or similar) persuasion and, as already described, it has long been thought that the biblical figure of Jesus came from the former of these two secretive groups. However, irrespective of whether that is so, it is also fairly clear that "someone" went public and started teaching and proselytizing an esoteric Buddhist form of gnosticism—that a true self-knowledge and understanding of suffering leads to liberation from both[29]—on a rather more extensive basis, at some time between the written works of Philo and Josephus. That "someone" seems to have taken the form of an individual known as Jesus (or rather, "Jeshua"), who, for his enlarged vision, was proscribed by the Jewish Sanhedrin at Jerusalem, which then politically engineered his execution at the perhaps unwilling hands of the local Roman governor. That much of the story would appear quite logical and consistent with other references.

It is well known, however, among scholars of the subject, that several of the early Christian bishops—Eusebius, Ireneus, Clement of Alexandria, and St. Jerome among them—mercilessly altered by editorial forgery the older texts of Josephus and others for political reasons, to provide a better-sounding theological foundation for early Christians in the second and third centuries CE. On this same subject of retrospective amendment, the author Edmond Bordeaux Szekely has a great deal to say in his work, *The Essene Origins of Christianity*. However, he lacks any basic esoteric perception, failing to understand the conceptual nature of the Word or the Holy Spirit, or to appreciate the factor of "overshadowing" of a disciple by a Master initiate. He thus considers the whole issue of the real Jesus from a purely materialistic viewpoint, although he does in passing mention a variety of highly important historical facts concerning the supposed background of the biblical Jesus.

One of these is that the town of Nazareth did not even exist until at least the eighth century CE, nor was there such a place-name until then. It appears that the Christian Church fathers of the time realized this fact and immediately had one selected and constructed so that "Jesus of Nazareth" was associated with a known location reasonably close to Bethlehem (where by prior Judaic tradition the Messiah was supposed to be born), rather than confirmed as being born among the Essene "Nazarenes" or "Nazirites."[30] A second is that the very word *nazar* (itself as n-z-r) meant "consecrated to Yahweh" and was applied to all the first-born sons of Jewish families under Mosaic law.[31] It is curious to learn that the term actually derives from the Sanskrit root *nag,* meaning "a serpent," but esoterically denoting an initiate, a *nagar.* Even more curiously, we learn that the same word, borrowed by the Arabic (as *nas'r*), means "one who is of the offspring of Muhammad"—hence also an initiate by inference rather than being of Muhammad's family bloodline. This latter fact is overlooked by modern historians and Islamic theologians alike.

It would then seem that, in the aftermath of his crucifixion—whether he survived it or not—this Buddhistic gnosticism survived and flourished (under the aggressive guidance of St. Paul), becoming "Christianized" because its followers saw Jeshua as a spiritual teacher—a "Krisna"—who had laid down his life for them. That they took this view would quite naturally have become well known and, as this was a rare example of a spiritual individual following a particular Path, it would not have been surprising to find elements of his personal life story becoming magnified in importance over succeeding decades and centuries to become the stuff of at least local legend. For example, the story of Krisna has him descending into the Underworld, just as Jesus is supposed to have done following his death. The wholesale adaptation of this story to Christ-hood by less knowledgeable and more politically orientated quasi-gnostics would thus prove very simple.

THE GNOSTIC ALTERNATIVE

Let us now look at the perhaps less obvious alternative. As David Fideler interestingly explains for us in his work *Jesus Christ, Sun of God,* the Greek version of the name Jesus amounts in terms of gematria to the number 888, which was mystically as well as mathematically related to the Spiritual Sun.[32] As the Greek alphabet was itself based on the octave, the further implication was that the name Jesus represented the alpha and omega and that it accordingly possessed an occult potency above all other possible names.[33] From a slightly different viewpoint, however, the number 8 (as ∞) mathematically represents an infinity, while in esoteric terms it is also the octave containing the septenary system. This, as we saw in earlier chapters, is also symbolic of the soul principle. The latter is similarly represented, whether in the human individual or as the Oversoul of a celestial body.

Following on from that in kabbalistic terms (Yah being the same as the Chaldeo-Babylonian god Ea), the soul principle is the same as the third sephiroth Binah, a name derived from the compound ben-Yah, meaning the "son of God." Hence the further implication arising in the minds of early gnostic Christians is that the 888 actually represented the united Trinity, which was emanated by the Deity—that is, as Divine Soul, Spiritual Soul, and terrestrial or human soul. In other words, the name Jesus was itself suggestive of God incarnate, as the avataric Christos.

From the rather more systematically hard-headed viewpoint of a real esotericist, however, this is nonsensical when applied to an individual and purely the result of wishful thinking. Nevertheless, in an intellectual and mystical "hothouse" atmosphere like that of Alexandria at the time of naturally great expectancy accompanying the change of zodiacal Age from Aries to Pisces, it would not have been altogether surprising to find such extreme "New Age" views being dramatically introduced to support a particular viewpoint to a mystically impressionable audience. As David Fideler further adds:

> As Christianity evolved into a collective belief system, it developed a political structure and creeds, teaching that Jesus came and left at a particular point in time . . . it outlawed other forms of religious expression. . . . The Church thereby proclaimed itself as the official mediator between man and God, thus usurping the original function of Christ the Logos.[34]

We otherwise know for a fact—because of the "gnostic gospels" in the Nag Hammadi texts—that the figures of Jesus, Mary Magdalene, and at least some of the disciples were well known in literary terms to the local gnostic community of the time. But whereas these documents have been taken by at least some of the modern Christian community as confirming the existence of the historical Jesus, others naturally reject the idea because the gnostic philosophy, which he is shown as teaching, was extensively allegorical in nature. This appears superficially unhelpful. But what if this particular gnostic literature and its teachings were historically rather older than our academics imagine? As already suggested, we know that various forms of gnostic philosophy were already being discussed and considered in Alexandria much earlier, by at least two centuries, as a result of the city having become a psycho-spiritual "melting pot" for all sorts of mystical, occult, and philosophical ideas drawn from around the Near East and Middle East, seemingly extending as far as India and China.

So what if the early Christians were indeed a breakaway (originally gnostic) group of misguided "fundamentalists" who had come to believe that the entirely mythical figure of Jesus in their Gospels "must" in fact have been a historical being? Would that perhaps not help to explain why so many of the "attached" characteristics of Jesus—which clearly (as acknowledged by historians) derive from Mithraic, Hindu, and other mythic philosophy—became part of the description surrounding him? Some of those "attachments" have already been mentioned earlier in this book. They include: the fact that the Hindu god Visvakarman was represented as a carpenter—hence Jesus being the "son of a carpenter"; the fact that the crucifixion and use of a crown of thorns were taken from the story of the god Indra; the fact that the "virgin birth" and the associated idea of his being the "Son of God" were associations common with all mythic gods in the ancient world, for example in the case of the Greek Dionysus.

The further associated idea of the Divine Trinity is itself a basically universal gnostic concept, while Mary, the supposed mother of Jesus, is already acknowledged by many scholars as a purely literal and anthropocentric parallel to the gnostic Sophia. However, the latter idea involves a very basic compound misconception because the gnostic Sophia represented the "wisdom-breath" of the Logos, which is a far cry from "the mother of God" in a strictly personalized sense.

It is perhaps worthwhile drawing a further parallel here, that between the kabbalistic Keter—the primordial emanation of Ain Soph—and the Greek term Logos. The latter, as David Fideler reminds us, conveys the meanings of order and pattern, or ratio, plus causation and mediation.[35] It is thus associated with Man, the "fallen" spirit who, as we saw in earlier chapters, represents the Higher Purpose that is to be imposed upon the kosmic Underworld. In the Greek system of Platonic philosophy, the term Logos signifies not only Divine Order but also, quite logically, the "son of God" emanated from the Unknowable GOOD (i.e., from Ain Soph in equivalent terms). This emanation thereby gave rise to the creative "Architect" or "Second God," which, in turn, gave rise to the originally Platonic concept of the Demiurge, which the later Christian gnostics so horrendously distorted. The Logos is otherwise directly related to the Nous or Universal Mind from which all possible forms are derived. It is also the Source of all existence, thereby being the origin of both life and light in the lower world system. Now, in the true gnostic tradition, the fully Self-realized man is a perfected expression of the Divine Mind. He, the initiate of the seventh degree (the Manushi Buddha), is the Christ who, as the "Son of the Father" acts as the avataric "Redeemer." However, instead of properly relating this to humanity as a whole, early political Christianity chose merely to idealize it by singular association with the supposedly historical Jesus and their own formative religion.

If the New Testament Jesus did not in fact exist and if the foregoing is indicative of the more accurate derivation of the story surrounding him, it clearly throws some large question marks over the actual theology of the Christian religion, just as literal (and unsupported) belief in the supposed historicity of the Hebrew patriarchs undermines the basis of the Judaic religion. However, as at least one modern British archbishop has openly declared that, even if Jesus did not exist, he would still remain a fully committed Christian, perhaps it is the gentle core of Christian philosophy (so akin to Jain and Buddhist philosophy) that is in any case the more important to our modern humanity in general. But then what of the alternative "Jesus" figure who seemingly became an Adept? It seems, from other information that has come my way, that something of the truth is known to at least some of the Sufi sheiks in the Middle East. However, at present, the Adept Brotherhood itself evidently sees fit to let the "waters" of public opinion and orthodoxy remain undisturbed by any further revelation.

Further puzzlement at the Adept Brotherhood's real attitude is otherwise provided by the many positive references to the sayings and nature of both Jesus and the Christ respectively in *The Secret Doctrine*. By way of example, we find such forthrightly emergent statements as: "For the teachings of Christ were occult teachings. . . . They were never intended for the masses"[36] and "Christos is the seventh principle, if anything." Blavatsky was also to add that "Neither Buddha nor 'Christ' ever wrote anything themselves, but both spoke in allegories."[37] From these it is clear that the Adept Brotherhood is not actually rejecting the reality of their existence at all, as so many "back-to-Blavatsky" enthusiasts make out through careless reading and assumption. The fact that Blavatsky refers to "Christ" in parenthesis even implies that the real Adept behind that title was in some degree comparable to or associated with the Buddha. We shall look at this idea in further detail a little later on, in the next chapter.

OTHER ADEPT TEACHERS OF THE TIME

Some further interesting parallels are to be found in the life of Apollonius of Tyana (see fig. 13.6), a neo-Pythagorean (hence also gnostic) ascetic and theurgist who was apparently a near contemporary of the real Jesus of Nazareth.[38] He was born in Cappadocia, seemingly during the early-to-mid

Fig. 13.6.
Apollonius of Tyana

first century CE, according to historians. The Adept DK openly states that Apollonius was the next (although not necessarily immediate) reincarnation of the historical Jesus, becoming a full Master in that incarnation,[39] after travelling to India to meet the Adept Hierarchy of the time.

We know something of his extraordinary story from the historian, his friend and travelling companion, Philostratus. From the latter we understand that Apollonius's birth was attended by "miracles and portents" and that at the age of sixteen he set out to adopt the type of monastic life ascribed to Pythagoras, renouncing wine, women, and the eating of flesh. As well as these he allowed his hair to grow long just like the Nazarenes, also wearing only a linen garment and never wearing shoes. He developed a widespread reputation as a deeply holy man, a social reformer, exorcist, and well-known healer. He was also known to have travelled to India, Persia, and Egypt, learning of the deep occult skills and philosophies of their Adepts, which he was himself thereafter able to demonstrate. Two of these involved the ability (at will) to suddenly disappear or reappear and otherwise to appear in two quite different and distant places at the same time (by psychic projection).[40]

It is otherwise interesting to note that Apollonius actually, in one sense, prepared the way for the wider development of Christianity although, rather curiously, Christian historians of the third century CE went out of their way to denigrate him, suggesting among other things that Apollonius had far fewer and less dramatic powers than had Jesus.[41] However, if nothing else, the story of Apollonius confirms that in the first century CE there were in objective or public existence very occasional individuals of Adept status so highly familiar with the theory and practice of occult philosophy that they left the deepest memory of their existence in the social traditions of the time. Temples and shrines to Apollonius were set up in different parts of Asia Minor as a rival to the Christian Jesus, and he is even reported by reliable authority to have attended before the Roman Emperors Vespasian and Titus.[42] It is also interesting to note that Apollonius himself, who could remember his previous lifetimes, neither claimed to be a reincarnation of Jesus nor even mentioned him. However, one could say with some degree of logic that, had he known of his supposedly previous incarnation as Jesus, it was probably the last thing that he would have wanted to make public anyway.

MESSIANIC DISCIPLESHIP

We are otherwise told not only that the Christ and the Islamic Imam Mahdi are one and the same, but also that the Islamic religion involves part of the continuing work of the Master Jesus (now himself apparently a Chohan). We are also told that the prophet Muhammad was supposedly one of his chelas or disciples,[43] albeit evidently unaware of the fact. Hence, it would appear that, by virtue of Jesus having apparently been a chela of the Christ, the Islamic religion—although founded on the (supposedly Hebrew) Old Testament—is or will become much more directly connected with Christianity than it currently is or appears to be. Bearing in mind the current problems in Palestine and Jerusalem between Islam and various mutually antagonistic forms of Christianity (quite apart from the input of Jewish Zionism), the development of this complex relationship should make for interesting observation during the next century or so. This is more especially the case as there is now a nascent school of academic thought querying whether much written about the character and personal history of Muhammad was itself merely a manufactured myth.[44] The parallel with the academic argument over the last century as to whether Jesus really existed is obvious.

Bearing in mind that the Jewish religion is itself a cultural leftover from the Age of Aries, it is clear that its incompatibility with the Age of Aquarius will need to be cleared up. So when the further comment by the Tibetan Adept DK—that the Chohan Jesus will probably adopt the role of the Hebrew "Messiah"[45]—is taken into account with that in mind, it perhaps gives some indication as to the Adept Hierarchy intending that these three religious belief systems should hopefully reach some sort of mutual rapprochement in the relative nearness of time. For that possibility to emerge, however, the influence of theological extremists in each of the three religious camps will perhaps have to be progressively sidelined by wider public opinion.

In concluding this section on the question of whether a human individual known as Jesus or Jeshua ever actually existed in fulfillment of the biblical story, however, it becomes fairly clear that there is still (at least at present) insufficient evidence to confirm matters conclusively one way or another. This is irrespective of the fact that the Adept Hierarchy—through Blavatsky's agency—have clearly confirmed that he was a gnostic Adept reformer and healer with a following of disciples, even if they have not confirmed exactly when he lived and died. For those concerned with history or theology this will undoubtedly continue to be frustratingly unsatisfactory. However, for the true esotericist who understands from experience something of the nature of how the Spiritual Ego overshadows the objective individual, it is of considerably less real importance. Nevertheless, let us now in the next chapter take a look at the further background to the corresponding mystery between the Christ, the Bodhisattva, and the Intelligence known to us as Maitreya Buddha.

FOURTEEN

THE CHRIST–MAITREYA
BUDDHA MYSTERY

In the last few chapters we have been made aware of the tradition that the consciousness of our planetary humanity during a prolonged series of zodiacal Ages is overshadowed, conditioned, and enlivened by the consciousness of a particular Buddha, or Planetary Spirit. He achieves this, we are told, through projecting an aspect of himself down into the field of human consciousness, manifesting and focusing his particular sense of evolutionary Purpose in the consciousness of a series of "chosen" individuals. They are thus effectively extensions of his own consciousness from birth. Such incarnations are known as Bodhisattva Avatars; they pass on the higher influence as best they can to their own circle of initiated human disciples, as well as conditioning the human psycho-spiritual "atmosphere" in general. However, in response to the question as to what the Buddha is and why he performs such a function, we should bear in mind that the Indo-Tibetan Buddha and the Egyptian Ptah are one and the same, both phonetically and actually. Both are Dhyani Buddhas, hence demiurgic Creator-Gods. They belong to the SELF-conscious hierarchy of celestial Intelligences, which are the literal expression of the Divine Mind, that which, as we saw in earlier chapters, itself both contains and informs the whole of our planetary Life.

In relation to the same question, we also otherwise need to have regard to the tradition that the spirits of humankind (the "divine sparks") are themselves the general animating factor in the kosmic etheric double of the Logos. Consequently, one might suggest that the (Dhyani) Buddha is himself the greater SELF-conscious projection or partial emanation of the Solar Logos from his own far higher plane of Being, which indirectly animates part of that same kosmic etheric double (associated with our planet) and invests it with a sense of Purpose. The Dhyani Buddha nature itself, however, because of its sheer power as the pure expression of Logoic Mind, can descend no lower than the Oversoul of the planet. It cannot normally descend into the kosmic etheric double itself. It must thus project mere aspects of itself down into the double. This it does through the emanating agency of Man, the spiritual Monad.

Objective humankind, on the other hand, because not divinely (or even spiritually) self-conscious, is not able to respond directly to the overall emanating sense of logoic Purpose, involving the Will-to-know. The latter must therefore be given out slowly, bit-by-bit, so that the consciousness of humanity is subjected to a consistent momentum of gradual change and awakening. Were this not done, it is suggested, the etheric double of the Logos would logically cease to function, and his objective body of manifestation would simply die from a process of attrition. The purpose of humankind is thus essentially to act en masse as the (initially unconscious) agent of the Buddha, in executing the objective Purpose of the Logos.

It follows, however, that while the vast majority have not attained to anything like real spiritual self-awareness, the objective logoic body must itself remain largely in a state of dormancy. This is more pronounced when there is no manifest Bodhisattva in incarnation. However, when a new Bodhisattva individuality is projected by the Dhyani Buddha and thus takes human incarnation—seemingly every seven hundred years or so—that Presence has a marked effect. It activates a fresh cycle of development through the agency of the most spiritually sensitive individuals (i.e., Adepts) who are capable of putting it into effect in the most practical way.

From Bailey's work we learn that the Intelligence otherwise objectively known to us as the Lord Gautama Sakyamuni Buddha held the position of our primary World Bodhisattva until it was taken over, some 2,000–2,500 years or so ago, by the Lord Maitreya,[1] the latter being himself, apparently, a "Buddha-in-waiting." His period of office, unlike that of his predecessors, will (so we are again told) cover two zodiacal eras, amounting to nearly 4,500 years.[2] However, Maitreya is otherwise defined by Blavatsky as "the secret name of the fifth Buddha and the Kalki Avatara of the Brahmins— the last Messiah who will come at the end of the Great Cycle."[3] Blavatsky also acknowledges that the Bodhisattva "will appear as Maitreya Buddha, the last of the Avataras and Buddhas, in the seventh Race" [of this Fourth Round],[4] which, according to *The Secret Doctrine,* will not appear for many tens of thousands of years to come. From this, it would certainly appear that Blavatsky and Bailey are in open conflict with each other. However, there are other associated issues to be considered as well before we make any final judgments as to whether this is really so. We shall now consider some of them.

Elsewhere in *The Secret Doctrine* we learn that "owing to the highest initiation [i.e., the seventh] performed by one overshadowed by the 'Spirit of Buddha' . . . a candidate becomes virtually a Bodhisattva, created such by the High Initiator."[5] In other words, Blavatsky here acknowledges the fact that the seventh initiation produces the self-generated human equivalent of the Bodhisattva, who is simultaneously a Manushi (i.e., human) Buddha. This attainment is achieved by virtue of his consciousness becoming at-one with (although not of anything like the same power as) that of the Dhyani Buddhas. The "High Initiator" referred to would appear to be Sanat Kumara, the direct representative of the Planetary Logos—himself a Dhyani Chohan. By virtue of the seventh solar state (*Adi*) being that of the "Fire Mist," the "Sea of Flame" from which the "parentless" human Monads themselves emerge (as we saw in earlier chapters), the Manushi Buddha is himself a "Son of Ad" or "Arhat of the Fire Mist." Concerning these Blavatsky comments that they are "but one remove from the Root-Base of their Hierarchy—the highest on Earth and our terrestrial chain."[6] As our humanity is apparently the ninth of the twelve solar Hierarchies,[7] this "Root Base" must itself be equivalent to the consciousness of the Demiurge of our planet, which is itself but one of the fohatic (i.e., kosmic mental) projections of the Amitabha Buddhas (one per planetary scheme) from the kosmic buddhic plane.

Concerning this same "Root Base," Blavatsky adds that it corresponds with the "Wondrous Being" [the "One Initiator"], which descended to Earth "in the early part of the Third Age, before the separation of the sexes of the Third [Lemurian] Race."[8] This same Being then devolved into "a group of semi-divine and semi-human beings. Set apart in Archaic genesis for certain purposes, they are those in whom are said to have incarnated the highest Dhyanis, Munis and Rishis from previous Manvantaras [eonic cycles]—to form the nursery for future human Adepts, on this Earth and during the present cycle."[9]

It is thus clear from this that the eighth state being referred to (the divine octave) comprises the fohatically enfolding kosmic mental consciousness of those (Nirmanakaya) Dhyani Buddhas, which contains the organism of our planet within its Ring-Pass-Not. However, the consciousness of the Dhyani Buddha is itself interplanetary and, being kosmic, extends as far as the Ring-Pass-Not of our immediate solar system. He cannot, however, roam throughout the other six solar systems of which ours is said to be but a fellow member within the local celestial scheme. This is permitted only to those imponderable Beings called "Lipika Lords" who are themselves the great Dhyani Lords of Karma for our entire solar system.[10]

MANUSHI BUDDHAS AND BODHISATTVAS

Furthermore, Blavatsky refers here also to the evidently many such Manushi Buddhas "appointed to govern the Earth in this Round." The inference is that two "parentless" Dhyani Buddhas "govern" the planet in some particular sense, developing its culture, during any one Root Race.[11] They do so through the agency of their human projections on Earth, of which there are many, doubtless appearing according to due cycle, as described in a moment. Each of the latter is then what we call the "Bodhisattva" of the historical era in question. In practical terms, the Dhyani Buddha (the "Buddha of Contemplation") would remain in governance from within the World Oversoul, periodically emanating or "overshadowing" human Bodhisattvas until the first of the evolving human Monads were themselves able to attain to a self-generated and thus Self-conscious Manushi Buddhahood. At that point, (divine) humanity would logically begin to become responsible for its own immediate governance. The previous system of external projection would then become progressively redundant.

Although all this might seem very complex, it is essentially logical when considered in relation to the already established principle that all human Monads are themselves derived from the mass emanation of the celestial Dhyani Buddhas who form the Logoic Nous. Thus it is that the Bodhisattva initiation—the last and highest of the seven planetary initiations—must come to each and every monadic "divine spark" before they can themselves become fully fledged and thus also SELF-conscious Dhyani Buddhas (albeit of the lower orders). It would also logically follow that the leading (originally human) Intelligence, which became the first Bodhisattva of our particular (Fourth) Round humanity, should itself "strike the note" for the future and thus perhaps also become the Dhyani Buddha responsible for the humanity of the next (i.e., Fifth) Round, first appearing in the Seventh Root Race of the present (Fourth) Round. Thus the idea of Maitreya Buddha fulfilling both these roles in turn is perhaps, after all, not in conflict with the statements in *The Secret Doctrine*.

OF FOURTH, FIFTH, AND SIXTH ROUNDERS
(See also appendix A)

Because the concept of planetary "Rounds" is of such complexity, a little further explanation would perhaps not go amiss here for those interested. This is particularly in view of the fact that the Masters of the Adept Hierarchy are themselves supposed to be "Fifth Rounders," while the mass of humanity are only "Fourth Rounders." A perception of past, present, and future as coexistent in the field of consciousness might here help us a little in the sense that the masses of Fourth Round humanity (representing the Present) are, in this cycle, trying to attain to Fifth Round (i.e., Adept) consciousness, thereby becoming the future humanity. The few who have already done so are themselves endeavoring to evolve yet further so that they literally "become the future" beyond even that.

However, according to the Adepts themselves, Gautama (representing that further future) was himself a "Sixth Rounder." He was thus an indirect manifestation or expression of the consciousness of the Amitabha Buddha hierarchy,[12] which was described in an earlier chapter as being of kosmic buddhic (mahatic) consciousness. Logically, therefore, he was a far more highly advanced being, relatively speaking, than even his predecessors in the same hierarchical position. The reason for this—although not specifically confirmed by them (and having been mentioned as highly esoteric)—seems to relate specifically to the further evolutionary advancement of the Adept Hierarchy itself rather than that of humanity (the latter representing the effects of the immediately past evolutionary cycle), along the following suggested lines.

To begin with, we need to bear in mind that the whole macro-kosmic evolutionary process necessarily involves the development of the various parts of the intended logoic organism to a certain point before they can be brought together to commence the process of their overall coordination. In other words, taking the human fetal organism by way of correspondence, the various organs of the baby's body have to be separately developed in the early stages of pregnancy before a specific point in the overall fetal cycle is reached. Then the various organs can be positively linked up (neurologically) to permit the next and greater stage of integrated development.

During this prolonged early natal stage in the Macrocosm, the Dhyani Buddhas cyclically project an aspect of themselves (i.e., a human Bodhisattva) into the organism in order to maintain the influence of their Will-to-know, which promotes the evolutionary instinct and the corresponding sequence of development. These cycles, so it would appear, coincide with the zodiacal Ages each of 2,160 years. However, in the case of our particular planetary Life, it would appear (and this is pure speculation) that, because it was approaching such an important cyclical nexus, the evolved spirit known to us as Gautama Buddha was brought in from an already far more highly developed part of the celestial organism (i.e., the Sixth Round) specifically in order to connect up the Fifth Round consciousness of our leading humanity with it. In this way, the fetal kosmic etheric vehicle of the Logos was being geared up to attain to a much greater degree of coordinated functional capacity than it had enjoyed and employed before that.

As already described, the Adepts of the Fifth Degree are said to constitute the nucleus of the forthcoming fifth kingdom in Nature; so it would appear that, in order for some of them to move on to the Sixth Degree (and thus form the nucleus of our future sixth kingdom of Nature), guided external assistance was logically needed from a yet higher group, in line with an occult principle previously enunciated by Blavatsky concerning evolution in general. Hence a Sixth Round Intelligence (Gautama) was brought or sent in from another already rather more advanced part of the planetary chain of evolution. This was to combine the taking of a human form with high Adept consciousness but also having other, semi-divine attributes. That combination would then act as a hugely dynamic example and thus actively influence the Adept Hierarchy toward their own next evolutionary step. According to what the Tibetan Adept DK tells us, the actual achievement of his human Buddhahood apparently took place in 592 BCE, when he was but twenty-eight or twenty-nine years of age.[13] It is suggested that this effectively confirms that the Buddha nature overshadowing Gautama Siddhartha had already passed through the same initiation in a much earlier incarnation and was thus merely reenacting that achievement (as far as reasonably possible) in a modern human body.

As also mentioned in an earlier chapter, the tradition otherwise implies that one of Gautama's chief responsibilities was to weld back together into a coherently unified body the spiritual Brotherhood of Adepts, which had become fragmented some ten thousand years before his appearance around 600 BCE. This fragmentation had apparently occurred as a result of the great planetary cataclysms that not only destroyed the final Atlantean island of Poseidonis but also changed much else of the world's geography, as I have sought to describe in my book *The Rise and Fall of Atlantis*.[14]

Notwithstanding this, the task of the Bodhisattva is commonly best known as encouraging enlightenment in humanity generally, supposedly so that all can reach nirvana. However, as nirvana (or *moksha* as it is more correctly known) essentially involves "final" liberation, one must then ask "liberation from precisely what?"—in metaphysical terms. The answer to this appears to be "from the kosmic physical state." This was itself depicted in several ancient traditions as a great Underworld mountain at the center of which exists a fiery state of lesser emanation—symbolized by the Greeks as the cavernous "forge" of the god Hephaestos. Thus, as the octave contains the sevenfold progression, it is the eighth initiation that logically generates that greatest liberation, as we saw in chapters 11 and 12. This coincides exactly with gnostic tradition.

Although our knowledge of Gautama and his work really only extends back as far as the sixth century BCE, it would seem that rather more may eventually become known of his historical influence before that, once the Adepts have again made themselves better known to the world. We are nevertheless assured by them (through both Blavatsky and Bailey) that Gautama was himself preceded by an untold number of prior human Buddhas in the Bodhisattva role, thereby confirming that the position of Bodhisattva is itself a hierarchical one, subject to cyclic change in line with the overall evolutionary process. This is important.

However, what is also important—and has never before been suggested or confirmed, as far as I am aware—is that the whole nature of the Bodhisattvas of our planet changed with the advent of Gautama, for the reasons just described. One might add that this also explains why it is that the present Adept Hierarchy regard Gautama as their particular "patron," rather than merely holding him in great respect as but the latest of the Bodhisattva line (which he was not). As a friend has reminded me, the more ancient Tibetan texts confirmed that the coming of Gautama was itself predicted long in advance and on repeated occasions by Dipankara, a rather more primordially historic human Buddha figure.

There is one further point worthy of consideration. Although in chapter 11 it was suggested that Gautama must have achieved Dhyani Buddhahood involving at least the eighth degree on the initiatory Path, there is a possibility that he might have attained to (but not completed) a yet higher degree as the Pali canon suggests. The tradition surrounding him and his supposedly "final" initiation—as described in the quotations from *The Light of Asia* given in chapter 11—describe him having to face up to all the conglomerate "fiends of Mara." The latter represented what Christians would regard as the Devil in his worst and most powerful possible manifestation. Now the eighth degree of initiation does not coincide with this, but the ninth does. We are told that it involves the initiate facing the huge reservoir of kosmic evil, which cyclically overflows the world, headed up by the massed Adepts of the Black Lodge (see appendix D for an explanation of the "Black Lodge"). In response, however, the Buddha nature refuses them all recognition—hence this being called the initiation of "refusal"—and thus passes on, rejecting all further contact with the kosmic physical plane altogether unless at the sixth initiatory degree (as a Chohan) he chose the Path of World Service.[15] This appears to be the sole exception to the general rule.

Still in relation to this, but from an historical viewpoint, we might also take into consideration the artistic image of the Buddha statuary found throughout Asia. The head of the Buddha figure (see fig. 6.9) is always shown with very tight hair curls and very long ears, which are definitely suggestive of a Fourth Root Race (i.e., Atlantean) human type, the long face and ears in particular being akin to those of the statues on Easter Island. It is thus suggested that the Manushi Buddha-Bodhisattva statue was only ever intended to signify a repetitive archetype rather than being directly associated with Gautama Sakyamuni himself. The latter was born of a Nepalese royal family and we can logically expect that he would thus have had definitely Indo-Caucasian features, with only wavy hair and a less fulsome mouth. As we have previously suggested that the ancient Tirthankaras of Jain religious tradition were actually Bodhisattvas or human Buddhas, this too makes quite logical sense. One might also mention that there are to be found all over Asia a variety of other Buddha statues—like the laughing Buddha—which are intended to exemplify particular kosmic or universal principles other than wisdom.

THE LORD MAITREYA

Returning to the persona of the Lord Maitreya, who we are told currently holds the position of the World Bodhisattva or Christ, there is a curious (although not well substantiated) tradition that he is himself of Indo-Caucasian stock. Jean Overton-Fuller recounts for us that when various Adepts passed through New York in the 1870s, at the time of the founding of the Theosophical Society, Blavatsky's cofounder Henry Olcott once mentioned "The Teacher of our Teachers, a paramahaguru" [i.e., an unnamed super-Adept] who had appeared before him, having blue eyes, fair hair, plus a European complexion and features.[16] This coincides with another story from

Tibet confirming that Maitreya was frequently portrayed as a European.[17] This is mentioned in passing, but it is of no spiritual concern whatsoever to us, because his given role is that of the World Teacher, not that of any particular ethnic or religious group. These personal details (even if true) are also otherwise of no real importance simply because the Adept of such high standing is supposedly able to change his physical body or appearance at will.

What is of importance is the suggestion that he is the first of our own humanity to have attained to true divinity. As this sounds both obscure and rather dramatic, it perhaps needs some more explanation along the following suggested lines. As already described, the phrase "our own humanity" is indicative of the fact that the objective human kingdom is itself cyclical in generation. That is to say, a new form or type of humanity (with an associated quality of consciousness) is generated in each planetary subcycle, the current preponderance of ours being of the fourth and fifth in a series of seven such "Root Races" (as described in greater detail in appendix A).

During the earlier "Round," the lesser "divine spark" (jiva) emanated by Man evolves through the various kingdoms of Nature before becoming a self-conscious human being. This evolution, as described in theosophical terms, takes place by unconscious emanation from the spiritual state, descending progressively to the objective state and then (upon attaining the human stage) gradually returning back to the spiritual state. In the latter case, it is with the fully evolved Self-consciousness of an Adept, the "Hero" of ancient Greek tradition. Subsequently, further and higher experience and training leads to the individuality attaining the consciousness and knowledge of a demigod and then (much later) a full god, as also explained earlier on. Semi-divinity coincides with attaining the consciousness of the highest two of the seven states within the field of planetary consciousness. Thus it is that *divinity* has to be seen as an entirely relative term. Man (i.e., the spiritual projection that descends in part into the human form) is essentially divine because of his kosmic origin, but (as mere man) he is entirely ignorant of the fact. It is only when a highly developed Self-consciousness has been achieved in his human nature, while simultaneously allowing Self-consciously perceptual function in the spiritual state, that a real and fully individualized divinity becomes potentially attainable.

THE ESOTERIC ROLES
OF GAUTAMA AND MAITREYA

It follows from this that the inspiring Intelligence behind the historical individual known to us as Gautama Siddhartha was, at his own high level (far, far beyond the human), the evolutionary product of the immediately preceding Round. His magnetic influence was thus necessary to provide the required subjective stimulation for the most advanced of the overall Fifth Race type of this Fourth Round—apparently headed by the Lord Maitreya—to take the sequentially next forward evolutionary leap. By virtue of this, so we are told, the Lord Maitreya became first a full Chohan of the sixth initiatory degree (some two thousand plus years ago) and then subsequently a human or "Manushi" Buddha of the seventh degree, thereby achieving union with the Life Consciousness of Shamballa—that of the Planetary Logos (the "Father"). By this time, so it would appear, the Lord Gautama had already taken the initiations of both the eighth and ninth degrees and thereby achieved almost fully Self-conscious liberation from planetary existence as the most superior type of Interplanetary Spirit known as a Dharmakaya Buddha. He had thereby become almost at-one with his own emanating Source, the hierarchy of Amitabha Buddhas. The latter achievement is itself openly acknowledged by the Adepts.[18] More than this one cannot (at present) really suggest other than to speculate that the joint achievement of the Lords Maitreya and Gautama Buddha (if as described) logically opened "the Higher Way" for the rest of our Fifth and Fourth Round humanity subsequently to follow. Hence the Christ's enigmatic statement in the New Testament "Nobody comes to the Father but through me,"[19] which the Christian church has managed to interpret in a wholly personalized sense.

The latter statement conclusively defines for us the fact that we (as evolving spirits) can only pass back to the state of consciousness of the Demiurge (i.e., "the Father") through the state already attained by the Lord Maitreya. One might conclude, however, by adding that the highest state in Pure Land Buddhism lies even beyond the seventh and highest state within our planetary field of consciousness to which the Lord Maitreya has evidently attained. It appears to relate to the fourth kosmic state (shown in fig. 3.4)—that of the Amitabha Dhyani Buddha hierarchy itself—which is known in kabbalism as the expression of Ain Soph (Aur), the "field of Boundless Light." As already described, it is from here that the downward spiritual emanations take place resulting in the planetary Rounds causing the formation of the sequential planetary chains of globes.[20] (See appendix A for further explanation of planetary Chains and Rounds.)

It would appear that the somewhat distorted Christian view of the Christ having taken upon his shoulders "the sins of the world" is directly connected with these initiations, as also perhaps the figurative concept of his "sitting at the right-hand side of God"—that is, the Demiurge—at Shamballa. The "sacrifice" connected with the seventh degree initiation, itself associated with the "Sea of Fire," as already described in chapter 11 and otherwise also in *The Voice of the Silence,* should perhaps help to explain this.[21] For it is at this point that "the Pilgrim" is said to have "returned back from the other shore," thereby becoming a future Savior of humankind in the mass. We are otherwise told, however, that the "tragedy" of the Christ mission of two thousand years ago was the result of three recognitions:

1. His discovery that humankind was then not yet ready for the influence that he brought and that much more time was necessary for humankind to respond to it
2. His realization that he needed many more trained workers to fulfill the needed work
3. His discovery that humankind was "not yet desperate enough to take the kingdom of Heaven by storm" and had thus to face further progressive initiation en masse[22]

Following on from this, we are told that when he completes his work during the next two thousand years or so, only then will he take "that stupendous initiation of which we know nothing except that the two divine aspects will blend and fuse in Him (as Love-Wisdom in full manifestation, motivated by Divine Will, or Power). Then the Buddha and the Christ will together pass before the Father . . . and eventually pass to higher service of a nature and calibre unknown to us."[23]

We might therefore approach the conclusion of this chapter with some consideration of the nature of the distinction between Love and Wisdom in relation to their expression by initiates of high degree, along the following lines.

THE LOVE-WISDOM PRINCIPLE

To begin with, these two aspects of the divine nature—Love and Wisdom—are regarded as fundamentally complementary, while it is otherwise seen that the Second Ray (of which they are the expression) is itself the foundational influence behind all sustainedly manifest existence in our solar system. However, we are otherwise told that the manifest universe is a phenomenon based on electro-magnetic principles, thereby giving rise to what we call the Law of Attraction and Repulsion. Now Love is fundamentally concerned with attraction and all-inclusiveness; so where does that place Wisdom? Does it have to do with separation and exclusiveness—or perhaps with the divine or spiritual equivalent?

In endeavoring to answer that question properly we first need to remove all personal, human associations from consideration, or we will learn nothing. Instead, we must look more closely at the way the wider universe functions, involving not only coherence but also dynamic inter-relationship. That is to say—following the descriptions of spirit and soul in the early chapters of this book—there is an incessant (although cyclical) interplay of influences between all celestial bodies, just as there is between all objective forms of life in Nature. All coherence in Universal Nature is maintained by the principle of soul, but all creative interplay between souls (resulting in karma) derives from the intelligent (or unnaturally forced) emanations of spirit.

As we also saw earlier, the lesser soul consciousness evolves through the partial "fall" (followed by the return) of a more highly evolved soul nature. Without this sacrifice, such evolutionary development becomes impossible. However, once the lesser soul nature has absorbed this and learned from the experience how to project itself outwardly, thereby achieving confidently self-generated relationships with the wider environment, its self-conscious individuality is progressively enhanced.

In a very real sense, the Love-Wisdom nature must on the one hand leave the past behind while consciously embracing the future—hence "Love" in this instance is actually based on assimilation of the higher and wider (i.e., kosmic) Ideal. Thus we might well understand how the Lord Buddha "culminated the Age of [objective] Knowledge" through his achievement of full Wisdom while the Lord Maitreya initiated a new and forthcoming "Age of more inclusive Reason"[24] by metaphorically "standing on the Buddha's shoulders" and reaching out yet further on behalf of the Causal Soul of humanity in general.

We might also add to this by suggesting that what is called "Love" is usually confused by we humans merely with degrees of personal affection. However, in the spiritual sense (even in the objective world), it is nothing of the sort. In the latter context it is essentially the recognition of the most profound bond of common inner identity. It thus involves the consequent taking up of a much greater field of responsibility (with associated senses of care and protectiveness of others) than previously perceived or experienced. It also necessarily involves an allied expansion of consciousness.

Hence the "organic" Christ nature is essentially self-sacrificial in the name of the greater Cause, yet Self-expansive because of the instinct to do more for that same Cause. However, to take up such a commitment involving a recognition of personal responsibility for the whole of humanity must have been terrifying in its enormity. Yet, one might suggest, the Wisdom of a prior understanding as to how the whole subliminal system of planetary consciousness works would have made the decision possible by giving the necessary strength of instinctively knowing how to deal with that increased responsibility.

By virtue of the fact (as we have already discussed) that a knowledge is a power, the Lord Maitreya would necessarily have had to rely upon his own Master—the Lord Buddha—to help absorb the vastly greater kosmic influence that he was essentially in the process of invoking. Thus the Wisdom of the Lord Buddha (overshadowing the Lord Maitreya, just as the latter overshadowed the Adept Jesus) might be regarded as having supplied knowledge from the planetary center of Shamballa, through the agency of his own consciousness, in a way that could then be adequately contained and adapted by their combined consciousness.

We suggested earlier that Gautama Buddha was/is the expression of the Amitabha Buddha hierarchy responsible for the Life of our solar system (our planetary scheme in particular); also that being a Sixth Rounder, he was himself the living expression of a previous cycle of achievement in the consciousness of our Logos. In other words, Gautama's dharma or spiritual responsibility was to create (or enhance) a direct link of yet higher (kosmic) consciousness by means of which the Purpose of the Amitabha Buddhas (the "Watchers") could subsequently motivate the objective solar scheme (the "body" of the Logos) more effectively. Thus he was the expression of their Wisdom as well as conveying "local" planetary knowledge to the Lord Maitreya from Shamballa. In a very real sense therefore, the Wisdom emanation (from the kosmic buddhic state) of the Amitabha Buddha hierarchy might be regarded as that of the Logos himself and, of this, Blavatsky has this to say:

> Whenever any particular individual [Adept] teacher reaches the highest state of spiritual culture, develops in himself all the virtues that alone entitle him to a union with the [Planetary] Logos and finally unites his soul with the Logos, there is, as it were, a sort of reaction emanating from that Logos for the good of humanity. . . . This influence may be conceived of as an invisible spiritual Grace that descends from heaven.[25]
>
> But this Light is [merely] the veil of the Logos in the sense that the Shekinah of the kabbalists is supposed to be the veil of Adonai. Verily, it is the Holy Ghost that seems to form the flesh and blood of the divine Christ.[26]

THE SPIRITUAL ROLE OF HUMANKIND

As humankind is the expression of the solar buddhic state of being (that of the Spiritual Soul), which is also the kosmic etheric double, all this makes perfectly logical sense. However, once the linking anchorage in the kosmic etheric double has been generated and "takes root," it is able to develop and maintain its own evolutionary link back toward its Source. In other words, it becomes the fully anchored (hence permanent) expression of that same Wisdom as a Higher Intelligence. At the same time, the Adept Hierarchy takes increasingly full responsibility for the Oversoul of our planetary Life as a whole, through the nature of its intelligently enhanced Love for all the other kingdoms of Nature. Consequently, the Maitreya Buddha—if indeed the first of our own Third, Fourth, and Fifth Race humanity to achieve the fully coordinated balance of such Love plus the higher Wisdom—must have, in a very real sense, opened the Higher Way for our humanity as a whole to follow via the initiatory Path.

This achievement, although immense, is as yet logically incomplete because, as we saw earlier, initiation always involves three progressive phases. When it is complete—some tens of thousands of years hence—humankind will effectively have "sealed the door where Evil dwells." That is for the simple reason that the Oversoul of our planetary Life will have come under the control of its own Causal Soul nature. Our planet will effectively become a "sacred planet" because a direct connection with its own higher Source will have been effected.

However, in the meantime, the elemental nature of our planet will battle to sustain its chaotic independence, in rejection of the necessary discipline that intelligent human nature will increasingly impose upon it. This is essentially no different than the way in which the elemental part of our own human nature battles against any form of discipline that we impose upon it in order to achieve our greater ideals and aims in life. It is thus entirely up to us at what speed we bring to bear our own intelligence in dominating our own lower nature. With all this in mind we can perhaps see why the Spiritual Hierarchy sees it as so important for humanity to develop a new and more direct perception of Divinity. We can also clearly see the logic of why the Adepts regard the time as being increasingly ripe for their own public externalization.

FOURTH AND FIFTH RACE BODHISATTVAS

In this chapter it has been suggested that the Maitreya Buddha Bodhisattva is (perhaps) a member of the Fifth Race, and this idea should accompany the following further suggestion that common sense would anticipate the overlap of one reign of responsibility with another, even in divine circles of existence where it would inevitably last thousands of years. Hence, apparently, the parallel fact that the Manu of the Fourth Race—responsible for retaining the essential coherence of the latter group—is himself still in existence, living somewhere in China,[27] while the Manu of the Fifth Race (Vaivasvata) has quite separate responsibilities. Thus we might suggest that while the appearances of the Lord (Gautama) Buddha and his predecessors (plus his further and seemingly last "incarnation" as Tzon-kha-pa)[28] were essentially expressions of the highest Wisdom aspects of Fourth Race consciousness, that of Maitreya Buddha is correspondingly representative of another succeeding but complementary divine principle, which is consequently capable of working in tandem with it. Is this perhaps why in the Bailey works so much emphasis is laid on the fact that the second great universal principle is the dual Love-Wisdom? Is it also why the same works describe Gautama as the greatest expression of the latter while Maitreya (building on Gautama's work) is presented as the greatest exponent of that further expression of Divine Reason and universal interrelationship to which we give the quite inadequately expressive and misleading titles "Love" and "the Will-to-good"?

Other than what is mentioned here, we are told almost nothing further whatsoever about these great Intelligences, despite confirmation that there were highly evolved initiates in the Fourth Race who took the sixth initiation and, in so doing, brought Atlantean civilization to an end.[29] With that in mind, paralleled by the further statement that a similar group of Chohans decided to bring about the end of the Piscean Age's materialism in the early twentieth century,[30] it seems not impossible that other Atlantean initiates may have attained to the seventh or even higher initiations. As the aim of the Fourth Race was the development throughout its more evolved humanity of the principle of creative imagination and spiritual idealism (involving mere desire in the masses), it might be useful to speculate somewhat along the following lines, in order to keep matters generally in reasonable perspective. In doing so, however, let us keep firmly in mind that the word *race* here is purely indicative of an expression of logoic consciousness and that it would therefore be entirely logical to conceive of an individual moving on in subjective evolutionary terms from one Race to another.

First of all then, why should there be apparently different Spiritual Hierarchies for these two Races, the Fourth comprising the ethnologically older oriental peoples of East and Southeast Asia (but not the Indian subcontinent), plus South America and the island peoples of Polynesia and Melanesia, as well as much of Africa? Why should the majority of souls of these peoples not have moved logically forward at the end of the Fourth Race, reincarnating into the Fifth? What could be the associated logic, particularly bearing in mind that some of their race (like the Tibetan Tzon-kha-pa of Kokonor), albeit in much later times, may have themselves attained to Bodhisattva-hood, if not to Buddha-hood itself?

The only possible answer appears to be one of free self-sacrifice of some of the more evolved and already initiated members of the Fourth Race, involving a decision to "stay behind" with those of their peoples not yet ready at that time to move on to the next stage, comprising the progressive development of the intellectual principle and its advancement in controlling the purely emotional faculty. This has itself resulted in the seemingly haphazard unfoldment, in the various Indo-Caucasian ethnological subtypes, not only of the lower mind in its various degrees, but also in conjunction with the emotional nature (kama-manas). It is this same only partial and often chaotically mixed development that, interacting clumsily with remaining Fourth Race consciousness, is causing so many cultural problems today throughout the world and has done so for many centuries past.

One might infer from this that the same principle—and the same cultural problems—will apply in relation to the Fifth Race when the time comes for its own final "Judgment Day." Quite clearly, only a proportion of the souls of the Race will quickly move on and reincarnate in the Sixth Race with its more instinctively intuitive bias. However, the remainder and their own subsequent spiritual development will still have to be looked after in line with their own further and later transitional development. This inevitably means that a proportion of the Spiritual Hierarchy of the Fifth Race will itself need to make that same personal sacrifice, remaining behind and assisting with the further (higher mental) development of the human race for at least the next greater cycle. But would this be fair and in line with an essential spiritual equality? The answer to that would be "yes," but it has to be considered in association with the next yet greater cycle of existence. In this, those who have taken longer to develop the astral or mental nature in the previous cycle would effectively have developed much more extensive familiarity with it and would thus also be the more advanced with its use in the next cycle. In other words, the whole process ultimately balances itself out in due course of time and no single group loses out. Interim appearances are merely deceptive.

THE PROBLEM OF
CHRISTHOOD PRESENTATION

In concluding this chapter, we might otherwise consider for a moment the deep psychological problem inevitably facing the Spiritual Hierarchy in persuading the vast mass of mainstream Christianity around the world that the concept of the "risen Christ" is of hugely greater importance than that of the "crucified Christ." From the most obvious viewpoint, the latter might appear to have a greater charismatic appeal simply because of the immediately reactive association with pain and suffering. The idea that one cannot hope to arrive at a spiritual realization or sense of beatitude without experiencing pain and suffering (although true in principle) is now being taken to an absurdly extreme extent. We even have some "fundamentalist" Catholic communities in Central and South America, and the Philippines, for example, pursuing the concept in an altogether literal fashion by allowing or encouraging individuals to be crucified.

From one viewpoint, this suggests that the old idea is already dying out. Hence some mistakenly believe that a pseudo-revival of the actual event is necessary to regalvanize the faith. However, such events do nothing in real terms other than stimulate the astral nature through either horror or crude fascination. It is effectively a symbolic blood ritual, which has no real place in modern human society. Today, passive suffering and the psychological negativity that it induces must give way to a compassionate determination to bring about a greater sense of sharing in all more positive and forward-looking fields of human endeavor, in all cultures. This is now becoming commonly accepted and is no longer considered to be a radical approach as it certainly would have been only a century or two ago.

One might well otherwise ask how such communities would respond to the actual reappearance of the Christ in our current day and age? For many, their morbid fascination with the crucifixion blood ritual would probably prevent them from regarding him as anything other than a human impostor because of his entirely new message. However, it has been made clear by the Spiritual Hierarchy that, on this next occasion, he will not be appearing alone or in an openly charismatic style involving any sort of sudden, avataric self-announcement. This time, he will undoubtedly appear much more quietly and be gradually recognized "by his own" who will then progressively bring the rest of human society around to fuller awareness of his new criteria for the Aquarian Age, through their own positively directed efforts on his behalf.

This time, they also say, he will clearly be preceded and his work accompanied not only by fellow Adepts and senior initiates, but also by literally worldwide generations of those (already visible today) already converted to the idea of an intelligently practical, universal compassion and sense of brotherhood. This will involve a vocational sense of common responsibility not just based on mysticism. Of those willing to leave behind the old God-fixation and accept the idea of the risen Buddha-Christ state as the aim for humanity in general, perhaps the majority would still see him from a largely devotional viewpoint.

However, at a time when the evolutionary impulse is supposed to be guiding humanity in general toward a more mentally reasoned approach to life, would this not involve a mere exchange of concepts? With that in mind, it is perhaps wiser to consider the wider ecumenical approach as being of greater immediate importance. Only when the three "Religions of the Book," plus Buddhism and Hinduism, are generally acknowledged as being complementary to each other, and sharing their underlying message with science as well, can we expect this apparent impasse to be resolved by newer and younger generations. It is therefore in the field of general education that the preliminary foundational work must be done, by those of a mentally polarized "New Age" outlook who are willing and able to project the common vision that suffering is based on ignorance, plus a willful failure to deal with it effectively, and thus that a common goodwill must form the basis of future human society.

One can see from all this that the concept of communal self-help (i.e., of service at all levels of human activity) is intrinsic to what is intended by the Spiritual Hierarchy. The whole movement toward a general increase in spiritual knowledge (not just spirituality per se) is dependent upon "grass roots" group effort spreading and interacting on a worldwide basis. It is not dependent upon large-scale political determination. In a very real sense, politics merely involves an institutionalized reaction and reorganization of social structures to accommodate what has already been decided upon (subjectively) "at ground level." It is for that reason that well-informed public opinion is so important in our day and age. At present, perennial ancient wisdom concepts are still not being well understood or implemented by the New Age movement in general because of the tendency to think in terms still of devotional or psychically exciting issues rather than objectively considered and well-constructed ones.

In the most practical terms, the forthcoming externalization of the Spiritual Hierarchy would be logically representative of that historic (astrologically determined) point where "Heaven comes closest to Earth." Such a time could not last forever, however. It could be only cyclical in nature and thus represents great evolutionary opportunity for the few great Lives of our planet who are occasionally able to make their liberated escape from the lowest of the seven kosmic states of Nature. This point is far too generally overlooked. However, the Buddha-Christ nature has also effectively acted as the first element of a permanent bridge, enabling far higher (i.e., kosmic) Intelligences to penetrate and influence our system in a much more direct fashion than ever before.

But that same bridging nature is, again quite logically, one that increasing numbers of initiated human beings will now progressively achieve and so strengthen, thereby rendering it permanent rather than cyclically temporary in nature. It is thus no longer a question of the Christ alone—or accompanied merely by Gautama Buddha—acting on behalf of humanity in the mass. It is now a question of humanity in the mass (irrespective of existing religious backgrounds or leanings) acting in concert as the spiritual and temporal bridge between the divine (i.e., kosmic) world and the lesser kingdoms of Nature.

That humanity in the mass does not yet consciously see or comprehend the underlying range of psychic and spiritual interrelationships, which make up the "bridge" that is thus now in process of forming, is relatively unimportant. The fact of it fast becoming a universally shared ideal in the minds of humankind's forthcoming generations is most significant. Once it is generally realized that this has already taken place, the speed of construction will inevitably accelerate very noticeably, and that will just as inevitably ensue upon the coming together of philosophy, religion, and science from the viewpoint of a common, underlying esotericism.

FIFTEEN

THE MODERN
RESTORATION OF THE
MYSTERIES

One of the major issues to be considered in terms of the future program of human development is the fact that, within the 25,920-year cycle of precession, we are fast approaching the celestial solstice (as described in earlier chapters) and the beginning of a major new astrological cycle. As a direct consequence—like the current of a river flowing toward a narrower elliptical bend in its course—our human society is experiencing a huge amount of turbulence during that approach. Much of the cultural experience of the last century is going around and around in ever faster subcycles, like localized whirlpools and eddies, thereby rendering our present social culture ever more repetitive and superficial from one angle.

In very real and practical terms, however, the "sediment" of historical mores and customs built up in our psychology (as instincts) over the last millennia or so is being shaken loose so that the inner current of intelligence can travel on faster and more freely to join the greater approaching cycle. This chaos will inevitably continue for the next several hundred years at least as the separated psychological sediment settles into its own slower cycle, leaving the faster spiritual flow to those capable of sustaining it and traveling onward with it. The acceleration away from the "bend" of the solstice will itself be substantial, effectively resulting in the psychological separation of a large part of our present human consciousness from the past.

In a very real sense, this approach to the forthcoming Age of Aquarius involves the protracted "Judgment Day" of our present greater cycle. Following this the faster-evolving spiritual nature of humankind will be allowed a period of unfettered progress, at least temporarily detached from the materialism of the immediately past cycle of centuries. Taking these latter issues into account, we shall make an attempt in this last chapter to consider the suggestion that it would be feasible to restore the Mysteries to mankind and, if so, on what basis. This is, self-evidently, a huge proposition, bearing in mind the considerably varied extent and range of human social tradition and religious culture in potential opposition to such change. So where does one start? Is there an existing foundation on which it might perhaps be possible to build? If so, where? Or is it necessary to start completely afresh? If so, how? From the viewpoint of esoteric and occult philosophy, these questions have to be considered first of all from the subjective and not the objective side, for the reasons to be explained in a moment. However, in addition to all this, we have to bear in mind that what is being discussed here applies largely to the Western or at least partially "Westernized" mind, which is more generally aware of the modern gnostic, kabbalistic, and theosophical approaches to esoteric philosophy. Fig. 15.1 may help to provide a common background for what we shall be considering in this chapter, at least by way of cross-correspondence.

One of the most important things to be ever borne in mind by the practicing esotericist-occultist concerned with the evolution of the human race as a whole is the considerable variation to be found in humankind's own psycho-spiritual makeup. The same applies in relation to the range of natural intelligence to be found—something that has nothing to do with academic IQ. Today's anthropological and bio-physiological sciences look at the human being from the angle of physical appearance and understandably see little difference, except in terms of color and particular facial characteristics. They then look at brain size and DNA makeup and make their judgments of intelligence based on that extraordinarily limited perspective. What they do not take into account, however, is that the physical human body today is

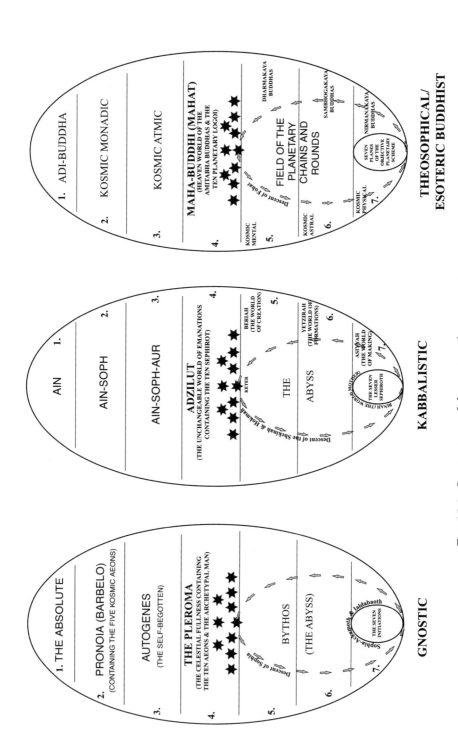

Fig. 15.1. Comparison of the various hermeneutic systems

merely the designed end-product of the last great evolutionary cycle, which is itself the result of long preceding psycho-spiritual causes. Even by reference to modern scientific data we can see that it was conceived and evolved many hundreds of thousands of years ago to provide the foundational "equipment" for the potential further development of the humanity of the current cycle, while also representing that which had already been developed prior to it.

With regard to the general human consciousness of the last (Atlantean) cycle, we are told that:

> The astral vehicle was the controlling factor. The mind was relatively quiescent except where the foremost members of the human race were concerned. The humanity of that world cycle were, however, all of them, extremely psychic and mediumistic. . . . They were in no way able to interpret that which they contacted; they were not able to distinguish astral phenomena from ordinary physical life. . . . The interpreting mind revealed nothing to them.[1]

These, however, are characteristics still very widely found throughout the world today, particularly when the emotions of the individual or group become aroused in conjunction with an only partially developed mind faculty, through mere reaction. Considered thought ceases to function. This is true of individuals and groups of all ethnological types—that is, of both Fourth and early Fifth Races (Third Race or Lemurian consciousness by now being virtually nonexistent)—but appears particularly so with all cultures of a tribal nature, even when found in the middle of modern urban society. (See appendix C for a presentation of the Root Races, which provides explanatory background for this discussion.) Associated physical appearances are of course deceptive (except for the quality of intelligence radiating out through the eyes of the individual) and anyone making generalizations as to evolutionary development based purely on ethnic or ethnological principles will almost certainly be wildly wrong.

However, there are fundamental subjective differences, which arise out of other considerations. For example, the Oriental mind-set is quite different from that of the Occidental, the former being "maternal" and quietly considered relative to the aggressively "paternal" and decisive nature of the latter.

The two are, however, complementary, and it is therefore fascinating from the viewpoint of a historian to observe how the influence of one relative to the other in different eras has brought about far-reaching changes in the social traditions of both. The most modern two-way (subjective and objective) results of such interchange are most obvious, for example, in relation to Britain and India, although the karmic flow-back from East to West is much more recent and, in fact, still very self-evidently in progress. Other European influences in their former African empires or colonies have otherwise produced very different results.

Even when it comes to considering the nature of the present Fifth (Indo-Caucasian) Race cycle and its objective human type—now to be found worldwide and of every race and color (or a colloidal mixture of them)—we find left-over characteristics. We are told, for example, that "the responsive sensitivity to creative impression was the outstanding quality of the later Atlantean consciousness and of the early Aryan period"[2]—the latter by now having extended throughout the world. Hence it is that

> although great creative monuments [such as the Egyptian pyramids perhaps?] appeared everywhere upon the planet, they were not the products of the minds of the men of the time, but were the imposition of the creative will of the planetary Hierarchy upon those who were sensitive to the higher impression.[3]

The inference arising out of this is that humankind in general, before the last great cycle, was subjectively incapable of instinctively independent mental creativity per se. It would thus appear that such creativity on any breadth of appreciable scale is something that has only appeared over the course of the last ten thousand years or so, understandably developed within the protective framework of the Sacred Mysteries. However, as we also saw in an earlier chapter, this creativity has itself became progressively split—starting about four to five thousand years ago—into the duality of subjective gnosis (which became what we call "philosophy") on the one hand and artistic "craft" on the other, the latter devolving in recent times into our modern "technology." Prior to this, all creative architectural and scientific or engineering knowledge had been contained by the Adept Brotherhood within its local ashramic centers—hence the supposedly different Mystery traditions of India, Persia, Egypt, Greece, and so on.

From one angle, that same division of sacred knowledge into subjective and objective faculty itself indicates a historically subjective progression on the part of humanity. In other words, through the wider development of an integrated human personality, there arose the inherent complementarity of craft and gnosis as a duality of which separate and objective advantage could be taken, for either commercial or social gain, or both.

Paradoxically, from the esoteric viewpoint, this attitude of "blind circumstance" giving rise to causes, which then give rise to effects, is fundamentally back-to-front. Everything has a causal base founded on choice or decision at some or other level of consciousness. However, humankind—that is, the intelligentsia of any particular cycle—only recognizes the inherently causal truths in things by coming at them in this retrogressive manner and thereby finding out, through the trial and error of direct experience producing mere effects, what in essence they are not. Thus, we may say, it is historically always the intelligentsia that generates the culture. It is the masses who, in following them, produce the consequent civilization, while all suffer the associated karmic problems.

In practical terms, the Mysteries provide informative knowledge concerning the still sacred. However, this is not given out, per se, simply through ritualized allegory, as is commonly supposed. It is these allegories that make man aware of a mechanism of revelation, which, if properly utilized, contains channels of activity that endow him with magnetic and radiatory (i.e., occult) powers, thereby drawing out and developing his spiritual individuality.[4] This is why so much emphasis has been placed in earlier chapters on the invocative and evocative development of human consciousness. Most importantly, from the esoteric and occult viewpoint, invocation and evocation are respectively associated with radiation and magnetism.[5] It naturally follows that the Mysteries are, historically speaking, a psychosocial mechanism capable of introducing a spectrum of knowledge and faculty to humanity as a whole, in a manner altogether higher than those to which it has become used over the many previous millennia. From that viewpoint, modern religion on its own is incapable of providing an adequate base for a new Mystery tradition, because it is itself based on purely devotional impulses of an astral character.

In a world where various forms and degrees of fundamentally competitive astral devotion—involving financial acquisitiveness, deific religion, and ancestor worship, plus various forms of tribalism—is still practiced by more than 80 percent of the planet's population, one has to ask what chance the Mysteries would have today of sheer survival; this is even if carefully and selectively restored, apart from the field of devotional religion. However, in order to answer that question, one must first look at the current state of all these various types of devotion, for they are by no means in a healthy condition and able to continue much longer of their own accord. Before we do that, however, let us first of all get rid of a fundamental misconception regarding the Mysteries and their return, supposedly as a result of the externalization of the Spiritual Hierarchy. This misconception is that the restoration of the Mysteries is purely being brought about for the sake of humanity, on the grounds that humanity has managed to raise itself to a point of evolutionary development that makes it worthwhile. This, however, is only a small part of the story.

THE HIERARCHICAL "CRISIS"

In fact, the evolutionary rhythms and cycles of humankind and those of the Spiritual Hierarchy, as well as their associated goals, are quite different. In this particular instance, therefore, the outward or externalizing movement by the Hierarchy is necessary because it is itself facing an internal crisis of decision, so we are told.[6] The rationale for this derives from the little recognized fact that the sixth initiation—whereby the Master becomes a Chohan—itself represents the equilibrium point between the processes of kosmic and systemic involution and evolution. This particular initiation has only become accessible to our humanity over the past 2,500 years, so it would seem. However, the pace of spiritual evolution of our humanity has now reached a point where appreciable numbers of our Adepts are apparently facing or potentially capable of making such a "leap" into the doorway of true kosmic consciousness.

The actual logic of this is quite straightforward. The greater involutionary cycle is determined by the Rays emanating from the plane of Kosmic Buddhi (*Mahat*) as we saw earlier. These pass into the sevenfold kosmic physical plane through the lens-like agency of the spiritual Monads of both man and deva, the latter more particularly. Consequently, when the Master becomes a Chohan, he recognizes (as a now Self-conscious Monad) where he actually stands from the greater perspective. So, with the powers thus engendered in him, he realizes that these same Rays no longer constrain him. He consequently becomes free to move "onward, upward, and outward," now aware of why the process of differentiation and its evolutionary reverse take place.[7] In so doing, upon the initiation being consummated, the Chohan must choose one of seven kosmic Paths,[8] only one of which (the Path of Earth Service) will see him remain within our immediate planetary scheme and involved with its direction through the planetary center at Shamballa. The others will take him to deal with responsibilities in other parts of the body of the Solar Logos. The capacity for the most senior members of the Spiritual Hierarchy to move on, however, must apparently involve their first demonstrating their capacity to control, all together, all the five kosmic physical elements—atma, buddhi, manas, kama, and the physical state—in their entirety, just as man on a lower turn of the spiral has to control the five corresponding planetary elements of aether, fire, air, water, and earth within his own nature. This, however, can only be done by their full and simultaneous expression of perfection in both the objective and subjective sense.[9] That in turn necessitates their coming out of their seclusion of the centuries and functioning as modern "demigods," although with great subtlety and not in the crudely obvious sense that some might consider likely.

It might be worthwhile inserting here a most important quote from one of the Masters regarding the further evolution of the divinity in man, as follows:

> [The Individuality in man] . . . to run successfully its sevenfold downward and upward course, has to assimilate to itself the eternal life-power residing but in the seventh [state] and then blend the three (the fourth, fifth and seventh) into one—the [Monadic] sixth. Those who succeed in doing so become Buddhas, Dhyan Chohans, etc. The chief object of our struggles and initiations is to achieve this union while yet on the Earth. Those who will be successful have nothing to fear [i.e., they will be free from "human" reincarnation] during the fifth, sixth and seventh Rounds.[10]

In effect, the members of the Spiritual Hierarchy must very clearly and effectively demonstrate their ability to be fully receptive to (and expressive of) real kosmic influences of great power while they are in physical manifestation, while not being overcome or in any way unbalanced by them. The natural effect of this, however, will be to render the whole of the objective planetary world hugely stimulated by their presence and activities, a potentially very problematic situation for the other kingdoms of Nature. Consequently, it is essential that the Mysteries are refounded (gradually) in order to ensure that such influences are properly "stepped down" by humanity, under self-control, so as to ensure no uncontrolled damaging side effects. It is also worth remembering here the old adage that "new wine and old bottles do not mix."

THE FURTHER EVOLUTION OF OUR HUMANITY

In conjunction with this, we perhaps need to deny one further common belief—that, given sufficient time, humanity will generate a real "Heaven on Earth" purely as a result of its own humanistically orientated efforts. As earlier indicated, the spiritual evolution of all kingdoms of Nature is actually derived through the influences received "from above," once that kingdom has itself reached a certain point of development—hence the "Judgment Day" in each greater cycle inevitably preceding any "New Age."[11] That same development, however, is itself achieved through due preparation (also "from above") of its more advanced types to become "vehicles" for such higher influences.

Then and only then does there take place an emanation from a higher state of being, enabling a small part of the latter's nature to manifest (as a new kingdom of Nature). That is because the greater Potency is itself far too powerful to manifest as a complete individuality in its own right. This is otherwise described for us in the tradition of our own humankind's first appearance on Earth, in Lemurian times.[12] The associated potency is in fact so great that such transitions are always accompanied by hugely disruptive events (e.g., cataclysms and electrical storms of vast magnitude) in the short term as the deva and elemental natures strive to adjust to the presence of the new influence.

It naturally follows, in relation to humankind, that the aim of the Spiritual Hierarchy is to anchor permanently on Earth certain immensely powerful kosmic Potencies, which can then be annually invoked and thus "tapped" to release their forces (in the ceremonials and rituals of the new world religion), mainly during the Taurean and Geminian full moon periods. These great Intelligences have already been contacted by the Hierarchy, so we are told, but the necessary further close link between the Hierarchy and humankind needed to bring them right through, thereby involving all the lower kingdoms of Nature, has not yet been established. Hence the need for the externalization of the Hierarchy, as a result of which the new Mysteries and the new world religion can be developed. Thus the forces required to bring about the great changes needed for the future world age(s)—including the objective appearance of new kingdoms of Nature—can be gradually and progressively drawn down.[13]

One might perhaps add that, by virtue of the principle that "Nature abhors a vacuum" (or evolutionary hiatus), the Spiritual Hierarchy of any great age has to provide for an alternative to take its place when its own superior members need to move on to fulfill their own evolutionary development and range of wider responsibilities (i.e., their destiny) within the body of the Logos. They effectively could not move on without doing so first in such a way that the overall evolutionary sequence in our planetary and solar system is not disrupted. Consequently, there is a straightforward logic in this next stage and our having previously been told that a major kosmic Potency was invoked during the Second World War. This was done in order to help overcome the "Powers of Darkness," the latter's instinctual involutionary aim being the maintenance of the world of form, at the expense of the evolutionary development of consciousness.[14]

CONSIDERING THE WIDER EFFECTS

The results on humanity of the Spiritual Hierarchy again becoming objective will inevitably vary according to the evolutionary development of those concerned. Those already "on the Path" (by now in the millions) will be highly stimulated by the spiritual potencies thus unfurled. Those of average to higher intelligence who have not yet developed a real spiritual orientation will become (at least temporarily) confused because of the large-scale social and cultural reorientation taking place in front of their very eyes. Those of undeveloped and still highly self-centered mentality will respond by subjectively "closing down" in a sort of inertial self-defense of resistance against change, thus automatically causing the retardation of their own intelligence during the remainder of the cycle in question.[15] They will need to be restimulated in a later cycle in order to continue their own further evolutionary progress.

It is perhaps also worth adding here the firm statement by the Adepts that

> peace is not the goal for our race or time, no matter what many men think. This is a cycle of steadily growing activity, with the aim in view of establishing right human relations, intelligently carried forward. Such activity and intense change is not consonant with what is usually understood as peace.[16]

That itself coincides with the biblical idea found in Revelations that the avataric "Rider on the White Horse" comes armed not with peace but "with a sword."

By virtue of international financial crashes arising out of modern "democratic" ideals of a high "quality of life," financial selfishness has by now widely come to be seen (at least in the more intelligent Western mind) as the unacceptable cause of all sorts of other basic problems in the world. However, in India, China, and Africa in particular—containing two-thirds of the world's population in a state of economic deprivation—this experience still has to be learned among the masses. But as their own internal economic development is necessary in order to generate a democratic stability, which will itself destroy the deeply embedded but now well out-of-date religious or other belief systems found there (e.g., the Hindu caste system), the one will logically have to follow the other over the next two thousand years or so. However, the Occidental world has itself a further major behavioral concern to relearn from the maternal Orient, involving the principle of caring and sharing inherent in its family traditions.

THE IMMEDIATE CRISIS
FACING ORTHODOX RELIGION

Where religion itself is concerned, major changes are already well under way. Christianity is already at a second major crossroads (the Reformation having been the first) by virtue of two things. First of all, Protestantism has temporarily lost its way in its pursuit of a "democracy" that has nothing whatsoever to do with spirituality. This has resulted in arguments over priestly homosexuality and the ordination of women priests while, despite the efforts of ecumenists, much vitality has been wasted in paying attention to completely superficial forms of so-called charismatic worship, which actually need to be shown as entirely superficial and self-centered in nature. Expansive evangelical (e.g., "Pentecostal") Christianity is, in fact, far more interested in the worldly returns supposedly to be provided by the Holy Spirit, in response to the overexuberant style of its invocative "worship," and associated commercial marketing, than it is in the development of quietly reflective pursuit of real Christian ethics and spiritual principles.

Roman Catholicism, with its foundations in secretive politics and banking commerce, plus its promotion across the world of objective educational ignorance in favor of blind faith, needs to "open up" generally. It has otherwise only recently suffered a major setback in relation to priestly sexual interference with children, from which it will never recover lost trust. Zionistic Judaism, with its essential separateness from all other religions and its consequently perennial paranoia about persecution, needs to move toward the liberal Jewish identity found in the West, and thus forget its spiritual self-isolation.

Islam, while appearing to be a growth religion (largely because of fascination with personal involvement in its forms of devotional ritual) is already in the very first throes of its own Reformation. Its insistence upon inconsistent Sharia law and suppression of women, its lack of internal discipline allowing constant infighting between Shias and Sunnis, plus widespread support of so-called jihadism supported by Gulf state finance (notwithstanding the foolish short-sightedness of American foreign policy), have all given it a widespread mantle of mistrust. It would not be too far-fetched to conceive of a Moslem equivalent of Martin Luther appearing (on behalf of the Spiritual

Hierarchy) during the next century to trigger major changes in Islamic belief and custom.

In the Far East, Hinduism will, through ever more widespread commercial force majeure, move progressively away from the caste system that has bound it in shackles for so many millennia. One can see this already beginning in and around the main cities all over the country, as "untouchables" are increasingly seen to possess useful commercial instincts. Furthermore, the spread of modern education (particularly where science is concerned) will slowly but progressively give rise to a general mistrust of the false "magic and miracles" of the exoteric yogi fraternity that still characterizes Indian culture today.

Even Buddhism now faces the need for a subjective adjustment, which must take into account the factor of worldwide business interplay. This will involve retention of its central principle of harmlessness to all, paradoxically in coordination with a major development of economic growth and intellectual (rather than devotional) stimulation. It is small wonder (particularly in view of direct Chinese influence in Tibet) that, though there has been for so long a tradition, the present Dalai Lama will be the last one. Although regarded by many as a religious and humanitarian disaster, in the longer term and from the wider viewpoint of the future of humankind in the mass, this may actually prove beneficial. Old-style Buddhism has quite self-evidently had its day and, other things considered, it seems not improbable that another form (and yet higher quality) of the Divine Avatar of Enlightenment will instead become the focus of attention and concern in the not-too-distant future.

THE PROBLEM OF "GOD"

It follows from everything already said that, if a new view of Divinity is to become universally accepted throughout the world, the problem of a "God" that is personal to some, impersonal to others, transcendent to some, and immanent to others, must be finally sorted out. Bearing in mind that the three "Religions of the Book"—Judaism, Christianity, and Islam—all take their standpoint on the foundation provided by Hebrew biblical tradition (itself founded on distorted earlier sacred traditions), we can make a start by understanding where and why these actually differ without actually understanding why.

Perhaps the most concise answer to the problem is given by Gershom Scholem in his book *The Messianic Idea in Judaism*. Here he tells us that the fundamental difference between Alexandrian gnostic philosophy and rabbinical Judaism was that "the impersonal First Cause"—which supposedly gave rise to the creative Demiurge—is (at least as regarded by Judaism) "not the concern of religion at all, for it has nothing to do with the affairs of this world or its creation and exerts no influence on it for good or bad."[17] Scholem then goes on rather remarkably to castigate several historical Jewish philosophers (such as the famous Maimonides) as misleading subsequent Jewish thought for centuries past in this very respect.[18]

Now both Christianity and Islam hold firmly to the idea of the "First Cause" as synonymous with the "One God" who is supposedly the "Creator of All," whereas ancient philosophy (even long before the Alexandrian gnostics) saw this as fundamentally illogical. To the latter, that which created a world or universe in which imperfections and evils of all sorts were self-evidently rampant could not be either perfect or ultimately "Good." Therefore, that aspect of Divinity that was only partial in its nature was also logically imperfect. Hence, the insistence by Judaic theology that its God was the sole Creator persuaded the Alexandrian gnostics—who had already otherwise completely misinterpreted its function—to regard it as evil.

The other curiosity—if Scholem is correct in otherwise stating that Judaism acknowledges "The Hidden Principle" or "First Cause"—is that Judaism is commonly regarded as monotheistic. The fact that it believes in only one god—that is, the tribal "God of Israel"—does not actually render it monotheistic in the commonly accepted sense adopted by Christians and Moslems, or otherwise by general public interpretation and acknowledgment. This should be much more widely appreciated.

If by reference to Plato (and the later gnostics) we acknowledge the existence of both "the Good" (i.e., the "Causeless First Cause") on the one hand and the creative Demiurge on the other, the latter as the primordial emanation of the former, there is no fundamental problem—except for those bent on devotional worship of a supposedly ultimate Deity. However, if we acknowledge the "Causeless First Cause" merely as a state (or the primary state) within a Universal Organism, of which we can have no faint conception, the problem is rather nearer resolution. From the viewpoint of esoteric philosophy we can say with conviction that Scholem's suggestion that the Causeless Cause "exerts no influence on the world for good or bad" is sheer nonsense. It may not do so directly. However, the Demiurge (the "God of Israel") is itself permanently dependent on the "First Cause" for the continuity of its very existence. This is quite apart from the fact that constant cyclical emanations of a celestial nature necessarily emanate from it and bring themselves to bear on the lesser entity, thereby forcing it to create or modify its creations on an ever-constant basis.

In short, modern orthodox Judaism does not understand its own Deity, while both Christianity and Islam have a complete misconception about theirs as well, each supposedly in its own favor. This altogether ludicrous situation, however, forms the very basis of all Western and much Middle-Eastern religious belief, both of which are essentially self-blinded in nature, through their own philosophical ignorance.

Having said all this, it would be frankly absurd to imagine that the forthcoming New Age is suddenly going to see the end of all devotion to a Deity. Those of a naturally humanistic tendency and those with the benefit of esoteric training will undoubtedly do so on the basis of understanding that an infinitude of celestial hierarchies of greater and greater Intelligence does not constitute an ultimate God figure. However, the vast majority of the world's population will not fit into either of these categories and will therefore seek a continuing focus for their religious observances, certainly still orientated toward a "personal" God.

With that in mind, it seems that the Spiritual Hierarchy might perhaps be quite willing to accept that the Planetary Logos should be regarded by the masses as fitting the role. This would explain why we find the Adept DK, in Bailey's works, constantly using the term "God" in this same sense when it had previously been made clear by both Blavatsky and the Chohans Morya and Kuthumi that the personal "God" concept was totally foreign to their way of thought and their own experience. The fact that many modern theosophists strongly object to the use of the term or concept of "God"—particularly when used in a personal religious sense—is neither here nor there. Neither does it constitute a proof that the esoteric philosophy contained in the Bailey works should automatically be considered suspect because of it. We have to accept the fact that not all our humanity moves forward at the same speed, or in precisely the same way. Therefore, it is up to those with a greater vision to show to others a rather more considerate and broadminded approach on this particular issue, so long as this causes no wider distortions.

One final thing to be taken into consideration here is the issue of anti-Semitism, or to be more precise, anti-Judaism, because the Jews are by no means the only Semites. This problem too must be dealt with before the Mysteries and any new world religion come happily into being. However, the issue needs to be properly understood, for it did not originate, as many seem to think, with the idea of deicide—that the Jews were responsible for killing the Avatar of the Christians, who is also bizarrely equated by the latter as their own God manifest. In fact, it seems to have started with the Jews/Hebrews themselves misinterpreting the ancient sacred philosophy (concerning divine mankind in general) and thereby coming to regard themselves as the "Chosen People," sacredly distinct from all others. One can safely suggest that this attitude would hardly have been likely to ingratiate them with anybody else.

However, when also taking the standpoint that their God (Jahve-Elohim) was effectively the creative Demiurge, it gave the less intelligent of the Alexandrian gnostics the perfect opportunity to label them effectively as self-confessed "children of a devilish deity." This plus the charge of deicide would then have been seen by early Christians, trying to set up their own religion but having as yet little or no supporting theology of their own, as perfect ammunition to downgrade the Jews and thereby hoist themselves upward in the divine scale. This tripartite historical foolishness needs to be openly recognized and come to terms with by all sides concerned. Otherwise the present political nonsense and bloodshed in Palestine and Israel will continue with eventually really dire results, because the rest of the world has lost patience.

The blind belief inherent in all orthodox (i.e., purely devotional) religion must thus come to an end, and it is here that the general adoption of science (or rather, of scientifically and esoterically orientated philosophy) must inevitably play a major, reconstructive part, although not in an atheistic sense. It will do so by confirming in ever-increasing detail that the universe is guided and maintained by an intelligently disciplined order, which necessitates the existence of moderation and sharing in all areas of life. It will also confirm the existence of a universal spectrum of Divine Intelligence quite distinct from the presumed Deity of theologians and the "gods" of untutored native belief. This progress is already well under way because mainstream science itself is at a point where it cannot resolve its many current paradoxes with merely materialistic reasoning. Similarly, the merely devotional approach of orthodox religion is already seen to be widely in denial of straightforward reason, while positive ecumenism is simultaneously on the rise.

Finally, in relation to ancestor worship—which is an Atlantean form of religion still practiced in native communities throughout Central and South America, Africa, China, and parts of Southeast Asia—we can reasonably suggest that, with a scientific approach, this too will die out gradually by mere attrition. Although associated with modern spiritualism, it has no philosophical or theological basis capable of standing on its own. At the same time, worship of other human beings (whether dead or alive)—particularly for reasons of supposedly continuing financial support—is no longer considered culturally acceptable.

WHAT FORMS WOULD THE FUTURE MYSTERIES TAKE?

In endeavoring to answer this question, we need first of all to ask what the ancient Mysteries were intended to achieve and whether this, resuscitated, would be appropriate in the modern era. Therefore, the first observation we can make is that the ancient Mysteries existed in a social environment quite different from our own with its immediately worldwide, media-driven capacities. The ancient outer Mysteries did not involve monotheism—devotion to a single God—simply because such a transcendent Deity would have been beyond all experience and imagination as far as the masses were concerned. Instead, on their behalf, various forms of ritualized devotional obeisance to "the gods" as a whole were devised, these rituals being orientated toward the varied phenomenal expression (as Universal Nature) of what was recognized by true initiates as the Unknowable Deity. In so doing, the masses were able to experience—through sacred metaphor and allegory used in ritual—a partial but personal, local involvement of a semi-spiritual nature, shared in common with their peers, thereby maintaining and regulating the coherence of their society.

That does not mean to say, however, that ancient religion ceased at this point. The more spiritually prescient or sensitive members of such societies were always encouraged to pursue a more direct involvement with less obvious aspects of Deity. Hence there arose the development of progressively more subtle forms of ritual and ascetic practice (including meditation) to stir the more spiritually subtle inner nature of the individual. This then is the whole basis of progressive initiatory practice in the Mysteries, a far cry from the blind belief attributed to ancient society by modern academic scholarship.

In a very real sense, the ancient orientation between the Spiritual Hierarchy and the masses of humankind involved the former sending out its disciples and agents (like Pythagoras and Plato) to stir and raise the consciousness of localized individuals in their own study groups or ashrams. However, that looks to be quite different to what is now evidently being considered. The orientation of effort is now to utilize those same groups—trained over previous incarnations—to act as coworkers in generating the invocative network needed to draw down higher (i.e., celestial) soul influences and anchor them permanently on Earth.[19] If one considers the analogical parallel of using many interconnected astronomical satellite dishes scattered over a large surface area to draw down and focus major celestial radio or other waves, the underlying idea will perhaps become more self-apparent. It is for this reason that the present reapproach by the Adept Hierarchy also lays such emphasis on group effort.

The second thing that we need to bear in mind is that there has never been a time when humankind in general was entirely on its own in a Darwinian sense, so to speak, in terms of lacking intelligent parental or pastoral care "from above." In the first place, so we are told, leaders—divine kings and priests—were provided by the Guides of our planetary Life from their own ranks.[20] Only much later, as our humanity began to progress creatively on the Path, were a few human individuals, here and there, allowed to participate in that leadership. Such participation inevitably expanded as time went on until eventually the Guides withdrew entirely into the background.

Then, as with our own human teenagers, almost the whole responsibility for such autonomous leadership and social management was passed over to humanity to test its powers of self-control and responsibility. The Guides meanwhile remained silently in the background, dealing with wider interplanetary affairs, yet ready to take action if any situation became seriously threatening or out of control. That is roughly where we stand today.

We otherwise need to bear in mind that the current aim of the Adept Hierarchy, as already explained, is to take humankind's general evolutionary development an important stage further. This will involve modern humankind's full emergence onto the Path at the stage of "accepted discipleship," details of which we considered in chapters 8 and 9. In some cultures this will inevitably prove far more difficult than in others. While comparisons are generally odious, let us by way of example consider some of those countries historically influenced by Spain and the Catholic Church—such as the Philippines and parts of Central and South America. Here the practice of Roman Catholic ritual is still strongly, even morbidly, orientated toward fascination with blood sacrifice. In most of western Europe, this is viewed with distaste and there is far greater, natural orientation toward the concept of resurrection and transcendence of death, although Christian priesthoods in general still seem rather apathetic in pursuing it more effectively.

Correspondingly, in Islam, there is such widespread dependence on the concept of "If Allah wills it" that psychological inertia is the main problem. In Hinduism, the caste system, plus an equally apathetic view of karma, still exerts the most powerful influence in inhibiting creative self-expression. However, this is just beginning to show definite signs of change as a result of the widespread arising of a creative business sense in all classes. This will destroy the caste system faster than any merely religious or legal form of insistence.

A yet further point of consideration is that human beings differ widely in their capacities for and qualities of spiritual response. In chapter 5, we saw that there are ten different stages of development of human intelligence apparent in the world today. Notwithstanding this, human society throughout the world is organized and run these days by the upper and lower middle classes, largely involving what we might call "the commercial intelligentsia," or professional and merchant classes. Not surprisingly therefore, the main orientation of human society tends to be toward financial comfort, with spiritual (i.e., religious) issues usually taking a second place. This is not quite the same in Islam, however, that fact being one of the main sources of contention between its followers and the world of Christianity.

The vast majority of humanity is so concerned with merely making a reasonable living in the face of generally quite intense market competition, or otherwise in the face of sheer environmental depredation, that spiritual concerns inevitably tend to become secondary. This has changed dramatically over the millennia. Originally, all surplus wealth was held in trust for society in general by the leaders of the temple and distributed accordingly as need required. There was no profiteering and, consequently, there was no need for theft. The latter has only developed as the leaders of human society developed personal political ambitions, necessitating their ability to maintain their followers by mercenary handouts of one sort or another. This in turn has produced its own range of also mercenary subcultures and psychologies.

As human society expanded and developed ever greater complexity, intercommunity trading inevitably expanded, thereby putting individualized wealth into the hands of the few. That in turn gave rise to the practice of material self-indulgence, with large houses (or palaces), retinues of servants, and the practice of self-centered political influence, which inevitably became interactively combative in nature. That in further turn gave rise to tribalism and, again inevitably, tribalism gave rise to the desire for personalized aspects of Deity and the sense of needing to subordinate other tribes to the same psychological orientations. Taken to the extreme of further development in historical terms, it is small wonder that human society today is so generally self-centered. Yet, peculiarly, this has also led to an internationalization of interest by the more intelligent in other cultures and the way they are run and have historically developed.

It is logical to assume that the future Mysteries—as with the ancient ones—will take a threefold form. That is to say, the lowest and most general form will involve universal practice by the whole community in every land and will thus take the form of a common, because universal, religion. This would perhaps, in some respects, be not unlike the Eleusynian Mysteries in Greece or the Rites of Osiris and Isis in Egypt, thereby involving an "ecological" orientation, concerned with involving the other kingdoms of Nature, as well as the human—although not possessing a wholly devotional approach as such. It would otherwise also involve baptismal and later confirmatory rituals acknowledging the point of spiritual development of the individual.

However, because of the eventually exoteric recognition of Shamballa and the Spiritual Hierarchy (rather than that of an unknown and purely theoretical "God"), it is suggested that the orientation of these progressive recognitions or acknowledgments would in fact be much more akin to the ritualistic approach of the Craft degrees in Freemasonry.[21] It follows almost without stating the obvious that this would involve major change from the style of the present, almost completely corrupted Masonic system. It would necessarily change into one involving processes of ritual invocation and evocation, which would themselves take the place of worship and prayer.[22] The first initiation in these revised Mysteries (equivalent to that of the Masonic "Entered Apprentice") would then logically form the common basis or ritualistic aim of the new world religion.[23] This is by virtue of the fact that humanity in the main would by then be regarded as firmly "on the Path" and thus to be seen as "accepted disciples" in the sense described earlier, in chapter 8.

Although the suggestion is entirely speculative, the two higher stages of the Mysteries (parallel to the Orphic Mysteries of Greece) would logically involve the second and third initiations. How soon these would become a more overt part of the new world religion is debatable. However, the highest (parallel to the Dionysian Mysteries of Greece), involving the fourth, fifth, and sixth initiations, would undoubtedly remain within the framework of the Inner Mysteries and thus well outside the immediate framework of the new world religion. The whole essence of world "religious" practice would in this sequentially organized manner again turn firmly in the direction of preparation for actual spiritual change in line with that evolutionary Purpose defined by the Higher Path.

RACE DIFFERENTIATION AND INTERNATIONAL COMMERCE

It was mentioned earlier on that the Occidental and Oriental natures are quite different and it would thus be quite fair to ask how that might itself make the emergence of a common Mystery tradition possible. We are told, however, that the Hierarchy of the Trans-Himalayan Adept Lodge attaches so much importance to the spiritual stimulation of humanity as a whole that one of its Adepts previously known as Confucius will incarnate in order to superintend the work as it affects those leading Egos of the Fourth Race,[24] the peak of this intended effort supposedly being in the middle of the twenty-first century.[25]

With that in mind, one can already see, within the past decade, a sudden and very marked acceleration of business-related development in Brazil and China in particular, and now India too, the latter two providing between them over one third of the world's total population. This acceleration will inevitably continue with the resultant emergence, over the next century or two, of a worldwide economy based on new principles, which will outstrip the present one by a huge extent and will just as inevitably bring the Oriental and Occidental races much closer together. As also mentioned earlier on, successful business necessitates trust, and trust forms the basis of all relationships in Nature.

One of the related effects of this will be to demonstrate that corporate internationalism will form one of the most important aspects of the world of the future—although very different in nature from the present, merely profit-orientated system with which we are so familiar. Nationalism (itself a rather more extended form of tribalism) will be increasingly seen as incapable of providing by itself an adequate politico-socio-economic base for human intercourse in general. This is already widely evident, many of the larger international corporations having a financial base of far greater strength and influence than many minor countries. The sense of internationalism and "family" generated by working within such organizations is itself what will gradually destroy all remaining sense of tribalism in human nature.

A vocational, socially concerned attitude and a much more professionally trained approach toward a business career will necessarily become prevalent, as also an accompanying international rule of law, which today is only manifest as a seed of what it must someday become. It is already apparent, and will necessarily become generally self-evident within the next two generations, that such a generally reliable, international legal framework is essential to maintain social as well as economic order throughout the world.

EFFECTS OF EXTERNALIZATION OF
SENIOR MEMBERS OF THE HIERARCHY

One might perhaps ask why it should be so important for even senior members of the Adept Hierarchy to incarnate and externalize, as apparently intended, and how this would be related to the Mysteries. Although we are not yet provided with any sort of detail, one might perhaps draw a speculative parallel from the world of physics, bearing in mind that our occult concerns involve the greater world of energies and forces, including the spiritual ones. So, bearing in mind that the seventh degree of the Adept Hierarchy in a sense represents the union of personal consciousness with the demiurgic Ring-Pass-Not of our planetary Life, we may reasonably suggest that their aim is to extend their field of influence beyond that, as a group on the Higher Way—something that must necessarily affect humanity too. Therefore, we may also infer that their physical incarnations and active existence in working with lesser initiates will put a terrific torsion (i.e., a compressed tension, like that of a coiled spring) into the whole field of world consciousness. That in turn will affect all the other kingdoms of Nature.

The associated intention is clearly to unite the consciousness of humankind much more closely with their own—which is itself already connected to Shamballa—for two reasons. First of all, as mentioned a little earlier, the prototypal fifth kingdom in Nature consciousness will begin to appear within the very next zodiacal era and it will need to be protected and encouraged in its development. Secondly, when the most senior Adepts decide that their own immediate work is done, their eventually final departure from Earth life will generate an immense expansion of consciousness of humanity as a whole, far beyond its natural limits at present. At the same time, it is inferred, Shamballa will correspondingly transfer its own existence to a yet higher state than that in which it is currently located. That will naturally also affect all the other kingdoms of Nature as well, thereby bringing about an almost unimaginable range of fundamental change.

In brief, and as already suggested, what is now already in process would seem to involve the eventual "Judgment Day" of our Fifth Race cycle within the course of the next two millennia or so. That itself will trigger the next planetary "Round," hundreds of thousands (if not millions) of years hence, involving the appearance of completely new types of form in all kingdoms of Nature. As well as this, it will (much later) enable many of today's domesticated and other advanced animal species to make the eventual leap of consciousness necessary to attain the primitively early human state, which our own humanity achieved in ancient Lemurian times.

Although many modern commentators in academia and the media conceive of the New Age fascination with mysticism, esotericism, and the occult merely as a historical phenomenon that has arisen in the light of failed orthodox religion, it can now be seen that the underlying reality extends far further. The sheer extent of associated numbers of lesser initiates today, right across the globe, tells us rather more. Whereas until the nineteenth century the numbers showing such interest were few and far between, they now exist literally in the millions, even if general esoteric understanding still remains publicly somewhat limited.

As a consequence of this, the Adept Hierarchy realized that the old and accepted style of teaching—privately in an ashram or, before that, in the caverns and rooms of the Mysteries—just could not accommodate such numbers. Consequently, spearheaded by major advances in public education and literacy in the West, it was evidently decided to open up the teachings on a grandly open scale, to see if self-education in esotericism and occult science could be achieved through book learning, allied to explanations given out more occasionally by advanced initiates.

It is to this end, essentially, that the works of Blavatsky and Bailey in particular have self-evidently been aimed by the Spiritual Hierarchy. Just as Blavatsky brought explanatory innovation with the concept that karma and reincarnation were essentially interlinked, so Bailey brought forth the illuminative teaching as to the Seven Rays, which condition the evolutionary purpose and development of humankind in general. The next stages will evidently involve a logical further progression, involving the mere mystic idealisms of the past giving way to the firm spiritual perceptions of the future.

There is no intention here to go into any further attempted detail concerning the prospective format and structure of the new world religion or the revived Mysteries that will form an intrinsic attachment to it. Much other information has already been provided in Bailey's works with such clarity that any further comment by this author at this present stage would be altogether superfluous. The intention here, so far, has been merely to provide a range of explanatory suggestions concerning the logic of what must happen next in our human world culture over the next few centuries, as a matter of natural progression. That progression will involve the "bringing down to earth" of spiritual knowledge and higher influences upon all in practical ways, rather than the attempted raising of consciousness to spiritual levels pursued by the few over so many past millennia. With that specifically in mind, it is important to understand that information concerning the Mysteries has to be considered in conjunction with the issue of world education in the New Age. This has been neglected in relation to the masses over thousands of years and that must change.

THE VITAL SIGNIFICANCE OF MASS EDUCATION

The separation of education from the original Mysteries, which has taken place over the last two thousand years or so, has from one angle been irrational, despite its usefulness in developing a real and perhaps more focused sense of greater human potential. During that time, it has involved concentration on developing the faculty of logically organized memory above all else. However, as observed in chapter 5, intellectual memory and its organization involve using merely the lowest two subplanes of matter of the mental plane. The third involves the analytic or discriminatively logical function, which enables the individual actually to think with any degree of rational coherence, while the fourth—that of the integrated personality—involves creative coordination of all the lower three, with real and considered thought.

A salutary example of the effects of misusing the mind function in religion is to be seen in the products of the Islamist mudrassahs. These misguided schools of extremism teach the memorization of nothing but the Qur'an—and even this in purely parrot fashion, without any attempt to consider or question the meaning of the verses in any breadth or depth (often without the young individual even understanding the associated Arabic). Consequently, the minds of those "schooled" in this way have no even basic cultural depth or breadth of perspective with which to face the world. Small wonder that fatalism and blind religious extremism are the result. But the same problem is to be found resulting from an overliteralistic approach to the Jewish Torah and the Christian Bible, the latter particularly in America, where it breeds just the same superficiality and extremism. In fact, so we are told, the whole problem of modern "fundamentalist" schools of thought—in religious, political, and even scientific environments—is due to psychically sensitive Sixth Ray devotees misusing early incoming Seventh Ray energies of which they are not even aware.[26] This influence will naturally pass and we must therefore be patient, while not allowing it to take further root.

The Mysteries, however, are concerned with spiritual orientation and thus with sensitivity to the influences of the higher mental subplanes, plus the buddhic state—that of the kosmic etheric double of the Logos, the importance of which has already been mentioned. Consequently, as reliable walls are only built on reliably strong foundations, the new approach to public education must necessarily involve a recognition of the fact that it is essentially subsidiary to the Mysteries and not just there for maximizing career intentions, as at present. Then, with the personality imbued with the understanding of its own self-discipline under the Spiritual Ego, the development of the higher mental path of consciousness (that of the antahkarana) will become far more straightforward than it is today.[27]

However, it is equally important to recognize that intellectual development should not be rushed. The average child is involved in a thoroughly natural sequence of astral/feeling development during the first fourteen years of life (between seven to fourteen in particular), when its senses of mystery and inner, imaginative creativity are at their most sensitive and where emotional balance, consistency, and order are developed. These are all of immense importance in the individual's overall range of developed faculty. It follows quite logically that real intellectual stimulation should not be attempted before the age of seventeen, nor real spiritual stimulation (via Higher Education) before the age of twenty-one. Similarly, no introduction to practical involvement in the Inner Mysteries should be considered before the twenty-eighth year. The latter is itself a really crucial age in the integrated relationship between the Spiritual Ego and its human expression. Having said all this, however, it must be acknowledged that there will always be a few unusual exceptions to the general rule.

It naturally follows from what has just been described in very general terms that New Age society (throughout the psychologically "Westernized" world) will itself have to change dramatically over the next few centuries in order to take full advantage of the incoming new spiritual influences on a large scale. However, as the old saying goes, "Many are called, but [relatively] few are actually chosen." The approach to the Mysteries has necessarily to be based upon an increasingly ascetic self-discipline (based, however, on common sense), and there is very little of that currently apparent in modern (especially Western) society.

Nevertheless, there is a huge expansion of idealism apparent in the worldwide younger generations of today (especially where politics is concerned). This—generating greater subjective freedom and creativity—must in turn be for the better in the long term, although in the shorter term it will inevitably result in much social strife through their trying to "kick over the traces." That is particularly so in relation to those who merely indulge in wealth and also those governmental political structures where the so-called "ruling classes" are corruptly self-concerned to maintain their own socioeconomic positions at the literal expense of the masses. In that respect we live in interestingly turbulent times of very real psychological and social crisis, which seem likely to continue for many generations yet to come.

ACTUAL REINTRODUCTION
OF THE MYSTERIES

The final point we have to deal with here involves the question "When will the Mysteries be reintroduced?" The answer, as given to us, is not precise, although we are told that later in this twenty-first century:

When the Seventh Ray has achieved complete manifestation and the Piscean influence is completely removed, the Seventh Ray Avatar will appear [and that] He will be largely instrumental in producing those conditions which will permit of the reappearance upon Earth of the Mysteries of Initiation, of which the Hierarchy is the custodian.[28]

To this we find added: "The work done during the next two centuries in the field of education is definitely temporary and balancing, and that out of the fulfillment of the task assigned to education will grow those more permanent systems which, in the new age, will be found flourishing everywhere."[29]

These comments were given out well over half a century ago, during the 1940s, but we can already see their practical development as more than mere theory. In addition, the implicit but fairly clear suggestion in all this is that, because of the time needed to clear up the worldwide political, religious, and socioeconomic mess in our present civilization, and also because of the aggressively retentive nature of the Sixth Ray influence, the Mysteries are unlikely to become in any degree seriously objective until at least the second half of the twenty-second century CE. That, however, involves a matter of only seven to eight generations from now, which means that a few of the grandchildren (if not also some of the children) of today's own youth may live to see the dawn of this great era unfold. However, one final complementary quote from the Masters needs to be borne in mind in conclusively answering this question:

> The Schools of the Mysteries . . . will come into being and practice; but this will be temporarily a secondary activity; the full expression of ashramic activity will be directed to practical world affairs, to the education of the general public, and not in the early stages to esoteric matters.[30]

Despite this, we are otherwise told that schools of esotericism will progressively be set up in the following areas:

Preparatory Grades, leading to . . . Advanced Schools	
1 Greece or Syria	Egypt
2 Midwest, USA	California
3 Southern France	Italy
4 Scotland or Wales	Ireland
5 Sweden	Russia
6 New Zealand	Australia[31]

Not altogether surprisingly, in conformity with occult principles, a seventh school is also intended, the preparatory part of which will be in Japan while the advanced part will be in western China, both of these being under the watchful supervisory eye of the Manu of the Fourth Race[32] (and his counterpart on the Teaching Ray). Perhaps surprisingly to some, it seems that no such schools are intended in either South America or southern Africa, these apparently being intended to follow at a much later date.[33] That is because the predominant (tribal) consciousness of the native peoples in either instance is quite different from that of the Western mind. Similarly, no such school is apparently intended for India, despite its immense historic background of learning in the fields of esotericism and occultism. This might at first seem highly illogical. However, the deep-rooted pride and intellectual inertia of the Brahmin tradition, regarding itself as the epitome of possible knowledge in these fields, plus the social intractability of the caste system, would probably render abortive all attempts at sowing any new thought there for some time yet. The ruthlessly self-concerned manner in which Buddhism (both exoteric and esoteric) was historically driven out of India by the Brahmins two thousand years ago might otherwise be partly responsible for this deliberate omission as well. However, the underlying instinct of so many of the peoples of India toward magic in all aspects of life would also make it potentially very dangerous indeed—and thus impossible for practical consideration for some time to come.

There will undoubtedly be those shallow or spiritually lazy commentators who will see in all this little but supposedly arbitrary wishful thinking. For them all truly radical forward thinking is based upon elitism, favoritism, and lack of egalitarian consideration. Yet it is quite logical that the students of these various schools—based on those Ray affiliations described in earlier chapters—will come from widely different ethnic groups all over the world, as they already do at university level today, to deal with particular academic subjects. However, in answer to these critics, one can probably do no better than provide the following Adept quote, which sweeps away all of the usual blind modern sentimentalism about true concern for human development in the round:

Search for the Path to Manhood both within and without yourself. It lies within, for within your nature all men and all things exist. It lies without, for the Life that is yours is the Life of the world also. It is within all things, but it cannot be found in any one thing alone, for each thing is a part of every other. You will seek it in many things and in many ways, and in all things and all ways united; but not until you and all become one will you find the Way to Manhood.[34]

EPILOGUE

A forthright statement by the Master Adept (now Chohan) Kuthumi provides us with two central descriptions as to what the work of the Spiritual Hierarchy of Adepts is apparently all about:

> Plato was right. Ideas rule the world; and, as men's minds will receive new ideas, laying aside the old and effete, the world will advance. Mighty revolutions will spring from them; creeds and even powers will crumble before their onward march, crushed by the irresistible force. It will be just as impossible to resist their influx, when the time comes, as to stay the progress of the tide. But all this will come gradually on and before it comes, we have a duty set before us; that of sweeping away as much as possible the dross left to us by our pious forefathers. New ideas have to be planted on clean places, for these ideas touch upon the most momentous subjects. It is not physical phenomena but these universal ideas that we study. . . . They touch man's true position in the universe in relation to his previous and future births; his origin and ultimate destiny; the relation of the mortal to the immortal; of the temporary to the eternal; of the finite to the infinite; ideas larger, grander, more comprehensive, recognising the reign of Immutable Law, unchanging and unchangeable, in regard to which there is only an ETERNAL NOW, while to uninitiated mortals time is past or future as related to their finite existence on this material speck of dirt. This is what we study and what many have solved.[1]

Taking into consideration that idea-forms are themselves groups of elemental entities, historically generated and conditioned by humankind's own subjective nature in response to long past spiritual innovation, it first of all involves the destruction and sweeping away of those same ideas when they are no longer of continuing use to humankind's future evolution. Secondly, it involves the study and wisely discriminating assimilation of those future spiritual influences, emanating literally from the Mind of the Solar Logos via the Planetary Spirits (Dhyani Buddhas and Dhyan Chohans), which will be of definite use to future generations of humanity. These two aspects of their work should be sufficient to demonstrate to us that the nature of the true Adept consciousness is far and away beyond that of the purely human, despite many of them retaining human bodies specifically in order to maintain adequate continuity of contact with humanity in general. The "New Age" views of the Adept Hierarchy as a group of merely spiritualized human beings to be worshipped from afar, or as otherwise completely absorbed (i.e., "ascended") into Universal Consciousness, are so far from practical reality that they are merely absurd.

As otherwise also mentioned, the main point behind the public resurgence of the sacred wisdom tradition was to introduce humankind in general to a new perspective in relation to Divinity itself. Through the work of humanism over the last several centuries (and even of its predecessors in Greek times) plus that of modern science, it has become increasingly obvious that the old religio-mystic idea of God has served its usefulness, that it now serves largely to divide rather than to unite, and that, despite the widening ecumenical movement, it no longer suffices to satisfy all human spiritual need. The "new" perspective revealed by nineteenth and twentieth century theosophy (supported by ancient tradition) has demonstrated why and how the "God" of the main religions is merely a demiurgic hierarchy of divine beings that owes its very existence to the emanations of far superior hierarchies of Intelligence, whose own existence lies on kosmic planes of existence far beyond our own. It has also shown how and why it is that Man in his innermost nature is the very alpha and omega of the universal evolutionary process.

Why should all this have been revealed? We are told that it is because our planetary Life as a whole—itself the vehicle of a divine hierarchy of

beings—has reached the point in its evolutionary progress where a great forward surge of development is naturally imminent. This will thereby bring
about a huge expansion of consciousness in all its kingdoms of Nature, not
just the human. Thus what humankind has been given over the last few centuries is merely a preparation for its accessing and absorption of far greater
celestial knowledge and responsibilities, provided that its improved mental
development is accompanied by emotional stability. To many this will appear
as mere wishful thinking—or a frightening threat. Yet it involves the quite
natural progression of the evolutionary process, viewed as a whole, even if as
yet beyond modern science's perceptions.

Indeed, the very nature and history of esoteric and occult philosophy as
something after all perhaps rational—by virtue of consciousness itself being
recognized as the basis of a science (psychology)—is now being openly considered by academia within university departments of the humanities and
of religion. It is also being increasingly acknowledged by steadily increasing numbers of research scientists, in their published books, as the necessary
"tool" of all metaphysical thought. This is as a direct result of the coherent
literary work of but a few practical researchers of original thought in each
of the past few centuries. The modern "New Age" movement is itself merely
the cloudy response of partial psychic recognition and much attendant wishful thinking that has sprung up around them. The idea that today's "New
Age" thinkers are those who have given rise to this movement is quite wrong.
It follows the equally false assumption that superstition gives rise to myth,
whereas the truth is that real myth is based on clearly formulated spiritual
metaphor and allegory that, through ignorant literalism, has lost its inner,
causal drive and thus degenerated into mere superstition and prejudice. As
Frithjof Schuon comments supportingly in his work *The Transcendent Unity
of Religions:*

> The exoteric viewpoint is in fact doomed to end by negating itself
> once it is no longer vivified by the presence within of the esoterism of
> which it is both the outward radiation and the veil. So it is that religion,
> according to the measure in which it denies metaphysical and initiatory
> realities and becomes crystallised in a literalistic dogmatism, inevitably
> engenders unbelief; the atrophy that overtakes dogmas when they are

deprived of their internal dimension recoils upon them from the outside, in the form of heretical and atheistic negations.[2]

H. P. Blavatsky's stupendous literary work—much if not most of it directly generated by the Adept Hierarchy—was undoubtedly the "engine" that has driven the leading human intelligence of the last century and a half into recognizing that philosophy, science, and religion are (or appear to be) merely aspects of the same field of universal knowledge. Blavatsky's work was thus foundational. The later work of A. A. Bailey, in the early-to-mid twentieth century—although as yet less generally acknowledged—provides the superstructure built (also by the Adept Hierarchy) on those same foundations, in preparation for the real New Age of human thought, of which only a few preceding shadows are as yet clearly apparent. To many this too might sound like complete wishful thinking. Yet careful consideration should logically suggest to us that a completely new and more direct view of Divinity, plus the rational application of esoteric and occult philosophy to the combined fields of philosophy, religion, and science—and even in some respects to all other fields of human life—must inevitably lead in that direction. All that is otherwise necessary involves the progressive giving up of those conflicting ancient thought forms that have been produced in response to the underlying involutionary processes in Nature.

The whole emphasis in this book has been on the proposition that the process of spiritual initiation in relation to humanity merely involves an acceleration of the general evolutionary process from within; that it is normally available only to the few because only the few have the drive and willingness to put up with the very real accompanying hardships. However, it is also because of the persistent work of the few that humanity as a whole has benefited and thus now reached a point where it can take a giant step forward as a complete kingdom of Nature. In relation to the latter we might perhaps draw the parallel of the ugly and destructive caterpillar, which becomes a beautiful butterfly, although one might hardly imagine at the outset that such a radical transformation could be in any way possible.

The view held by some critics that the initiatory process was ever "elitist" misses the point completely. That is because they themselves completely fail to understand what the whole underlying process involves and they thus arrive at superficial judgments purely based on normally self-centered human social standards. This needs to be much more clearly acknowledged and put across to the wider public, together with the concept that the long term will-to-good is much more important than the short term will-to-peace (or rather, the desire-for-peace-and-quiet).

That relates to another proposition this work has striven to highlight—that initiation involves not only progressive expansions of consciousness and spiritual faculty, but also a progressively parallel capacity to access and maintain an equivalent psycho-spiritual tension, with its associated focus. Without this capacity—necessitating really great persistence and psychological (as well as physical) effort—no such initiation (or any other form of forward subjective movement) would be possible; nor would it be possible to assess general human experience in any proper perspective. From this proposition, it then becomes rather more possible to analyze human history in retrospect from a wider angle than historians are generally wont to do. It thus becomes an issue of seeing crisis itself as an inevitably necessary part of the movement to forward change—and as a fundamental part of the transitional cyclic process.

Scientists and historians have yet to acknowledge that such cycles exist or have any material impact upon human society, although many theorists have certainly speculated on the subject in relation to economics. However, as astrology is also now becoming an academically acceptable subject at university level (even though largely based on historical grounds as yet), this too may change in due course of time. The fact that our modern science has already begun to realize from its own research and observation that an underlying order of harmonic (i.e., ecologically balanced) interrelationships is apparent throughout Nature, at all levels, will ultimately render the cyclical issue as unavoidably primary.

Referring back to what was said in the first few chapters about the progressively sequential involutionary–evolutionary–devolutionary process, it should thus also become obvious to us that our humanity is increasingly more closely approaching the inevitable "Day of Judgment" of the greater current cycle. The evolutionary consciousness phase necessarily involves a progressive synthesizing of past human knowledge and experience. The involutionary cycle of persistent fragmentation and differentiation is thus at or very closely nearing its end. The "Aristotelian" reductive approach, using purely objective classifications to arrive at inner perceptions, is increasingly being seen as leading us down a path to nowhere.

Having said this, nothing in the way of change in Nature moves very fast. It only appears to do so when it reaches a climax of progressively acquired tension. Our present era certainly contains and expresses a huge amount of psychological tension (globally considered) by reference to previous political history. Before the twentieth century, such tension could only be considered on a locally international basis, at best, as one leading only to unwelcome sociopolitical frictions. However, the present era—which will certainly continue for the next century and a half at least—is actually one of tremendous opportunity, if taken in the right spirit. The great problem for the Adept Hierarchy and the Guides of our world is clearly to ensure that the tension can be maintained productively, leading to a general public recognition that the new perspective is inevitable and, in any case, much more inherently attractive than the one just past, from which we are currently in the process of emerging.

That such an effort naturally involves great challenges, when considered in instinctively racial and nationalistic terms, is obvious. That is why the international mixing of racial identities and cultures—a purely external phenomenon—is so important. Just as important, however, is the increasingly general recognition (also among scientists) of a universality of existence in greater Nature, in which we are all ecologically interdependent facilitators, irrespective of genus, race, creed, gender, or color. It is not a question of losing identity. It is a question of sharing it by inner recognition of the same inner values being superficially obscured by outer forms. The great instinctive fear on many parts is that of losing something that has taken centuries or even millennia to develop. Yet, just as human marriage necessitates a yielding up of some established individualism, to develop an ideal of far greater family potential, so the family of individual human races and nations must be prepared to consider doing the same thing, yet on a far greater scale than hitherto.

Even if we do not realize it, our objective planetary world is a very localized venue or "school of life." That which lies beyond it—the psychospiritual world—is of staggeringly greater perspective and potentiality. Yet, because our instinctive association is almost entirely within the framework of consciousness of the objective world, we are blind to the character of what lies beyond (or rather, parallel to) it. This is the great paradox. Only by a progressive experiencing of the fragmented limitations of the objective world can our inner, more expansive spiritual nature progressively learn to reject them. By so doing so it must thus insist upon the outer being replaced by the more inclusive (because interdisciplinary) spiritual principles of which we are increasingly aware, even if we cannot as yet perceive their full detail.

Because our sense of association is naturally that of a very brief single lifetime (in which the sense of a reincarnating continuity is as yet indifferently present), we also fail to perceive the longer cycle of experience of our Higher Soul-Self. Yet it is the latter recognition that the whole process of expansive spiritual education by the Adept Hierarchy is trying to encourage. However, as in any school, it is up to us how much attention we individually pay and how much general effort we are individually prepared to put in to changing ourselves by acknowledging our own previous limitations of effort.

In addition to developing a general participatory "school" sense along with all others, it is of tremendous help to us individually to understand (in all silent modesty) at what level or in which class of the "school" we personally stand. This must include an understanding of conditioning Ray influences. That, however, can only be done by adopting (or at least exploring) the wider metaphysical and hermeneutic perspective that the philosophy of the modern worldwide theosophical movement presents. In that way we will come to see that there also exists in life's greater field a "junior school," a "senior school," and a "university"—and that it is the latter toward which our inner strivings are ultimately taking us all, if we so will it.

PLANETARY CHAINS AND ROUNDS

One of the most interestingly new and intellectually challenging concepts introduced by the Adept Hierarchy and later detailed by Blavatsky in *The Secret Doctrine,* in introducing deeper theosophical ideas to the world, was this particular subject, itself derived from esoteric Buddhism. It concerns the "fall" of Man the archangel (as the agent of kosmic Mind) from vastly higher planes of being and his progressively sequential involvement in a succession of objective forms as he cyclically passes, in involutionary and evolutionary sequences, through the lesser states of planetary experience. To describe these sequences in simple terms is not at all easy because we lack a really adequate English vocabulary for the various associated states of consciousness and thus have to depend, to some extent at least, on the Sanskrit terminology.

However, because it has a direct and immensely important relationship with the greater evolutionary process (involving humanity as a whole), let us try in general terms, as follows. As Blavatsky puts it concerning the involutionary–evolutionary "Round" cycle:

Our Earth, as the visible representative of its invisible, superior fellow globes . . . has to live, as have the others, through seven Rounds. During the first three, it forms and consolidates, during the fourth it settles and hardens, during the last three it gradually returns to its first ethereal form; it is spiritualised, so to say. Its humanity develops fully only in the fourth—our present—Round. Up to this fourth life cycle, it is referred to as "humanity" only for lack of a more appropriate term. . . . Arrived on our Earth at the commencement of the Fourth [Round] . . . [proto-typal] "man" is the first form that appears thereon, being preceded only by the mineral and vegetable kingdoms. . . . During the three Rounds to come, humanity will be ever tending to reassume its primeval form, that of a Dhyani Chohanic [archangelic] host.[1]

In noting that this concept is derived from esoteric Buddhism, it is perhaps worth actually quoting from Evans-Wentz's well-known work *The Tibetan Book of the Dead* the following statement:

According to occult teachings common to Northern Buddhism and to that Higher Hinduism which the Hindu-born Bodhisattva who became the Gautama Buddha, the reformer of the lower Hinduism and the codi-fier of the Secret Lore, never repudiated, there are seven worlds or seven degrees of Maya within the Sangsara, constituted as seven globes of a planetary chain. On each globe, there are seven rounds of evolution, mak-ing the forty-nine stations of active existence. As in the embryonic state in the human species the foetus passes through every form of organic struc-ture from the amoeba to man, the highest mammal, so in the after-death state, the embryonic state of the psychic world, the Knower or principle of consciousness anterior to its re-emergence in gross matter, analogously experiences purely psychic conditions. In other words, in both these inter-dependent embryonic processes—the one physical the other psychical—the evolutionary and involutionary attainments, corresponding to the forty-nine stations of existence are passed through.[2]

However, it should be borne in mind by the student of this subject that not all planetary globes are man-bearing.[3]

What has just been described self-evidently involves a huge and complex process, which modern astrophysics conceives of in purely materialistic form as the objective "Big Bang." However, what esoteric Buddhism describes involves a much more all-encompassing process involving the generation and unfolding of kosmic consciousness into an increasingly objective series of celestial forms, the last and most evolved of which is that of the human being. Our modern science cannot as yet conceive of consciousness on such a vast scale and thus makes no attempt to incorporate any suggestion of it in its current paradigms, even though it now openly acknowledges that the human body (like all forms on our planet) is actually made up of "star matter." In simple terms, all such forms are made up of "crystallized light"—the objective appearance of which we recognize as carbon; hence the importance of the carbon cycle in the creation of organic forms on our Earth—although that is another story altogether.

Where humankind as a whole is concerned, the wider concept thus described apparently involves the derivation of an impulse in the (kosmic) Mind of the Solar Logos giving rise to a (progressively objective) sevenfold form of lesser expression. The latter then involves the gradual appearance of seven planetary schemes, which are themselves intended to give compound expression to all those lives that we associate with the various kingdoms of Nature throughout our solar system. In each planetary scheme, this then produces a sevenfold, involutionary–evolutionary duality of expression (called a planetary "Chain" of globes), the progressively objective appearance and densification of which Blavatsky describes as follows:

1. A merely homogeneous mass
2. That of a nebulously aeriform and radiant cloud
3. A curd-like, nebulous form
4. Atomic yet still ethereal, involving primary differentiation
5. Germinal and fiery in appearance—comprising the germs of the elements in their early states
6. Fourfold and vapory—the future Earth globe
7. Cold and depending on the Sun— as we know it today[4]

THE TRUE NATURE OF THE SUN

Let us go back a stage, however, commencing logically with the origin of the Sun itself—the first objective manifestation of the Solar Logos—as this is itself necessarily parent to all the planetary schemes. In doing so we need to bear in mind that the objective Sun is said to be a gigantic ball of (living) electromagnetic plasma, an effect generated at the center of the field of homogeneous primordial substance contained by the solar Oversoul.[5] The latter is the sphere of kosmic consciousness, which is itself the first celestial phenomenon in the Creation sequence. Following the sequence described at the outset, that spheroidal field is itself contained by a peripheral Mind-sheath emanated by the Solar Logos through the agency of the Elohim. The latter are otherwise referred to in *The Secret Doctrine* as the Ah-hi—hence the later Greek name Aion (the god of a celestial cycle) derived from Ah-hi-on. The Mind-sheath itself is symbolically referred to in the *Book of Genesis* as a "firmament"—the "event horizon" of modern quantum physics. In the Hindu tradition the same concept involves the symbolic "Ring of Fire" surrounding the figure of the god Siva Natarajah who represents the divine Will-to-be.

Rather interestingly, modern astrophysics recognizes that celestial bodies are contained by "fields," which arrest the "dark matter" contained by them from spinning centrifugally off into space in the process of axial rotation. However, they self-admittedly do not know what these "fields" are or otherwise what actually causes them—not surprisingly, as they do not yet conceive of the science of what we might call "occult metaphysics." Nor do they understand (or conceive of) the suggestion that there is a logical sequence of coordinated celestial expression in the various planetary schemes. That, in fact, is only possible through the study of esoteric astrology, which is not even acknowledged by most "orthodox" practitioners of today's astrology.

Into that same causal field (that of the solar system-to-be) is then projected or emanated a mass of ten celestial influences or Powers, which are themselves the equivalent of the kabbalistic sephiroth, or the ten points of the Pythagorean tetraktys. These ten influences are the very essences of the core of the Sun—that which the Hindu metaphysicist calls the Adi-tattva, or *Aditi*. This is otherwise known to theosophists as "Root Substance" (*mulaprakriti* in Sanskrit), while the objectively visible Sun is Aditya, the mere "son of Aditi." The substance of the latter, we are told, comprises the foundational nature of the "bodies" of the highest angelic hierarchs (archons) of the solar scheme. These, in response to the force of meditative concentration by the celestial Intelligences informing the logoic Oversoul, then form (by the power of *Adi-krit*) ten planetary schemes out of the initially chaotic plasmic mass contained within its field. The latter is itself the celestial *linga sarira,* or kosmic etheric double. These ten schemes—all thus "brothers" of one parent entity—are themselves organized objectively in the involutionary–evolutionary–devolutionary sequence of planets shown earlier in fig. 5.2.

As a result of this involutionary–evolutionary progression, both hierarchically identifiable forms and an associated consciousness are produced in each planetary scheme, each of the first four overall globe-states becoming, as a result, increasingly dense and objective. In the second half of the Round cycle, however—that is, from the latter part of the Fourth Round back to the Seventh Round—every such form and its associated consciousness re-becomes increasingly etherealized and spiritual. The overall effect is somewhat like the emanation of a musical sound, which increases in volume to full pitch as a melodic chord and then recedes back into a contentedly fulsome quietude, which we assimilate. Thus all the planetary schemes taken together are producing a combination of such sounds, all together comprising an equivalent choral chord, or greater "Divine Word." Our own planetary scheme (Earth itself the fourth of the ten planetary schemes) being just over halfway through its own Fourth Round, is at its densest possible point and state. From here back to its archangelic point of origin, all will become increasingly spiritual, even though this will undoubtedly take untold millions of years.

In relation to the solar scheme as a whole, the involutionary–evolutionary cycle is primarily concerned with the sequence of planetary schemes from Vulcan to Jupiter. The hierarchical groups of Lives within these that succeed to a certain given evolutionary point (as Adepts and human Buddhas) will then apparently transfer to the devolutionary (i.e., synthesizing) schemes of Saturn, Uranus, and Neptune, in preparation for much later onward transmission to the next (third) solar system. Those that do not will presumably be transferred instead to the lesser planetoidal schemes attached to Jupiter, that is, its twelve "moons."

It follows logically from this that the final involutionary–evolutionary cycle of the three synthesizing schemes of Saturn, Uranus, and Neptune will only positively commence their own later evolutionary sequences when each Round has already been completed on all of the seven lesser planetary schemes. These seemingly include that which has yet to take form in what is still known merely as the "asteroid belt." The latter is an astrophysical and occult mystery regarding which no explanatory comment has yet been advanced by the Adept Hierarchy. There remains another mystery in relation to the planet Pluto, but that is another story that needs to be addressed within the context of a work on esoteric astrology in general.

THE ISSUE OF SHAMBALLA

David Frawley tells us:

> According to the Tibetan Buddhists, there was an earlier Buddhist kingdom in Central Asia from which their teaching derives, called Shamballa, which appears to have been in the Tarim Basin, northwest of Tibet. . . . This earlier Buddhist culture in Central Asia was, by Tibetan accounts, also a culture in which Sanskrit [originally Zendskrit], the "language of the gods," was spoken.[1]

Here, according to the most ancient tradition, lived those great Intelligences (Kumaras) who are the real Guides of our planetary Life as a whole—not just of man. These same Intelligences, so we are told, are those who have literally eons ago passed beyond the stage of human existence and are now identifiable as fully liberated "Planetary Spirits." Now mere desert, the original Shamballa was apparently a beautiful island in the middle of a vast inland lake, rather like the huge fresh water Lake Baikal, further to the north in modern Russia. From here, these Intelligences kept watch over the evolution of all the various kingdoms of our planetary Nature, seen and unseen.

We are also told that there was a time, many millions of years ago, when at least some of the inhabitants of Shamballa took physical bodies and moved openly among the prototypal (Lemurian) humanity of the time in order to bring about the nurturing of the full human type.[2] This was at a time, apparently, when an earlier equivalent of Shamballa existed in the area of what is now central South America.[3] Once the full individualization of self-conscious man had been achieved, however, they moved their location to the other side of the world, there awaiting the development of the next great racial types, the Atlanteans and the Aryans (or Indo-Caucasians). At some stage in between, the objectively visible land of Shamballa and its inhabitants seemingly moved into a higher state of being, which, to us, is invisible.[4] Modern travelers and archaeologists have found no objective trace of it.

The three massive but differently-sized statues of Bamian in Afghanistan, adjacent to the Hindu Kush mountain range—stupidly destroyed by the Islamist Taliban in recent years—although supposedly of the Buddha, may perhaps have been connected with Shamballa. Blavatsky tells us that they were originally erected in immensely ancient times and were supposed to be symbolic of the three Root Races of humanity to date.[5] However, other sources suggest that all the various gigantic statues of Buddha found around the Far East are indicative of a far more ancient esoteric "Buddhism," which long preceded that derived from the better known and more modern teachings of Gautama Sakyamuni. One of these refers to them as associated with Agharti (originally Akh-Urti perhaps, meaning "the heavenly land of self-sacrificing, divine spirits"), the allegorically "underground" kingdom of the inhabitants of Shamballa, as follows:

> The various gigantic statues of Buddha do not represent the human Gautama but rather those subterranean supermen who came up to teach and help humanity at remote times in the past. These Buddhas all taught the same universal, scientific religion as emissaries of Agharti, the subterranean Paradise which it is the goal of all true Buddhists to reach.[6]

This curious suggestion of Agharti being an "underground" kingdom seems to be the result of a misunderstanding of the ancient concept that our planetary world of existence is itself a solar "Underworld," by virtue of it existing in the seventh and lowest state of kosmic matter. Notwithstanding this, its inhabitants are said to continue even today with their task of closely overshadowing and looking after all the various kingdoms of our planetary world. These great Intelligences were known in ancient times as Lhas, from which the Islamic god-name, Allah, is derived. The name Shamballa is itself an agglutinative compound: derived from either T'schamba-Lha or Skambha-Lha. Skambha is, according to some, supposed to denote the axial "pole" of our planet.[7] There is another suggestion that our modern English word *chamber*—meaning a ceremonially orientated room and itself derived from the French *chambre*—comes from the same source.

It would appear that the supposedly current location of the Spiritual Adept Hierarchy in the southwestern foothills of the Himalayas is itself due to their need to be within reasonably close range of the influences emanating from Shamballa, so as to facilitate the highest telepathic sensitivity to the spiritual currents emanating from there. However, the suggestion put forward by some that there are tunnels directly connecting Shamballa with Shigatse (the place in Tibet where some at least of the Adepts are actually

THREE SUPERIOR (UNSEEN) KUMARAS
Governing the higher Kingdoms of our planetary Nature
comprising the three hierarchies of Dhyani-Buddhas

SHAMBALLA
(Tcham- b'Allah)

FOURTH (SANAT) KUMARA

FIFTH KUMARA

SIXTH KUMARA

SEVENTH KUMARA

Governing the
Human Kingdom
via the Adept Hierarchy
& the Element of Fire
via the Devas

Governing the
Animal Kingdom
& Element of Air
(via the Devas)

Governing the
Plant Kingdom &
Element of Water
(via the Devas)

Governing the
Mineral Kingdom
& Element of Earth
(via the Devas)

Fig. App.B.1. Structure of Shamballa

supposed to live, or have lived) seems somewhat overimaginative, despite the historic tradition of extensive tunnels under the Himalayas.

THE KUMARAS

The Kumaras are the primary (although apparently not the only) inhabitants of Shamballa. They are those four immensely evolved celestial Intelligences said to be the actual governing principals of our planetary Life as a whole. However, there are said to be seven of them in all, three being of such high degree that they are unmanifest within the immediate aura of our planet. Of the lesser four, three—referred to as "Buddhas of Activity"—are described as being in charge of the overall evolution of the mineral, plant, and animal kingdoms through their control over the various archangelic and deva kingdoms, which are these kingdoms' day-to-day administrators. The fourth Kumara, called Sanat Kumara, is described as the earthly representative and regent of our Planetary Logos. His immediate concern is the subjective evolution of the human kingdom over which his "personal" influence occurs via the three most senior members of the Adept Hierarchy, the Manu, Bodhisattva, and Mahachohan, each of whom is an initiated Adept of the seventh degree.

In very real terms, the Adept Hierarchy itself seemingly represents an intermediate evolutionary staging point between the human state and the state of divinity, or kosmic consciousness which the superior Lhas and the Kumaras themselves inhabit. The Adepts thus act like electrical transformers—they have learned how to step down the higher vibratory influences of Shamballa, which would otherwise be far too destructive in their direct effect upon humanity. Hence it is that the evolutionary aim of the Adepts themselves is to attain Shamballa consciousness.

When all of our humanity has done this, so we are told, we shall in turn and quite logically become the divine administrators of this planet, assisting its yet-to-appear proto-humanity of another age in their own evolutionary progression. The superior planetary Lhas and the Kumaras will themselves then move on in evolutionary terms to take charge of yet other and even greater planetary schemes and even whole solar systems—a future that awaits us too (although as also divinized post-human beings), in far distant eons to come.

THE PUZZLE CONCERNING
THE RELATIONSHIP BETWEEN EARTH
AND ITS MOON

This same progression may help to explain the also amazing description by Blavatsky in *The Secret Doctrine* of an identifiable proportion of the spirits of our more advanced humanity having arrived on this planet by transfer from its Moon, thereby leaving the Moon as a dead planet in orbit around ours. The essence of the idea is that each celestial system—as the "body" of an inconceivable Logos—generates "Mind sparks" within its various solar schemes. These then provide individual planetary schemes, which act as the fields of experience that enable the "sparks" to develop an autonomous creative intelligence. Once the full potential of each such solar scheme has been achieved, the mass of intelligent consciousness thus derived is then passed on via the most developed planetary scheme within it to the next solar scheme in the overall sequence. Hence the donating planetary scheme becomes a dead "moon" at a specific point within the next solar scheme. And so on. In fact, while Blavatsky openly suggests that our planet (being of later origin) was actually the satellite of the Moon, modern science has confirmed that both revolve around a point between them called the "barycenter."

So we are otherwise told, the three "Buddhas of Activity" who (with Sanat Kumara) are the highest Intelligences informing our planetary Life, are not from this solar system at all.[8] The clear inference is that they were the Planetary Logoi of the three synthesizing planetary schemes of the solar system prior to this one (ours being the second in a series of three).[9] Just as Saturn, Uranus, and Neptune represent those same synthesizing planetary schemes within our own solar system, so theirs represented the highest aspects of logoic "personality" development of that last system. All three Buddhas of Activity appear to have transferred their informing lives en masse to this planet via its Moon (which itself appears to have been the last planet of the previous solar system), bringing with them all the lesser hierarchies of life that now animate the mineral, plant, and animal kingdoms of this Earth—plus some of the human as well.

In relation to our own overall planetary consciousness, these Dhyani Buddhas now seemingly represent the kosmic correspondence to the instinctual nature of the physical senses, the feeling/desire nature, and the concrete mind of the human being. Hence they also logically have a particular association with the Lemurian, Atlantean, and Indo-Aryan root races. To the initiate, however, they represent a sort of Higher Triad. Consequently, they are, in a very real sense, a trinitarian focus of the whole evolutionary process on our planet. That being the case, their own particular higher association in our solar system is quite logically with the Saturnian scheme.[10] This suggestion and its (esoteric) astrological implications need to be rather carefully considered.

With all this in mind, it follows that the "heaven world" of Shamballa needs to be kept by us in sensible and logical perspective rather than in forms of adulatory worship and outright awe. The spiritual energies and forces of which its inhabitants are evidently long past masters are those we are already learning to deal with on a minor scale. They too are acting as electrical transformers, of a yet higher kosmic consciousness down into the solar and planetary world systems;[11] and their capacity to fulfill that function must to some definite extent lie in the developed capacity of humanity to respond intelligently (i.e., knowingly) to their influence, rather than keeping it at a distance by the merely devotional worship involved in orthodox religions. It is seemingly for that reason above all that a new perception of Divinity (leading to a new world religion) is now called for on the part of our own humanity.

THE EVOLUTION OF THE HUMAN RACIAL TYPE

From the very outset of this book the point has been made that esotericism concerns itself really only with the evolution of consciousness. All objective forms are derived from consciousness and are therefore only of secondary importance in Nature generally. However, for the sake of "rounding out" our descriptions of how this process might work, let us spend a moment or two looking at the past anthropological history of humankind (from the viewpoint of the Ancient Wisdom tradition) as a prelude to what might perhaps lie in the future.

As otherwise mentioned in an earlier chapter, the esoteric philosophy of the Ancient Wisdom tradition posits the idea that the soul, cell, and atom are all expressions of the very same principle in Universal Nature. It is therefore quite logical that the very first proto-human forms that appeared on our planet are described by *The Secret Doctrine* as having been gigantic cellular entities with no limbs. The latter only developed as the consciousness within the cellular soul entity developed and caused an outward expansion within the mass of ethereal matter (the Greek *hyle*) contained by it, having been borrowed from the astral light of the planet. Thus these early entities were themselves very ethereal in nature to begin with, only developing progressive solidity as evolutionary development itself progressed. That same solidifying development then also caused a generally marked reduction in size.

The changing evolutionary type of our planet's humanity has been described in modern theosophical literature (vide Blavatsky's seminal work *The Secret Doctrine*) as "Root Races." There is a sequence of seven such Races, only five of which have so far been developed. These have been given the following names:

The First Root Race:	the Perennial Race
The Second Race:	the Hyperborean Race
The Third Race:	the Lemurian Race
The Fourth Race:	the Atlantean Race
The Fifth Race:	the Indo-Aryan (Indo-Caucasian) Race

Of these Races, perhaps the most immediately interesting is the Third Race, during which, we are told, the early progenitors of the future mammalian type not only split into two sexes but also separated from each other as the unselfconscious animal type on the one hand and self-conscious humankind on the other.[1] This would suggest that, as Darwin hypothesized, man and animal both derived (in the Tertiary Age) from a common ancestor. However, one might suggest that Darwin's concept is only partially correct, for the following reasons.

As described in chapters 1 and 2, the animal genus has only one soul—the "astral" or terrestrial soul—whereas man has two, the second being what we have described as the "Causal Soul." The latter contains the projected emanation of the "divine spark," which is of a vastly more evolved nature than the "lesser spark" animating the animal nature. This then endows the human being with the faculty of a dual "self" consciousness and a highly subtle creative objectivity. In the case of the prototypal mammalian creatures of the Third (Lemurian) Race, the "astral" souls of the relative few that had evolved to sufficiently high degree were contained by the projected Causal Soul, a phenomenon brought about by the psychic work of the Kumaras, although allegorically described since.[2] This resulted in the Causal nature projecting a tiny aspect of itself downward into the entity's heart center. It was this, fundamentally, which seemingly caused the original separation of the human from the animal type.

When we consider the type of evolutionary development achieved in the various Races, we find the following correspondences as between the masses of the Race in question and its most advanced types.

Race	Racial Evolutionary Development	Most Advanced Types
First Race	Formation of the etheric double from local astral light matter.	Proto-humanoid and deva group hierarchies separate.
Second Race	Appearance of first primitive physical body types plus desire feelings and primitive emotions.	Proto-humanoid types of the First Race mutate. The devas generate the first reptile, fish, and bird forms.
Third Race	Primitive (Cyclopean) faculty of sight develops, plus first lower mental capacities appear in the most advanced types.	Separation of the sexes followed by appearance of first mammalian types in response to generation of the Causal Soul Body. Animals react against the new proto-humans with violence.
Fourth Race	First responsiveness to the Higher Mind principle by the most advanced human types.	First true human types appear. Mass devotional religion appears. Appearance of the first Mystery Schools and the formation of the Spiritual Hierarchy.
Fifth Race	First responsiveness to buddhic intuitive consciousness by the most advanced types, following fully active grasp of the Higher/Abstract Mind faculty.	Mass religion is reoriented toward scientific approach to Divinity. Externalization of the Spiritual Hierarchy takes place and new Mystery Schools founded. Humanity as a whole embarks on the Path of "accepted discipleship."
Sixth Race	First responsiveness to monadic Will nature by the most advanced human types who thereby become Adepts of the fourth or fifth degree.	Large majority of the human race achieve initiatory third degree by the end of the Race period.
Seventh Race	Full responsiveness to kosmic influence by the most advanced human types who thereby become Manushi Buddhas.	Mass majority of the human race achieves initiatory fifth degree by the end of the Race period.

Touching on the issue of associated Egoic Ray types during the earlier Races of humankind, we are told that in later Lemurian times (following individualization) approximately 75 percent were of Second Ray quality while the other roughly 25 percent were of culture-orientated Third Ray association, with a very few First Ray types also being present.[3]

In Atlantean times, however, we are further told, a very large influx of First Ray types came in (before the "door" was closed to the animal kingdom), thereby altering the proportions (and the overall culture) very markedly. So it seems that about 80 percent of those entering the human evolutionary process at that stage were of the First Ray while only 20 percent were Second Ray types.[4] At the same time, others of a Third Ray type were seemingly still entering our planetary scheme from the subtler states of the dying Moon Chain. With all this in mind, it is perhaps unsurprising that Atlantean civilization came to a rapidly progressive and cataclysmic end in conjunction with the development of a completely new type of consciousness and, consequent upon this, a prospectively new (semi-mentally orientated) racial type.

By virtue of the principle of concentration of consciousness leading to evolutionary development, it naturally follows that the planetary Oversoul began to reduce in size from the beginning of the current major ("Round") cycle, as did the physical planet itself. Consequently, the first gigantic cellular entities, which comprised the future mammalian types of the animal and human kingdom also gradually diminished in size, in sympathy, as that evolutionary development progressed. Thus, so we are told, by the time of the mid-Third (Lemurian) Race, the average height of proto-humankind was around thirty-three feet, reducing by around half in the next Atlantean cycle and then again by half or more in the present Indo-Caucasian cycle.

As the soul consciousness of man is now again expanding, with a far greater degree of quality inherent in his nature, one presumes that the most advanced human types of the next Race will be of equivalent height and quality of appearance, as well as quality of mind. One must again stress, however, that appearances are naturally misleading; thus, to spend much time considering them is a complete and utter waste of effort.

While mentioning the Third (Lemurian) Race, the following highly important quote from Bailey's work *A Treatise on Cosmic Fire* should be noted specifically in relation to the first appearance of self-conscious humankind.

> The advent of the Lords of the Flame [Kumaras], [and] the electrical storm which ushered in the period of man [i.e., self-conscious proto-humanity], was distinguished by disaster, chaos and the destruction of many in the third kingdom of Nature. The spark of Mind was implanted and the strength of its vibration and the immediate effect of its presence caused the [widespread] death of the animal form, thus producing the immediate possibility of the newly vitalised Causal Bodies vibrating to such purpose that new [specifically human] physical vehicles were taken.[5]

These "Causal Bodies" or "Causal Souls" are as described in the earlier chapters of this book. As G. R. S. Mead reminds us, according to St. Paul, the yet higher spiritual body of man (the "body of glory") is not a body of pure spirit but a body capable by its purity of manifesting the immediate power of the spirit.[6] In the first place—that is, when the first self-conscious humanity appeared in Lemurian times—these same ethereal "bodies" would have been pure and clear, their beautiful coloring and radiance only appearing after millions of years of evolutionary development leading to initiation on the spiritual Path.

It is otherwise worth mentioning the further suggestion that, coincident with the huge influx of spiritual energy now influencing our planet—involving a crisis as great as the actual individualization of man in Lemurian times—a new kingdom of Nature will (in due course) emerge into objectivity as a direct result.[7] That new (fifth) kingdom will comprise a far more spiritualized type of humanity whose consciousness is entirely higher mental-cum intuitional-cum will-orientated in nature (i.e., that of the lesser Adept), although itself a direct progression from the present emotional-mental nature of our humanity. The result of this progression will, quite naturally, involve an initiation of our planetary Life as a whole, thereby rendering it esoterically "sacred" and thus bringing about a more direct association with the Greater Adept Brotherhood of the star Sirius, hence also with the Life and consciousness of the Greater Logos.[8] With that in mind, it is again very clear why our present Adept Brotherhood should wish to inaugurate in humanity's consciousness a completely new but entirely rational perspective as to the actual nature of Divinity.

THE THREE SOLAR SYSTEMS AND THE FAILURE OF THE MOON CHAIN

Why, you might ask, should we concern ourselves with kosmic issues that are so far beyond our human powers of comprehension that they make little or no rational sense? The answer to that lies in the fact that the great celestial Intelligences who populate and control the universe were themselves once mere human spirits, so we are assured. In line with that, those high initiates of our present humanity (our "Elder Brothers") who achieve moksha (liberation from our world-state) are themselves en route to fulfilling a similar function. Therefore, our own evolutionary future, long eons hence, must lie in the very same direction and we should be aware of that. We are all but cells in the organism of the greater Logos.

We are told, as otherwise also mentioned a little earlier, that our present solar system is the second in a series of three,[1] within a larger kosmic system of seven solar schemes, which themselves comprise the seven primary chakras in the objective body of a Logos whose unimaginably evolved Intelligence would be light years in advance of that of our own Solar Logos. That superior Logos would appear to be directly associated with the Pleiades. Although this sounds frighteningly complex, it is less so if following the hermeneutic system also described earlier. That threefold progression would then make reasonably logical sense. It would do so in terms of an overall involutionary–evolutionary–devolutionary development. That would then seem to infer that our solar system may be representative, in equivalent terms, of the eye or throat chakra in the etheric body of the greater Logos. That in turn would perhaps suggest the first solar system to have been correspondingly representative of the logoic sacral chakra, its lesser counterpart.

The implied follow-on from this is that the Moon Chain (parent to the Earth) represented the most developed planetary scheme in the first solar system, which could go no further in its own evolutionary development—hence the fact that its most evolved humanity was transferred to this planet, Earth. The groups thus transferred were, in a sense, relative "failures," which had not already achieved full spiritual Self-consciousness. Therefore, under karmic Divine Law, according to *The Secret Doctrine*, they were forced back into the next available cycle of human experience[2]—which coincided with the Fourth or Atlantean Root Race on our Earth. So we are also told in *The Secret Doctrine*, even the Kumaras were relative "failures" from a previous solar cycle.[3] However, by virtue of their evolution being so far advanced, as relative "gods," they could not be thrown back. They were instead projected into the aura of our world in a latent state, as a single group, there to await the due time when they could "awaken" and begin the alchemical process of turning merely prototypal humanity into self-consciously reasoning human beings, as supposedly took place in very ancient Lemurian times.

The "failure" of the Planetary Logos of the Moon Chain seems to have been merely relative. That is to say, the fact of only a part of its humanity achieving spiritual Self-consciousness was inevitable. So, having achieved a high degree of materialistic mentality on the Moon Chain—the desire-to-know (the lesser "Brahma" nature) apparently being the primary evolutionary influence on the Moon—these same human soul groups were transferred to our solar system and our Earth, which is itself primarily influenced by the Will-to-know (the Visnu nature). As a direct consequence, the duality generated by these two groups coming together produced inevitable conflict during the Atlantean period. That same conflict eventually resulted in the materialistic influence giving rise to the formation of the Lodge of Black Adepts (of the Left-Hand Path) while the "organic" influence of the Will-to-know produced by the Planetary Logos of the Earth resulted in the formation of the Great White Lodge (of Adepts of the Right-Hand Path).

The whole issue of "white" and "black" magic has arisen in the popular mind as a result of these historic issues. However, the problem is one that has evidently to be resolved by the Spiritual Hierarchy, not by mere human beings. We human beings certainly need to be aware of the influence of the "Brothers of the Left-Hand Path" as one that mistakenly seeks to promote material benefits and purely selfish individualism as its overriding priorities. However, to think of the issue as one pertaining only to the supposed Devil via ritual magic (a.k.a. the books of Denis Wheatley or Aleister Crowley) would be quite wrong.

The real problem lies in the completely false but widespread assumption that a high level of material welfare (or so-called "quality of life") should be our prime concern before we even consider spiritual issues. This is manifestly not so, irrespective of what our worldly gurus of Western society have to say on the subject. A basic level of material welfare and comfort (involving shelter and food) for all is indeed necessary—after all, one cannot reasonably expect homeless, starving, or unhealthy people to focus on important subjective issues. However, a high level of consumption or ownership of belongings becomes a mere distraction. That is why the spiritual Path inculcates a reasonable degree of personal asceticism, so that the elemental nature is kept under disciplined control by the Higher Self. Failure to recognize this is why so many mystically orientated idealists come to grief so quickly.

As already mentioned, a great part of the work of the Adept Hierarchy (since 1775 at least)[4] involves the intentional destruction of redundant and materialistically orientated thought-forms, as well as those getting out of control like rampant weeds in a garden. These exist within the field of what Jung called the "collective unconscious," and they are constantly and perniciously (although unconsciously) being regenerated by human beings, particularly through the medium of such agencies as the modern advertising industry. This, in conjunction with the modern worldwide stock market, functions on the basis of greed and fear, these supposedly being the two factors that alone drive consumption. Yet even recent experience has shown us that this need not be so.

It is a fact that human beings in the mass allow themselves to fall prey to unconscious and ill-thought-through fears of losing their means of living or their cultural status quo. That is largely due to worries about unexpected natural forces or to anxiety about other human beings taking unfair advantage. Hence it is that the Adept Hierarchy finds it necessary to bring about those occasional social crises that force people (i.e., via public opinion) to stop and think—particularly where both psychological and material profit margins are concerned. The human Spiritual Ego is involved in precisely the same process in watching over the evolution of each individual human being. Were it not for this constant process of cultural renewal engineered by the Spiritual Hierarchy from behind the scenes, human civilization would be in a perpetual and thoroughly unacceptable state of unregenerate chaos or stagnation. Thus it is that the Hierarchy uses its disciple-agents (such as the humanist Jean-Jacques Rousseau, for example) as agents-provocateurs to stimulate humanity into new orientations of thought and fresh channels of creative cultural activity.

However, although humanity alone makes the decision as to which direction it will actually follow, the planetary Powers-that-Be will not allow humankind to cause the planetary ruin that many fear because there is far too much in the way of a far higher Purpose at stake. Mankind must itself realize that crisis is necessarily of a temporary yet necessary nature to ensure that forward progress (through associated psychological testing as to strength of character) is possible. Hence it is that those mass elements of human society that do not come up to cyclical par must automatically be withdrawn from incarnation, largely via pandemics and natural disasters involving earthquakes, tsunamis, and volcanic activity. These temporary "failures" will then not be allowed to reincarnate during the present cycle, as they would otherwise slow its development down to an unacceptable degree.

As regards the remainder, the Adepts—once they have telepathically projected their suggestions to lesser initiates for the future development of human culture and civilization—can only watch and hope that progressive evolutionary common sense will prevail before they give any further assistance. The rest, as they say, is up to us.

APPENDIX E

SPIRITUAL AVATARS

Although this subject has been lightly touched upon in the main text of the book, the subject needs to be put into a context other than a mystic one in order for it to be understood in perspective with everything else so far suggested. The primary consideration must therefore be to remind ourselves that we exist within the "body" of a great Intelligence (Logos) "in Whom we live and move and have our being." Within this great organism, which comprises and thus extends throughout our local universe, the stars fulfill the function of greater and lesser chakras, while the planetary schemes are in a corresponding sense like the greater and lesser organs of the human body. Like our own human organism, this "body" functions according to sensed need, which is necessarily invocative in nature.

As already described, the whole of this great logoic organism is united by the kosmic etheric state (known to us by the Sanskrit terms Maha-Buddhi or Mahat) and it is throughout this state that the main flow of kosmic energies are to be found. However, just as in our own human organism there are non-physical forces lying apparently dormant until specifically called upon, so in the kosmic etheric double (and in the kosmic astral and mental states as well) there exist direct correspondences. As the logoic organism progresses toward its own eventually full birth in the kosmos, all of these celestial potentials have to come into proper working order. However, they can only do so by virtue of Man's involvement.

Now, as we suggested at the outset, Man is essentially a divine being that has "fallen" en masse into the kosmic Underworld of celestial objectivity within our and other adjacent solar systems. He has done so as the latent coordinating expression of logoic Purpose. This has itself to work out in functional terms by consciously coordinating the animal, plant, and mineral kingdoms (comprising the kosmic gaseous, liquid, and dense states of the logoic body), as well as the lesser elemental subkingdoms. That can only ultimately be done, however, by his achieving Adept consciousness, which involves a progression of spiritual, semi-divine, and ultimately divine Self-consciousness in the creative and administrative process. Thus as Man achieves this, so the Logos himself achieves increasing degrees of SELF-consciousness in his own objective body. This, it is suggested, is the overall purpose of Creation.

By virtue of many of the auxiliary forces inherent in the compound logoic body organism being found latently circulating outside the celestial environs of the various planetary bodies, they have to be directly supplicated or called upon if their powers are to be usefully employed. This, however, can only be done by the Adept Hierarchy of each planetary scheme, for it is they who constitute its local center of animating and directing intelligence; but in order for them to do so, they must themselves develop increasingly greater and ever more subtle powers of invocation. Those greater powers of invocation come about as the direct result of an increasing number of human beings developing spiritual self-awareness and then spiritual Self-consciousness.

As the masses develop, thereby providing an increasingly strong foundational capacity for actual containment of higher energies, so the Adept Hierarchy itself evolves a greater coordinated power, which is itself the living SELF-expression of the Logos. It can then quite logically invoke interplanetary Avatars (in due cycle) to assist with the carrying out of progressively greater degrees of logoic function, by the use in our world of greater power and knowledge, as and when required. When humankind eventually realizes its true Purpose in this regard, then and only then will Evil (very logically) cease to exist.

It would appear that there have been three great kosmically related events in the life experience of our own Planetary Logos, all related to avataric involvement on a major scale and all involving the "Day of Judgment" of the associated era. The first was that of the "coming of the Kumaras" as a latent force in Nature to begin with,[1] resulting in the founding of the original Shamballa. This was followed by the separation of the animal and human kingdoms, the appearance of dual gender, and finally the appearance of egoic self-consciousness in primeval humanity. This all took place during the Third (Lemurian) Race. The second occurred during the Fourth (Atlantean) Race and involved the final separation of higher astral from physical consciousness, thereby generating higher and lower types of human idealism and the first organic progression of members of our humanity into the lower echelons of the Spiritual Hierarchy of the planet. The third has only just taken place, involving (to begin with) the release of atomic/nuclear energy in this Fifth Race, during the twentieth century.[2]

Although generally regarded by humankind as merely associated with warfare, the capacity to generate atomic and now nuclear energy has a far higher, even spiritual association. The latter is concerned, one might suggest, with liberation from the threatened bondage of personality-driven human culture and the desire-orientated profit motive. From that viewpoint, even though the effects may not yet be widely or even clearly apparent, because of their mainly subjective nature, there is now taking place a fundamental separation of the lower mind principle from the astral nature in human consciousness generally.

Although atomic energy per se is a low form of energy associated with base matter, the occult principle involved is that its so-called "fission" could only take place as a result of sympathetic association. That is to say, only by virtue of the same thing taking place at the correspondingly higher level of Being could it then occur at the physical level. From this angle, it might be seen as representative of a downflow of kosmic etheric energy, thereby generating in due sequence an inflow of buddhic consciousness into the field of the human Higher Mind principle. That in turn results in the generation of a wave of higher Egoic Self-consciousness throughout our humanity. It is this, one might further suggest, which caused the superficial stimulus resulting in the appearance of the 1950s and 1960s "New Age" consciousness in a generation overshadowed by the presence of the planet Pluto in the zodiacal sign of Leo.

This third avataric event is of the same magnitude as the first, it is suggested, by virtue of the Fifth Race being the venue of the "Judgment Day" of the greater cycle involving the whole series of Fourth Round Root Races. This will be more understandable by reference to fig. 2.7 related to the cyclic movement of the Life wave. From this we can see that at each rising stage there occurs a "failure," which itself results in a "fall." That thereby generates a lesser, involutionary wave cycle, while the rest continues onward and upward. With that in mind, the implication is that the release of atomic energy heralded only the first stage of the current "Judgment Day"; so the rest must now follow. As such powerfully occult events otherwise inevitably result in corresponding cataclysms, the probability naturally follows that such will appear in increasing degree. As already suggested in a preceding chapter, one of the objectively more obvious results to be expected from this is that there will now progressively come about a very substantial reduction in the by now rather overcrowded population of our planet.

Consequent upon this, so we are told, a great Seventh Ray Avatar will appear in the not-too-distant future, in order to initiate the reappearance of the Mysteries.[3] The latter will obviously take a somewhat different form than that of the ancient Mysteries, but the general principles are likely to remain the same, thereby forming the basis not only of public religion but also of higher philosophical teachings. That is to say, they will probably involve three different levels of Mysteries, each related to particular ranges of initiatory experience. However, instead of being founded on a purely mystic (i.e., astral) orientation, they will be based upon mental recognition of scientific laws, but with a properly spiritual orientation.

NOTES

PROLOGUE

1. A. T. Barker, ed., *The Mahatma Letters to A. P. Sinnett* (Adyar, India: Theosophical Publishing House, 1998), 118.
2. A. A. Bailey, *Esoteric Psychology,* vol. 2 (London: Lucis Press, 1981), 218–19.
3. D. Fideler, *Jesus Christ, Sun of God* (Wheaton, Ill.: Quest Books, 1993), xvi.

INTRODUCTION

1. N. Goodrick-Clarke, *The Western Esoteric Traditions* (Oxford: Oxford University Press, 2008), 35ff.
2. In this book I have made no attempt to deal in any detail with the many and varied subbranches of modern theosophical thought pursued by such as Besant, Leadbeater, and Steiner (and many others). That is simply because very few of their concepts or lines of thought were actually original.
3. A. A. Bailey, *The Rays and the Initiations* (London: Lucis Publishing, 1971), 538.
4. A. T. Barker, ed., *The Mahatma Letters to A. P. Sinnett.*

CHAPTER ONE.
ON SPIRIT, SOUL, AND CONSCIOUSNESS IN GENERAL

1. C. G. Jung, *Analytical Psychology: Its Theory and Practice* (London: Routledge and Kegan Paul, 1970), 4, 66, 81, 99, 106, 110.

2. W. J. Hanegraaff, *New Age Religion and Western Culture* (New York: SUNY Press, 1998), 126.

3. Ibid., 145.

4. Ibid., 163–67.

5. B. Reynolds, ed., *Embracing Reality: The Integral Vision of Ken Wilber* (New York: Penguin, 2004), 45–46.

6. K. Wilber, *Quantum Questions* (Boston: Shambhala, 2001), 3.

7. D. Lindorff, *Jung and Pauli—The Meeting of Two Great Minds* (Wheaton, Ill.: Quest Books, 2004), 2.

8. A. Faivre quoting a paper by F. B. Nicolescu titled "The Metamorphosis of Hermes," *Access to Western Esotericism* (New York: SUNY Press, 1994), 281.

9. A. Goswami, *The Self-Aware Universe* (London and New York: Penguin Putnam, 1995), 10.

10. Ibid., 61.

11. A. Goswami, *The Visionary Window* (Wheaton, Ill.: Quest Books, 2006), 18.

12. Ibid., 96.

13. Ibid., 42–48.

14. H. P. Blavatsky, *The Voice of the Silence* (Los Angeles: The Theosophy Co., 1987), 2.

15. Plotinus, *The Enneads* 4.3 (London: Penguin Classics, 1991), 1–2.

16. B. P. Copenhaver, ed., *Hermetica* (Cambridge: Cambridge University Press, 1992), 34.

17. Ibid., 46.

18. H. P. Blavatsky, *The Secret Doctrine* (Adyar, India: Theosophical Publishing House, 1979), vol. 1, 568, and vol. 2, 672.

19. B. P. Copenhaver, ed., *Hermetica,* 175.

20. Ibid., 499.

21. Iamblichus, *Theurgia—De Mysteriis,* trans. A. Wilder (London: Rider, 1911), 44.

22. Plato's *Phaedo* from J. M. Cooper, *The Complete Works of Plato* (Indianapolis, Ill.: Hackett Publishing Co., 1997), 79.

23. A. Goswami, *The Visionary Window,* 46.

24. B. Lipton, *Spontaneous Evolution* (London: Hay House, 2001), 7–42. See also Rupert Sheldrake's *A New Science of Life.*

25. Ibid.

26. Plato, *Phaedra,* 250c6, from *The Complete Works of Plato.*

27. H. P. Blavatsky, *The Secret Doctrine,* vol. 1, 147.

28. B. P. Copenhaver, ed., *Hermetica,* 6 and 13.

29. Iamblichus, *Theurgia—De Mysteriis,* 245.

30. G. Scholem, *Zohar—The Book of Splendour* (London: Rider and Co., 1977), 79.

31. B. P. Copenhaver, ed., *Hermetica,* 2.

32. Iamblichus, *Theurgia—De Mysteriis,* 29.

33. W. Y. Evans-Wentz, *The Tibetan Book of the Dead* (Oxford: Oxford University Press, 1927), xiii.

34. Iamblichus, *Theurgia—De Mysteriis,* 33.

35. Eliphas Levi, *The Key of the Mysteries* (London: Rider and Co., 1969), 96.

36. H. P. Blavatsky, *The Secret Doctrine,* 373 and 572.

37. Plato, *The Banquet,* v. 189–190.

38. Plato, *The Republic,* Bk. 7, v. 514–20.

39. Plato, *Timaeus,* 83.

40. Ibid., 62.

41. A. A. Bailey, *A Treatise on Cosmic Fire* (New York: Lucis Press, 1964), 1097.

42. G. R. S. Mead, *Echoes from the Gnosis* (Wheaton, Ill.: Quest Books, 2006), 76.

43. B. P. Copenhaver, ed., *Hermetica,* 199.

CHAPTER TWO.
HUMAN CONSCIOUSNESS

1. B. P. Copenhaver, ed., *Hermetica,* 32.

2. A. Bailey, *The Rays and the Initiations,* 489.

3. Ibid., 490.

4. A. Bailey, *A Treatise on Cosmic Fire,* 132.

5. Proclus, *Commentary on the Timaeus of Plato,* Bk. 2, 561.

6. B. P. Copenhaver, ed., *Hermetica,* 2.

7. A. Bailey, *A Treatise on Cosmic Fire,* 689.

8. Ibid., 92.

9. G. de Santillana and H. von Dechend, *Hamlet's Mill* (Boston: D. R. Godine, 1977), 308–9.

10. H. P. Blavatsky, *The Secret Doctrine,* vol. 1, 184–85, and vol. 2, 185, 1195, and 200.

11. B. P. Copenhaver, ed., *Hermetica,* 36.

12. Ibid., 43.

13. Ibid., 363.

14. Herodotus, *The Histories* (London: Penguin Classics, 1983), 157.

15. H. P. Blavatsky, *The Secret Doctrine,* vol. 1, 109.

16. S. A. Hoeller, *The Gnostic Jung and the Seven Sermons to the Dead* (Wheaton, Ill.: Quest Books, 1982), 195.

17. H. P. Blavatsky, *The Secret Doctrine,* vol. 1, 197.

18. S. A. Hoeller, *The Gnostic Jung,* 91.

19. A. A. Bailey, *Education in the New Age* (London: Lucis Press 1954), 67.

20. Ibid., 111–12. See also *Esoteric Psychology,* vol. 2, 576–78.

21. A. A. Bailey, *Initiation, Human and Solar* (London: Lucis Press, 1977), 63–70.

22. The Holy Bible, 1 Corinthians VI: 3.

CHAPTER THREE.
THE UNSEEN KINGDOMS OF NATURE AND THEIR ROLES

1. A. A. Bailey, *A Treatise on Cosmic Fire,* 244, 251, and 270.

2. Ibid., 488–89.

3. Ibid., 654.

4. H. P. Blavatsky, *The Secret Doctrine,* vol. 1, 626, and vol. 2, 633.

5. A. A. Bailey, *A Treatise on Cosmic Fire,* 245.

6. Ibid., 629–31.

7. Ibid., 951–52.

8. B. P. Copenhaver, ed., *Hermetica,* 36.

9. H. P. Blavatsky, *The Secret Doctrine,* vol. 1, 406.

10. A. A. Bailey, *Initiation, Human and Solar,* 97.

11. A. A. Bailey, *A Treatise on Cosmic Fire,* 489.

12. Iamblichus, *Theurgia—De Mysteriis,* 105.

13. H. P. Blavatsky, *The Secret Doctrine,* vol. 1, 280.

14. A. A. Bailey, *A Treatise on Cosmic Fire,* 489.

15. Iamblichus, *Theurgia—De Mysteriis,* 21.

16. Ibid.

17. Ibid., 23.

18. B. P. Copenhaver, ed., *Hermetica,* 36.

19. Iamblichus, *Theurgia—De Mysteriis,* 29.

20. Ibid., 259, and 319–21.

21. A. T. Barker, ed., *The Mahatma Letters to A. P. Sinnett,* 257.

22. A. A. Bailey, *The Externalisation of the Hierarchy,* 2nd ed. (New York: Lucis Press, 1958), 505.

23. Ibid.

24. Ibid., 506–7.

25. Iamblichus, *Theurgia—De Mysteriis,* 87.

26. Ibid., 89.

27. Ibid., 95.

28. J. S. Gordon, *The Rise and Fall of Atlantis* (London: Watkins Books, 2008), 86–87.

29. A. A. Bailey, *A Treatise on Cosmic Fire,* 589.

CHAPTER FOUR.
ON KARMA AND REINCARNATION

1. B. P. Copenhaver, ed., *Hermetica,* 9.

2. Ibid., 85.

3. G. Hodson, *The Kingdom of the Gods* (Adyar, India: Theosophical Publishing House, 1987), 39–49.

4. W. Y. Evans-Wentz, *The Tibetan Book of the Dead,* 10–15.

5. A. Besant and B. Das, *Bhagvad Gita* (Ninth Discourse) (Adyar, India: Theosophical Publishing House, 1926), 161.

6. A. A. Bailey, *A Treatise on Cosmic Fire,* 715.

7. Ibid., 692.

8. H. P. Blavatsky, *The Secret Doctrine,* vol. 1, 457, and vol. 2, 281.

9. A. A. Bailey, *A Treatise on Cosmic Fire,* 188.

10. Ibid., 545.

11. W. J. Hanegraaff, *New Age Religion and Western Culture,* 276–301.

12. J. S. Gordon, *The Rise and Fall of Atlantis,* 192ff.

CHAPTER FIVE.
EVOLUTION AND INITIATION IN NATURE

1. W. Y. Evans-Wentz, *The Tibetan Book of the Dead,* 6.
2. Ibid. See also H. P. Blavatsky, *The Theosophical Glossary* (Los Angeles: The Theosophy Co., 1990), 278.
3. A. A. Bailey, *The Externalisation of the Hierarchy,* 107–8 and 126–27.
4. A. A. Bailey, *A Treatise on Cosmic Fire,* 188.
5. H. P. Blavatsky, *The Secret Doctrine,* vol. 1, 181.
6. Ibid., vol. 2, 172 and 260.
7. G. Hodson, *The Kingdom of the Gods,* 98.
8. Ibid., 115.
9. H. P. Blavatsky, *The Secret Doctrine,* vol. 1, 295.
10. A. A. Bailey, *A Treatise on Cosmic Fire,* 286.
11. A. A. Bailey, *The Soul: The Quality of Life* (London: Lucis Press, 1974), 176–78.
12. A. A. Bailey, *The Rays and the Initiations,* 364.
13. H. P. Blavatsky, *The Voice of the Silence,* 61–62.
14. Ibid.

CHAPTER SIX.
SACRED METAPHOR AND ALLEGORY IN RELATION TO THE ANCIENT MYSTERY TRADITIONS AND ASSOCIATED INITIATION

1. J. S. Gordon, *Land of the Fallen Star Gods* (subsequently republished by Inner Traditions as *Egypt, Child of Atlantis*).
2. G. R. S. Mead, *Echoes from the Gnosis,* 41.
3. B. P. Copenhaver, ed. *Hermetica,* 87–88.
4. J. Naydler, *Temple of the Cosmos* (Rochester, Vt.: Inner Traditions, 2005), 193–286.
5. E. A. Wallis Budge, *Egyptian Religion* (London: Bell Publishing, 1959), 61–84.
6. R. T. Rundle Clark, *Myth and Symbol in Ancient Egypt* (London: Thames and Hudson, 1959), 109–12 and 195–208.
7. J. Naydler, *Temple of the Cosmos,* 160 and 280.
8. Iamblichus, *Theurgia—De Mysteriis,* 254.

9. A. E. Waite, *The Occult Sciences* (Reprint, London: Kegan Paul, 1972), 11.

10. D. A. Mackenzie, *Myths of Babylonia and Assyria* (London: The Gresham Publishing Co., 1915), 342.

11. Ibid., 138ff.

12. Ibid., 75.

13. Ibid., 171ff.

14. Ibid., 53 and 84ff.

15. Y. Stoyanov, *The Other God* (New Haven: Yale University Press, 2000), 72–83.

16. S. H. Nasr, *The Islamic Intellectual Tradition in Persia* (London: Curzon Press, 1996), 73.

17. Ibid., 14.

18. P. Nabarz, *The Mysteries of Mithras* (Rochester, Vt.: Inner Traditions, 2005), 80–89.

19. Ibid., 30–41.

20. Ibid., 78.

21. H. P. Blavatsky, *The Secret Doctrine,* vol. 1, 268 and 322, and vol. 2, 269 and 559.

22. R. Graves, *The Greek Myths* (London: Penguin Books, 1960), 27–41.

23. Ibid., 89–92.

24. J. Yarker, *The Arcane Schools* (Belfast: W. Tait, 1909), 175ff.

25. T. Taylor, *Hymns and Initiations* (Frome, England: Prometheus Trust, 1994), 10–11.

26. A. David-Neel, *Initiations and Initiates in Tibet* (London: Rider and Co., 1970), 15.

27. W. Y. Evans-Wentz, *The Tibetan Book of the Dead.*

28. D. Frawley, *Gods, Sages and Kings* (Salt Lake City, Utah: Passage Press, 1991), 281.

29. S. Sand, *The Invention of the Jewish People* (London: Verso, 2009), 98 and 118–22.

30. H. P. Blavatsky, *The Secret Doctrine,* vol. 1, 313, vol. 2, 200 and 471.

31. N. Glatzer, *The Judaic Tradition* (New York: Behrman House, 1969) 4.

32. G. R. S. Mead, *Echoes from the Gnosis,* 186–99.

33. G. Scholem, *Zohar—Book of Splendour,* 79.

34. G. Scholem, *Origins of the Kabbala* (Princeton: Princeton University Press, 1987), 134, 136, and 361.

35. G. Scholem, *On the Kabbala and Its Symbolism* (London: Routledge and Kegan Paul, 1965), 25.

36. C. H. Kahn, *Pythagoras and the Pythagoreans* (Cambridge, Mass.: Hackett Publishing Co., 2001), 55.

37. T. Taylor, *Collected Writings on the Gods and the Worlds* (Westbury, England: Prometheus Trust, 1994), 206.

38. H. P. Blavatsky, *The Secret Doctrine,* vol. 1, 27ff.

39. D. Fideler, *The Pythagorean Sourcebook and Library* (Grand Rapids, Mich.: Phanes Press, 1987), 30–31 and 51.

40. Ibid., 37.

41. I. Shah, *Oriental Magic* (London: Octagon Press, 1956), 78–86.

42. I. Shah, *The Sufis* (London: Octagon Press, 1977), 108–10.

43. B. Jowett, *Plato's Republic and Other Works* (London: Anchor Press, 1973), 312. See also Copenhaver, *Hermetica,* 306–7.

44. Proclus, *Commentary on the Timaeus of Plato* (Frome, England: Prometheus Trust, 1998), 17–18.

45. Plato, *The Banquet,* v. 189–90.

46. H. P. Blavatsky, *The Secret Doctrine,* vol. 1, 86ff.

47. B. P. Copenhaver, ed., *Hermetica,* 25.

48. Ibid., 2.

49. A. Faivre and J. Needleman, eds., *Modern Esoteric Spirituality* (New York: Crossroad Publishing Co., 1992), 3.

50. Editors, *The Chaldean Oracles* (Fintry, England: Shrine of Wisdom, 1936), 13.

51. Ibid., 52.

52. Ibid., 28.

53. S. A. Hoeller, *The Gnostic Jung,* 22.

54. W. J. Hanegraaff, "On the Construction of Esoteric Traditions," in Faivre and Hanegraaff, *Western Esotericism and the Science of Religion* (Leuven, Belgium: Peeters, 1998), 20.

55. S. H. Nasr, *The Islamic Intellectual Tradition in Persia,* 128.

56. S. Hoeller, *Gnosticism: New Light on the Ancient Tradition of Inner Knowing* (Wheaton, Ill.: Quest Books, 2002), 38–40.

57. D. A. Mackenzie, *Myths of Babylonia and Syria,* 332.

58. The Acts of the Apostles, Matthew XIII:11; Mark IV:11; and Luke VIII:10.

59. J. Yarker, *The Arcane Schools,* 163.

60. Origen, *Philocalia,* trans. G. Lewis (Edinburgh: T and T Clark, 1911), 1, 17.

61. Ibid.

62. J. Yarker, *The Arcane Schools,* 159–60.

63. K. Nabarz, *The Mysteries of Mithras,* 48–49.

64. Y. Stoyanov, *The Other God,* 122.

65. Ibid., 104.

66. Ibid., 105.

67. J. Yarker, *The Arcane Schools,* 169.

68. K. Armstrong, *Muhammad—A Biography of the Prophet* (London: Phoenix Press, 1991), 45ff.

69. Ibid., 110.

CHAPTER SEVEN.
THE "DARK AGES" AND THE RISE OF WESTERN ESOTERICISM

1. R. H. Allen, *Star Names: Their Lore and Meaning* (New York: Dover Publications, 1980), 393.

2. R. Bauval and G. Hancock, *Keeper of Genesis* (London: Random House, 1997), 65, 79, and 140–43.

3. Herodotus, *The Histories,* 149.

4. H. P. Blavatsky, *The Secret Doctrine,* vol. 1, 750, vol. 2, 746. See also her *Collected Writings,* vol. 5, 286, and vol. 11, 227 and 263.

5. Plato, *Timaeus and Critias,* 131–45.

6. Y. Stoyanov, *The Other God,* 67.

7. A. T. Barker, ed., *The Mahatma Letters to A. P. Sinnett,* 62.

8. A. A. Bailey, *The Rays and the Initiations,* 369. See also *Esoteric Psychology,* vol. 2, 15–210.

9. A. T. Barker, ed., *The Mahatma Letters to A. P. Sinnett,* 62.

10. A. A. Bailey, *The Rays and the Initiations,* 697.

11. S. A. Hoeller, *Gnosticism,* 74 and 112.

12. Y. Stoyanov, *The Other God,* 75.

13. J. Godwin, *The Golden Thread* (Wheaton, Ill.: Quest Books, 2007), 67. See also Faivre and Needleman's *Modern Esoteric Spirituality,* 23.

14. J. Godwin, *The Golden Thread,* 69 and 118.

15. Faivre and Needleman, *Modern Esoteric Spirituality,* 65.

16. S. A. Hoeller, *The Gnostic Jung,* 97.

17. J. Jacobi, ed., *Paracelsus: Selected Writings* (London: Routledge and Kegan Paul, 1951), 45–46.

18. J. S. Gordon, *The Rise and Fall of Atlantis,* 238–40 and 322–23.

19. A. A. Bailey, *The Rays and the Initiations,* 254.

20. G. Scholem, *The Messianic Idea in Judaism* (New York: Schocken Books, 1971), 41.

21. S. Sand, *The Invention of the Jewish People,* 75ff. and 280ff.

22. D. Frawley, *Gods, Sages and Kings,* 282.

23. H. P. Blavatsky, *The Secret Doctrine,* vol. 2, 463.

24. N. Goodrick-Clarke, *The Western Esoteric Traditions,* 34ff.

25. A. E. Waite, *The Occult Sciences,* 7.

26. Ibid., 212–25.

27. A. A. Bailey, *The Externalisation of the Hierarchy,* 401 and 418.

CHAPTER EIGHT.
MODERN SPIRITUAL PROBATION AND DISCIPLESHIP

1. B. P. Copenhaver, ed., *Hermetica,* 43.

2. C. H. Kahn, *Pythagoras and the Pythagoreans,* 8.

3. H. P. Blavatsky, *Practical Occultism* (London: Theosophical Publishing Society, n.d.), 4–5.

4. A. A. Bailey, *Initiation, Human and Solar,* 71.

5. Ibid.

6. Ibid., 76.

7. Ibid., 84.

8. A. A. Bailey, *The Rays and the Initiations,* 498.

9. H. P. Blavatsky, *Five Years of Theosophy,* facsimile edn. (Los Angeles: The Theosophy Co. 1980), 223–24.

10. A. A. Bailey, *The Rays and the Initiations,* 498.

11. Ibid., 682.

12. A. A. Bailey, *The Externalisation of the Hierarchy,* 539.

13. Ibid., 562–63.

14. A. A. Bailey, *A Treatise on Cosmic Fire,* 651.

15. A. A. Bailey, *The Reappearance of the Christ* (London: Lucis Press, 1969), 18–19 and 480.

16. H. P. Blavatsky, *Practical Occultism,* 64.

17. A. A. Bailey, *Letters on Occult Meditation* (New York: Lucis Press, 1973), 3.

18. Ibid., 2.

19. Ibid., 3.

20. A. A. Bailey, *The Rays and the Initiations,* 453.

21. Ibid., 455.

22. H. P. Blavatsky, *The Secret Doctrine,* vol. 1, 206.

CHAPTER NINE.
INITIATIONS OF THE THRESHOLD

1. A. A. Bailey, *Esoteric Astrology,* 475.

2. A. A. Bailey, *The Rays and the Initiations,* 585.

3. The Holy Bible, Romans VII:15.

4. H. P. Blavatsky, *The Voice of the Silence,* 18.

5. Ibid., 57.

6. A. A. Bailey, *Initiation, Human and Solar,* 82.

7. Ibid., 84.

8. H. P. Blavatsky, *The Voice of the Silence,* 58.

9. A. A. Bailey, *Initiation, Human and Solar,* 85.

10. Ibid.

11. A. A. Bailey, *Esoteric Healing,* 406.

12. Ibid.

13. H. P. Blavatsky, *The Voice of the Silence,* 13.

14. A. A. Bailey, *Discipleship in the New Age* (London: Lucis Press, 1980), vol. 2, 337 and 375.

CHAPTER TEN.
THE GREAT TRANSITION

1. A. A. Bailey, *The Rays and the Initiations,* 600.

2. A. T. Barker, ed., *The Mahatma Letters to A. P. Sinnett,* 401.

3. A. A. Bailey, *Initiation, Human and Solar,* 86.

4. H. P. Blavatsky, *The Voice of the Silence,* 60.

5. A. A. Bailey, *Initiation, Human and Solar,* 88.

6. A. A. Bailey, *The Rays and the Initiations,* 589–602.

7. Ibid., 522. See also her *Discipleship in the New Age,* vol. 2, 388.

8. H. P. Blavatsky, *The Voice of the Silence,* 60–61.

9. A. A. Bailey, *The Rays and the Initiations,* 197.

10. A. A. Bailey, *Initiation, Human and Solar,* 89.

11. A. A. Bailey, *Serving Humanity,* 210–12.

12. A. A. Bailey, *Esoteric Astrology,* 194 and 208.

13. A. A. Bailey, *The Rays and the Initiations,* 494.

14. Ibid., 495.

15. Ibid.

16. A. A. Bailey, *Esoteric Healing,* 406.

17. A. A. Bailey, *The Rays and the Initiations,* 539.

18. H. P. Blavatsky, *The Voice of the Silence,* 62.

19. B. Copenhaver, ed., *Hermetica,* 16.

20. A. A. Bailey, *Esoteric Astrology,* 208.

21. A. A. Bailey, *The Rays and the Initiations,* 162.

22. Ibid., 523.

23. H. P. Blavatsky, *The Voice of the Silence,* 62.

24. A. A. Bailey, *A Treatise on Cosmic Fire,* 118–20.

25. A. A. Bailey, *The Rays and the Initiations,* 46.

26. H. P. Blavatsky, *The Voice of the Silence,* 59.

27. A. A. Bailey, *The Rays and the Initiations,* 486–95.

28. Ibid., 585.

29. H. P. Blavatsky, *The Voice of the Silence,* 67.

30. A. T. Barker, ed. *The Mahatma Letters to A. P. Sinnett,* 48.

31. M. Eliade, *Myths, Dreams and Mysteries* (London: Collins Fontana, 1957), 238.

32. H. P. Blavatsky, *The Voice of the Silence,* 68.

33. A. A. Bailey, *Letters on Occult Meditation,* 37.

34. H. P. Blavatsky, *The Voice of the Silence,* 20.

35. H. P. Blavatsky, *The Secret Doctrine,* vol. 1, 273.

36. A. A. Bailey, *The Rays and the Initiations,* 341.

37. G. R. S. Mead, *The Subtle Body* (London: Stuart and Watkins, 1919), 99.

38. Ibid., 66–67.

39. Ibid., 66.

40. A. A. Bailey, *Initiation, Human and Solar,* 118.

CHAPTER ELEVEN.
THE VARIOUS STAGES OF ADEPTSHIP

1. A. T. Barker, ed., *The Mahatma Letters to A. P. Sinnett,* 123.

2. H. P. Blavatsky, *The Voice of the Silence,* 52–53.

3. Ibid., 65–66.

4. A. A. Bailey, *The Externalisation of the Hierarchy,* 568–69.

5. A. T. Barker, ed., *The Mahatma Letters to A. P. Sinnett,* 257.

6. H. P. Blavatsky, *The Voice of the Silence,* 66–67.

7. Ibid., 67–68.

8. A. A. Bailey, *A Treatise on Cosmic Fire,* 572.

9. A. T. Barker, ed., *The Mahatma Letters to A. P. Sinnett,* 31.

10. A. A Bailey, *A Treatise on Cosmic Fire,* 699.

11. A. A. Bailey, *Esoteric Astrology,* 422 and 589.

12. A. A. Bailey, *A Treatise on Cosmic Fire,* 244 and 251.

13. H. P. Blavatsky, *The Secret Doctrine,* vol. 2, 668.

14. A. A. Bailey, *A Treatise on Cosmic Fire,* 245.

15. A. A. Bailey, *The Rays and the Initiations,* 721–22.

16. Ibid., 719.

17. A. A. Bailey, *A Treatise on Cosmic Fire,* 739.

18. A. A. Bailey, *The Rays and the Initiations,* 722.

19. A. A. Bailey, *The Externalisation of the Hierarchy,* 222–24 and 302–12.

20. H. P. Blavatsky, *The Voice of the Silence,* 70.

21. A. A. Bailey, *A Treatise on Cosmic Fire,* 696.

22. H. P. Blavatsky, *The Secret Doctrine,* vol. 1, 75.

23. H. P. Blavatsky, *The Voice of the Silence,* 71.

24. J. Naydler, *Temple of the Cosmos,* 242.

25. A. A. Bailey, *The Rays and the Initiations,* 395ff. and 729–30.

26. A. A. Bailey, *A Treatise on Cosmic Fire*, 121.

27. A. A. Bailey, *The Rays and the Initiations*, 363.

28. H. P. Blavatsky, *The Secret Doctrine*, vol. 1, 289–90.

29. Ibid.

30. A. A. Bailey, *A Treatise on Cosmic Fire*, 577. See also *The Rays and the Initiations*, 688.

31. H. P. Blavatsky, *The Voice of the Silence*, 72–73.

32. Ibid., 73–74.

33. A. T. Barker, ed., *The Mahatma Letters to A. P. Sinnett*, 62.

34. Ibid., 63.

35. Ibid., 59.

36. S. A. Hoeller, *Gnosticism*, 87.

37. Ibid., 88.

38. G. Scholem, *Zohar—The Book of Splendour*, 79.

39. S. A. Hoeller, *Gnosticism*, 91.

40. E. Arnold, *The Light of Asia* (Adyar, India: Theosophical Publishing House, 1997), 154–62.

41. B. Copenhaver, ed., *Hermetica*, 6.

42. Proclus, *Commentary on the Timaeus of Plato*, 577.

43. E. Arnold, *The Light of Asia*, 163.

44. A. A. Bailey, *The Rays and the Initiations*, 535.

45. A. A. Bailey, *A Treatise on Cosmic Fire*, 1157.

46. Ibid., 904.

47. H. Corbin, *Temps Cyclique et Gnose Ismailienne* (Oxford: Berg International, 1982), 65.

48. A. A. Bailey, *The Rays and the Initiations*, 197.

49. G. R. S. Mead, *Echoes from the Gnosis*, 49.

50. S. A. Hoeller, *The Gnostic Jung*, 191.

51. Ibid., 70–71.

52. H. S. Olcott, *Old Diary Leaves* (Wheaton, Ill.: Theosophical Publishing House, 2002), 236–54.

53. A. A. Bailey, *A Treatise on Cosmic Fire*, 392, 829.

54. Ibid., 618–19, 686, and 847.

55. Ibid., 364.

56. D. Frawley, *Gods, Sages and Kings,* 41.

57. Ibid., 41.

CHAPTER TWELVE.
THE "MASTERS" OF THE MODERN THEOSOPHICAL MOVEMENT

1. K. Johnson, *The Masters Revealed: Madame Blavatsky and the Myth of the Great White Lodge* (New York: SUNY Press, 1994).

2. K. Johnson, *Initiates of Theosophical Masters* (New York: SUNY Press, 1995).

3. Ibid., 12.

4. K. Johnson, *The Masters Revealed,* 4–15.

5. A. T. Barker, ed. *The Mahatma Letters to A. P. Sinnett,* 91.

6. A. A. Bailey, *Discipleship in the New Age,* 787.

7. Ibid., 788.

8. A. A. Bailey, *The Externalisation of the Hierarchy,* 410–11.

9. A. T. Barker, ed., *The Mahatma Letters to A. P. Sinnett,* 87.

10. Ibid., 129.

11. H. P. Blavatsky, *The Secret Doctrine,* vol. 1, 248 and 442.

12. A. T. Barker, ed., *The Mahatma Letters to A. P. Sinnett,* 31.

13. H. P. Blavatsky, *The Secret Doctrine,* vol. 1, 573.

14. Ibid., vol. 1, 63 and 235.

15. A. A. Bailey, *Letters on Occult Meditation,* 189 (see also her *A Treatise on Cosmic Fire,* 436).

16. A. A. Bailey, *The Externalisation of the Hierarchy,* 451.

17. H. P. Blavatsky, *The Secret Doctrine,* vol. 1, 250 and 321, vol. 2, 146ff.

18. A. A. Bailey, *The Rays and the Initiations,* 241. See also *Initiation, Human and Solar,* 54.

19. A. A. Bailey, *The Externalisation of the Hierarchy,* 662–63.

20. Ibid., 479–80. See also *Initiation, Human and Solar,* 54.

21. H. P. Blavatsky, *The Secret Doctrine,* vol. 1, 108.

22. A. A. Bailey, *The Rays and the Initiations,* 83–84.

23. A. A. Bailey, *The Externalisation of the Hierarchy,* 505 and 644.

24. A. A. Bailey, *Initiation, Human and Solar,* 55.

25. A. T. Barker, ed., *The Mahatma Letters to A. P. Sinnett*, 411, 416, and 434.

26. Ibid., 129.

27. A. A. Bailey, *Discipleship in the New Age*, vol. 2, 383.

28. A. T. Barker, ed., *The Mahatma Letters to A. P. Sinnett*, 27. See also A. A. Bailey, *Discipleship in the New Age*, 135.

29. A. A. Bailey, *The Externalisation of the Hierarchy*, 541.

30. Ibid., 644 and 667–69.

31. A. A. Bailey, *Initiation, Human and Solar*, 59–60. See also her *The Externalisation of the Hierarchy*, 664–67.

32. A. A. Bailey, *Telepathy and the Etheric Vehicle* (New York: Lucis Press, 1950), 4.

33. A. A. Bailey, *Initiation, Human and Solar*, 46. See also her *A Treatise on Cosmic Fire*, 1259.

34. A. A. Bailey, *The Externalisation of the Hierarchy*, 682.

35. A. A. Bailey, *Initiation Human and Solar*, 59.

36. A. A. Bailey, *Letters on Occult Meditation*, 305.

37. A. A. Bailey, *A Treatise on Cosmic Fire*, 1259. See also Manly Hall, *The Most Holy Trinosophia of the Complete St. Germain* (Los Angeles: Philosophical Research Society, 1933), xiii.

38. A. A. Bailey, *Initiation, Human and Solar*, 56–57.

39. A. T. Barker, ed., *The Mahatma Letters to A. P. Sinnett*, 109.

40. H. P. Blavatsky, *The Secret Doctrine*, vol. 2, 504.

41. H. S. Olcott, *Old Diary Leaves*, vol. 1, 236–54.

42. A. A. Bailey, *A Treatise on Cosmic Fire*, 1193.

43. A. A. Bailey, *Education in the New Age*, 52–54 and 225.

44. A. A. Bailey, *A Treatise on Cosmic Fire*, 442–48.

45. A. A. Bailey, *The Rays and the Initiations*, 586.

46. A. A. Bailey, *Initiation, Human and Solar*, 57–58.

47. A. A. Bailey, *The Externalisation of the Hierarchy*, 507. See also her *Initiation, Human and Solar*, 53.

48. M. K. Neff, *Personal Memories of H. P. Blavatsky* (London: Rider and Co., 1937), 222 and 279.

49. A. A. Bailey, *A Treatise on Cosmic Fire*, 758.

50. A. A. Bailey, *Letters on Occult Meditation*, 304–5.

51. A. A. Bailey, *A Treatise on Cosmic Fire*, 1080.

52. A. T. Barker, ed., *The Mahatma Letters to A. P. Sinnett,* 410.

53. A. A. Bailey, *Letters on Occult Meditation,* 304–5.

54. A. A. Bailey, *The Externalisation of the Hierarchy,* 527.

55. A. A. Bailey, *Esoteric Psychology,* vol. 2, 33.

56. A. A. Bailey, *The Rays and the Initiations,* 206 and 387.

57. A. A. Bailey, *A Treatise on Cosmic Fire,* 753.

58. A. A. Bailey, *The Rays and the Initiations,* 531.

59. A. A. Bailey, *Initiation Human and Solar,* 88–89.

60. A. A. Bailey, *The Destiny of the Nations,* 17–20.

61. A. A. Bailey, *The Rays and the Initiations,* 523.

62. H. P. Blavatsky, *The Voice of the Silence,* 67.

63. A. T. Barker, ed. *The Mahatma Letters to A. P. Sinnett,* 70.

64. A. A. Bailey, *The Externalisation of the Hierarchy,* 519.

65. Ibid.

66. Ibid.

67. Ibid., 113.

68. A. A. Bailey, *Discipleship in the New Age,* vol. 2, 201–18.

69. Ibid., 201.

70. A. T. Barker, ed., *The Mahatma Letters to A. P. Sinnett,* 73.

71. Ibid., 19.

72. A. A. Bailey, *The Externalisation of the Hierarchy,* 530.

73. Ibid., 107–8.

74. A. A. Bailey, *Discipleship in the New Age,* vol. 2, 326.

75. A. A. Bailey, *The Externalisation of the Hierarchy,* 568.

76. Ibid., 567.

CHAPTER THIRTEEN.
THE JESUS-AS-CHRIST MYSTERY

1. A. T. Barker, ed., *The Mahatma Letters to A. P. Sinnett,* 377.

2. W. Whiston, trans., *The Works of Flavius Josephus: Antiquities of the Jews* (London: T. Nelson and Sons, 1883), Bk. VIII ch. Iii.

3. A. A. Bailey, *The Rays and the Initiations,* 524.

4. A. T. Barker, ed., *The Mahatma Letters to A. P. Sinnett,* 182.

5. J. Yarker, *The Arcane Schools,* 151.

6. H. P. Blavatsky, *Isis Unveiled,* vol. 2 (Los Angeles: The Theosophy Co., 1982), 155.

7. J. Yarker, *The Arcane Schools,* 154. (See also *The Works of Philo* regarding the Therapeutai.)

8. C. Ginsburg, *The Essenes: Their Histories and Doctrines* (London: Routledge and Kegan Paul, 1864), 7.

9. Ibid., 10–15.

10. Ibid., 15–16.

11. Ibid., 40–49 (echoing the ancient Jewish historian Josephus in his book *The Works of Flavius Josephus: The Jewish War,* Bk II Ch. 8, sections 2–18).

12. H. P. Blavatsky, *The Theosophical Glossary,* 108, and *Isis Unveiled,* vol. 2, 180.

13. J. Yarker, *The Arcane Schools,* 149.

14. Ibid., 98.

15. Ibid., 154.

16. H. P. Blavatsky, *The Secret Doctrine,* vol. 1, 198.

17. J. Yarker, *The Arcane Schools,* 157–58.

18. D. Fideler, *Jesus Christ, Sun of God* (Wheaton, Ill.: Quest Books, 1993), 176.

19. J. Yarker, *The Arcane Schools,* 159–60.

20. H. P. Blavatsky, *Isis Unveiled,* vol. 2, 204.

21. Ibid., 386, referring to the *Sepher Toledoth Jeshu.*

22. A. A. Bailey, *Initiation, Human and Solar,* 56.

23. H. P. Blavatsky, *Isis Unveiled,* vol. 2, 548.

24. Ibid., 132.

25. J. Yarker, *The Arcane Schools,* 158.

26. H. P. Blavatsky, *Isis Unveiled,* vol. 2, 197–98.

27. H. P. Blavatsky, *Collected Writings,* vol. vi (Wheaton, Ill.: Theosophical Publishing House, 2002), 265.

28. M. Meyer, *The Secret Gospels of Jesus* (London: Darton, Longman and Todd, 2005), xxi and xxvii.

29. E. B. Szekely, *The Essene Origins of Christianity* (Nelson, Canada: International Biogenic Society, 1993), 110.

30. Ibid., 109.

31. D. Fideler, *Jesus Christ, Sun of God,* 29–30.

32. Ibid.

33. Ibid., 51.

34. Ibid., 38.

35. H. P. Blavatsky, *The Secret Doctrine*, vol. 2, 231.

36. H. P. Blavatsky, *The Key to Theosophy*, 79.

37. H. P. Blavatsky, *Isis Unveiled*, vol. 2, 341.

38. A. A. Bailey, *Initiation, Human and Solar*, 56.

39. Philostratus, *The Life of Apollonius of Tyana* (Peabody, Mass.: Hendrickson Publishers, 1993), Bk. I, xi–xvii.

40. Ibid.

41. Ibid., xiii–xiv.

42. A. A. Bailey, *The Rays and the Initiations*, 254.

43. See J. Wansborough, *Quranic Studies* (Oxford: Oxford University Press, 1977), and also Ibn Warraq, *The Quest for the Historical Muhammad* (New York: Prometheus Books, 2000).

44. A. A. Bailey, *The Rays and the Initiations*, 706.

45. Ibid., 706, and A. A. Bailey, *Esoteric Astrology*, 564.

CHAPTER FOURTEEN.
THE CHRIST–MAITREYA BUDDHA MYSTERY

1. A. A. Bailey, *A Treatise on Cosmic Fire*, 120 and 211.

2. A. A. Bailey, *The Reappearance of the Christ*, 82–83.

3. H. P. Blavatsky, *The Secret Doctrine*, vol. 1, 384.

4. Ibid., 470.

5. Ibid., 109.

6. Ibid., vol. 2, 207.

7. A. A. Bailey, *A Treatise on Cosmic Fire*, 1195ff. and 1224–26.

8. H. P. Blavatsky, *The Secret Doctrine*, vol. 2, 207.

9. Ibid.

10. Ibid., vol. 1, 129–32.

11. Ibid., vol. 1, 108.

12. Ibid., 108 and 162.

13. A. A. Bailey, *Letters on Occult Meditation*, 351.

14. J. S. Gordon, *The Rise and Fall of Atlantis,* 219ff.

15. A. A. Bailey, *The Rays and the Initiations,* 696–98.

16. J. Overton Fuller, *Blavatsky and Her Teachers,* 113.

17. Ibid., 114.

18. A. T. Barker, ed., *The Mahatma Letters to A. P. Sinnett,* 62 and 275.

19. The Holy Bible, John XIV:6. See also A. A. Bailey's *Education in the New Age,* 52–53.

20. See H. J. Spierenberg, *The Buddhism of H. P. Blavatsky* (San Diego, Calif.: Point Loma Publishing, 1991).

21. H. P. Blavatsky, *The Voice of the Silence,* 70–79.

22. A. A. Bailey, *The Reappearance of the Christ,* 96–97.

23. Ibid., 40.

24. A. A. Bailey, *Education in the New Age,* 53.

25. H. J. Spierenberg, *The Vedanta Commentaries of H. P. Blavatsky* (San Diego, Calif.: Point Loma Publishing, 1992), 90.

26. Ibid., 110.

27. A. A. Bailey, *Letters on Occult Meditation,* 305.

28. H. P. Blavatsky, *The Secret Doctrine,* vol. 1, 108.

29. A. A. Bailey, *The Rays and the Initiations,* 555.

30. Ibid., 553–54.

CHAPTER FIFTEEN.
THE MODERN RESTORATION
OF THE MYSTERIES

1. A. A. Bailey, *The Rays and the Initiations,* 477.

2. Ibid., 478.

3. Ibid.

4. Ibid., 18–357.

5. Ibid., 383–84.

6. Ibid., 334–35.

7. A. A. Bailey, *The Rays and the Initiations,* 333–35 and 372.

8. Ibid., 399.

9. Ibid., 334.

10. A. T, Barker, ed., *The Mahatma Letters to A. P. Sinnett,* 124.

11. A. A. Bailey, *The Externalisation of the Hierarchy,* 230.

12. H. P. Blavatsky, *The Secret Doctrine,* vol. 2, 46 and 680.

13. A. A. Bailey, *The Externalisation of the Hierarchy,* 225–26 and 230.

14. Ibid., 437–38.

15. A. A. Bailey, *The Rays and the Initiations,* 374.

16. A. A. Bailey, *The Externalisation of the Hierarchy,* 277.

17. G. Scholem, *The Messianic Idea in Judaism,* 105.

18. Ibid.

19. A. A. Bailey, *The Externalisation of the Hierarchy,* 30.

20. H. P. Blavatsky, *The Secret Doctrine,* vol. 1, 266–67.

21. A. A. Bailey, *The Reappearance of the Christ,* 122.

22. Ibid., 151.

23. Ibid., 86.

24. A. A. Bailey, *Education in the New Age,* 119.

25. A. A. Bailey, *A Treatise on Cosmic Fire,* 1079–80.

26. A. A. Bailey, *Education in the New Age,* 4–7.

27. A. A. Bailey, *The Externalisation of the Hierarchy,* 298–99.

28. A. A. Bailey, *Education in the New Age,* 94–95.

29. A. A. Bailey, *The Externalisation of the Hierarchy,* 582.

30. A. A. Bailey, *Letters on Occult Meditation,* 307–8.

31. Ibid., 309.

32. Ibid.

33. P. G. Bowen, *The Sayings of the Ancient One* (Wheaton, Ill.: Theosophical Publishing House, 1985), 38.

34. A. A. Bailey, *The Externalisation of the Hierarchy.*

EPILOGUE

1. A. T. Barker, ed., *The Mahatma Letters to A. P. Sinnett,* 39.

2. F. Schuon, *The Transcendent Unity of Religions* (Wheaton, Ill.: Quest Books, 1984), 9.

APPENDIX A.
PLANETARY CHAINS AND ROUNDS

1. H. P. Blavatsky, *The Secret Doctrine,* vol. 1, 159.
2. W. Y, Evans-Wentz, *The Tibetan Book of the Dead,* 6–7.
3. A. T. Barker, ed., *The Mahatma Letters to A. P. Sinnett,* 180.
4. H. P. Blavatsky, *The Secret Doctrine,* vol. 1, 198–207.
5. Hence the suggestion made by the Adepts themselves that the Sun would be "the first to disintegrate at the solar pralaya" (*The Mahatma Letters to A. P. Sinnett,* 188).

APPENDIX B.
THE ISSUE OF SHAMBALLA

1. D. Frawley, *Gods, Sages and Kings,* 295.
2. H. P. Blavatsky, *The Secret Doctrine,* vol. 2, 161ff. (See also A. A. Bailey, *A Treatise on White Magic,* 378.)
3. A. A. Bailey, *A Treatise on White Magic,* 379–80.
4. A. A. Bailey, *Initiation, Human and Solar,* 33.
5. H. P. Blavatsky, *The Secret Doctrine,* vol. 2, 224 and 337–40.
6. R. Bernard, *Agharta: The Subterranean World,* n.p., 1960.
7. G. de Santillan and H. von Dechend, *Hamlet's Mill,* 227 and 232–33.
8. A. A. Bailey, *The Rays and the Initiations,* 267–68.
9. Ibid., 268.
10. Ibid., 269.
11. A. A. Bailey, *Telepathy and the Etheric Vehicle,* 41–51.

APPENDIX C.
THE EVOLUTION OF THE HUMAN RACIAL TYPE

1. H. P. Blavatsky, *The Secret Doctrine,* vol. 2, 184ff.
2. Ibid., 227ff.
3. A. A. Bailey, *Esoteric Psychology,* vol. 2, 111.
4. Ibid.
5. A. A. Bailey, *A Treatise on Cosmic Fire,* 425.

6. G. R. S. Mead, *The Subtle Body,* 9.

7. A. A. Bailey, *Esoteric Psychology,* vol. 2, 213ff.

8. Ibid.

APPENDIX D.
THE THREE SOLAR SYSTEMS AND
THE FAILURE OF THE MOON CHAIN

1. A. A. Bailey, *A Treatise on Cosmic Fire,* 618–19, 686–87, and 847.

2. A. A. Bailey, *Initiation, Human and Solar,* 33. (See also *A Treatise on Cosmic Fire,* 700.)

3. A. T. Barker, ed. *The Mahatma Letters to A. P. Sinnett,* 179.

4. A. A. Bailey, *The Externalisation of the Hierarchy,* 556.

APPENDIX E.
SPIRITUAL AVATARS

1. H. P. Blavatsky, *The Secret Doctrine,* vol. 2, 233.

2. A. A. Bailey, *The Externalisation of the Hierarchy,* 491.

3. Ibid., 299.

GLOSSARY

Adept: A highly evolved Intelligence who, entirely through sustained self-effort in developing his spiritual faculties, has passed out of the human kingdom into the fifth kingdom in Nature.

Adi (Sanskrit): The highest of the seven states of being contained by the demiurgic Oversoul of the world; pure primeval or divine substance.

Aeon: A member of the hierarchies of celestial Intelligence that contain the Oversoul of our solar system within their consciousness, from which all cycles of lesser (planetary) existence and their associated kingdoms of Nature are then generated.

Aether: The highest of the five natural elements, from which the lesser four—fire, air, water, and earth—are themselves generated.

Ahi: The (apparently Tibetan) name given by H. P. Blavatsky in *The Secret Doctrine,* signifying the creative hierarchies of Elohim.

Ain Soph Aur: The Boundless Light of the kosmic buddhic plane/state (Mahat) from which the planetary Chains and Rounds are emanated.

Akasa (Sanskrit): The spiritual essence that pervades Space. Also, the monadic state within which All-Knowledge of the system in question exists. Derived from Akh-as, the semi-divine state from which all purposefully creative, "downward" emanation takes place within a field of Creation in response to logoic intent.

Amshaspends: The Persian equivalent of the Judaic Elohim.

Anima Mundi (Latin): The World Soul, the divine essence of which permeates and animates the forms of the smallest atom to those of the highest celestial beings.

Antahkarana (Sanskrit): The "path" of consciousness between the lower and Higher Mind principles.

Anupadaka (Sanskrit): The pregenetic state of the "self-born," "divine spark" and also of its parent, the Dhyani Buddha.

Apollonius of Tyana: The Pythagorean philosopher and highly reputed Adept-theurgist born in Cappadocia in the early first century CE, who during the latter part of his long life founded a school of esotericism in Ephesus.

Archon: The highest form of planetary archangel.

Arhat: A self-evolved spiritual Adept, there being four stages of Adeptship, the last culminating in the high initiate becoming a human Buddha or Bodhisattva.

Aristotelian Thought: The process of logical deduction used by the Greek philosopher Aristotle, involving classification of forms of appearance and associated function. In modern terms, it is reductionism, that is, interpretation through a sum of the parts.

Ashram: A sacred place of learning controlled by a spiritual guru (in India).

Astral light: The mass of subatmospheric etheric substance contained by the Oversoul of our planet, from which all planetary forms are generated and to which they return following their natural degeneration. Otherwise known as the planet's *linga sarira* (Sanskrit) or its "etheric double."

Atma (Sanskrit): The principle of Divine Will emanated by the Monad; the higher, spiritual equivalent of *prana* (life force).

Avatar: A divine being who, despite having himself passed beyond the necessity of personal reincarnation, nevertheless does so self-sacrificially for a specific purpose in connection with furthering the evolution of mankind.

Berber: Otherwise known as the Irmazigh, the original Berber peoples are of naturally tall, Indo-Caucasian appearance, with fair hair and blue eyes. They comprise the indigenous ethnic tribes of northwest Africa (the Mahgreb) geographically westward of the Siwa oasis, in Egypt, and extending from the Mediterranean to the Atlantic. The Berber language forms the "Berber branch" of the Afro-Asiatic language family. Today, most Berber-speaking people live in Morocco and Algeria, although smaller populations are also to be found scattered throughout Tunisia, Libya, and Mauritania.

Bhagavad Gita: The "Lord's Song"—a part of the *Mahabharata,* the great epic poem of ancient India, involving a dialogue between Arjuna (man) and Krisna (the Spiritual Ego).

Bharaka: The Arabic term meaning "spiritual Grace," as used in the Islamic world.

Bodhisattva: The highest potential state of achievement within our field of planetary consciousness, wherein the Adept becomes at-one with the nature of the demiurgic Deity (Logos) and thus becomes his agent of expression in the lower world system.

Buddhi (Sanskrit): The kosmic "etheric double" of our solar system; the higher, spiritual equivalent of the "astral light" of the planet.

Causal Soul: The intermediate, semi-spiritual soul that provides the human being with his sense of self-consciousness and his Higher Mind faculty.

Chakra (Sanskrit): A psychic force center in the etheric body of an organism—the human being having seven main such centers and a variety of lesser ones.

Chaos: The wholly unorganized and homogeneous universal state that preexists all Creation and to which all Creation eventually returns.

Chohan: The third stage of spiritual Adeptship.

Confucius (551–479 BCE): A Chinese philosopher and politician whose philosophy emphasized personal and governmental morality, correctness of social relationships, justice, and sincerity. He championed strong family loyalty, ancestor worship, respect of elders by their children and of husbands by their wives. He also recommended family as a basis for ideal government. He espoused the well-known principle "Do not do to others what you do not want done to yourself."

Council of Nicaea: A council of Christian bishops convened in Nicaea in Bithynia by the Roman Emperor Constantine I in CE 325. This involved the first ecumenical effort to attain consensus in the church through an assembly representing all of Christendom. Its main accomplishments involved settlement of the Trinitarian issue of the nature of Christ as the only Divine Son and his relationship to God the Father, plus the promulgation of early canon law.

Craft Masonry: Ancient Craft Masonry—one of the world's oldest and largest fraternal organizations with meetings based on sacred allegory and ritual—refers to the first three degrees of modern Freemasonry. It is known by many names including "the Blue Lodge," "Symbolic Masonry," or simply as "the Craft." It involves three initiatory degrees: Entered Apprentice, Fellow Craft, and Master Mason. Hermetic philosophy, Kabbala, and Alchemy, for example, share many of the same symbolisms.

Creationism: The rabid system of completely literal belief in the apparent wording of the Christian Bible, which rejects any suggestion of such wording being perhaps merely allegorical or metaphorical in nature.

Darwinism: The scientific anthropological theory developed by Charles Darwin in the nineteenth century suggesting (a) that all evolution occurs through the strength of survival of the fittest and (b) that the human being and the anthropoid ape are both evolved from a simian ancestor.

Demiurge: The Creator-God (or hierarchy of gods) responsible for generating the actual forms of worlds and their inhabitants/kingdoms of Nature in response to an impulse from higher kosmic sources, in response to sensed Divine Purpose.

Deva: An angelic member of the hierarchy of beings parallel to Man, responsible for acting as the memory of the Logos but having no sense of choice as does Man.

Dharma (Sanskrit): Duty or purpose of a spiritual nature.

Dhyani Buddha: A kosmic Intelligence comprising an aspect of the creative Intelligence (imagination) and memory of the Logos.

Dhyani Chohan: A kosmic Intelligence beyond the highest stage of human Adeptship.

Dionysian Mysteries: The highest and most sacred of the three ancient Greek Mystery Schools, erroneously believed by most modern historians to be founded on rituals involving "wine, women, and song" in unbridled orgiastic license. In fact, the associated philosophy involved the highest spiritual asceticism.

Dionysus: The Greek demigod, son of Zeus, who esoterically represents the human Monad.

Dipankara ("the Lamp bearer"): One of the early historic Buddhas said to have predicted the later incarnation of one of his own disciples as Gautama Buddha.

"Divine Spark": An alternative term for the monadic unit, which represents an aspect of the divine Mind of the Logos.

Dravidian: Pertaining to the ancient civilization of India, which preceded the Indo-Caucasian, now associated with the peoples and culture of southern India and Sri Lanka.

Druze: A religious sect of Sufis, the "disciples of Hamsa," living on and around Mount Lebanon in Syria.

Dweller-on-the-Threshold: The elemental entity comprising the semi-individualized synthesis of all the worst aspects of the human persona, generated and accrued over many lifetimes.

Elemental: A low-grade psychic entity still working its way along the involutionary scale of consciousness development.

Elohim: The Hebrew/Jewish word (derived from the much earlier "Elu") for the archangelic groups responsible for Creation out of their own nature.

Epigenetics: A field of modern science within the field of biology, and specifically genetics. It involves the study of inheritable changes or modifications by genes or cellular phenotype caused by environmental influences or mechanisms other than changes in the naturally underlying DNA sequence.

Eros: A Greek word denoting the universal creative principle emanated by the Titan god Ouranos to fertilize the area of Space (Gaia) in which Creation is to take place.

Esoteric: Derived from the Greek word *soter* meaning "obscure," it means that which is *spiritually* obscure for intentional reasons related to protecting its sacred nature.

Essene: A mysterious sect (supposedly of Hebrews) who, according to Pliny, had lived near the Dead Sea for many millennia. Their traditions and practices were clearly of mixed Pythagorean and Buddhist origin in nature.

Ether: The invisible plasma underlying and supporting the gaseous atmosphere of our planet. Otherwise known to some esotericists as the "astral light."

Event horizon: A modern scientific term used to denote the peripheral field of a celestial body. In esoteric terms, it denotes the Ring-Pass-Not of the soul or Oversoul.

Fohat: The electric energy of the Mind principle, which, as H. P. Blavatsky describes, "digs holes in Space," thereby generating the first stage of Creation through spiral-cyclic isolation of a field of potential existence.

Freemasonry: A fraternal organization derived from the ancient Mystery Tradition, the modern version of which arose in Europe from obscure origins in late sixteenth to early seventeenth century Craft Masonry. The (worldwide) fraternity is itself administratively organized as independent Grand Lodges or sometimes Orients, each of which governs its own jurisdiction comprising subordinate local Lodges.

Gematria: A division of the sacred Kabbala involving the numerological value of Hebrew words and phrases through adding up the value of all the associated letters.

Gnosticism: The philosophy of "Sacred Knowledge," usually associated by historians with development in Alexandria around the turn of the Aries-Pisces millennium, but actually of far older origin.

Golden Dawn: The Hermetic Order of the Golden Dawn was an influential sacred magic orientated cult, active in Great Britain during the late nineteenth and early twentieth centuries. Its ritualized system involved the practice of theurgy, supposedly in relation to wished-for spiritual development. The Golden Dawn system—involving three internal Orders—was based on hierarchy and initiation like Masonic Lodges. However, women were admitted to it on an equal basis with men.

Group soul: The as-yet-unindividualized mass Intelligence that, emanated by the Logos down in the objective world state, will progressively incarnate as the various kingdoms of Nature, eventually becoming self-conscious man.

Hebdomad: A septenary form or system.

Hermeneutic: A structured system of planes of consciousness such as that found in the modern theosophical system of thought.

Herodotus: The Greek historian of antiquity (fifth century BCE) known for his famous classical work, *The Histories.*

Hermetica: The sacred Greco-Egyptian writings rediscovered in 1460 and translated into Latin at the court of Cosimo de Medici in Florence.

Hologram: An apparently three-dimensional image derived from holography, a technique involving the use of a laser, interference, diffraction, and light intensity plus associated illumination of the whole process.

Humanist: Follower of a body of philosophies and ethical principles that emphasize the value of humanity, individually and collectively, ascribing greater value to rational thought derived from classical, pre-Christian sources than to religious faith.

Hylozoism: The concept that there is no such thing as dead matter, all matter in the omniverse being imbued with the principle of Life.

Hypatia: The highly regarded female neo-Platonist philosopher and teacher of mathematics and astronomy, head of the Platonist school in Alexandria during the early fifth century CE, who was murdered and dismembered by a Christian mob, motivated by jealous local Christian theologians.

Iamblichus: The great and learned philosopher and mystic of the third-fourth centuries CE, born in Syria, disciple of Porphyry and revitalizer of theurgical magic among the neo-Platonic fraternity of his time.

Imam Mahdi: The Islamic equivalent of the Christ, or the Judaic Messiah, similarly seen as a cultural-cum-spiritual Avatar.

Jiva (Sanskrit): The lesser "divine spark" emanated by the Monad—that which animates the human intelligence.

Judgment Day: That part of the astrological cycle in question when a decision is made by the directing Adept Hierarchy or Guides of the race as between those groups of humanity ready for imminent onward progressive spiritual development and those who are not, the opportunity for the latter being deferred to the next cycle.

Kabbala: The esoteric philosophy (historically but erroneously regarded as derived from Judaism) that is structured around the concept of the ten emanations of Elohim groups. The name itself appears to have been derived by phonetic corruption from Geb-Allah, "the Word of God."

Kama (Sanskrit): The principle or state of desire.

Karma (Sanskrit): The Law of Cause and Effect in Universal Nature.

Kosmos/kosmic: Refers to the visible and invisible (that is, the objective and subjective) universe, involving the principles of Unitary Being and Universal Consciousness.

Krisna: The divine Avatar of Hinduism.

Kumara: An ever-virgin divine youth; a Planetary Spirit responsible (with others) for the overall command and running of a planetary globe.

Lethe: Greek word signifying the sleep that overcomes the spiritual nature when descending into incarnation.

Logos: Greek word meaning "the Intelligent Light emanated by a divine Being in charge of a planet or solar system."

Magi: Plural noun, derived from the Latin Magus, indicating a "wise man."

Mahachohan: Great Chohan; also a title within the Spiritual Hierarchy given to the highest Adept with overall responsibility for the Third Ray influence on our planet.

Mahatma (Sanskrit): One who, as a Master, has attained at least the second of the four stages of Adeptship.

Manas (Sanskrit): The Mind principle.

Manu: A divine being who, in the Vedic tradition, is representative of the perfect Man.

Mayavirupa: The illusive and immaterial psycho-spiritual form projected at a distance by an accomplished Adept.

Mesmerism: The practice of healing through the projection of personal magnetism in such a manner as to affect the etheric double of the human being or animal.

Messiah: In the Hebrew Bible a *messiah* is understood as an anointed king or high priest. However, messiahs were not exclusively Jewish kings. For example, the Hebrew Bible refers to Cyrus the Great, king of Persia, as a messiah. In later Jewish messianic tradition and eschatology, the messiah became a leader anointed by God (i.e., an Avatar), effectively a future king of Israel, descended from King David, who will supposedly herald the age of global peace.

Metaphysics: Originally from *metaphysis,* literally, "beyond the *physis,*" the latter being a Greek word for the state of the fifth element (aether).

Monad: The "divine spark"; derived by Leibnitz from the Pythagorean *monas,* itself derived from the Sanskrit *manas,* meaning "the Mind principle."

Morphic: The taking of shape or form of a particular structure.

Morphogenetic: The telepathically transmitted impulse that gives rise to the generation of particular forms, usually as between species of plants or animals.

Mysteries: Ancient sacred observances and rituals connected with initiation, mostly kept secret from the profane or uninitiated masses.

Nag Hammadi: A collection of early Christian gnostic texts discovered in central Egypt in 1945.

Nature spirit: An angelic entity of the lower deva hierarchies, concerned with building and maintaining the various forms of the plant and mineral kingdoms, as well as helping to control the elements of fire, air, water, and earth.

Nirmanakaya: The psycho-spiritual post mortem state chosen by the Adept who wishes to continue his work for the Spiritual Hierarchy within the limitations of our world state, rather than leaving it to attain a complete personal *nirvana.*

Nirvana: A state of (individualized) liberation from and renunciation of all involvement in human affairs, resulting in the highest spiritual bliss.

Occult Science: Concealed or secret knowledge of Nature's energies and forces and how they can be controlled and manipulated.

Ogdoad: The eightfold entity, form, or state that enclosed seven lesser states.

Orphic Mysteries: Orphism involved religious beliefs and ritualized practices originating in the ancient Greek and the Hellenistic world, associated with sacred literature ascribed to the mythical poet Orpheus, who descended into Hades to recover his wife Persephone but returned without her. The associated allegory is symbolic of the incarnation of the human Spiritual Ego endeavoring to raise its lesser (terrestrial) soul to spiritual heights.

Oversoul: A name ascribed to the Greek philosopher Plotinus, meaning the greater or macrocosmic soul body enclosing and giving rise to the lesser soul.

Pagan: According to the dictionary, "a heathen person without a religion." However, most modern "pagans" are believers in Earth Mystery traditions of a psycho-spiritual nature.

Pali canon: The ancient and most sacred religious texts of India, which preceded the Sanskrit, based on the language of the prehistoric civilization of Magadha. The original Buddhist scriptures are all written in Pali.

Permanent Atom: A term originated by Annie Besant and Charles Leadbeater during their clairvoyant research into the etheric nature of the atom, as described in their subsequently published theosophical book *Occult Chemistry*.

Piezo-electric: The production of electric polarity by applying mechanical stress to crystal structures.

Pistis Sophia: An important sacred gnostic text (re)discovered in the eighteenth century, possibly originating in the second century CE. It deals with the supposedly post-resurrection gnostic teachings of Jesus to the assembled disciples (including his mother Mary, Mary Magdalene, and Martha), after the risen Christ had accomplished eleven years speaking with his disciples. In it, the complex structures and hierarchies of the heaven world are revealed.

Planetary Spirit: A highly evolved (divine) Intelligence, which, although once human, has subsequently progressed beyond even the fifth kingdom in Nature and has thus developed a pan-solar or kosmic consciousness.

Plasm: A colloidal or fluidic precellular mass of pregenetic substance, which gives rise to organic forms. Germ plasm is a zone found in the cytoplasm of the egg cells of some organisms, which contains determinants that will give rise to cell lineage. The term "germ plasm" was first used by the German biologist August Weismann (1834–1914), whose theory states that multicellular organisms consist of germ cells, which contain and transmit heritable information, plus somatic cells, which carry out ordinary bodily functions.

Plotinus: The major third century CE Greek neo-Platonic philosopher, pupil of the Alexandrian Ammonius Saccas, who first used the term *theosophy*. In Plotinus's system of thought there are three dominant principles: the One, the Intellect, and the Soul. He also originated the idea of the Oversoul. His metaphysical writings have inspired centuries of Pagan, Christian, Jewish, Islamic, and gnostic philosophers.

Poseidonis: A term given by H. P. Blavatsky to the last remaining island of northern Atlantis, described in Plato's work *Timaeus and Critias* as having been located facing the modern Straits of Gibraltar and having disappeared in a mighty cataclysm some nine thousand years before his own time (i.e., around 12,500 years ago).

Post-Modernism: Despite there being no consensus among scholars as to a precise definition, the term indicates any interpretation of reality by the human mind in objection to the paradigms of orthodox science.

Precession (of equinoxes): The cycle of 25,920 years during which our Earth appears to revolve backward through the Zodiac, at the rate of one degree every seventy-two years.

Protoplasm: The first inchoate form of precellular existence.

Ptah: The ancient Egyptian creator god known as "the Great Architect." The name Ptah is another form of Buddha.

Quadrivium: In the system of medieval education, the teaching of arithmetic, geometry, astronomy, and music.

Quantum theory: Quantum theory is about the very nature of matter. It evolved as a new branch of theoretical physics during the first few decades of the twentieth century in an endeavor to understand those fundamental properties of matter associated with the tiny particles of which atoms are made, as opposed to Einstein's relativity theory, which dealt with the largest phenomena in the universe. It began with the study of the interactions of matter and radiation that could not be explained by either classical mechanics or the theory of electromagnetism.

Qumran texts: Otherwise known as "The Dead Sea Scrolls," these are a collection of 972 texts consisting of biblical manuscripts from what is now known as the Hebrew Bible, plus various extra-biblical documents, discovered on the northwest shore of the Dead Sea. These scrolls are traditionally identified with the ancient Jewish gnostic sect called the Essenes.

Rig Veda: The first and most important of the four Vedas of ancient India, great literary works of Hindu philosophy, compiled many thousands of years BCE.

Ring-pass-not: The peripheral field surrounding a celestial body, otherwise known as an "Oversoul."

Rosicrucian: Member of a school of hermetic philosophy that appeared in the early seventeenth century in western Europe, orientated around the mystic figure of one Christian Rosenkreutz and having as its glyph a red rose superimposed on a white cross. Rosicrucianism involves an allegorical literary work orientated toward revealing esoteric truths of the ancient past, which had been previously revealed to spiritual Adepts, although concealed from access by the average man. The work was contained in two "Manifestos"—the *Fama Fraternitatis* and the *Confessio Fraternitatis,* both of which were openly antagonistic to Roman Catholicism and called for a general spiritual reformation of mankind.

Round (Planetary): The immense evolutionary cycle during and through which the Monad passes round the complete chain of a planetary scheme of seven globes.

Saracen: Saracen was a term for heavy cavalry Muslim warriors widely used throughout Europe during the later medieval era. However, during the early centuries CE among the Greeks and Latins, it referred to a people who lived in desert areas around northern Arabia but who were specifically quite distinct from the Arabian peoples. In Byzantium and later in Europe during the early medieval era, the term began to be used to describe Arab tribes as well, and by the twelfth century, the term had become synonymous with any Muslim. Wider research suggests that the original Saracens were perhaps of distantly colonizing Tuareg origin, from the Mahgreb and Saharan areas, hence (phonetically) the origin of the "Turk-ish" (i.e., Tuareg-ish) Ottoman empire.

Sepher ha Zohar: The "Book of Splendor," which appeared in Europe during the thirteenth century but which appears to be of pre-CE Aramaic origin, is the foundational book of Jewish mystical thought known as Kabbala. It is a group of literary works that include commentary on the mystical aspects of the sacred Torah. It also contains a discussion of the nature of Deity and of the soul, the origins and composition of the universe, spiritual redemption, the relationship of the "true self" or Ego to "The Light of God," plus the relationship between man and the divine Universal Force that animates the kosmos.

Sephiroth: One of the ten kosmic emanations in the kabbalistic system of creative deities.

Serapean Mysteries: The late Greco-Egyptian form of belief adopted by Ptolemy in order to regenerate religion in Egypt following the death of Alexander the Great and the separation of his empire into three parts.

Shaman: A "witch doctor" or exponent of native community cult magic, who exercises his art through psycho-spiritual ritual in which he/she is literally taken over by elemental spirits in order to generate specific theurgical or thaumaturgical effects.

Shamballa: The fabled dwelling place of the divine Kumaras, said to exist in invisibly ethereal substance somewhere to the north of the Tibetan plateau.

Skandha: One of a group of (five) psychic attributes, which act as the coordinated memory from previous lifetimes, giving rise to reincarnation as a defined human personality.

Socratic thought: Socrates was a classical Greek Athenian philosopher of the fifth–sixth centuries BCE. Acknowledged as one of the founders of Western philosophy, he was himself the enigmatic teacher of Plato, many of whose writings are clearly dedicated to him and his ethical philosophy. Much of the latter was expressed through irony and serially logical query in order to highlight the fundamental but underlying issues related to any particular subject.

Sophia: From Suf-Ea, the "divine breath of knowledge" emanating from the Kosmic Mind.

Soul: The coordination of a group of spirits having a common sense of identity (or "selfhood") into a peripheral field of isolated existence, which then acts as a space within which Creation can take place.

Sufism: An initiation-based "Mystery" philosophy of life, the term itself being derived from the same root as *suf* (breath) and Sophia (Wisdom). Now recognized as merely the esoteric aspect of Islam, Sufism is actually far older and dates back to ancient Indo-Persia.

Sutratma (Sanskrit): The ethereal "life thread" connecting the physical human being to his animating Spiritual Ego.

Tabula Smagdarina: The "Emerald Tablet" of Hermes Trismegistus, according to the hermetic tradition, it is a supposedly alchemical text (which has never been found, however) purporting to reveal the secret of the primordial substance and its transmutations.

Tetraktys: The ten living points making up a sacred equilateral triangle, as an expression of a manifesting Divinity, ascribed to the philosophy of Pythagoras.

Theophany: The subjectively visual perception of divine organization.

Theosophical: From *theos-sophia,* "the knowledge of the gods." Modern theosophy involves a metaphysically structured concept of the psycho-spiritual "mechanics and dynamics" behind all objective existence.

Therapeutai: An inner school of esotericists orientated toward healing, based in Alexandria and supposedly comprising Hellenistic Jews.

Theurgy: The knowledge and capacity of how discriminatingly to invoke higher beings and being able to communicate consciously with them, a faculty necessitating a very high degree of self-conscious spirituality.

Titan: A member of the supreme family of kosmic gods in the ancient Greek Mystery tradition.

Transpersonal psychology: That school of psychology that studies the self-transcendent or spiritual aspects of the human experience. Transpersonal experiences may thus be defined as experiences in which the sense of self extends beyond the individual or personal to encompass recognition and realization of the highest subjective potential of humankind.

Trivium: In the medieval educational system, the teaching of grammar, rhetoric, and logic.

Tuareg: Member of an originally late Atlantean tribe based in northwestern Africa, having reddish skins and being unusually tall in physique. The men folk were characterized by their (usually blue) turbans and masked faces while also being generally known for their long-distance camel-borne incursions over vast Saharan desert areas to attack and plunder towns, cities, and caravan trains.

Upadhi (Sanskrit): An ethereal base or vehicle of consciousness within the psycho-spiritual consciousness of the human organism.

Umayyad Caliphate: The Umayyad Caliphate (ca. 661–750 CE) was the second of the four major Islamic caliphates established after the death of Muhammad. Although the Umayyad family originally came from the city of Mecca, its capital was Damascus. After the Umayyads were overthrown by the Abbasid Caliphate, they fled across North Africa to the Iberian Peninsula (Al-Andalus), where they established the Caliphate of Córdoba, which lasted until 1031 before coming to an end.

Wahabi Islam: An eighteenth-century form of Islam, named after its scholarly founder, but adopted and radically altered in style by modern religious extremists, aiming at literal return to the Qur'an and the Hadeeth, plus sole reliance on interpretation of Islamic theology and philosophy by trained scholars.

World Mother: The planetary "Oversoul."

Yin-yang: The Chinese term for the duality of shadow and light that in their ancient philosophy concerned itself with the magnetic polarity between all things in Nature.

Ziggurat: The ancient form of stepped pyramid found in both Babylon and Central America, used as a temple involving celestial religious orientation and initiatory ritual.

Zionism: The extreme form of Judaic theology, which concerns itself with (a) purity in all respects, and (b) the supposed return to Zion, a phonetically corrupted term, derived from the Indo-Tibetan *dhzyan,* intimating the semi-divine state of the Monad, not a geographical location as supposed by modern adherents of "orthodox" Judaic theology.

Zoroastrianism: The so-called "fire-worshipping" religion of ancient Persia of which Zoroaster (seemingly derived from the Vedic "Zeru-Ishtar") or Zarathustra was the founder.

BIBLIOGRAPHY

Allen, R. H. *Star Names: Their Lore and Meaning*. New York: Dover Publications, 1980.

Armstrong, K. *Muhammed—A Biography of the Prophet*. London: Phoenix Press, 1991.

Arnold, E. *The Light of Asia*. Adyar, India: Theosophical Publishing House, 1997.

Bailey, A. A. *Discipleship in the New Age*. London: Lucis Press, 1980.

———. *Esoteric Psychology*. London: Lucis Press, 1981.

———. *The Externalisation of the Hierarchy*. 2nd ed. New York: Lucis Press, 1958.

———. *Initiation, Human and Solar*. London: Lucis Press, 1977.

———. *Letters on Occult Meditation*. New York: Lucis Press, 1973.

———. *The Reappearance of the Christ*. London: Lucis Press, 1969.

———. *The Soul: The Quality of Life*. London: Lucis Press, 1974.

———. *Telepathy and the Etheric Vehicle*. New York: Lucis Press, 1950.

———. *A Treatise on Cosmic Fire*. New York: Lucis Press, 1964.

———. *A Treatise on the Seven Rays Vols. I–X*. New York: Lucis Press, 1936.

Barker, A. T., ed. *The Mahatma Letters to A. P. Sinnett*. Adyar, India: Theosophical Publishing House, 1998.

Bauval, R., and G. Hancock. *Keeper of Genesis*. London: Random House, 1997.

Besant, A., and B. Das. *Bhagvad Gita*. Adyar, India: Theosophical Publishing House, 1926.

Blavatsky, H. P. *Collected Writings Vols. I – XV*. 3rd ed. Wheaton, Ill.: Theosophical Publishing House, 2002.

———. *Five Years of Theosophy*. Los Angeles: The Theosophy Co., 1980.

———. *Isis Unveiled*. Los Angeles: The Theosophy Co., 1982.

———. *Practical Occultism*. London: The Theosophical Publishing Society, n.d.

———. *The Secret Doctrine*. Adyar, India: Theosophical Publishing House, 1979.

———. *The Theosophical Glossary*. Los Angeles: The Theosophy Co., 1990.

———. *The Voice of the Silence*. Los Angeles: The Theosophy Co., 1987.

Bowen, P. G. *The Sayings of the Ancient One*. Wheaton, Ill.: Theosophical Publishing House, 1985.

Budge, E. W. *Egyptian Religion*. New York: Gramercy Books, 1959.

Churton, T. *Gnostic Philosophy*. Rochester, Vt.: Inner Traditions, 2005.

Clark, G. *Iamblichus: On the Pythagorean Life*. Liverpool: Liverpool University Press, 1989.

Cohn-Sherbok, D. *Jewish Mysticism—An Anthology*. London: One World Publications, 1995.

Cooper, J. M. *The Complete Works of Plato*. Indianapolis, Ill.: Hackett Publishing Co., 1997.

Copenhaver, B. P., ed. *Hermetica*. Cambridge: Cambridge University Press, 1992.

Corbin, H. *Temps Cyclique et Gnose Ismailienne*. Oxford: Berg International, 1982.

David-Neel, A. *Initiations and Initiates in Tibet*. London: Rider and Co., 1970.

———. *Magic and Mystery in Tibet*. London: Unwin Paperbacks, 1986.

De Santillana, G., and H. Von Dechend. *Hamlet's Mill*. Boston: D. R. Godine, 1977.

Dyer, C. *Symbolism in Craft Freemasonry*. Hersham, England: Lewis Masonic, 2003.

Editors. *The Chaldean Oracles*. Fintry, England: Shrine of Wisdom, 1979.

———. *The Human Soul in the Myths of Plato*. Fintry, England: Shrine of Wisdom, 1936.

Eliade, M. *Myths, Dreams and Mysteries*. London: Collins Fontana, 1957.

Evans-Wentz, W. Y. *The Tibetan Book of the Dead*. Oxford: Oxford University Press, 1927.

———. *Tibet's Great Yogi Milarepa*. Oxford: Oxford University Press, 1969.

Everard, Dr. *The Divine Pymander*. Michigan: Wizard Bookshelf, 2000.

Faivre, A. *Access to Western Esotericism*. New York: SUNY Press, 1994.

Faivre, A., and W. J. Hanegraaff. *Western Esotericism and the Science of Religion*. Leuven, Belgium: Peeters, 1998.

Faivre, A., and J. Needleman, eds. *Modern Esoteric Spirituality*. New York: Crossroad Publishing Co., 1992.

Fideler, D. *Jesus Christ, Sun of God*. Wheaton, Ill.: Quest Books, 1993.

———. *The Pythagorean Sourcebook and Library*. Grand Rapids, Mich.: Phanes Press, 1987.

Frawley, D. *Gods, Sages and Kings*. Salt Lake City, Utah: Passage Press, 1991.

Ginsburg, G. *The Essenes: Their History and Doctrines*. London: Routledge and Kegan Paul, 1864.

Glatzer, N. *The Judaic Tradition*. New York: Behrman House, 1960.

Godwin, J. *The Golden Thread*. Wheaton, Ill.: Quest Books, 2007.

Goodrick-Clarke, N. *The Western Esoteric Traditions*. Oxford: Oxford University Press, 2008.

Goodrick-Clarke, C. and N., eds. *GRS Mead and the Gnostic Quest*. Berkeley, Calif.: North Atlantic Books, 2005.

Gordon, J. S. *The Rise and Fall of Atlantis*. London: Watkins Books, 2008.

Gorman, P. *Pythagoras: A Life*. London: Routledge and Kegan Paul, 1979.

Goswami, A. *The Self-Aware Universe*. London and New York: Penguin Putnam, 1995.

———. *The Visionary Window*. Wheaton, Ill.: Quest Books, 2006.

Graves, R. *The Greek Myths*. London: Penguin Books, 1960.

Graves, R., and R. Patai. *Hebrew Myths—The Book of Genesis*. London: Cassel and Co., 1964.

Guthrie, K. S. *The Pythagorean Sourcebook and Library*. Grand Rapids. Mich.: Phanes Press, 1988.

Hall, M. P., ed. *The Most Holy Trinosophia of the Comte de St. Germain*. Los Angeles: Philosophical Research Society, 1933.

Hanegraaff, W. J. *New Age Religion and Western Culture*. New York: SUNY Press, 1998.

Herodotus. *The Histories*. London: Penguin Classics, 1983.

Hodson, G. *The Kingdom of the Gods*. Adyar, India: Theosophical Publishing House, 1987.

Hoeller, S. A. *Gnosticism: New Light on the Ancient Tradition of Inner Knowing*. Wheaton, Ill.: Quest Books, 2002.

———. *The Gnostic Jung and the Seven Sermons to the Dead*. Wheaton, Ill.: Quest Books, 1982.

Jacobi, J., ed. *Paracelsus: Selected Writings*. London: Routledge and Kegan Paul, 1951.

Johnson, K. P. *Initiates of Theosophical Masters*. New York: SUNY Press, 1995.

————. *The Masters Revealed: Madame Blavatsky and the Myth of the Great White Lodge*. New York: SUNY Press, 1994.

Jowett, B., trans. *Plato's Republic and Other Works*. London: Anchor Press, 1973.

Jung, C. G. *Analytical Psychology: Its Theory and Practice*. London: Routledge and Kegan Paul, 1970.

Judge, W. Q. *The Bhagvad Gita*. Los Angeles: The Theosophy Co., 1986.

Kahn, C. H. *Pythagoras and the Pythagoreans*. Cambridge, Mass.: Hackett Publishing Co., 2001.

Kersten, H. *Jesus Lived in India*. England: Element Books, 1994.

Lau, D. C. *Lao Tzu: Tao Te Ching*. London: Penguin Classics, 1963.

Leclerc, I., ed. *The Philosophy of Leibnitz and the Modern World*. Nashville, Tenn.: Vanderbilt University Press, 1973.

Levi, E. *The Key of the Mysteries*. London: Rider and Co., 1969.

Lindorff, D. *Jung and Pauli—The Meeting of Two Great Minds*. Wheaton, Ill.: Quest Books, 2004.

Lipton, B. *A New Biology of Life*. London: Hay House, 2005.

————. *Spontaneous Evolution*. London: Hay House, 2001.

Mackenzie, D. A. *Myths of Babylonia and Assyria*. London: The Gresham Publishing Co., 1915.

Mead, G. R. S. *Echoes from the Gnosis*. Wheaton, Ill.: Quest Books, 2006.

————. *The Subtle Body*. London: Stuart and Watkins, 1919.

————. *Thrice Greatest Hermes*. Boston: Weiser Books, 2001.

Meyer, M. *The Secret Gospels of Jesus*. London: Darton, Longman and Todd, 2005.

Milner, D. *Kosmos: An Evolutionary-Wholistic Account of Creation*. Authors Online.

Nabarz, P. *The Mysteries of Mithras—The Pagan Belief That Shaped the Christian World*. Rochester, Vt.: Inner Traditions, 2005.

Nasr, S. H. *The Islamic Intellectual Tradition in Persia*. London: Curzon Press, 1996.

Naydler, J. *Temple of the Cosmos*. Rochester, Vt.: Inner Traditions, 2005.

Neff, M. K. *Personal Memories of H. P. Blavatsky*. London: Rider and Co., 1937.

Oliveti, V. *Terrror's Source*. Birmingham, U.K.: Amadeus Books, 2002.

Pagels, E. *The Gnostic Gospels*. London: Penguin Books, 1979.

Parrinder, G. *Jesus in the Qur'an*. London: Faber and Faber, 1965.

De Purucker, G. *Galaxies and Solar Systems*. San Diego, Calif.: Point Loma Publishing, 1987.

———. *Hierarchies and the Doctrine of Emanations*. San Diego, Calif.: Point Loma Publishing, 1987.

———. *Invisible Worlds and Their Inhabitants*. San Diego, Calif.: Point Loma Publishing, 1987.

Philo. *The Works of Philo*. Peabody, Mass.: Hendrickson Publishers, 1993.

Philostratus. *The Life of Apollonius of Tyana*. London: Loeb Classical Library, 1989.

Plato. *Timaeus and Critias*. London: Penguin Classics, 1977.

Plotinus. *The Enneads*. London: Penguin Classics, 1991.

Reynolds, B., ed. *Embracing Reality: The Integral Vision of Ken Wilber*. New York: Penguin, 2004.

Rowe, N., ed. *Commentary of Hierocles on the Golden Verses of Pythagoras*. London: Theosophical Publishing House, 1971.

Rundle Clark, R. T. *Myth and Symbol in Ancient Egypt*. London: Thames and Hudson, 1959.

Sand, S. *The Invention of the Jewish People*. London: Verso, 2009.

Scholem, G. *The Messianic Idea in Judaism*. New York: Schocken Books, 1971.

———. *On the Kabbala and Its Symbolism*. London: Routledge and Kegan Paul, 1965.

———. *Origins of the Kabbala*. Princeton: Princeton University Press, 1987.

———. *Zohar—The Book of Splendour*. London: Rider and Co., 1977.

Sheldrake, R. *A New Science of Life*. London: Paladin, 1984.

Scott, Sir Walter. *Hermetica*. Bath, England: Solos Press, 1993.

Shah, I. *Oriental Magic*. London: Octagon Press, 1956.

———. *A Perfumed Scorpion—The Way to the Way*. London: Harper and Row, 1982.

———. *The Sufis*. London: Octagon Press, 1977.

Schuon, F. *The Transcendent Unity of Religions*. Wheaton, Ill.: Quest Books, 1984.

Smith, M. *Jesus The Magician*. London: Aquarian Press, 1978.

Spierenberg, H. J. *The Buddhism of H. P. Blavatsky*. San Diego, Calif.: Point Loma Publishing, 1991.

———. *H. P. Blavatsky on the Gnostics*. San Diego, Calif.: Point Loma Publishing, 1994.

———. *The New Testament Commentaries of H. P. Blavatsky.* San Diego, Calif.: Point Loma Publishing, 1987.

———. *The Vedanta Commentaries of H. P. Blavatsky.* San Diego, Calif.: Point Loma Publishing, 1992.

Stoyanov, Y. *The Other God.* New Haven: Yale University Press, 2000.

Szekely, E. B. *The Essene Origins of Christianity.* Nelson, Canada: International Biogenic Society, 1993.

Taylor, T. *Collected Writings on the Gods and the World.* Westbury, England: Prometheus Trust, 1994.

———. *Proclus: Commentary on the Timaeus of Plato.* Westbury, England: Prometheus Trust 1998.

Taylor, T., ed. *Iamblichus' Life of Pythagoras.* London: J. M. Watkins, 1918.

Thurman, R., ed. *The Life and Teachings of Tsong Khapa.* Dharamsala: Library of Tibetan Works and Archives, 1982.

Van den Broek, R., and W. J. Hanegraaff. *Gnosis and Hermeticism—From Antiquity to Modern Times.* New York: SUNY Press, 1998.

Waite, A. E. *The Holy Kabbalah.* London: Williams and Norgate, 1929.

———. *The Occult Sciences.* 1891. Reprint, London: Kegan Paul, 1972.

Wansbrough, J. *Quranic Studies.* Oxford: Oxford University Press, 1977.

Warraq, Ibn. *The Quest for the Historical Muhammad.* New York: Prometheus Books, 2000.

Whiston, W. *The Works of Flavius Josephus: Antiquities of the Jews,* London: T. Nelson and Sons, 1883.

Wilber, K. *Quantum Questions.* Boston: Shambhala, 2001.

Yarker, J. *The Arcane Schools.* Belfast: W. Tait, 1909.

INDEX

BOOKS OF RELATED INTEREST

Land of the Fallen Star Gods
The Celestial Origins of Ancient Egypt
by J. S. Gordon

The Morning of the Magicians
Secret Societies, Conspiracies, and Vanished Civilizations
by Louis Pauwels and Jacques Bergier

Stones of the Seven Rays
The Science of the Seven Facets of the Soul
by Michel Coquet

Music and Its Secret Influence
Throughout the Ages
by Cyril Scott

Lords of the Left-Hand Path
Forbidden Practices and Spiritual Heresies
by Stephen E. Flowers, Ph.D.

Introduction to Magic
Rituals and Practical Techniques for the Magus
by Julius Evola and the UR Group

Gnostic Philosophy
From Ancient Persia to Modern Times
by Tobias Churton

Grail Alchemy
Initiation in the Celtic Mystery Tradition
by Mara Freeman

INNER TRADITIONS • BEAR & COMPANY
P.O. Box 388
Rochester, VT 05767
1-800-246-8648
www.InnerTraditions.com

Or contact your local bookseller